THE WORLD OF LOVE

THE WORLD OF

LOVE

Edited with Introductions by

ISIDOR SCHNEIDER

I

THE MEANINGS OF LOVE

George Braziller   New York

ACKNOWLEDGMENTS

During the months in which I was engaged on this project I could not keep it out of conversations at home and with friends. This was helpful not only for the specific suggestions it evoked but because the patient attention I received served me as an effective sounding board for proposed approaches. I take this opportunity to thank them all who provided such direct and indirect assistance. Above all I wish to acknowledge with admiration and gratitude the able and sensitive editing of George Brante.

I also wish to thank the following for permission to reprint the material in this volume:

George Allen & Unwin Ltd.—for *Thus Spake Zarathustra* by Friedrich Nietzsche;—and for *Rūmī,* tr. by R. A. Nicholson.

Appleton-Century-Crofts—for *The Study of Man* by Ralph Linton. Copyright 1936, D. Appleton-Century Co., Inc. Reprinted by permission of Appleton-Century-Crofts.

Edward Arnold (Publishers) Ltd.—for *The Waning of the Middle Ages* by Johan Huizinga.

Augsburg Publishing House—for *Faith Active in Love* by George Wolfgang Forell, 1954. Used by permission of Augsburg Publishing House, Minneapolis, Minnesota, copyright owner.

A. & C. Black Ltd. and Barnes & Noble, Inc.—for *Early Greek Philosophy* by John Burnet.

Basil Blackwell, Publisher—for *Epicurus and his Gods* by A. J. Festugiere, tr. by C. W. Chilton.

George Braziller, Inc.—for *Saint Genêt* by Jean-Paul Sartre, tr. by Bernard Frechtman. © 1963 by George Braziller, Inc.;—and for "The Star-Jazzer" from *The Green Crow* by Sean O'Casey. Copyright © 1956 by Sean O'Casey. Reprinted by permission of George Braziller, Inc.

Chatto and Windus Ltd.—for *Héloïse, A Biography* by Enid McLeod.

E. P. Dutton & Co., Inc.—for "Altruism" by Sir Charles Sherrington from *An Analysis of the Kinsey Report,* ed. by Donald Porter Geddes. Copyright © 1954 by The New American Library of World Literature, Inc. Reprinted by permission of the New American Library of World Literature. "Altruism" originally appeared in *Man On his Nature* by Sir Charles Sherrington, published by Cambridge University Press;—and J. M. Dent & Sons Ltd. Publishers for *Poems and Translations* by Dante Gabriel Rossetti. Published by E. P. Dutton & Co., Inc.; for *Offices and Select Letters* by Cicero, tr. by William Melmoth. Everyman's Library; for *Ethics* by Aristotle, tr. by D. P. Chase. Everyman's Library; for *Ethics* by Spinoza, tr. by Andrew Boyle. Everyman's Library; and for *Of the Nature of Things* by Lucretius, tr. by William Ellery Leonard. Everyman's Library. All selections reprinted by permission of E. P. Dutton & Co., Inc.

Emerson Books, Inc.—for *Psychology of Sex* by Havelock Ellis, Copyright 1933, 1938, by Havelock Ellis, © 1960 by Françoise Lafitte-Cyon, Edith Gertrude Ellis, and Mneme Kirkland. Reprinted by permission of the publishers, Emerson Books, Inc.

v

Farrar, Straus & Co., Inc.—for *Of Love and Lust* by Theodor Reik, Copyright © 1941, 1944, 1957 by Theodor Reik; copyright 1949 by Farrar, Straus & Co.;—and Martin Secker & Warburg Ltd. for *The Adolescents* by Alberto Moravia, Copyright 1950 by Valentino Bompiani & Co. S. A.; and for *Chéri and The Last of Chéri* by Colette, Copyright 1951 by Farrar, Straus & Young;—and for *Of Fear and Freedom* by Carlo Levi, Copyright 1950 by Farrar, Straus & Co., Inc. All selections reprinted by permission of Farrar, Straus & Co., Inc.

Jules Feiffer—for his cartoon on love.

Free Press of Glencoe—for *Love Is Not Enough* by Bruno Bettelheim. Copyright 1950 by The Free Press, A Corporation. Reprinted with permission of the publisher, Free Press of Glencoe.

Harcourt, Brace & World, Inc.—for *Chance, Love and Logic* by Charles S. Peirce;—and Geoffrey Bles Ltd. for *The Four Loves* by C. S. Lewis, © 1960 by Helen Joy Lewis;—and The Hogarth Press Ltd. and Leonard Woolf for "The Legacy" from *A Haunted House and Other Stories* by Virginia Woolf, copyright 1944 by Harcourt, Brace & World, Inc.;—and Philosophical Library, Publishers and Curtis Brown Ltd. for "De Profundis" from *The Letters of Oscar Wilde* ed. by Rupert Hart-Davis, © 1962 by Vyvan Holland and Rupert Hart-Davis;—for *Love Against Hate* by Karl Menninger, copyright 1942 by Karl Menninger and Jeanetta Lyle Menninger;—for "The Whole World Knows" from *The Golden Apples* by Eudora Welty. Copyright 1947 by Eudora Welty;—and for *The Warriors* by J. Glenn Gray, © 1959, by J. Glenn Gray. All selections reprinted by permission of Harcourt, Brace & World, Inc.

Harper & Row, Publishers—for *Works of Love* by Soren Kierkegaard, tr. by Howard and Edna Hong. Copyright © 1963 by Howard Hong;—for "Sex and Character" by Erich Fromm from *The Family: Its Function and Destiny* ed. by Ruth Nanda Anshen. Copyright 1949 by Harper & Brothers;—for "The Diary of Adam and Eve" from *The Complete Short Stories of Mark Twain* ed. by Charles Neider;—for "How to Tell Love From Passion" by E. B. White from *Is Sex Necessary?* by James Thurber and E. B. White. Copyright 1929 by Harper & Brothers;—for *The Direction of Human Development* by Ashley Montagu. Copyright © 1955 by Harper & Brothers;—and for *The Art of Loving* by Erich Fromm. Copyright © 1956 by Erich Fromm. All selections reprinted with the permission of Harper & Row, Publishers, Inc.

A. M. Heath & Co., Ltd.—for *R.U.R.* by Karel Čapek. Reprinted by permission of A. M. Heath & Co., Ltd. and the estate of the author.

Hodder & Stoughton Ltd.—for *Amor Dei* by John Burnaby.

Holt, Rinehart & Winston, Inc.—for "Crisis in Modern Marriage" from *The Christian Opportunity* by Denis de Rougemont, tr. by Donald Lehmkuhl. Copyright © 1963 by Denis de Rougemont;—and Faber and Faber Ltd. for *The Mind and Heart of Love* by Martin C. D'Arcy, S. J. Copyright 1947 by Holt, Rinehart & Winston, Inc.;—and for *Out of My Life and Thought* by Albert Schweitzer. Copyright 1933, 1949 by Holt, Rinehart & Winston, Inc. All selections reprinted by permission of Holt, Rinehart & Winston, Inc.

Sir Julian Huxley and Harper & Row, Publishers—for "What Do We Know About Love" from *New Bottles for New Wine* by Sir Julian Huxley. By permission of A. D. Peters, literary agents for Sir Julian Huxley.

Indiana University Press—for *The Moral Decision* by Edmond Cahn. Copyright © 1955 by Indiana University Press. All rights reserved.

The Julian Press, Inc., Publishers and Routledge & Kegan Paul Ltd.—for *The Origins of Love and Hate* by Ian D. Suttie. Copyright 1935, 1952 by The Julian Press, Inc. All rights reserved.

Liveright Publishing Corp. and George Allen & Unwin Ltd.—for *Marriage and Morals* by Bertrand Russell. Copyright © R—1957 by Bertrand Russell. Reprinted by permission of Liveright Publishers, New York.

The Macmillan Co., Macmillan & Co. Ltd. and The Macmillan Co. of Canada Ltd.—for *Inishfallen, Fare Thee Well* by Sean O'Casey. Copyright 1949 by Sean O'Casey. Reprinted with permission of The Macmillan Co.

Macmillan & Co. Ltd.—for *Tragic Sense of Life* by Miguel de Unamuno, tr. by J. E. Crawford Flitch. Reprinted by permission of The Executors of the Estate of the late J. E. Crawford Flitch, Dover Publications Inc., and Macmillan & Co. Ltd.

National Psychological Association for Psychoanalysis, Inc.—for "First Dreams in Analysis" by Bernard Bressler from *Psychoanalysis and the Psychoanalytic Review*, Vol. 48, No. 4, Winter 1961-62;—and for "Beauty and the Beast" by Jacques Barchilon from *Psychoanalysis and the Psychoanalytic Review*, Vol. 46, No. 4, Winter 1959-60. Reprinted through the courtesy of the editors and publisher, National Psychological Association for Psychoanalysis, Inc.

New Directions—for "Erostratus" from *Intimacy and Other Stories* by Jean-Paul Sartre, tr. by Lloyd Alexander. Copyright 1948 by New Directions;—and for "Night Watch" from *Nightwood* by Djuna Barnes. Copyright 1937 by Djuna Barnes. Selections reprinted by permission of New Directions, Publishers.

New Education Fellowship—for "The Family: Past and Present" by Bronislaw Malinowski from *The New Era in Home and School*, Nov. 1934 (Vol. XV), pp. 203-206, ed. by M. Myers, Mall Cottage, Chiswick Mall, London, W. 4, England. Reprinted by permission of The New Education Fellowship.

W. W. Norton & Co. Inc. and Sidgwick & Jackson Ltd.—for *Letters to a Young Poet* by Rainer Maria Rilke. Rev. ed. tr. by M. D. Herter Norton. Copyright 1934 by W. W. Norton & Co., Inc. Renewed 1962 by M. D. Herter Norton. Rev. ed. copyright 1954 by W. W. Norton & Co., Inc. Reprinted by permission of the Author's Representatives and of the Publishers Sidgwick & Jackson Ltd.;—and The Hogarth Press Ltd. for *Civilization and Its Discontents* by Sigmund Freud, newly tr. from the German and ed. by James Strachey. Copyright © 1961 by James Strachey, from *The Standard Edition of the Complete Psychological Works of Sigmund Freud*, Vol. XXI;—for *Behaviorism* by John B. Watson. Copyright 1925 & 1953 by John B. Watson;—for *Man's Search for Himself* by Rollo May. Copyright 1953 by W. W. Norton & Co., Inc.;—and for *Neurosis and Human Growth* by Karen Horney. Copyright 1950 by W. W. Norton & Co., Inc. All selections reprinted by permission of W. W. Norton & Co., Inc.

Pocket Books, Inc.—for *The Confessions of Jean Jacques Rousseau*, ed. by L. G. Crocker. Copyright © 1956 by Pocket Books, Inc. Reprinted by permission of Pocket Books, Inc.

Psychoanalytic Quarterly, Inc. and May E. Romm—for "Some Dynamics in Fetishism" by May E. Romm from *The Psychoanalytic Quarterly*, Vol. XVIII, No. 2.

G. P. Putnam's Sons and Elek Books Ltd.—for *Memoirs of Casanova*, tr. by Arthur Machen. All rights reserved.

Random House, Inc.—for "The Darling" by Anton Chekhov, "The Christmas Tree and the Wedding" by Fëdor Dostoevsky and "Her Lover" by Maxim Gorky from *Best Russian Short Stories*, ed. by Thomas Seltzer. Copyright 1917 by Boni and Liveright, Inc. Copyright 1925 by The Modern Library, Inc. Published by Random House, Inc.;—for "A Country Excursion" and "Ball-of-Fat" from *The Best Short Stories of Guy de Maupassant*. Published by Random House, Inc.;—for *Mind and Body* (rev. ed.), by Flanders Dunbar. Copyright 1947, 1955 by Flanders

Dunbar. Reprinted by permission of Random House, Inc.;—for *Nature, Man and Woman* by Alan W. Watts. © Copyright 1958 by Pantheon Books, Inc. Reprinted by permission of Random House, Inc.;—and Faber and Faber Ltd. for *Love Declared* by Denis de Rougemont. © Copyright 1963 by Random House, Inc. Reprinted by permission of Pantheon Books; and for *Love in the Western World* by Denis de Rougemont. © Copyright 1940, 1956 by Pantheon Books, Inc. Reprinted by permission of Random House, Inc.;—for *The Second Sex* by Simone de Beauvoir. Copyright 1952 by Alfred A. Knopf, Inc. Reprinted by permission;—and Chatto & Windus Ltd. for "Swann's Way" by Marcel Proust. Copyright 1928 and renewed 1956 by The Modern Library, Inc. Reprinted from *Remembrance of Things Past* by Marcel Proust, tr. by C. K. Scott Moncrieff, by permission of Random House, Inc.

Routledge & Kegan Paul Ltd.—for *The Practice and Theory of Individual Psychology* by Alfred Adler.

Charles Scribner's Sons—for "Love" from *Reason in Society* by George Santayana. Reprinted with the permission of Charles Scribner's Sons.

Sheed & Ward, Inc. of New York and Sheed & Ward Ltd.—for *An Augustine Synthesis* by Erich Przywara.

The Society of Authors and the Public Trustee—for *Getting Married* and *Man and Superman* by George Bernard Shaw.

University of Chicago Press—for *The Human Animal* by Weston La Barre. Copyright 1954 by The University of Chicago. All rights reserved. Copyright 1954 under the International Copyright Union;—and for "Sex Differences in Play Configurations of American Pre-Adolescents" by Erik H. Erikson from *Childhood in Contemporary Cultures* ed. by Margaret Mead and Martha Wolfenstein. Copyright 1955 by The University of Chicago. © The University of Chicago, 1955. All rights reserved. Copyright 1955 under the International Copyright Union. All selections reprinted by permission of the University of Chicago Press.

The Viking Press, Inc.—for "Love" from *The Portable Voltaire*, ed. by Ben Ray Redman;—for "The Blind Man" from *The Complete Short Stories of D. H. Lawrence*, Vol. 2. Copyright 1922 by Thomas Seltzer, Inc.; 1950 by Frieda Lawrence;—and for *Wayward Youth* by August Aichhorn. Copyright © 1935, by The Viking Press, Inc. All selections reprinted by permission of The Viking Press, Inc.

Westminster Press and the Society for Promoting Christian Knowledge—for *Agape and Eros* by Anders Nygren, tr. by Philip S. Watson. Published 1953, The Westminster Press. Used by permission.

Williams & Norgate Ltd.—for *The Poems of Sappho*, tr. by E. M. Cox. By permission of Ernest Benn Ltd.

Mrs. Fritz Wittels—for *Sex Habits of American Women* by Fritz Wittels, M.D., in collaboration with Herbert C. Rosenthal. Copyright 1951. Reprinted by permission.

Hugh Ross Williamson and Faber & Faber Ltd.—for *The Arrow and the Sword* by Hugh Ross Williamson. Reprinted by permission.

The World Publishing Co.—for *On Love: Aspects of a Single Theme* by José Ortega y Gasset, tr. by Tony Talbot; published by Meridian Books, The World Publishing Co., Cleveland and New York. Copyright © 1957 by The World Publishing Co. Used by permission of the publisher.

PREFACE

PROBABLY THE first association evoked in the majority of readers by the word "love" is with the sexual relationship. Indeed, so far as I know, this is the first general anthology that does not restrict love to that relationship. Had another word existed which more directly expressed the great diversity of relationships comprehended in the word "love" I would have used it. Since there is no such alternative term, "love" is used here, but in its most inclusive sense, with the sexual as one among many love relationships.

My intention here is to bring together examples from fiction and non-fiction which illustrate the many aspects of the human experience which we call love.

In that broader sense of the word, one who embarks on a study of love is immediately awed by its boundlessness. For love is the universal subject of literature; it has become the core of the social sciences; through the recognition of emotional factors in disease it has formally entered into medicine as "Psychosomatics" (it had always been there, empirically, in the physician's practice); its presence has been postulated in the physical sciences as well, from the time of Empedocles to the present atomic age, in the mysterious communions of atoms and in the attractions and repulsions of magnetic fields. Consequently, to comprehend in a single compilation all that love comprises is manifestly impossible; and generally the scope of this anthology, which, so far as I am aware, is more comprehensive than any previously attempted, may best be indicated by the limitations I have found it necessary to set.

First of all, except for allusions in some of the sections to natural forces, I have restricted this anthology to human love, to man's relationships with and within his own kind and with the images projected by his mind. Secondly, with one or two exceptions, I have made no attempt, though in some selections other cultures are reflected upon, to give representation to the lore of other major cultures than those of the West. To adequately represent other cultures would have required additional large compilations, and linguistic and other knowledges that no one person in our time can even aspire to. Moreover, ethnologists and other specialists in comparative culture are in virtually unanimous agreement that, while cultural differences are significant, they are not conclusive but are subject to change and development; and it is valid to assume that the basics of one culture apply to all.

Neither can I claim that what is offered here is a comprehensive presentation of all Western contributions to the subject. It would require large volumes merely to represent *all* the schools of psychoanalysis, not to speak of the other schools of psychology; or to represent the whole literature on the subject, amassed in Western theology; or to provide the selections necessary to trace all the changes in attitudes toward and relationships of love as these are recorded in historical and sociological studies and reflected in literature. One would wish to illustrate not only the changes wrought by the rise and fall of empires but such more transforming changes as the end of human slavery, the breakdown of castes, the extension of individual identity to the masses, and the great industrial revolutions which have been bringing to an end division of labor according to sex and class and, correspondingly, of economic and legal status according to sex and class.

Within these limitations and in the generous space provided by the publisher, I have made the representation as full and varied as I could. It should be added that, to keep it representative, pieces have been included whose viewpoints I do not personally share.

I am certain that I have missed some important works and that I might have made better choices from some that I have drawn upon. But this is only to acknowledge one's human limitations of capacity and time. The perfect compilation would require a lifetime of continuous reading and sifting instead of the many months I have been able to spend. Yet in the course of this absorbing task, as I drew upon my past reading in the light of my special reading for the project, I experienced a refreshed and enlarged understanding of what I had read and felt before. I trust that, to some degree, these volumes will serve the reader in the same way. It is with this hope that I leave them now in the reader's hands.

ISIDOR SCHNEIDER

New York, 1963

CONTENTS

xi

IV. The Flight from the Other: Homosexuality 511

V. Master and Slave: Sadism-Masochism

PART THREE   THE MEANINGS OF LOVE— TWO SUMMATIONS

VOLUME I

THE MEANINGS OF LOVE

From its first appearances in the recorded speculations of man love has been related to concepts of unity and the ideal. Growth into a maturity that realizes union among men and that does not distort the ideal may therefore be regarded as the health of love. But this is seldom fully and never easily achieved. To grow in love one must grow as a person. Where growth is thwarted, the person becomes ill and his love becomes pathological. This volume deals with the meanings that men have given to love and the pathologies to which frustrated growth subjects their love.

PART ONE

THE WAYS OF LOVE

Philosophical, scientific, theological and literary approaches to love may each use a different dialogue or a specialized terminology, yet are in essential agreement, today, on the nature and growth of love. All see it as a principle in which forces are exerted for unification and growth against opposing forces of hatred and disintegration. Psychoanalysis, itself, is veering toward this concept and according recognition to other mutualities beside mutual sexual satisfaction as the basis of love.

The stages of love have been frequently defined by the classic terms Eros, Agape and Philia, the first to denote love in the sense in which the self and its demands and needs are emphasized; the second in the sense in which others are acknowledged and their needs and demands are taken into account; the third in the sense of a fusion and fulfillment of the two. This implies a developmental process which, it will immediately be recognized, coincides with healthy human growth, from childhood with its need and taking, through adolescence with its growing awareness of others and its growing capacity to give to others, into maturity, the stage of mutual taking and giving.

However, the words Eros, Agape and Philia have acquired such diverse and even contradictory connotations that they could

17

not be used without elaborate explication, as can be seen in the contributions here which do make use of them. It seemed best, therefore, in these brief introductory comments, to turn to the simpler terms "need-love," "gift-love" and "mature love." Around these terms fewer, if any, conflicting associations have clustered, at least in the connotations called for here.

Plato, the outstanding classical writer on the subject, uses approximations of these terms. He makes of love a "child of need," which seeks to be replenished from the fullness of others; and a "child of fullness" which seeks completion in overflow into the needs of others. This is close to the modern concepts "need-love" and "gift-love" expressed by writers like C. S. Lewis. We are using these terms here together with the concept "mature love" to denote that experience which comprehends both and transcends them.

It must be borne in mind that varying concepts of love throughout history reflect the social structure and the cultural practices which condition all the ways of love. Underneath the variations, in most societies, as the anthropologists have found, marriage has been the approved and preferred situation for mature love. This is the obvious consequence of the complementary needs of the two sexes and of the added mutualities of family life in the common concern of child-rearing. But conditioning influences may limit the role of marriage or may introduce and sanction competing forms of love. Thus in hierarchical societies in which aristocracies have determined the cultural values and shaped the conventions, or in societies where monasticism is practiced, the "good life," which is always centered on love, was often sought by many outside the family.

In ancient Greece it was frequently sought in outright homosexual relationships or in non-sexual friendships—what has come to be called "Platonic love." In feudal aristocracies perfect love was sought either in passionate extra-marital love or in romanticized non-sexual relationships such as was avowed by Dante for his Beatrice and Petrarch for his Laura. The classical tradition experienced several revivals. Montaigne, as will be seen, spoke of friendship in a manner not far different from that of Plato, Aristotle and Cicero. Similarly the medieval tradition has experienced revivals of a sort in romantic and neo-romantic passion love, Byronic and totally egoistic at one extreme and Werther-like self-denying and self-immolating at the other extreme.

Behind these manifestations, however, were complex influences. Among the ancient Greeks, for example, a complicating factor was the near-idolization of the beauty of athletes. Another contributing factor was the bias that the free-born gentleman of leisure who dominated Athenian culture held against any form of laborious responsibility, because labor was associated with slavery. Unfortunately this association extended to the home, with its house slaves and arduous housekeeping functions, so that fulfillments, including those of love, were sought outside the home.

In medieval societies, where, similarly, a leisured aristocracy set the social course, romantic love was made part of the knightly discipline; "courts of love" were sometimes held where such judgments were rendered as that perfect love was attainable only outside marriage or, on the other hand, only if the lover and his lady avoided sexual communion. Here the complicating factors were survivals or resurgences of Paganism expressed in what were masked rituals of sex-worship in the contrasted forms of total indulgence or total abstinence.

The excesses noted in some of these manifestations return us to our starting points. One who does not progress beyond need-love remains emotionally infantile; he can only take and never give and cannot, therefore, experience fulfillment. One who does not progress beyond gift-love, whose recognition of the needs of others ends in his being overwhelmed by them, who can take nothing from others, who knows no other way of love except self-effacement and self-denial, may have advanced a stage but is no better off. The maturity of love remains beyond him. The development must be completed by both giving and taking, the reciprocal and complementary interchange of need and fullness. Without it there is conflict.

I

The Cosmic Pattern:
Love and Strife

The conflict between love as the drive for unification and order and hate as the drive for disintegration may be called the cosmic pattern. It appears in almost every generalizing concept, in the earliest myths and the latest speculations of philosophers. The myths depict gods bringing order out of chaos or light triumphing over darkness. The cosmic pattern was advanced by Empedocles twenty-five centuries ago and we meet with it in the thinking of today's atomic scientists. We find it in the theories of Epicurus and in the final works of Freud such as "Civilization and Its Discontents." The source of love is the growth toward unity in all relationships. The source of hatred is the arrest of such growth and the consequent frustrations and hostility. This pattern can also be perceived in the civilizations of man, in the evolution of species and, on the grandest scale, in the order and disorders of the cosmos. We begin then with considerations of this cosmic pattern.

FRANCIS BACON: The Myth of Cupid*

THE PARTICULARS related by the poets of Cupid, or Love, do not properly agree to the same person; yet they differ only so far, that if the confusion of persons be rejected, the correspondence may hold. They say, that Love was the most ancient of all the gods, and existed before everything else, except Chaos, which is held coeval therewith. But for Chaos, the ancients never paid divine honours, nor gave the title of a god thereto. Love is represented absolutely without progenitor, excepting only that he is said to have proceeded from the egg of Nox; but that himself begot the gods, and all things else, on Chaos. His attributes are four, viz.: 1, perpetual infancy; 2, blindness; 3, nakedness; and 4, archery.

There was also another Cupid, or Love, the youngest son of the gods, born of Venus; and upon him the attributes of the elder are transferred with some degree of correspondence.

This fable points at, and enters, the cradle of nature. Love seems to be the appetite, or incentive, of the primitive matter; or, to speak more distinctly, the natural motion, or moving principle, of the original corpuscles, or atoms; this being the most ancient and only power that made and wrought all things out of matter. It is absolutely without parent, that is, without cause; for causes are as parents to effects; but this power or efficacy could have no natural cause; for, excepting God, nothing was before it; and therefore it could have no efficient in nature. And as nothing is more inward with nature, it can neither be a genius nor a form; and, therefore, whatever it is, it must be somewhat positive, though inexpressible. And if it were possible to conceive its modus and process, yet it could not be known from its cause, as being, next to God, the cause of causes, and itself without a cause. And perhaps we are not to hope that the modus of it should fall or be comprehended, under human inquiry. Whence it is properly feigned to be the egg of Nox, or laid in the dark.

The divine philosopher declares that "God has made everything beautiful in its season: and has given over the world to our disputes and inquiries: but that man cannot find out the work which God has wrought, from its beginning up to its end." Thus the summary or collective law of nature, or the principle of love, impressed by God upon the original particles of all things, so as to make them attack each other and come together, by the repetition and multiplication whereof all the variety in the universe is

* Reprinted from *The Works of Francis Bacon*.

produced, can scarce possibly find full admittance into the thoughts
of men, though some faint notion may be had thereof. The Greek
philosophy is subtile, and busied in discovering the material principles of things, but negligent and languid in discovering the
principles of motion, in which the energy and efficacy of every
operation consists. And here the Greek philosophers seem perfectly blind and childish: for the opinion of the Peripatetics, as
to the stimulus of matter, by privation, is little more than words,
or rather sound than signification. And they who refer it to God,
though they do well therein, yet they do it by a start, and not by
proper degrees of assent; for doubtless there is one summary, or
capital law, in which nature meets, subordinate to God, viz., the
law mentioned in the passage above quoted from Solomon; or the
work which God has wrought from its beginning up to its end.

Democritus, who further considered this subject having first
supposed an atom, or corpuscle, of some dimension or figure,
attributed thereto an appetite, desire, or first motion simply, and
another comparatively, imagining that all things properly tended
to the centre of the world; those containing more matter falling
faster to the centre, and thereby removing, and in the shock driving away, such as held less. But this is a slender conceit, and regards too few particulars; for neither the revolutions of the celestial bodies, nor the contractions and expansions of things, can be
reduced to this principle. And for the opinion of Epicurus, as to
the declination and fortuitous agitation of atoms, this only brings
the matter back again to a trifle, and wraps it up in ignorance and
night.

Cupid is elegantly drawn a perpetual child; for compounds
are larger things, and have their periods of age; but the first seeds
or atoms of bodies are small, and remain in a perpetual infant
state.

He is again justly represented naked; as all compounds
may properly be said to be dressed and clothed, or to assume a
personage; whence nothing remains truly naked, but the original
particles of things.

The blindness of Cupid contains a deep allegory; for this
same Cupid, Love, or appetite of the world, seems to have very
little foresight, but directs his steps and motions conformably to
what he finds next him, as blind men do when they feel out their
way; which rends the divine and overruling Providence and foresight the more surprising; as by a certain steady law, it brings
such a beautiful order and regularity of things out of what seems
extremely casual, void of design, and, as it were, really blind.

The last attribute of Cupid is archery, viz., a virtue of
power operating at a distance; for everything that operates at a

distance may seem, as it were, to dart, or shoot with arrows. And whoever allows of atoms and vacuity, necessarily supposes that the virtue of atoms operates at a distance; for without this operation, no motion could be excited, on account of the vacuum interposing, but all things would remain sluggish and unmoved.

As to the other Cupid, he is properly said to be the youngest son of the gods, as his power could not take place before the formation of species, or particular bodies. The description given us of him transfers the allegory to morality, though he still retains some resemblance with the ancient Cupid; for as Venus universally excites the affection of association and the desire of procreation, her son Cupid applies the affection to individuals; so that the general disposition proceeds from Venus, but the more close sympathy from Cupid. The former depends upon a near approximation of causes, but the latter upon deeper, more necessitating, and uncontrollable principles, as if they proceeded from the ancient Cupid, on whom all exquisite sympathies depend.

EMPEDOCLES: Love and Strife

I SHALL TELL thee a twofold tale. At one time it grew to be one only out of many; at another, it divided up to be many instead of one. There is a double becoming of perishable things and a double passing away. The coming together of all things brings one generation into being and destroys it; the other grows up and is scattered as things become divided. And these things never cease continually changing places, at one time all uniting in one through Love, at another each borne in different directions by the repulsion of Strife. Thus, as far as it is their nature to grow into one out of many, and to become many once more when the one is parted asunder, so far they come into being and their life abides not. But, inasmuch as they never cease changing their places continually, so far they are ever immovable as they go round the circle of existence.

CHARLES S. PEIRCE: Evolutionary Love*

AT FIRST BLUSH. COUNTER-GOSPELS

PHILOSOPHY, when just escaping from its golden pupa-skin, mythology, proclaimed the great evolutionary agency of the universe to be Love. Or, since this pirate-lingo, English, is poor in such-like words, let us say Eros, the exuberance-love. Afterwards, Empedocles set up passionate-love and hate as the two co-ordinate powers of the universe. In some passages, kindness is the word. But certainly, in any sense in which it has an opposite, to be senior partner of that opposite, is the highest position that love can attain. Nevertheless, the ontological gospeller, in whose days those views were familiar topics, made the One Supreme Being, by whom all things have been made out of nothing, to be cherishing-love. What, then, can he say to hate? Never mind, at this time, what the scribe of the apocalypse, if he were John, stung at length by persecution into a range unable to distinguish suggestions of evil from visions of heaven, and so become the Slanderer of God to men, may have dreamed. The question is rather what the sane John thought, or ought to have thought, in order to carry out his idea consistently. His statement that God is love seems aimed at that saying of Ecclesiastes that we cannot tell whether God bears us love or hatred. "Nay," says John, "we can tell, and very simply! We know and have trusted the love which God hath in us. God is love." There is no logic in this, unless it means that God loves all men. In the preceding paragraph, he had said, "God is light and in him is no darkness at all." We are to understand, then, that as darkness is merely the defect of light, so hatred and evil are mere imperfect stages of ἀγάπη and ἀγαθόν, love and loveliness. This concords with that utterance reported in John's Gospel: "God sent not the Son into the world to judge the world; but that the world should through him be saved. He that believeth on him is not judged: he that believeth not hath been judged already. . . . And this is the judgment, that the light is come into the world, and that men loved darkness rather than the light." That is to say, God visits no punishment on them; they punish themselves by their natural affinity for the defective. Thus, the love that God is, is not a love of which hatred is the contrary; otherwise Satan would be a co-ordinate power; but it is a love which embraces hatred as an imperfect stage of it, an Anteros—yea, even needs hatred and hatefulness as its object. For self-love is no love; so if

* Reprinted from *Chance, Love, and Logic*. First appeared in *The Monist*, January, 1893.

God's self is love, that which he loves must be defect of love; just as a luminary can light up only that which otherwise would be dark. Henry James, the Swedenborgian, says: "It is no doubt very tolerable finite or creaturely love to love one's own in another, to love another for his conformity to one's self: but nothing can be in more flagrant contrast with the creative Love, all whose tenderness *ex vi termini* must be reserved only for what intrinsically is most bitterly hostile and negative to itself." This is from *Substance and Shadow:* an *Essay on the Physics of Creation.* It is a pity he had not filled his pages with things like this, as he was able easily to do, instead of scolding at his reader and at people generally, until the physics of creation was well-nigh forgot. I must deduct, however, from what I just wrote: obviously no genius could make his every sentence as sublime as one which discloses for the problem of evil its everlasting solution.

The movement of love is circular, at one and the same impulse projecting creations into independency and drawing them into harmony. This seems complicated when stated so; but it is fully summed up in the simple formula we call the Golden Rule. This does not, of course, say, Do everything possible to gratify the egoistic impulses of others, but it says, Sacrifice your own perfection to the perfectionment of your neighbor. Nor must it for a moment be confounded with the Benthamite, or Helvetian, or Beccarian motto, Act for the greatest good of the greatest number. Love is not directed to abstractions but to persons; not to persons we do not know, nor to numbers of people, but to our own dear ones, our family and neighbors. "Our neighbor," we remember, is one whom we live near, not locally perhaps, but in life and feeling.

Everybody can see that the statement of St. John is the formula of an evolutionary philosophy, which teaches that growth comes only from love, from—I will not say self-*sacrifice*, but from the ardent impulse to fulfil another's highest impulse. Suppose, for example, that I have an idea that interests me. It is my creation. It is my creature; for as shown in last July's *Monist*, it is a little person. I love it; and I will sink myself in perfecting it. It is not by dealing out cold justice to the circle of my ideas that I can make them grow, but by cherishing and tending them as I would the flowers in my garden. The philosophy we draw from John's gospel is that this is the way mind develops; and as for the cosmos, only so far as it yet is mind, and so has life, is it capable of further evolution. Love, recognizing germs of loveliness in the hateful, gradually warms it into life, and makes it lovely. That is the sort of evolution which every careful student of my essay *The Law of Mind*, must see that *synechism* calls for.

The nineteenth century is now fast sinking into the grave, and we all begin to review its doings and to think what character it is destined to bear as compared with other centuries in the minds of future historians. It will be called, I guess, the Economical Century; for political economy has more direct relations with all the branches of its activity than has any other science. Well, political economy has its formula of redemption, too. It is this: Intelligence in the service of greed ensures the justest prices, the fairest contracts, the most enlightened conduct of all the dealings between men, and leads to the *summum bonum*, food in plenty and perfect comfort. Food for whom? Why, for the greedy master of intelligence. I do not mean to say that this is one of the legitimate conclusions of political economy, the scientific character of which I fully acknowledge. But the study of doctrines, themselves true, will often temporarily encourage generalizations extremely false, as the study of physics has encouraged necessitarianism. What I say, then, is that the great attention paid to economical questions during our century has induced an exaggeration of the beneficial effects of greed and of the unfortunate results of sentiment, until there has resulted a philosophy which comes unwittingly to this, that greed is the great agent in the elevation of the human race and in the evolution of the universe.

I open a handbook of political economy,—the most typical and middling one I have at hand,—and there find some remarks of which I will here make a brief analysis. I omit qualifications, sops thrown to Cerberus, phrases to placate Christian prejudice, trappings which serve to hide from author and reader alike the ugly nakedness of the greed-god. But I have surveyed my position. The author enumerates "three motives of human action:

The love of self;

The love of a limited class having common interests and feelings with one's self;

The love of mankind at large."

Remark, at the outset, what obsequious title is bestowed on greed,—"the love of self." Love! The second motive *is* love. In place of "a limited class" put "certain persons," and you have a fair description. Taking "class" in the old-fashioned sense, a weak kind of love is described. In the sequel, there seems to be some haziness as to the delimitation of this motive. By the love of mankind at large, the author does not mean that deep, subconscious passion that is properly so called; but merely public-spirit, perhaps little more than a fidget about pushing ideas. The author proceeds to a comparative estimate of the worth of these motives. Greed, says he, but using, of course, another word, "is not so great an evil as is commonly supposed. . . . Every man can promote his own interests a great deal more effectively than he can promote any one else's, or than any one else can promote his." Besides, as he remarks on another page, the more miserly a man is, the more good he does. The second motive "is the most dangerous one to which society is exposed." Love is all very pretty: "no higher or purer source of human happiness exists." (Ahem!) But it is a "source of enduring injury," and, in short, should be overruled by something wiser. What is this wiser motive? We shall see.

As for public spirit, it is rendered nugatory by the "difficulties in the way of its effective operation." For example, it might suggest putting checks upon the fecundity of the poor and the vicious; and "no measure of repression would be too severe," in the case of criminals. The hint is broad. But unfortunately, you cannot induce legislatures to take such measures, owing to the pestiferous "tender sentiments of man towards man." It thus appears, that public-spirit, or Benthamism, is not strong enough to be the effective tutor of love, (I am skipping to another page), which must, therefore, be handed over to "the motives which animate men in the pursuit of wealth," in which alone we can confide, and which "are in the highest degree beneficent."[1] Yes, in the "highest degree" without exception are they beneficent to the being upon whom all their blessings are poured out, namely, the Self, whose "sole object," says the writer in accumulating wealth is his individual "sustenance and enjoyment." Plainly, the author holds the notion that some other motive might be in a higher degree beneficent even for the man's self to be a paradox wanting in good sense. He seeks to gloze and modify his doctrine; but he lets the perspicacious reader see what his animating principle is; and when, holding the opinions I have repeated, he at the same time acknowledges that society could not exist upon a basis of intelligent greed alone, he simply pigeon-holes himself as one of the eclectics of inharmonious opinions. He wants his mammon flavored with a *soupçon* of god.

The economists accuse those to whom the enunciation of their atrocious villainies communicates a thrill of horror of being *sentimentalists*. It may be so: I willingly confess to having some tincture of sentimentalism in me, God be thanked! Ever since the French Revolution brought this leaning of thought into ill-repute,—and not altogether undeservedly, I must admit, true, beautiful, and good as that great movement was,—it has been the tradition to picture sentimentalists as persons incapable of logical thought and unwilling to look facts in the eyes. This tradition may be classed with the French tradition that an Englishman says *godam* at every second sentence, the English tradition that an American talks about "Britishers," and the American tradition that a Frenchman carries forms of etiquette to an inconvenient extreme, in short with all those traditions which survive simply because the men who use their eyes and ears are few and far between. Doubtless some excuse there was for all those opinions in days gone by; and sentimentalism, when it was the fashionable amusement to spend one's evenings in a flood of tears over a woeful performance on a candlelitten stage, sometimes made itself a little ridiculous. But what after all is sentimentalism? It is an *ism*, a doctrine, namely, the doctrine that great respect should be paid to the natural judgments of the sensible heart. This is what sentimentalism precisely is; and I entreat the reader to consider whether to contemn it is not of all blasphemies the most degrading. Yet the nineteenth century has steadily contemned it, because it brought about the Reign of Terror. That it did so is true. Still, the whole question is one of *how much*. The Reign of Terror was very bad; but now the Gradgrind banner has been this century long flaunting in the face of heaven, with an insolence to provoke the very skies to scowl and rumble. Soon a flash and quick peal will shake economists quite out of their complacency, too late. The twentieth century, in its latter half, shall surely see the deluge-tempest burst upon the social order,—to clear upon a world as deep in ruin as that greed-philosophy has long plunged it into guilt. No post-thermidorian high jinks then!

So a miser is a beneficent power in a community, is he? With the same reason precisely, only in a much higher degree, you might pronounce the Wall Street sharp to be a good angel, who takes money from heedless persons not likely to guard it properly, who wrecks feeble enterprises better stopped, and who administers wholesome lessons to unwary scientific men, by passing worthless checks upon them,—as you did, the other day, to me, my millionaire Master in glomery, when you thought you saw your way to using my process without paying for it, and of so bequeathing to your children something to boast of their father about,—and who by a thousand wiles puts money at the service of intelligent greed, in his own person. Bernard Mandeville, in his *Fable of the Bees*, maintains that private vices of all descriptions are public benefits, and proves it, too, quite as cogently as the economist proves his point concerning the miser. He even argues, with no slight force, that but for vice civilization would never have existed. In the same spirit, it has been strongly maintained and is to-day widely believed that all acts of charity and benevolence, private and public, go seriously to degrade the human race.

The *Origin of Species* of Darwin merely extends politico-economic views of progress to the entire realm of animal and vegetable life. The vast majority of our contemporary naturalists

hold the opinion that the true cause of those exquisite and marvellous adaptations of nature for which, when I was a boy, men
used to extol the divine wisdom is that creatures are so crowded
together that those of them that happen to have the slightest advantage force those less pushing into situations unfavorable to
multiplication or even kill them before they reach the age of reproduction. Among animals, the mere mechanical individualism
is vastly reënforced as a power making for good by the animal's
ruthless greed. As Darwin puts it on his title-page, it is the struggle
for existence; and he should have added for his motto: Every
individual for himself, and the Devil take the hindmost! Jesus, in
his sermon on the Mount, expressed a different opinion.

Here, then, is the issue. The gospel of Christ says that
progress comes from every individual merging his individuality
in sympathy with his neighbors. On the other side, the conviction
of the nineteenth century is that progress takes place by virtue of
every individual's striving for himself with all his might and
trampling his neighbor under foot whenever he gets a chance to
do so. This may accurately be called the Gospel of Greed.

Much is to be said on both sides. I have not concealed, I
could not conceal, my own passionate predilection. Such a confession will probably shock my scientific brethren. Yet the strong
feeling is in itself, I think, an argument of some weight in favor
of the agapastic theory of evolution,—so far as it may be presumed
to bespeak the normal judgment of the Sensible Heart. Certainly,
if it were possible to believe in agapasm without believing it
warmly, that fact would be an argument against the truth of the
doctrine. At any rate, since the warmth of feeling exists, it should
on every account be candidly confessed; especially since it creates
a liability to onesidedness on my part against which it behooves
my readers and me to be severally on our guard.

SECOND THOUGHTS. IRENICA.

Let us try to define the logical affinities of the different
theories of evolution. Natural selection, as conceived by Darwin,
is a mode of evolution in which the only positive agent of change
in the whole passage from moner to man is fortuitous variation.
To secure advance in a definite direction chance has to be sec-
onded by some action that shall hinder the propagation of some
varieties or stimulate that of others. In natural selection, strictly
so called, it is the crowding out of the weak. In sexual selection,
it is the attraction of beauty, mainly.

The *Origin of Species* was published toward the end of the
year 1859. The preceding years since 1846 had been one of the

most productive seasons,—or if extended so as to cover the great book we are considering, *the* most productive period of equal length in the entire history of science from its beginnings until now. The idea that chance begets order, which is one of the corner-stones of modern physics (although Dr. Carus considers it "the weakest point in Mr. Peirce's system,") was at that time put into its clearest light. Quetelet had opened the discussion by his *Letters on the Application of Probabilities to the Moral and Political Sciences*, a work which deeply impressed the best minds of that day, and to which Sir John Herschel had drawn general attention in Great Britain. In 1857, the first volume of Buckle's *History of Civilisation* had created a tremendous sensation, owing to the use he made of this same idea. Meantime, the "statistical method" had, under that very name, been applied with brilliant success to molecular physics. Dr. John Herapath, an English chemist, had in 1847 outlined the kinetical theory of gases in his *Mathematical Physics*; and the interest the theory excited had been refreshed in 1856 by notable memoirs by Clausius and Krönig. In the very sum-mer preceding Darwin's publication, Maxwell had read before the British Association the first and most important of his researches on this subject. The consequence was that the idea that fortuitous events may result in a physical law, and further that this is the way in which those laws which appear to conflict with the princi-ple of the conservation of energy are to be explained, had taken a strong hold upon the minds of all who were abreast of the leaders of thought. By such minds, it was inevitable that the *Origin of Species*, whose teaching was simply the application of the same principle to the explanation of another "non-conserva-tive" action, that of organic development, should be hailed and welcomed. The sublime discovery of the conservation of energy by Helmholtz in 1847, and that of the mechanical theory of heat by Clausius and by Rankine, independently, in 1850, had decid-edly overawed all those who might have been inclined to sneer at physical science. Thereafter a belated poet still harping upon "science peddling with the names of things" would fail of his effect. Mechanism was now known to be all, or very nearly so. All this time, utilitarianism,—that improved substitute for the Gospel, —was in its fullest feather; and was a natural ally of an individu-alistic theory. Dean Mansell's injudicious advocacy had led to mutiny among the bondsmen of Sir William Hamilton, and the nominalism of Mill had profited accordingly; and although the real science that Darwin was leading men to was sure some day to give a death-blow to the sham-science of Mill, yet there were several elements of the Darwinian theory which were sure to charm the followers of Mill. Another thing: anaesthetics had been in use for thirteen years. Already, people's acquaintance with suffering had dropped off very much; and as a consequence, that unlovely hardness by which our times are so contrasted with those that immediately preceded them, had already set in, and inclined people to relish a ruthless theory. The reader would quite mistake the drift of what I am saying if he were to understand me as wishing to suggest that any of those things (except perhaps Malthus) influenced Darwin himself. What I mean is that his hypothesis, while without dispute one of the most ingenious and pretty ever devised, and while argued with a wealth of knowledge, a strength of logic, a charm of rhetoric, and above all with a certain magnetic genuineness that was almost irresistible, did not appear, at first, at all near to being proved; and to a sober mind its case looks less hopeful now than it did twenty years ago; but the extraordinarily favorable reception it met with was plainly owing, in large measure, to its ideas being those toward which the age was favorably disposed, especially, because of the encouragement it gave to the greed-philosophy.

Diametrically opposed to evolution by chance, are those theories which attribute all progress to an inward necessary principle, or other form of necessity. Many naturalists have thought that if an egg is destined to go through a certain series of embryological transformations, from which it is perfectly certain not to deviate, and if in geological time almost exactly the same forms appear successively, one replacing another in the same order, the strong presumption is that this latter succession was as predeterminate and certain to take place as the former. So, Nägeli, for instance, conceives that it somehow follows from the first law of motion and the peculiar, but unknown, molecular constitution of protoplasm, that forms must complicate themselves more and more. Kölliker makes one form generate another after a certain maturation has been accomplished. Weismann, too, though he calls himself a Darwinian, holds that nothing is due to chance, but that all forms are simple mechanical resultants of the heredity from two parents.[2] It is very noticeable that all these different sectaries seek to import into their science a mechanical necessity to which the facts that come under their observation do not point. Those geologists who think that the variation of species is due to cataclysmic alterations of climate or of the chemical constitution of the air and water are also making mechanical necessity chief factor of evolution.

Evolution by sporting and evolution by mechanical necessity are conceptions warring against one another. A third method, which supersedes their strife, lies enwrapped in the theory of Lamarck. According to his view, all that distinguishes the highest

organic forms from the most rudimentary has been brought about
by little hypertrophies or atrophies which have affected individuals early in their lives, and have been transmitted to their offspring. Such a transmission of acquired characters is of the general
nature of habit-taking, and this is the representative and derivative within the physiological domain of the law of mind. Its action
is essentially dissimilar to that of a physical force; and that is the
secret of the repugnance of such necessitarians as Weismann to
admitting its existence. The Lamarckians further suppose that
although some of the modifications of form so transmitted were
originally due to mechanical causes, yet the chief factors of their
first production were the straining of endeavor and the over-
growth superinduced by exercise, together with the opposite actions. Now, endeavor, since it is directed toward an end, is essentially physical, even though it be sometimes unconscious; and the
growth due to exercise, as I argued in my last paper, follows a law
of a character quite contrary to that of mechanics.

Lamarckian evolution is thus evolution by the force of
habit.—That sentence slipped off my pen while one of those neighbors whose function in the social cosmos seems to be that of an
Interrupter, was asking me a question. Of course, it is nonsense.
Habit is mere inertia, a resting on one's oars, not a propulsion.
Now it is energetic projaculation (lucky there is such a word, or
this untried hand might have been put to inventing one) by
which in the typical instances of Lamarckian evolution the new
elements of form are first created. Habit, however, forces them to
take practical shapes, compatible with the structures they affect,
and in the form of heredity and otherwise, gradually replaces the
spontaneous energy that sustains them. Thus, habit plays a double
part; it serves to establish the new features, and also to bring them
into harmony with the general morphology and function of the
animals and plants to which they belong. But if the reader will
now kindly give himself the trouble of turning back a page or
two, he will see that this account of Lamarckian evolution coincides with the general description of the action of love, to which,
I suppose, he yielded his assent.

Remembering that all matter is really mind, remembering,
too, the continuity of mind, let us ask what aspect Lamarckian
evolution takes on within the domain of consciousness. Direct
endeavor can achieve almost nothing. It is as easy by taking
thought to add a cubit to one's stature, as it is to produce an idea
acceptable to any of the Muses by merely straining for it, before
it is ready to come. We haunt in vain the sacred well and throne
of Mnemosyne; the deeper workings of the spirit take place in
their own slow way, without our connivance. Let but their bugle

sound, and we may then make our effort, sure of an oblation for the altar of whatsoever divinity its savor gratifies. Besides this inward process, there is the operation of the environment, which goes to break up habits destined to be broken up and so to render the mind lively. Everybody knows that the long continuance of a routine of habit makes us lethargic, while a succession of surprises wonderfully brightens the ideas. Where there is a motion, where history is a-making, there is the focus of mental activity, and it has been said that the arts and sciences reside within the temple of Janus, waking when that is open, but slumbering when it is closed. Few psychologists have perceived how fundamental a fact this is. A portion of mind abundantly commissured to other portions works almost mechanically. It sinks to a condition of a railway junction. But a portion of mind almost isolated, a spiritual peninsula, or *cul-de-sac*, is like a railway terminus. Now mental commissures are habits. Where they abound, originality is not needed and is not found; but where they are in defect, spontaneity is set free. Thus, the first step in the Lamarckian evolution of mind is the putting of sundry thoughts into situations in which they are free to play. As to growth by exercise, I have already shown, in discussing *Man's Glassy Essence*, in last October's *Monist*, what its *modus operandi* must be conceived to be, at least, until a second equally definite hypothesis shall have been offered. Namely, it consists of the flying asunder of molecules, and the reparation of the parts by new matter. It is, thus, a sort of reproduction. It takes place only during exercise, because the activity of protoplasm consists in the molecular disturbance which is its necessary condition. Growth by exercise takes place also in the mind. Indeed, that is what it is to *learn*. But the most perfect illustration is the development of a philosophical idea by being put into practice. The conception which appeared, at first, as unitary, splits up into special cases; and into each of these new thought must enter to make a practicable idea. This new thought, however, follows pretty closely the model of the parent conception; and thus a homogeneous development takes place. The parallel between this and the course of molecular occurrences is apparent. Patient attention will be able to trace all these elements in the transaction called learning.

Three modes of evolution have thus been brought before us; evolution by fortuitous variation, evolution by mechanical necessity, and evolution by creative love. We may term them *tychastic* evolution, or *tychasm*, *anancastic* evolution, or *anancasm*, and *agapastic evolution*, or *agapasm*. The doctrines which represent these as severally of principal importance, we may term *tychasticism*, *anancasticism*, and *agapasticism*. On the other hand the mere propositions that absolute chance, mechanical necessity, and the law of love, are severally operative in the cosmos, may receive the names of *tychism, anancism,* and *agapism.*

All three modes of evolution are composed of the same general elements. Agapasm exhibits them the most clearly. The good result is here brought to pass, first, by the bestowal of spontaneous energy by the parent upon the offspring, and, second, by the disposition of the latter to catch the general idea of those about it and thus to subserve the general purpose. In order to express the relation that tychasm and anancasm bear to agapasm, let me borrow a word from geometry. An ellipse crossed by a straight line is a sort of cubic curve; for a cubic is a curve which is cut thrice by a straight line; now a straight line might cut the ellipse twice and its associated straight line a third time. Still the ellipse with the straight line across it would not have the characteristics of a cubic. It would have, for instance, no contrary flexure, which no true cubic wants; and it would have two nodes, which no true cubic has. The geometers say that it is a *degenerate* cubic. Just so, tychasm and anancasm are degenerate forms of agapasm.

Men who seek to reconcile the Darwinian idea with Christianity will remark that tychastic evolution, like the agapastic, depends upon a reproductive creation, the forms preserved being those that use the spontaneity conferred upon them in such wise as to be drawn into harmony with their original, quite after the Christian scheme. Very good! This only shows that just as love cannot have a contrary, but must embrace what is most opposed to it, as a degenerate case of it, so tychasm is a kind of agapasm. Only, in the tychastic evolution progress is solely owing to the distribution of the napkin-hidden talent of the rejected servant among those not rejected, just as ruined gamesters leave their money on the table to make those not yet ruined so much the richer. It makes the felicity of the lambs just the damnation of the goats, transposed to the other side of the equation. In genuine agapasm, on the other hand, advance takes place by virtue of a positive sympathy among the created springing from continuity of mind. This is the idea which tychasticism knows not how to manage.

The anancasticist might here interpose, claiming that the mode of evolution for which he contends agrees with agapasm at the point at which tychasm departs from it. For it makes development go through certain phases, having its inevitable ebbs and flows, yet tending on the whole to a foreordained perfection. Bare existence by this its destiny betrays an intrinsic affinity for the good. Herein, it must be admitted, anancasm shows itself to be in a broad acception a species of agapasm. Some forms of it might easily be mistaken for the genuine agapasm. The Hegelian philosophy is such an anancasticism. With its revelatory religion, with its synechism (however imperfectly set forth), with its "reflection," the whole idea of the theory is superb, almost sublime. Yet, after all, living freedom is practically omitted from its method. The whole movement is that of a vast engine, impelled by a *vis a tergo*, with a blind and mysterious fate of arriving at a lofty goal. I mean that such an engine it *would* be, if it really worked; but in point of fact, it is a Keely motor. Grant that it really acts as it professes to act, and there is nothing to do but accept the philosophy. But never was there seen such an example of a long chain of reasoning,—shall I say with a flaw in every link?—no, with every link a handful of sand, squeezed into shape in a dream. Or say, it is a pasteboard model of a philosophy that in reality does not exist. If we use the one precious thing it contains, the idea of it, introducing the tychism which the arbitrariness of its every step suggests, and make that the support of a vital freedom which is the breath of the spirit of love, we may be able to produce that genuine agapasticism, at which Hegel was aiming.

NOTES

1. How can a writer have any respect for science, as such, who is capable of confounding with the scientific propositions of political economy, which have nothing to say concerning what is "beneficent," such brummagem generalisations as this?

2. I am happy to find that Dr. Carus, too, ranks Weismann among the opponents of Darwin, notwithstanding his flying that flag.

SIGMUND FREUD: Civilization and Its Discontents

IN NONE of my previous writings have I had so strong a feeling as now that what I am describing is common knowledge and that I am using up paper and ink and, in due course, the compositor's and printer's work and material in order to expound things which are, in fact, self-evident. For that reason I should be glad to seize the point if it were to appear that the recognition of a special, independent aggressive instinct means an alteration of the psycho-analytic theory of the instincts.

We shall see, however, that this is not so and that it is merely a matter of bringing into sharper focus a turn of thought arrived at long ago and of following out its consequences. Of all the slowly developed parts of analytic theory, the theory of the instincts is the one that has felt its way the most painfully forward.[1] And yet that theory was so indispensable to the whole structure that something had to be put in its place. In what was at first my utter perplexity, I took as my starting-point a saying of the poet-philosopher, Schiller, that 'hunger and love are what moves the world'.[2] Hunger could be taken to represent the instincts which aim at preserving the individual; while love strives after objects, and its chief function, favoured in every way by nature, is the preservation of the species. Thus, to begin with, ego-instincts and object-instincts confronted each other. It was to denote the energy of the latter and only the latter instincts that I introduced the term 'libido'.[3] Thus the antithesis was between the ego-instincts and the 'libidinal' instincts of love (in its widest sense[4]) which were directed to an object. One of these object-instincts, the sadistic instinct, stood out from the rest, it is true, in that its aim was so very far from being loving. Moreover it was obviously in some respects attached to the ego-instincts: it could not hide its close affinity with instincts of mastery which have no libidinal purpose. But these discrepancies were got over; after all, sadism was clearly a part of sexual life, in the activities of which affection could be replaced by cruelty. Neurosis was regarded as the outcome of a struggle between the interest of self-preservation and the demands of the libido, a struggle in which the ego had been victorious but at the price of severe sufferings and renunciations.

Every analyst will admit that even to-day this view has not the sound of a long-discarded error. Nevertheless, alterations in it became essential, as our enquiries advanced from the repressed to the repressing forces, from the object-instincts to the ego. The decisive step forward was the introduction of the concept of narcissism—that is to say, the discovery that the ego itself is cathected with libido, that the ego, indeed, is the libido's original home, and remains to some extent its headquarters.[5] This narcissistic libido turns towards objects, and thus becomes object-libido; and it can change back into narcissistic libido once more. The concept of narcissism made it possible to obtain an analytic understanding of the traumatic neuroses and of many of the affections bordering on the psychoses, as well as of the latter themselves. It was not necessary to give up our interpretation of the transference neuroses as attempts made by the ego to defend itself against sexuality; but the concept of libido was endangered. Since the ego-instincts, too, were libidinal, it seemed for a time inevitable that we should make libido coincide with instinctual energy in general, as C. G. Jung had already advocated earlier. Nevertheless, there still remained in me a kind of conviction, for which I was not as yet able to find reasons, that the instincts could not all be of the same kind. My next step was taken in *Beyond the Pleasure Principle* (1920g), when the compulsion to repeat and the conservative character of instinctual life first attracted my attention. Starting from speculations on the beginning of life and from biological parallels, I drew the conclusion that, besides the instinct to preserve living substance and to join it into ever larger units,[6] there must exist another, contrary instinct seeking to dissolve those units and to bring them back to their primaeval, inorganic state. That is to say, as well as Eros there was an instinct of death. The phenomena of life could be explained from the concurrent or mutually opposing action of these two instincts. It was not easy, however, to demonstrate the activities of this supposed death instinct. The manifestations of Eros were conspicuous and noisy enough. It might be assumed that the death instinct operated silently within the organism towards its dissolution, but that, of course, was no proof. A more fruitful idea was that a portion of the instinct is diverted towards the external world and comes to light as an instinct of aggressiveness and destructiveness. In this way the instinct itself could be pressed into the service of Eros, in that the organism was destroying some other thing, whether animate or inanimate, instead of destroying its own self. Conversely, any restriction of this aggressiveness directed outwards would be bound to increase the self-destruction, which is in any case proceeding. At the same time one can suspect from this example that the two kinds of instinct seldom—perhaps never—appear in isolation from each other, but are alloyed with each other in varying and very different proportions and so become unrecognizable to our judgement. In sadism, long since known to us as a component instinct of sexuality, we should have before us a particularly strong alloy of this kind between trends of love and the destructive instinct; while its counterpart, masochism, would be a union between destructiveness directed inwards and sexuality—a union which makes what is otherwise an imperceptible trend into a conspicuous and tangible one.

The assumption of the existence of an instinct of death or destruction has met with resistance even in analytic circles; I am aware that there is a frequent inclination rather to ascribe whatever is dangerous and hostile in love to an original bipolarity in its own nature. To begin with it was only tentatively that I put forward the views I have developed here,[7] but in the course of time they have gained such a hold upon me that I can no longer think in any other way. To my mind, they are far more serviceable from a theoretical standpoint than any other possible ones; they provide that simplification, without either ignoring or doing violence to the facts, for which we strive in scientific work. I know that in sadism and masochism we have always seen before us manifestations of the destructive instinct (directed outwards and inwards), strongly alloyed with erotism; but I can no longer understand how we can have overlooked the ubiquity of non-erotic aggressivity and destructiveness and can have failed to give it its due place in our interpretation of life. (The desire for destruction when it is directed *inwards* mostly eludes our perception, of course, unless it is tinged with erotism.) I remember my own defensive attitude when the idea of an instinct of destruction first emerged in psycho-analytic literature, and how long it took before I became receptive to it.[8] That others should have shown, and still show, the same attitude of rejection surprises me less. For 'little children do not like it'[9] when there is talk of the inborn human inclination to 'badness', to aggressiveness and destructiveness, and so to cruelty as well. God has made them in the image of His own perfection; nobody wants to be reminded how hard it is to reconcile the undeniable existence of evil—despite the protestations of Christian Science—with His all-powerfulness or His all-goodness. The Devil would be the best way out as an excuse for God; in that way he would be playing the same part as an agent of economic discharge as the Jew does in the world of the Aryan ideal.[10] But even so, one can hold God responsible for the existence of the Devil just as well as for the existence of the wickedness which the Devil embodies. In view of these difficulties, each of us will be well advised, on some suitable occasion, to make a low bow to the deeply moral nature of mankind; it will help us to be generally popular and much will be forgiven us for it.[11]

The name 'libido' can once more be used to denote the manifestations of the power of Eros in order to distinguish them from the energy of the death instinct.[12] It must be confessed that we have much greater difficulty in grasping that instinct; we can only suspect it, as it were, as something in the background behind Eros, and it escapes detection unless its presence is betrayed by its being alloyed with Eros. It is in sadism, where the death instinct twists the erotic aim in its own sense and yet at the same time fully satisfies the erotic urge, that we succeed in obtaining the clearest insight into its nature and its relation to Eros. But even where it emerges without any sexual purpose, in the blindest fury of destructiveness, we cannot fail to recognize that the satisfaction of the instinct is accompanied by an extraordinarily high degree of narcissistic enjoyment, owing to its presenting the ego with a fulfilment of the latter's old wishes for omnipotence. The instinct of destruction, moderated and tamed, and, as it were, inhibited in its aim, must, when it is directed towards objects, provide the ego with the satisfaction of its vital needs and with control over nature. Since the assumption of the existence of the instinct is mainly based on theoretical grounds, we must also admit that it is not entirely proof against theoretical objections. But this is how things appear to us now, in the present state of our knowledge; future research and reflection will no doubt bring further light which will decide the matter.

In all that follows I adopt the standpoint, therefore, that the inclination to aggression is an original, self-subsisting instinctual disposition in man, and I return to my view [p. 112] that it constitutes the greatest impediment to civilization. At one point in the course of this enquiry [p. 96] I was led to the idea that civilization was a special process which mankind undergoes, and I am still under the influence of that idea. I may now add that civilization is a process in the service of Eros, whose purpose is to combine single human individuals, and after that families, then races, peoples and nations, into one great unity, the unity of mankind. Why this has to happen, we do not know; the work of Eros is precisely this.[13] These collections of men are to be libidinally bound to one another. Necessity alone, the advantages of work in common, will not hold them together. But man's natural aggressive instinct, the hostility of each against all and all against each, opposes this programme of civilization. This aggressive instinct is the derivative and the main representative of the death instinct which we have found alongside of Eros and which shares world-dominion with it. And now, I think, the meaning of the evolution of civilization is no longer obscure to us. It must present the struggle between Eros and Death, between the instinct of life and the instinct of destruction, as it works itself out in the human species. This struggle is what all life essentially consists of, and the evolution of civilization may therefore be simply described as the struggle for life of the human species.[14] And it is this battle of the giants that our nurse-maids try to appease with their lullaby about Heaven.[15]

NOTES

1. [Some account of the history of Freud's theory of the instincts will be found in the Editor's Note to his paper 'Instincts and their Vicissitudes' (1915c), *Standard Ed.*, 14, 113 ff.]

2. ['Die Weltweisen.']

3. [In Section II of the first paper on anxiety neurosis (1895b).]

4. [I.e. as used by Plato. See Chapter IV of *Group Psychology* (1921c), *Standard Ed.*, 18, 99.]

5. [Cf. in this connection the editorial Appendix B to *The Ego and the Id*, *Standard Ed.*, 19, 63.]

6. The opposition which thus emerges between the ceaseless trend by Eros towards extension and the general conservative nature of the instincts is striking, and it may become the starting-point for the study of further problems.

7. [Cf. *Beyond the Pleasure Principle* (1920g), *Standard Ed.*, 18, 59.]

8. [See some comments on this in the Editor's Introduction, p. 61 ff. above.]

9. ['Denn die Kindlein, Sie hören es nicht gerne.' A quotation from Goethe's poem 'Die Ballade vom vertriebenen und heimgekehrten Grafen'.]

10. [Cf. p. 114 above.]

11. In Goethe's Mephistopheles we have a quite exceptionally convincing identification of the principle of evil with the destructive instinct:

> *Den alles, was entsteht,*
> *Ist wert, dass es zu Grunde geht . . .*
> *So ist dann alles, was Ihr Sünde,*
> *Zerstörung, kurz das Böse nennt,*
> *Mein eigentliches Element.*

> [For all things, from the Void
> Called forth, deserve to be destroyed . . .
> Thus, all which you as Sin have rated—
> Destruction,—aught with Evil blent,—
> That is my proper element.]

The Devil himself names as his adversary, not what is holy and good, but Nature's power to create, to multiply life—that is, Eros:

> *Der Luft, dem Wasser, wie der Erden*
> *Entwinden tausend Keime sich,*
> *Im Trocknen, Feuchten, Warmen, Kalten!*
> *Hätt' ich mir nicht die Flamme vorbehalten,*
> *Ich hätte nichts Aparts für mich.*

> [From Water, Earth, and Air unfolding,
> A thousand germs break forth and grow,
> In dry, and wet, and warm, and chilly:
> And had I not the Flame reserved, why, really,
> There's nothing special of my own to show.]

Both passages are from Goethe's *Faust*, Part I, Scene 3. Translated by Bayard Taylor. There is a passing allusion to the second passage in Chapter 1 (G) of *The Interpretation of Dreams* (1900a), *Standard Ed.*, 4, 78.]

12. Our present point of view can be roughly expressed in the statement that libido has a share in every instinctual manifestation, but that not everything in that manifestation is libido.

13. [See *Beyond the Pleasure Principle* (1920g) passim.]

14. And we may probably add more precisely, a struggle for life in the shape it was bound to assume after a certain event which still remains to be discovered.

15. ['*Eiapopeia vom Himmel.*' A quotation from Heine's poem *Deutschland*, Caput I.]

II

The Problem of Love

One's own experiences, not to speak of the voluminous testimony of literature and the social sciences, are enough to keep one constantly aware of the problem of love. It arises out of the multiplicity of love-objects and their conflicts, and is reflected in the confusingly diverse concepts of love. In the growth from self-love to other-love and, in turn, from familial love to the multiple loves evoked by the community and its institutions, man proceeds over many stages, each confronting him with problems. Philosophers have sought to centralize them on the pivotal issue of self-interest versus altruism. Plato provided a perceptive and poetic presentation of the issue; Aristotle's conception of friendship sought to resolve it.

PLATO: The Symposium

ARISTOPHANES PROFESSED to open another vein of discourse; he had a mind to praise Love in another way, unlike that either of Pausanias or Eryximachus. Mankind, he said, judging by their neglect of him, have never, as I think, at all understood the power of Love. For if they had understood him they would surely have built noble temples and altars, and offered solemn sacrifices in his honour; but this is not done, and most certainly ought to be done: since of all the gods he is the best friend of men, the helper and the healer of the ills which are the great impediment to the happiness of the race. I will try to describe his power to you, and you shall teach the rest of the world what I am teaching you. In the first place, let me treat of the nature of man and what has happened to it; for the original human nature was not like the present, but different. The sexes were not two as they are now, but originally three in number; there was man, woman, and the union of the two, having a name corresponding to this double nature, which had once a real existence, but is now lost, and the word 'Androgynous' is only preserved as a term of reproach. In the second place, the primeval man was round, his back and sides forming a circle; and he had four hands and four feet, one head with two faces, looking opposite ways, set on a round neck and precisely alike; also four ears, two privy members, and the remainder to correspond. He could walk upright as men now do, backwards or forwards as he pleased, and he could also roll over and over at a great pace, turning on his four hands and four feet, eight in all, like tumblers going over and over with their legs in the air; this was when he wanted to run fast. Now the sexes were three, and such as I have described them; because the sun, moon, and earth are three; and the man was originally the child of the sun, the woman of the earth, and the man-woman of the moon which is made up of sun and earth, and they were all round and moved round and round like their parents. Terrible was their might and strength, and the thoughts of their hearts were great, and they made an attack upon the gods; of them is told the tale of Otys and Ephialtes who, as Homer says, dared to scale heaven, and would have laid hands upon the gods. Doubt reigned in the celestial councils. Should they kill them and annihilate the race with thunderbolts, as they had done the giants, then there would be an end of the sacrifices and worship which men offered to them; but, on the other hand, the gods could not suffer their insolence to be unrestrained. At last, after a good deal of reflection, Zeus discovered a way. He said: 'Methinks I have a plan which will humble their pride and improve their manners; men shall continue to exist, but I will cut them in two and then they will be diminished in strength and increased in numbers; this will have the advantage of making them more profitable to us. They shall walk upright on two legs, and if they continue insolent and will not be quiet, I will split them again and they shall hop about on a single leg.' He spoke and cut men in two, like a sorb-apple which is halved for pickling, or as you might divide an egg with a hair; and as he cut them one after another, he bade Apollo give the face and the half of the neck a turn in order that the man might contemplate the section of himself: he would thus learn a lesson of humility. Apollo was also bidden to heal their wounds and compose their forms. So he gave a turn to the face and pulled the skin from the sides all over that which in our language is called the belly, like the purses which draw in, and he made one mouth at the centre, which he fastened in a knot (the same which is called the navel); he also moulded the breast and took out most of the wrinkles, much as a shoemaker might smooth leather upon a last; he left a few, however, in the region of the belly and navel, as a memorial of the primeval state. After the division the two parts of man, each desiring his other half, came together, and throwing their arms about one another, entwined in mutual embraces, longing to grow into one, they were on the point of dying from hunger and self-neglect, because they did not like to do anything apart; and when one of the halves died and the other survived, the survivor sought another mate, man or woman as we call them,—being the sections of entire men or women,—and clung to that. They were being destroyed, when Zeus in pity of them invented a new plan: he turned the parts of generation round to the front, for this had not been always their position, and they sowed the seed no longer as hitherto like grasshoppers in the ground, but in one another; and after the transposition the male generated in the female in order that by the mutual embraces of man and woman they might breed, and the race might continue; or if man came to man they might be satisfied, and rest, and go their ways to the business of life: so ancient is the desire of one another which is implanted in us, reuniting our original nature, making one of two, and healing the state of man. Each of us when separated, having one side only, like a flat fish, is but the indenture of a man, and he is always looking for his other half. Men who are a section of that double nature which was once called Androgynous are lovers of women; adulterers are generally of this breed, and also adulterous women who lust after men: the women who are a section of the woman do not care for men, but have female attachments; the female companions are of this sort.

But they who are a section of the male follow the male, and while they are young, being slices of the original man, they hang about men and embrace them, and they are themselves the best of boys and youths, because they have the most manly nature. Some indeed assert that they are shameless, but this is not true; for they do not act thus from any want of shame, but because they are valiant and manly, and have a manly countenance, and they embrace that which is like them. And these when they grow up become our statesmen, and these only, which is a great proof of the truth of what I am saying. When they reach manhood they are lovers of youth, and are not naturally inclined to marry or beget children,—if at all, they do so only in obedience to the law; but they are satisfied if they may be allowed to live with one another unwedded; and such a nature is prone to love and ready to return love, always embracing that which is akin to him. And when one of them meets with his other half, the actual half of himself, whether he be a lover of youth or a lover of another sort, the pair are lost in an amazement of love and friendship and intimacy, and will not be out of the other's sight, as I may say, even for a moment: these are the people who pass their whole lives together; yet they could not explain what they desire of one another. For the intense yearning which each of them has towards the other does not appear to be the desire of lover's intercourse, but of something else which the soul of either evidently desires and cannot tell, and of which she has only a dark and doubtful presentiment. Suppose Hephaestus, with his instruments, to come to the pair who are lying side by side and to say to them, 'What do you people want of one another?' they would be unable to explain. And suppose further, that when he saw their perplexity he said: 'Do you desire to be wholly one; always day and night to be in one another's company? for if this is what you desire, I am ready to melt you into one and let you grow together, so that being two you shall become one, and while you live live a common life as if you were a single man, and after your death in the world below still be one departed soul instead of two—I ask whether this is what you lovingly desire, and whether you are satisfied to attain this?'—there is not a man of them who when he heard the proposal would deny or would not acknowledge that this meeting and melting into one another, this becoming one instead of two, was the very expression of his ancient need. And the reason is that human nature was originally one and we were a whole, and the desire and pursuit of the whole is called love. There was a time, I say, when we were one, but now because of the wickedness of mankind God has dispersed us, as the Arcadians were dispersed into villages by the Lacedaemonians. And if we are not obedient to the gods, there is a danger that we shall be split up again and go about in basso-relievo, like the profile figures having only half a nose which are sculptured on monuments, and that we shall be like tallies. Wherefore let us exhort all men to piety, that we may avoid evil, and obtain the good, of which Love is to us the lord and minister; and let no one oppose him—he is the enemy of the gods who oppose him. For if we are friends of the God and at peace with him we shall find our own true loves, which rarely happens in this world at present. I am serious, and therefore I must beg Eryximachus not to make fun or to find any allusion in what I am saying to Pausanias and Agathon, who, as I suspect, are both of the manly nature, and belong to the class which I have been describing. But my words have a wider application—they include men and women everywhere; and I believe that if our loves were perfectly accomplished, and each one returning to his primeval nature had his original true love, then our race would be happy. And if this would be best of all, the best in the next degree and under present circumstances must be the nearest approach to such an union; and that will be the attainment of a congenial love. Wherefore, if we would praise him who has given to us the benefit, we must praise the god Love, who is our greatest benefactor, both leading us in this life back to our own nature, and giving us high hopes for the future, for he promises that if we are pious, he will restore us to our original state, and heal us and make us happy and blessed. . . .

[Socrates] In the magnificent oration which you have just uttered, I think that you were right, my dear Agathon, in proposing to speak of the nature of Love first and afterwards of his works—that is a way of beginning which I very much approve. And as you have spoken so eloquently of his nature, may I ask you further, Whether love is the love of something or of nothing? And here I must explain myself: I do not want you to say that love is the love of a father or the love of a mother—that would be ridiculous; but to answer as you would, if I asked is a father a father of something? to which you would find no difficulty in replying, of a son or daughter: and the answer would be right.

Very true, said Agathon.

And you would say the same of a mother?

He assented.

Yet let me ask you one more question in order to illustrate my meaning: Is not a brother to be regarded essentially as a brother of something?

Certainly, he replied.

That is, of a brother or sister?

Yes, he said.

And now, said Socrates, I will ask about Love:—Is Love of something or of nothing?

Of something, surely, he replied.

Keep in mind what this is, and tell me what I want to know—whether Love desires that of which love is.

Yes, surely.

And does he possess, or does he not possess, that which he loves and desires?

Probably not, I should say.

Nay, replied Socrates, I would have you consider whether 'necessarily' is not rather the word. The inference that he who desires something is in want of something, and that he who desires nothing is in want of nothing, is in my judgment, Agathon, absolutely and necessarily true. What do you think?

I agree with you, said Agathon.

Very good. Would he who is great, desire to be great, or he who is strong, desire to be strong?

That would be inconsistent with our previous admissions.

True. For he who is anything cannot want to be that which he is?

Very true.

And yet, added Socrates, if a man being strong desired to be strong, or being swift desired to be swift, or being healthy desired to be healthy, in that case he might be thought to desire something which he already has or is. I give the example in order that we may avoid misconception. For the possessors of these qualities, Agathon, must be supposed to have their respective advantages at the time, whether they choose or not; and who can desire that which he has? Therefore, when a person says, I am well and wish to be well, or I am rich and wish to be rich, and I desire simply to have what I have—to him we shall reply: 'You, my friend, having wealth and health and strength, want to have the continuance of them; for at this moment, whether you choose or not, you have them. And when you say, I desire that which I have and nothing else, is not your meaning that you want to have what you now have in the future?' He must agree with us—must he not?

He must, replied Agathon.

Then, said Socrates, he desires that what he has at present may be preserved to him in the future, which is equivalent to saying that he desires something which is non-existent to him, and which as yet he has not got.

Very true, he said.

Then he and every one who desires, desires that which he has not already, and which is future and not present, and which he has not, and is not, and of which he is in want;—these are the sort of things which love and desire seek.

Very true, he said.

Then now, said Socrates, let us recapitulate the argument. First, is not love of something, and of something too which is wanting to a man?

Yes, he replied.

Remember further what you said in your speech, or if you do not remember I will remind you: you said that the love of the beautiful set in order the empire of the gods, for that of deformed things there is no love—did you not say something of that kind?

Yes, said Agathon.

Yes, my friend, and the remark was a just one. And if this is true, Love is the love of beauty and not of deformity?

He assented.

And the admission has been already made that Love is of something which a man wants and has not?

True, he said.

Then Love wants and has not beauty?

Certainly, he replied.

And would you call that beautiful which wants and does not possess beauty?

Certainly not.

Then would you still say that love is beautiful?

Agathon replied: I fear that I did not understand what I was saying.

You made a very good speech, Agathon, replied Socrates; but there is yet one small question which I would fain ask:—Is not the good also the beautiful?

Yes.

Then in wanting the beautiful, love wants also the good?

I cannot refute you, Socrates, said Agathon:—Let us assume that what you say is true.

Say rather, beloved Agathon, that you cannot refute the truth; for Socrates is easily refuted.

And now, taking my leave of you, I will rehearse a tale of love which I heard from Diotima of Mantineia, a woman wise in this and in many other kinds of knowledge, who in the days of old, when the Athenians offered sacrifice before the coming of the plague, delayed the disease ten years. She was my instructress in the art of love, and I shall repeat to you what she said to me, beginning with the admissions made by Agathon, which are nearly if not quite the same which I made to the wise woman when she questioned me: I think that this will be the easiest way, and I shall take both parts myself as well as I can. As you, Agathon, suggested, I must speak first of the being and nature of Love, and then of his works. First I said to her in nearly the same words which he used to me, that Love was a mighty god, and likewise

fair; and she proved to me as I proved to him that, by my own
showing, Love was neither fair nor good. 'What do you mean,
Diotima,' I said, 'is love then evil and foul?' 'Hush,' she cried;
'must that be foul which is not fair?' 'Certainly,' I said. 'And is
that which is not wise, ignorant? do you not see that there is a
mean between wisdom and ignorance?' 'And what may that be?'
I said. 'Right opinion,' she replied; 'which, as you know, being
incapable of giving a reason, is not knowledge (for how can
knowledge be devoid of reason? nor again, ignorance, for neither
can ignorance attain the truth), but is clearly something which is
a mean between ignorance and wisdom.' 'Quite true,' I replied.
'Do not then insist,' she said, 'that what is not fair is of necessity
foul, or what is not good evil; or infer that because love is not fair
and good he is therefore foul and evil; for he is in a mean between
them.' 'Well,' I said, 'Love is surely admitted by all to be a great
god.' 'By those who know or by those who do not know?' 'By all.'
'And how, Socrates,' she said with a smile, 'can Love be acknowledged to be a great god by those who say that he is not a god at
all?' 'And who are they?' I said. 'You and I are two of them,' she
replied. 'How can that be?' I said. 'It is quite intelligible,' she
replied; 'for you yourself would acknowledge that the gods are
happy and fair—of course you would—would you dare to say that
any god was not?' 'Certainly not,' I replied. 'And you mean by
the happy, those who are the possessors of things good or fair?'
'Yes.' 'And you admitted that Love, because he was in want,
desires those good and fair things of which he is in want?' 'Yes, I
did.' 'But how can he be a god who has no portion in what is
either good or fair?' 'Impossible.' 'Then you see that you also
deny the divinity of Love.'

'What then is Love?' I asked; 'Is he mortal?' 'No.' 'What
then?' 'As in the former instance, he is neither mortal nor immortal, but in a mean between the two.' 'What is he, Diotima?'
'He is a great spirit (δαίμων), and like all spirits he is intermediate
between the divine and the mortal.' 'And what,' I said, 'is his
power?' 'He interprets,' she replied, 'between gods and men, conveying and taking across to the gods the prayers and sacrifices of
men, and to men the commands and replies of the gods; he is the
mediator who spans the chasm which divides them, and therefore
in him all is bound together, and through him the arts of the
prophet and the priest, their sacrifices and mysteries and charms,
and all prophecy and incantation, find their way. For God min-
gles not with man; but through Love all the intercourse and converse of god with man, whether awake or asleep, is carried on.
The wisdom which understands this is spiritual; all other wisdom,
such as that of arts and handicrafts, is mean and vulgar. Now

these spirits or intermediate powers are many and diverse, and one of them is Love.' 'And who,' I said, 'was his father, and who his mother?' 'The tale,' she said, 'will take time; nevertheless I will tell you. On the birthday of Aphrodite there was a feast of the gods, at which the god Poros or Plenty, who is the son of Metis or Discretion, was one of the guests. When the feast was over, Penia or Poverty, as the manner is on such occasions, came about the doors to beg. Now Plenty, who was the worse for nectar (there was no wine in those days), went into the garden of Zeus and fell into a heavy sleep; and Poverty considering her own straitened circumstances, plotted to have a child by him, and accordingly she lay down at his side and conceived Love, who partly because he is naturally a lover of the beautiful, and because Aphrodite is herself beautiful, and also because he was born on her birthday, is her follower and attendant. And as his parentage is, so also are his fortunes. In the first place he is always poor, and anything but tender and fair, as the many imagine him; and he is rough and squalid, and has no shoes, nor a house to dwell in; on the bare earth exposed he lies under the open heaven, in the streets, or at the doors of houses, taking his rest; and like his mother he is always in distress. Like his father too, whom he also partly resembles, he is always plotting against the fair and good; he is bold, enterprising, strong, a mighty hunter, always weaving some intrigue or other, keen in the pursuit of wisdom, fertile in resources: a philosopher at all times, terrible as an enchanter, sorcerer, sophist. He is by nature neither mortal nor immortal, but alive and flourishing at one moment when he is in plenty, and dead at another moment, and again alive by reason of his father's nature. But that which is always flowing in is always flowing out, and so he is never in want and never in wealth; and, further, he is in a mean between ignorance and knowledge. The truth of the matter is this: No god is a philosopher or seeker after wisdom, for he is wise already; nor does any man who is wise seek after wisdom. Neither do the ignorant seek after wisdom. For herein is the evil of ignorance, that he who is neither good nor wise is nevertheless satisfied with himself: he has no desire for that of which he feels no want.' 'But who then, Diotima,' I said, 'are the lovers of wisdom, if they are neither the wise nor the foolish?' 'A child may answer that question,' she replied; 'they are those who are in a mean between the two; Love is one of them. For wisdom is a most beautiful thing, and Love is of the beautiful; and therefore Love is also a philosopher or lover of wisdom, and being a lover of wisdom is in a mean between the wise and the ignorant. And of this too his birth is the cause; for his father is wealthy and wise, and his mother poor and foolish. Such, my dear Socrates, is the

nature of the spirit Love. The error in your conception of him
was very natural, and as I imagine from what you say, has arisen
out of a confusion of love and the beloved, which made you think
that love was all beautiful. For the beloved is the truly beautiful,
and delicate, and perfect, and blessed; but the principle of love
is of another nature, and is such as I have described.'

I said: 'O thou stranger woman, thou sayest well; but, assuming Love to be such as you say, what is the use of him to men?'
'That, Socrates,' she replied, 'I will attempt to unfold: of his nature and birth I have already spoken; and you acknowledge that
love is of the beautiful. But some one will say: Of the beautiful
in what, Socrates and Diotima?—or rather let me put the question
more clearly, and ask: When a man loves the beautiful, what does
he desire?' I answered her 'That the beautiful may be his.' 'Still,'
she said, 'the answer suggests a further question: What is given by
the possession of beauty?' 'To what you have asked,' I replied, 'I
have no answer ready.' 'Then,' she said, 'let me put the word
"good" in the place of the beautiful, and repeat the question once
more: If he who loves loves the good, what is it then that he loves?'
'The possession of the good,' I said. 'And what does he gain who
possesses the good?' 'Happiness,' I replied; 'there is less difficulty
in answering that question.' 'Yes,' she said, 'the happy are made
happy by the acquisition of good things. Nor is there any need
to ask why a man desires happiness; the answer is already final.'
'You are right,' I said. 'And is this wish and this desire common
to all? and do all men always desire their own good, or only some
men?—what say you?' 'All men,' I replied; 'the desire is common
to all.' 'Why, then,' she rejoined, 'are not all men, Socrates, said
to love, but only some of them? whereas you say that all men are
always loving the same things.' 'I myself wonder,' I said, 'why this
is.' 'There is nothing to wonder at,' she replied; 'the reason is that
one part of love is separated off and receives the name of the
whole, but the other parts have other names.' 'Give an illustration,' I said. She answered me as follows: 'There is poetry, which,
as you know, is complex and manifold. All creation or passage of
non-being into being is poetry or making, and the processes of all
art are creative; and the masters of arts are all poets or makers.'
'Very true.' 'Still,' she said, 'you know that they are not called
poets, but have other names; only that portion of the art which
is separated off from the rest, and is concerned with music and
metre, is termed poetry, and they who possess poetry in this sense
of the word are called poets.' 'Very true,' I said. 'And the same holds
of love. For you may say generally that all desire of good and
happiness is only the great and subtle power of love; but they who
are drawn towards him by any other path, whether the path of

money-making or gymnastics or philosophy, are not called lovers—
the name of the whole is appropriated to those whose affection
takes one form only—they alone are said to love, or to be lovers.'
'I dare say,' I replied, 'that you are right.' 'Yes,' she added, 'and
you hear people say that lovers are seeking for their other half;
but I say that they are seeking neither for the half of themselves,
nor for the whole, unless the half or the whole be also a good.
And they will cut off their own hands and feet and cast them
away, if they are evil; for they love not what is their own, unless
perchance there be some one who calls what belongs to him the
good, and what belongs to another the evil. For there is nothing
which men love but the good. Is there anything?' 'Certainly, I
should say, that there is nothing.' 'Then,' she said, 'the simple
truth is, that men love the good.' 'Yes,' I said. 'To which must be
added that they love the possession of the good?' 'Yes, that must
be added.' 'And not only the possession, but the everlasting possession of the good?' 'That must be added too.' 'Then love,' she
said, 'may be described generally as the love of the everlasting
possession of the good?' 'That is most true.'

'Then if this be the nature of love, can you tell me further,'
she said, 'what is the manner of the pursuit? what are they
doing who show all this eagerness and heat which is called love?
and what is the object which they have in view? Answer me.' 'Nay,
Diotima,' I replied, 'if I had known, I should not have wondered
at your wisdom, neither should I have come to learn from you
about this very matter.' 'Well,' she said, 'I will teach you:—The
object which they have in view is birth in beauty, whether of body
or soul.' 'I do not understand you,' I said; 'the oracle requires an
explanation.' 'I will make my meaning clearer,' she replied. 'I
mean to say, that all men are bringing to the birth in their bodies
and in their souls. There is a certain age at which human nature
is desirous of procreation—procreation which must be in beauty
and not in deformity; and this procreation is the union of man
and woman, and is a divine thing; for conception and generation
are an immortal principle in the mortal creature, and in the inharmonious they can never be. But the deformed is always inharmonious with the divine, and the beautiful harmonious. Beauty,
then, is the destiny or goddess of parturition who presides at birth,
and therefore, when approaching beauty, the conceiving power
is propitious, and diffusive, and benign, and begets and bears
fruit: at the sight of ugliness she frowns and contracts and has a
sense of pain, and turns away, and shrivels up, and not without
a pang refrains from conception. And this is the reason why, when
the hour of conception arrives, and the teeming nature is full,
there is such a flutter and ecstasy about beauty whose approach is

the alleviation of the pain of travail. For love, Socrates, is not, as you imagine, the love of the beautiful only.' 'What then?' 'The love of generation and of birth in beauty.' 'Yes,' I said. 'Yes, indeed,' she replied. 'But why of generation?' 'Because to the mortal creature, generation is a sort of eternity and immortality,' she replied; 'and if, as has been already admitted, love is of the everlasting possession of the good, all men will necessarily desire immortality together with good: Wherefore love is of immortality.'

All this she taught me at various times when she spoke of love. And I remember her once saying to me, 'What is the cause, Socrates, of love, and the attendant desire? See you not how all animals, birds, as well as beasts, in their desire of procreation, are in agony when they take the infection of love, which begins with the desire of union; whereto is added the care of offspring, on whose behalf the weakest are ready to battle against the strongest even to the uttermost, and to die for them, and will let themselves be tormented with hunger or suffer anything in order to maintain their young. Man may be supposed to act thus from reason; but why should animals have these passionate feelings? Can you tell me why? Again I replied that I did not know. She said to me: 'And do you expect ever to become a master in the art of love, if you do not know this?' 'But I have told you already, Diotima, that my ignorance is the reason why I come to you; for I am conscious that I want a teacher; tell me then the cause of this and of the other mysteries of love.' 'Marvel not,' she said, 'if you believe that love is of the immortal, as we have several times acknowledged; for here again, and on the same principle too, the mortal nature is seeking as far as is possible to be everlasting and immortal: and this is only to be attained by generation, because generation always leaves behind a new existence in the place of the old. Nay even in the life of the same individual there is succession and not absolute unity: a man is called the same, and yet in the short interval which elapses between youth and age, and in which every animal is said to have life and identity, he is undergoing a perpetual process of loss and reparation—hair, flesh, bones, blood, and the whole body are always changing. Which is true not only of the body, but also of the soul, whose habits, tempers, opinions, desires, pleasures, pains, fears, never remain the same in any one of us, but are always coming and going; and equally true of knowledge, and what is still more surprising to us mortals, not only do the sciences in general spring up and decay, so that in respect of them we are never the same; but each of them individually experiences a like change. For what is implied in the word "recollection," but the departure of knowledge, which is ever being forgotten, and is renewed and preserved by recollection, and appears to be the same although in reality new, according to that law of succession by which all mortal things are preserved, not absolutely the same, but by substitution, the old worn-out mortality leaving another new and similar existence behind—unlike the divine, which is always the same and not another? And in this way, Socrates, the mortal body, or mortal anything, partakes of immortality; but the immortal in another way. Marvel not then at the love which all men have of their offspring; for that universal love and interest is for the sake of immortality.'

I was astonished at her words, and said: 'Is this really true, O thou wise Diotima?' And she answered with all the authority of an accomplished sophist: 'Of that, Socrates, you may be assured;—think only of the ambition of men, and you will wonder at the senselessness of their ways, unless you consider how they are stirred by the love of an immortality of fame. They are ready to run all risks greater far than they would have run for their children, and to spend money and undergo any sort of toil, and even to die, for the sake of leaving behind them a name which shall be eternal. Do you imagine that Alcestis would have died to save Admetus, or Achilles to avenge Patroclus, or your own Codrus in order to preserve the kingdom for his sons, if they had not imagined that the memory of their virtues, which still survives among us, would be immortal? Nay,' she said, 'I am persuaded that all men do all things, and the better they are the more they do them, in hope of the glorious fame of immortal virtue; for they desire the immortal.

'Those who are pregnant in the body only, betake themselves to women and beget children—this is the character of their love; their offspring, as they hope, will preserve their memory and give them the blessedness and immortality which they desire in the future. But souls which are pregnant—for there certainly are men who are more creative in their souls than in their bodies—conceive that which is proper for the soul to conceive or contain. And what are these conceptions?—wisdom and virtue in general. And such creators are poets and all artists who are deserving of the name inventor. But the greatest and fairest sort of wisdom by far is that which is concerned with the ordering of states and families, and which is called temperance and justice. And he who in youth has the seed of these implanted in him and is himself inspired, when he comes to maturity desires to beget and generate. He wanders about seeking beauty that he may beget offspring—for in deformity he will beget nothing—and naturally embraces the beautiful rather than the deformed body; above all when he finds a fair and noble and well-nurtured soul, he embraces the two in one person, and to such an one he is full of speech about virtue and the nature and pursuits of a good man; and he tries to edu-

cate him; and at the touch of the beautiful which is ever present
to his memory, even when absent, he brings forth that which he
had conceived long before, and in company with him tends that
which he brings forth; and they are married by a far nearer tie
and have a closer friendship than those who beget mortal children, for the children who are their common offspring are fairer
and more immortal. Who, when he thinks of Homer and Hesiod
and other great poets, would not rather have their children than
ordinary human ones? who would not emulate them in the creation of children such as theirs, which have preserved their memory
and given them everlasting glory? Or who would not have such
children as Lycurgus left behind him to be the saviours, not only
of Lacedaemon, but of Hellas, as one may say? There is Solon, too,
who is the revered father of Athenian laws; and many others there
are in many other places, both among Hellenes and barbarians,
who have given to the world many noble works, and have been
the parents of virtue of every kind; and many temples have been
raised in their honour for the sake of children such as theirs;
which were never raised in honour of any one, for the sake of his
mortal children.

'These are the lesser mysteries of love, into which even you,
Socrates, may enter; to the greater and more hidden ones which
are the crown of these, and to which, if you pursue them in a
right spirit, they will lead, I know not whether you will be able
to attain. But I will do my utmost to inform you, and do you
follow if you can. For he who would proceed aright in this matter
should begin in youth to visit beautiful forms; and first, if he be
guided by his instructor aright, to love one such form only—out of
that he should create fair thoughts; and soon he will of himself
perceive that the beauty of one form is akin to the beauty of another; and then if beauty of form in general is his pursuit, how
foolish would he be not to recognize that the beauty in every
form is one and the same! And when he perceives this he will
abate his violent love of the one, which he will despise and deem
a small thing, and will become a lover of all beautiful forms; in
the next stage he will consider that the beauty of the mind is
more honourable than the beauty of the outward form. So that if
a virtuous soul have but a little comeliness, he will be content to
love and tend him, and will search out and bring to the birth
thoughts which may improve the young, until he is compelled to
contemplate and see the beauty of institutions and laws, and to
understand that the beauty of them all is of one family, and that
personal beauty is a trifle; and after laws and institutions he will
go on to the sciences, that he may see their beauty, being not like
a servant in love with the beauty of one youth or man or institu-

tion, himself a slave mean and narrow-minded, but drawing towards and contemplating the vast sea of beauty, he will create many fair and noble thoughts and notions in boundless love of wisdom; until on that shore he grows and waxes strong, and at last the vision is revealed to him of a single science, which is the science of beauty everywhere. To this I will proceed; please to give me your very best attention:

'He who has been instructed thus far in the things of love, and who has learned to see the beautiful in due order and succession, when he comes toward the end will suddenly perceive a nature of wondrous beauty (and this, Socrates, is the final cause of all our former toils)—a nature which in the first place is everlasting, not growing and decaying, or waxing and waning; secondly, not fair in one point of view and foul in another, or at one time or in one relation or at one place fair, at another time or in another relation or at another place foul, as if fair to some and foul to others, or in the likeness of a face or hands or any other part of the bodily frame, or in any form of speech or knowledge, or existing in any other being, as for example, in an animal, or in heaven, or in earth, or in any other place; but beauty absolute, separate, simple, and everlasting, which without diminution and without increase, or any change, is imparted to the ever-growing and perishing beauties of all other things. He who from these ascending under the influence of true love, begins to perceive that beauty, is not far from the end. And the true order of going, or being led by another, to the things of love, is to begin from the beauties of earth and mount upwards for the sake of that other beauty, using these as steps only, and from one going on to two, and from two to all fair forms, and from fair forms to fair practices, and from fair practices to fair notions, until from fair notions he arrives at the notion of absolute beauty, and at last knows what the essence of beauty is. This, my dear Socrates,' said the stranger of Mantineia, 'is that life above all others which man should live, in the contemplation of beauty absolute; a beauty which if you once beheld, you would see not to be after the measure of gold, and garments, and fair boys and youths, whose presence now entrances you; and you and many a one would be content to live seeing them only and conversing with them without meat or drink, if that were possible—you only want to look at them and to be with them. But what if man had eyes to see the true beauty—the divine beauty, I mean, pure and clear and unalloyed, not clogged with the pollutions of mortality and all the colours and vanities of human life—thither looking, and holding converse with the true beauty simple and divine? Remember how in that communion only, beholding beauty with the eye of the

mind, he will be enabled to bring forth, not images of beauty, but
realities (for he has hold not of an image but of a reality), and
bringing forth and nourishing true virtue to become the friend of
God and be immortal, if mortal man may. Would that be an
ignoble life?' . . .

ARISTOTLE: Ethics

NEXT WOULD seem properly to follow a disserta-
tion on friendship: because, in the first place, it is either itself a
virtue or connected with virtue; and next it is a thing most necessary for life, since no one would choose to live without friends
though he should have all the other good things in the world: and,
in fact, men who are rich or possessed of authority and influence
are thought to have special need of friends: for where is the use of
such prosperity if there be taken away the doing of kindnesses of
which friends are the most usual and most commendable objects?
Or how can it be kept or preserved without friends? because the
greater it is so much the more slippery and hazardous: in poverty
moreover and all other adversities men think friends to be their
only refuge.

Furthermore, Friendship helps the young to keep from
error: the old, in respect of attention and such deficiencies in
action as their weakness makes them liable to; and those who are
in their prime, in respect of noble deeds ("They *two* together
going," Homer says, you may remember), because they are thus
more able to devise plans and carry them out.

Again, it seems to be implanted in us by Nature: as, for
instance, in the parent towards the offspring and the offspring
towards the parent (not merely in the human species but likewise
in birds and most animals), and in those of the same tribe towards
one another, and specially in men of the same nation; for which
reason we commend those men who love their fellows: and one
may see in the course of travel how close of kin and how friendly
man is to man.

Furthermore, Friendship seems to be the bond of Social
Communities, and legislators seem to be more anxious to secure
it than Justice even. I mean, Unanimity is somewhat like to
Friendship, and this they certainly aim at and specially drive out
faction as being inimical.

Again, where people are in Friendship Justice is not required; but, on the other hand, though they are just they need

Friendship in addition, and that principle which is most truly just is thought to partake of the nature of Friendship.

Lastly, not only is it a thing necessary but honourable likewise: since we praise those who are fond of friends, and the having numerous friends is thought a matter of credit to a man; some go so far as to hold, that "good man" and "friend" are terms synonymous.

Yet the disputed points respecting it are not few: some men lay down that it is a kind of resemblance, and that men who are like one another are friends: whence come the common sayings, "Like will to like," "Birds of a feather," and so on. Others, on the contrary, say, that all such come under maxims, "Two of a trade never agree."

Again, some men push their inquiries on these points higher and reason physically: as Euripides, who says,

"The earth by drought consumed doth love the rain,
And the great heaven, overcharged with rain,
Doth love to fall in showers upon the earth."

Heraclitus, again, maintains, that "contrariety is expedient, and that the best agreement arises from things differing, and that all things come into being in the way of the principle of antagonism."

Empedocles, among others, in direct opposition to these, affirms, that "like aims at like."

These physical questions we will take leave to omit, inasmuch as they are foreign to the present inquiry; and we will examine such as are proper to man and concern moral characters and feelings: as, for instance, "Does Friendship arise among all without distinction, or is it impossible for bad men to be friends?" and, "Is there but one species of Friendship, or several?" for they who ground the opinion that there is but one on the fact that Friendship admits of degrees hold that upon insufficient proof; because things which are different in species admit likewise of degrees (on this point we have spoken before).

Our view will soon be cleared on these points when we have ascertained what is properly the object-matter of Friendship: for it is thought that not everything indiscriminately, but some peculiar matter alone, is the object of this affection; that is to say, what is good, or pleasurable, or useful. Now it would seem that that is useful through which accrues any good or pleasure, and so the objects of Friendship, as absolute Ends, are the good and the pleasurable.

A question here arises; whether it is good absolutely or that which is good to the individuals, for which men feel Friendship (these two being sometimes distinct): and similarly in respect of the pleasurable. It seems then that each individual feels it towards that which is good to himself, and that abstractedly it is the real good which is the object of Friendship, and to each individual that which is good to each. It comes then to this; that each individual feels Friendship not for what *is* but for that which *conveys to his mind the impression of being* good to himself. But this will make no real difference, because that which is truly the object of Friendship will also convey this impression to the mind.

There are then three causes from which men feel Friendship: but the term is not applied to the case of fondness for things inanimate because there is no requital of the affection nor desire for the good of those objects: it certainly savours of the ridiculous to say that a man fond of wine wishes well to it: the only sense in which it is true being that he wishes it to be kept safe and sound for his own use and benefit. But to the friend they say one should wish all good for his sake. And when men do thus wish good to another (he not reciprocating the feeling), people call them Kindly; because Friendship they describe as being "Kindliness between persons who reciprocate it." But must they not add that the feeling must be mutually known? for many men are kindly disposed towards those whom they have never seen but whom they conceive to be amiable or useful: and this notion amounts to the same things as a real feeling between them.

Well, these are plainly Kindly-disposed towards one another: but how can one call them friends while their mutual feelings are unknown to one another? to complete the idea of Friendship, then, it is requisite that they have kindly feelings towards one another, and wish one another good from one of the aforementioned causes, and that these kindly feelings should be mutually known.

As the motives to Friendship differ in kind so do the respective feelings and Friendships. The species then of Friendship are three, in number equal to the objects of it, since in the line of each there may be "mutual affection mutually known."

Now they who have Friendship for one another desire one another's good according to the motive of their Friendship; accordingly they whose motive is utility have no Friendship for one another really, but only in so far as some good arises to them from one another.

And they whose motive is pleasure are in like case: I mean, they have Friendship for men of easy pleasantry, not because they are of a given character but because they are pleasant to themselves. So then they whose motive to Friendship is utility love their friends for what is good to themselves; they whose motive is pleasure do so for what is pleasurable to themselves; that is to say, not in so far as the friend beloved *is* but in so far as he is useful or pleasurable. These Friendships then are a matter of result: since the object is not beloved in that he is the man he is but in that he furnishes advantage or pleasure as the case may be.

Such Friendships are of course very liable to dissolution if the parties do not continue alike: I mean, that the others cease to have any Friendship for them when they are no longer pleasurable or useful. Now it is the nature of utility not to be permanent but constantly varying: so, of course, when the motive which made them friends is vanished, the Friendship likewise dissolves; since it existed only relatively to those circumstances.

Friendship of this kind is thought to exist principally among the old (because men at that time of life pursue not what is pleasurable but what is profitable); and in such, of men in their prime and of the young, as are given to the pursuit of profit. They that are such have no intimate intercourse with one another; for sometimes they are not even pleasurable to one another: nor, in fact, do they desire such intercourse unless their friends are profitable to them, because they are pleasurable only in so far as they have hopes of advantage. With these Friendships is commonly ranked that of hospitality.

But the Friendship of the young is thought to be based on the motive of pleasure: because they live at the beck and call of passion and generally pursue what is pleasurable to themselves and the object of the present moment: and as their age changes so likewise do their pleasures.

This is the reason why they form and dissolve Friendships rapidly: since the Friendship changes with the pleasurable object and such pleasure changes quickly.

The young are also much given up to Love; this passion being in great measure, a matter of impulse and based on pleasure: for which cause they conceive Friendships and quickly drop them, changing often in the same day: but these wish for society and intimate intercourse with their friends, since they thus attain the object of their Friendship.

That then is perfect Friendship which subsists between those who are good and whose similarity consists in their goodness: for these men wish one another's good in similar ways; in so far as they are good (and good they are in themselves); and those are specially friends who wish good to their friends for their sakes, because they feel thus towards them on their own account and not as a mere matter of result; so the Friendship between these men continues to subsist so long as they are good; and goodness, we know, has in it a principle of permanence.

Moreover, each party is good abstractedly and also relatively to his friend, for all good men are not only abstractedly good but also useful to one another. Such friends are also mutually pleasurable because all good men are so abstractedly, and also relatively to one another, inasmuch as to each individual those actions are pleasurable which correspond to his nature, and all such as are like them. Now when men are good these will be always the same, or at least similar. . . .

But there is another form of Friendship, that, namely, in which the one party is superior to the other; as between father and son, elder and younger, husband and wife, ruler and ruled. These also differ one from another: I mean, the Friendship between parents and children is not the same as between ruler and the ruled, nor has the father the same towards the son as the son towards the father, nor the husband towards the wife as she towards him; because the work, and therefore the excellence, of each of these is different, and different therefore are the causes of their feeling Friendship; distinct and different therefore are their feelings and states of Friendship.

And the same results do not accrue to each from the other, nor in fact ought they to be looked for: but, when children render to their parents what they ought to the authors of their being, and parents to their sons what they ought to their offspring, the Friendship between such parties will be permanent and equitable.

Further; the feeling of Friendship should be in a due proportion in all Friendships which are between superior and inferior; I mean, the better man, or the more profitable, and so forth, should be the object of a stronger feeling than he himself entertains, because when the feeling of Friendship comes to be after a certain rate then equality in a certain sense is produced, which is thought to be a requisite in Friendship.

(It must be remembered, however, that the equal is not in the same case as regards Justice and Friendship: for in strict Justice the exactly proportioned equal ranks first, and the actual numerically equal ranks second, while in Friendship this is exactly reversed.)

And that equality is thus requisite is plainly shown by the occurrence of a great difference of goodness or badness, or prosperity, or something else: for in this case, people are not any longer friends, nay they do not even feel that they ought to be. The clearest illustration is perhaps the case of the gods, because they are most superior in all good things. It is obvious too, in the case of kings, for they who are greatly their inferiors do not feel entitled to be friends to them; nor do people very insignificant to be friends to those of very high excellence or wisdom. Of course, in such cases it is out of the question to attempt to define up to what point they may continue friends: for you may remove many points of agreement and the Friendship last nevertheless; but when one of the parties is very far separated (as a god from men), it cannot continue any longer.

This has given room for a doubt, whether friends do really wish to their friends the very highest goods, as that they may be gods: because, in case the wish were accomplished, they would no longer have them for friends, nor in fact would they have the good things they had, because friends are good things. If then it has been rightly said that a friend wishes to his friend good things for that friend's sake, it must be understood that he is to remain such as he now is: that is to say, he will wish the greatest good to him of which as man he is capable: yet perhaps not all, because each man desires good for himself most of all.

It is thought that desire for honour makes the mass of men wish rather to be the objects of the feeling of Friendship than to entertain it themselves (and for this reason they are fond of flatterers, a flatterer being a friend inferior or at least pretending to be such and rather to entertain towards another the feeling of Friendship than to be himself the object of it), since the former is thought to be nearly the same as being honoured, which the mass of men desire. And yet men seem to choose honour, not for its own sake, but incidentally: I mean, the common run of men delight to be honoured by those in power because of the hope it raises; that is, they think they shall get from them anything they may happen to be in want of, so they delight in honour as an earnest of future benefit. They again who grasp at honour at the hands of the good and those who are really acquainted with their merits desire to confirm their own opinion about themselves: so they take pleasure in the conviction that they are good, which is based on the sentence of those who assert it. But in being the objects of Friendship men delight for its own sake, and so this may be judged to be higher than being honoured and Friendship to be in itself choiceworthy. Friendship, moreover, is thought to consist in feeling, rather than being the object of, the sentiment of Friendship, which is proved by the delight mothers have in the feeling: some there are who gave their children to be adopted and brought up by others, and knowing them bear this feeling towards them never seeking to have it returned, if both are not possible; but seeming to be content with seeing them well off and bearing this feeling themselves towards them, even though they, by reason of ignorance, never render to them any filial regard or love.

Since then Friendship stands rather in the entertaining, than in being the object of, the sentiment, and they are praised who are fond of their friends, it seems that entertaining the sentiment is the Excellence of friends; and so, in whomsoever this exists in due proportion these are stable friends and their Friendship is permanent. And in this way they who are unequal best be friends, because they may thus be made equal.

Equality, then, and similarity are a tie to Friendship, and specially the similarity of goodness, because good men, being stable in themselves, are also stable as regards others, and neither ask degrading services nor render them, but, so to say, rather prevent them: for it is the part of the good neither to do wrong themselves nor to allow their friends in so doing. . . .

Attendant then on each form of Political Constitution there plainly is Friendship exactly co-extensive with the principle of Justice; that between a King and his Subjects being in the relation of a superiority of benefit, inasmuch as he benefits his subjects; it being assumed that he is a good king and takes care of their welfare as a shepherd tends his flock; whence Homer (to quote him again) calls Agamemnon, "shepherd of the people." And of this same kind is the Paternal Friendship, only that it exceeds the former in the greatness of the benefits done; because the father is the author of being (which is esteemed the greatest benefit) and of maintenance and education (these things are also, by the way, ascribed to ancestors generally): and by the law of nature the father has the right of rule over his sons, ancestors over their descendants, and the king over his subjects.

These friendships are also between superiors and inferiors, for which reason parents are not merely loved but also honoured. The principle of Justice also between these parties is not exactly the same but according to proportion, because so also is the Friendship.

Now between Husband and Wife there is the same Friendship as in Aristocracy: for the relation is determined by relative excellence, and the better person has the greater good, and each has what befits: so too also is the principle of Justice between them.

The Fraternal Friendship is like that of Companions, because brothers are equal and much of an age, and such persons have generally like feelings and like dispositions. Like to this also is the Friendship of a Timocracy, because the citizens are intended to be equal and equitable: rule, therefore, passes from hand to hand, and is distributed on equal terms: so too is the Friendship accordingly.

In the deflections from the constitutional forms, just as the principle of Justice is but small so is the Friendship also: and least of all in the most perverted form: in Despotism there is little or no Friendship. For generally wherever the ruler and the ruled have nothing in common there is no Friendship because there is no Justice; but the case is as between an artisan and his tool, or between soul and body, and master and slave; all these are benefited by those who use them, but towards things inanimate there is neither Friendship nor Justice: nor even towards a horse or an ox, or a slave *quâ* slave, because there is nothing in common: a slave as such is an animate tool, a tool an inanimate slave. *Quâ* slave, then, there is no Friendship towards him, only *quâ* man: for it is thought that there is some principle of Justice between every man, and every other who can share in law and be a party to an agreement; and so somewhat of Friendship, in so far as he is man. So in Despotisms the Friendships and the principle of Justice are inconsiderable in extent, but in Democracies they are most considerable because they who are equal have much in common.

Now of course all Friendship is based upon Communion, as has been already stated: but one would be inclined to separate off from the rest the Friendship of Kindred, and that of Companions: whereas those of men of the same city, or tribe, or crew, and all such, are more peculiarly, it would seem, based upon Communion, inasmuch as they plainly exist in right of some agreement expressed or implied: among these one may rank also the Friendship of Hospitality.

The Friendship of Kindred is likewise of many kinds, and appears in all its varieties to depend on the Parental: parents, I mean, love their children as being a part of themselves, children love their parents as being themselves somewhat derived from them. But parents know their offspring more than these know that they are from the parents, and the source is more closely bound to that which is produced than that which is produced is to that which formed it: of course, whatever is derived from one's self is proper to that from which it is so derived (as, for instance, a tooth or a hair or any other thing whatever to him that has it): but the source to it is in no degree proper, or in an inferior degree at least.

Then again the greater length of time comes in: the parents love their offspring from the first moment of their being, but their offspring them only after a lapse of time when they have attained intelligence or instinct. These considerations serve also to show why mothers have greater strength of affection than fathers.

Now parents love their children as themselves (since what is derived from themselves becomes a kind of other Self by the fact of separation), but children their parents as being sprung from them. And brothers love one another from being sprung from the same; that is, their sameness with the common stock creates a sameness with one another; whence come the phrases, "same blood," "root," and so on. In fact they are the same, in a sense, even in the separate distinct individuals.

Then again the being brought up together, and the nearness of age, are a great help towards Friendship, for a man likes one of his own age and persons who are used to one another are companions, which accounts for the resemblance between the Friendship of Brothers and that of Companions.

And cousins and all other relatives derive their bond of union from these, that is to say, from their community of origin; and the strength of this bond varies according to their respective distances from the common ancestor.

Further: the Friendship felt by children towards parents, and by men towards the gods, is as towards something good and above them; because these have conferred the greatest possible benefits, in that they are the causes of their being and being nourished, and of their having been educated after they were brought into being.

And Friendship of this kind has also the pleasurable and the profitable more than that between persons unconnected by blood, in proportion as their life is also more shared in common. Then again in the Fraternal Friendship there is all that there is in that of Companions, and more in the good, and generally in those who are alike; in proportion as they are more closely tied and from their very birth have a feeling of affection for one another to begin with, and as they are more like in disposition who spring from the same stock and have grown up together and been educated alike: and besides this they have the greatest opportunities in respect of time for proving one another, and can therefore depend most securely upon the trial. The elements of Friendship between other consanguinities will be of course proportionably similar.

Between Husband and Wife there is thought to be Friendship by a law of nature: man being by nature disposed to pair, more than to associate in Communities: in proportion as the family is prior in order of time and more absolutely necessary than the Community. And procreation is more common to him with other animals; all the other animals have Communion thus far, but human creatures cohabit not merely for the sake of procreation but also with a view to life in general: because in this connection the works are immediately divided, and some belong to the man, others to the woman: thus they help one the other, putting what is peculiar to each into the common stock.

And for these reasons this Friendship is thought to combine the profitable and the pleasurable: it will be also based upon virtue if they are good people; because each has goodness, and they may take delight in this quality in each other. Children too are thought to be a tie: accordingly the childless sooner separate, for the children are a good common to both and anything in common is a bond of union.

The question how a man is to live with his wife, or (more generally) one friend with another, appears to be no more than this, how it is just that they should: because plainly there is not the same principle of Justice between a friend and friend, as between strangers, or companions, or mere chance fellow-travellers.

III

The Stages of Love

Man's potential for love is conditioned by his growth. All the potentials of love may be reached in the achievement of mature love, but fully mature love is seldom achieved. At each stage of growth there are conflicts which may distort or prevent further growth. Growth begins with the love response toward another, arising from dependence, the need for fulfillment, for gratification, for idealization. From this relationship develops concern for the necessary "other" and the desire to give to the "other" the fostering regard that can put self in the background. In the mature relationship, if it is truly mature, these stages are transcended; mutual love is a union within which the dialogue of need and fullness, the mutual give and take, occurs.

JOHN BURNABY: The Analogy of Love*

Although John Burnaby's Amor Dei *is a theological work, I have chosen to introduce this section with the following extract because of his clear and eloquent statement of the stages of human love.*
—Ed.

IT IS NOT only the disciple of Luther to whom all consideration of man's love to God is apt to seem a waste of time, or worse. When Dom Chapman of Downside, sketching out in a letter to a Jesuit his ample theory of Catholic truth, came to speak of Charity, he marked it as 'God's, not ours, which is not worth considering'.[1] *Herein is love, not that we loved God, but that He loved us.* Yet if we can say nothing at all of God but in the forms of our human thought and experience, that confession itself can have no meaning apart from the whole human context within which love has been understood or misunderstood.

There are two possible ways of understanding or misunderstanding it. We may either attempt to reduce the complexity and vagueness of the term to a single 'clear and distinct idea', by analysing, isolating, defining: this and this and this is called love, is confused with love, but Love itself, Auto-Agape, is none of these, it is That and That alone. Or we may, provisionally, acquiesce in the multiplicity, the apparent hotch-potch of dissimilarities which strive to cover themselves with Love's mantle, and ask whether after all they may be parts of an organic whole, aspects of a single spiritual reality.

Let us follow this second course. In whatever sense love may be taken in common usage, it will be in some relation to good. (*a*) Love may be subordinate to good, created, caused, or evoked by good; or (*b*) the relation may be reversed, and love may be the cause, good the effect; or (*c*) love and good may coalesce: love may be a kind of good, there may even be no way of explaining good except as love. The spiritual development of the ordinary human being does in fact seem to disclose, successively or concurrently, these three relations between love and good.

The child begins its life in complete dependence. Its needs are few but insistent, and it is helpless to satisfy them: it cannot even find its way to its mother's breast. What is 'good' for it is to be fed, warmed, and washed; and it 'loves' all three processes. Very soon it is more than a little animal. The mind, its distinctive humanity, awakes and grows—an awakening and a growth only in part determined by the actual human environment. The physical

* Reprinted from *Amor Dei*.

67

needs remain, but they are no longer the only needs: the child wants not only the breast or the bottle, but its mother, and it wants, more generally, to be amused. Still, all its good comes to it from outside: if it 'enjoys itself' at all, that is because it has been given what it needs. Its love is purely reactive to external sources of gratification, to the 'not-self' which answers to desire and gives delight.

But sooner or later comes the new stage, in which memory and imagination turn the passive recipient into an active originator. The child makes the great discovery that he need not always be asking for what he wants, that he has in himself a certain power of realising the good which from its station in the outside world has stepped in the form of an idea across the threshold of his mind and become at home within him. In fancy or in fact, in the endowing of a toy with life and character or in the building of houses in the sand, he can reproduce for himself the imagined good. The observer can become the artist, the enjoyer a quasi-creator. He is still dependent upon the given, for his creative activity presupposes vision. It is not true that he seeks to 'express himself', or that he makes just for the sake of making. He seeks to express something which is *not* himself, to make something that he has seen and that has value for him. Apart from its value he would not want to make it. The making is at first a travail, a struggle with difficulties, and only when a certain degree of mastery over the material has been achieved does the actual process of creation become enjoyable. But in the process love, without losing its old form, has taken on a new one. It is no longer *only* a reaction to presented good, but also a *causa efficiens*, summoning new good into existence.

Now it is true that the creative impulse opens a door of escape from self-centredness, inasmuch as in creation there is activity of the self *for* a good to be realised, instead of more or less passive intake of all good as *for* the self. But the new impulse can and at first does accentuate egoism rather than diminish it. What I have made is mine, and no one else has a right to its enjoyment. Before the self can begin to take its place in a wider world, the consequences must be drawn from another discovery. At first other people were so many objects in an environment upon which the child depended for the satisfaction of his needs. But he does not take very long to find that some of these objects (and one of them in particular) have a peculiar interest in him which he can turn to a good account. They show a concern for him which is not unlike his own concern for his own product or possession. They behave as though he were valuable to them, and he proves that he is aware of the fact by his ingenuity in trading upon it. But his parents' love is much more than a convenience to be used, more even than a value to be enjoyed. It evokes response in kind, and he finds himself loving them because they first loved him, and impelled continually to reinforce the bond which makes them his as he is theirs, by the little displays of love, of pure delight in pleasing, which are the sweetest of all parenthood's rewards. Love itself has become a peculiar good, a thing as precious as it is fragile —for faults and failures on either side can interrupt it. Moreover, it contains within itself, no less than the creative impulse, the seeds of mischief. The child, in realising his own value to another, is led for the first time to a conscious attribution of value to himself. He becomes an important person in his own eyes—a *more* important person than the visitor, the nurse, or the brother or sister, whom his parents do not or must not be allowed to love as well as him. Through the very experience that begins his emancipation from self-centredness, he becomes infected with the pride which is a far more serious obstacle than natural egoism to the progress and the perfection of love.

Let us suppose that our child is growing up as he should in a society of fellow-children. He is constantly confronted by the claims of partnership, and he assumes the validity of the axiom: 'the more there is of yours, the less there is of mine'—an axiom which is true enough of the particular kind of good which at this stage has most apparent value for him. Daily experience of an enjoyment which is in fact the keener for being shared fails to convince him that he would not be happier if he had all the good things to himself. Daily experience of the discomfort of quarrelling fails to prove that peace is better secured by concession or compromise than by victory. For the jealousy which is pride's inseparable companion is actually stronger than the desire of good things themselves. He does not 'want equals', and he cannot understand that the struggle for superiority is a waste of the energies which should be directed towards creation and enjoyment. Fellowship in love, a natural growth between child and parent, manifests its value much less easily between brother and sister. But this manifestation is the indispensable condition for the security of all other values. The lesson has to be learnt, not only that jealousy poisons creation, that sharing intensifies enjoyment, but that brotherly love is to be sought for its own sake, and that its enemy is not the desire for any other competing good, but the pride which is in declared and deliberate opposition to the unity of the Spirit in the bond of peace.

The lesson is too large to be learnt in the nursery: indeed the measure of its appropriation is the measure in which the child has become the man. Spiritual growth means, first, the testing and

correction of childhood's values, the recognition that abiding good
is not to be found in anything which cannot be shared or is diminished by participation. It means, next, the purification of the
creative impulse, so that the maker is moved not by the attraction
of novelty nor to satisfy a conceit of power, but simply by the call
of good to be let into the world through any door that can be
opened to it. And it means, above all, the discovery of supreme
power in humility, in the charity which seeketh not her own, is
not easily provoked, hopeth all things, believeth all things, endureth all things. That discovery is never made by taking thought: it
is never a deduction from abstract principles. The truth to be
found has always to be seen somewhere in actual embodiment.
We learn the possibility of love only when it is at work before our
eyes in concrete and visible form.

So much may serve as an outline, commonplace enough, of
the developing functions of human love. It appears first as reaction to the given good, then as impulse to embody the good idea,
and finally as purpose to be served in patient devotion. If we now
attempt to trace a corresponding pattern in the love which is
God's own nature, it will be in the faith common to St. Augustine
and St. Thomas, that His invisible things are understood through
the things that are made, that there is a relation not of identity
but of analogy between the natural and the supernatural, between
the changing and the changeless Good.

For all human apprehension, the good is in some sense a
thing given. The noblest achievements of human creativity are
never 'out of nothing': the richest soil is barren until the seed
of the 'word' has fallen upon it. God's grace is everywhere
prevenient; and that is why our creating is at most an analogue
of His. He is the only true Creator, for He alone needs no
model, no vision of a good that is not His own: He alone is
dependent upon no imperfect medium. In all that is good, there
is a likeness of Him: the orders of space and time reveal His
glory; and if for us to whom the revelation is given there is one
glory of the sun, another of the moon, another of the stars, if to
our partial vision there is more of God here than there, now than
then, the apparent inequalities are grounded in the Revealer's
design to keep us on tip-toe, to nourish our thirst for Himself.
It is good for us that our reach should exceed our grasp, that
enjoyment should never quench desire. But for the Creator we
may surely believe that His 'ancient rapture' is eternal: that
the universe in all its tragi-comic magnificence reflects a divine
self-enjoyment in which God will have us share whenever we
look into the tiniest corner of His creation and see that it is good.
Not all the suffering through which love must pass to be made

perfect should blind us to the truth that love is consummated in delight; for greater than the pain of childbirth is the joy that a man is born into the world. And a thought of the infinite love of God which gives no place to delight can hardly claim kinship with the mind of One who traced that love in the glorious arraying of the lilies. There must be a sense in which whatsoever things are lovely are lovely *for* their Maker as well as, nay far more than, for us to whom they reveal Him.

But they would not be so, were not He Himself revealed in them. And if it is true that no solitary enjoyment is perfect, that no good is equal to the good of fellowship, it will follow that the love which unites men to one another, the *vinculum perfectionis,* must also and pre-eminently have its analogue in the love of God. God has made men apt to find their completion in communion, because such communion is a likeness of the mutual love in which and through which Three Persons are One God. We could conceive of a divine Agape that was nothing but a sheer giving of itself, only if God's existence were wholly dependent on the existence of the world, and His Kingdom, not Himself, were the Supreme Good. What St. Augustine's doctrine of the Holy Spirit means is that the perfection of love is spiritual κοινωνία or fellowship, that love belongs to the eternal Being of God because the divine Life is itself not bare unity but community, and that love can have no other purpose, as it can have no other source, but the mutual 'inherence' of persons, life in one another.

What then are we to say of the charity which endureth all things? If our deepest insight into the divine purpose shows us the will of God to unite us to Himself as children to their Father, and if there is nothing but sin that separates us from God, no obstacle to communion but pride, we must acknowledge our responsibility for the Cross. We cannot say that *all* suffering is the consequence of sin. It may be true that part of the pain in which the whole creation groans and travails together is an inevitable accompaniment of creation as such; that to make a world at all, a world that should be *other* than God, involved a self-limitation of the Infinite of which pain, and pain of which He could not and would not escape the burden for Himself, is a necessary aspect. We do not know enough to speak confidently of these mysteries; though we could not love the Creator of such a world as this, were we not sure of His compassion, of His presence in the sparrow that falls to the ground as well as in every crying child that is the victim of man's wickedness. But we do know that nothing but the sight of the anguish it inflicts upon love has power to break down pride.

The love which endures, which offers itself to the unloving,

is always the servant of its own high purpose—not to rest till the
sundered fellowship is restored, till rejection is changed to
response. Calvary is for the sake of Pentecost: *It is expedient
for you that I go away:* the Body of Christ is broken in the
Eucharist, to be made whole in its partakers. So long as there
is sin in the world, the breaking must go on: membership
of Christ must mean communion in His sufferings. The 'merci-
fulness' which is literally *com*-passion is the way in which we
are called to imitate the divine perfection in a world still to
be redeemed. Yet suffering can be the end neither for God nor
man. We are not yet come to the Perfect Man; but that is the
unseen reality on which we lay hold in faith, the consummation
to which we look forward. Charity believeth all things, hopeth
all things; and its faith and hope no less than its endurance are
creative of that unity of the Spirit which is its end.

NOTES

1. *Spiritual Letters of Dom John Chapman,* p. 226.

1. LOVE, THE CHILD OF NEED

*"Love, the child of need," to use Plato's term, is not only mani-
fested in childhood, where its nature is clearest in the dependence
of the child on loving parental care, but in many other relationships. As the subdivisions of this section indicate—"the search for
fulfillment," "romantic love and the search for the ideal,"—need-
love proceeds from the need for the love object to its idealization.
Idealization has an extreme expression in romantic love, medieval
and modern. Need-love is also a progression from the self toward
the other who complements his need and in unity with whom he
can achieve fruition. Where need-love remains pure self-interest
and does not grow into recognition and concern for the good of
the other, love itself is distorted and becomes pathological.*

A. The Search for Fulfillment

VOLTAIRE: Love*

THERE ARE so many sorts of love that one does not know where to seek a definition of it. The name of "love" is given boldly to a caprice of a few days' duration; to a sentiment devoid of esteem; to a casual liaison; to the affectations of a cicisbeo; to a frigid habit; to a romantic fantasy; to relish followed by prompt disrelish:—yes, people give this name to a thousand chimeras.

If philosophers wish to probe to the bottom this hardly philosophical matter, let them meditate on Plato's *Symposium,* in which Socrates, the honorable lover of Alcibiades and Agathon, converses with them on the metaphysics of love.

Lucretius deals with it more from the point of view of a natural philosopher: Virgil follows in the steps of Lucretius; *amor omnibus idem.*

It is the stuff of nature embroidered by imagination. Do you want an idea of love? look at the sparrows in your garden; look at your pigeons; look at the bull which is brought to the heifer. Look at this proud horse which two of your grooms lead to the quiet mare awaiting him; she draws aside her tail to welcome him; see how her eyes sparkle; hark to the neighing; watch the prancing, the curvetting, the ears pricked, the mouth opening with little convulsions, the swelling nostrils, the fiery breath, the manes rising and floating, the impetuous movement with which he hurls himself on the object which nature has destined for him. But do not be jealous of him. Think of the advantages of the human species; love compensates them for all those qualities that nature has given to the animals—strength, beauty, nimbleness, and speed.

There are even animals who do not know the joy of intercourse. Scale fish are deprived of this delight: the female throws millions of eggs on the mud; the male who encounters them swims over them, and fertilizes them with his seed, without troubling about the female to whom they belong.

Most animals that couple, taste pleasure only by a single sense, and as soon as the appetite is satisfied, everything is extinguished. You are the only animal who knows what kissing is. The whole of your body is sensitive, but your lips especially are capable of a pleasure that is tireless; and this pleasure belongs to no species

* Reprinted from *Philosophical Dictionary.*

but yours. You can give yourself up to love at any time, and the animals have but a fixed time. If you reflect on these superiorities, you will say with the earl of Rochester: "In a country of atheists, love would cause the Deity to be worshiped."

As men have received the gift of perfecting all the gifts of nature, they have perfected love. Cleanliness and the care of oneself, by making the skin more delicate, increase the pleasure of contact; and attention to one's health renders the organs of pleasure more sensitive. All the other sentiments enter into that of love, just like metals which amalgamate with gold: friendship and esteem come to help; the faculties of mind and body are still further chains.

Self-love, above all, tightens all these bonds. One applauds oneself for one's choice, and a crowd of illusions form the decoration of the building of which nature has laid the foundations.

There are the advantages you have over the animals. But if you taste so many pleasures unknown to them, how many sorrows, too, are there of which the beasts have no idea! How terrible for you that over three-fourths of the earth nature has poisoned the pleasures of love and the sources of life with an appalling disease to which man alone is subject, and by which only man's organs of generation are infected!

This plague is not like so many other maladies which are caused by our excesses. It was not debauch that introduced it into the world. Phryne, Lais, Flora, Messalina and those like them, were not attacked by it. It was born in some islands where men lived in innocence, and thence spread itself over the ancient world.

If ever one could accuse nature of despising her work, of contradicting her plans, of acting against her designs, it is in this detestable scourge which has soiled the earth with horror and filth. Is this the best of all possible worlds? Even if Caesar, Antony, Octavius never had this disease, might it not have been possible for it to spare François I? "No," people say, "things were ordered thus for the best." I should like to think so; but it is sad for those to whom Rabelais dedicated his book.

Erotic philosophers have often debated the question of whether Heloise could still really love Abelard when he was both a monk and a eunuch. One of these qualities did great harm to the other. But console yourself, Abelard, you were loved. The root of the hewn tree still retains a remnant of sap; the imagination aids the heart. One can still be happy at table even though one eats no longer. Is it love? Is it simply a memory? Is it friendship? It is an indefinable complex of all these elements. It is an obscure feeling resembling the fantastic passions retained by the dead in the Elysian fields. The heroes who, during their lifetime, shone in the chariot races, drove imaginary chariots when they were dead. Heloise lived with you on illusions and memories. She kissed you sometimes, and with all the more pleasure because she had taken a vow at the Paraclete to love you no longer, which made her kisses thereby more precious as they were more culpable. A woman can hardly be seized with a passion for a eunuch: but she can keep her passion for a lover who has become a eunuch, provided that he remains lovable.

It is not the same, ladies, for a lover who has grown old in service. The externals no longer remain the same. The wrinkles horrify, the white eyebrows shock, the lost teeth disgust, the infirmities estrange. All that one can do is to enjoy the virtue of playing nurse, and of tolerating what one once loved. It is burying a dead man.

WILLIAM HAZLITT: *Liber Amoris**

UNALTERED LOVE

"Love is not love that alteration finds:
Oh no! it is an ever-fixed mark,
That looks on tempests and is never shaken."

SHALL I not love her for herself alone, in spite of fickleness and folly? To love her for her regard to me, is not to love her, but myself. She has robbed me of herself: shall she also rob me of my love of her? Did I not live on her smile? Is it less sweet because it is withdrawn from me? Did I not adore her every grace? Does she bend less enchantingly, because she has turned from me to another? Is my love then in the power of fortune, or of her caprice? No, I will have it lasting as it is pure; and I will make a Goddess of her, and build a temple to her in my heart, and worship her on indestructible altars, and raise statues to her: and my homage shall be unblemished as her unrivalled symmetry of form; and when that fails, the memory of it shall survive; and my bosom shall be proof to scorn, as hers has been to pity; and I will pursue her with an unrelenting love, and sue to be her slave, and tend her steps without notice and without reward; and serve her living, and mourn for her when dead. And thus my love will have shewn itself superior to her hate; and I shall triumph and then die. This is my idea of the only true and heroic love! Such is mine for her.

* Reprinted from *Selected Essays*.

PERFECT LOVE

Perfect love has this advantage in it, that it leaves the possessor of it nothing farther to desire. There is one object (at least) in which the soul finds absolute content, for which it seeks to live, or dares to die. The heart has as it were filled up the moulds of the imagination. The truth of passion keeps pace with and outvies the extravagance of mere language. There are no words so fine, no flattery so soft, that there is not a sentiment beyond them, that it is impossible to express, at the bottom of the heart where true love is. What idle sounds the common phrases, *adorable creature, angel, divinity,* are! What a proud reflection it is to have a feeling answering to all these, rooted in the breast, unalterable, unutterable, to which all other feelings are light and vain! Perfect love reposes on the object of its choice, like the halcyon on the wave; and the air of heaven is around it.

IAN D. SUTTIE: The Biology of Love and Interest*

MODERN PSYCHOLOGY is concerned with the motives of human conduct and the sources of enjoyment, happiness and misery. This contrasts rather sharply with what is called Academic Psychology which affords us rather a *description* of the adult self-conscious mind, and gives us little assistance in predicting or influencing behaviour and still less in the understanding of mental development and its aberrations. For all *practical* purposes we are dependent upon this modern "dynamic" and genetic psychology, which, broadly speaking, we owe to the pioneer work of Freud. Indeed twenty years ago we could have said with substantial truth that the only useful psychology was Freud's. Since then, however, there have been important developments and divergences of opinion. Other schools of thought have developed their own systems with independence more or less artificial. Even within the Freudian movement itself important dissensions have recently arisen, largely through the work of the child psychologists. Many vital tenets and conceptions, confidently held ten or fifteen years ago, are now formally abandoned. Freud himself has said, "We shall have to abandon the universality of the dictum that the Oedipus Complex is the nucleus of the Neurosis." Everyday life and mental illness alike are now regarded as

---

* Reprinted from *The Origins of Love and Hate.*

an attempt to "master anxiety", and this anxiety itself is no longer considered to be merely frustrated sexual desire but is regarded as largely due to hatred and aggressive wishes. The task of healthy development is even described by Dr. Brierly as "overcoming hatred with love", and in many devious ways Psycho-analytic Theory is recognizing more clearly the social nature of man, and is no longer presenting his psychology as that of a self-contained entity independent of his fellows except in so far as his bodily appetites and gratifications demand their services. Psychoanalysis in fact is losing much that made it obnoxious to European philosophy, good sense and good feeling, but it still fails to take a wide enough view of its subject matter. This statement may seem outrageous to many who are acquainted with Psycho-analytic studies of Art, Biography, Primitive Custom, etc., but it must be remembered that psycho-analytic ideas are merely *applied* in these fields; they are *developed* and *tested* almost exclusively in the consulting room.

From the widest scientific and philosophic standpoint we must consider the human mind as the product of evolution—that is to say as having had its definite function to serve in the survival of our species and in the attainment of our present dominant position. Later we shall find it necessary to consider mind from two other points of view also—namely as the result of the child's contact with members of its own family, and as the result of its parents' social and cultural relationships. The evolution of cultures and civilizations cannot be explained in terms of the individual minds which are its members. Nor should mind be considered in isolation from its social contacts. Psychologists are prone to describe a Mind as if it were an independent self-contained but standardized entity, a number of which, grouped together in some mysterious way, constitutes a Society. Anthropologists frequently make the opposite mistake and describe social organizations and behaviour with little reference to the minds which produce and are moulded by these institutions. The separation of the science of Mind from that of Society is arbitrary and was originally dictated by practical convenience and the tastes and fancy of the student. The two scientists must be pursued in relation to each other, for mind is social and society is mental. Finally the whole study of human behaviour must be correlated with that of the social animals both on the grounds of the evolutionary relationship of species and of the common purposes in life and the different means of attaining these.

We must first, then, direct our study to the relationship between the Human Mind and those of animals which *might* be similar to those of our remote ancestors. Formerly, Comparative

Psychology was the playground of the Victorian Arm-chair Theorists who cheerfully attributed much of their own ill-understood mentality to the higher animals and even the social insects. Mind in those days was regarded as mainly concerned with the intelligent pursuit of rational purposes and/or with the instinctive performance of some biological task satisfying some need or *condition of survival*. Worse still, these old psychologists reconstructed the mind of the *infant* in terms of this false conception of *animal* mind. The child and primitive adults, they supposed, were alike and but a stage removed from our pre-human ancestors who in turn were regarded as very similar to the higher animals, although, as we shall see, the very opposite is the case. Accordingly the infant's "disposition" was regarded as a bundle of instincts some of which, like sex, remained latent till adult life (!), while others had to be disciplined and held in control by education and civilization.

If ever a doubt arose as to the forces which brought about this supposed *subjection of animal impulses*, one or other of three different explanations was offered.

(1) Religion and the Will of God was cited, though it did not well explain *animal* society or the fact that primitive peoples conform far more closely and rigorously to tribal custom and moral codes than civilized Christians do.

(2) "Reason and Utility" were popular as an alternative explanation; though here again it was difficult to understand how a species of animals like our pre-social ancestors could foresee the advantage of social co-operation without culture or experience, could negotiate such a social contract without language, and could adhere to the bargain without moral impulses.

A third type of explanation of man's social character suggested that a change had occurred in his inherited constitution; in other words a chemical change in the germ plasm. According to this "herd instinct" theory, man is different from birth from non-social animals. The theory however really explains nothing and has been utterly useless, adding nothing to our knowledge and presenting an illusory solution to the problem. Further it presents the difficulty of forcing us to suppose that the same variation has occurred in at least twenty-five different species of insect and in a very great number of species of birds and mammals; whereas man, the most social of all, has the greatest difficulty in maintaining his adjustment to social life.

It will be no matter for surprise that, with such conceptions of the infant mind and of the forces moulding upbringing, no progress was made in the understanding either of the child or of society. Such conclusions as these early speculators arrived at were wrong in every material respect and wholly useless as work-ing hypotheses for further investigation. When we actually study the facts of social life comparatively, in order to see if social differ from "solitary" animals in any respect *other than this habit*, the important fact emerges that social animals as a rule nurture their young and conversely that nurtured animals tend to be more or less social. The social disposition seems to be a modified continu-ance of the infant's need for the nurtural parent's presence (even when the material need is outgrown). Into it enters also nurtural or parental impulses, but there is no need to postulate a special social instinct.

We need in fact only suppose the child is born with a mind and instincts *adapted to infancy*; or, in other words, so disposed as to profit by parental nurture. This is not an unreasonable sup-position, but it implies the conclusion that the child mind is *less* like that of primitive animals than is the adult mind. It is less like animal mind since it is adapted to a milieu and mode of behaving vastly different from that of free-living, self-supporting animals. Instead of an armament of instincts—latent or otherwise—which would lead it to attempt on its own account things impossible to its powers or even undesirable—it is born with a simple attach-ment-to-mother who is the sole source of food and protection. Instincts of self-preservation such as would be appropriate in an animal which has to fend for itself would be positively destructive to the dependent infant, whose impulses *must* be adapted to its mode of livelihood, namely a pseudo-parasitism.

We can reject therefore once and for all the notion of the infant mind being a bundle of co-operating or competing in-stincts, and suppose instead that it is dominated from the begin-ning by the need to retain the mother—a need which, if thwarted, must produce the utmost extreme of terror and rage, since the loss of mother is, under natural conditions, but the precursor of death itself. We have now to consider whether this attachment-to-mother is merely the sum of the infantile bodily needs and satis-factions which refer to her, or whether the *need for a mother is primarily presented to the child mind as a need for company and as a discomfort in isolation*. I can see no way of settling this ques-tion conclusively, but the fact is indisputable that a need for company, moral encouragement, attention, protectiveness, leader-ship, etc., remains after all the sensory gratifications connected with the mother's body have become superfluous and have been surrendered. In my view this is a direct development of the primal attachment-to-mother, and, further, I think that play, co-operation, competition and culture-interests generally are substitutes for the mutually caressing relationship of child and mother. *By these sub-*

*stitutes we put the whole social environment in the place once
occupied by mother*—maintaining with it a mental or cultural
rapport in lieu of the bodily relationship of caresses, etc., formerly
enjoyed with the mother. A joint interest in *things* has replaced
the reciprocal interest in *persons*; friendship has developed out of
love. True, the personal love and sympathy is preserved in *friendship*; but this differs from love in so far as it comes about by the
direction of attention upon the same things (rather than upon
each other), or by the pursuit of *the same activities even if these
are not intrinsically useful* and gratifying, as is the case with much
ritual and dance, etc. The interest is intensified even if it is not
entirely created (artificial) by being *shared*; while the fact of
sharing interest deepens the appreciation of the other person's
presence even while it deprives it of sensual (or better of sensorial)
qualities.

This is my view of the process of sublimation; but it differs
very greatly from that of Freud and his enormous "team" of
expert specialists. As far as anyone can tell, Freud considers that
all the infant's desires for the mother, and the gratification it
receives from her, are of a sexual nature. Indeed it is probable
that a strict Freudian would define all pleasure or satisfaction as
"sexual". These longings and urges are called "skin", "eye",
"mouth", and other "erotisms" to indicate their essentially *sexual*
nature. At a certain age, Freud tells us, they become organized
under the supremacy of "the genital zone". That is to say they
become "sexual" in the "proper" and popular meaning of the
word. Having become sexual—according to Freud—they have also
become incestuous (directed towards other members of the same
family) and hence lead to jealousy. The Oedipus Complex is
thereby established. Undergoing repression next from fear of the
rival's displeasure and revenge, these sexual wishes (for the parent
of opposite sex) become goal-inhibited; that is to say become a
de-sexualized love. Or they may be deflected to the parent of the
same sex, thereby constituting homo-sexuality, and then sublimated as friendship. The wishes themselves may be altered, distorted or symbolized *beyond recognition* and this "displacement"
from the original biological objective is imagined as the basis of
culture-interest in the race and (presumably) of sublimation in
the individual. (Freud, *Introductory Lectures*, p. 290.)

Freud's view seems to me inadequate to explain the mechanism of the development of interest or its very early appearance in
childhood, that is to say, its appearance before the maturation,
repression and sublimation of sexuality can be imagined to have
taken place. Further it is certain that the Freudian ideas in these
matters cannot explain the constitution of society. Society in fact

never was instituted by an aggregation of independent adult individuals, nor even by the growth of a single family by polygamy, group marriage, exogamy or otherwise. Society exists already in the group of the children of the same mother and develops by the addition of others to this original love-group. Neither does culture arise by the thwarting of sex-impulse and its deflection to symbolic ends. (Freudian Sublimation.) Still less does it arise through rational co-operation in the pursuit of the material necessities of life. Necessity is not "the mother of invention"; Play is.

Play is a necessity, not merely to develop the bodily and mental faculties, but to give to the individual that reassuring contact with his fellows which he has lost when the mother's nurtural services are no longer required or offered. Conversation is mental play, but it is long before the child completely outgrows the need for bodily contact. Even many adults retain the need for caresses apart from sexual intentions and gratifications. Nevertheless cultural interests do ultimately form a powerful antidote to loneliness even where there is no participator present in person; that is to say, cultural pursuits have a social value even where "the other person" is imagined or left unspecified.

We can now clearly understand why man has become virtually the only cultural animal and hence by far the most sociable. We can also understand from the same considerations why Man has developed an aggressiveness, a competitiveness and a complex morality in which also he is unique. The neo-Freudians, approaching this point of view, no longer refer to human life as a struggle for pleasure, sense-gratification or self-expression (detensioning) as formerly. They see the master-motive of humanity as the "struggle to master anxiety" and further recognize this dread to be one of "separation". Still, they endeavour to retain a materialistic, individualistic interpretation of separation-anxiety; but, more and more, psychologists are convinced that it is really a dread of loneliness which is the *conscious expression of the human form of the instinct of self-preservation* which originally attached the infant to its mother.

It is as if the process of evolution had taken back with one hand a portion of the benefits conferred by the other. Man has to be thankful for,

(1) his prolonged and sheltered immaturity which provides leisure and a respite from the struggle for existence, in which to *experiment* with development and with behaviour;

(2) he has to thank the extreme plasticity of his instinct of self-preservation, not only for his adaptation to infancy, but for his capacity to deflect interest from the satisfaction of appetite and from the procuring of defense and the means of existence, to

activities we call cultural, which in turn have *incidentally* procured for him a tremendous mastery over all nature except his
own. Against these benefits (of the opportunity to develop and to
learn and the interest-disposition to do so) we must set the very
equivocal power to love and the need for love. While this provides the incentive and conditions for *learning* by experience and
for accumulating knowledge from generation to generation and
so of building up an immortal tradition, at the same time it drives
man so hard as to make him anxious, aggressive and inhibited.
Man is the only *anxious* animal. When nature produced him she
found herself with an "explosive" on her hands which she did not
know how to handle. For all our language, cultural achievements
and our family life, our love-need is still seeking new techniques
of social relationship. In this search for the security and satisfaction of social integration (fellowship) we are constantly driven
into false channels which we will have to study presently.

To sum up the evolutionary antecedents of man, we may
say the principal features that distinguish him from other (even
social) animals are:

(*a*) The extreme degree to which the definite, stereotyped,
specific, instincts of "self-preservation" of his pre-human ancestors are "melted down" or unfocussed into a dependent love-for-
mother, which in turn becomes need for others and finally
parental "love" and interest, social feeling, etc.

(*b*) The prolongation of the period of immaturity between organically nurtured infancy and matehood and parenthood. This, as I said, along with the social need, affords both the
opportunity and the incentive to co-operative activities not concerned with the material necessities of existence, and which may
therefore develop indefinitely on free *playful* and *experimental*
lines. The organic bodily relationships of infancy, matehood and
parenthood can be imagined as affording security and satiety to
this social need, and in them, moreover, the interest of each party
is absorbed in the other *person* rather than directed upon "things"
and *joint pursuits*. Further, adulthood has its practical, material
cares that demand close attention to business and the rigorous
adherence to well-tried customary methods of getting things done.
The practical man is notoriously stereotyped—a creature of habit
and opposed to all innovation. Practical shipbuilders told us a
century ago that iron ships could not float. We can therefore conclude that the period of *youth* is not only that of mental development in the individual, but is the reason for the development of
that distinctively human product, Culture.

(*c*) The fact (mentioned in (*a*)) that in man a collection of
instincts is replaced by a relatively aimless and plastic curiosity,

attachments and interest, is of course the reason why this play period can be turned to such account. Non-appetitive "interest" combined with need-for-company (they may even have the same origin) to apply the drive to the cultural pursuits of knowledge for its own sake, and to the development of a tradition which can be accumulated indefinitely.

These three characteristics then represent the advantages that the course of evolution has conferred upon man. Respectively they make him *social, educable* and *progressive*. At the same time evolution has left man with so little definite biological guidance in the form of instinct and with so much drive towards association and experiment that he has become *unstable and pervertible*. Other distinctively human characteristics are thus accounted for, namely man's anxiety, his arbitrary social customs and his liability to psychogenic mental disorder. Now we can see why man has been set a peculiar task which to some seems to offset his advantages—namely the task of understanding and mastering himself. This is what gives to modern psychology its peculiar importance and makes it a matter of urgency that it should be widely and critically studied by every citizen and not relegated to the specialist.

Having presented a synoptical picture of the fundamentals of human nature as I see it, it is, therefore, only fair to show how this compares with the broad outlines of the Freudian view. The difference will be found to turn largely, but by no means wholly, on the meaning attached to the word sexual.

I see in the infant's longing for the mother an expression of what in free-living animals we call the self-preservative instinct. Consistently with this, I see in anxiety and hate an expression of apprehension or discomfort at the frustration, or threatened frustration, of this all-important motive: Freud sees the infantile attachment as sexual and indeed sensual, while he regards anxiety and hate as proceeding from a separate independent instinct for destruction *which even aims to destroy its possessor*. The latter theory of Death-Instinct has produced the greatest dissensions in the ranks of Psychoanalysts themselves, and has been shown to be completely untenable and self-contradictory in many ways.[1]

Again the period between infancy and adulthood appears to me to be dominated by an almost insatiable social need, which uses the plastic energy of human interest for its satisfaction in play. Freud sees this period as one of repression of the (by now definitely *genital*) sex impulses on account of their incestuous aims. Interest for Freud is just a substitute for *or sublimation* of sexual yearnings, and friendship is sexuality which has become "goal-inhibited" by the definitely genital wish becoming repressed. He accounts for the supposed stronger cultural "drive" in the male sex on the supposition that the Oedipus Wish (sexual desire for mother) is stronger and better repressed than is the girl's corresponding desire for her father. It seems to me that man's cultural need is greater than woman's, inasmuch as he can never look forward to the bodily functions of maternity and lactation by which evolution has conferred upon women the virtual monopoly of the child. In a later chapter I will deal with the evidence of this and other jealousies which are much neglected by Freudians.

Further comparison of views must be deferred until after a consideration of the subjective aspect of the infant's mind.

NOTES

1. "The Mother: Agent or Object" (with Dr. J. I. Suttie), Pts. I and II. *Brit. Jl. of Med. Psych.*, 1932–3. And, "Metapsychology and Biology." *Jl. of Neurol. and Psychopath.*, 1924.

JOHN B. WATSON: Behaviorism

. . . THERE ARE many other types of conditioned emotional responses, such as those connected with *love*, where the mother by petting the child, rocking it, stimulating its sex organs in bathing, and the like, calls out the embrace, gurgling and crowing as an unlearned original response. Soon this response becomes conditioned. The mere sight of the mother calls out the same kind of response as actual bodily contacts. In *rage* we get a similar set of facts. The stimulus of holding the infant's moving members brings out the original unlearned response we call rage. Soon the mere sight of a nurse who handles a child badly throws the child into a fit. Thus we see how relatively simple our emotional responses are in the beginning and how terribly complicated home life soon makes them. . . .

Love: The study of this emotion in the infant is beset with a great many difficulties on the conventional side. Our observations consequently have been incidental rather than directly experimental. The stimulus to *love responses* apparently is stroking of the skin, tickling, gentle rocking, patting. The responses are especially easy to bring out by the stimulation of what, for lack of a better term, we may call the erogenous zones, such as the nipples, the lips and the sex organs. The response in an infant depends upon its state; when crying the crying will cease and a smile begin. Gurgling and cooing appear. Violent movement of arms and trunk with pronounced laughter occur in even 6–8 months old infants when tickled. It is thus seen that we used the term "love" in a much broader sense than it is popularly used. The responses we intend to mark off here are those popularly called "affectionate," "good natured," "kindly." The term "love" embraces all of these as well as the responses we see in adults between the sexes.

JOSÉ ORTEGA Y GASSET: On Love

THERE ARE situations, moments in life, in which, unawares, the human being confesses great portions of his ultimate personality, of his true nature. One of these situations is love. In their choice of lovers both the male and the female reveal their essential nature. The type of human being which we prefer reveals the contours of our heart. Love is an impulse which springs from the most profound depths of our beings, and upon reaching the visible surface of life carries with it an alluvium of shells and seaweed from the inner abyss. A skilled naturalist, by filing these materials, can reconstruct the oceanic depths from which they have been uprooted.

Someone may wish to refute this with the presumed experience that frequently a woman whom we consider to be of an eminent nature fixes her enthusiasm upon a stupid, vulgar man. But I suspect that those who make this judgment almost always suffer from an optical illusion: they speak from too great a distance, and love, being a gossamer of such delicate wool, can only be observed close up. In many instances, this enthusiasm is only apparent: in reality it does not exist. Genuine and false love comport themselves—when seen from afar—with similar movements. But let us imagine a case in which the enthusiasm is real: what ought we to think? One of two things: either that the man is not so contemptible as we think, or that the woman was not, really, of so select a temperament as we imagined.

In conversations and in university courses (when the occasion arises to define the meaning of what we call "character") I have repeatedly expounded this belief, and I have observed that it almost automatically provokes an initial reaction of protest and resistance. It is as if the idea itself contains some irritating or acid ingredient—why, as a general thesis, should we not flatter ourselves that our loves are a manifestation of our concealed beings?

—and it is that automatic resistance which is tantamount to confirmation of its truth. The individual feels that he is caught by
surprise, out in the open, because of a breach which he failed to
close. We are always annoyed when someone judges us by some
facet of our personality revealed by our negligence. They take us
unawares, and this irritates us. We should like to be judged with
forewarning and to pose, as for a photograph, with postures which
we can control at will. (A terror of what is "instantaneous.") Of
course, from the point of view of the investigator of the human
heart, the most interesting adventure is to penetrate one's fellow
man where he least expects it and to catch him *in flagranti*.

If man's will could completely supplant his spontaneity
there would be no reason for delving into the recondite recesses
of his personality. But the will can suspend the vigor of spontaneity only for a few moments at a time. In the course of a whole
life, the intervention of will over character is practically nil. Our
being tolerates a certain amount of falsification through the will:
within this measure it is legitimate to say that, rather than falsify,
it completes and perfects us. It is the finishing stroke which the
mind—intelligence and will—gives to our primogenital clay. Long
may this divine intervention of spiritual power remain in all its
glory. It is necessary to modify one's illusions about it, however,
and not believe that this marvelous influence can exceed a certain
limit. Beyond this limit real falsification begins. The fact is that
a man who goes against his instinctive inclinations during his
entire life is as a consequence instinctively inclined to falseness.
There are those who are sincerely hypocritical or naturally
affected.

The more present-day psychology penetrates the mechanism of the human being, the more evident it becomes that the
role of the will and, in general, of the mind, is not creative, but
merely corrective. The will does not incite, but rather deters this
or that involuntary impulse which animalistically rises from the
subconscious. Its intervention is, then, negative. If it sometimes
seems the contrary, it is for the following reason: it constantly
occurs that, in the intricacy of our inclinations, appetites, and
desires, one acts as a restraint upon the other. The will, when it
defers to this restraint, allows the previously shackled inclination
to flow and extend itself completely. It seems that our "wanting"
has an active power when, actually, all that it has done is open the
floodgates that restrained an already existing impulse.

The greatest error, from the Renaissance to our own day,
lay in believing—with Descartes—that we live out of our consciousness, that slight portion of our being that we see clearly and
upon which our will operates. To say that a man is rational and

free is, I think, a statement very close to being false. We actually do possess reason and freedom; but both powers form only a tenuous film which envelops our being, the interior of which is neither rational nor free. The ideas, of which reason is composed, come to us readymade from a vast, obscure source located beneath our consciousness. Likewise, desires appear upon the stage of our clear minds like actors who appear from the shadowy, mysterious wings, in their costumes, reciting their lines. And just as it would be incorrect to confuse the theater with the play performed upon its illuminated stage, so I think it is at least inaccurate to claim that man lives out of his consciousness, out of his spirit. The fact is that, except for the superficial intervention of our will, we live an irrational life, which empties into our consciousness and which originates from our hidden source, the invisible depths which really define us. For the preceding reasons, the psychologist must be transformed into a diver and submerge himself beneath the words, acts, and thoughts of his fellow being, for they are but the surface that conceals the deeps. The things which are important lie behind the things that are apparent. For the spectator it is enough to see Hamlet dragging his neurasthenia through the fictitious garden. The psychologist, however, waits for him when he leaves the stage, and, in the penumbra of the curtain and the stage riggings, he wishes to know who the *actor* is that plays Hamlet.

It is natural, then, for him to look for trap doors and crevices through which he can slip into the hidden aspect of an individual. Love is one of these trap doors. It is in vain for the lady, who is trying to appear so exquisite, to attempt to deceive us. We have seen that she once loved so-and-so. So-and-so is stupid and coarse, and worries only about the perfection of his tie and the shine of his Rolls-Royce . . .

There are innumerable objections to the idea that we reveal our most authentic inner selves by our choice of lovers. Possibly there are among them some which are strong enough to destroy the truth of the assertion. However, I think those which one usually hears are inoperative, inexact, and improvised by hasty judgment. It is forgotten that the psychology of eroticism can only proceed microscopically.

The more inward the psychological theme with which one deals, the greater will be the influence of detail. The need for love is one of the most inward. Probably, there is only one other theme more inward than love: that which may be called "metaphysical sentiment," or the essential, ultimate, and basic impression which we have of the universe. This acts as a foundation and support for our other activities, whatever they may be. No one lives without it, although its degree of clarity varies from person to person. It encompasses our primary, decisive attitude toward all of reality, the pleasure which the world and life hold for us. Our other feelings, thoughts, and desires are activated by this primary attitude and are sustained and colored by it. Of necessity, the complexion of our love affairs is one of the most telling symptoms of this primogenital sensation. By observing our neighbor in love we are able to deduce his vision or goal in life. And this is the most interesting thing to ascertain: not anecdotes about his existence, but the card upon which he stakes his life. We all realize to some extent that the kind of life to which we are committed is already determined in areas deeper than those in which our will is active. Turning experiences and arguments over and over in our minds is futile: our hearts, with the obstinacy of a star, are committed to a predetermined orbit, which will revolve by its own gravitation toward art, political ambition, sexual pleasure, or money. Many times, the surface existence of an individual rubs against the grain of his inner destiny, and surprising disguises are the result of this friction: the businessman who conceals a sensualist, or the writer whose only real ambition is political power.

The normal man "likes" almost every woman he encounters. This fact permits the nature of profound choice, which love possesses, to stand out all the more. It is necessary, however, that one not confuse liking and loving. The good-looking girl who passes by produces an excitation in the periphery of masculine sensibility, which is much more impressionable—let it be said to his credit—than that of a woman. This excitation automatically produces his first move in her direction. So automatic and mechanical is this reaction that not even the Church dares to consider it as a form of sin. In former times the Church was an excellent psychologist. It is a pity that it has fallen behind during the last two centuries. The fact is that the Church clairvoyantly recognized the innocence of "first moves." Thus it is that the male feels attracted and lured on by the woman who clicks along on high heels in front of him. Without these preliminaries there would be none of the rest—neither the good nor the bad, neither the virtue nor the vice. The expression "first move" does not say, however, all that it should. It is "first," because it emerges from the periphery where it has received the stimulus, without the person's inner self having participated in it.

The attraction which almost every woman exerts upon a man and which amounts to a sort of instinctual call to the profound core of our personality is, in fact, usually not followed by any response, or only by a negative response. The response would be positive if a feeling of involvement with what has just attracted our periphery burst forth from our utterly personal core. Such a feeling, when it arises, joins the core or axis of our souls to that external sensation; or, said in another way: we are not only attracted at our periphery, but, by ourselves, go toward that attraction, and put our whole being at its disposal. In sum: we are not only attracted, but we show interest. One is as different from the other as being dragged is different from moving voluntarily.

This interest is love. It acts upon the innumerable attractions which are experienced, eliminating most of them and focusing only upon one. Therefore, it produces selection in the extremely broad area of instinct, whose role is thereby recognized and at the same time limited. Nothing is more needed, in order to clarify the better the workings of love, than to define with some exactness the role which sexual instinct plays in them. If it is an absurdity to say that a man's or woman's true love for one another has nothing sexual about it, it is another absurdity to believe that love can be equated with sexuality. Among many characteristics which make the two different, is this fundamental one: instinct tends to amplify indefinitely the number of objects which satisfy it, whereas love tends toward exclusivism. These contrasting tendencies are clearly manifested in the fact that nothing immunizes a male against other sexual attractions so well as amorous enthusiasm for a *certain* woman.

Love, then, in its very essence, is choice. And since it springs from the personal core—the spiritual depths—the selective principles which determine it are at the same time the most mysterious preferences which form our individual character.

I have indicated that love, living on details, proceeds microscopically. Instinct, on the other hand, is macroscopic and is active in the presence of the whole. One could say that both operate from two different distances. The kind of beauty which attracts one is seldom the kind of beauty which makes one fall in love. If the indifferent man and the lover could compare what beauty means to each of them or what constitutes the charm of one and the same woman, they would be amazed at the incongruity. The indifferent man will find beauty in the broad lines of her face and figure—what, in fact, is usually called beauty. For the lover these sweeping lines—the architecture of the beloved person as seen from afar—do not exist; they have disappeared. If he is sincere, he will find beauty in separate little unrelated aspects: the color of her eyes, the way her mouth turns, the sound of her voice, etc.

When he analyzes his feeling and follows its course from within himself to his beloved, he notes that the thread of love is inextricably bound up with these little aspects, and constantly receives sustenance from them. There is no doubt that love is continually being fed; it derives nourishment from the beloved's charms, which it beholds either in reality or in imagination. It lives in the realm of ceaseless confirmation. (Love is monotonous, incessant, boring; no one would stand for anyone's repeating the most ingenious statement so many times and, yet, the lover demands unending reiteration that his beloved loves him. And vice versa: when someone is not in love, love bestowed upon him oppresses him and drives him mad by its utter plodding quality.)

It is important to emphasize the role which facial details and gesture play in love, because they are the most expressive means of revealing a person's true character, and hence are instrumental in our choice. That kind of beauty which, when viewed from a distance, reveals not only a personal character and a mode of being, but also an independent esthetic value—an objective plastic charm—is what we allude to by the noun *beauty*. It would be a mistake, I think, to believe that it is this plastic beauty which incites a man's ardor. I have always noticed that men seldom fall in love with the most plastically beautiful women. There are a few "official beauties" in every society, whom people point to with their fingers in theaters and at parties, as if they were public monuments; however, personal masculine ardor is rarely directed toward them. Such beauty is so decidedly esthetic that it converts the woman into an artistic object, and, by isolating her, places her at a distance. She is admired—a sentiment which implies distance —but she is not loved. The desire for intimacy, which acts as love's advance guard, is rendered impossible by mere admiration.

The expressive charm of a certain manner of being, and not correctness or plastic perfection, is, in my opinion, the quality which effectively inspires love. And vice versa: when an individual finds himself involved in a false instead of true love—whether for reasons of self-love, curiosity, or pigheadedness—the mute incompatibility which he feels with certain aspects of the other person is the first indication that he is not in love. On the other hand, a lack of correctness or perfection of appearance, from the point of view of pure beauty, is not an obstacle to love if it is not of grotesque proportions.

The idea of beauty, like a slab of magnificent marble, has crushed all possible refinement and vitality from the psychology of love. People think that in saying that a man has fallen in love with a woman whom he thinks good-looking they have said everything. This error has its origin in the Platonic inheritance. (No one can estimate the penetration of concepts of ancient philosophy into the ranks of western civilization. The most uneducated man uses words and concepts from Plato, Aristotle, and the Stoics.) It was Plato who made the everlasting connection between love and beauty; although by beauty he did not mean precisely physical perfection. Beauty was, rather, the name for all perfection, the form, to put it another way, in which anything worthy appeared to the Greeks. Beauty was superiority. This peculiarity in vocabulary has led subsequent thinking on eroticism astray.

Loving is something more serious and significant than being excited by the lines of a face and the color of a cheek; it is a decision on a certain type of human being, symbolically presented in the details of the face, voice and gestures.

"Love is a desire for generation and birth in beauty (*tiktein en tô kalô*)," Plato said. Generation is creation of a future. Beauty is the good life. Love implies an inner adherence to a certain type of humanity which to us seems the best and which we find preconceived, inherent in another being.

And this, my dear madame, probably sounds abstract, abstruse, and removed from concrete reality. Nevertheless, guided by this abstraction, I have just discovered in the look you gave to X what life means to you. Let's have another cocktail!

In most cases a man is in love several times during his lifetime. This fact raises a number of theoretical problems, in addition to the practical ones which the lover will have to solve on his own. For example: is this successive continuum of love affairs part of masculine nature, or is it a defect, a licentious remnant of primitivism and barbarism which still survives? Would a single love be the ideal, perfect and desirable thing? Is there any difference, in this matter, between the normal woman and the normal man?

For the moment we are going to avoid every attempt to answer such dangerous questions. Without allowing ourselves to take a stand on them, we accept, without much ado, the indisputable fact that the male is almost always pluralistic in love. Since we are discussing, however, the pure forms of this sentiment, the simultaneous existence of several love affairs is excluded and we are left with those which occur successively.

Does the fact of male pluralism present a serious objection to our thesis that choice in love reveals the essential nature of a person? Perhaps; but first it is worthwhile to remind the reader of the trivial observation that this diversity of love affairs can be of two classes. There are individuals who in the course of their lives love several women; but with clear persistency each one is a repetition of a single feminine type. Sometimes, the coincidence is so great that these women even share the same physical features. This kind of masked fidelity, in which actually a single generic woman is loved under the guise of many women, is exceedingly frequent and constitutes the most direct proof of the idea which we hold.

But in other cases, the women successively loved by a man, or the men preferred by a woman, are, in truth, very different types. If this fact is considered from the point of view of our previous idea, it would mean that the man's essential nature had changed from one time to another. Is such a change in the very roots of our being possible? The problem is of a crucial, and perhaps decisive, nature in any study of character. During the second half of the nineteenth century it was customary to think that the direction of character formation moved from the outside inwards. The experience of life, the habits they engender, the influences of the environment, the vicissitudes of fortune, physiological conditions, would, like a well, decant that essence which we call character. There would not be, then, an essential nature of an individual, there would not be any inner structure prior to and independent of the happenings of existence. We would be formed, like a snowball, from the dust on the road which we travel. According to this way of thinking, which obviates any radical nucleus in the personality, there does not exist, of course, the problem of radical changes. So-called character would be constantly modified: in the same way as it is being made it is also being unmade.

Arguments of sufficient weight, which this is not the time to enumerate, make me lean to the opposite belief: it seems more exact to say that we live from the inside outwards. The essential lines of our inner character are already formed prior to the occurrence of external contingencies, and although the events of one's existence do have some influence upon character, the influence which character exercises upon events is much greater. We are incredibly impervious to what befalls us when it is not in harmony with that innate "character" which, in the final analysis, we are. "In that case," you will say, "there is no point in even talking about fundamental character changes. What we were when we were born we will be at the hour of our death."

Indeed not. This opinion possesses enough flexibility to be adaptable to situations of every variety. It allows us to distinguish between the slight modifications which external events introduce into our mode of being and other deeper changes which are not founded on those grounds of chance, but on the very nature of character itself. I would say that character does change, if change is properly understood to be an evolution. And this evolution, like that of any organism, is induced and guided by internal reasons, inherent in the person himself and as innate as his character. The reader has most probably had betimes the impression that his neighbor's transformations are frivolous and unjustified, that they are foreign to his innermost self, but that in other instances the change possesses complete dignity and every visible sign of growth. It is like the seedling which becomes a tree; it is the naked tree before the leaves; it is the fruit which follows the foliage.

This is my answer to the former objection. There are people who do not develop, who, relatively speaking, are mentally stagnant (in general, those with little vitality: the prototype, the "good bourgeois"). They will persist in an invariable scheme of amorous choice. There are, however, individuals of a fertile nature, rich in possibilities and destinies, who patiently await their moment of blossoming. You can almost say that this is the normal case. A personality experiences in the course of its life two or three great transformations, which are like different stages of the same moral trajectory. Without losing solidarity, or even the fundamental homogeneity of yesterday's feelings, we notice one day that we have entered upon a new phase or modulation of our characters. Such modulation we call a fundamental change. It is nothing more, and nothing less.[1] Our innermost being seems, in each one of these two or three phases, to rotate a few degrees upon its axis, to shift toward another quadrant of the universe and to orient itself toward new constellations.

Is it not a meaningful coincidence that the number of true loves which the normal man usually experiences is almost always the same in number: two or three? And, moreover, that each of these loves appears chronologically localized in each of these stages in character? Therefore, I do not think it extravagant to see in the plurality of loves the sharpest confirmation of the doctrine I am suggesting. A new mode of reacting to life results in a vigorous change, and it is but a normal consequence that a different type of woman should be preferred. Our system of values has been altered to a greater or lesser degree—always in potential harmony with the old one; qualities which we previously did not value and of which we may not even have been aware, emerge into the foreground, and a new pattern of erotic selection is interposed between the man and passing woman.

Only the novel offers an adequate vehicle to illustrate this idea. I have read selections from one—which perhaps will never be published—whose theme is precisely this: the profound evolution of a masculine character seen through his loves. The author —and this is what is interesting—also insists on showing the continuity of the character in the course of his changes and the divergent contours which these changes possess, thus elucidating, with living logic, their inevitable genesis. At each step the rays of that evolving vitality are gathered and concentrated in the figure of one woman, like the images formed by light in a dense atmosphere.

NOTES

1. The most curious and extreme phenomenon is "conversion," the sudden tumultuous change which a person sometimes undergoes. Allow me to leave this difficult subject untouched for now.

C. S. LEWIS: Gift-love and Need-love*

"GOD IS LOVE," says St. John. When I first tried to write this book I thought that his maxim would provide me with a very plain highroad through the whole subject. I thought I should be able to say that human loves deserved to be called loves at all just in so far as they resembled that Love which is God. The first distinction I made was therefore between what I called Gift-love and Need-love. The typical example of Gift-love would be that love which moves a man to work and plan and save for the future well-being of his family which he will die without sharing or seeing; of the second, that which sends a lonely or frightened child to its mother's arms.

There was no doubt which was more like Love Himself. Divine Love is Gift-love. The Father gives all He is and has to the Son. The Son gives Himself back to the Father, and gives Himself to the world, and for the world to the Father, and thus gives the world (in Himself) back to the Father too.

And what, on the other hand, can be less like anything we believe of God's life than Need-love? He lacks nothing, but our Need-love, as Plato saw, is "the son of Poverty." It is the accurate reflection in consciousness of our actual nature. We are born helpless. As soon as we are fully conscious we discover loneliness. We need others physically, emotionally, intellectually; we need them if we are to know anything, even ourselves.

I was looking forward to writing some fairly easy panegyrics on the first sort of love and disparagements of the second. And much of what I was going to say still seems to me to be true. I still think that if all we mean by our love is a craving to be loved, we are in a very deplorable state. But I would not now say (with my master, MacDonald) that if we mean only this craving we are mistaking for love something that is not love at all. I can-

* Reprinted from *The Four Loves.*

not now deny the name *love* to Need-love. Every time I have tried to think the thing out along those lines I have ended in puzzles and contradictions. The reality is more complicated than I supposed.

First of all, we do violence to most languages, including our own, if we do not call Need-love "love." Of course language is not an infallible guide, but it contains, with all its defects, a good deal of stored insight and experience. If you begin by flouting it, it has a way of avenging itself later on. We had better not follow Humpty Dumpty in making words mean whatever we please.

Secondly, we must be cautious about calling Need-love "mere selfishness." *Mere* is always a dangerous word. No doubt Need-love, like all our impulses, can be selfishly indulged. A tyrannous and gluttonous demand for affection can be a horrible thing. But in ordinary life no one calls a child selfish because it turns for comfort to its mother; nor an adult who turns to his fellow "for company." Those, whether children or adults, who do so least are not usually the most selfless. Where Need-love is felt there may be reasons for denying or totally mortifying it; but not to feel it is in general the mark of the cold egoist. Since we do in reality need one another ("it is not good for man to be alone"), then the failure of this need to appear as Need-love in consciousness—in other words, the illusory feeling that it *is* good for us to be alone—is a bad spiritual symptom; just as lack of appetite is a bad medical symptom because men do really need food.

MAXIM GORKY: Her Lover

AN ACQUAINTANCE of mine once told me the following story.

When I was a student at Moscow I happened to live alongside one of those ladies whose repute is questionable. She was a Pole, and they called her Teresa. She was a tallish, powerfully-built brunette, with black, bushy eyebrows and a large coarse face as if carved out by a hatchet—the bestial gleam of her dark eyes, her thick bass voice, her cabman-like gait and her immense muscular vigour, worthy of a fishwife, inspired me with horror. I lived on the top flight and her garret was opposite to mine. I never left my door open when I knew her to be at home. But this, after all, was a very rare occurrence. Sometimes I chanced to meet her on the staircase or in the yard, and she would smile upon me with a smile which seemed to me to be sly and cynical. Occasionally, I saw her drunk, with bleary eyes, tousled hair, and a particularly hideous grin. On such occasions she would speak to me.

"How d'ye do, Mr. Student!" and her stupid laugh would still further intensify my loathing of her. I should have liked to have changed my quarters in order to have avoided such encounters and greetings; but my little chamber was a nice one, and there was such a wide view from the window, and it was always so quiet in the street below—so I endured.

And one morning I was sprawling on my couch, trying to find some sort of excuse for not attending my class, when the door opened, and the bass voice of Teresa the loathsome resounded from my threshold:

"Good health to you, Mr. Student!"

"What do you want?" I said. I saw that her face was confused and supplicatory. . . . It was a very unusual sort of face for her.

"Sir! I want to beg a favour of you. Will you grant it me?"

I lay there silent, and thought to myself:

"Gracious! . . . Courage, my boy!"

"I want to send a letter home, that's what it is," she said; her voice was beseeching, soft, timid.

"Deuce take you!" I thought; but up I jumped, sat down at my table, took a sheet of paper, and said:

"Come here, sit down, and dictate!"

She came, sat down very gingerly on a chair, and looked at me with a guilty look.

"Well, to whom do you want to write?"

"To Boleslav Kashput, at the town of Svieptziana, on the Warsaw Road. . . ."

"Well, fire away!"

"My dear Boles . . . my darling . . . my faithful lover. May the Mother of God protect thee! Thou heart of gold, why hast thou not written for such a long time to thy sorrowing little dove, Teresa?"

I very nearly burst out laughing. "A sorrowing little dove!" more than five feet high, with fists a stone and more in weight, and as black a face as if the little dove had lived all its life in a chimney, and had never once washed itself! Restraining myself somehow, I asked:

"Who is this Bolest?"

"Boles, Mr. Student," she said, as if offended with me for blundering over the name, "he is Boles—my young man."

"Young man!"

"Why are you so surprised, sir? Cannot I, a girl, have a young man?"

She? A girl? Well!

"Oh, why not?" I said. "All things are possible. And has he been your young man long?"

"Six years."

"Oh, ho!" I thought. "Well, let us write your letter. . . ."

And I tell you plainly that I would willingly have changed places with this Boles if his fair correspondent had been not Teresa but something less than she.

"I thank you most heartily, sir, for your kind services," said Teresa to me, with a curtsey. "Perhaps *I* can show *you* some service, eh?"

"No, I most humbly thank you all the same."

"Perhaps, sir, your shirts or your trousers may want a little mending?"

I felt that this mastodon in petticoats had made me grow quite red with shame, and I told her pretty sharply that I had no need whatever of her services.

She departed.

A week or two passed away. It was evening. I was sitting at my window whistling and thinking of some expedient for enabling me to get away from myself. I was bored; the weather was dirty. I didn't want to go out, and out of sheer ennui I began a course of self-analysis and reflection. This also was dull enough work, but I didn't care about doing anything else. Then the door opened. Heaven be praised! Some one came in.

"Oh, Mr. Student, you have no pressing business, I hope?"

It was Teresa. Humph!

"No. What is it?"

"I was going to ask you, sir, to write me another letter."

"Very well! To Boles, eh?"

"No, this time it is from him."

"Wha-at?"

"Stupid that I am! It is not for me, Mr. Student, I beg your pardon. It is for a friend of mine, that is to say, not a friend but an acquaintance—a man acquaintance. He has a sweetheart just like me here, Teresa. That's how it is. Will you, sir, write a letter to this Teresa?"

I looked at her—her face was troubled, her fingers were trembling. I was a bit fogged at first—and then I guessed how it was.

"Look here, my lady," I said, "there are no Boleses or Teresas at all, and you've been telling me a pack of lies. Don't you come sneaking about me any longer. I have no wish whatever to cultivate your acquaintance. Do you understand?"

And suddenly she grew strangely terrified and distraught; she began to shift from foot to foot without moving from the place, and spluttered comically, as if she wanted to say something and couldn't. I waited to see what would come of all this, and I saw and felt that, apparently, I had made a great mistake in suspecting her of wishing to draw me from the path of righteousness. It was evidently something very different.

"Mr. Student!" she began, and suddenly, waving her hand, she turned abruptly towards the door and went out. I remained with a very unpleasant feeling in my mind. I listened. Her door was flung violently to—plainly the poor wench was very angry. . . . I thought it over, and resolved to go to her, and, inviting her to come in here, write everything she wanted.

I entered her apartment. I looked round. She was sitting at the table, leaning on her elbows, with her head in her hands.

"Listen to me," I said.

Now, whenever I come to this point in my story, I always feel horribly awkward and idiotic. Well, well!

"Listen to me," I said.

She leaped from her seat, came towards me with flashing eyes, and laying her hands on my shoulders, began to whisper, or rather to hum in her peculiar bass voice:

"Look you, now! It's like this. There's no Boles at all, and there's no Teresa either. But what's that to you? Is it a hard thing for you to draw your pen over paper? Eh? Ah, and *you*, too! Still such a little fair-haired boy! There's nobody at all, neither Boles, nor Teresa, only me. There you have it, and much good may it do you!"

"Pardon me!" said I, altogether flabbergasted by such a reception, "what is it all about? There's no Boles, you say?"

"No. So it is."

"And no Teresa either?"

"And no Teresa. I'm Teresa."

I didn't understand it at all. I fixed my eyes upon her, and tried to make out which of us was taking leave of his or her senses. But she went again to the table, searched about for something, came back to me, and said in an offended tone:

"If it was so hard for you to write to Boles, look, there's your letter, take it! Others will write for me."

I looked. In her hand was my letter to Boles. Phew!

"Listen, Teresa! What is the meaning of all this? Why must you get others to write for you when I have already written it, and you haven't sent it?"

"Sent it where?"

"Why, to this—Boles."

"There's no such person."

I absolutely did not understand it. There was nothing for me but to spit and go. Then she explained.

"What is it?" she said, still offended. "There's no such person, I tell you," and she extended her arms as if she herself did not understand why there should be no such person. "But I wanted him to be. . . . Am I then not a human creature like the rest of them? Yes, yes, I know, I know, of course. . . . Yet no harm was done to any one by my writing to him that I can see. . . ."

"Pardon me—to whom?"

"To Boles, of course."

"But he doesn't exist."

"Alas! alas! But what if he doesn't? He doesn't exist, but he *might!* I write to him, and it looks as if he did exist. And Teresa—that's me, and he replies to me, and then I write to him again. . . ."

I understood at last. And I felt so sick, so miserable, so ashamed, somehow. Alongside of me, not three yards away, lived a human creature who had nobody in the world to treat her kindly, affectionately, and this human being had invented a friend for herself!

"Look, now! you wrote me a letter to Boles, and I gave it to some one else to read it to me; and when they read it to me I listened and fancied that Boles was there. And I asked you to write me a letter from Boles to Teresa—that is to me. When they write such a letter for me, and read it to me, I feel quite sure that Boles is there. And life grows easier for me in consequence."

"Deuce take you for a blockhead!" said I to myself when I heard this.

And from thenceforth, regularly, twice a week, I wrote a letter to Boles, and an answer from Boles to Teresa. I wrote those answers well. . . . She, of course, listened to them, and wept like anything, roared, I should say, with her bass voice. And in return for my thus moving her to tears by real letters from the imaginary Boles, she began to mend the holes I had in my socks, shirts, and other articles of clothing. Subsequently, about three months after this history began, they put her in prison for something or other. No doubt by this time she is dead.

My acquaintance shook the ash from his cigarette, looked pensively up at the sky, and thus concluded:

Well, well, the more a human creature has tasted of bitter things the more it hungers after the sweet things of life. And we, wrapped round in the rags of our virtues, and regarding others through the mist of our self-sufficiency, and persuaded of our universal impeccability, do not understand this.

And the whole thing turns out pretty stupidly—and very

cruelly. The fallen classes, we say. And who are the fallen classes,
I should like to know? They are, first of all, people with the same
bones, flesh, and blood and nerves as ourselves. We have been told
this day after day for ages. And we actually listen—and the devil
only knows how hideous the whole thing is. Or are we completely
depraved by the loud sermonising of humanism? In reality, we
also are fallen folks, and, so far as I can see, very deeply fallen
into the abyss of self-sufficiency and the conviction of our own
superiority. But enough of this. It is all as old as the hills—so old
that it is a shame to speak of it. Very old indeed—yes, that's what
it is!

B. Romantic Love and the Search
for the Ideal

ST. AUGUSTINE: Spiritual Eros*

AN IMPURE love inflames the mind and summons
the soul destined to perish to lust after earthly things, and to
follow what is perishable, and precipitates it into the lowest
places, and sinks it in the abyss; so holy love raiseth us to supernal
things, and inflames us to what is eternal, and excites the soul to
those things which do not pass away and die, and from the depths
of hell raiseth it to heaven. Yet all love hath a power of its own,
nor can love in the soul of the lover be idle; it must needs draw
it on. But dost thou wish to know of what sort love is? See whither
it leadeth. We do not therefore warn you to love nothing; but
that you love not the world, that you may freely love Him who
made the world. For the soul when bound by the love of the
earth, hath as it were birdlime on its wings; it cannot fly. But
when purged from the sordid affections of the world, extending
as it were its pair of wings, and freeing them from every impediment, flieth upon them, that is to say, upon the two commandments of love unto God and our neighbour. Whither will it fly,
but by rising in its flight to God? For it riseth by loving. Before
it can do this, it groaneth on earth, if it hath already in it the
desire for flight; and saith, 'who will give me wings like a dove,
and I will fly and be at rest' (Ps. liv, 7). . . . From the midst of
offences, then, from the medley of evil men, from the chaff mingled with the grain, it longeth to fly, where it may not suffer the

* Reprinted from *Enarrationes* in *Psalmos* **CXXI**, 1.

society of any wicked one, but may live in the holy company of angels, the citizens of the eternal Jerusalem.

RALPH WALDO EMERSON: Love*

EVERY PROMISE of the soul has innumerable ful-filments; each of its joys ripens into a new want. Nature, uncontainable, flowing, forelooking, in the first sentiment of kindness anticipates already a benevolence which shall lose all particular regards in its general light. The introduction to this felicity is in a private and tender relation of one to one, which is the enchantment of human life; which, like a certain divine rage and enthusiasm, seizes on man at one period and works a revolution in his mind and body; unites him to his race, pledges him to the domestic and civic relations, carries him with new sympathy into nature, enhances the power of the senses, opens the imagination, adds to his character heroic and sacred attributes, establishes marriage and gives permanence to human society.

The natural association of the sentiment of love with the heyday of the blood seems to require that in order to portray it in vivid tints, which every youth and maid should confess to be true to their throbbing experience, one must not be too old. The delicious fancies of youth reject the least savor of a mature philosophy, as chilling with age and pedantry their purple bloom. And therefore I know I incur the imputation of unnecessary hardness and stoicism from those who compose the Court and Parliament of Love. But from these formidable censors I shall appeal to my seniors. For it is to be considered that this passion of which we speak, though it begin with the young, yet forsakes not the old, or rather suffers no one who is its servant to grow old, but makes the aged participators of it not less than the tender maiden, though in a different and nobler sort. For it is a fire that kindling its first embers in the narrow nook of a private bosom, caught from a wandering spark out of another private heart, glows and enlarges until it warms and beams upon multitudes of men and women, upon the universal heart of all, and so lights up the whole world and all nature with its generous flames. It matters not therefore whether we attempt to describe the passion at twenty, thirty, or at eighty years. He who paints it at the first period will lose some of its later, he who paints it at the last, some of its earlier traits. Only it is to be hoped that by patience and the Muses' aid

* Reprinted from *Essays*.

we may attain to that inward view of the law which shall describe
a truth ever young and beautiful, so central that it shall commend
itself to the eye at whatever angle beholden.

And the first condition is that we must leave a too close and
lingering adherence to facts, and study the sentiment as it appeared in hope, and not in history. For each man sees his own life
defaced and disfigured, as the life of man is not to his imagination. Each man sees over his own experience a certain stain of
error, whilst that of other men looks fair and ideal. Let any man
go back to those delicious relations which make the beauty of his
life, which have given him sincerest instruction and nourishment,
he will shrink and moan. Alas! I know not why, but infinite com-
punctions embitter in mature life the remembrances of budding
joy, and cover every beloved name. Every thing is beautiful seen
from the point of the intellect, or as truth. But all is sour if
seen as experience. Details are melancholy; the plan is seemly
and noble. In the actual world—the painful kingdom of time and
place—dwell care and canker and fear. With thought, with the
ideal, is immortal hilarity, the rose of joy. Round it all the Muses
sing. But grief cleaves to names and persons and the partial interests of to-day and yesterday.

The strong bent of nature is seen in the proportion which
this topic of personal relations usurps in the conversation of
society. What do we wish to know of any worthy person so much
as how he has sped in the history of this sentiment? What books
in the circulating library circulate? How we glow over these novels
of passion, when the story is told with any spark of truth and
nature! And what fastens attention, in the intercourse of life, like
any passage betraying affection between two parties? Perhaps we
never saw them before and never shall meet them again. But we
see them exchange a glance or betray a deep emotion, and we are
no longer strangers. We understand them and take the warmest
interest in the development of the romance. All mankind love a
lover. The earliest demonstrations of complacency and kindness
are nature's most winning pictures. It is the dawn of civility and
grace in the coarse and rustic. The rude village boy teases the
girls about the school-house door;—but to-day he comes running
into the entry and meets one fair child disposing her satchel; he
holds her books to help her, and instantly it seems to him as if she
removed herself from him infinitely, and was a sacred precinct.
Among the throng of girls he runs rudely enough, but one alone
distances him; and these two little neighbors, that were so close
just now, have learned to respect each other's personality. Or who
can avert his eyes from the engaging, half-artful, half-artless ways
of school-girls who go into the country shops to buy a skein of silk

or a sheet of paper, and talk half an hour about nothing with the broad-faced, good-natured shop-boy. In the village they are on a perfect equality, which love delights in, and without any co-quetry the happy, affectionate nature of woman flows out in this pretty gossip. The girls may have little beauty, yet plainly do they establish between them and the good boy the most agreeable, con-fiding relations; what with their fun and their earnest, about Edgar and Jonas and Almira, and who was invited to the party, and who danced at the dancing-school, and when the singing-school would begin, and other nothings concerning which the parties cooed. By and by that boy wants a wife, and very truly and heartily will he know where to find a sincere and sweet mate, without any risk such as Milton deplores as incident to scholars and great men.

I have been told that in some public discourses of mine my reverence for the intellect has made me unjustly cold to the personal relations. But now I almost shrink at the remembrance of such disparaging words. For persons are love's world, and the coldest philosopher cannot recount the debt of the young soul wandering here in nature to the power of love, without being tempted to unsay, as treasonable to nature, aught derogatory to the social instincts. For though the celestial rapture falling out of heaven seizes only upon those of tender age, and although a beauty overpowering all analysis or comparison and putting us quite beside ourselves we can seldom see after thirty years, yet the remembrance of these visions outlasts all other remembrances, and is a wreath of flowers on the oldest brows. But here is a strange fact; it may seem to many men, in revising their experience, that they have no fairer page in their life's book than the delicious memory of some passages wherein affection contrived to give a witchcraft, surpassing the deep attraction of its own truth, to a parcel of accidental and trivial circumstances. In looking back-ward they may find that several things which were not the charm have more reality to this groping memory than the charm itself which embalmed them. But be our experience in particulars what it may, no man ever forgot the visitations of that power to his heart and brain, which created all things anew; which was the dawn in him of music, poetry and art; which made the face of nature radiant with purple light, the morning and the night varied enchantments; when a single tone of one voice could make the heart bound, and the most trivial circumstance associated with one form is put in the amber of memory; when he became all eye when one was present, and all memory when one was gone; when the youth becomes a watcher of windows and studious of a glove, a veil, a ribbon, or the wheels of a carriage; when no place is too

solitary and none too silent for him who has richer company and
sweeter conversation in his new thoughts than any old friends,
though best and purest, can give him; for the figures, the motions,
the words of the beloved object are not, like other images, written
in water, but, as Plutarch said, "enamelled in fire," and make the
study of midnight:—

> "Thou art not gone being gone, where'er thou art,
>   Thou leav'st in him thy watchful eyes, in him thy loving
>   heart."

In the noon and the afternoon of life we still throb at the recollection of days when happiness was not happy enough, but must
be drugged with the relish of pain and fear; for he touched the
secret of the matter who said of love,—

> "All other pleasures are not worth its pains:"

and when the day was not long enough, but the night too must be
consumed in keen recollections; when the head boiled all night on
the pillow with the generous deed it resolved on; when the moonlight was a pleasing fever and the stars were letters and the flowers
ciphers and the air was coined into song; when all business seemed
an impertinence, and all the men and women running to and fro
in the streets, mere pictures.

The passion rebuilds the world for the youth. It makes all
things alive and significant. Nature grows conscious. Every bird
on the boughs of the tree sings now to his heart and soul. The
notes are almost articulate. The clouds have faces as he looks on
them. The trees of the forest, the waving grass and the peeping
flowers have grown intelligent; and he almost fears to trust them
with the secret which they seem to invite. Yet nature soothes and
sympathizes. In the green solitude he finds a dearer home than
with men:—

> "Fountain-heads and pathless groves,
>   Places which pale passion loves,
>   Moonlight walks, when all the fowls
>   Are safely housed, save bats and owls,
>   A midnight bell, a passing groan,—
>   These are the sounds we feed upon."

Behold there in the wood the fine madman! He is a palace
of sweet sounds and sights; he dilates; he is twice a man; he walks
with arms akimbo; he soliloquizes; he accosts the grass and the
trees; he feels the blood of the violet, the clover and the lily in his
veins; and he talks with the brook that wets his foot.

The heats that have opened his perceptions of natural
beauty have made him love music and verse. It is a fact often

observed, that men have written good verses under the inspiration of passion who cannot write well under any other circumstances.

The like force has the passion over all his nature. It expands the sentiment; it makes the clown gentle and gives the coward heart. Into the most pitiful and abject it will infuse a heart and courage to defy the world, so only it have the countenance of the beloved object. In giving him to another it still more gives him to himself. He is a new man, with new perceptions, new and keener purposes, and a religious solemnity of character and aims. He does not longer appertain to his family and society; *he* is somewhat; *he* is a person; *he* is a soul.

And here let us examine a little nearer the nature of that influence which is thus potent over the human youth. Beauty, whose revelation to man we now celebrate, welcome as the sun wherever it pleases to shine, which pleases everybody with it and with themselves, seems sufficient to itself. The lover cannot paint his maiden to his fancy poor and solitary. Like a tree in flower, so much soft, budding, informing loveliness is society for itself; and she teaches his eye why Beauty was pictured with Loves and Graces attending her steps. Her existence makes the world rich. Though she extrudes all other persons from his attention as cheap and unworthy, she indemnifies him by carrying out her own being into somewhat impersonal, large, mundane, so that the maiden stands to him for a representative of all select things and virtues. For that reason the lover never sees personal resemblances in his mistress to her kindred or to others. His friends find in her a likeness to her mother, or her sisters, or to persons not of her blood. The lover sees no resemblance except to summer evenings and diamond mornings, to rainbows and the song of birds.

The ancients called beauty the flowering of virtue. Who can analyze the nameless charm which glances from one and another face and form? We are touched with emotions of tenderness and complacency, but we cannot find whereat this dainty emotion, this wandering gleam, points. It is destroyed for the imagination by any attempt to refer it to organization. Nor does it point to any relations of friendship or love known and described in society, but, as it seems to me, to a quite other and unattainable sphere, to relations of transcendent delicacy and sweetness, to what roses and violets hint and foreshow. We cannot approach beauty. Its nature is like opaline doves'-neck lustres, hovering and evanescent. Herein it resembles the most excellent things, which all have this rainbow character, defying all attempts at appropriation and use. What else did Jean Paul Richter signify, when he said to music, "Away! away! thou speakest to me of things which in all my endless life I have not found and shall not find." The same fluency may be observed in every work of the plastic arts. The statue is then beautiful when it begins to be incomprehensible, when it is passing out of criticism and can no longer be defined by compass and measuring-wand, but demands an active imagination to go with it and to say what it is in the act of doing. The god or hero of the sculptor is always represented in a transition *from* that which is representable to the senses, *to* that which is not. Then first it ceases to be a stone. The same remark holds of painting. And of poetry the success is not attained when it lulls and satisfies, but when it astonishes and fires us with new endeavors after the unattainable. Concerning it Landor inquires "whether it is not to be referred to some purer state of sensation and existence."

In like manner, personal beauty is then first charming and itself when it dissatisfies us with any end; when it becomes a story without an end; when it suggests gleams and visions and not earthly satisfactions; when it makes the beholder feel his unworthiness; when he cannot feel his right to it, though he were Caesar; he cannot feel more right to it than to the firmament and the splendors of a sunset.

Hence arose the saying, "If I love you, what is that to you?" We say so because we feel that what we love is not in your will, but above it. It is not you, but your radiance. It is that which you know not in yourself and can never know.

This agrees well with that high philosophy of Beauty which the ancient writers delighted in; for they said that the soul of man, embodied here on earth, went roaming up and down in quest of that other world of its own out of which it came into this, but was soon stupefied by the light of the natural sun, and unable to see any other objects than those of this world, which are but shadows of real things. Therefore the Deity sends the glory of youth before the soul, that it may avail itself of beautiful bodies as aids to its recollection of the celestial good and fair; and the man beholding such a person in the female sex runs to her and finds the highest joy in contemplating the form, movement and intelligence of this person, because it suggests to him the presence of that which indeed is within the beauty, and the cause of the beauty.

If however, from too much conversing with material objects, the soul was gross, and misplaced its satisfaction in the body, it reaped nothing but sorrow; body being unable to fulfil the promise which beauty holds out; but if, accepting the hint of these visions and suggestions which beauty makes to his mind, the soul passes through the body and falls to admire strokes of character, and the lovers contemplate one another in their discourses and their actions, then they pass to the true palace of beauty, more and more inflame their love of it, and by this love extinguishing the base affection, as the sun puts out fire by shining on the hearth, they become pure and hallowed. By conversation with that which is in itself excellent, magnanimous, lowly, and just, the lover comes to a warmer love of these nobilities, and a quicker apprehension of them. Then he passes from loving them in one to loving them in all, and so is the one beautiful soul only the door through which he enters to the society of all true and pure souls. In the particular society of his mate he attains a clearer sight of any spot, any taint which her beauty has contracted from this world, and is able to point it out, and this with mutual joy that they are now able, without offence, to indicate blemishes and hindrances in each other, and give to each all help and comfort in curing the same. And beholding in many souls the traits of the divine beauty, and separating in each soul that which is divine from the taint which it has contracted in the world, the lover ascends to the highest beauty, to the love and knowledge of the Divinity, by steps on this ladder of created souls.

Somewhat like this have the truly wise told us of love in all ages. The doctrine is not old, nor is it new. If Plato, Plutarch and Apuleius taught it, so have Petrarch, Angelo and Milton. It awaits a truer unfolding in opposition and rebuke to that subterranean prudence which presides at marriages with words that take hold of the upper world, whilst one eye is prowling in the cellar; so that its gravest discourse has a savor of hams and powdering-tubs. Worst, when this sensualism intrudes into the education of young women, and withers the hope and affection of human nature by teaching that marriage signifies nothing but a housewife's thrift, and that woman's life has no other aim.

But this dream of love, though beautiful, is only one scene in our play. In the procession of the soul from within outward, it enlarges its circles ever, like the pebble thrown into the pond, or the light proceeding from an orb. The rays of the soul alight first on things nearest, on every utensil and toy, on nurses and domestics, on the house and yard and passengers, on the circle of household acquaintance, on politics and geography and history. But things are ever grouping themselves according to higher or more interior laws. Neighborhood, size, numbers, habits, persons, lose by degrees their power over us. Cause and effect, real affinities, the longing for harmony between the soul and the circumstance, the progressive, idealizing instinct, predominate later, and the step backward from the higher to the lower relations is impossible. Thus even love, which is the deification of persons, must become more impersonal every day. Of this at first it gives no hint. Little think the youth and maiden who are glancing at each other across crowded rooms with eyes so full of mutual intelligence, of the precious fruit long hereafter to proceed from this new, quite external stimulus. The work of vegetation begins first in the irritability of the bark and leaf-buds. From exchanging glances, they advance to acts of courtesy, of gallantry, then to fiery passion, to plighting troth and marriage. Passion beholds its object as a perfect unit. The soul is wholly embodied, and the body is wholly ensouled:—

> "Her pure and eloquent blood
> Spoke in her cheeks, and so distinctly wrought,
> That one might almost say her body thought."

Romeo, if dead, should be cut up into little stars to make the heavens fine. Life, with this pair, has no other aim, asks no more, than Juliet,—than Romeo. Night, day, studies, talents, kingdoms, religion, are all contained in this form full of soul, in this soul which is all form. The lovers delight in endearments, in avowals of love, in comparisons of their regards. When alone, they solace themselves with the remembered image of the other. Does that other see the same star, the same melting cloud, read the same book, feel the same emotion, that now delights me? They try and weigh their affection, and adding up costly advantages, friends, opportunities, properties, exult in discovering that willingly, joyfully, they would give all as a ransom for the beautiful, the beloved head, not one hair of which shall be harmed. But the lot of humanity is on these children. Danger, sorrow and pain arrive to them as to all. Love prays. It makes covenants with Eternal Power in behalf of this dear mate. The union which is thus effected and which adds a new value to every atom in nature—for it transmutes every thread throughout the whole web of relation into a golden ray, and bathes the soul in a new and sweeter element—is yet a temporary state. Not always can flowers, pearls, poetry, protestations, nor even home in another heart, content the awful soul that dwells in clay. It arouses itself at last from these endearments, as toys, and puts on the harness and aspires to vast and universal aims. The soul which is in the soul of each, craving a perfect beatitude, detects incongruities, defects and disproportion in the behavior of the other. Hence arise surprise, expostulation and plain. Yet that which drew them to each other was signs of loveliness, signs of virtue; and these virtues are there, however eclipsed. They appear and reappear and continue to attract; but the regard changes, quits the sign and attaches to the substance. This repairs the wounded affection. Meantime, as life wears on, it proves a game of permutation and combination of all possible positions of the parties, to employ all the resources of each and acquaint each with the strength and weakness of the other. For it is the nature and end of this relation, that they should represent the human race to each other. All that is in the world, which is or ought to be known, is cunningly wrought into the texture of man, of woman:—

> "The person love does to us fit,
> Like manna, has the taste of all in it."

The world rolls; the circumstances vary every hour. The angels that inhabit this temple of the body appear at the windows, and the gnomes and vices also. By all the virtues they are united. If there be virtue, all the vices are known as such; they confess and flee. Their once flaming regard is sobered by time in either breast, and losing in violence what it gains in extent, it becomes a thorough good understanding. They resign each other without complaint to the good offices which man and woman are severally appointed to discharge in time, and exchange the passion which once could not lose sight of its object, for a cheerful disengaged furtherance, whether present or absent, of each other's designs. At last they discover that all which at first drew them together,—those once sacred features, that magical play of charms,—was deciduous, had a prospective end, like the scaffolding by which the house was built; and the purification of the intellect and the heart from year to year is the real marriage, foreseen and prepared from the first, and wholly above their consciousness. Looking at these aims with which two persons, a man and a woman, so variously and correlatively gifted, are shut up in one house to spend in the nuptial society forty or fifty years, I do not wonder at the emphasis with which the heart prophesies this crisis from early infancy, at the profuse beauty with which the instincts deck the nuptial bower, and nature and intellect and art emulate each other in the gifts and the melody they bring to the epithalamium.

Thus are we put in training for a love which knows not sex, nor person, nor partiality, but which seeks virtue and wisdom everywhere, to the end of increasing virtue and wisdom. We are by nature observers, and thereby learners. That is our permanent state. But we are often made to feel that our affections are but tents of a night. Though slowly and with pain, the objects of the affections change, as the objects of thought do. There are moments when the affections rule and absorb the man and make his happiness dependent on a person or persons. But in health the mind is presently seen again,—its overarching vault, bright with galaxies of immutable lights, and the warm loves and fears, that swept over us as clouds, must lose their finite character and blend with God, to attain their own perfection. But we need not fear that we can

lose any thing by the progress of the soul. The soul may be trusted
to the end. That which is so beautiful and attractive as these relations, must be succeeded and supplanted only by what is more
beautiful, and so on for ever.

STENDHAL: The Salzburg Bough*

IN THE salt mines of Hallein near Salzburg, the
miners throw into the deepest unused caverns a winter-killed tree
branch; two or three months later, when the salt particles in the
water have moistened the bough and then withdrawn leaving it to
dry, it is found covered with brilliant crystals. The smallest twigs,
those no larger than a chickadee's claw, are shimmering and dazzling, encrusted with an infinite number of small crystals. One
cannot recognize the original bough; it has become a child's pretty
plaything. When there is bright sun and perfectly dry air, the
miners of Hallein always offer these diamond boughs to travellers
preparing to go down into the mine. This descent is a unique
operation. The travellers sit astride the trunks of huge fir trees
sloping downward end to end. The fir trunks are enormous and
their use as horses for over a century has left them quite glossy. In
front of the saddle which holds you while you glide down the path
of fir trunks, a miner sits on a leather platform, sliding ahead of
you to prevent your descending too rapidly.

Before undertaking this rapid trip, the miners instruct the
ladies to cover themselves with immense bloomers of grey serge.
Bundling their dresses inside, they give a highly comical appearance. I visited these picturesque mines at Hallein in the summer
of 18— with Signora Gherardi. At first, it had only been a question of the unbearable heat we were enduring at Bologna and the
thought of the cool air at Mt. St. Gothard. In the night we crossed
the disease-ridden marshes of Mantone and lovely Lake Garda and
arrived at Riva, Bolzano and Innsbruck.

Signora Gherardi found these mountains so beautiful that,
although we set out for a short trip, we made a lengthy journey.
Following the banks of the Inn River and then of the Salza, we
came to Salzburg. The brisk air north of the Alps, compared to
the stifling heat we had left on the dusty plains of Lombardy, gave
us daily delight and persuaded us to go further. At Golling we
bought peasant clothing to wear. Frequently we had trouble in
lodging, or even feeding, such a large party; but these obstacles
and difficulties added to our pleasure.

* Translated by Ruth Parrish.

We came from Golling to Hallein, not knowing of the existence of these mines of which I was just speaking. There we found a large number of curious people in whose midst we appeared in our peasant garb with our ladies covered in the peasant cloaks they had bought. We went to the mines without the slightest intention of going into the underground pits; the thought of sliding astride a horse of wood for a trip of three quarters of a league seemed odd and we were afraid of suffocating at the bottom of this deep black hole. Signora Gherardi pondered for a moment and decided that, for her part, she was going to go down and we were free to do as we wished.

During the lengthy preparations and while we searched for dinner before being swallowed in this deep cavity, I entertained myself by observing what was passing in the mind of a handsome, blond young officer of the Bavarian Light Horse. Recently we had become acquainted with this pleasant young man who spoke French and was most helpful to us in meeting the German peasants of Hallein. The young officer was handsome but not foppish; he seemed to be highly intelligent. This was first noticed by Signora Gherardi. I observed the officer falling in love before my eyes with the charming Italian, who was delighted with the idea of going into a mine and being five hundred feet underground. Signora Gherardi was totally absorbed in the beauty of the pits, the wide galleries and the obstacles that had been overcome. She was a thousand leagues from dreaming of attracting anyone and even further from being attracted by anyone. Soon I was astonished at the strange confidence of the Bavarian officer entrusted to me without being aware of it. He was so absorbed with the heavenly countenance lighted by an angelic spirit which he found at the same table in a small mountain inn shadowed by its green-paneled windows that I noticed how often he spoke without knowing to whom or what he said. I informed Signora Gherardi who, without my words, would have missed this happening, although a young lady can never be wholly unaware of such actions. I was most amazed by the air of madness which pervaded the reflections of the officer; he was incessantly finding in this woman perfections unseen by me. What he said bore continually less resemblance to the woman he was beginning to love. I said to myself: La Ghita is surely not the cause of all the ecstasy of this poor German. For example, he began to praise Signora Gherardi's hand which had been strangely spotted with small pox when she was a child and still appeared marked and brown as a result.

How can I explain what I see, I asked myself. Where can I find a comparison to clarify my thoughts?

At that moment Signora Gherardi was playing with the

lovely diamond-covered branch which the miners had given to her. It was bright sunlight; this was the third of August and the little salt crystals glittered as brightly as diamonds in a lighted ball-room. The Bavarian officer, who had received a branch even odder and more brilliant, asked Signora Gherardi to exchange with him. She agreed; when he received her branch he pressed it to his heart with a gesture so ridiculous that all the Italians burst out laugh-ing. The embarrassed officer paid the most exaggerated and ardent compliments to Signora Gherardi. As I had taken him under my protection, I sought to justify the folly of these praises. I said to Ghita:

"The effect on this young man of the beauty of your Italian features and of your eyes which are unlike any he has seen before is exactly the same process as the crystallization working on this little branch of yoke-elm which you are holding and finding so beautiful. Stripped of its leaves by winter, it was anything but a splendid sight. The crystallization of the salt has coated the black-ened twigs of this branch with such a number of brilliant dia-monds that one can only see the original branch at very few places."

"So! what do you wish to deduce from that?" asked Signora Gherardi.

"That this branch faithfully represents La Ghita, as the imagination of this young man sees her."

"So it appears to you, sir, that the difference between the reality of me and the way this young man sees me is the same as that between this withered twig of yoke-elm and the gorgeous diamond plume which the miners gave you."

"Signora, the young officer discerned qualities in you which your old friends have never seen. For instance, we could never perceive an air of tender compassion. As the young man is Ger-man, the finest quality of a woman in his opinion, is kindness and immediately he discovers in your face a look of kindness. If he were English, he would have seen the aristocratic great-lady air of a duchess, but if he were I, he would see you as you are, since for a long while, to my sorrow, I can imagine nothing more seductive."

"Oh! I understand," said Ghita. "At the moment you begin to be absorbed in a woman, you see her not as she is, but as you would like her to be. You are comparing these lovely diamonds concealing the winter-killed branch of yoke-elm to the favorable allusions which grow from this beginning interest and which, you will note, are only visible to the young man who is falling in love."

"That is why," I replied, "the speeches of lovers seem so foolish to the wise people who are ignorant of the phenomenon of crystallization."

"Oh, you call it *crystallization*," said Ghita; "well, sir, crystallize for me."

This singular image struck the imagination of Signora Gherardi; when we arrived at the great pit of the mines, lighted by a hundred little lamps which seemed like ten thousand because of the salt crystals covering the sides, she said to the young Bavarian:

"Oh, this is so lovely. I crystallize for this pit. I feel that I am exaggerating its beauty; are you crystallizing?"

"Yes, Signora," innocently replied the young officer, delighted to have a feeling in common with the beautiful Italian lady although it gave him no understanding of what she was saying. His simple answer made us burst out laughing, because it stirred the jealousy of the dullard whom Ghita loved so that he began to be very suspicious of the Bavarian officer. He looked on the word *crystallization* with dislike.

When we left the Hallein mines, my new friend, the Bavarian officer, whose involuntary confidences were far more interesting to me than details on salt mining, learned from me that Signora's name was Ghita and that proper form in Italy was to address her as La Ghita. The excited boy ventured to call her La Ghita, and Signora Gherardi, amused by the young man's air of fearful passion and the deep irritation on another person's face, invited the officer to dinner the next day before our return to Italy. When he had gone, the irritated person demanded of her: "Explain to me, dear friend, why you are giving us the companionship of this mawkish blond with the stupefied eyes?"

"Because, sir, after ten days of travelling with me constantly, you all see me as I am and those gentle eyes you call stupefied see me as perfect. Filippo," she addressed me directly, "don't his eyes cover me with a shining crystallization; to them I am perfection; the most enjoyable part is that whatever I do, whatever stupid remarks I may make, in the eyes of the handsome German, I lose no perfection. That is comforting. For example, Annibalino, (the lover whom we find a little dull) I will wager that just now you do not find me quite perfect. You think that I am making a mistake in allowing this young man into my company. Do you know what is happening to you, my dear? For me you are no longer crystallizing."

The word *crystallization* became a frequent one with us. It so appealed to the lovely Ghita's imagination that she used it constantly.

On our return to Bologna, one could scarcely tell a story of love without her asking: "Does this incident verify or disprove such and such of our theories?" The many foolish acts by which a lover sees every perfection in the woman with whom he is falling in love we always called by the name "crystallization." The word recalled our pleasant journey. In all my life I had never felt so keenly the moving, haunting beauty of the shores of Lake Garda; we spent delightful mornings boating on the lake, despite the ever-present heat. We enjoyed unforgettable moments; it was one of the most memorable times of our youth.

One evening someone came to give us the news that the Princess Lanfranchi and the beautiful Florenza were vying for the love of a young painter Oldofredi. The poor Princess seemed to be truly in love while the young Milanese artist seemed absorbed with the charms of Florenza. We wondered: Is Oldofredi really in love with her?

But I beg the reader to believe that I am not trying to justify this kind of conversation, in which one has the impertinence to ignore the established rules of French conversation. I do not know why that evening our self-conceit insisted on trying to guess whether the Milanese artist was in love with the beautiful Florentine.

We became lost in the discussion of a great number of trivialities. When we were weary of centering our attention on the almost imperceptible shades of feeling which were yet by no means conclusive, Signora Gherardi began to tell us the little romance which she believed was passing in Oldofredi's heart. At the beginning of her story, she used the unfortunate word "crystallization"; Colonel Annibal, who had still in mind the handsome figure of the Bavarian officer, pretended not to understand and demanded of us for the hundredth time what the word "crystallization" meant.

"It is a feeling I do not have for you," Signora Gherardi answered him quickly.

After that, leaving him in his corner in a black humour, she said to us:

"I believe a man to be falling in love when I see him sad."

We objected instantly. "What, *love, that delicious feeling that begins so well . . .*"

"And which sometimes ends so badly, in ill humour and quarrels," said Signora Gherardi laughing and looking at Annibal. "I understand your objection. You men, with your less sensitive nature, see only one thing in the birth of love; one loves or one does not love. Just as ordinary people think all nightingales sing alike when we who delight in listening to them know there are more than ten different tones from one to another."

"All the same, Signora," someone said, "it seems to me that one loves or one does not love."

"Not at all, Sir; it is as if you said that a man who leaves Bologna en route to Rome has arrived at the gates of Rome when

from high in the Apennines, he can still look back to Garisenda
Tower. It is quite far from one of these cities to the other, and
when one can go a quarter or half or three fourths of this distance
without having arrived in Rome, we do not say that he is still in
Bologna."

"In this analogy," I said, "Bologna seems to represent in-
differences and Rome perfect love."

"When you are in Bologna," said Signora Gherardi, "you
are entirely indifferent, you do not dream of admiring in a special
manner the woman with whom a day later you will be madly in
love. Your imagination is even less likely to exaggerate her merits.
In a word, as we said at Hallein, crystallization has not yet begun."

At the words, Annibal rose angrily and left saying, "I will
return when you speak Italian."

Immediately we began to converse in French. Everyone was
laughing, even Signora Gherardi.

"Oh, well, there goes love," she said, and we laughed again.
"You leave Bologna, climb the Apennine Mountains, and take the
road toward Rome. . . ."

"But, Signora," someone said, "we have gone a long way
from the painter Oldofredi," which caused her to move impa-
tiently and probably put Annibal's brusque departure from her
mind.

"Do you wish to know," she said to us, "what happens
when you leave Bologna? In the first place, I believe this departure is not of volition but of necessity. I am not suggesting that it
is not accompanied by considerable pleasure. First you admire,
then you think: What joy to be loved by that charming woman!
Then hope appears; after hope (often conceived without much
basis, because one is never doubtful if he has a little warmth in
his blood), after hope, I say, you delight in exaggerating the
beauty and merits of the woman by whom you hope to be loved."

While Signora Gherardi was speaking, I took a playing
card on the back of which I drew Rome on one side, Bologna on
the other and between Bologna and Rome, the four stages which
Signora Gherardi had listed.
1. Admiration.
2. You come to the second point on the road when you think
"What joy to be loved by that charming woman!"
3. The third stage is marked by the birth of hope.
4. You arrive at the fourth when you exaggerate with delight the
beauty and merits of the woman you love. It is this which we old
experts call by the name of "crystallization," a word which puts
the Carthaginians to flight. In truth, it is difficult to understand.

Signora Gherardi went on: "During these four movements
of the mind or manners of being which Filippo has outlined, I do

not see any reason for our traveller to be sad. The fact is that one's
pleasure is vivid, that it claims all the attention the mind can
give. You are serious, but not sad; there is a great difference."

"We understand, Signora," said one of her listeners, "you
are not speaking of those commonplace people for whom all nightingales sing the same notes."

"The difference between being serious and being sad
(*l'esser serio e l'esser mesto*)," continued Signora Gherardi, "is decisive when it is a question of solving a problem such as: Does
Oldofredi love the beautiful Florenza? I believe that Oldofredi
is in love, because I have seen that after being occupied by
thoughts of La Florenza, he has become sad and not just serious.
He is sad, because this is what happened to him. After exaggerating the pleasure which he might enjoy from that nature with its
Raphaelesque features—the lovely shoulders, the beautiful arms,
in a word, the figure worthy of Canova in the beautiful Florenza,
he has probably tried to obtain confirmation of the hopes he had
conceived. Quite likely, also, La Florenza, afraid to love a stranger
who might leave Bologna at any minute and especially irritated
that he should have conceived such hopes so quickly, has destroyed
them for him most cruelly."

We had the pleasure of seeing Signora Gherardi daily. A
perfect intimacy governed our group; each understood the slightest hint. We often laughed together at jokes which had needed no
word to explain them, a glance was enough. Here, a French reader
will notice that a beautiful lady in Italy gives herself with abandon
to every bizarre idea that comes to mind. In Rome, Bologna or
Venice, a beautiful woman is an absolute queen. There is nothing
more tyrannical than her rule over her society. In Paris a beautiful woman is always concerned with public opinion and that hang-
man of reputation, ridicule. Deep in her heart lies a constant fear
of being laughed at, just as an absolute ruler hides his fear of a
Magna Charta. This is the secret fear that troubles her in the
midst of her pleasure and suddenly gives her a serious expression.
To an Italian woman the limited authority of a Parisian in her
drawing room would seem ridiculous. She is all-powerful over the
men who approach her and whose happiness, in the evening at
least, depends on her caprice. I speak of the happiness of simple
friendship. If you annoy a reigning lady in her box, you will see
annoyance in her eyes and you will do well to absent yourself for
that day.

One day when I was riding with Signora Gherardi on the
way to the Cascata del Reno, we met Oldofredi, alone, quite animated and absorbed, but not all somber. Signora Gherardi called
him and spoke with him to be better able to observe him.

"If I am not mistaken," I said to Signora Gherardi, "poor Oldofredi has completely succumbed to his passion for La Florenza. Explain, please, to me, your devoted servant, at what stage in the sickness of love do you think he has arrived?"

"I see him," said Signora Gherardi, "walking alone and saying to himself repeatedly, 'Yes, she loves me.' Then he busies himself in finding new charms in her to give himself new reason to love her so madly."

"I do not believe he can be as happy as you think. Oldofredi must often have cruel doubts: he cannot be sure of La Florenza's love; he does not know, as we do, to what little degree she considers wealth, rank and position in love affairs. Oldofredi is delightful, it is true, but he is only a poor stranger."

"Even so," said Signora Gherardi, "I would wager that when we met him just now, he felt that he had reason to hope."

"But," I said, "he had a profoundly troubled air. He must have moments of frightful misery. He must say to himself: Can it be that she loves me?"

"I avow," said Signora Gherardi, forgetting to whom she was speaking, "that when the answer one gives to oneself is satisfactory, there are moments of divine happiness and nothing in the world can compare with them. It is without doubt one of the best things in life. When, at last, the soul, weary with such violent sentiments returns to reason, that which survives after all these opposing movements is this certitude: I will find in *him* a happiness which *he alone* can give me."

Little by little I allowed my horse to withdraw from Signora Gherardi's. We finished the three miles to Bologna without saying another word, practising the virtue of discretion.

STENDHAL: Ernestine*

AN INTELLIGENT, worldly woman was maintaining one day that love is not born suddenly, as people often say. "It seems to me," she said, "that in the birth of love I can find seven entirely distinct periods." To prove this, she related the following story. We were in the country, it was pouring rain, so we were more than happy to listen.

In an entirely unformed mind, like that of a young girl living in an isolated chateau deep in the countryside, the slightest

* Translated by Ruth Parrish.

unforeseen event arouses the deepest interest. Let us suppose that she were to meet a young horseman unexpectedly in the forest near her home. It was through such a simple event that the misfortunes of Ernestine de S—— began. The house where she lived alone with her elderly uncle, the Count de S—— had been built in medieval times near the banks of the Drac, on one of the enormous rocks that determine the bending course of this torrential stream; it overlooked one of the finest views in Dauphiny. The young horseman whom she chanced to meet seemed to her to have an air of nobility. His face returned often to her thoughts, for what else had she to think about in that ancient house? She lived a life of magnificence, she directed a large number of servants, but in the twenty years since they and their master had grown old, everything was done by routine; there was no conversation except to criticize current events and to lament even the simplest changes. One spring evening as the day came to a close, Ernestine was at her window, gazing at the lake and the outlying woods; the deep beauty of the countryside moved her to a moody reverie. Suddenly she saw again the young horseman she had noticed some days earlier. Again he was standing in the woods beyond the lake holding a bouquet of flowers. He paused as if he saw her. Then she saw him kiss the flowers and with tender care place them in the hollow of an old oak tree near the lake.

What thoughts this little action brought to her mind! and how such vivid thoughts compared to the monotonous emotions that previously filled her life! A new existence began for her; did she dare to go see the flowers? Dear God! how imprudent, she thought fearfully. What if just as I came to the old oak tree, the young horseman were to emerge from the nearby thickets? How embarrassing! What would he think of me? True, this lovely tree was often her destination on her solitary walks. Often she sat on the platform made by the giant roots winding around its trunk; they formed a natural bench in the shade of its dense foliage.

That night Ernestine could scarcely sleep. At five in the morning, as soon as it was light, she climbed to the tower rooms of the house. Her eyes sought the great oak beyond the lake; as soon as she saw it, she became still and breathless. The exciting joy of passion was replacing the aimless and almost unconscious happiness of her youth.

Ten days passed, with Ernestine counting the days. Once only she saw the young horseman; he carried a bouquet of flowers to her beloved tree and placed it in the same way as the first one. The old Count de S—— thought that she was spending her days caring for a dove-cot located in the turrets of the house. As she sat at a little window with the shutter closed, she could see clearly to the tree beyond the lake. She was quite sure that the stranger could not see her, so she could think of him constantly without embarrassment. One thought continually tormented her. If he believed that she paid no attention to his flowers, he would decide that his homage, which was only simple courtesy, was unwanted, and if he were of sensitive character, he would not come again. Four days passed, but oh so slowly. On the fifth day, Ernestine, passing by chance near the old oak, could not resist the temptation to look toward the hollow where she had seen the flowers placed. She was accompanied by her governess and so was not afraid. She expected to find only a few faded flowers; to her inexpressible delight, she saw a bouquet of rare and lovely flowers, sparkling in their freshness; not even a petal of the most delicate flower was faded. All this she saw at a glance and then, keeping her governess in sight, she ran with the speed of a deer through the woods a hundred feet around the tree. She saw no one. Sure that she was unseen, she returned to the great oak and ventured to gaze with joy on the charming flowers. Heavens! there was a barely visible slip of paper fastened to the bow on the basket.

"What is it, Ernestine?" asked her governess, startled by her companion's cry of discovery.

"Nothing, dear friend," replied Ernestine. "A partridge flew up at my feet."

A fortnight earlier, Ernestine would not have thought of lying. She came nearer to the charming flowers; she bent her head and, redcheeked, she read on the little piece of paper:

"For a month I have brought flowers each morning. Will these be fortunate enough to be seen?"

The little note was fascinating. The English fashion of writing the letters was most elegant. In the four years since she had left Paris and the fashionable convent of Faubourg Saint-Germain, Ernestine had had nothing so exquisite. Blushing suddenly, she joined her governess and urged her to return to the house. To arrive there most quickly, instead of passing through the valley and circling the lake as usual, Ernestine took the path to a small bridge in a straight line with the house. Thoughtfully, she resolved never to return to that place, for suddenly she had realized that this was a love letter he had dared to write to her. "Still, it was not sealed," she said softly. From then on, her life was disturbed by her anxious concern. Could she not gaze at her beloved tree from a distance? Her sense of propriety forbade this indulgence.

"If I go to the other side of the lake, I cannot trust my resolution."

Toward eight o'clock the sound of the porter closing the

iron gate of the little bridge removed her last hope and seemed to free her mind from a heavy burden, for now she could not fail to conquer her desire, even if she were weak enough to consent to it.

The next day, nothing could cheer her from a deep depression. She was so somber and pale, that her uncle took notice, ordered the horses to be harnessed to the ancient coach, and took her for a drive in the area as far as the avenue in front of Mme. Dayssin's house. On the way home, the Count order a halt at the thicket by the lake; the coach came toward it over the grass. The count wished to revisit the huge oak which he always called Charlemagne's contemporary.

"The great emperor may have seen it while crossing our mountains to go to Lombardy to defeat King Desiderius." The thought of such a long life seemed to rejuvenate the almost eighty-year old man. Ernestine was far from following her uncle's thoughts. She was blushing deeply; she was going to be near the old oak another time, but she resolved not to look in the small hiding place. But an instinctive, almost unconscious, movement, a glance—and she saw the bouquet and turned pale. It was made of red roses shading toward darkest red. Written on the paper attached to the bouquet were the words: "I am so miserable, I must leave forever. The lady I love will not deign to accept my homage." Ernestine read them without even trying to stop herself from looking at the paper. She was so shaken that she was obliged to lean against the tree; soon she wept. That evening she said to herself: "He will go away and I will never see him again."

At noon the next day in the hot sun of August, as she was walking with her uncle under the avenue of plane trees bordering the lake, she saw on the opposite bank the young man going to the old oak. He seized his flowers, threw them into the lake and departed. Ernestine supposed that it was an angry gesture and presently she was sure of it. She was surprised that she had ever doubted his anger. It was clear that, seeing himself unwanted, he was going away; she would never see him again.

That day was an anxious one in the house, where she was the only one ever to show gaiety. Her uncle insisted that she was ill. A deep pallor and a tension in her face had replaced her usual sweet expression, which until then had only reflected the tranquillity of happy youth. That evening, at the time of their walk, Ernestine did not offer any objection to her uncle's leading her toward the thicket by the lake. She looked as they passed with heavy, tear-filled eyes, sure that the hiding place three feet from the ground would be empty; she had certainly seen him throw the bouquet into the lake. But what a surprise! there was another bouquet.

"Have pity on my wretched unhappiness and deign to take the white rose."

While she read these amazing words, her hand, almost unconsciously, removed the white rose from the middle of the bouquet.

"He is so unhappy," she told herself.

Just then her uncle called and she followed him happily. She held the white rose in her little batiste handkerchief which was so sheer that for the rest of the walk, she could see the color through the fine material. Carefully she held her handkerchief so no harm could come to the beloved rose.

As soon as they returned home, she ran up the steep stairway which led to the turret at the corner of the house. At last she dared to look freely at her cherished rose, gazing at it through happy tears. What did her tears mean? Ernestine did not know. Had she been able to divine the sentiment that caused them, she would have had the courage to sacrifice the rose that she had placed with such care in the crystal vase on her mahogany table. But if the reader has any regret for his lost youth, he will know that these tears, far from denoting sorrow, are the inseparable companions of sudden glimpses of great joy. They say, "How sweet it is to be loved." It was at a moment when the excitement of the first happiness in her life clouded her judgment that Ernestine made the mistake of taking the flower. But she was not yet able to understand and to regret her inconsistency.

For us, with fewer illusions, the third stage in the birth of love is clear: the appearance of hope. Ernestine did not know that as she gazed at the rose, she was saying in her heart, "Now I am sure he loves me."

But how can it be that Ernestine was about to fall in love? Would not this emotion break all rules of common sense? Listen! only three times had she seen the man who was causing her tears. And even then she had only seen him across the lake at a distance of five hundred paces or more. And, indeed, had she met him without his gun and his riding-jacket, she might not have recognized him. She did not know his name or his family, yet she spent her days nourishing passionate sentiments, which I will give but briefly as I have neither space nor the wish to write a novel. Her thoughts were only a variation of the idea: "How wonderful to be loved!" Or else, she pondered the other question of extreme importance: "Dare I hope to be truly loved? Perhaps it is only in jest that he says he loves me."

Although she lived in a chateau built by Lesdiguieres, and belonged to the family of one of the bravest companions of that great Constable, Ernestine never thought of one other objection: "Perhaps he is the son of a neighborhood peasant."

Why? She lived in such deep solitude. Certainly Ernestine was far from realizing the nature of the sentiments controlling her heart. If she had been able to see where they led, she might have escaped their domination. A young German, English or Italian girl would have recognized love; our wise education having taken the course of denying to maidens the existence of love, Ernestine was only slightly dismayed over what was going on in her heart; even when she thought deeply, it was of simple friendship. She took the rose, so she believed, only from fear of hurting her new friend and losing him.

"And, too," she said to herself after thinking a while, "one must not be lacking in courtesy."

Ernestine's heart was disturbed by violent emotions. For four days which seemed like four centuries to the lonely girl, an indefinable fear restrained her from leaving the house. On the fifth day her uncle, still concerned for her health, insisted that she accompany him to the woods; she came near the fatal tree, she read the little paper hidden in the bouquet.

"If you will take the pink and white camellia, I will be in the village church on Sunday."

At church Ernestine saw a man of about thirty-five dressed in very simple style. She noticed that he did not even wear a cross. He read from his prayerbook, holding it in such a way that his eyes scarcely left her. Of course, throughout the service, Ernestine was in a state of anxiety. Her prayer-book fell as she left the ancient manorial pew and she tripped in picking it up. She blushed deeply at her awkwardness.

"He will think me so clumsy that he will take no more notice of me," she said to herself.

Indeed, from the moment of this accident, she did not see the stranger any more. After entering the carriage, she paused in vain, distributing coins to the poor village lads; she could not see, among the groups of peasants chattering around the church door, the person she had been afraid to look at during Mass. She, who had formerly been the soul of honesty, pretended to have lost her handkerchief. A servant returned to the church and looked some time in the Count's pew for the handkerchief he had no chance of finding. But the delay occasioned by this ruse was useless; she did not see the horseman again.

"It is easy to see why," she told herself, "Mlle. de C——— told me that I was not pretty and that my manner was arrogant and forbidding. Besides, he could not have missed my awkward-ness; I am sure that he despises me."

These sad thoughts occupied her through two or three calls her uncle made during their return to the chateau. As soon as they reached home toward four o'clock, she ran along the row of plane trees toward the lake. The iron gate was closed on Sunday; luckily she saw a gardener whom she called to bring the boat and row her to the other shore. She reached the land near the great oak. The boat stayed near enough the bank to reassure her. The low, nearly horizontal branches of the great oak reached almost to the lake. Walking decidedly, she approached the tree, with a somber melancholy as if going to her death. She was certain she would find nothing in the hiding-place and, sure enough, there she could see only a withered flower left from an old bouquet.

"If he had been pleased with me," she said, "he would not have failed to thank me with flowers."

She was rowed back to the house, ran upstairs to her rooms and once in her turret, free from interruption, she burst into tears.

"Mlle. de C—— was right," she sobbed. "The only way to think me pretty is to be five hundred paces away. In this land of freedom where my uncle never sees anyone but peasants and priests, my manners have become awkward and even gross. Then, too, I have a forbidding and arrogant expression." She went to her mirror to look at her expression and saw blue eyes filled with tears.

"At this time," she said, "I cannot have an imperious look which makes it impossible for me to please."

The dinner bell rang and with difficulty she dried her tears. She came into the drawing room and found M. Villars, an aged botanist who spent a week of each year with Count de S——, to the annoyance of her nurse-turned-governess, who lost her place at the count's table during these visits. All went well until time for champagne. The wine-cooler was placed before Ernestine. The ice had melted, so she called a servant, saying, "Throw this water away and put ice in it quickly."

"That little imperious tone is becoming to you," laughed the great-uncle kindly.

At the word "imperious" Ernestine's eyes filled with tears so that she could not hide them. She was obliged to leave the dining room and as she closed the door, they could hear her choking sobs. The elderly gentlemen were totally at a loss.

Two days later she passed by the old oak. She went close and looked in the hiding place as if to recall the spot where she had been so happy. Great was her joy in finding two nose-gays there. She seized them with their little notes, hid them in her handkerchief and ran to the house, without wondering whether the stranger might have hidden in the woods, observing her actions, a consideration that she had never before overlooked. Breathless and unable to run further, she had to stop about half-way home. As soon as she was able to breathe again, she started running at top speed. At last, she was in her bedroom. She took the flowers from the handkerchief and without reading the notes, began to kiss the flowers rapturously, blushing when she realized what she was doing.

"Oh, I will never be imperious again," she said. "I will correct myself."

At last when she had lavished all her tenderness on the little bouquets, made of the rarest flowers, she read the notes. (A man would have done that first.) The first one, dated Sunday at five o'clock, said:

"I denied myself the pleasure of seeing you after the service. I could not be alone; I feared that everyone would see in my eyes the love with which I yearn for you."

She reread three times the words "the love with which I yearn for you" and then she went to see in her mirror if she had an imperious air; she continued: "the love with which I yearn for you. If your heart is free, I beg you to take away this note which might compromise us."

The second, dated Monday, was in pencil and rather badly written, but Ernestine had passed the point where the graceful English script of the stranger was charming to her eyes; she was concerned with more serious matters than such details.

"I came. I had been fortunate enough to hear you spoken of in my presence. They told me that you crossed the lake yesterday. I see that you did not deign to take the note which I left. That dictates my destiny. You love someone and that one is not me. It was folly for a man of my age to fall in love with a girl of yours. Farewell forever. I will not add the misery of being importunate to that of having occupied you too long with a passion that is perhaps ridiculous in your eyes."

"What a passion!" said Ernestine, raising her eyes to heaven. The moment was so sweet. This young girl of remarkable beauty and youth, cried out "He deigns to love me. Dear God, how happy I am." She fell on her knees before a charming Carlo Dolci Madonna brought back from Italy by one of her ancestors.

"Oh, yes, I will be good and virtuous," she cried with tears. "My God, grant that I may have my faults shown to me so that I may correct them, for now anything is possible."

She rose to reread the notes twenty times. The second especially left her ecstatic. Soon she became aware of a truth that had grown in her mind for some time, that she would never be attracted by a man under forty. (The stranger had spoken of his age.) She recalled that in the church, as his hair was a little sparse, he had seemed to be thirty-four or thirty-five years old. But she was not sure about this as she had been afraid to look at him. And she had been so worried! During the night Ernestine did not sleep. In her life, she had never anticipated such happiness. She rose to write in English in her Book of Hours: *I will never be imperious*. I make this vow Sept. 30, 18——.

During the night she became more and more certain of this fact: It is impossible to love a man under forty. As she contemplated the good qualities of the stranger, it struck her that in addition to the advantage of being over forty, he might well have that of poverty. He was so simply dressed at church that he was doubtless poor. She could hardly contain her joy at this discovery.

"He would never be complacent and dull like our friends, M. So-and-so and So-and-so when they came at St. Hubert's Day to honor my father by hunting his stags and at the table narrate their youthful exploits unasked. May it be so, dear God, that he is poor. In that case, nothing is lacking for my happiness." She rose a second time to light the candle in her night-light and look for an estimate of her fortune which a cousin had written down one day in her books. She found that she would have seventeen thousand francs a year if she married and later on, forty or fifty thousand. When she thought of this income, the clock struck four. She shivered. "Perhaps it is light enough for me to see my dear tree."

She opened the shutters. She could indeed see the old oak with its dense foliage, but she saw by moonlight and not by the aid of the first light of dawn which was still far off.

Dressing in the morning, she said to herself: "The friend of a man of forty should not dress like a child." So for an hour she looked through her wardrobe for a dress, hat and belt which made such an unusual outfit that when she came into the dining room, her uncle, governess and the old botanist burst out laughing.

"Come to me," said the old Count de S——, a former horseman of St. Louis, wounded at Quiberion. "Come here, Ernestine; you look as if you wanted to disguise yourself as a forty year old woman this morning." At these words she blushed and a happy youthful look came into her eyes.

"God forgive me," said the good uncle to the old botanist at the close of the meal, "it is a joke; is it not true, sir, that Ernestine has all the manners of a thirty-year old this morning? She has a positively maternal way of speaking to the servants that is charmingly ridiculous. I have laid two or three traps for her to see if I was right."

This remark redoubled Ernestine's happiness, if it is possible to use this word in speaking of a happiness already overflowing.

With difficulty she left the others after lunch. Her uncle and his botanist friend could not stop teasing her about her little old lady airs. She went to her room and looked at the oak. For the first time in twenty hours, a small cloud shaded her happiness although she was unable to account for the sudden change. The happiness she had felt since the moment when, despairing, she had found the bouquets in the tree, was dimmed by the question she asked:

"How should I behave with my friend so he will admire me? Such an intelligent man with the advantage of being forty, must be very discriminating. His regard for me will fail if I make any false steps."

As Ernestine was saying this to herself in the most suitable position for the serious meditations of a young girl, she realized with horror that she was wearing at her belt a gold hook with small chains attached, holding a thimble, a pair of scissors and a needlecase. It was a charming piece of jewelry which she had been admiring wholeheartedly the day before and which her uncle had given her for her name day less than a fortnight earlier. She looked on the jewelry with dismay and removed it hastily, remembering her maid telling her that it cost eight hundred and fifty francs at Laurencot's, the most expensive jewelers in Paris. "What would he think of me, he who has the honor of being poor, if he saw me wearing jewelry of such a ridiculous price? What could be more absurd than to advertise in this way my taste for housekeeping; for this is what I am saying with these scissors, thimble and needlecase which I always carry with me. And this good housewife never thinks that this jewel wastes each year the interest on the money it cost."

Carefully, she calculated and found that the jewel cost nearly fifty francs a year. This tidy reflection on domestic economics which Ernestine owed to the excellent education she received from an outlaw who had hidden for many years in her uncle's house—this reflection only served to postpone another problem. When she locked the extravagant jewel in her chest, she returned to the embarrassing question: how to behave so as not to lose the respect of such an intelligent man.

Ernestine's reflections (which we may recognize simply as the fifth stage in the birth of love) could lead us quite far. This girl had intelligence, sound and vivid as the mountain air. Her uncle, who had been intelligent and still was in regard to the two or three subjects that interested him, observed that she perceived spontaneously all the delineations of an idea. It was the good man's custom, when he was in a gay mood (the governess had remarked that this joke of his was a sure sign of his mood) to tease

Ernestine about what he called her military outlook. Perhaps it was this quality which later, when she went into the world and was unafraid to speak, made her play so brilliant a role. But at the time we are concerned with, Ernestine, in spite of intelligence, was mistaken entirely in her reasoning. Twenty times she hesitated about going to walk near the tree.

"A single gaucherie, showing the childishness of a very young girl, may cost me my friend's respect."

But in spite of all the subtle arguments which she used with all her mental powers, she did not yet possess the difficult art of controlling her passions by reason. The love which was transporting this girl had unknowingly clouded her reason and persuaded her, too soon for her happiness, to go to the tree. After much hesitation, she found herself there one day about one o'clock with her maid. She drew away from the servant and approached the tree, shining with delight, poor child. She seemed to float on the grass and not to walk. The old botanist who was walking with them commented on this to the maid as the girl ran away from them.

All of Ernestine's happiness was gone in a twinkling of an eye. It was not that there was no bouquet in the hollow of the tree; there was a charming fresh bouquet which gave her vivid pleasure. It had not been long since her friend stood in precisely the spot she was standing. She searched the grass to trace his footsteps; then she was charmed to find that in place of a simple piece of paper there was a letter, a long letter. She looked for the signature. She read it. The letter fell from her hands, along with the flowers. A deadly chill shook her. She had seen at the bottom of the page the name of Philip Astezan. M. Astezan was known in the house of the Count de S—— as the lover of Mme. Dayssin, a rich and elegant Parisian who scandalized the province by daring to pass four months alone in the country with a man not her husband. To increase Ernestine's sorrow, she was a widow, young, pretty and able to marry M. Astezan. All these sad facts, which were true as related, seemed much more appalling in the discourses of the gloomy people and their criticisms of the errors of youth—she heard them sometimes when they came to visit at the ancient manor of Ernestine's great-uncle. Never, in so few seconds had happiness so pure and so pristine, the first in her life, been replaced by such hopeless misery.

"Cruel man! he wanted to mock me," said Ernestine. "He wanted to give himself something to do on hunting trips, to turn the head of a young girl, perhaps in order to amuse Mme. Dayssin. And that I should dream of marrying him. What childishness! what humiliation!"

When she came to this terrible thought, Ernestine fell fainting beside the fatal tree which she had gazed on so often in the last three months. Half an hour later, the maid and the old botanist found her lying there. To sharpen her pain, when she was revived, Ernestine saw at her feet the letter from Astezan, opened so that the signature was visible. Quickly she rose and covered the letter with her foot.

She explained her accident away and unobserved, picked up the fatal letter. For a long time it was impossible to read it as her governess insisted that she sit down and would not leave her. The botanist called a peasant from the fields to bring the carriage from the house. Ernestine, to spare herself from answering questions about her accident, pretended to be unable to speak; a frightful headache served as a pretext for keeping her handkerchief to her eyes. The carriage came and feeling more like herself once she was riding in it, she succumbed to the indescribable sorrow penetrating her mind while the carriage returned to the house. Most frightful to her mind was the feeling that she ought to despise herself. The fatal letter which she could feel in her handkerchief burned her hand. Night came while they were on the way so she could open her eyes without being noticed. The view of the brilliant stars of a beautiful night in the South of France comforted her a little. Suffering all the effects of these passionate emotions, she was still prevented by her youthful innocence from understanding them. After two hours of acute mental grief Ernestine found her first moment of respite in a brave resolution: I will not read the letter of which I saw only the signature. I will burn it when I reach home.

Thus she could credit herself with having courage, for her love, although apparently defeated, had not failed to suggest to her that the letter might explain satisfactorily the relations between M. Astezan and Mme. Dayssin.

Entering her room, Ernestine threw the letter into the fire. The next morning at eight, she returned to practise her piano which she had not touched for the last two months. She took down the collection of Memoirs on the History of France, published by Petitot, and once again began making long extracts from the sanguinary Montluc. She was adroit enough to have the old botanist renew his offer to teach her Natural History. After a fortnight this good man, as simple as his plants, could not stop talking of the amazing application shown by his pupil; he was truly astonished. She herself was quite indifferent; all her thoughts led equally to despair. Her uncle was worried; Ernestine was visibly growing more ill. As she had, by chance, a cold, the good old man thought she must be suffering from consumption. Ernestine believed this, too, and owed to this idea the only endurable moments of this period. The hope that she was going to die soon made her bear life patiently. During this long month, she had no other feeling but a sorrow that was deepened by the self-contempt she felt; since she had had no experience of life, she could not comfort herself by saying that no one could have any suspicion of what had passed in her heart and that probably the cruel man who had caused it could not guess the slightest part of her love for him. In the depths of her misery, she never lost courage. It was no trouble to throw into the fire the two other letters addressed in that fine English handwriting.

She also resolved never to look at the lawn beyond the lake; in the drawing room, she never lifted her gaze to the windows opening on that side. One day, about six weeks after she learned the name of Philip Astezan, the good M. Villars, her teacher of Natural History, thought of giving a lesson on aquatic plants. He took her in the boat and had them rowed to an arm of the lake running up into the valley. As Ernestine entered the boat, a side glance cast almost without volition, assured her that there was no one near the old oak; she did notice that part of the bark of the tree was of a lighter grey than the rest. Two hours later, when she had returned from the lesson, she was startled to realize that what she had taken for an oddity of shading in the bark of the tree was the color of the hunting jacket worn by Philip Astezan and that for two hours he had been seated on the tree roots, as still as if he were dead. In making a comparison, Ernestine had used the words "as if he were dead" and it struck her that if he were dead, there would be no harm in thinking of him.

For some time, this thought gave her an excuse for surrendering herself to the dream of love which had engulfed her at the sight of her lover. This discovery was very upsetting to her. The next evening a neighborhood priest, who was calling at the house, asked Count de S—— to lend him the *Moniteur*. While the old servant went to bring the library collection of the *Moniteur* for the month, the Count said:

"But, M. le Cure, you have not been curious this year. This is the first time that you asked me for the *Moniteur*."

"M. le Comte," replied the priest, "Mme. Dayssin, my neighbor, loaned it to me while she was here, but she has been away a fortnight."

This casual remark disturbed Ernestine so much that she was afraid of being ill; she was mortified to feel her heart tremble at the priest's words.

"So this is the way I have succeeded in forgetting him!"

That evening for the first time in a long while, she began to smile.

"Even so," she thought, "he has remained in the country,

a hundred and fifty leagues from Paris and allowed Mme. Dayssin to go back alone."

His stillness on the roots of the oak came to her mind and she allowed her thoughts to dwell on this idea. For the last month, her only comfort had been the thought that she had consumption. The next day she was surprised to find herself thinking that as snow was beginning to cover the mountain peaks, it would be quite cool in the evening; she would be wise to prepare warmer clothing. Any ordinary person would not fail to take this precaution; Ernestine only thought of it after the priest had spoken.

The feast of St. Hubert was approaching and with it the occasion of the only important dinner given in the chateau during the year. Ernestine's piano was brought down to the drawing room. Opening it the next day, she found on the keys a slip of paper with these words: Do not cry out when you see me. It was so short that she read it before the handwriting of the author struck her—it was disguised. As Ernestine owed to fate, or perhaps the mountain air of the Dauphiny, a resolute character, prior to hearing the priest's words on Mme. Dayssin's departure, she would have locked herself in her room, not to be seen till after the party.

Two days later the grand annual St. Hubert's Day dinner party was held. At the table, Ernestine did the honors opposite her uncle; she was dressed with great elegance. The guest list was composed almost entirely of neighboring priests or mayors of the area with five or six local gentry, boasting of themselves and their exploits in war, the hunt, in love, and especially of the antiquity of their ancestry. They had never had the misfortune to make less of an impression on the heiress of the manor. Ernestine's deep pallor, coupled with her beautiful features, gave her an air of disdain. The fops who sought to speak with her felt cowed as soon as they began. For her part, she never thought of wasting her time on them.

The early part of the dinner passed without her noticing anything extraordinary. She was beginning to breathe calmly when, raising her eyes, she met the gaze of a mature peasant, who seemed to be the footman of a mayor from the banks of the Drac. She experienced the same odd sensation in her heart that she had felt when the priest spoke; yet she was certain of nothing. This peasant did not resemble Philip. She dared to look a second time. There was no doubt, it was he. He was disguised in a manner that made him quite ugly.

It is time to speak briefly of Philip Astezan, for he was acting like a man in love and perhaps we can find in his story the verification of the theory of seven stages of love. When he had come to the Chateau de Lafrey with Mme. Dayssin five months before, one of the priests she entertained at her house to keep up good relations with the clergy, told a witty story. Philip was surprised to hear wit in the speech of such a man and asked who had originated the story.

"The niece of Count de S———," said the priest, "a girl who will be very rich but has been given a bad education. She never passes a year without receiving a case of books from Paris. I fear she will turn out badly and may not even be able to make a good marriage. Who wants to burden himself with such a wife? etc., etc."

Philip asked questions and the priest continued to lament Ernestine's great beauty which would certainly contribute to her downfall. He described so exactly the tedium of the life at the count's chateau that Mme. Dayssin cried:

"Oh, please stop, M. le Cure, you will make me dislike your beautiful mountains."

"One cannot help loving a country for which one does good," replied the priest, "and the money Mme. has given to help us buy our third bell for the church guarantees. . . ."

Philip listened no longer, thinking of Ernestine and what must pass in the heart of a girl confined to a house that seemed boring by the standards of a country priest.

"I must amuse her," he said to himself. "I will make love to her in a romantic manner; this will give the poor girl something to think about." The next day he went hunting near the count's chateau by a little lake. He had the idea of doing honor to Ernestine with a bouquet; we already know what happened with the flowers and the notes. When he hunted by the great oak, he would place them himself; other days he sent his servant. Philip did this in kindness and never even thought of seeing Ernestine; it would have been difficult and boring to be presented at her uncle's house. When Philip saw Ernestine at the church, his first thought was that he was too old to be pleasing to a girl of eighteen or twenty. He was moved by the beauty of her features and by a certain dignified simplicity in her expression.

"There is naïveté in her character," he told himself and from then on he found her charming. When she left her prayer book fall as she left the manorial pew and stooped to pick it up with sweet gaucherie, he began to think of love, because he had hope. He remained in the church when she left; he was meditating on a subject distasteful to a man falling in love. He was thirty-five and his hair was beginning to grow sparse; according to Dr. Gall this would give him a fine forehead but it certainly added three or four years to his appearance.

"If my age has not spoiled everything at first sight," he said to himself, "she will have to doubt my feelings for her before she can forget it."

Looking from a little Gothic window opening on the square, he saw Ernestine enter the carriage; he found her figure and foot charming as she gave out alms. It seemed to him that she was looking for someone.

"Why," he wondered, "is she looking so far off while she is giving money close to the carriage. Can it be that I have piqued her curiosity?"

He saw Ernestine give an order to a footman; meanwhile he was gazing at her beauty. He saw her blush, as his eyes were near her—the carriage was less than ten paces from the Gothic window. He saw the servant re-enter the church and hunt for something in the manorial pew. While the servant was absent, he was certain that Ernestine's eyes were looking for someone over the heads of the crowd, but this might not be Philip Astezan. In this girl's eyes, he might seem fifty, sixty years old, who knows. At her age and with her fortune, was there not a suitor among the country squires? "However, I saw no one during Mass."

When the Count's carriage had gone, Astezan mounted and made a detour in the woods to avoid meeting her. Hastily he went to the grass plot and to his satisfaction, he was able to reach the oak before Ernestine had seen the bouquet and the note which he had sent that morning; he removed the bouquet, tied his horse in the wood and began to walk about. He was totally upset; he seized on the idea of hiding himself in the thickest part of the woods a hundred feet from the tree. From this lookout, which hid him from all eyes, he could see through a clearing in the woods to the oak and the lake.

Imagine his delight when a short time later he saw the little boat with Ernestine coming across the placid lake as the noonday breeze gently ruffled it. It was a moment of decision. The view of the lake and the loveliness of Ernestine, whom he had just seen in church, were graven on his heart. From that moment, Ernestine had something which set her apart from all other women in his eyes and all he needed to be madly in love with her was hope. He saw her approach the tree eagerly; he saw her sadness at not finding a bouquet. The moment was so delightful to him and so vivid that when Ernestine ran away, Philip believed he must have been mistaken in thinking he saw sadness in her glance when she did not find a bouquet in the hollow of the tree. The whole outcome of his love depended on this circumstance. He said to himself,

"She had a sad air about her when she came from the boat, even before she reached the tree."

"But," his hopes replied, "she did not look sad in church; on the contrary, she was brilliant with fresh color, beauty and youth and just a trifle nervous; a great animation showed in her face."

When Philip Astezan could see Ernestine no longer, as she had disembarked at the plane-tree walk on the other side of the lake, he left his hiding place quite another man from the one who had entered it. Returning at a gallop to the house of Mme. Dayssin, he had only two thoughts:

"Was the sadness she showed caused by not finding a bouquet in the tree? Or was it caused by wounded vanity?"

This probable supposition won out in his mind and allowed the return of rational ideas to a man of thirty-five. He became very serious. There were many people at Mme. Dayssin's house; in the course of the evening, she teased him about his grave manner and his conceit. She said that he never passed a mirror without glancing in it.

"I have a horror of this habit of worldly young men," said Mme. Dayssin. "It is a custom you did not always have; try to get rid of it, or I will punish you by having all the mirrors removed."

Philip was embarrassed; he did not know how to explain an absence he was planning. Besides it was true that he kept looking into mirrors to see if he appeared old.

The next day he resumed his position on the hillock we have mentioned, from which he had a good view of the lake; he settled himself there with a telescope and remained there till nightfall. The following day he brought a book; he could not have said what he read, but if he had not had a book, he would have wished for one. Finally, about three o'clock, to his great delight, he saw Ernestine go slowly down the plane tree walk to the lake; she came along the avenue wearing a large hat of Italian straw. She approached the fatal tree with a very dejected air. With the help of his telescope, he was positively amazed at her depressed manner. She took the two nosegays which he had put there in the morning, put them in her handkerchief and left running with the speed of lightning. This simple act conquered his heart completely. So vivid and swift was her action that it did not leave him time to see if Ernestine still had the air of sadness or whether joy was showing in her eyes. What could he think of her odd behavior? Was she about to show the flowers to her governess? In that case, Ernestine was only a child, and he was even more childish to lose his heart to a little girl.

"Fortunately," he told himself, "she does not know my

name; only I know of my folly and it is far from the first one I have forgiven myself."

Philip left his hideout, thoughtfully seeking out his horse which he had left with a peasant a half-mile away.

"I must grant that I am a great fool," he said to himself, as he left his horse in the courtyard of Mme. Dayssin's house. Entering the drawing room, his face was still, tense and frigid. He was no longer in love.

The following morning as he tied his tie, Philip felt that he looked very old. He had no desire to ride three leagues and hide out in a thicket to stare at a tree, but he did not wish to do anything else.

"This is completely ridiculous," he scolded himself.

Yes, but ridiculous to whose eyes? Besides, it never does to argue with destiny. He wrote an excellent letter, in which, like another Lindor, he declared his name and his qualities. This well-written letter, as we recall, had the misfortune of being burnt without being read by anyone. The words of the letter which our hero wrote with least thought, his name Philip Astezan, were the only ones honored by being read. In spite of his rational arguments, this reasonable man was again hidden in his usual place when his name caused such a dramatic effect; he saw Ernestine faint when she opened the letter; he was totally baffled.

A day later, he had to admit that he was in love—his own actions were proof. He returned each day to the thicket where he had felt such sweet emotion. Mme. Dayssin was planning to return to Paris so Philip had a letter written to himself and then said that he was leaving Dauphiny to spend a fortnight in Burgundy with a sick uncle. He took the stage and returned in a round-about fashion so well-planned that he missed being at the lake only one day. He settled in the wilds of Crossey, about two leagues from Count de S——'s house on the opposite side from Mme. Dayssin's chateau. From there he went daily to the lake shore. For thirty-three days he came without seeing Ernestine. She did not come to the church; Mass was said at the chateau. In disguise he went to the house and twice was happy to see Ernestine. In his eyes nothing could equal her dignified expression, at once noble and naïve. He said to himself: I could never grow weary of such a woman. To Astezan the young girl's extreme pallor and look of suffering were most touching. I could write ten volumes like Richardson, if I undertook to note all the ways in which this man, so sensible and experienced, explained Ernestine's fainting and her sadness. Finally he resolved to have an understanding with her and to enter the house to do so. Timidity (imagine being timid at age thirty-five!), timidity restrained him for a long while.

He took measures most wisely and yet, if fate had not put in the mouth of a casual visitor the announcement of Mme. Dayssin's departure, all efforts of Philip would only have succeeded in showing him Ernestine's love through her anger. Likely he would have interpreted that anger as astonishment at being loved by a man of his age. He would have considered himself rejected and in order to forget that painful sensation, he would have had recourse to the gambling halls or the stage door of the Opera and would have become more egotistical and insensitive in thinking that youth was finished for him.

A fine man, mayor of a commune in the mountain and a deer-hunting companion of Philip's, agreed to take him, in disguise as his footman, to the great dinner at the Chateau of S———. Here Ernestine recognized him.

Ernestine, feeling that she was blushing madly, had a frightening thought: he is going to think that I love him madly, without knowing it; he will consider me a child and return to Paris to rejoin Mme. Dayssin. I shall never see him again.

Such a painful idea gave her courage to rise and go to her rooms. She had been there about two minutes when she heard the door of the foyer open. Thinking it was the governess, she rose seeking a pretext for sending her away. As she walked toward the door, it opened. Philip was at her feet.

"In God's name, forgive my attempts," he begged her, "but I have been in despair for two months; will you be my wife?"

The moment was exquisite for Ernestine.

"He is asking me to marry him," she said to herself; "I need no longer fear Mme. Dayssin."

She searched her mind for a severe reply but in spite of her best efforts, she might never have found one. Her two months of despair were forgotten; she was at the peak of happiness. Fortunately, at this moment they heard the opening of the foyer door. Ernestine said to him:

"You have disgraced me."

"Admit nothing," muttered Philip and hastily slid himself between the wall and the pink and white bed. It was the governess, concerned about her pupil's health and even more troubled by the state in which she found her. This lady was slow in leaving the room. During her stay, Ernestine had time to grow accustomed to her delight; she became composed once more. When the governess had gone and Philip ventured out again, she made him an excellent reply.

Ernestine was so beautiful in his sight and her expression so severe as she began to speak to him that he became convinced that all his thoughts had been illusions and that she did not love him. His expression changed quickly and showed only despair. Ernestine, though moved to the depths of her being by his hopeless air, was able to send him away. All that she remembered of that strange encounter was that, when he begged permission to ask for her hand, she replied that business matters, as well as his affections, must be calling him to Paris. He insisted that his only business was to win Ernestine's heart, that he swore on his knees not to leave Dauphiny while she lived there and never to return to the house where he had lived before he met her.

Ernestine was overwhelmed with joy. The following day she went on foot to the old oak, well chaperoned by her governess and the old botanist. She did not fail to find a bouquet and a letter. At the end of a week she had almost decided to reply to Philip's letter, but the next week she learned that Mme. Dayssin had returned from Paris to Dauphiny. A great uncertainty replaced Ernestine's other sentiments. It was the village gossips who at this time, unintentionally, decided her future life; for she never lost an opportunity to let them gossip and finally they said that Mme. Dayssin, angry and jealous, had come to seek her former lover, Philip Astezan; he, according to rumor, had remained in the country with the plan of becoming a Carthusian monk. To prepare for the austerities of that order, he had withdrawn into solitude in Crossey, leaving Mme. Dayssin in despair.

Ernestine soon learned that Mme. Dayssin, unsuccessful in her effort to see Philip, had returned angrily to Paris.

While Ernestine was trying to confirm these sweet tidings, Philip was in despair; he loved her madly and believed that she did not love him. He crossed her path several times but was received so coldly that he thought that his ardor had offended his beloved's pride. Twice he left for Paris; twice after going twenty leagues or so, he returned to his cabin in the rocks of Crossey. After flattering himself with hope, which now he felt was without foundation, he sought to renounce love, but found that the other pleasures of life were spoiled for him.

Ernestine was more fortunate than he: she loved and was loved. Love ruled her heart which we have seen passing through the seven stages separating indifference from passion. An ordinary mind sees this as a simple change, whose nature it cannot understand.

As for Philip Astezan, to punish him for abandoning a former mistress as she approached what is called old age for women, we leave him tormented by one of the cruelest states of mind possible to a human being. He was loved by Ernestine but could not gain her hand in marriage. The next year she was married to an old Lieutenant General, a very rich man and a Knight of many Orders.

GEORGE SANTAYANA: Ideal Love*

FLUID EXISTENCES HAVE NONE BUT IDEAL GOALS.

IF MAN were a static or intelligible being, such as angels are thought to be, his life would have a single guiding interest, under which all other interests would be subsumed. His acts would explain themselves without looking beyond his given essence, and his soul would be like a musical composition, which once written out cannot grow different and once rendered can ask for nothing but, at most, to be rendered over again. In truth, however, man is an animal, a portion of the natural flux; and the consequence is that his nature has a moving centre, his functions an external reference, and his ideal a true ideality. What he strives to preserve, in preserving himself, is something which he never has been at any particular moment. He maintains his equilibrium by motion. His goal is in a sense beyond him, since it is not his experience, but a form which all experience ought to receive. The inmost texture of his being is propulsive, and there is nothing more intimately bound up with his success than mobility and devotion to transcendent aims. If there is a transitive function in knowledge and an unselfish purpose in love, that is only because, at bottom, there is a self-reproductive, flying essence in all existence.

If the equilibrium of man's being were stable he would need neither nutrition, reproduction, nor sense. As it is, sense must renew his ideas and guide his instincts otherwise than as their inner evolution would demand; and regenerative processes must strive to repair beneath the constant irreparable lapse of his substance. His business is to create and remodel those organisms in which ideals are bred. In order to have a soul to save he must perpetually form it anew; he must, so to speak, *earn his own living*. In this vital labour, we may ask, is nutrition or reproduction the deeper function? Or, to put the corresponding moral question, is the body or the state the primary good?

NUTRITION AND REPRODUCTION.

If we view the situation from the individual's side, as self-consciousness might view it, we may reply that nutrition is fundamental, for if the body were not nourished every faculty would decay. Could nutrition only succeed and keep the body young, reproduction would be unnecessary, with its poor pretence at maintaining the mobile human form in a series of examples. On

* Reprinted from *Reason in Society*.

the other hand, if we view the matter from above, as science and philosophy should, we may say that nutrition is but germination of a pervasive sort, that the body is a tabernacle in which the transmissible human spirit is carried for a while, a shell for the immortal seed that dwells in it and has created it. This seed, however, for rational estimation, is merely a means to the existence and happiness of individuals. Transpersonal and continuous in its own fluid being, the potential grows personal in its ideal fulfilments. In other words, this potentiality is material (though called sometimes an idea) and has its only value in the particular creatures it may produce.

PRIORITY OF THE LATTER.

Reproduction is accordingly primary and more completely instrumental than nutrition is, since it serves a soul as yet nonexistent, while nutrition is useful to a soul that already has some actuality. Reproduction initiates life and remains at life's core, a function without which no other, in the end, would be possible. It is more central, crucial, and representative than nutrition, which is in a way peripheral only; it is a more typical and rudimentary act, marking the ideal's first victory over the universal flux, before any higher function than reproduction itself has accrued to the animal. To nourish an existing being is to presuppose a pause in generation; the nucleus, before it dissolves into other individuals, gathers about itself, for its own glory, certain temporal and personal faculties. It lives for itself; while in procreation it signs its own death-warrant, makes its will, and institutes its heir.

LOVE CELEBRATES THE INITIAL TRIUMPH OF FORM AND IS DEEPLY IDEAL.

This situation has its counterpart in feeling. Replenishment is a sort of delayed breathing, as if the animal had to hunt for air: it necessitates more activity than it contains; it engages external senses in its service and promotes intelligence. After securing a dumb satisfaction, or even in preparing it, it leaves the habits it employed free for observation and ideal exercise. Reproduction, on the contrary, depletes; it is an expense of spirit, a drag on physical and mental life; it entangles rather than liberates; it fuses the soul again into the impersonal, blind flux. Yet, since it constitutes the primary and central triumph of life, it is in itself more ideal and generous than nutrition; it fascinates the will in an absolute fashion, and the pleasures it brings are largely spiritual. For though the instrumentalities of reproduction may seem gross and trivial from a conventional point of view, its essence is really ideal, the perfect type, indeed, of ideality, since form and an identical life are therein sustained successfully by a more rhythmical flux of matter.

It may seem fanciful, even if not unmeaning, to say that a man's soul more truly survives in his son's youth than in his own decrepitude; but this principle grows more obvious as we descend to simpler beings, in which individual life is less elaborated and has not intrenched itself in so many adventitious and somewhat permanent organs. In vegetables soul and seed go forth together and leave nothing but a husk behind. In the human individual love may seem a mere incident of youth and a sentimental madness; but that episode, if we consider the race, is indispensable to the whole drama; and if we look to the order in which ideal interests have grown up and to their superposition in moral experience, love will seem the truly primitive and initiatory passion. Consciousness, amused ordinarily by the most superficial processes, itself bears witness to the underlying claims of reproduction and is drawn by it for a moment into life's central vortex; and love, while it betrays its deep roots by the imperative force it exerts and the silence it imposes on all current passions, betrays also its ideal mission by casting an altogether novel and poetic spell over the mind.

DIFFICULTY IN DESCRIBING LOVE.

The conscious quality of this passion differs so much in various races and individuals, and at various points in the same life, that no account of it will ever satisfy everybody.[1] Poets and novelists never tire of depicting it anew; but although the experience they tell of is fresh and unparalleled in every individual, their rendering suffers, on the whole, from a great monotony. Love's gesture and symptoms are noted and unvarying; its vocabulary is poor and worn. Even a poet, therefore, can give of love but a meagre expression, while the philosopher, who renounces dramatic representation, is condemned to be avowedly inadequate. Love, to the lover, is a noble and immense inspiration; to the naturalist it is a thin veil and prelude to the self-assertion of lust. This opposition has prevented philosophers from doing justice to the subject. Two things need to be admitted by anyone who would not go wholly astray in such speculation: one, that love has an animal basis; the other, that it has an ideal object. Since these two propositions have usually been thought contradictory, no

writer has ventured to present more than half the truth, and that
half out of its true relations.

ONE-SIDED OR INVERTED THEORIES ABOUT IT.

Plato, who gave eloquent expression to the ideal burden
of the passion, and divined its political and cosmic message, passed
over its natural history with a few mythical fancies; and Schopen-
hauer, into whose system a naturalistic treatment would have fitted
so easily, allowed his metaphysics to carry him at this point into
verbal inanities; while, of course, like all profane writers on the
subject, he failed to appreciate the oracles which Plato had delivered. In popular feeling, where sentiment and observation must
both make themselves felt somehow or other, the tendency is to
imagine that love is an absolute, non-natural energy which, for
some unknown reason, or for none at all, lights upon particular
persons, and rests there eternally, as on its ultimate goal. In other
words, it makes the origin of love divine and its object natural:
which is the exact opposite of the truth. If it were once seen, however, that every ideal expresses some natural function, and that
no natural function is incapable, in its free exercise, of evolving
some ideal and finding justification, not in some collateral animal,
but in an inherent operation like life or thought, which being
transmissible in its form is also eternal, then the philosophy of
love should not prove permanently barren. For love is a brilliant
illustration of a principle everywhere discoverable: namely, that
human reason lives by turning the friction of material forces into
the light of ideal goods. There can be no philosophic interest in
disguising the animal basis of love, or in denying its spiritual sub-
limations, since all life is animal in its origin and all spiritual in
its possible fruits.

SEXUAL FUNCTIONS ITS BASIS.

Plastic matter, in transmitting its organisation, takes various courses which it is the part of natural history to describe.
Even after reproduction has become sexual, it will offer no basis
for love if it does not require a union of the two parent bodies.
Did germinal substances, unconsciously diffused, meet by chance
in the external medium and unite there, it is obvious that whatever obsessions or pleasures maturity might bring they would not
have the quality which men call love. But when an individual of
the opposite sex must be met with, recognized, and pursued, and
must prove responsive, then each is haunted by the possible other.
Each feels in a generic way the presence and attraction of his fel-

lows; he vibrates to their touch, he dreams of their image, he is restless and wistful if alone. When the vague need that solicits him is met by the presence of a possible mate it is extraordinarily kindled. Then, if it reaches fruition, it subsides immediately, and after an interval, perhaps, of stupor and vital recuperation, the animal regains his independence, his peace, and his impartial curiosity. You might think him on the way to becoming intelligent; but the renewed nutrition and cravings of the sexual machinery soon engross his attention again; all his sprightly indifference vanishes before nature's categorical imperative. That fierce and turbid pleasure, by which his obedience is rewarded, hastens his dissolution; every day the ensuing lassitude and emptiness give him a clearer premonition of death. It is not figuratively only that his soul has passed into his offspring. The vocation to produce them was a chief part of his being and when that function is sufficiently fulfilled he is superfluous in the world and becomes partly superfluous even to himself. The confines of his dream are narrowed. He moves apathetically and dies forlorn.

Some echo of the vital rhythm which pervades not merely the generations of animals, but the seasons and the stars, emerges sometimes in consciousness; or reaching the tropics in the mortal ecliptic, which the human individual may touch many times without much change in his outer fortunes, the soul may occasionally divine that it is passing through a supreme crisis. Passion, when vehement, may bring atavistic sentiments. When love is absolute it feels a profound impulse to welcome death, and even, by a transcendental confusion, to invoke the end of the universe.[2] The human soul reverts at such a moment to what an ephemeral insect might feel, buzzing till it finds its mate in the noon. Its whole destiny was wooing, and, that mission accomplished, it sings its *Nunc dimittis*, renouncing heartily all irrelevant things, now that the one fated and all-satisfying good has been achieved. Where parental instincts exist also, nature soon shifts her loom: a milder impulse succeeds, and a satisfaction of a gentler sort follows in the birth of children. The transcendental illusion is here corrected, and it is seen that the extinction the lovers had accepted needed not to be complete. The death they welcomed was not without its little resurrection. The feeble worm they had generated bore their immortality within it.

The varieties of sexual economy are many and to each may correspond, for all we know, a special sentiment. Sometimes the union established is intermittent; sometimes it crowns the end of life and dissolves it altogether; sometimes it remains, while it lasts, monogamous; sometimes the sexual and social alertness is constant in the male, only periodic in the female. Sometimes the group established for procreation endures throughout the seasons, and from year to year; sometimes the males herd together, as if normally they preferred their own society, until the time of rut comes, when war arises between them for the possession of what they have just discovered to be the fair.

STRUCTURE THE GROUND OF FACULTY AND FACULTY OF DUTY.

A naturalist not ashamed to indulge his poetic imagination might easily paint for us the drama of these diverse loves. It suffices for our purpose to observe that the varying passions and duties which life can contain depend upon the organic functions of the animal. A fish incapable of coition, absolved from all care for its young, which it never sees or never distinguishes from the casual swimmers darting across its path, such a fish, being without social faculties or calls to co-operation, cannot have the instincts, perceptions, or emotions which belong to social beings. A male of some higher species that feels only once a year the sudden solicitations of love cannot be sentimental in all the four seasons: his headlong passion, exhausted upon its present object and dismissed at once without remainder, leaves his senses perfectly free and colourless to scrutinise his residual world. Whatever further fears or desires may haunt him will have nothing mystical or sentimental about them. He will be a man of business all the year round, and a lover only on May-day. A female that does not suffice for the rearing of her young will expect and normally receive her mate's aid long after the pleasures of love are forgotten by him. Disinterested fidelity on his part will then be her right and his duty. But a female that, once pregnant, needs, like the hen, no further co-operation on the male's part will turn from him at once with absolute indifference to brood perpetually on her eggs, undisturbed by the least sense of solitude or jealousy. And the chicks that at first follow her and find shelter under her wings will soon be forgotten also and relegated to the mechanical landscape. There is no pain in the timely snapping of the dearest bonds where society has not become a permanent organism, and perpetual friendship is not one of its possible modes.

Transcendent and ideal passions may well judge themselves to have an incomparable dignity. Yet that dignity is hardly more than what every passion, were it articulate, would assign to itself and to its objects. The dumbness of a passion may accordingly, from one point of view, be called the index of its baseness; for if it cannot ally itself with ideas its affinities can hardly lie in the rational mind nor its advocates be among the poets. But if we listen to the master-passion itself rather than to the loquacious arts it may have enlisted in its service, we shall understand that it is not self-condemned because it is silent, nor an anomaly in nature because inharmonious with human life. The fish's heartlessness is his virtue; the male bee's lasciviousness is his vocation; and if these functions were retrenched or encumbered in order to assimilate them to human excellence they would be merely dislocated. We should not produce virtue where there was vice, but defeat a possible arrangement which would have had its own vitality and order.

GLORY OF ANIMAL LOVE.

Animal love is a marvellous force; and while it issues in acts that may be followed by a revulsion of feeling, it yet deserves a more sympathetic treatment than art and morals have known how to accord it. Erotic poets, to hide their want of ability to make the dumb passion speak, have played feebly with veiled insinuations and comic effects; while more serious sonneteers have harped exclusively on secondary and somewhat literary emotions, abstractly conjugating the verb to love. Lucretius, in spite of his didactic turns, has been on this subject, too, the most ingenuous and magnificent of poets, although he chose to confine his description to the external history of sexual desire. It is a pity that he did not turn, with his sublime sincerity, to the inner side of it also, and write the drama of the awakened senses, the poignant suasion of beauty, when it clouds the brain, and makes the conventional earth, seen through that bright haze, seem a sorry fable. Western poets should not have despised what the Orientals, in their fugitive stanzas, seem often to have sung most exquisitely: the joy of gazing on the beloved, of following or being followed, of tacit understandings and avowals, of flight together into some solitude to people it with those ineffable confidences which so naturally follow the outward proofs of love. All this makes the brightest page of many a life, the only bright page in the thin biography of many a human animal; while if the beasts could speak they would give us, no doubt, endless versions of the only joy in which, as we may fancy, the blood of the universe flows consciously through their hearts.

The darkness which conventionally covers this passion is one of the saddest consequences of Adam's fall. It was a terrible misfortune in man's development that he should not have been able to acquire the higher functions without deranging the lower. Why should the depths of his being be thus polluted and the most delightful of nature's mysteries be an occasion not for communion with her, as it should have remained, but for depravity and sorrow?

This question, asked in moral perplexity, admits of a scientific answer. Man, in becoming more complex, becomes less stably organised. His sexual instinct, instead of being intermittent, but violent and boldly declared, becomes practically constant, but is entangled in many cross-currents of desire, in many other equally imperfect adaptations of structure to various ends. Indulgence in any impulse can then easily become excessive and thwart the rest; for it may be aroused artificially and maintained from without, so that in turn it disturbs its neighbours. Sometimes the sexual instinct may be stimulated out of season by example, by a too wakeful fancy, by language, by pride—for all these forces are now working in the same field and intermingling their suggestions. At the same time the same instinct may derange others, and make them fail at their proper and pressing occasions.

MORAL CENSURE PROVOKED.

In consequence of such derangements, reflection and public opinion will come to condemn what in itself was perfectly innocent. The corruption of a given instinct by others and of others by it, becomes the ground for long attempts to suppress or enslave it. With the haste and formalism natural to language and to law, external and arbitrary limits are set to its operation. As no inward adjustment can possibly correspond to these conventional barriers and compartments of life, a war between nature and morality breaks out both in society and in each particular bosom—a war in which every victory is a sorrow and every defeat a dishonour. As one instinct after another becomes furious or disorganised, cowardly or criminal, under these artificial restrictions, the public and private conscience turns against it all its forces, necessarily without much nice discrimination; the frank passions of youth are met with a grimace of horror on all sides, with *rumores senum severiorum*, with an insistence on reticence and hypocrisy. Such suppression is favourable to corruption: the fancy with a sort of idiotic ingenuity comes to supply the place of experience; and nature is rendered vicious and overlaid with pruriency, artifice, and the love of novelty. Hereupon the authorities that rule in such matters naturally redouble their vigilance and exaggerate their reasonable censure: chastity begins to seem essentially holy and perpetual virginity ends by becoming an absolute ideal. Thus the disorder in man's life and disposition, when grown intolerable, leads him to condemn the very elements out of which order might have been constituted, and to mistake his total confusion for his total depravity.

THE HEART ALIENATED FROM THE WORLD.

Banished from the open day, covered with mockery, and publicly ignored, this necessary pleasure flourishes none the less in dark places and in the secret soul. Its familiar presence there, its intimate habitation in what is most oneself, helps to cut the world in two and to separate the inner from the outer life. In that mysticism which cannot disguise its erotic affinities this disruption reaches an absolute and theoretic form; but in many a youth little suspected of mysticism it produces estrangement from the conventional moralising world, which he instinctively regards as artificial and alien. It prepares him for excursions into the private fairy-land in which unthought-of joys will blossom amid friendlier magic forces. The truly good then seems to be the fantastic, the sensuous, the prodigally unreal. He gladly forgets the dreary world he lives in to listen for a thousand and one nights to his dreams.

CHILDISH IDEALS.

This is the region where those who have no conception of the Life of Reason place the ideal; and an ideal is indeed there but the ideal of a single and inordinate impulse. A rational mind, on the contrary, moves by preference in the real world, cultivating all human interests in due proportion. The love-sick and luxurious dream-land dear to irrational poets is a distorted image of the ideal world; but this distortion has still an ideal motive, since it is made to satisfy the cravings of a forgotten part of the soul and to make a home for those elements in human nature which have been denied overt existence. If the ideal is meantime so sadly caricatured, the fault lies with the circumstances of life that have not allowed the sane will adequate exercise. Lack of strength and of opportunity makes it impossible for man to preserve all his interests in a just harmony; and his conscious ideal, springing up as it too often does in protest against suffering and tyranny, has not scope and range enough to include the actual opportunities for action. Nature herself, by making a slave of the body, has thus made a tyrant of the soul.

THEIR LIGHT ALL FOCUSSED ON THE OBJECT OF LOVE.

Fairy-land and a mystical heaven contain many other factors besides that furnished by unsatisfied and objectless love. All
sensuous and verbal images may breed after their own kind in an
empty brain; but these fantasies are often supported and directed
by sexual longings and vaguely luxurious thoughts. An Oriental
Paradise, with its delicate but mindless aestheticism, is above
everything a garden for love. To brood on such an Elysium is a
likely prelude and fertile preparation for romantic passion. When
the passion takes form it calls fancy back from its loose reveries
and fixes it upon a single object. Then the ideal seems at last to
have been brought down to earth. Its embodiment has been discovered amongst the children of men. Imagination narrows her
range. Instead of all sorts of flatteries to sense and improbable
delicious adventures, the lover imagines but a single joy: to be
master of his love in body and soul. Jealousy pursues him. Even
if he dreads no physical betrayal, he suffers from terror and
morbid sensitiveness at every hint of mental estrangement.

This attachment is often the more absorbing the more un-
accountable it seems; and as in hypnotism the subject is dead to
all influences but that of the operator, so in love the heart sur-
renders itself entirely to the one being that has known how to
touch it. That being is not selected; it is recognised and obeyed.
Pre-arranged reactions in the system respond to whatever stimulus, at a propitious moment, happens to break through and arouse
them pervasively.

THREE ENVIRONMENTS FOR LOVE.

Nature has opened various avenues to that passion in
whose successful operation she has so much at stake. Sometimes
the magic influence asserts itself suddenly, sometimes gently and
unawares. One approach, which in poetry has usurped more than
its share of attention, is through beauty; another, less glorious,
but often more efficacious, through surprised sense and premoni-
tions of pleasure; a third through social sympathy and moral
affinities. Contemplation, sense, and association are none of them
the essence nor even the seed of love; but any of them may be its
soil and supply it with a propitious background. It would be mere
sophistry to pretend, for instance, that love is or should be nothing
but a moral bond, the sympathy of two kindred spirits or the
union of two lives. For such an effort no passion would be
needed, as none is needed to perceive beauty or to feel pleasure.

What Aristotle calls friendships of utility, pleasure, or virtue, all resting on common interests of some impersonal sort, are far from possessing the quality of love, its thrill, flutter, and absolute sway over happiness and misery. But it may well fall to such influences to awaken or feed the passion where it actually arises. Whatever circumstances pave the way, love does not itself appear until a sexual affinity is declared. When a woman, for instance, contemplating marriage, asks herself whether she really loves her suitor or merely accepts him, the test is the possibility of awakening a sexual affinity. For this reason women of the world often love their husbands more truly than they did their lovers, because marriage has evoked an elementary feeling which before lay smothered under a heap of coquetries, vanities, and conventions.

SUBJECTIVITY OF THE PASSION.

Man, on the contrary, is polygamous by instinct, although often kept faithful by habit no less than by duty. If his fancy is left free, it is apt to wander. We observe this in romantic passion no less than in a life of mere gallantry and pleasure. Sentimental illusions may become a habit, and the shorter the dream is the more often it is repeated, so that any susceptible poet may find that he, like Alfred de Musset, "must love incessantly, who once has loved." Love is indeed much less exacting than it thinks itself. Nine-tenths of its cause are in the lover, for one-tenth that may be in the object. Were the latter not accidentally at hand, an almost identical passion would probably have been felt for someone else; for although with acquaintance the quality of an attachment naturally adapts itself to the person loved, and makes that person its standard and ideal, the first assault and mysterious glow of the passion is much the same for every object. What really affects the character of love is the lover's temperament, age, and experience. The objects that appeal to each man reveal his nature; but those unparalleled virtues and that unique divinity which the lover discovers there are reflections of his own adoration, things that ecstasy is very cunning in. He loves what he imagines and worships what he creates.

MACHINERY REGULATING CHOICE.

Those who do not consider these matters so curiously may feel that to refer love in this way chiefly to inner processes is at once ignominious and fantastic. But nothing could be more natural; the soul accurately renders, in this experience, what is going

on in the body and in the race. Nature had a problem to solve
in sexual reproduction which would have daunted a less ruthless
experimenter. She had to bring together automatically, and at the
dictation, as they felt, of their irresponsible wills, just the creatures that by uniting might reproduce the species. The complete
sexual reaction had to be woven together out of many incomplete
reactions to various stimuli, reactions not specifically sexual. The
outer senses had to be engaged, and many secondary characters
found in bodies had to be used to attract attention, until the
deeper instinctive response should have time to gather itself together and assert itself openly. Many mechanical preformations
and reflexes must conspire to constitute a determinate instinct.
We name this instinct after its ultimate function, looking forward
to the uses we observe it to have; and it seems to us in consequence
an inexplicable anomaly that many a time the instinct is set in
motion when its alleged purpose cannot be fulfilled; as when love
appears prematurely or too late, or fixes upon a creature of the
wrong age or sex. These anomalies show us how nature is built up
and, far from being inexplicable, are hints that tend to make
everything clear, when once a verbal and mythical philosophy has
been abandoned.

Responses which we may call sexual in view of results to
which they may ultimately lead are thus often quite independent,
and exist before they are drawn into the vortex of a complete and
actually generative act. External stimulus and present idea will
consequently be altogether inadequate to explain the profound
upheaval which may ensue, if, as we say, we actually fall in love.
That the senses should be played upon is nothing, if no deeper
reaction is aroused. All depends on the juncture at which, so to
speak, the sexual circuit is completed and the emotional currents
begin to circulate. Whatever object, at such a critical moment,
fills the field of consciousness becomes a signal and associate for
the whole sexual mood. It is breathlessly devoured in that pause
and concentration of attention, that rearrangement of the soul,
which love is conceived in; and the whole new life which that
image is engulfed in is foolishly supposed to be its effect. For the
image is in consciousness, but not the profound predispositions
which gave it place and power.

THE CHOICE UNSTABLE.

This association between passion and its signals may be
merely momentary, or it may be perpetual: a Don Juan and a
Dante are both genuine lovers. In a gay society the gallant addresses every woman as if she charmed him, and perhaps actually
finds any kind of beauty, or mere femininity anywhere, a sufficient

spur to his desire. These momentary fascinations are not necessarily false: they may for an instant be quite absorbing and irresistible; they may genuinely suffuse the whole mind. Such mercu-
rial fire will indeed require a certain imaginative temperament;
and there are many persons who, short of a life-long domestic
attachment, can conceive of nothing but sordid vice. But even an
inconstant flame may burn brightly, if the soul is naturally com-
bustible. Indeed these sparks and glints of passion, just because
they come and vary so quickly, offer admirable illustrations of it,
in which it may be viewed, so to speak, under the microscope and
in its formative stage.

Thus Plato did not hesitate to make the love of all wines,
under whatever guise, excuse, or occasion, the test of a true taste
for wine and an unfeigned adoration of Bacchus; and, like
Lucretius after him, he wittily compiled a list of names, by which
the lover will flatter the most opposite qualities, if they only succeed in arousing his inclination. To be omnivorous is one pole of
true love: to be exclusive is the other. A man whose heart, if I
may say so, lies deeper, hidden under a thicker coat of mail, will
have less play of fancy, and will be far from finding every charm
charming, or every sort of beauty a stimulus to love. Yet he may
not be less prone to the tender passion, and when once smitten
may be so penetrated by an unimagined tenderness and joy, that
he will declare himself incapable of ever loving again, and may
actually be so. Having no rivals and a deeper soil, love can ripen
better in such a constant spirit; it will not waste itself in a continual patter of little pleasures and illusions. But unless the passion of it is to die down, it must somehow assert its universality:
what it loses in diversity it must gain in applicability. It must
become a principle of action and an influence colouring everything that is dreamt of; otherwise it would have lost its dignity
and sunk into a dead memory or a domestic bond.

INSTINCTIVE ESSENCE OF LOVE.

True love, it used to be said, is love at first sight. Manners
have much to do with such incidents, and the race which happens
to set, at a given time, the fashion in literature makes its temperament public and exercises a sort of contagion over all men's
fancies. If women are rarely seen and ordinarily not to be spoken
to; if all imagination has to build upon is a furtive glance or
casual motion, people fall in love at first sight. For they must fall
in love somehow, and any stimulus is enough if none more powerful is forthcoming. When society, on the contrary, allows constant
and easy intercourse between the sexes, a first impression, if not
reinforced, will soon be hidden and obliterated by others. Ac-

quaintance becomes necessary for love when it is necessary for
memory. But what makes true love is not the information con-
veyed by acquaintance, not any circumstantial charms that may be
therein discovered: it is still a deep and dumb instinctive affinity,
an inexplicable emotion seizing the heart, an influence organising
the world, like a luminous crystal, about one magic point. So that
although love seldom springs up suddenly in these days into anything like a full-blown passion, it is sight, it is presence, that
makes in time a conquest over the heart; for all virtues, sympathies, confidences will fail to move a man to tenderness and to
worship, unless a poignant effluence from the object envelop
him, so that he begins to walk, as it were, in a dream.

Not to believe in love is a great sign of dullness. There are
some people so indirect and lumbering that they think all real
affection must rest on circumstantial evidence. But a finely constituted being is sensitive to its deepest affinities. This is precisely
what refinement consists in, that we may feel in things immediate
and infinitesimal a sure premonition of things ultimate and important. Fine senses vibrate at once to harmonies which it may
take long to verify; so sight is finer than touch, and thought than
sensation. Well-bred instinct meets reason half way, and is prepared for the consonances that may follow. Beautiful things, when
taste is formed, are obviously and unaccountably beautiful. The
grounds we may bring ourselves to assign for our preferences are
discovered by analysing those preferences, and articulate judgments follow upon emotions which they ought to express, but
which they sometimes sophisticate. So, too, the reasons we give for
love either express what it feels or else are insincere, attempting
to justify at the bar of reason and convention something which is
far more primitive than they and underlies them both. True
instinct can dispense with such excuses. It appeals to the event
and is justified by the response which nature makes to it. It is, of
course, far from infallible; it cannot dominate circumstances, and
has no discursive knowledge; but it is presumably true, and what
it foreknows is always essentially possible. Unrealisable it may
indeed be in the jumbled context of this world, where the Fates,
like an absent-minded printer, seldom allow a single line to stand
perfect and unmarred.

The profoundest affinities are those most readily felt, and
though a thousand later considerations may overlay and override
them, they remain a background and standard for all happiness.
If we trace them out we succeed. If we put them by, although in
other respects we may call ourselves happy, we inwardly know
that we have dismissed the ideal, and all that was essentially possible has not been realised. Love in that case still owns a hidden
and potential object, and we sanctify, perhaps, whatever kind-

nesses or partialities we indulge in by a secret loyalty to something impersonal and unseen. Such reserve, such religion, would not have been necessary had things responded to our first expectations. We might then have identified the ideal with the object that happened to call it forth. The Life of Reason might have been led instinctively, and we might have been guided by nature herself into the ways of peace.

ITS IDEALITY.

As it is, circumstances, false steps, or the mere lapse of time, force us to shuffle our affections and take them as they come, or as we are suffered to indulge them. A mother is followed by a boyish friend, a friend by a girl, a girl by a wife, a wife by a child, a child by an idea. A divinity passes through these various temples; they may all remain standing, and we may continue our cult in them without outward change, long after the god has fled from the last into his native heaven. We may try to convince ourselves that we have lost nothing when we have lost all. We may take comfort in praising the mixed and perfunctory attachments which cling to us by force of habit and duty, repeating the empty names of creatures that have long ceased to be what we once could love, and assuring ourselves that we have remained constant, without admitting that the world, which is in irreparable flux, has from the first been betraying us.

Ashamed of being so deeply deceived, we may try to smile cynically at the glory that once shone upon us, and call it a dream. But cynicism is wasted on the ideal. There is indeed no idol ever identified with the ideal which honest experience, even without cynicism, will not some day unmask and discredit. Every real object must cease to be what it seemed, and none could ever be what the whole soul desired. Yet what the soul desires is nothing arbitrary. Life is no objectless dream, but continually embodies, with varying success, the potentialities it contains and that prompt desire. Everything that satisfies at all, even if partially and for an instant, justifies aspiration and rewards it. Existence, however, cannot be arrested; and only the transmissible forms of things can endure, to match the transmissible faculties which living beings hand down to one another. The ideal is accordingly significant, perpetual, and as constant as the nature it expresses; but it can never itself exist, nor can its particular embodiments endure.

ITS UNIVERSAL SCOPE.

Love is accordingly only half an illusion; the lover, but not his love, is deceived. His madness, as Plato taught, is divine; for though it be folly to identify the idol with the god, faith in the god is inwardly justified. That egregious idolatry may therefore be interpreted ideally and given a symbolic scope worthy of its natural causes and of the mystery it comes to celebrate. The lover knows much more about absolute good and universal beauty than any logician or theologian, unless the latter, too, be lovers in disguise. Logical universals are terms in discourse, without vital ideality, while traditional gods are at best natural existences, more or less indifferent facts. What the lover comes upon, on the contrary, is truly persuasive, and witnesses to itself, so that he worships from the heart and beholds what he worships. That the true object is no natural being, but an ideal form essentially eternal and capable of endless embodiments, is far from abolishing its worth; on the contrary, this fact makes love ideally relevant to generation, by which the human soul and body may be for ever renewed, and at the same time makes it a thing for large thoughts to be focussed upon, a thing representing all rational aims.

Whenever this ideality is absent and a lover sees nothing in his mistress but what everyone else may find in her, loving her honestly in her unvarnished and accidental person, there is a friendly and humorous affection, admirable in itself, but no passion or bewitchment of love; she is a member of his group, not a spirit in his pantheon. Such an affection may be altogether what it should be; it may bring a happiness all the more stable because the heart is quite whole, and no divine shaft has pierced it. It is hard to stanch wounds inflicted by a god. The glance of an ideal love is terrible and glorious, foreboding death and immortality together. Love could not be called divine without platitude if it regarded nothing but its nominal object; to be divine it must not envisage an accidental good but the principle of goodness, that which gives other goods their ultimate meaning and makes all functions useful. Love is a true natural religion; it has a visible cult, it is kindled by natural beauties and bows to the best symbol it may find for its hope; it sanctifies a natural mystery; and, finally, when understood, it recognises that what it worshipped under a figure was truly the principle of all good.

The loftiest edifices need the deepest foundations. Love would never take so high a flight unless it sprung from something profound and elementary. It is accordingly most truly love when it is irresistible and fatal. The substance of all passion, if we could gather it together, would be the basis of all ideals, to which all goods would have to refer. Love actually accomplishes something of the sort; being primordial it underlies other demands, and can be wholly satisfied only by a happiness which is ultimate and comprehensive. Lovers are vividly aware of this fact: their ideal, apparently so inarticulate, seems to them to include everything. It shares the mystical quality of all primitive life. Sophisticated people can hardly understand how vague experience is at bottom, and how truly that vagueness supports whatever clearness is afterward attained. They cling to the notion that nothing can have a spiritual scope that does not spring from reflection. But in that case life itself, which brings reflection about, would never support spiritual interests, and all that is moral would be unnatural and consequently self-destructive. In truth, all spiritual interests are supported by animal life; in this the generative function is fundamental; and it is therefore no paradox, but something altogether fitting, that if that function realised all it comprises, nothing human would remain outside. Such an ultimate fulfilment would differ, of course, from a first satisfaction, just as all that reproduction reproduces differs from the reproductive function itself, and vastly exceeds it. All organs and activities which are inherited, in a sense, grow out of the reproductive process and serve to clothe it; so that when the generative energy is awakened all that can ever be is virtually called up and, so to speak, made consciously potential; and love yearns for the universe of values.

ITS EUTHANASIA.

This secret is gradually revealed to those who are inwardly attentive and allow love to teach them something. A man who has truly loved, though he may come to recognise the thousand incidental illusions into which love may have led him, will not recant its essential faith. He will keep his sense for the ideal and his power to worship. The further objects by which these gifts will be entertained will vary with the situation. A philosopher, a soldier, and a courtesan will express the same religion in different ways. In fortunate cases love may glide imperceptibly into settled domestic affections, giving them henceforth a touch of ideality; for when love dies in the odour of sanctity people venerate his relics. In other cases allegiance to the ideal may appear more sullenly, breaking out in whims, or in little sentimental practices which might seem half-conventional. Again it may inspire a religious conversion, charitable works, or even artistic labours. In all these ways people attempt more or less seriously to lead the Life of Reason, expressing outwardly allegiance to whatever in their minds has come to stand for the ideal. If to create was love's impulse originally, to create is its effort still, after it has been chastened and has received some rational extension. The machinery which serves reproduction thus finds kindred but higher uses, as every organ does in a liberal life; and what Plato called a desire for birth in beauty may be sublimated even more, until it yearns for an ideal immortality in a transfigured world, a world made worthy of that love which its children have so often lavished on it in their dreams.

NOTES

1. The wide uses of the English word love add to the difficulty. I shall take the liberty of limiting the term here to imaginative passion, to being in love, excluding all other ways of loving. It follows that love—like its shadow, jealousy—will often be merely an ingredient in an actual state of feeling; friendship and confidence, with satisfaction at being liked in return, will often be mingled with it. We shall have to separate physiologically things which in consciousness exist undivided, since a philosophic description is bound to be analytic and cannot render everything at once. Where a poet might conceive a new composite, making it live, a moralist must dissect the experience and rest in its eternal elements.

2. One example, among a thousand, is the cry of Siegfried and Brünhilde in Wagner:

> Lachend lass' uns verderben,
> Lachend zu Grunde geh'n.
> Fahr hin, Walhall's
> Leuchtende Welt! . . .
> Leb' wohl, pragende
> Götter Pracht!
> Ende in Wonne,
> Du ewig Geschlecht!

JOHAN HUIZINGA: Heroism and Love*

A CONCEPTION of military life resembling that of medieval chivalry is found nearly everywhere, notably with the Hindus of the *Mahâbhârata* and in Japan. Warlike aristocracies need an ideal form of manly perfection. The aspiration to a pure and beautiful life, expressed in the *Kalokagathia* of the Hellenes, in the Middle Ages gives birth to chivalry. And during several centuries that ideal remains a source of energy, and at the same time a cloak for a whole world of violence and self-interest.

The ascetic element is never absent from it. It is most accentuated in the times when the function of knighthood is most vital, as in the times of the early crusades. The noble warrior has to be poor and exempt from worldly ties. "This ideal of the well-born man without possessions"—say William James—"was embodied in knight-errantry and templardom, and, hideously corrupted as it has always been, it still dominates sentimentally, if not practically, the military and aristocratic view of life. We

* Reprinted from *The Waning of The Middle Ages.*

glorify the soldier as the man absolutely unincumbered. Owning nothing but his bare life, and willing to toss that up at any moment when the cause commands him, he is the representative of unhampered freedom in ideal directions." Medieval chivalry, in its first bloom, was bound to blend with monachism. From this union were born the military orders of the Templars, of Saint John, of the Teutonic knights, and also those of Spain. Soon, however, or rather from the very beginning, reality gives the lie to the ideal, and accordingly the ideal will soar more and more towards the regions of fantasy, there to preserve the traits of asceticism and sacrifice too rarely visible in real life. The knight-errant, fantastic and useless, will always be poor and without ties, as the first Templars had been.

It would thus be unjust to regard as factitious or superficial the religious elements of chivalry, such as compassion, fidelity, justice. They are essential to it. Yet the complex of aspirations and imaginings, forming the idea of chivalry, in spite of its strong ethical foundation and the combative instinct of man, would never have made so solid a frame for the life beautiful if love had not been the source of its constantly revived ardour.

These very traits, moreover, of compassion, of sacrifice, and of fidelity, which characterize chivalry, are not purely religious; they are erotic at the same time. Here, again, it must be remembered that the desire of bestowing a form, a style, on sentiment, is not expressed exclusively in art and literature; it also unfolds in life itself: in courtly conversation, in games, in sports. There, too, love incessantly seeks a sublime and romantic expression. If, therefore, life borrows motifs and forms from literature, literature, after all, is only copying life. The chivalrous aspect of love had somehow to make its appearance in life before it expressed itself in literature.

The knight and his lady, that is to say, the hero who serves for love, this is the primary and invariable motif from which erotic fantasy will always start. It is sensuality transformed into the craving for self-sacrifice, into the desire of the man to show his courage, to incur danger, to be strong, to suffer and to bleed before his lady-love.

From the moment when the dream of heroism through love has intoxicated the yearning heart, fantasy grows and overflows. The first simple theme is soon left behind, the soul thirsts for new fancies, and passion colours the dream of suffering and of renunciation. The man will not be content merely to suffer, he will want to save from danger, or from suffering, the object of his desire. A more vehement stimulus is added to the primary motif: its chief feature will be that of defending imperilled virginity—in other words, that of ousting the rival. This, then, is the essential theme of chivalrous love poetry: the young hero, delivering the virgin. The sexual motif is always behind it, even when the aggressor is only an artless dragon; a glance at Burne-Jones's famous picture suffices to prove it.

One is surprised that comparative mythology should have looked so indefatigably to meteorological phenomena for the explanation of such an immediate and perpetual motif as the deliverance of the virgin, which is the oldest of literary motifs, and one which can never grow antiquated. It may from time to time become stale from overmuch repetition, and yet it will reappear, adapting itself to all times and surroundings. New romantic types will arise, just as the cowboy has succeeded the corsair.

The Middle Ages cultivated these motifs of a primitive romanticism with a youthful insatiability. Whereas in some higher genres of literature, such as lyrical poetry, the expression of desire and fulfilment became more refined, the romance of adventure always preserved it in its crude and naïve form, without ever losing its charm to its contemporaries. We might have expected that the last centuries of the Middle Ages would have lost their relish for these childish fancies. We are inclined to suppose that *Méliador*, the super-romantic novel by Froissart, or *Perceforest*, those belated fruits of chivalrous romance, were anachronisms even in their own day. They were no more so than the sensational novel is at present. Erotic imagination always requires similar models, and it finds them here. In the heyday of the Renaissance we see them revive in the cycle of Amadis of Gaul. When, a good while after the middle of the sixteenth century, François de la Noue affirms that the novels of Amadis had caused "un esprit de vertige" among his generation—the generation of the Huguenots, which had passed through humanism with its vein of rationalism— we can imagine what must have been the romantic susceptibility of the ill-balanced and ignorant generation of 1400.

Literature did not suffice for the almost insatiable needs of the romantic imagination of the age. Some more active form of expression was required. Dramatic art might have supplied it, but the medieval drama in the real sense of the word treated love matters only exceptionally; sacred subjects were its substance. There was, however, another form of representation, namely, noble sports, tourneys and jousts. Sportive struggles always and everywhere contain a strong dramatic element and an erotic element. In the medieval tournament these two elements had so much got the upper hand, that its character of a contest of force and courage had been almost obliterated by its romantic purport. With its bizarre accoutrements and pompous staging, its poetical illusion and pathos, it filled the place of the drama of a later age.

The life of aristocracies when they are still strong, though of small utility, tends to become an all-round game. In order to forget the painful imperfection of reality, the nobles turn to the continual illusion of a high and heroic life. They wear the mask of Lancelot and of Tristram. It is an amazing self-deception. The crying falsehood of it can only be borne by treating it with some amount of raillery. The whole chivalrous culture of the last centuries of the Middle Ages is marked by an unstable equilibrium between sentimentality and mockery. Honour, fidelity and love are treated with unimpeachable seriousness; only from time to time the solemn rigidity relaxes into a smile, but downright parody never prevails. Even after the *Morgante* of Pulci and the *Orlando Innamorato* of Boiardo had made the heroic pose ridiculous, Ariosto recaptured the absolute serenity of chivalrous sentiment.

In French circles, of about 1400, the cult of chivalry was treated with perfect gravity. It is not easy for us to understand this seriousness, and not to be startled by the contrast between the literary note of a Boucicaut and the facts of his career. He is represented as the indefatigable defender of courtesy and of chivalry, serving his lady according to the old rules of courteous love. "He served all, he honoured all, for the love of one. His speech was graceful, courteous and diffident before his lady." During his travels in the Near East in 1388, he and his companions in arms amuse themselves by composing a poetical defence of the faithful and chaste love of a knight—the *Livre des Cent Ballades*. One might have supposed him cured of all chivalrous delusions after the catastrophe of Nicopolis. There he had seen the lamentable consequences of statecraft recklessly embarking on an enterprise of vital import in the spirit of a chivalrous adventure. His companions of the *Cent Ballades* had perished. That would suffice, one would think, to make him turn his back on old-fashioned forms of courtesy. Yet he remains devoted to them and resumes his moral task in founding the order "de la dame blanche à l'escu vert."

Like all romantic forms that are worn out as an instrument of passion, this apparatus of chivalry and of courtesy affects us at first sight as a silly and ridiculous thing. The accents of passion are heard in it no more save in some rare products of literary genius. Still, all these costly elaborated forms of social conduct have played their part as a decoration of life, as a framework for a living passion. In reading this antiquated love poetry, or the clumsy descriptions of tournaments, no exact knowledge of historical details avails without the vision of the smiling eyes, long

turned to dust, which at one time were infinitely more important
than the written word that remains.

Only a stray glimmer now reminds us of the passionate
significance of these cultural forms. In the *Vœu du Héron* the
unknown author makes Jean de Beaumont speak:

> *"Quant sommes ès tavernes, de ces fors vins buvant,*
> *Et ces dames delès qui nous vont regardant,*
> *A ces gorgues polies, ces coliés tirant,*
> *Chil œil vair resplendissent de biauté souriant,*
> *Nature nous semont d'avoir cœur désirant,*
> *. . . Adonc conquerons-nous Yaumont et Agoulant*
> *Et li autre conquierrent Olivier et Rollant.*
> *Mais, quant sommes as camps sus nos destriers courans,*
> *Nos escus à no col et nos lansses bais(s)ans,*
> *Et le froidure grande nous va tout engelant,*
> *Li membres nous effondrent, et derrière et devant,*
> *Et nos ennemies sont envers nous approchant,*
> *Adonc vorrièmes estre en un chélier si grant*
> *Que jamais ne fussions veu tant ne quant."*[1]

Nowhere does the erotic element of the tournament appear
more clearly than in the custom of the knight's wearing the veil
or the dress of his lady. In *Perceforest* we read how the lady spectators of the combat take off their finery, one article after another,
to throw them to the knights in the lists. At the end of the fight
they are bareheaded and without sleeves. A poem of the thirteenth
century, the work of a Picard or a Hainaut minstrel, entitled *Des
trois Chevaliers et del Chainse*,[2] has worked out this motif in all
its force. The wife of a nobleman of great liberality, but not very
fond of fighting, sends her shirt to three knights who serve her for
love, that one of them at the tournament which her husband is
going to give may wear it as a coat-armour, without any mail
underneath. The first and the second knights excuse themselves.
The third, who is poor, takes the shirt in his arms at night, and
kisses it passionately. He appears at the tournament, dressed in the
shirt and without a coat of mail; he is grievously wounded, the
shirt, stained with his blood, is torn. Then his extraordinary
bravery is perceived and he is awarded the prize. The lady gives
him her heart. The lover asks something in his turn. He sends
back the garment, all blood-stained, to the lady, that she may wear
it over her gown at the meal which is to conclude the feast. She
embraces it tenderly and shows herself dressed in the shirt as the
knight had demanded. The majority of those present blame her,
the husband is confounded, and the minstrel winds up by asking
the question: Which of the two lovers sacrificed most for the sake
of the other?

The Church was openly hostile to tournaments; it repeatedly prohibited them, and there is no doubt that the fear of the passionate character of this noble game, and of the abuses resulting from it, had a great share in this hostility. Moralists were not favourably disposed towards tournaments, neither were the humanists. Where do we read, Petrarch asks, that Cicero or Scipio jousted? The burghers thought them useless and ridiculous. Only the world of the nobility continued to cultivate all that regarded tournaments and jousts, as things of the highest importance. Monuments were erected on the sites of famous combats, as the Pélerine Cross near Saint Omer, in remembrance of the Passage of Arms of la Pélerine, and of the exploits of the bastard of Saint Pol and a Spanish knight. Bayard piously went to visit this cross, as if on a pilgrimage. In the church of Notre Dame of Boulogne were preserved the decorations of the Passage of Arms of the Fontaine des Pleurs, solemnly dedicated to the Holy Virgin.

The warlike sports of the Middle Ages differ from Greek and modern athletics by being far less simple and natural. Pride, honour, love and art give additional stimulus to the competition itself. Overloaded with pomp and decoration, full of heroic fancy, they serve to express romantic needs too strong for mere literature to satisfy. The realities of court life or a military career offered too little opportunity for the fine make-belief of heroism and love, which filled the soul. So they had to be acted. The staging of the tournament, therefore, had to be that of romance; that is to say, the imaginary world of Arthur, where the fancy of a fairy-tale was enhanced by the sentimentality of courtly love.

A Passage of Arms of the fifteenth century is based on a fictitious case of chivalrous adventure, connected with an artificial scene called by a romantic name, as, for instance, *La fontaine des pleurs, L'arbre Charlemagne*. A fountain is expressly constructed, and beside it a pavilion, where during a whole year a lady is to reside (in effigy, be it understood), holding a unicorn which bears three shields. The first day of each month knights come to touch the shields, and in this way to pledge themselves for a combat of which the "Chapters" of the Passage of Arms lay down the rules. They will find horses in readiness, for the shields have to be touched on horseback. Or, in the case of the *Emprise du dragon*, four knights will be stationed at a cross-road where, unless she gives a gage, no lady may pass without a knight breaking two lances for her. There is an unmistakable connection between these primitive forms of warlike and erotic sport and the children's play of forfeits. One of the rules of the "Chapters" of the *Fontaine des pleurs* runs thus: he who, in a combat, is unhorsed, will during a year wear a gold bracelet, until he finds the lady who holds the

key to it and who can free him, on condition that he shall
serve her.

The nobles liked to throw a veil of mystery and melancholy over the procedure. The knight should be unknown. He is
called "le blanc chevalier," "le chevalier mesconnu," or he wears
the crest of Lancelot or Palamedes. The shields of the Fount of
Tears are white, violet and black, and overspread with white
tears; those of the Tree of Charlemagne are sable and violet, with
gold and sable tears. At the *Emprise du dragon*, celebrated on the
occasion of the departure of his daughter Margaret for England,
King René was present, dressed all in black, and his whole outfit,
caparison, horse and all, down to the wood of his lance, was of
the same colour.

NOTES

1. When we are in the tavern, drinking strong wines, And the ladies pass
and look at us, With those white throats, and tight bodices, Those sparkling eyes
resplendent with smiling beauty, Then nature urges us to have a desiring heart,...
Then we could overcome Yaumont and Agoulant And the others would conquer
Oliver and Roland. But when we are in camp on our trotting chargers, Our
bucklers round our necks and our lances lowered, And the great cold is congealing
us altogether, And our limbs are crushed before and behind, And our enemies are
approaching us, Then we should wish to be in a cellar so large That we might
never be seen by any means.
2. Of the three knights and the shirt.

DENIS DE ROUGEMONT: The Tristan Myth*

TOPICALITY OF THE MYTH, OR REASONS FOR ITS
ANALYSIS

THERE IS no need to have read Béroul's *Tristan*
or M. Bédier's, and no need to have heard Wagner's opera, in
order to undergo in the course of everyday life the nostalgic
dominion of such a myth. It is manifested in the majority of
novels and films, in the popularity these enjoy with the masses,
the acceptance which they meet with in the hearts of middle-class
people, from poets, from ill-assorted couples, and from the seam-
stresses who dream of having a miraculous love-affair. The myth
operates wherever passion is dreamed of as an ideal instead of

* Reprinted from *Love in the Western World*.

being feared like a malignant fever; wherever its fatal character is welcomed, invoked, or imagined as a magnificent and desirable disaster instead of as simply a disaster. It lives upon the lives of people who think that love is their fate (and as unavoidable as the effect of the love-potion is in the Romance); that it swoops upon powerless and ravished men and women in order to consume them in a pure flame; or that it is stronger and more real than happiness, society, or morality. It lives upon the very life of the romanticism within us; it is the great mystery of that religion of which the poets of the nineteenth century made themselves the priests and prophets.

Of this influence, and that it is the influence of a myth, there is immediate evidence, evidence provided in this very place by the reader's reluctance to face squarely what it is I am proposing to do. The Romance of Tristan is 'sacred' for us precisely to the extent that it seems 'sacrilegious' on my part to attempt to analyse it. No doubt the charge of sacrilege now has a very mild quality. In primitive societies it resulted, not in the reluctance which I anticipate, but in the execution of the guilty person. The sacred which is involved here amounts to no more than an obscure and weak survival. The only risk I run is that the reader may close the book at this point, and not open it again. True, the unconscious intent of such an act does not fall short of getting me put to death, but the intent is without effect. However, supposing you spare me, dear Reader, am I to conclude that the passion is not sacred for you? Possibly people are nowadays as feeble in passion as in acts of reproof. In the absence of open foes, perhaps it is against themselves that writers must show the daring which is being demanded of them, and perhaps it is only the enemy in our own breasts that we can really contend with.

I confess I was vexed to find one commentator describing the Tristan legend as 'an epic of adultery'. The phrase may be accurate enough in respect of the dry bones of the Romance. That does not make it any the less vexatious and 'prosaically' narrow. I doubt if it can be maintained that the real subject of the legend is the moral fault. How assert that Wagner's *Tristan*, for example, is no more than an opera about adultery? For that matter, is adultery but a nasty word, or a breach of contract? Adultery is that too, and in all too many cases no more than that. But it often is a great deal more—a passionate and tragic atmosphere beyond good and evil, and a drama either lofty or dreadful; in short, a drama—a *romance*. And 'romanticism' derives from 'romance'.

The problem expands splendidly—and my case worsens proportionately. I shall set out my reasons for going on, and it can then be decided if they are diabolical. First, social confusion has now reached a point at which the pursuit of immorality turns out to be more exhausting than compliance with the old moral codes. The cult of passionate love has been *democratized* so far as to have lost its aesthetic virtues together with its spiritual and tragic values; and we are left with a dull and diluted pain, something unclean and gloomy. In profaning the falsely sacred causes of this, I cannot believe that we have anything to lose. The literature dealing with passion, the advertising which passion gets, the business-like 'vogue' of what used to be a religious secret—all that needs to be attacked and made war upon, if only to rescue the myth from being abused in its excessive popularization. And whatever sacrilege we may thereby commit will not matter; for poetry has other outlets.

My second reason is a desire to be quite clear about contemporary life. I fasten upon the Tristan myth because it enables me to offer a *simple explanation* of our present confusion and at the same time to set forth certain *permanent relations* which the scrupulous vulgarities of current psychologies submerge. Furthermore, I can lay bare a particular *dilemma,* the stern reality of which we are in process of overlooking as a result of our frenzied living, the state of our culture, and the purr of current moral doctrines.

To raise up the myth of passion in its primitive and sacred vigour and in its monumental integrity, as a salutary comment upon our tortuous connivances and inability to choose boldly between the Norm of Day and the Passion of Night—such is my first purpose. It means raising up that image of the Dying Lovers which is excited by the disturbing and vampire-like crescendo of Wagner's second act. And what I aim at is to bring the reader to the point of declaring frankly, either that 'That is what I wanted!' or else 'God forbid!'

I am not certain that complete self-awareness is useful either in a general way or *per se.* I do not hold that practical truths can be made plain in the market place. But whatever the 'usefulness' of my undertaking, we who dwell in the Western world are destined to become more and more aware of the illusions on which we subsist. And possibly it is the job of philosophers, moralists, and creators of ideal forms, simply to increase our self-awareness—the consciousness which is of course also a bad conscience.

With that I pass to the promised analysis. Remaining deaf and blind to the 'charms' of the tale, I am going to try to summarize 'objectively' the events it relates and the reasons which it either gives for these events or very oddly omits.

WHAT THE TRISTAN ROMANCE[1] SEEMS TO BE ABOUT

*Amors par force vos demeine!—*BÉROUL.

Tristan is born in misfortune. His father has just died, and Blanchefleur, his mother, does not survive his birth. Hence his name, the sombre hue of his life, and the lowering stormy sky that hangs over the legend. King Mark of Cornwall, Blanchefleur's brother, takes the orphan into his castle at Tintagel and brings him up there.

Tristan presently performs an early feat of prowess. He vanquishes the Morholt. This Irish giant has come like a Minotaur to exact his tribute of Cornish maidens or youths. Tristan is of an age for knighthood—that is, he has just reached puberty—and he obtains leave to fight him. The Morholt is killed, but not before he has wounded Tristan with a poisoned barb. Having no hope of recovery, Tristan begs to be put on board a boat that is cast adrift with neither sail nor oar. He takes his sword and harp with him.

He lands in Ireland. There is only one remedy that can save him, and, as it happens, the Queen of Ireland is alone in knowing its secret. But the giant Morholt was this queen's brother, and so Tristan is careful not to disclose his name or to explain how he has come by his wound. Iseult, the queen's daughter, nurses him and restores him to health. That is the Prologue.

A few years later a bird has brought to King Mark a golden hair. The king determines to marry the woman from whose head the hair has come. It is Tristan whom he selects to go in quest of her. A storm causes the hero to be cast ashore once again in Ireland. There he fights and kills a dragon that was threatening the capital. (This is the conventional motif of a virgin delivered by a young paladin.) Having been wounded by the dragon, Tristan is again nursed by Iseult. One day she learns that the wounded stranger is no other than the man who killed her uncle. She seizes Tristan's sword and threatens to transfix him in his bath. It is then that he tells her of the mission on which he has been sent by King Mark. And Iseult spares him, for she would like to be a queen. (According to some of the authors, she spares him also because she then finds him handsome.)

Tristan and the princess set sail for Cromwall. At sea the wind drops and the heat grows oppressive. They are thirsty. Brengain, Iseult's maid, gives them a drink. But by mistake she pours out the 'wine of herbs' which the queen, Iseult's mother, has brewed for King Mark and his bride after they shall have wed. Tristan and Iseult drink it. The effect is to commit them to a fate from 'which they can never escape during the remainder of their lives, *for they have drunk their destruction and death'*. They confess that they are now in love, and fall into one another's arms.

(Let it be noted here that according to the archetypal version, which Béroul alone has followed, the effect of the love-potion is limited to three years.[2] Thomas, a sensitive psychologist and highly suspicious of marvels, which he considers crude, minimizes the importance of the love-potion as far as possible, and depicts the love of Tristan and Iseult as having occurred spontaneously. Its first signs he places as early as the episode of the bath. On the other hand, Eilhart, Gottfried, and most of the others attribute unlimited effect to the magic wine. Nothing could be more significant than these variations, as we shall see.)

Thus the fault is perpetrated. *Yet Tristan is still in duty bound to fulfil the mission with which King Mark has entrusted him.* So, notwithstanding his betrayal of the king, he delivers Iseult to him. On the wedding night Brengain, thanks to a ruse, takes Iseult's place in the royal bed, thus saving her mistress from dishonour and at the same time expiating the irretrievable mistake she made in pouring out the love-potion.

Presently, however, four 'felon' barons of the king's go and tell their sovereign that Tristan and Iseult are lovers. Tristan is banished to Tintagel town. But thanks to another trick—the episode of the pine-tree in the orchard—Mark is convinced of his innocence and allows him to return to the castle. Then Frocin the Dwarf, who is in league with the barons, lays a trap in order to establish the lovers' guilt. In the spear-length between Tristan's bed and the queen's he scatters flour, and persuades Mark to order Tristan to ride to King Arthur at Carduel the next morning at dawn. Tristan is determined to embrace his mistress once more before he rides away. To avoid leaving his foot-marks in the flour he leaps across from his own bed to the queen's. But the effort reopens a wound in his leg inflicted the previous day by a boar. Led by Frocin, the king and the barons burst into the bed-chamber. They find the flour blood-stained. Mark is satisfied with this evidence of adultery. Iseult is handed over to a party of a hundred lepers, and Tristan is sentenced to the stake. On the way to execution, however, he is allowed to go into a chantry on the cliff's edge. He forces a window and leaps over the cliff, thus effecting his escape. He rescues Iseult from the lepers, and together they go and hide in the depths of the Forest of Morrois. There for three years they lead a life 'harsh and hard'. It happens one day that Mark comes upon them while they are asleep. But on this occasion Tristan has put between Iseult and himself his drawn sword. Moved by this evidence of innocence, as he supposes it to be, the king spares them. Without waking them, he takes up Tristan's sword and sets his own in its place.

At the end of three years the potency of the love-potion wears off (according to Béroul and the common ancestor of the five versions). It is only then that Tristan repents, and that Iseult wishes she were a queen again. Together they seek out the hermit Ogrin, through whom Tristan offers peace to the king, saying he will surrender Iseult. Mark promises forgiveness. As the royal procession approaches, the lovers part. But before this happens Iseult has besought Tristan to stay in the neighbourhood till he has made certain that Mark is treating her well. Then, with a final display of feminine wiles, she follows up her advantage in having persuaded Tristan to agree to this, and declares she will join him at the first sign he makes, for nothing shall stop her from doing his will, 'neither tower, nor wall, nor stronghold'.

They have several secret meetings in the hut of Orri the Woodman. But the felon barons are keeping watch and ward over the queen's virtue. She asks and is granted 'a Judgement of God'. Thanks to a subterfuge, the ordeal is a success. Before she grasps the red-hot iron which will not harm one who has spoken the truth, she swears that no man has ever held her in his arms except the king and a poor pilgrim who has just carried her ashore from a boat. And the poor pilgrim is Tristan in disguise.

However, fresh adventures carry Tristan far away from Iseult, and he then comes to suppose that she no longer loves him. So he agrees to marry 'for her beauty and her name'[3] another Iseult, Iseult 'of the White Hand'. And indeed this Iseult remains unstained, for after their marriage Tristan still sighs for 'Iseult the Fair'.

At last, wounded by a poisoned spear and about to die, Tristan sends for the queen from Cornwall, she who alone can save his life. She comes and as her ship draws near it hoists a white sail as a sign of hope. But Iseult of the White Hand has been on the look-out, and, tormented by jealousy, she runs to Tristan and tells him that the sail is black. Tristan dies. As he does so, Iseult the Fair lands, and on arriving at the castle, she lies down beside her dead lover and clasps him close. Then she dies too.

SOME RIDDLES

Thus summarized, and with all the 'charm' destroyed, the most absorbing of poems appears, on cool consideration, to be straightforward neither in its matter nor in its progression. I have passed over numerous accessory episodes, but over none of the motives alleged for the central action. Indeed, these motives I have rather stressed. They have been seen not to amount to much. Tristan delivers up Iseult to the king, *because* bound by the fealty of a knight. At the end of the three years spent in the forest, the lovers part, *because* the love-potion has lost its potency. Tristan marries Iseult of the White Hand *'for her beauty and her name'*. If these 'reasons' are discounted—although we shall return to them—the Romance turns out to depend on a series of puzzling contradictions.

I have been struck by the passing comment of one recent editor of the legend. All through the Romance Tristan is made to appear the physical superior of all his foes and particularly of the king. It follows that no external power prevents him from carrying off Iseult and thus fulfilling his fate. The manners of the time sanctioned the rights of the stronger; they made these rights divine without qualification; and this was especially the case with a man's rights over a woman. *Why does Tristan not take advantage of these rights?*

Put on the alert by this first question, our critical suspicions lead us to discover other riddles, no less curious and obscure. *Why has the sword of chastity been placed between the two sleepers in the forest?* The lovers have already sinned, and they refuse to repent just then. Furthermore, they do not expect that the king will discover them. Yet in all five versions there is neither a line nor a word to explain the sword.[4] Again, *why does Tristan restore the queen to Mark*, even in those versions where at that time the love-potion is still active? If, as some say, the lovers part because they now sincerely repent, why do they promise one another to meet again in the moment they undertake to part? And why later does Tristan go forth upon fresh adventures when he and Iseult have made a tryst in the forest? Why does the guilty queen ask for 'a Judgement of God'? She must know that the ordeal is bound to go against her. It is only successful thanks to a trick improvised at the last moment; and this trick, it is implied, deceives God Himself, since the miracle ensues.[5] Moreover, the judgement having gone in the queen's favour, her innocence is thereupon taken for granted. But if she is innocent, so is Tristan; and it becomes quite impossible to see what prevents his return to the king's castle, and *hence to Iseult's side*.

At the same time it is surely very odd that thirteenth-century poets—so punctilious in matters of honour and suzerain fealty—should let pass without a word of comment so much thoroughly indefensible behaviour. How can they hold up Tristan as a model of chivalry when he betrays his king with the most shameless cunning, or the queen as a virtuous lady when she is not only an adulteress, but does not shrink from committing an astute blasphemy? On the other hand, why do they call 'felons' the four barons who defend Mark's honour and who, even if actuated by jealousy, neither deceive nor betray (which is more than can be said of Tristan)?

Even the validity of what few motives are mentioned remains open to question. For if the rule of suzerain fealty required that Tristan should deliver to Mark the betrothed he had been to fetch,[6] his compliance with this rule must seem both very belated and hardly sincere, inasmuch as once he has delivered up Iseult he knows no rest till he has contrived to get back into the castle and is with her again. And as the love-potion was brewed for Mark and his queen, it must be wondered why its potency is not permanent. Three years of married bliss are not much. And when Tristan marries another Iseult 'for her beauty and her name', but does not touch her, it is surely obvious that nothing has compelled him either to marry or to be guilty of his insulting chastity, and that by marrying a woman whom he cannot make his wife he has put himself into a position from which the only way out is death.

CHIVALRY V. MARRIAGE

The Romance of *Tristan and Iseult* brings home to us the antagonism which grew up in the second half of the twelfth century between the rule of chivalry and feudal custom. Perhaps the extent to which the Arthurian romances reflect and foster this antagonism has not hitherto attracted the notice it deserves. In all likelihood, courtly chivalry was never more than an ideal. The earliest writers to mention it commonly lament its decay, but in doing so they overlook that in the form which they would like it to assume it has only just come into existence in their dreams. It is of the essence of an ideal that its decay should be lamented in the very moment it is clumsily striving for fulfilment. Moreover, to contrast the *fiction* of some ideal of living with tyrannical reality is precisely something possible in a romance. A preliminary answer to several of the riddles propounded by the legend can be sought in this direction. Once it is granted that Tristan's experience was intended to illustrate a conflict between chivalry and feudal society—and hence a conflict between two kinds of *duty* and even between 'two religions'—a number of episodes are made intelligible. At any rate, even if not disposing of every difficulty, the hypothesis significantly delays a solution.

Arthurian romance, which supplanted the *chanson de geste* with astonishing swiftness in the middle of the twelfth century, differs from this *chanson* in that it allots to a woman the part formerly taken by a suzerain. An Arthurian knight, exactly like a

troubadour of the South, regarded himself as the vassal of some
chosen Lady, when actually, he remained the vassal of a lord; and
this gave rise to a number of conflicting claims of which the
Romance supplies examples.

Let me go back to the three 'felon' barons. According to
feudal morals, it was the duty of a vassal to warn his lord of anything that might endanger the latter's rights or honour. He was
a 'felon' if he did not. Now, in *Tristan* the barons go and tell
King Mark how Iseult is behaving. They should therefore be considered feal and true. If, then, the author refers to them as 'felons',
he must evidently do so in virtue of some other code, which can
only be the code of southern chivalry. For instance, according to
a well-known judgement delivered by the Gascon courts of love,
whosoever discloses the secrets of courtly love is a felon. The
single instance is enough to show that the authors of the different
versions of the Romance were deliberately siding with 'courtly'
chivalry against feudal law. But there are further grounds for
thinking so. Alone the view of fidelity and of marriage that was
adopted in courtly love will explain some of the striking contradictions in the tale.

According to the theory officially received, courtly love
arose as a reaction to the brutal lawlessness of feudal manners.
It is well known that the nobles in the twelfth century made of
marriage simply a means of enriching themselves, either through
the annexation of dower estates or through expectations of inheritance. When a 'deal' turned out badly, the wife was repudiated.
The plea of incest was exploited in curious ways, and in the face
of it the Church was powerless. To allege a consanguinity of even
the fourth degree, no matter on what slender evidence, was
enough to secure an annulment. In order to counteract these
abuses, which led to much quarrelling and to warring, courtly love
established a *fealty* that was independent of legal marriage and
of which the sole basis was love. It was even contended—for example, in the famous judgement delivered by a court of love in the
house of the Countess of Champagne[7]—that love and marriage
were incompatible. If such is the view of both Tristan and the
author of the Romance, the sense given to the terms 'felony' and
'adultery' is thereby justified—indeed, more than justified, ex-
tolled, inasmuch as it implies an intrepid loyalty to the higher
law of the *donnoi* or court love. (*Donnoi*, or *domnei*, is the
Provençal name for the vassal-relation set up between a knight-
lover and his lady, or *domina*.)

As has been said, this loyalty was incompatible with the
fidelity of marriage. The Romance misses no opportunity of disparaging the social institution of marriage and of humiliating

husbands—e.g. the king with horse's ears who is always being so easily deceived—as well as of glorifying the virtue of men and women who love outside, and in despite of, marriage. This courtly loyalty, however, displays one curious feature. It is opposed to the 'satisfaction' of love as much as to marriage. 'Of *donnoi* he knows truly nothing who wants fully to possess his lady. *Whatever turns into a reality is no longer love.*'[8] Here is something that puts us on the track of a preliminary explanation of such episodes as that of the sword of chastity, of Iseult's return to her lord after staying in the Forest of Morrois, and even of Tristan's nominal marriage.

The 'claims of passion', as understood today, would entitle Tristan to carry off Iseult as soon as he and she had drunk the love-potion. Instead he delivers her to Mark, and he does so because the rule of courtly love did not allow a passion of this kind 'to turn into a reality', to result in the 'full possession of his lady'. Accordingly, Tristan chooses to respect feudal fealty, which is thus made to disguise and equivocally to abet courtly fealty. He chooses quite freely; for, as was noted above, being stronger than the king and the barons, he could—*on the feudal plane upon which he puts himself*—resort to the right of force.

What a strange love (it will be thought) that thus conforms to laws whereby it stands condemned in order the better to preserve itself! Whence arises this preference for whatever *thwarts* passion, hinders the lovers' 'happiness', and parts and torments them? To reply that so courtly love required is only to reply superficially; for this still leaves it to be ascertained why love of this kind is preferred to the other, the love that gets 'fulfilled' and 'satisfied'. With the help of the highly plausible theory that the Romance illustrates a conflict between 'religions', we have been able to specify and set forth the main difficulties raised by the plot; but really we have only succeeded in deferring a solution of the problem. . . .

THE LOVE OF LOVE

'De tous les maux, le mien diffère; il me plaît; je me réjouis de lui; mon mal est ce que je veux et ma douleur est ma santé. Je ne vois donc pas de quoi je me plains; car mon mal me vient de ma volonté; c'est mon vouloir qui devient mon mal; mais j'ai tant d'aise à vouloir ainsi que je souffre agréablement, et tant de joie dans me douleur que je suis malade avec délices.'—
CHRESTIEN DE TROYES.[9]

It is only 'silly' questions that can enlighten us; for behind whatever seems obvious lurks something that is not. Let us then boldly ask: Does Tristan care for Iseult, and she for him? The lovers do not seem to be brought together in any normal *human* way. On the contrary, at their first encounter they confine themselves to having ordinary polite relations; and later, when Tristan returns to Ireland to fetch Iseult, the politeness, it will be remembered, gives place to open hostility. Everything goes to show that they would never have chosen one another were they acting *freely*. But no sooner have they drunk the love-potion than passion flares between them. Yet that any fondness supervenes to unite them as a result of the magic spell I have found, among the thousands of lines of the Romance, only a single indication. When, following Tristan's escape, it has been told how they have gone to live in the Forest of Morrois, there occur these lines:

> *Aspre vie meinent et dure:*
> *Tant s'entraiment de bone amor*
> *L'un por l'autre ne sent dolor.*[10]

If it should be imagined that poets in the Middle Ages were less emotional than we have grown to be and felt no need to insist on what goes without saying, let the account of the three years in the forest be read attentively. Its two finest passages—which are no doubt also the most profound passages in the whole legend—describe the lovers' two visits to the hermit Ogrin. The first time they go to see him, it is in order to make confession. But instead of confessing their sin and asking for absolution, they do their best to convince him that they are not to blame for what has befallen, since after all *they do not care for one another!*

> *Q'el m'aime, c'est par la poison*
> *Ge ne me pus de lié partir,*
> *N'ele de moi———*[11]

So speaks Tristan, and Iseult says after him:

> *Sire, por Deu omnipotent,*
> *Il ne m'aime pas, ne je lui,*
> *Fors par un herbé dont je bui*
> *Et il en but: ce fu pechiez.*[12]

They are thus in a thrillingly contradictory position. They love, but not one another. They have sinned, but cannot repent; for they are not to blame. They make confession, but wish neither to reform nor even to beg forgiveness. Actually, then, like all other great lovers, they imagine that they have been ravished 'beyond good and evil' into a kind of transcendental state outside ordinary human experience, into an ineffable absolute irreconcilable with the world, but that they feel to be *more real than the world*. Their oppressive fate, even though they yield to it with wailings, obliterates the antithesis of good and evil, and carries them away beyond the source of moral values, beyond pleasure and pain, beyond the realm of distinctions—into a realm where opposites cancel out.

Their admission is explicit enough: 'Il ne m'aime pas, ne je lui.' Everything happens as if they could neither see nor recognize one another. They are the prisoners of 'exquisite anguish' owing to something which neither controls—some alien power independent of their capacities, or at any rate of their conscious wishes, and of their being in so far as they are aware of being. Both characters, the man as much as the woman, are depicted physically and psychologically in an entirely conventional and rhetorical manner. He is 'the strongest'; she, 'the most beautiful'; he, the knight; she, the princess; and so on. It is impossible to believe that any human feeling can grow between two such rudimentary characters. The friendship mentioned in connexion with the length of time the effect of the love-potion lasts is the opposite of a true friendship; and, what is still more striking, if moral friendship does at last appear, it is at the moment their passion declines. And the immediate consequence of their nascent friendship, far from being to knit them more closely together, is to make them feel that they have everything to gain from a separation. This last point deserves to be considered more closely.

> L'endemain de la saint Jehan
> Aconpli furent li troi an.[13]

Tristan is out in the forest after game. Suddenly he is reminded of the world. He sees in his mind's eye King Mark's castle. He sighs for 'the vair and grey' and for the pomp of chivalry. He thinks of the high rank he might hold among his uncle's barons. He thinks too of his beloved—apparently for the first time! But for him she might be 'in fine rooms . . . hung with cloth of silk'. Simultaneously Iseult is filled with similar regrets. In the evening they are together and they confess to one another what is newly agitating them—'en mal uson nostre jovente'. It does not take them long to agree to part. Tristan talks of making off to Brittany. But first they will seek out Ogrin the Hermit and beg his forgiveness—and at the same time King Mark's forgiveness of Iseult.

It is at this point that there occurs a highly dramatic short dialogue between the hermit and the two penitents:

> Amors par force vos demeine![14]
> Conbien durra vostre folie?
> Trop avez mené ceste vie.

So Ogrin admonishes them.

> *Tristan li dist: or escoutez*[15]
> *Si longuement l'avons menee*
> *Itel fu nostre destinee.*

On top of this comes one more feature. When Tristan hears that the king agrees to Iseult's return:

> *Dex! dist Tristan, quel departie!*[16]
> *Molt est dolenz qui pert s'amie!*

It is with his own pain that he commiserates; not a thought for 's'amie'! And she too, we are made to feel, finds it much more pleasant to be back with the king than she ever did with her lover—happier in the unhappiness of love than she ever was in the life they led together in the Morrois.

For that matter, later on—as we have seen—passion seizes the lovers again, notwithstanding that the effect of the love-potion has worn off, and this time they are so carried away that they die —'he by her, she by him'. The seeming *selfishness* of their love is enough to account for the many 'chance' happenings and tricks of fate that obstruct their attainment of happiness. But this self-ishness, in its profound ambiguity, still wants explaining. Selfish-ness, it is said, always ends in death. But that is as a final defeat. Theirs, on the contrary, requires death for its perfect fulfilment and triumph. To the problem this raises there is only one answer worthy of the myth.

Tristan and Iseult do not love one another. They say they don't and everything goes to prove it. *What they love is love and being in love.* They behave as if aware that whatever obstructs love must ensure and consolidate it in the heart of each and in-tensify it infinitely in the moment they reach the absolute ob-stacle, which is death. Tristan loves the awareness that he is loving far more than he loves Iseult the Fair. And Iseult does nothing to hold Tristan. All she needs is her passionate dream. Their need of one another is in order to be aflame, and they do not need one another as they are. What they need is not one another's presence, but one another's absence. *Thus the partings of the lovers are dic-tated by their passion itself,* and by the love they bestow on their passion rather than on its satisfaction or on its living object. That is why the Romance abounds in obstructions, why when mutually encouraging their joint dream in which each remains solitary they show such astounding indifference, and why events work up in a romantic climax to a fatal apotheosis.

The duality is at once irrevocable and deliberate. 'Mot est dolenz qui pert s'amie,' Tristan sighs: and yet he then already sees, glimmering in the depths of the approaching night, that hidden flame which absence rekindles.

THE LOVE OF DEATH

But we must push on further still. Augustine's *amabam amare* is a poignant phrase with which he himself was not content. I have repeatedly referred to *obstruction*, and there is the way in which the passion of the two lovers *creates obstruction*, its effects coinciding with those of narrative necessity and of the reader's suspense. Is this obstruction not simply a *pretext* needed in order to enable the passion to progress, or is it connected with the passion in some far more profound manner? If we delve into the recesses of the myth, we see that this obstruction is what passion really *wants*—its true object.

I have shown that the Romance is given its motive power by the repeated partings and reunions of the lovers. For convenience, here once more, briefly, is what happens. Tristan, having landed in Ireland, meets Iseult and then parts from her without being in love. He turns up in Ireland again, and this time Iseult wants to kill him. They take ship together and drink the love-potion, and then sin. Next, Iseult is delivered up to Mark, and Tristan is banished from the castle. He and Iseult meet under a pine-tree, their talk being overheard by Mark. Tristan comes back to the castle, and Frocin and the barons discover evidence of his crime. They are parted. They meet again, and for three years go to live in the forest. Then, once more, they part. They meet at the hut of Orri the Woodman. Tristan goes away. He comes back, disguised as a poor pilgrim. He goes away again. The separation this time is prolonged, and he marries Iseult of the White Hand. Iseult the Fair is about to rejoin him when he dies. She dies too. More briefly still: They have one long spell together ('L'aspre vie'—'The harsh life'), to which corresponds a lengthy separation—and Tristan's marriage. First, the love-potion; lastly, the death of both. In between, furtive meetings.

They are led to part so often either by adverse external circumstances or by hindrances which Tristan devises; and it is to be noted that Tristan's behavior varies according to which kind of cause is operating. When social circumstances—for example, Mark's presence, the barons' suspiciousness, the Judgement of God—threaten the lovers, Tristan leaps over the obstruction (this is symbolized by his leap from his own bed to the queen's). He then does not mind pain (his wound reopens) nor the danger to his life (he knows he is being spied upon). Passion is then so violent—so brutish, it might be said—that in the intoxication of his *déduit* (or delight) he is oblivious to pain and perils alike. Nevertheless, the blood flowing from his wound betrays him. This is the 'red stain' that apprises the king of what is happening. And it also apprises the reader of the lovers' secret—that they are seeking peril for its own sake. But so long as the peril comes from without, Tristan's prowess in overcoming it is an affirmation of life. At this stage Tristan is simply complying with the feudal practice of knights. He has to prove his 'valour' and show he is either the stronger or the more wily. We have seen that if he persevered in this direction he would carry off the queen, and that established law is only respected here because this gives the tale an excuse to rebound.

But the knight's demeanour becomes quite different when nothing external any longer separates the two lovers. Indeed, it becomes the opposite of what it has been. When Tristan puts his drawn sword between himself and Iseult although they are lying down fully clothed, this is again prowess, but on this occasion against himself, *to his own cost*. Since he himself has set up the obstruction, it is no longer one *he can overcome!* It must not be overlooked that the hierarchy of events corresponds closely to the hierarchy of both the story-teller's and the reader's *preferences*. The most serious obstruction is thus the one preferred above all. It is the one most suited to intensifying passion. At this extreme, furthermore, the wish to part assumes an emotional value *greater than that of passion itself*. Death, in being the goal of passion, kills it.

Yet the drawn sword is not the ultimate expression of the dark desire and of the actual *end* of passion (in both senses of the word 'end'). The admirable episode of the exchange of swords makes this clear. When the king comes upon the lovers lying asleep in the cave, he substitutes his own sword for that of his rival. The meaning of this is that in place of the obstruction which the lovers have wanted and have deliberately set up he puts the sign of his social prerogative, a legal and objective obstruction. Tristan accepts the challenge, and thereby enables the *action* of the tale to rebound. At this point the word 'action' takes on a symbolical meaning. Action prevents 'passion' from being complete, for passion is 'what is suffered'—and its limit is death. In other words, the action here is a fresh postponement of passion, which means a delaying of Death.

There is the same shift as regards the two marriages in the Romance, that of Iseult the Fair to the king and that of Iseult of the White Hand to Tristan. The first is an obstruction in fact. The concrete existence of a *husband* symbolizes its character, husbands being despised in courtly love. Making the obstruction that leads to adultery a husband is unimaginative, the excuse most readily thought of, and most in keeping with everyday experience.[17] See how Tristan shoves the husband aside, and enjoys making sport of him! But for the existence of a husband, the love of Tristan and Iseult would not have lasted beyond three years! And old Béroul showed his good sense in limiting the effect of the love-potion to that length of time:

> *La mere Yseut, qui le bolli,*
> *A trois anz d'amistié le fist.*

But for the existence of a husband, the lovers would have had to get married; and it is unbelievable that Tristan should ever be in a position to marry Iseult. She typifies the woman a man does not marry; for once she became his wife she would no longer be what she is, and he would no longer love her. Just think of a Mme Tristan! It would be the negation of passion—at least of the passion we are concerned with here. The spontaneous ardour of a love crowned and not thwarted is essentially of short duration. It is a flare-up doomed not to survive the effulgence of its fulfilment. But its *branding* remains, and this is what the lovers want to prolong and indefinitely to renew. That is why they go on summoning fresh perils. But these the knight's valour drives him to overcome, and so he has to go away, in quest of more profound and more intimate—and it even seems, more interior—experiences.

When Tristan is sighing quietly for his lost Iseult, the brother of Iseult of the White Hand thinks his friend must be in love with his sister. This confusion—produced by identity of name—is the sole 'cause' of Tristan's marrying. It is obvious that he could easily have cleared up the misunderstanding. But here again honour supervenes—of course, as a mere pretext—to prevent him from drawing back. The reason is that he foresees, in this new ordeal which is *self-imposed*, the opportunity of a decisive advance. This merely formal marriage with a woman he finds beautiful is an obstruction which he can remove only by achieving a victory *over himself* (as well as over the institution of marriage, which he thus damages from within). This time his prowess goes against him. His chastity now he is married corresponds to the placing of the drawn sword between himself and the other Iseult. But a self-imposed chastity is a symbolical suicide (here is the hidden meaning of the sword)—a victory for the courtly ideal over the sturdy Celtic tradition which proclaimed its pride in life. It is a way of purifying desire of the spontaneous, brutish, and active elements still encumbering it. 'Passion' triumphs over desire. Death triumphs over life.

Hence Tristan's inclination for a *deliberate obstruction* turns out to be a desire for death and an advance in the direction of Death! But this death is for love, a deliberate death coming at the end of a series of ordeals thanks to which he will have been purified; a death that means transfiguration, and is in no way the result of some violent chance. Hence the aim is still to unite an external with an internal fate, which the lovers deliberately embrace. *In dying for love they redeem their destiny and are avenged for the love-potion.* So that at the last the struggle between passion and obstruction is inverted. At this point the obstruction is no longer serving irresistible passion, but has itself become the goal and end wished for for its own sake. Passion has thus only played the part of a purifying ordeal, it might almost be said of a penance, in the service of this transfiguring death. Here we are within sight of the ultimate secret.

The love of love itself has concealed a far more awful passion, a desire altogether unavowable, something that could only be 'betrayed' by means of symbols such as that of the drawn sword and that of perilous chastity. Unawares and in spite of themselves, the lovers have never had but one desire—the desire for death! Unawares, and passionately deceiving themselves, they have been seeking all the time simply to be redeemed and avenged for 'what they have suffered'—the passion unloosed by the love-potion. In the innermost recesses of their hearts they have been obeying the fatal dictates of a wish for death; they have been in the throes of *the active passion of Darkness.*

NOTES

1. In summing up the chief episodes of the Romance, I shall make use (except here and there) of M. Bédier's *Concordance* (contained in his study of Thomas's poem) for the five twelfth-century versions—those by Béroul, Thomas and Eilhart together with *La Folie Tristan* and *Le Roman en prose.* The later versions by Gottfried of Strasbourg, or by German, Italian, Danish, Russian, Czech, and other imitators, are all derived from those five. I also take into account the more recent critical undertakings of Messrs. E. Muret and E. Vinaver.

2. Verses 2137-2140:

> *A conbien fu determinez*
> *Li lovendrins, li vin herbez:*
> *La mere Yseut, qui le bolli,*
> *A trois anz d'amistié le fist.*

The quotation is from Béroul, as are those in Chapter 8, below. I follow A. Ewert's text (*The Romance of Tristan* (Oxford, Blackwell, 1939)), which is later than E. Muret, and I am also indebted to Ewert's glossary for my translations. 'For how long was the love potion, the herb wine? Mother Yseut, who brewed it, made it to three years of love.'—Translator's Note.

3. '*Pur belté e pur nun d'Isolt*' (Thomas).

4. It is true that in Bédier's edition of Thomas's poem (Vol. I, p. 240), the king's huntsman is said to have gone to the lovers' retreat, where he has seen 'Tristan' lying asleep, and across the cave was Iseult. The lovers were resting from the great heat, and lay apart from one another because . . . .' At this point the text

breaks off! And Bédier notes: 'An unintelligible passage.' What diabolical agency can have partly destroyed *the one text* likely to have solved the riddle?

5. Gottfried of Strasbourg brazenly insists:

'Twas thus made manifest
And averr'd before all
That Christ most glorious
Will mould like cloth for garments.
. . . He complies with ev'ry one's wish
Whether honest or deceitful.
He ever is as we would have Him be.

6. But to whom he had won a full title *himself* by delivering her from the dragon, as Thomas does not omit to stress.

7. The judgement reads as follows: 'We declare and affirm, by the tenour of these presents, that love cannot extend its rights over two married persons. For indeed lovers grant one another all things mutually and freely, without being impelled by any motive of necessity, whereas husband and wife are held by their duty to submit their wills to each other and to refuse each other nothing.

'May this judgement, which we have delivered with extreme caution, and after consulting with a great number of other ladies, be for you a constant and unassailable truth, Delivered in this year 1174, on the third day before the Kalends of May, Proclamation VII.'

8. Claude Fauriel, *Histoire de la poésie provençale* (Paris, 1846), I, p. 512.

9. 'From all other ills doth mine differ. It pleaseth me; I rejoice at it; my ill is what I want and my suffering is my health. So I do not see what I am complaining about; for my ill comes to me by my will; it is my willing that becomes my ill; but I am so pleased to want thus that I suffer agreeably, and have so much joy in my pain that I am sick with delight.'

10. 'Harsh life led they and hard, so entertaining good love for one another. One by the other was ne'er exposed to pain.'

11. 'If she loves me, it is by the poison which holds me from leaving her and her from leaving me.'

12. 'Lord, by almighty God, he loves me not, nor I him; except for a herb potion which I drank and which he drank; it was a sin.'

13. 'On the morrow of St John's Day, the three years were accomplished.'

14. 'Love by force dominates you. How long will your folly last? Too long you have been leading this life.' *Amors par force vos demeine*—the most poignant description of passion ever penned by a poet! We must pause to admire it. In a single line the whole of passion is summed up with a vigour of expression making all romanticism look pallid! Shall we ever recover this sturdy 'dialect of the heart'?

15. 'Tristan quoth to him: "Now hearken, if for long we have been leading this life, that is because it was our destiny."'

16. 'God!' quoth Tristan, 'What a fate! Wretched he who loseth his mistress.'

17. Romanticism was later on to devise more refined excuses.

DANTE ALIGHIERI: Beatrice*

IN THAT part of the book of my memory before the which is little that can be read, there is a rubric, saying, *Incipit Vita Nova*.[1] Under such rubric I find written many things; and among them the words which I purpose to copy into this little book; if not all of them, at the least their substance.

* Reprinted from *The New Life*.

Nine times already since my birth had the heaven of light returned to the selfsame point almost, as concerns its own revolution, when first the glorious Lady of my mind was made manifest to mine eyes; even she who was called Beatrice by many who knew not wherefore.[2] She had already been in this life for so long as that, within her time, the starry heaven had moved towards the Eastern quarter one of the twelve parts of a degree; so that she appeared to me at the beginning of her ninth year almost, and I saw her almost at the end of my ninth year. Her dress, on that day, was of a most noble colour, a subdued and goodly crimson, girdled and adorned in such sort as best suited with her very tender age. At that moment, I say most truly that the spirit of life, which hath its dwelling in the secretest chamber of the heart, began to tremble so violently that the least pulses of my body shook therewith; and in trembling it said these words: *Ecce deus fortior me, qui veniens dominabitur mihi.*[3] At that moment the animate spirit, which dwelleth in the lofty chamber whither all the senses carry their perceptions, was filled with wonder, and speaking more especially unto the spirits of the eyes, said these words: *Apparuit jam beatitudo vestra.*[4] At that moment the natural spirit, which dwelleth there where our nourishment is administered, began to weep, and in weeping said these words. *Heu miser! quia frequenter impeditus ero deinceps.*[5]

I say that, from that time forward, Love quite governed my soul; which was immediately espoused to him, and with so safe and undisputed a lordship (by virtue of strong imagination), that I had nothing left for it but to do all his bidding continually. He oftentimes commanded me to seek if I might see his youngest of the Angels: wherefore I in my boyhood often went in search of her, and found her so noble and praiseworthy that certainly of her might have been said those words of the poet Homer, "She seemed not to be the daughter of a mortal man, but of God."[6] And albeit her image, that was with me always, was an exultation of Love to subdue me, it was yet of so perfect a quality that it never allowed me to be overruled by Love without the faithful counsel of reason, whensoever such counsel was useful to be heard. But seeing that were I to dwell overmuch on the passions and doings of such early youth, my words might be counted something fabulous, I will therefore put them aside; and passing many things that may be conceived by the pattern of these, I will come to such as are writ in my memory with a better distinctness.

After the lapse of so many days that nine years exactly were completed since the above-written appearance of this most gracious being, on the last of those days it happened that the same wonderful lady appeared to me dressed all in pure white, between

two gentle ladies elder than she. And passing through a street, she
turned her eyes thither where I stood sorely abashed: and by her
unspeakable courtesy, which is now guerdoned in the Great Cycle,
she saluted me with so virtuous a bearing that I seemed then and
there to behold the very limits of blessedness. The hour of her
most sweet salutation was certainly the ninth of that day; and because it was the first time that any words from her reached mine
ears, I came into such sweetness that I parted thence as one intoxicated. And betaking me to the loneliness of mine own room, I fell
to thinking of this most courteous lady, thinking of whom I was
overtaken by a pleasant slumber, wherein a marvellous vision was
presented to me: for there appeared to be in my room a mist of
the colour of fire, within the which I discerned the figure of a lord
of terrible aspect to such as should gaze upon him, but who seemed
therewithal to rejoice inwardly that it was a marvel to see. Speaking he said many things, among the which I could understand but
few; and of these, this: *Ego dominus tuus.*[7] In his arms it seemed
to me that a person was sleeping, covered only with a blood-
coloured cloth; upon whom looking very attentively, I knew that
it was the lady of the salutation who had deigned the day before
to salute me. And he who held her held also in his hand a thing
that was burning in flames; and he said to me, *Vide cor tuum.*[8]
But when he had remained with me a little while, I thought that
he set himself to awaken her that slept; after the which he made
her to eat that thing which flamed in his hand; and she ate as one
fearing. Then, having waited again a space, all his joy was turned
into most bitter weeping; and as he wept he gathered the lady into
his arms, and it seemed to me that he went with her up towards
heaven; whereby such a great anguish came upon me that my light
slumber could not endure through it, but was suddenly broken.
And immediately having considered, I knew that the hour wherein this vision had been made manifest to me was the fourth hour
(which is to say, the first of the nine last hours) of the night.

Then, musing on what I had seen, I proposed to relate the
same to many poets who were famous in that day: and for that I
had myself in some sort the art of discoursing with rhyme, I resolved on making a sonnet, in the which, having saluted all such
as are subject unto Love, and entreated them to expound my
vision, I should write unto them those things which I had seen in
my sleep. And the sonnet I made was this:—

> To every heart which the sweet pain doth move,
>   And unto which these words may now be brought
>   For true interpretation and kind thought,
> Be greeting in our Lord's name, which is Love.
> Of those long hours wherein the stars, above.

Wake and keep watch, the third was almost nought
When Love was shown me with such terrors fraught
As may not carelessly be spoken of.

He seem'd like one who is full of joy, and had
My heart within his hand, and on his arm
My lady, with a mantle round her, slept;
Whom (having waken'd her) anon he made
To eat that heart; she ate, as fearing harm.
Then he went out; and as he went, he wept.

. . . There rose up in me on a certain day, about the ninth
hour, a strong visible phantasy, wherein I seemed to behold the
most gracious Beatrice, habited in that crimson raiment which
she had worn when I had first beheld her; also she appeared
to me of the same tender age as then. Whereupon I fell into a
deep thought of her: and my memory ran back according to the
order of time, unto all those matters in the which she had borne
a part: and my heart began painfully to repent of the desire by
which it had so basely let itself be possessed during so many days,
contrary to the constancy of reason.

And then, this evil desire being quite gone from me, all
my thoughts turned again unto their excellent Beatrice. And I say
most truly that from that hour I thought constantly of her with
the whole humbled and ashamed heart; the which became often
manifest in sighs, that had among them the name of that most
gracious creature, and how she departed from us. Also it would
come to pass very often, through the bitter anguish of some one
thought, that I forgot both it, and myself, and where I was. By
this increase of sighs, my weeping, which before had been somewhat lessened, increased in like manner; so that mine eyes seemed
to long only for tears and to cherish them, and came at last to be
circled about with red as though they had suffered martyrdom;
neither were they able to look again upon the beauty of any face
that might again bring them to shame and evil: from which things
it will appear that they were fitly guerdoned for their unsteadfast-
ness. Wherefore I (wishing that mine abandonment of all such
evil desires and vain temptations should be certified and made
manifest, beyond all doubts which might have been suggested by
the rhymes aforewritten) proposed to write a sonnet, wherein I
should express this purport. And I then wrote, "Woe's me!" . . .

After writing this sonnet, it was given unto me to behold a
very wonderful vision;[9] wherein I saw things which determined
me that I would say nothing further of this most blessed one, until
such time as I could discourse more worthily concerning her. And
to this end I labour all I can; as she well knoweth. Wherefore if it

be His pleasure through whom is the life of all things, that my life continue with me a few years, it is my hope that I shall yet write concerning her what hath not before been written of any woman. After the which, may it seem good unto Him who is the Master of Grace, that my spirit should go hence to behold the glory of its lady: to wit, of that blessed Beatrice who now gazeth continually on His countenance *qui est per omnia sæcula benedictus.*[10] *Laus Deo.*

NOTES

1. "Here beginneth the new life."
2. In reference to the meaning of the name, "She who confers blessing." We learn from Boccaccio that this first meeting took place at a May Feast, given in the year 1274 by Folco Portinari, father of Beatrice, who ranked among the principal citizens of Florence: to which feast Dante accompanied his father, Alighiero Alighieri.
3. "Here is a deity stronger than I; who, coming, shall rule over me."
4. "Your beatitude hath now been made manifest unto you."
5. "Alas! how often shall I be disturbed from this time forth!"
6.
$$\text{Οὐδὲ ἐῴκει Ἀνδρός γε θνητοῦ παῖς ἔμμεναι, ἀλλὰ θεοῖο.}$$
(*Iliad*, xxiv. 258.)
7. "I am thy master."
8. "Behold thy heart."
9. This we may believe to have been the Vision of Hell, Purgatory, and Paradise, which furnished the triple argument of the *Divina Commedia*. The Latin words ending the *Vita Nuova* are almost identical with those at the close of the letter in which Dante, on concluding the *Paradise*, and accomplishing the hope here expressed, dedicates his great work to Can Grande della Scala.
10. "Who is blessed throughout all ages."

JOHANN WOLFGANG VON GOETHE: The Sorrows of Young Werther

. . . A STREAM of tears, which gushed from Lotte's eyes and afforded relief to her oppressed heart, interrupted Werther's reading. He threw down the sheets, seized her hand and wept bitterly. Lotte supported herself on her other arm and hid her eyes in her handkerchief. The agitation of both of them was terrible. They felt their own misery in the fate of those noble ones, felt it together, and their tears mingled. Werther's lips and eyes burned on Lotte's arms, a tremor ran through her, she tried to withdraw, and all her grief, all her pity lay heavy as lead upon her. She took a deep breath to recover herself and begged him with a sob to continue, begged him with the whole voice of

Heaven. Werther trembled, his heart felt as though it would burst, he picked up the sheet and read in a broken voice:[1]

"Why dost thou awake me, O breath of Spring, thou dost woo me and say: 'I cover thee with the drops of heaven,' But the time of my fading is near, the blast that shall scatter my leaves. To-morrow shall the traveller come; he that saw me in my beauty shall come. His eyes will search the field, but they will not find me."

The whole force of these words deprived the unhappy man of his self-possession. He threw himself at Lotte's feet in utter despair, seized her hands, pressed them against his eyes, against his forehead, and a foreboding of his dreadful intention appeared to flash through her soul. Her mind grew confused, she clasped his hands, pressed them against her breast, bent over him with a sorrowful air, and their burning cheeks touched. They were lost to the world, he twined his arms round her, pressed her to his breast, and covered her trembling, stammering lips with frenzied kisses. "Werther!" she cried in a suffocating voice, turning away her face, "Werther!", and she thrust him away from her breast with a nerveless hand. "Werther!" she cried in a calm tone with noble dignity. He did not resist, released her from his embrace, and threw himself madly at her feet. She got up hastily and, in nervous confusion, trembling between love and anger, she said, "This is the last time, Werther! You shall not see me again." With a look, fraught with love, at the unhappy man, she rushed into the next room and locked the door behind her. Werther stretched his arms out towards her, not daring to hold her back. He lay on the ground, his head on the sofa, and in this attitude he remained for half an hour, until a sound recalled him to himself. It was the maid who wanted to lay the table. He walked up and down the room and, when he saw that he was alone again, went to the door of the cabinet and called gently, "Lotte! Lotte! only one word more, in farewell!"—She was silent, he waited—and begged—and waited, then tore himself away and cried, "Farewell, Lotte! Farewell for ever!"

He came to the town gate. The watchmen, who were used to him, let him out without a word. There was a drizzle, half rain half snow, and it was getting on for eleven when he knocked at the gate again. His servant noticed, when Werther returned home, that he was without his hat. He did not venture to say anything and undressed him. Everything was wet. The hat was found afterwards on a rock, on the slope of the hill towards the valley, and it is inconceivable how he managed to climb up there on a wet dark night without falling headlong.

He lay down in bed and slept for many hours. His servant

found him writing, when, at his call, he brought in his coffee next morning. He added the following to the letter to Lotte:

For the last time then, for the last time I open these eyes. They are alas! to see the sun no more; it is hidden by a dark and misty day. Mourn then, Nature! thy son, thy friend, thy lover nears his end. Lotte, it is a feeling without compare, and yet it is most akin to a twilight dream, to say to oneself, 'This is the last morning.' The last! Lotte, I have no conception of the word—the last! Do I not stand here in all my strength, and to-morrow I shall lie stretched out and inert on the ground! Die! What does that mean? We are dreaming when we speak of death. I have seen many people die, yet humanity is so limited that it has no conception of the beginning and end of its existence. Still mine, thine! thine! beloved, and the next moment— separated, parted—perhaps for ever.—No, Lotte, no.—How can I pass away, how can you pass away, do we not exist!—Pass away!—What does that mean? It is again a word! an empty sound, that awakes no echo in my heart.—Dead, Lotte! Interred in the cold earth, so narrow, so dark!—There was a girl who was everything to me in my helpless youth; she died, and I followed her corpse and stood beside her grave. As they let down the coffin and pulled up the whirring ropes again from under it, as the first shovelful of earth thudded down and the fearful shell gave back a muffled sound, becoming more and more muffled till it was at last entirely covered—I sank down beside the grave—moved, shaken, in anguish, my soul torn, but I knew not what had happened to me—what will happen to me—Death! The grave! I do not understand the words!

Oh, forgive me! Yesterday! It should have been the last hour of my life. Oh, you angel! for the first time, for the first time there glowed through the depths of my soul, without room for doubt, the feeling of rapture: She loves me! She loves me! The sacred fire that streamed from your lips still burns on mine, a fresh rapturous warmth is in my heart. Forgive me, forgive me.

Oh, I knew that you loved me, knew from the first soulful glances, the first hand pressure, and yet when I went away again, when I saw Albert at your side, I again despaired with feverish doubtings.

Do you remember the flowers you sent me, when you were unable to say a word to me, or give me your hand, at that odious party? Oh! I have knelt in front of them half the night and they put the seal on your love for me. But alas! these impressions faded, as the believer gradually loses the sense of his God's loving kindness which was accorded him with all Heaven's abundance in sacred and visible symbols.

All this is transitory, but no eternity can extinguish the glowing essence that I imbibed yesterday from your lips, that I feel within me. She loves me! This arm has embraced her, these lips have trembled on her lips, this mouth has stammered against hers. She is mine! You are mine! Yes, Lotte, for ever!

And what does it mean, that Albert is your husband? Husband!—That is to say in this world—and in this world it is a sin that

I love you, that I would like to snatch you from his arms into mine? A sin? Good! I am punishing myself for it. I have tasted this sin in all its divine rapture, have drunk restoring balsam and strength into my heart. From that moment you were mine! mine, Lotte! I go ahead! to my Father and to yours. To Him I will bring my plaint, and He will solace me till you come and I can fly to you, clasp you, stay with you before the face of the Infinite in an eternal embrace.

This is no dream, no delusion! On the verge of the grave I saw more clearly. We *shall* exist! We shall see one another again! See your mother! I shall see her, find her, and oh! pour out all my heart before her. Your mother, bearing the semblance of yourself.

Towards eleven o'clock Werther enquired of his servant whether Albert had yet returned. The servant said that he had, for he had seen his horse being led. His master then gave him an unsealed note with the following contents:

Would you lend me your pistols for a journey I am about to undertake? Farewell.

Lotte had slept little that night; she was in a state of feverish agitation, and her heart was ravaged with a thousand emotions. In spite of herself, she felt deep within her breast the passion of Werther's embraces, and at the same time she saw with double beauty the days of her artless innocence, of her care-free confidence in herself. She already feared beforehand her husband's gaze and his half-vexed, half-mocking questions, when he should hear of Werther's visit. She had never dissembled, she had never lied, and now she was faced, for the first time, with the unavoidable necessity of doing so. The reluctance, the embarrassment she felt, made the fault all the greater in her eyes, and yet she could neither hate him who was the cause of it nor promise herself never to see him again. She wept till morning, when she sank into a sleep of exhaustion, from which she had hardly risen and dressed when her husband returned, whose presence for the first time she found quite unbearable. For she trembled lest he should discover in her the traces of a sleepless night spent in tears, and this increased her confusion, so that she greeted him with an impetuous embrace which was more expressive of consternation and remorse than passionate delight, thereby attracting the attention of Albert, who asked her curtly, after he had opened some letters and packets, whether anything had happened, whether any one had called. She answered hesitatingly that Werther had been there for an hour on the previous day.—"He chooses his time well," he replied, and went to his study. Lotte remained alone for a quarter of an hour. The presence of her husband, whom she loved and honoured, had made a fresh impression on her heart. She remembered all his kindness, generosity and affection, and reproached herself for having so ill requited them. An obscure impulse made her follow him; she took her work, as she was sometimes wont to do, and went to his room. She asked him whether he needed anything, but he said that he did not and sat down at his desk to write, while she sat down to do her knitting. They had been together for an hour in this way, when Albert began to walk up and down the room. Lotte spoke to him, but he made little or no reply, only sitting down at his desk again, and she fell into a train of melancholy thoughts which were all the more distressing since she tried to hide them and to stay her tears.

The appearance of Werther's boy plunged her in the greatest embarrassment. He handed the note to Albert, who turned coldly to his wife and said, "Give him the pistols."—"I wish him a good journey," he said to the youth. This was like a thunderclap to her. She faltered in an attempt to rise. She could not understand her feelings. Slowly she went to the wall, took them down trembling, wiped off the dust and hesitated, and would have delayed still more if Albert's enquiring glance had not impelled her. She gave the fatal weapons to the boy, without being able to utter a word, and when he had gone she gathered her work together and went to her room in a state of the most inexpressible anguish. Her heart prophesied all sorts of catastrophes. At first she was on the verge of throwing herself at her husband's feet and revealing everything—what had happened on the previous evening, her own fault and forebodings. Then she could not see what would be the advantage of such a step. Least of all could she hope to persuade her husband to go to Werther. The table was laid, and a friend of Lotte's, who only came to make some enquiry but was not allowed by Lotte to leave, made conversation bearable during the meal. They constrained themselves, discussed sundry matters, and were able to forget.

The boy brought the pistols to Werther, who took them from him in a transport of delight when he heard that they had been handed to him by Lotte. He had bread and wine brought in, told the boy to go and have his dinner, and sat down to write.

They have passed through your hands, you have wiped the dust from them, I kiss them a thousand times for you have touched them. Thou, Spirit of Heaven, dost favour my resolve! And you, Lotte, offer me the weapon, you, at whose hands I wished to encounter death and alas! now encounter it! Oh! I made my servant tell me everything —you trembled when you handed them to him, you bade me no farewell!—Alas! Alas!—no farewell! Is it possible that you have closed your heart to me on account of the moment which sealed me to you for ever? Lotte, a thousand years cannot wipe out the impress! And I feel that you cannot hate him who burns for you thus.

After the meal he ordered his boy to finish packing everything, destroyed a number of papers, and went out to settle some small debts. He returned home, went out again beyond the gate, in spite of the rain, as far as the Count's garden, roved about the neighbourhood, came back as night fell, and wrote:

I have seen field, wood and sky for the last time, Wilhelm. I bid you farewell, also! Forgive me, mother! Console her, Wilhelm. God bless you both! My affairs are all in order. Farewell! We shall meet again in happier circumstances.

I have ill rewarded you, Albert, but you will forgive me. I have ruined the peace of your house and sowed distrust between you. Farewell, I am about to make an end. Oh! that my death might restore your happiness! Albert! Albert! Make the angel happy. And may God's blessing rest upon you!

He spent much time turning out his papers during the evening, tore many of them up and threw them in the stove, and sealed a number of packages which he addressed to Wilhelm. They contained small essays and disconnected ideas, several of which I have seen. After having the fire made up and a flask of wine brought in, he sent his servant, who slept some distance away, as did the other domestics, to bed. The boy lay down in his clothes in order to be at hand at an early hour, for his master had told him that the coach horses would be at the door before six.

after eleven.

All is so still around me and my soul so calm. I thank thee, Lord, for these last moments of strength and ardour.

I step to the window, my dearest, and still see some stars shining through the fleeting storm-clouds. No, you will not fall! The Eternal One bears you at his heart, and me. I saw the wheeler stars of Charles's Wain, the loveliest of all the constellations. When I left you at night, as I went out at the gate, it was in front of me. With what intoxication have I so often gazed at it, raised aloft my hands and made it a symbol, a sacred token of the bliss I felt, and still—Oh! Lotte, what is there that does not remind me of you! Are you not about me always! And have I not always, like a child, insatiably, seized every trifle that your saintly hands had touched!

Beloved silhouette! I now return it to you at my death, Lotte, and beg you to hold it in honour. I have pressed a thousand, thousand kisses on it, waved a thousand greetings to it when I went out or returned.

I have left a note for your father entreating him to protect my body. In the churchyard there are two lime trees, at the back in a corner, towards the field, and there I wish to lie. He can and will do this for his friend. Add your entreaties to mine. I will not ask pious Christians to allow their bodies to rest beside that of a poor wretch. Oh! I could wish to be buried by the wayside, or in the lonely valley, that priest and Levite might cross themselves as they passed by the stone which marked the spot, and the Samaritan shed a tear.

Here, Lotte! I do not shudder to take the dread cold cup from which I am to drink the ecstasy of death! It is you who have handed it to me, and I do not fear. All! All! thus are all the desires and hopes of my life fulfilled! To knock so cold, so stiff, at the brazen gate of death.

That I might have been granted the happiness to die for you! To sacrifice myself for you, Lotte! I would die with a stout heart, I would die gladly, if I could restore the tranquillity, the rapture of your life. But alas! it was granted to but few noble souls to shed their blood for those they loved, and by their deaths to kindle for them a new life enhanced an hundredfold.

I wish to be buried in these clothes, Lotte. You have touched and sanctified them. I have asked your father to grant me this favour. My soul will hover over my coffin. Let them not search my pockets. This pink bow which you wore on your bosom, when I met you first among your children—Oh! kiss them a thousand times and tell them the fate of their unhappy friend. The darlings, how they swarm about me. Oh! how I attached myself to you, could not keep away from you from the first moment! Let this bow be buried with me. You gave it me on my birthday! How eagerly I accepted it all!—Alas, I did not think that the way would lead to this!—Be calm! I beg you, be calm!—

They are loaded—it is striking twelve!—So be it then—Lotte! Lotte, farewell! Farewell!

A neighbour saw the flash of the powder and heard the shot, but as everything remained still he paid no more attention.

At six next morning the servant entered with a candle and found his master stretched on the floor, with blood about and the pistol by him. He called to him, seized hold of him, but there was no answer, only a rattling in the throat. He ran for a doctor, for Albert. Lotte heard the bell, all her limbs began to tremble. She woke her husband, they got up, the servant stammered the news amid sobs, Lotte sank to the ground in a swoon in front of Albert.

When the physician arrived, he found the unhappy youth on the floor beyond all hope; his pulse was still beating but all his limbs were paralysed. He had shot himself through the head above the right eye, and his brains were protruding. He was bled in the arm, the blood flowed and he still breathed.

From the blood on the arm of his chair it was concluded that he had committed the deed sitting at his desk. He had then sunk down and twisted convulsively round the chair. He lay on his back in the direction of the window, deprived of strength, fully dressed in boots, blue coat and yellow waistcoat.

The house, the neighbours, the whole town were in a turmoil. Albert entered. Werther had been laid on the bed, his forehead tied up, his face already like that of a dead man, without moving a limb. A dreadful rattling noise still came from his lungs, now faintly, now more loudly; the end was near.

He had only drunk one glass of the wine. *Emilia Galotti* lay open on his desk.

I cannot describe Albert's dismay, Lotte's grief.

The old bailiff came galloping up at the news, and he kissed the dying youth as the hot tears coursed down his cheeks. His eldest sons arrived soon afterwards on foot and sank beside the bed with expressions of the most unrestrained sorrow, kissed his hands and mouth, and the eldest, of whom he had been the most fond, clung to his lips and had to be torn away by force. He died at noon. The presence of the bailiff and the arrangements he made prevented a crowd from assembling. He had him buried towards eleven o'clock at night at the spot that he had chosen. The old man and his sons followed the body. Albert could not. Lotte's life was in danger. He was carried by workmen. There was no pastor present.

NOTES

1. From Ossian's *Berrathon*. (Translator's note).

SAMUEL TAYLOR COLERIDGE: Passion and Order*

PERHAPS THERE is no more sure criterion of refinement in moral character, of the purity of intellectual intention, and of the deep conviction and perfect sense of what our own nature really is in all its combinations, than the different definitions different men would give of love. I will not detain you by stating the various known definitions, some of which it may be better not to repeat: I will rather give you one of my own, which, I apprehend, is equally free from the extravagance of pretended Platonism (which, like other things which super-moralise, is sure to demoralise) and from its grosser opposite.

Consider myself and my fellow-men as a sort of link between heaven and earth, being composed of body and soul, with power to reason and to will, and with that perpetual aspiration which tells us that this is ours for a while, but it is not ourselves;

* Reprinted from *Literary Criticism*.

considering man, I say, in this two-fold character yet united in one person, I conceive that there can be no correct definition of love which does not correspond with our being, and with that subordination of one part to another which constitutes our perfection. I would say therefore that—

"Love is a desire of the whole being to be united to some thing, or some being, felt necessary to its completeness, by the most perfect means that nature permits, and reason dictates."

It is inevitable to every noble mind, whether man or woman, to feel itself, of itself, imperfect and insufficient, not as an animal only, but as a moral being. How wonderfully, then, has Providence contrived for us, by making that which is necessary to us a step in our exaltation to a higher and nobler state! The Creator has ordained that one should possess qualities which the other has not, and the union of both is the most complete ideal of human character. In everything the blending of the similar with the dissimilar is the secret of all pure delight. Who shall dare to stand alone, and vaunt himself, in himself, sufficient? In poetry it is the blending of passion with order that constitutes perfection: this is still more the case in morals, and more than all in the exclusive attachment of the sexes.

True it is, that the world and its business may be carried on without marriage; but it is so evident that Providence intended man (the only animal of all climates, and whose reason is preeminent over instinct) to be the master of the world, that marriage, or the knitting together of society by the tenderest, yet firmest ties, seems ordained to render him capable of maintaining his superiority over the brute creation. Man alone has been privileged to clothe himself, and to do all things so as to make him, as it were, a secondary creator of himself, and of his own happiness or misery: in this, as in all, the image of the Deity is impressed upon him.

Providence, then, has not left us to prudence only; for the power of calculation, which prudence implies, cannot have existed, but in a state which pre-supposes marriage. If God has done this, shall we suppose that he has given us no moral sense, no yearning, which is something more than animal, to secure that, without which man might form a herd, but could not be a society? The very idea seems to breathe absurdity.

From this union arise the paternal, filial, brotherly and sisterly relations of life; and every state is but a family magnified. All the operations of mind, in short, all that distinguishes us from brutes, originate in the more perfect state of domestic life.—One infallible criterion in forming an opinion of a man is the reverence in which he holds women. Plato has said, that in this way we rise from sensuality to affection, from affection to love, and from love to the pure intellectual delight by which we become worthy to conceive that infinite in ourselves, without which it is impossible for man to believe in a God. In a word, the grandest and most delightful of all promises has been expressed to us by this practical state—our marriage with the Redeemer of mankind.

I might safely appeal to every man who hears me, who in youth has been accustomed to abandon himself to his animal passions, whether when he first really fell in love, the earliest symptom was not a complete change in his manners, a contempt and a hatred of himself for having excused his conduct by asserting, that he acted according to the dictates of nature, that his vices were the inevitable consequences of youth, and that his passions at that period of life could not be conquered? The surest friend of chastity is love: it leads us, not to sink the mind in the body, but to draw up the body to the mind—the immortal part of our nature. See how contrasted in this respect are some portions of the works of writers, whom I need not name, with other portions of the same works: the ebullitions of comic humour have at times, by a lamentable confusion, been made the means of debasing our nature, while at other times, even in the same volume, we are happy to notice the utmost purity, such as the purity of love, which above all other qualities renders us most pure and lovely.

Love is not, like hunger, a mere selfish appetite: it is an associative quality. The hungry savage is nothing but an animal, thinking only of the satisfaction of his stomach: what is the first effect of love, but to associate the feeling with every object in nature? the trees whisper, the roses exhale their perfumes, the nightingales sing, nay the very skies smile in unison with the feeling of true and pure love. It gives to every object in nature a power of the heart, without which it would indeed be spiritless.

PERCY BYSSHE SHELLEY: Love Is a Powerful Attraction

WHAT IS LOVE? Ask him who lives, what is life? ask him who adores, what is God?

I know not the internal constitution of other men, nor even thine, whom I now address. I see that in some external attributes they resemble me, but when, misled by that appearance, I have thought to appeal to something in common, and unburthen

my inmost soul to them, I have found my language misunderstood, like one in a distant and savage land. The more opportunities they have afforded me for experience, the wider has appeared
the interval between us, and to a greater distance have the points
of sympathy been withdrawn. With a spirit ill fitted to sustain
such proof, trembling and feeble through its tenderness, I have
everywhere sought sympathy and have found only repulse and
disappointment.

Thou demandest what is love? It is that powerful attraction
towards all that we conceive, or fear, or hope beyond ourselves,
when we find within our own thoughts the chasm of an insufficient void, and seek to awaken in all things that are, a community
with what we experience within ourselves. If we reason, we would
be understood; if we imagine, we would that the airy children of
our brain were born anew within another's; if we feel, we would
that another's nerves should vibrate to our own, that the beams
of their eyes should kindle at once and mix and melt into our
own, that lips of motionless ice should not reply to lips quivering
and burning with the heart's best blood. This is Love. This is the
bond and the sanction which connects not only man with man,
but with everything which exists. We are born into the world,
and there is something within us, from the instant that we live,
that more and more thirsts after its likeness. It is probably in correspondence with this law that the infant drains milk from the
bosom of its mother; this propensity develops itself with the development of our nature. We dimly see within our intellectual
nature a minimum as it were of our entire self, yet deprived of
all that we condemn or despise, the ideal prototype of everything
excellent or lovely that we are capable of conceiving as belonging
to the nature of man. Not only the portrait of our external being,
but an assemblage of the minutest particles of which our nature
is composed; a mirror whose surface reflects only the forms of
purity and brightness; a soul within our soul that describes a
circle around its proper paradise, which pain, and sorrow, and
evil dare not overleap. To this we eagerly refer all sensations,
thirsting that they should resemble or correspond with it. The
discovery of its antitype; the meeting with an understanding capable of clearly estimating our own; and imagination which should
enter into and seize upon the subtle and delicate peculiarities
which we have delighted to cherish and unfold in secret; with a
frame whose nerves, like the chords of two exquisite lyres, strung
to the accompaniment of one delightful voice, vibrate with the
vibrations of our own; and of a combination of all these in such
proportion as the type within demands; this is the invisible and
unattainable point to which Love tends; and to attain which, it

urges forth the powers of man to arrest the faintest shadow of that, without the possession of which there is no rest nor respite to the heart over which it rules. Hence in solitude, or in that deserted state when we are surrounded by human beings, and yet they sympathize not with us, we love the flowers, the grass, and the waters, and the sky. In the motion of the very leaves of spring, in the blue air, there is then found a secret correspondence with our heart. There is eloquence in the tongueless wind, and a melody in the flowing brooks and the rustling of the reeds beside them, which by their inconceivable relation to something within the soul, awaken the spirits to a dance of breathless rapture, and bring tears of mysterious tenderness to the eyes, like the enthusiasm of patriotic success, or the voice of one beloved singing to you alone. Sterne says that, if he were in a desert, he would love some cypress. So soon as this want or power is dead, man becomes the living sepulchre of himself, and what yet survives is the mere husk of what once he was.

BENJAMIN FRANKLIN, NAPOLEON, LORD BYRON: Love Letters

Benjamin Franklin to Madame Helvetius

MORTIFIED at the barbarous resolution pronounced by you so positively yesterday evening, that you would remain single the rest of your life, as a compliment due to the memory of your husband, I retired to my chamber. Throwing myself upon my bed, I dreamt that I was dead, and was transported to the Elysian Fields.

I was asked whether I wished to see any persons in particular; to which I replied, that I wished to see the philosophers. "There are two who live here at hand in this garden; they are good neighbors, and very friendly towards one another." "Who are they?" "Socrates and Helvetius." "I esteem them both highly; but let me see Helvetius first, because I understand a little of French, but not a word of Greek." I was conducted to him; he received me with much courtesy, having known me, he said, by character, some time past. He asked me a thousand questions relative to the war, the present state of religion, of liberty, of the government in France. "You do not inquire, then," said I, "after your dear friend, Madame Helvetius; yet she loves you exceedingly; I was in her company not more than an hour ago." "Ah," said he, "you make me recur to my past happiness, which ought to be forgotten in order to be happy here. For many years I could think of nothing but her, though at length I am consoled. I have taken another wife, the most like her that I could find; she is not indeed altogether so handsome, but she has a great fund of wit and good sense; and her whole study is to please me. She is at this moment gone to fetch the best nectar and ambrosia to regale me; stay here awhile and you will see her." "I perceive," said I, "that your former friend is more faithful to you than you are to her; she has had several good offers, but refused them all. I will confess to you that I loved her extremely; but she was cruel to me, and rejected me peremptorily for your sake." "I pity you sincerely," said he, "for she is an excellent woman, handsome and amiable. But do not the Abbé de la Roche and the Abbé Morelett visit her?" "Certainly they do; not one of your friends has dropped her acquaintance." "If you had gained the Abbé Morelett with a bribe of good coffee and cream, perhaps you would have succeeded; for he is as deep a reasoner as Duns Scotus or St. Thomas; he arranges and methodizes his arguments in such a manner that they are almost irresistible. Or, if by a fine edition of some old classic, you had gained the Abbé de la Roche to speak *against* you, that would have been still better; as I always observed, that when he recommended anything to her, she had a great inclination to do directly the contrary." As he finished these words the new Madame Helvetius entered with the nectar, and I recognized her immediately as my former American friend, Mrs. Franklin! I reclaimed her, but she answered me coldly: "I was a good wife to you for forty-nine years and four months, nearly half a century; let that content you. I have formed a new connection here, which will last to eternity."

Indignant at this refusal of my Eurydice, I immediately resolved to quit those ungrateful shades, and return to this good world again, to behold the sun and you! Here I am: let us *avenge ourselves!*

Napoleon Bonaparte to Josephine

Chanceaux Post House
March 14th, 1796

I wrote to you at Chatillon, and sent you the power of attorney to enable you to receive various sums of money in course of remittance to me. Every moment separates me further from you, my beloved, and every moment I am less able to exist so far from you. You are the constant object of my thoughts; I exhaust my imagination in thinking of what you are doing. If I see you unhappy my heart is torn, and my grief grows greater. If you are gay and lively among your friends, male and female, I reproach you with having so soon forgotten our sorrowful separation of three days ago; therefore you must be fickle, and not lastingly stirred by deep emotions. So you see I am not easy to satisfy; but, my dear, I have quite different sensations when I fear that your health may be affected, or that you have cause to be annoyed; then I regret the haste with which I was separated from my darling. I feel, in fact, that your natural kindness of heart exists no longer for me, and it is only when I am quite sure you are not vexed that I am satisfied. If I were asked how I slept, I feel that before replying I should have to get a message to tell me that you had had a good night. The vices, the passions of men influence me only when I imagine they may affect you, my dear.

May my good genius, which has always preserved me in the midst of great dangers, surround you, enfold you, while I face my fate unguarded. Ah, be not too gay, but a trifle melancholy; and especially may your mind be free from worries, as your body from illness: you know what our good Ossian says on this subject. Write me, dear, and at full length, and accept a thousand and one kisses from your most devoted and faithful friend.

Verona, November 13th, 1796

I don't love you, not at all; on the contrary, I detest you—You're a naughty, gawky, foolish Cinderella. You never write me; you don't love your husband; you know what pleasure your letters give him, and yet you haven't written him six lines, dashed off casually!

What do you do all day, Madam? What is the affair so important as to leave you no time to write to your devoted lover? What affection stifles and puts to one side the love, the tender and constant love you promised him? Of what sort can be that marvelous being, that new lover who absorbs every moment, tyrannizes over your days, and prevents your giving any attention to your husband? Josephine, take care! Some fine night, the doors will be broken open, and there I'll be.

Indeed, I am very uneasy, my love, at receiving no news of you; write me quickly four pages, pages full of agreeable things which shall fill my heart with the pleasantest feelings.

I hope before long to crush you in my arms and cover you with a million kisses burning as though beneath the equator.

Bonaparte

Milan, November 27th, 1796, three o'clock afternoon

I arrive at Milan, I rush into your apartment, I have left everything to see you, to press you in my arms. . . you were not there;

you run to town where there are festivities; you leave me when I arrive, you do not care anymore for your dear Napoleon. It was a caprice, your loving him; fickleness makes you indifferent to him. Accustomed to dangers, I know the remedy for the worries and ills of life. The misfortune that overtakes me is incalculable; I had the right to be spared this.

I shall be here till the 9th in the evening. Do not put yourself out; run after pleasures; happiness is made for you. The entire world is too glad to be able to please you, and only your husband is very, very unhappy.

Bonaparte

Lord Byron to the Countess Guiccioli

Bologna, Aug. 25, 1819

MY DEAREST TERESA,—I have read this book in your garden. My love, you were absent, or else I could not have read it. It is a favourite book of yours, and the writer was a friend of mine. You will not understand these English words, and others will not understand them, which is the reason I have not scrawled them in Italian; but you will recognize the handwriting of him who passionately loved you, and you will divine that over a book which was yours he could only think of love. In that word, beautiful in all languages, but most so in yours,—*Amor mio,*—is comprised my existence here and hereafter. I feel I exist here, and I fear that I shall exist hereafter—to what purpose you will decide; my destiny rests with you, and you are a woman, eighteen years of age, and two out of a convent. I wish that you had stayed there, with all my heart,—or, at least, that I had never met you in your married state.

But all this is too late. I love you and you love me,—at least, you say so and act as if you did so, which last is a great consolation in all events. But I more than you, and cannot cease to love you.

Think of me sometimes when the Alps and the ocean divide us; but they never will, unless you wish it.

Byron

Venice, December 3rd, 1819

YOU are, and ever will be, my first thought, but at this moment, I am in a state most dreadful, not knowing which way to decide:— on the one hand, fearing that I should compromise you forever, by my return to Ravenna, and the consequences of such a step, and, on the other, dreading that I shall lose both you and myself, and all that I have ever known or tasted of happiness, by never seeing you more, I pray of you, I implore you to be comforted, and to believe that I cannot cease to love you but with my life. . . .

I go to save you, and leave a country insupportable to me without you. Your letters to F. and myself do wrong to my motives—but you will yet see your injustice. It is not enough that I must leave you—from motives of which ere long you will be convinced—it is not enough that I must fly from Italy, with a heart deeply wounded, after having passed all my days in solitude since your departure, sick both in body and mind—but I must also have to endure your reproaches without answering them and without deserving them. Farewell!—In that one word is comprised the death of my happiness.

Venice, December 9th, 1819

F. will already have told you, *with her accustomed sublimity*, that Love has gained the victory. I could not summon up resolution enough to leave the country where you are, without at least once more seeing you. On *yourself*, perhaps, it will depend, whether I ever again shall leave you. Of the rest we shall speak when we meet. You ought, by this time, to know which is most conducive to your welfare, my presence or my absence. For myself, I am a citizen of the world—all countries are alike to me. You have ever been, since our first acquaintance, *the sole object of my thoughts*. My opinion was, that the best course I could adopt, both for your peace and that of all your family, would have been to depart and go far, *far* away from you;—since to have been near and not approach you would have been, for me, impossible. You have, however, decided that I am to return to Ravenna. I shall accordingly return—and shall *do*—and *be* all that you wish. I cannot say more.

IVAN TURGENEV: First Love

My "PASSION" dated from that day. I think my feelings must have been something like those of a man starting upon a career of service. I was no longer just a young boy; I was a lover. I have said that my passion dated from that day, but I ought to add that my sufferings, too, began on that day. I pined when I was away from Zinaida; I could not concentrate, I could do nothing but think of her all day long. . . . I pined when I was away from her . . . but her presence brought me no relief, either.

I was jealous, conscious of my own insignificance, sulked foolishly, and prostrated myself before her no less foolishly; but an irresistible force drew me to her, and every time I could not cross the threshold of her room without a joyous pang. Zinaida very soon divined that I was in love with her, indeed I had no thought of concealment; she made merry over my infatuation, fooled, petted and tormented me in turns. It is sweet to be the sole source, the absolute and unchallengeable cause of the greatest happiness or the profoundest grief of another—and Zinaida found me as wax in her hands. But I was not the only one in love with her: all the men who visited the house raved about her, and she kept them all on a tether—at her feet. It amused her to excite in them hopes and misgivings by turns, to twist them round her little finger (she called it knocking people against one another), and they had no thought of resistance and submitted gladly to her will. Her vivacious and lovely being was imbued with an entrancing blend of cunning and recklessness, of artificiality and simplicity, of tranquility and animal spirits; over everything she said or did, over all her movements, there seemed to hover a light, subtle grace; a peculiar power was in play everywhere. And her face, which changed constantly, also seemed to be in play; it expressed almost instantaneously derision, thought and fervour. The most conflicting emotions, light and swift as the shadows of clouds on a sunny windy day, seemed to be ever chasing one another over her eyes and lips.

Each of her admirers was necessary to her. Belovzorov, whom she called "My Beast," or sometimes simply "Mine," would have rushed into the flames for her; not relying upon his mental powers or other qualities, he kept offering her his hand, hinting that the others were not serious. Maidanov answered to the poetic strain in her; though, like most authors, cold by nature, he assured her earnestly, and himself too, perhaps, that he adored her, eulogizing her in endless poetic effusions, which he recited to her with a kind of ecstasy that was at once affected and sincere. And she, while feeling a certain sympathy for him, treated him with a shade of mockery; she had not much faith in him, and after listening to his effusions, made him recite Pushkin, to clear the atmosphere, as she said. Lushin, the droll doctor, whose words sounded so cynical, understood her better and loved her more than all the rest, though he abused her, both to her face and behind her back. She respected him, but showed him no mercy and found a malicious delight in letting him see that he, too, was in her power. "I am a flirt, I have no heart, I am an actress by nature," she once said to him in my presence. "Very well, then! Give me your hand, now, and I will stick a pin into it; you will feel humiliated

before the young man here, you will feel pain, and yet you will
be so good as to laugh, Monsieur Truthful." Lushin flushed up,
averted his face, bit his lip, but ended by stretching his hand out
to her. She pricked it, and he actually laughed . . . and she
laughed too, thrusting the pin deep into his flesh and looking into
his eyes, which he vainly tried to keep away from her face. . . .
Least of all could I understand her relations with Count Malevsky.
He was good-looking, alert, and intelligent, but there was something dubious, something false about him which even I, a lad of
sixteen, could feel, and I could not help marvelling that Zinaida
failed to notice it. But who knows—perhaps she noticed the falseness and did not mind it! The defects of her education, her
strange acquaintances and habits, the constant presence of her
mother, the poverty and disorder in the house, everything, from
the freedom which this young girl enjoyed to the consciousness
of her superiority over those surrounding her, had developed a
kind of half-contemptuous negligence and moral callousness in
her. Whatever happened in their household, whether Vonifaty
came to announce there was no sugar, or some shabby piece of
gossip came to light, or her guests quarrelled among themselves,
she only tossed her curls and said: "Nonsense!" refusing to be
moved.

     As for me, my blood boiled whenever Malevsky stole up
to her, sly as a fox, lolled elegantly over the back of her chair,
and began whispering in her ear with a complacent and unctuous
simper, while she, her arms folded, looked at him gravely, smiling
and shaking her head from side to side.

     "What makes you receive Count Malevsky?" I once
asked her.

     "He has such a darling little moustache, you see," she
answered. "But of course you wouldn't understand that."

     "You don't mean to say you think I'm in love with him?"
she volunteered another time. "No, I could never love a man like
that, a man I can't help looking down on. I need someone capable
of breaking my will. But I shall never come across such a person,
thank God! I'm not going to fall into anyone's talons, not I!"

     "Does that mean you will never love anyone?"

     "What about you? Don't I love you?" she retorted, flicking
my nose with her glove.

     Oh yes, Zinaida got a lot of entertainment at my expense.
For three weeks I saw her every day, and the life she led me
during that time! She did not often come to our house, and I was
not sorry for it, for whenever she did, she acted the young lady,
the Princess, and I turned shy. I was afraid of giving myself away
before my mother, who thoroughly disapproved of Zinaida and
watched us with hostile eyes.

I did not mind my father nearly as much; he ignored me, and scarcely spoke to her, but when he did, it was always to say something clever and pointed. I gave up study and reading, I even gave up my country rambles and my riding. Like a beetle fastened by the leg I spun around the beloved annex; I would have stayed there forever, if that had been possible . . . but my mother grumbled and Zinaida herself sometimes drove me away. When she did this, I locked myself up in my room or went to the farthest end of the garden, where I clambered up on to the crumbling wall of the high, brick-built conservatory and sat there for hours, my legs dangling over the wall on the side facing the road, gazing in front of me with unseeing eyes. While butterflies fluttered languidly over the dusty nettles; a perky little sparrow alighted on a broken brick near by, chirruping exasperatingly, turning round and round, and spreading its tail; the crows, who still regarded me with suspicion, cawed now and then from the bare top of a birch, and the sun and wind played among its thin branches; sometimes the calm, austere boom of the bells from the Donskoi Monastery reached my ears, and I would sit there looking and listening, my heart overflowing with a sensation I could not define; it embraced everything—sadness and joy, anxious forebodings, desire for life, and fear of life. But I understood nothing of all this at the time, and would not have been able to put a name to what was fermenting within me, or, if I had tried, would have found one name for it all—Zinaida.

And all the while Zinaida played with me as a cat plays with a mouse. She flirted with me, and I immediately melted and became agitated, or she suddenly repulsed me, and I did not dare to approach her or even look at her.

I remember she was very distant with me for several days running; I lost heart, and sneaking timidly into the annex, tried to keep near the old Princess, although she was in the worst of tempers at the time; her financial affairs were very bad, and she had twice been obliged to explain her situation at the local police station.

Once, passing the familiar garden-fence, I caught sight of Zinaida; she was sitting motionless on the grass, leaning back on her hands. I made as if to go quietly away, but she suddenly lifted her head, motioning to me imperiously. I stood rooted to the ground; I was not quite sure what her gesture meant. She repeated it. I promptly leaped over the palings and ran joyously towards her; but she stopped me with her eyes, pointing towards the path two paces from where she was sitting. Perplexed and abashed, I knelt at the side of the path. She was so pale, every feature of her face breathed such bitter grief, such profound weariness that it wrung my heart, and I could not help asking:

"What's the matter?"

Zinaida stretched out her hand, plucked a blade of grass, chewed it, and flung it away from her.

"You love me very much, don't you?" she asked at last. "You do, don't you?"

I did not answer, there was no need to do so.

"Yes," she said, still looking at me, "I know you do. The same eyes," she added, turning thoughtful and covering her face with her hands. "I'm sick of it all," she whispered. "I'd like to go to the end of the world, I can't stand it any longer, I can't bear it. . . . And what's in store for me? . . . Oh, I'm so unhappy, so unhappy!"

"But why?" I asked timidly.

For all answer, Zinaida shrugged her shoulders. I remained kneeling, gazing at her in profound misery. Every word she said pierced my heart. I would have given my life at that moment to relieve her sorrow. I looked at her, still unable to think what could have made her so unhappy, and vividly imagined how, in a fit of uncontrollable sadness, she had gone out into the garden and dropped to the ground as if shot. All around was so green, so radiant; a breeze ruffled the leaves, every now and then shaking the raspberry canes above Zinaida's head.

Doves cooed in the distance, and the bees murmured, flying low over the sparse grass. The blue sky shed its kindly radiance from above, but I felt so melancholy. . . .

"Do you feel like reciting some poetry?" asked Zinaida gently, supporting herself on one elbow. "I like to hear you recite. You chant, rather, it's true, but I don't mind it, it's so very young. Recite 'The Hills of Georgia.' Only do sit down, first."

I sat down and recited "The Hills of Georgia."

" 'For not to love is quite beyond its powers,' " Zinaida repeated the last line. "That is what we love poetry for: it treats of unreal things and makes them sound not only better but even more real than real things. . . . 'For not to love is quite beyond its powers'—that's it, the heart would like not to love, but it can't help loving." She fell silent again, then with a sudden start got on to her feet. "Come on! Maidanov is sitting with my mother; he brought me his poem, and I went away. He's upset, too. . . . But it can't be helped! One day you'll know all . . . don't be angry with me, now!"

Giving a quick pressure to my hand, Zinaida ran ahead. We went back to the annex together. Maidanov began reading us his *Assassin*, which had just come out, but I did not listen to him. He declaimed his four-foot iambics in a sing-song voice, the rhymes alternating and jingling like sleigh-bells, loud and empty, while I studied Zinaida's face, trying to probe the meaning of what she had been saying to me.

> Or is it that a secret rival
> Has overwhelmed you all at once?

Maidanov suddenly declaimed in nasal accents, and my eyes met Zinaida's. She lowered hers, reddening slightly. I saw her flush and went numb with fear. I had been jealous before, but never before had the idea that she might have fallen in love crossed my mind. "Why! She is in love!"

. . . My father was in the habit of taking a ride every day; he had a fine English russet stallion with a long thin neck and long legs; it was a savage, indomitable animal; its name was Electric. Nobody but my father could manage it. One day he came into my room in a good-natured mood, a rare thing with him of late; he was going out riding and had his spurs on. I begged him to take me with him.

"We'd better play leap-frog, instead," my father answered, "you won't be able to keep up with me on your little German nag."

"Oh yes, I will; I'll put on spurs."

"Come on, then!"

We set out. I had a shaggy black pony, sure-footed and spirited; true, it had to go at a gallop to keep up with Electric's trot, but I did not fall behind. I have never seen a horseman like my father; his seat was so carelessly easy, so elegant, and the horse seemed to feel it and to be proud of its rider. We rode through the boulevards, spent some time on the Devichye Polye, jumped several fences (at first I had been afraid of jumping, but my father despised timid people—and so I had stopped being afraid), crossed the Moscow River twice, and I was beginning to think we were going back, especially as my father remarked that my horse seemed tired, when he suddenly turned sharply from me and made for the Krymsky ford, sending his horse at a gallop along the bank. I galloped after him. When we reached a towering pile of old logs, he jumped lightly off Electric, bade me dismount, threw the reins of his horse into my hands, and told me to wait there, by the logs; then he turned into a narrow side-street and disappeared from my sight. I began pacing backwards and forwards along the bank, leading the horses and scolding Electric, who kept tossing his head, shaking all over, snorting and neighing; whenever I stood still, he pawed the ground, squealed and bit my nag on the neck, in a word, behaved like the spoilt thoroughbred he was. Still my father did not come back. An unpleasant dampness rose from the river; a drizzling rain fell soundlessly, mottling with tiny dark patches those tiresome grey logs, around which I kept wandering till heartily sick of them. I felt bored and dejected, and still my father did not come. A policeman, evidently a Finn, as grey as the logs, with an enormous potlike shako on his head, and carrying a halberd (and what on earth was a policeman doing on the bank of the Moscow River?), approached me, and turning a face like that of a wrinkled beldame towards me, asked:

"What are you doing here with those horses, Master? Let me hold them for you."

I did not answer him; he begged for some tobacco. To get rid of him (and also because my impatience was becoming intolerable), I took a few paces in the direction in which my father had gone; then I went down the side-street, turned the corner—and stopped short. About forty paces away, at the open window of a small wooden house, stood my father, his back to me; he was leaning against the window-sill, and inside, half concealed by the curtain, sat a woman in a dark dress, talking to my father; the woman was Zinaida.

I was dumbfounded. I had certainly not expected this. My first impulse was to turn tail. "If my father looks back, I am lost," I thought. But a strange feeling, which was stronger than curiosity, stronger even than jealousy, stronger than fear, kept me rooted to the spot. I stood gazing and straining my ears to catch their words. My father seemed to be insisting on something to which Zinaida would not consent. I can still see her face—sorrowful, grave, beautiful, stamped with an indescribable blend of devotion, sadness, and love, and with a kind of despair—I can find no other word for it. She spoke in monosyllables, never raising her eyes, merely smiling humbly and stubbornly. The smile alone would have told me it was Zinaida. My father shrugged his shoulders and straightened his hat—a sure sign of impatience with him. . . . Then I made out the words: *"Vous devez vous séparer de cette. . . ."* Zinaida drew herself up and stretched out her arm. . . . An extraordinary scene was enacted before my eyes: my father lifted his riding-crop, with which he had been flicking the dust from the skirts of his coat, and brought it down with a smart crack on that bared forearm. It was all I could do not to cry out, but Zinaida only started, looked at my father in silence, lifted her arm slowly up to her lips, kissing the weal crimsoning on it. Flinging away the riding-crop, my father rushed up the steps of the porch and burst into the house. . . . Zinaida turned away from the window, her arms outstretched and her head thrown back. . . .

I retreated, faint with fear, my heart filled with an anguish of amazement; I ran to the end of the side-street, almost letting

Electric break loose from the halter, and returned to the river-bank. My thoughts were in utter confusion. I had known before that my father, usually so cool and reserved, was given to sudden fits of fury, and yet I found it impossible to realize what it was I had just witnessed. . . . But I knew I should never be able to forget, as long as I lived, Zinaida's gesture, look, smile; I knew that her image, so suddenly revealed to me in this new aspect, would be engraved forever on my memory. I gazed vacantly at the river, unconscious of the tears trickling down my cheeks. "He beat her," I kept repeating, "beat her, beat her. . . ."

"Come on, give me the reins, won't you?" It was my father's voice behind me.

I handed him the reins mechanically. He leaped on to Electric's back. . . . The horse, chilled from the long wait, reared, and then sprang forward ten feet or so. But my father soon got the better of it, plunging his spurs into the animal's sides and striking it on the neck with his fist. . . . "Ah—I haven't got my whip!" he muttered.

I thought of the crack with which the riding-crop had come down, and shuddered.

"What have you done with it?" I asked my father after a short pause.

He galloped ahead without answering. I overtook him. I felt I simply must see his face.

"Did you get tired waiting?" my father asked through his teeth.

"Rather. But where did you drop your whip?" I insisted.

My father darted a swift glance at me.

"I didn't drop it," he said, "I threw it away."

He turned thoughtful and bent his head . . . and it was then, for the first and probably last time, that I saw what kindness and compassion his severe features were capable of expressing.

Again he set his horse at a gallop, and this time I was not able to overtake him. I arrived home a quarter of an hour after he did.

"That's what love is!" I told myself once more that night, seated at my desk, on which books and note-books were gradually accumulating. "That's passion! You would think *anyone* would be roused to anger, *no one* would submit to a blow, however dear the hand which dealt it! But apparently even this can be endured by one who loves. . . . And I . . . and I thought. . . ."

This last month had matured me considerably, and my own love, with its agitation and sufferings, now seemed to me petty, childish, insignificant, in comparison with that other unknown thing as to which I could only form vague surmises, that thing which was as terrifying to me as an unfamiliar countenance, beautiful but stern, which one seeks in vain to make out through the gloom. . . .

I had a strange and terrible dream that night. I dreamed I went into a dark, low-ceilinged room. . . . My father stood there, whip in hand, stamping his foot; Zinaida crouched in the corner, and there was a red gash, not on her arm, but across her brow. Behind them both rose the figure of Belovzorov, covered with blood. He opened his pale lips and uttered angry threats at my father. . . .

Two months later I entered the University, and six months after that my father died (of a stroke) in Petersburg, where we had just moved. A few days before his death he received a letter from Moscow which caused him great agitation. He went to my mother and asked her for something, they say he actually wept—my father wept! On the morning of the day when he had his stroke, he began a letter to me in French: "My son," he wrote, "beware of the love of woman, beware of that joy, that poison. . . ." After his death, my mother sent a considerable sum of money to Moscow.

OSCAR WILDE: The Nightingale and the Rose

"She said that she would dance with me if I brought her red roses," cried the young Student; "but in all my garden there is no red rose."

From her nest in the holm-oak tree the Nightingale heard him, and she looked out through the leaves, and wondered.

"No red rose in all my garden!" he cried, and his beautiful eyes filled with tears. "Ah, on what little things does happiness depend! I have read all that the wise men have written, and all the secrets of philosophy are mine, yet for want of a red rose is my life made wretched."

"Here at last is a true lover," said the Nightingale. "Night after night have I sung to him, though I knew him not: night after night have I told his story to the stars, and now I see him. His hair is dark as the hyacinth-blossom, and his lips are red as the rose of his desire; but passion has made his face like pale ivory, and sorrow has set her seal upon his brow."

"The Prince gives a ball to-morrow night," murmured the young Student, "and my love will be of the company. If I bring her a red rose she will dance with me till dawn. If I bring her a red rose, I shall hold her in my arms, and she will lean her head upon my shoulder, and her hand will be clasped in mine. But there is no red rose in my garden, so I shall sit lonely, and she will pass me by. She will have no heed of me, and my heart will break."

"Here indeed is the true lover," said the Nightingale. "What I sing of, he suffers: what is joy to me, to him is pain. Surely Love is a wonderful thing. It is more precious than emeralds, and dearer than fine opals. Pearls and pomegranates cannot buy it, nor is it set forth in the market-place. It may not be purchased of the merchants, nor can it be weighed out in the balance of gold."

"The musicians will sit in their gallery," said the young Student, "and play upon their stringed instruments, and my love will dance to the sound of the harp and the violin. She will dance so lightly that her feet will not touch the floor, and the courtiers in their gay dresses will throng round her. But with me she will not dance, for I have no red rose to give her"; and he flung himself down on the grass, and buried his face in his hands, and wept.

"Why is he weeping?" asked a little Green Lizard as he ran past him with his tail in the air.

"Why, indeed?" said a Butterfly, who was fluttering about after a sunbeam.

"Why, indeed?" whispered a Daisy to his neighbour, in a soft, low voice.

"He is weeping for a red rose," said the Nightingale.

"For a red rose!" they cried; "how very ridiculous!" and the little Lizard, who was something of a cynic, laughed outright.

But the Nightingale understood the secret of the Student's sorrow, and she sat silent in the oak-tree, and thought about the mystery of Love.

Suddenly she spread her brown wings for flight, and soared into the air. She passed through the grove like a shadow, and like a shadow she sailed across the garden.

In the centre of the grass-plot was standing a beautiful Rose-tree, and when she saw it, she flew over to it, and lit upon a spray.

"Give me a red rose," she cried, "and I will sing you my sweetest song."

But the Tree shook its head.

"My roses are white," it answered; "as white as the foam of the sea, and whiter than the snow upon the mountain. But go to my brother who grows round the old sun-dial, and perhaps he will give you what you want."

So the Nightingale flew over to the Rose-tree that was growing round the old sun-dial.

"Give me a red rose," she cried, "and I will sing you my sweetest song."

But the Tree shook its head.

"My roses are yellow," it answered; "as yellow as the hair of the mermaiden who sits upon an amber throne, and yellower than the daffodil that blooms in the meadow before the mower comes with his scythe. But go to my brother who grows beneath the Student's window, and perhaps he will give you what you want."

So the Nightingale flew over to the Rose-tree that was growing beneath the Student's window.

"Give me a red rose," she cried, "and I will sing you my sweetest song."

But the Tree shook its head.

"My roses are red," it answered; "as red as the feet of the dove, and redder than the great fans of coral that wave and wave in the ocean cavern. But the winter has chilled my veins, and the frost has nipped my buds, and the storm has broken my branches, and I shall have no roses at all this year."

"One red rose is all I want," cried the Nightingale. "Only one red rose! Is there any way by which I can get it?"

"There is a way," answered the Tree; "but it is so terrible that I dare not tell it to you."

"Tell it to me," said the Nightingale, "I am not afraid."

"If you want a red rose," said the Tree, "you must build it out of music by moonlight, and stain it with your own heart's-blood. You must sing to me with your breast against a thorn. All night long you must sing to me, and the thorn must pierce your heart, and your life-blood must flow into my veins, and become mine."

"Death is a great price to pay for a red rose," cried the Nightingale, "and Life is very dear to all. It is pleasant to sit in the green wood, and to watch the Sun in his chariot of gold, and the Moon in her chariot of pearl. Sweet is the scent of the hawthorn, and sweet are the bluebells that hide in the valley, and the heather that blows on the hill. Yet Love is better than Life, and what is the heart of a bird compared to the heart of a man?"

So she spread her brown wings for flight, and soared into the air. She swept over the garden like a shadow, and like a shadow she sailed through the grove.

The young Student was still lying on the grass, where she had left him, and the tears were not yet dry in his beautiful eyes.

"Be happy," cried the Nightingale, "be happy; you shall have your red rose. I will build it out of music by moonlight, and stain it with my own heart's-blood. All that I ask of you in return is that you will be a true lover, for Love is wiser than Philosophy, though she is wise, and mightier than Power, though he is mighty. Flame-coloured are his wings, and coloured like flame is his body. His lips are sweet as honey, and his breath is like frankincense."

The Student looked up from the grass, and listened, but he could not understand what the Nightingale was saying to him, for he only knew the things that are written down in books.

But the Oak-tree understood, and felt sad, for he was very fond of the little Nightingale who had built her nest in his branches.

"Sing me one last song," he whispered; "I shall feel very lonely when you are gone."

So the Nightingale sang to the Oak-tree, and her voice was like water bubbling from a silver jar.

When she had finished her song the Student got up, and pulled a notebook and a lead-pencil out of his pocket.

"She has form," he said to himself, as he walked away through the grove—"that cannot be denied her; but has she got feeling? I am afraid not. In fact, she is like most artists; she is all style, without any sincerity. She would not sacrifice herself for others. She thinks merely of music, and everybody knows that the arts are selfish. Still, it must be admitted that she has some beautiful notes in her voice. What a pity it is that they do not mean anything, or do any practical good." And he went into his room, and lay down on his little pallet-bed, and began to think of his love; and, after a time, he fell asleep.

And when the Moon shone in the heavens the Nightingale flew to the Rose-tree, and set her breast against the thorn. All night long she sang with her breast against the thorn, and the cold crystal Moon leaned down and listened. All night long she sang, and the thorn went deeper and deeper into her breast, and her life-blood ebbed away from her.

She sang first of the birth of love in the heart of a boy and a girl. And on the topmost spray of the Rose-tree there blossomed a marvellous rose, petal followed petal, as song followed song. Pale was it, at first, as the mist that hangs over the river—pale as the feet of the morning, and silver as the wings of the dawn. As the shadow of a rose in a mirror of silver, as the shadow of a rose in a water-pool, so was the rose that blossomed on the topmost spray of the Tree.

But the Tree cried to the Nightingale to press closer against the thorn. "Press closer, little Nightingale," cried the Tree, "or the Day will come before the rose is finished."

So the Nightingale pressed closer against the thorn, and louder and louder grew her song, for she sang of the birth of passion in the soul of a man and a maid.

And a delicate flush of pink came into the leaves of the

rose, like the flush in the face of the bridegroom when he kisses
the lips of the bride. But the thorn had not yet reached her heart,
so the rose's heart remained white, for only a Nightingale's heart's-
blood can crimson the heart of a rose.

And the Tree cried to the Nightingale to press closer
against the thorn. "Press closer, little Nightingale," cried the
Tree, "or the Day will come before the rose is finished."

So the Nightingale pressed closer against the thorn, and the
thorn touched her heart, and a fierce pang of pain shot through
her. Bitter, bitter was the pain, and wilder and wilder grew her
song, for she sang of the Love that is perfected by Death, of the
Love that dies not in the tomb.

And the marvellous rose became crimson, like the rose of
the eastern sky. Crimson was the girdle of petals, and crimson as
a ruby was the heart.

But the Nightingale's voice grew fainter, and her little
wings began to beat, and a film came over her eyes. Fainter and
fainter grew her song, and she felt something choking her in her
throat.

Then she gave one last burst of music. The white Moon
heard it, and she forgot the dawn, and lingered on in the sky. The
red rose heard it, and it trembled all over with ecstasy, and opened
its petals to the cold morning air. Echo bore it to her purple
cavern in the hills, and woke the sleeping shepherds from their
dreams. It floated through the reeds of the river, and they carried
its message to the sea.

"Look, look! cried the Tree, "the rose is finished now";
but the Nightingale made no answer, for she was lying dead in
the long grass, with the thorn in her heart.

And at noon the Student opened his window and looked
out.

"Why, what a wonderful piece of luck!" he cried; "here is
a red rose! I have never seen any rose like it in all my life. It is so
beautiful that I am sure it has a long Latin name"; and he leaned
down and plucked it.

Then he put on his hat, and ran up to the Professor's house
with the rose in his hand.

The daughter of the Professor was sitting in the doorway
winding blue silk on a reel, and her little dog was lying at her
feet.

"You said that you would dance with me if I brought you
a red rose," cried the Student. "Here is the reddest rose in all the
world. You will wear it to-night next your heart, and as we dance
together it will tell you how I love you."

But the girl frowned.

"I am afraid it will not go with my dress," she answered; "and, besides, the Chamberlain's nephew has sent me some real jewels, and everybody knows that jewels cost far more than flowers."

"Well, upon my word, you are very ungrateful," said the Student angrily; and he threw the rose into the street, where it fell into the gutter, and a cart-wheel went over it.

"Ungrateful!" said the girl. "I tell you what, you are very rude; and, after all, who are you? Only a Student. Why, I don't believe you have even got silver buckles to your shoes as the Chamberlain's nephew has"; and she got up from her chair and went into the house.

"What a silly thing Love is," said the Student as he walked away. "It is not half as useful as Logic, for it does not prove anything, and it is always telling one of things that are not going to happen, and making one believe things that are not true. In fact, it is quite unpractical, and, as in this age to be practical is everything, I shall go back to Philosophy and study Metaphysics."

So he returned to his room and pulled out a great dusty book, and began to read.

2. *LOVE, THE CHILD OF FULLNESS*

First in one's awareness of love is, of course, one's own need. Yet it is a need for the other, and the consequent awareness of the other soon makes possible loving regard for the other, a creative development of love which evokes and fosters good in the other. This takes many forms—familial love, friendship, love of the good and the ideal. As a concept it had early formulations in classic philosophy, and its latest formulations in the work of modern social scientists go far to confirm those of the classic philosophers and the Christian theologians, in whose extensive debate, still going on, the fullest speculations on this aspect of love have been advanced. It is for this reason that the selections in this section are mainly drawn from the theological tradition.

CICERO: On Friendship

FRIENDSHIP MAY be shortly defined, "a perfect conformity of opinions upon all religious and civil subjects, united with the highest degree of mutual esteem and affection;" and yet from these simple circumstances results the most desirable blessing (virtue alone excepted) that the gods have bestowed on mankind. I am sensible that in this opinion I shall not be universally supported—health and riches, honours and power, have each of them their distinct admirers, and are respectively pursued as the supreme felicity of human life; whilst some there are (and the number is by no means inconsiderable) who contend that it is to be found only in the sensual gratifications. But the latter place their principal happiness on the same low enjoyments which constitute the chief good of brutes, and the former on those very precarious possessions that depend much less on our own merit than on the caprice of fortune. They, indeed, who maintain that the ultimate good of man consists in the knowledge and practice of virtue, fix it, undoubtedly, upon its truest and most glorious foundation; but let it be remembered, at the same time, that virtue is at once both the parent and the support of friendship.

I have already declared that by virtue I do not mean, with the philosophers before alluded to, that ideal strain of perfection which is nowhere to be found but in the pompous language of enthusiastic declamation; I mean only that attainable degree of moral merit which is understood by the term in common discourse, and may be exemplified in actual practice. . . .

"Life would be utterly lifeless," as old Ennius expresses it, without a friend on whose kindness and fidelity one might confidently repose. Can there be a more real complacency, indeed, than to lay open to another the most secret thoughts of one's heart with the same confidence and security as if they were still concealed in his own? Would not the fruits of prosperity lose much of their relish were there none who equally rejoiced with the possessor in the satisfaction he received from them? And how difficult must it prove to bear up under the pressure of misfortunes unsupported by a generous associate who more than equally divides their load? In short, the several occasions to which friendship extends its kindly offices are unbounded, while the advantage of every other object of human desires is confined within certain specific and determinate limits, beyond which it is of no avail. Thus wealth is pursued for the particular uses to which it is solely applicable; power, in order to receive worship; honours, for the sake of fame; sensual indulgences, on account of the gratifications that attend them; and health, as the means of living exempt from pain and possessing the unobstructed exercise of all our corporeal faculties. Whereas Friendship (I repeat again) is adapted by its nature to an infinite number of different ends, accommodates itself to all circumstances and situations of human life, and can at no season prove either unsuitable or inconvenient—in a word, not even fire and water (to use a proverbial illustration) are capable of being converted to a greater variety of beneficial purposes.

I desire it may be understood, however, that I am now speaking, not of that inferior species of amity which occurs in the common intercourse of the world (although this, too, is not without its pleasures and advantages), but of that genuine and perfect friendship, examples of which are so extremely rare as to be rendered memorable by their singularity. It is this sort alone that can truly be said to heighten the joys of prosperity, and mitigate the sorrows of adversity, by a generous participation of both; indeed, one of the chief among the many important offices of this connection is exerted in the day of affliction, by dispelling the gloom that overcasts the mind, encouraging the hope of happier times, and preventing the depressed spirits from sinking into a state of weak and unmanly despondence. Whoever is in possession of a true friend sees the exact counterpart of his own soul. In consequence of this moral resemblance between them, they are so intimately one that no advantage can attend either which does not equally communicate itself to both; they are strong in the strength, rich in the opulence and powerful in the power of each other. They can scarcely, indeed, be considered in any respect as separate individuals, and wherever the one appears the other is virtually present. I will venture even a bolder assertion, and affirm that in despite of death they must both continue to exist so long as either of them shall remain alive; for the deceased may, in a certain sense, be said still to live whose memory is preserved with the highest veneration and the most tender regret in the bosom of the survivor, a circumstance which renders the former happy in death, and the latter honoured in life.

If that benevolent principle which thus intimately unites two persons in the bands of amity were to be struck out of the human heart, it would be impossible that either private families or public communities should subsist—even the land itself would lie waste, and desolation overspread the earth. Should this assertion stand in need of a proof, it will appear evident by considering the ruinous consequences which ensue from discord and dissension; for what family is so securely established, or what government fixed upon so firm a basis, that it would not be overturned and utterly destroyed were a general spirit of enmity and malevolence to break forth amongst its members?—a sufficient argument, surely, of the inestimable benefits which flow from the kind and friendly affections.

I have been informed that a certain learned bard of Agrigentum published a philosophic poem in Greek, in which he asserted that the several bodies which compose the physical system of the universe preserve the consistence of their respective forms, or are dispersed into their primitive atoms, as a principle of amity, or of discord, becomes predominant in their composition. It is certain, at least, that the powerful effects of these opposite agents in the moral world is universally perceived and acknowledged. Agreeable to this general sentiment, who is there, when he beholds a man generously exposing himself to certain danger, for the sake of rescuing his distressed friend, that can forbear expressing the warmest approbation? Accordingly, what repeated acclamations lately echoed through the theatre at the new play of my host and friend Pacuvius, in that scene where Pylades and Orestes are introduced before the king; who being ignorant which of them was Orestes, whom he had determined to put to death, each insists, in order to save the life of his associate, that he himself is the real person in question. If the mere fictitious representation of such a magnanimous and heroic contention was thus universally applauded by the spectators, what impression must it have made upon their minds had they seen it actually displayed in real life! The general effect produced upon this occasion, clearly shows how deeply nature hath impressed on the human heart a sense of moral beauty; since a whole audience thus unanimously conspired in admiring an instance of sublime generosity in another's conduct, which not one of them, perhaps, was capable of exhibiting in his own. . . .

Having frequently, then, turned my thoughts on this subject, the principal question that has always occurred to me is, whether Friendship takes its rise from the wants and weaknesses of man, and is cultivated solely in order to obtain, by a mutual exchange of good offices, those advantages which he could not otherwise acquire? Or whether nature, notwithstanding this beneficial intercourse is inseparable from the connection, previously disposes the heart to engage in it upon a nobler and more generous inducement? In order to determine this question, it must be observed that love is a leading and essential principle in constituting that particular species of benevolence which is termed amity; and although this sentiment may be feigned, indeed, by the followers of those who are courted merely with a view to interest, yet it cannot possibly be produced by a motive of interest alone. There is a truth and simplicity in genuine friendship, an unconstrained and spontaneous emotion, altogether incompatible with every kind and degree of artifice and simulation. I am persuaded, therefore, that it derives its origin not from the indigence of human nature, but from a distinct principle implanted in the breast of man; from a certain instinctive tendency, which draws congenial minds into union, and not from a cool calculation of the advantages with which it is pregnant.

The wonderful force, indeed, of innate propensities of the benevolent kind is observable even among brutes, in that tender attachment which prevails during a certain period between the dam and her young. But their strongest effects are more particularly conspicuous in the human species; as appears, in the first place, from that powerful endearment which subsists between parents and children, and which cannot be eradicated or counteracted without the most detestable impiety; and in the next, from those sentiments of secret approbation which arise on the very first interview with a man whose manners and temper seem to harmonise with our own, and in whom we think we discover symptoms of an honest and virtuous mind. In reality, nothing is so beautiful as virtue; and nothing makes its way more directly to the heart: we feel a certain degree of affection even towards those meritorious persons whom we have never seen, and whose characters are known to us only from history. . . .

LAELIUS.—I will lay before you the result of frequent conversations which Scipio and I have formerly held together upon the subject. He used to say that nothing is so difficult as to preserve a lasting and unbroken friendship to the end of life. For it may frequently happen not only that the interest of the parties shall considerably interfere, or their opinions concerning political measures widely differ, but age, infirmities, or misfortunes are apt to produce very extraordinary changes in the tempers and dispositions of men. He illustrated this general instability of common friendships by tracing the revolutions they are liable to undergo from the earliest period in which this kind of connection can commence. Accordingly, he observed that those strong attachments which are sometimes formed in childhood were generally renounced with the puerile robe. But should a particular affection contracted in this tender age happen to continue to riper years, it is nothing unusual to see it afterwards interrupted, either by rivalship in a matrimonial pursuit, or some other object of youthful competition, in which both cannot possibly succeed. If these common dangers, however, should be happily escaped, yet others no less fatal may hereafter rise up to its ruin, especially if they should become opposite candidates for the same dignities of the state. For as with the generality of mankind, an immoderate desire of wealth, so among those of a more liberal and exalted spirit, an inordinate thirst of glory is usually the strongest bane of amity; and each of them have proved the occasion of converting the warmest friends into the most implacable enemies.

He added, that great and just dissensions had arisen also in numberless instances on account of improper requests—where a man has solicited his friend to assist him, for example, in his lawless gallantries, or to support him in some other act of equal dishonour and injustice. A denial upon such occasions, though certainly laudable, is generally deemed by the party refused to be a violation of the rights of amity; and he will probably resent it the more, as applications of this nature necessarily imply that the person who breaks through all restraints in urging them is equally disposed to make the same unwarrantable concessions on his own part. Disagreements of this kind have not only caused irreparable breaches between the closest connections, but have even kindled unextinguishable animosities. In short, the common friendships of the world are liable to be broken to pieces by such a variety of accidents, that Scipio thought it required a more than common portion, not only of good sense, but of good fortune, to steer entirely clear of those numerous and fatal rocks.

Our first inquiry therefore, if you please, shall be, "How far the claims of friendship may reasonably extend?" For instance, ought the bosom friends of Coriolanus (if any intimacies of that kind he had) to have joined him in turning his arms against his country; or those of Viscellinus, or Spurius Maelius, to have assisted them in their designs of usurping the sovereign power?

In those public commotions which were raised by Tiberius Gracchus, it appeared that neither Quintus Tubero, nor any other of those persons with whom he lived upon terms of the greatest intimacy, engaged in his faction, one only excepted, who was related to your family, Scaevola, by the ties of hospitality: I mean Blosius, of Cumae. This man (as I was appointed an assessor with the two consuls Laenas and Rupilius) applied to me to obtain his pardon, alleging, in his justification, that he entertained so high an esteem and affection for Gracchus, as to hold himself obliged to concur with him in any measure he might propose. What! if he had even desired you to set fire to the Capitol? "Such a request, I am confident," replied Blosius, "he never would have made." But admitting that he had, how would you have determined? "In that case," returned Blosius, "I should most certainly have complied." Infamous as this confession was, he acted agreeably to it; or rather, indeed, his conduct exceeded even the impiety of his professions, for, not contented with encouraging the seditious schemes of Tiberius Gracchus, he actually took the lead in them, and was an instigator as well as an associate in all the madness of his measures. In consequence of these extravagant proceedings, and alarmed to find that extraordinary judges were appointed for his trial, he made his escape into Asia, where, entering into the service of our enemies, he met with the fate he so justly merited for the injuries he had done to the commonwealth.

I lay it down, then, as a rule without exception, "that no degree of friendship can either justify or excuse the commission of a criminal action." For true amity being founded on an opinion of virtue in the object of our affection, it is scarcely possible that those sentiments should remain, after an avowed and open violation of the principles which originally produced them. . . .

The first and great axiom therefore in the laws of amity should invariably be—"never to require from a friend what he cannot grant without a breach of his honour; and always to be ready to assist him upon every occasion consistent with that principle." So long as we shall act under the secure guard of this sacred barrier, it will not be sufficient merely to yield a ready compliance with all his desires; we ought to anticipate and prevent them. Another rule likewise of indispensable obligation upon all who would approve themselves true friends, is, "to be ever ready to offer their advice, with an unreserved and honest frankness of heart." The counsels of a faithful and friendly monitor carry with them an authority which ought to have great influence, and they should be urged not only with freedom, but even with severity, if the occasion should appear to require it.

I am informed that certain Greek writers (philosophers, it seems, in the opinion of their countrymen), have advanced some very extraordinary positions relating to the subject of our present inquiry; as, indeed, what subject is there which these subtle geniuses have not tortured with their sophistry? The authors to whom I allude dissuade their disciples from entering into any strong attachments, as unavoidably creating supernumerary disquietudes to those who engage in them, and as every man has more than sufficient to call forth his solicitude in the course of his own affairs, it is a weakness, they contend, anxiously to involve himself in the concerns of others. They recommend it also in all connections of this kind to hold the bands of union extremely loose, so as always to have it in one's power to straiten or relax them as circumstances and situations shall render most expedient. They add, as a capital article of their doctrine, that "to live exempt from cares is an essential ingredient to constitute human happiness, but an ingredient, however, which he who voluntarily distresses himself with cares in which he has no necessary and personal interest, must never hope to possess."

I have been told, likewise, that there is another set of pretended philosophers of the same country, whose tenets concerning this subject are of a still more illiberal and ungenerous cast,
and I have already, in the course of this conversation, slightly
animadverted upon their principles. The proposition they attempt
to establish is that "friendship is an affair of self-interest entirely,
and that the proper motive for engaging in it is, not in order to
gratify the kind and benevolent affections, but for the benefit of
that assistance and support which is to be derived from the connection." Accordingly they assert that those persons are most disposed to have recourse to auxiliary alliances of this kind who are
least qualified by nature or fortune to depend upon their own
strength and powers; the weaker sex, for instance, being generally
more inclined to engage in friendships than the male part of our
species; and those who are depressed by indigence, or labouring
under misfortunes, than the wealthy and the prosperous.

Excellent and obliging sages these, undoubtedly. To strike
out the friendly affections from the moral world would be like
extinguishing the sun in the natural, each of them being the
source of the best and most grateful satisfactions that the gods
have conferred on the sons of men. But I should be glad to know
what the real value of this boasted exemption from care, which
they promise their disciples, justly amounts to? an exemption
flattering to self-love, I confess, but which, upon many occurrences
in human life, should be rejected with the utmost disdain. For
nothing, surely, can be more inconsistent with a well-poised and
manly spirit, than to decline engaging in any laudable action, or
to be discouraged from persevering in it, by an apprehension of
the trouble and solicitude with which it may probably be attended. Virtue herself, indeed, ought to be totally renounced, if
it be right to avoid every possible means that may be productive
of uneasiness; for who that is actuated by her principles can observe the conduct of an opposite character, without being affected
with some degree of secret dissatisfaction? Are not the just, the
brave, and the good necessarily exposed to the disagreeable emotions of dislike and aversion when they respectively meet with
instances of fraud, of cowardice, or of villainy? It is an essential
property of every well-constituted mind to be affected with pain,
or pleasure, according to the nature of those moral appearances
that present themselves to observation.

If sensibility, therefore, be not incompatible with true wisdom (and it surely is not, unless we suppose that philosophy
deadens every finer feeling of our nature) what just reason can be
assigned why the sympathetic sufferings, which may result from
friendship, should be a sufficient inducement for banishing that
generous affection from the human breast? Extinguish all emo-

tions of the heart and what difference will remain, I do not say between man and brute, but between man and a mere inanimate clod? Away then with those austere philosophers who represent virtue as hardening the soul against all the softer impressions of humanity. The fact, certainly, is much otherwise; a truly good man is upon many occasions extremely susceptible of tender sentiments, and his heart expands with joy or shrinks with sorrow, as good or ill fortune accompanies his friend. Upon the whole, then, it may fairly be concluded, that as in the case of virtue, so in that of friendship, those painful sensations which may sometimes be produced by the one, as well as by the other, are equally insufficient for excluding either of them from taking possession of our bosoms.

There is a charm in virtue, as I have already had occasion to remark, that by a secret and irresistible bias draws the general affection of those persons towards each other in whom it appears to reside, and this instantaneous goodwill is mutually attended with a desire of entering into a nearer and more intimate correspondence; sentiments which, at length, by a natural and necessary consequence, give rise to particular friendships. Strange, indeed, would it be that exalted honours, magnificent mansions, or sumptuous apparel, not to mention other splendid objects of general admiration, should have power to captivate the greater part of our species, and that the beauty of a virtuous mind, capable of meeting our affection with an equal return, should not have sufficient allurements to inspire the most ardent passion. I said "capable of meeting our affection with an equal return;" for nothing, surely, can be more delightful than to live in a constant interchange and vicissitude of reciprocal good offices. If we add to this, as with truth we may, that a similitude of manners is the most powerful of all attractions, it must be granted that the virtuous are strongly impelled towards each other by that moral tendency and natural relationship which subsists between them.

No proposition therefore can be more evident, I think, than that the virtuous must necessarily, and by an implanted sense in the human heart, receive impressions of goodwill towards each other, and these are the natural source from whence genuine friendship can only flow. Not that a good man's benevolence is by any means confined to a single object; he extends it to every individual. For true virtue, incapable of partial and contracted exceptions to the exercise of her benign spirit, enlarges the soul with sentiments of universal philanthropy. How, indeed, could it be consistent with her character to take whole nations under her protection, if even the lowest ranks of mankind, as well as the highest, were not the proper objects of beneficence?

But to return to the more immediate object of our present

consideration. They who insist that "utility is the first and prevailing motive which induces mankind to enter into particular friendships," appear to me to divest the associations of its most amiable and engaging principle. For to a mind rightly composed it is not so much the benefits received as the affectionate zeal from which they flow, that gives them their best and most valuable recommendation. It is so far, indeed, from being verified by fact, that a sense of our wants is the original cause of forming these amicable alliances; that, on the contrary, it is observable that none have been more distinguished in their friendships than those whose power and opulence, but above all, whose superior virtue (a much firmer support) have raised them above every necessity of having recourse to the assistance of others. Perhaps, however, it may admit of a question, whether it were desirable that one's friend should be so absolutely sufficient for himself, as to have no wants of any kind to which his own powers were not abundantly adequate. I am sure, at least, I should have been deprived of a most exquisite satisfaction if no opportunity had ever offered to approve the affectionate zeal of my heart towards Scipio, and he had never had occasion, either in his civil or military transactions, to make use of my counsel or my aid.

The true distinction, then, in this question is, that "although friendship is certainly productive of utility, yet utility is not the primary motive of friendship."

THE NEW TESTAMENT: The Commandment To Love

As the Father hath loved me, I also have loved you. Abide in my love.

If you keep my commandments, you shall abide in my love: as I also have kept my Father's commandments and do abide in his love. . . .

This is my commandment, that you love one another, as I have loved you.

Greater love than this no man hath, that a man lay down his life for his friends.

You are my friends, if you do the things I command you.

John 15: 9–10; 12–14.

If I speak with the tongues of men and of angels and have not charity, I am become as sounding brass or a tinkling cymbal.

And if I should have prophecy and should know all mysteries and all knowledge, and if I should have all faith, so that I could remove mountains, and have not charity, I am nothing.

And if I should distribute all my goods to feed the poor, and if I should deliver my body to be burned, and have not charity, it profiteth me nothing.

Charity is patient, is kind: charity envieth not, dealeth not perversely, is not puffed up.

Is not ambitious, seeketh not her own, is not provoked to anger, thinketh no evil:

Rejoiceth not in iniquity, but rejoiceth with the truth: Beareth all things, believeth all things, hopeth all things, endureth all things.

Charity never falleth away: whether prophecies shall be made void or tongues shall cease or knowledge shall be destroyed.

For we know in part, and we prophesy in part.

But when that which is perfect is come, that which is in part shall be done away.

When I was a child, I spoke as a child. I understood as a child, I thought as a child. But, when I became a man, I put away the things of a child.

We see now through a glass in a dark manner: but then face to face. Now I know in part: but then I shall know even as I am known.

And now there remain faith, hope and charity, these three: but the greatest of these is charity.

I Cor. 13.

ST. AUGUSTINE: Charity, the Law of God

THERE [on Sinai] the people were deterred by a terrible fear from approaching the place where the law was being given (Exod. xix); but here at [Pentecost] the Holy Ghost came upon them as they were gathered together in one place waiting for His promised coming (Acts ii). On the former occasion it was on tables of stone that the finger of God operated; on the latter it was on the hearts of men. There the law was laid down outwardly, that the unjust might be terrified; here it was given inwardly, that they might be justified. For . . . 'if there be any other commandment,' such of course as was written on those tables, 'it is,' saith the Apostle, 'comprised in this word: Thou shalt love thy neighbour as thyself. The love of our neighbour worketh no evil. Love therefore is the fulfilling of the law' (Rom.

xiii, 9, 10). This was not written on tables of stone, but 'poured forth in our hearts, by the Holy Ghost who is given to us' (*id.* v, 5). Charity, therefore, is the law of God.

De spiritu et littera, xvii, 29.

In order that we might receive that love whereby we should love, we were ourselves loved, while as yet we had it not. . . . For we would not have wherewithal to love Him, unless we received it from Him by His first loving us.

De gratia Christi, xxvi, 27 (NF).

The love of a created thing to be enjoyed without the love of God is not from God. The love of God (however) by which we attain to God, is not, except it be from God the Father through Jesus Christ with the Holy Ghost. Through this love of the Creator, every one can make a good use even of created things.

Contra Julianum, IV, iii, 33 (TM).

Love, and do what thou wilt; whether thou hold thy peace, of love hold thy peace; whether thou cry out, of love cry out; whether thou correct, of love correct; whether thou spare, through love do thou spare; let the root of love be within, of this root can nothing spring but what is good.

In Epistulam Joannis ad Parthos, Tr. vii, 8 (LF) .

GEORGE WOLFGANG FORELL: Martin Luther— Faith Active in Love

LUTHER KNEW that, following Augustine, Peter Lombard had claimed that the biblical commandment of love meant that first God is to be loved, then our soul, next our neighbor's soul, and lastly our body.[1] Luther was familiar with this doctrine of ordered love, and knew that it included and justified self-love.[2] Nevertheless, he objected emphatically, and openly opposed what had been considered the proper interpretation of Christian love for more than a thousand years, saying, "Saving the judgment of others and with due respect to the Fathers, in my opinion—I speak as a fool—that interpretation does not seem to be sound which is alleged concerning the precept of loving one's neighbor, whereby it is said that in the precept itself is the loving form with which one loves the neighbor, in that it says 'as thyself.' Therefore, they conclude: It is necessary that thou first love thyself and then after the pattern of thy love for thyself, love also thy neighbor."[3] On the contrary, he said, "I believe that by this precept, 'as thyself,' man is not bidden to love himself, but the vicious love is exposed wherewith he loves himself in fact; that is to say, thou art wholly bent upon thyself and turned to love of thyself, from which thou shalt not be made straight, except thou entirely cease to love thyself and, forgetful of thyself, love the neighbor alone. For it is perversity that we wish to be loved by all, and in all to seek our own; but rectitude is as if thou shouldst do to all men that which thou perversely wishest to be done to thyself."[4] Breaking all precedent and destroying a very practical and comfortable interpretation, Luther said: "Thou shalt love thy neighbor as thyself. Not as if thou oughtest to love thyself; for if that had been the meaning, then it would have been commanded. But so far is it from being commanded, that the commandment (of love to one's neighbor) is, on the contrary, based on the prohibition (of self-love). So thou dost ill in loving thyself. From this evil thou art delivered only when thou lovest thy neighbor in like manner—that is when thou ceasest to love thyself."[5] It is important to realize that Luther brought about a complete change in the generally accepted definition of love. Up to his time, theologians, guided by the principles of philosophical ethics, had interpreted love in essentially egocentric and eudaimonistic terms, even if these concepts were used in a sublimated sense. Love had been acquisitive love. Now Luther defined Christian love as self-giving, spontaneous, overflowing as the love of God. This love does not ask after the worthiness of the object, it is not concerned with the love-value of man, but "maketh the sun to rise on the evil and the good, and sendeth rain on the just and the unjust."[6]

It is on the basis of this definition of love, as overflowing, spontaneous love that Luther's ethical principle must be understood.[7] If love is really formed by faith, if it is the active tool of faith, then this love must be more than the prudential desire for the highest good. The love which is Christian faith in action must be part of the divine love given to man by God in order that man may pass it on to his fellow man.[8] For Luther, the love which is faith active towards the fellow man was a gift of God. He considered man merely the tube or channel through which God's love flows. While even Augustine spoke of "using one's neighbor in order to enjoy God,"[9] Luther spoke of faith and love as "placing man between God and his neighbor," as a medium which receives from above and gives out again below, and which is like "a vessel or tube through which the stream of divine blessings must flow without intermission to other people." And he continued: "See, those are then truly godlike men, who receive from

God all that He has in Christ, and in turn show themselves also by their well-doing to be, as it were, the gods of their neighbors."[10] This clearly shows what Luther meant by faith active in love: in faith man receives God's love and passes it on to his neighbor. The Christian as a child of God is used by God to mediate the divine love to other men.

It is to the needy neighbor that God wants man to show his love: "It is there God is to be found and loved, there He is to be served and ministered to, whoever wishes to minister to Him and serve Him; so that the commandment of the love of God is brought down in its entirety into the love of the neighbor. . . . For this was the reason why He put off the form of God and took on the form of a servant, that He might draw down our love for Him and fasten it on our neighbor."[11]

According to Luther, all ethics, individual as well as social, must be understood from the key-principle of love. "Faith brings you to Christ and makes Him your own with all that He has; Love gives you to your neighbor with all that you have."[12] Faith and hope are man's attitudes in regard to God, but love is the resulting attitude of man towards his fellow man.[13] But since love has its source not in man himself but in the relationship that God has established with man, it does not depend upon the reaction it elicits from the neighbor.[14] Luther considered love not a means to an end but the ethical end itself.[15]

NOTES

1. Augustine, *City*, II, 89 (XV, 12): "But we love the Creator truly if He be beloved for Himself, and nothing that is not of His essence be loved, for of Him we cannot love anything amiss. For that very love, whereby we love what is to be loved, is itself to be moderately loved in ourselves, as being virtue directing us in honest courses. And therefore I think that the best and briefest definition of virtue is this. It is an order of love." See also, ibid., XIX, 14; XII, 8, and Peter Lombard, as quoted in W.A., 56, 517, note 5.

2. W.A., 56, 516, 32 ff. (Comm. Romans, 1515-16): "In the comment I have said that love (caritas) is love (amor) not to oneself, but to one's neighbor. . . . Thus, to please one's neighbor is not to please oneself. But this statement of Gregory and of ours seems to be contradicted by that famous distinction and order of loving. For, according to the blessed Augustine, even the Master teaches that 'first God is to be loved, then our soul, next our neighbor's soul, and lastly our body.' Thus, ordered love begins with itself. The answer is that just this is one of those things by which we have been carried away from love (caritate)." Cf. Nygren, p. 493.

3. W.A., 56, 517, 17 ff.

4. W.A., 56, 518, 4 ff. (Comm. Romans 15:2, 1515-16). Cf. Nygren, p. 494. See also W.A., 2, 580, 24 ff. (Comm. Gal. 5:14, 1519): "This, too, deserves our careful attention, that some of the Fathers gathered from the words of this commandment (You shall love your neighbor as yourself) the opinion that 'ordered love' starts with oneself. They said that self-love defines the standard according to which you ought to love your neighbor. . . . But I understand that this command-

ment does not command self-love but love of the neighbor. It shows that self-love is already in all of us. For if He had wanted this 'ordered love' He would have said, 'love yourself and your neighbor as yourself.' . . . As far as I can see, this commandment speaks of the perverse love with which everybody, forgetting the neighbor, seeks only his own. This becomes again a right love when man forgets about himself and only wants to serve the neighbor. This is shown also by the members of the body where each serves the other, risking his own safety. For the hand fights for the head and receives injuries in its stead, the feet step into the mud and into the water to save the body. But through this ordered self-love, which Christ wanted to destroy through his commandment, the most dangerous desire to seek our own is nourished."

5. W.A., 56, 518, 14 ff. (Comm. Romans, 1515-16). Cf. Nygren, p. 494. See also W. A., 1, 654, 14 ff. (Against Silvester Prierias, 1518): "And this the words of Christ contain: 'He that loseth his life for My sake, shall find it.' Accordingly, when Christ says that we are to love our neighbor as we love ourselves, in my judgment He is speaking of the perverse and crooked love wherewith a man seeks nothing but his own; which love is not made straight unless it ceases to seek what is its own, and seeks what is its neighbor's. This is the opinion of the blessed Paul, Phil. 2: 'Not looking each of you to his own things, but to the things of others.' And I Cor. XIII: 'Love seeketh not its own.' With these words he manifestly forbids self-love."

6. Matthew 5:45. See also W.A., 1, 354, 35 (Heidelberg Disputation): "God's love does not find, but creates its lovable object; man's love is caused by its lovable object. The second clause is evident and it is agreed by all philosophers and theologians that the object is the cause of the love. They assume with Aristotle that every power of the soul is passive and 'matter' and that it acts by receiving—whereby he also testifies that his philosophy is contrary to theology—inasmuch as in all things it seeks its own and receives rather than confers good. The first clause is evident, since God's love living in man loves sinners, the evil, the foolish, the weak, that it may make them righteous, good, wise, and strong, and so it rather flows forth and confers good. For sinners are lovely because they are loved, they are not loved because they are lovely. So man's love shuns sinners and evil men. But thus Christ: 'I came not to call the righteous but sinners.' And this is the love of the Cross born of the Cross, which betakes itself not where it finds a good to enjoy, but where it may confer good upon the evil and the needy. For it is more blessed to give than to receive, says the Apostle. And so Psalm 41:2: 'Blessed is he that considereth the poor and needy.' Yet since the object of the understanding naturally cannot be that which is nothing, i.e., the poor or needy, but that which is, the true, the good, therefore, it judges according to appearance and accepts the person of men and judges according to the things which appear, etc." Cf. Nygren, p. 507 ff. W.A., 36, 358, 35 (Sermon, Nov. 24, 1532): "This is a knavish love, if I am friend to him only who serves me, can help me and honors me, and hate him who despises me and does not go along with me. Such love does not come from a heart which is good and pure towards everybody but comes from a heart that only seeks its own and is full of love to itself and not to others. For such a man loves nobody for his own self but figures what is in his interest and what he can get out of it. He is not interested in the neighbor."

7. W.A.T., 5, 397, 7 (5906): "To love God is to love the neighbor." See also W.A., 36, 360, 11 (Sermon on I Tim. 1:5, 1532): "This, however, must be an over-flowing love welling forth from within out of the heart like a fresh streamlet or brook which ever flows on and cannot be stopped or dried up or fail, which says: I love thee, not because thou art good or bad, for I draw my love not from thy goodness as from an alien spring, but from mine own well-spring—namely from the Word which is grafted into my heart."

8. Ibid., 360, 17: "Then it goes out lavishly and open to everyone who needs it, and meets both good and bad, friend and foe. Indeed, it is ready for enemies well-nigh most of all, as they have more need that I should pray for them and do all that I can, that they also may become godly and be redeemed from sin and the devil. See, that is a love welling out of the heart, not drawn into it, for he finds in that man nothing from which he might draw it; but because he is a

Christian and grasps the Word which in himself is quite pure, the same makes his heart also so pure and full of honest love, that he lets his love flow out unimpeded towards everyone, be the person who or what he may." Cf. Nygren, p. 513.

9. Ibid., p. 517.

10. W.A., 10, I, 100, 9 (Kirchenpostille, 1522, Titus 3:4-7).

11. W.A., 17, II, 99, 18 (Fastenpostille, 1525, Romans 13:8); cf. Nygren, p. 518

12. W.A., 10, I, (2), 38, 2 (Adventpostille, 1522, Matthew 21:1-9). See also Tr. Lenker of this sermon: "You ask, perhaps, what are the good works you are to do to your neighbor? Answer: They have no name. As the good works Christ does to you have no name, so your good works are to have no name. Whereby do you know them? Answer: They have no name, so that there may be no distinction made and they be not divided, that you might do some and leave others undone. You shall give yourself up to him altogether, with all you have. . . . Thus it is not your good work that you give alms or that you pray, but that you offer yourself to your neighbor and serve him, wherever he needs you and every way you can, be it with alms, prayer, work, fasting, counsel, comfort, instruction, admonition, punishment, apologizing, clothing, food, and lastly with suffering and dying for him."

13. W.A., 17, II, 278, 11 (Festpostille, 1527, Luke 12:35-40): "These are the most important three parts of the Christian life: faith, hope, and love. The first two look to God and belong above, the third looks to the neighbor and belongs down here. But our papists and work-righteous men have reversed it, go with their works before God and trade with Him, but with their faith they remain below with mankind."

14. W.A., 36, 358, 23 (Sermon, Nov. 24, 1532): "God has commanded me that I should show my love to my neighbor and favor everybody, be he friend or foe. Just as our Heavenly Father does by letting His sun rise and shine over the evil and the good. And He does good unto those who blaspheme Him day and night and who abuse His gifts through disobedience, blasphemy, sin, and shame. Similarly, He lets it rain for the grateful and the ungrateful alike, gives the gifts of the soil, money, property to even the worst knaves on earth. Why does He do it? Because of His pure love, which fills His heart to overflowing and which is outpoured freely to everybody without exception, be he good or bad, worthy or unworthy."

15. Ibid., 359, 36: "When God commands me to love the neighbor, He excludes nobody, neither friend nor foe, good nor evil. For even if a man is evil and does evil to you he does not lose the name 'neighbor.' He remains your flesh and blood and belongs in the commandment, 'Love thy neighbor.' . . . For a Christian must not derive his love from the person, as the love of this world does, e.g., a young fellow from a pretty girl, a miser from money and property, a lord or prince from honor and power, etc. This is all a derived or borrowed love, that cleaves outwardly to the good which it sees in a person, and lasts only so long as that same is there and can be enjoyed."

ST. FRANCIS DE SALES: Love of Neighbor*

GOD, who created man in His own image, commands us to love all men with a love similar to the love which should influence hearts for his divine Majesty. "Thou shalt love thy God" (Matt. 22:37-39).

Why do we love God? St. Bernard replies: "The motive for which we love God is God Himself" (De Diligendo Deo);

* Reprinted from A Treatise on Love of God.

thereby he insinuates that we love God because He is the sovereign and infinite goodness. But why do we love ourselves with a love of charity. Because we are the image and likeness of God. The dignity of resembling the Almighty is common to all men; we should then love them all as ourselves, as living images of the Deity. It is on this title that we belong to God; it is this which forms the strict alliance we have contracted with him and that bond of dependence by which we have become the children of God who assumes the tender name of parent. It is as images of God that we are capable of being united to His divine essence, of enjoying His sovereign goodness and of being happy with the bliss of God himself. It is in this quality that grace is communicated to us, that our soul is closely united with that of God and that according to the expression of St. Leo, we participate in some degree in the divine nature. The acts of love of God and our neighbor both proceed from the same charity. One end of the ladder seen by Jacob touched the heavens and the other rested on the earth, as if to enable the angels to descend and man to ascend. Thus the same love extends to God and our neighbor; by it we are elevated to union with the Divinity and descend to man, to live in union with him; yet by this love we always consider our neighbor as created to the image of God and thereby communicate with the goodness of God, participating in His graces and destined to enjoy His glory.

Whence it follows that to love our neighbor with a love of charity is to love God in man or man in God and consequently, to love God alone for His own sake and creatures for the love of God.

When we behold in our neighbor the lively image of God, should we not love him tenderly and wish him every blessing; not for his own sake, as I suppose that we are yet ignorant of his personal qualities; but for the love of God, who has created him to His own image, and consequently rendered him capable of participating in the effects of his goodness, both in the order of grace and of glory; for the love of that God whose hands have formed his being, to Whom he belongs, by Whom he subsists, in Whom he lives, for Whom he has been created and Whom he particularly resembles.

Therefore, the love of God not only frequently commands love of our neighbor, but produces and diffuses it in the heart, as its image and likeness. For as man is the image of God, so the perfect and holy love of our neighbor is the image of the love which inflames the heart of man for God.

SÖREN KIERKEGAARD: *You* Shall Love Your Neighbor*

Go, THEN, and do this—take away distinctions and similarities of distinctions—so that you can love your neighbour. Take away the distinctions of preference so that you can love your neighbour. But you are not to cease loving the beloved because of this—far from it. If this were so, the word *neighbour* would be the greatest fraud ever discovered, if you, in order to love your neighbour, must begin by ceasing to love those for whom you have a preference. Moreover, it would also be a contradiction, for, if one's neighbour is all men, then no one can be excluded—shall we now say, least of all the beloved? No, for this is the language of preference. Consequently, it is only the partiality which should be taken away—and yet it is not to be introduced again into the relationship with one's neighbour so that with extravagant preference you love your neighbour in contrast to your beloved. No, as they say to the solitary person, "Take care that you are not led into the snare of self-love," so it is necessary to say to the two lovers, "Take care that you are not led by erotic love itself into the snare of self-love." For the more decisively and exclusively preference centres upon one single person, the farther it is from loving the neighbour. You, husband, do not lead your wife into the temptation of forgetting your neighbour because of love for you; you, wife, do not lead your husband into this temptation! The lovers think that in erotic love they have the highest good, but it is not so, for therein they still do not have the eternal secured by the eternal. To be sure, the poet promises the lovers immortality if they are true lovers, but who is the poet; how good is his signature—he who cannot vouch for himself? The *royal law,* on the other hand, the love-command, promises life, eternal life, and this command simply says, "You shall love your neighbour." Just as this command will teach every man how he ought to love himself, likewise will it also teach erotic love and friendship what genuine love is: in love towards yourself preserve love to your neighbour, in erotic love and friendship preserve love to your neighbour. It may perhaps offend you—well, you know it anyway, that Christianity is always accompanied by signs of offence. Nevertheless believe it. Do not believe that the teacher who never extinguished a single smoking candle would extinguish any noble fire within a man; believe that he who was love will teach every man to love; believe that if all the song writers united in one song to the praise of erotic love and friendship, what they would have to

* Reprinted from *Works of Love.*

say would be nothing in comparison with the command, "You shall love; you shall love your neighbour as yourself!" Do not stop believing because the command almost offends you, because the discourse does not sound as flattering as that of the poet who courts your favour with his songs, because it repels and terrifies as if it would frighten you out of the beloved haunts of preference—do not for that reason cease to believe in it. Consider that just because the command and the discourse are what they are, for that very reason the object can be the object of faith! Do not give yourself over to the notion that you might compromise, that by loving some men, relatives and friends, you would love your neighbour—for this would mean giving up the poet without grasping what is Christian, and it was to prevent this compromise that the discourse set you between the poet's pride, which scorns all compromise, and the divine majesty of the royal command, which regards any compromise as blameworthy. No, love your beloved faithfully and tenderly, but let love to your neighbour be the sanctifier in your covenant of union with God; love your friend honestly and devotedly, but let love to your neighbour be what you learn from each other in the intimacy of friendship with God! Death erases all distinctions, but preference is always related to distinctions; yet the way to life and to the eternal goes through death and through the extinction of distinctions. Therefore only love to one's neighbour truly leads to life. As Christianity's glad proclamation is contained in the doctrine about man's kinship with God, so its task is man's likeness to God. But God is love; therefore we can resemble God only in loving, just as, according to the apostle's words, we can only "be God's co-workers—in love." Insofar as you love your beloved, you are not like unto God, for in God there is no partiality, something you have reflected on many times to your humiliation, and also at times to your rehabilitation. Insofar as you love your friend, you are not like unto God, because before God there is no distinction. But when you love your neighbour, then you are like unto God.

Therefore go and do likewise. Forsake all distinctions so that you can love your neighbour. Alas, perhaps it is not necessary to say this to you at all. Perhaps you have found no beloved in this world, no friend along the way, and you walk alone. Or perhaps God took from your side and gave you a beloved, but death came and took her from your side; it came again and took your friend but gave you none in return, and now you walk alone; you have no beloved to cover your weak side and no friend at your right hand. Or perhaps life separated you, even though all of you remained unchanged—in the solitariness of separation. Or, alas, perhaps change separated you and you walk sorrowfully alone because you found what you sought but then found that what you found—changed! How inconsolable! Yes, just ask the poet how inconsolable it is to live alone, to have lived alone, without being loved and without having any beloved. Just ask the poet if he knows of anything other than comfortlessness when death comes between the lovers, or when life separates friend from friend, or when change separates them as enemies from each other. For doubtless the poet loves solitude—he loves it so that in solitude he may discover the lost happiness of erotic love and friendship, just as one goes to a dark place in order to see the wonder of the stars. And yet, if a man were blameless in not having found a beloved, if he were blameless in having looked in vain for a friend, if the loss, the separation, and the change were not his fault, does the poet know of anything else than comfortlessness? But the poet himself has succumbed to change when he, the prophet of joy, does not know of anything else on the day of need than the mournful lament of comfortlessness. Or would you not call it change? Would you call it fidelity on the part of the poet that he inconsolably sorrows with the inconsolably sorrowing— well, we won't quarrel about that! But if you will compare this human fidelity with the faithfulness of heaven and the eternal, you will certainly concede that there is a change. For heaven not only rejoices—above any poet—with the joyful; heaven not only sorrows with the sorrowing—no, heaven has something new, a holier joy, in readiness for the sorrowing. Thus Christianity always has consolation, and its consolation is different from all human consolation in that human consolation recognises itself to be a substitute for lost joy—and Christian consolation *is joy itself*. Humanly speaking, consolation is a more recent invention. First came pain and suffering and the loss of joy, and then, afterwards, alas, after a long time, man hit upon the way of consolation. The same is true in the life of the individual. First comes pain and suffering and the loss of joy, and then afterward, alas, sometimes long afterward, comes consolation. But Christian consolation can never be said to come afterward, for since it is the consolation of the eternal, it is older than all temporal joy. As soon as this consolation comes, it comes with the head-start of the eternal and swallows up, as it were, pain, for pain and the loss of joy are momentary—even if the moment were a year—and the momentary is drowned in the eternal. Neither is Christian consolation a substitute compensation for lost joy, since it is joy itself. All other joy is essentially only disconsolateness in comparison with Christianity's consolation. Man's life was not and is not so perfect on this earth that the joy of the eternal could be proclaimed to him simply as joy which he had and which he has wasted. For that reason the joy of the eternal can be proclaimed to him only as consolation. As the human eye cannot bear to look directly at the sun except through dark glasses, so man cannot bear the joy of the eternal except through the dimness of being proclaimed as consolation.—Consequently, whatever your fate in erotic love and friendship, whatever your privation, whatever your loss, whatever the desolation of your life which you confide to the poet, the highest still stands: love your neighbour! As already shown, you can easily find him; him you can never lose. The beloved can treat you in such a way that he is lost to you, and you can lose a friend, but whatever a neighbour does to you, you can never lose him. To be sure, you can also continue to love your beloved and your friend no matter how they treat you, but you cannot truthfully continue to call them beloved and friend when they, sorry to say, have really changed. No change, however, can take your neighbour from you, for it is not your neighbour who holds you fast— it is your love which holds your neighbour fast. If your love for your neighbour remains unchanged, then your neighbour also remains unchanged just by being. Death itself cannot deprive you of your neighbour either, for if it takes one, life immediately gives you another. Death can deprive you of a friend, because in loving a friend you really cling to your friend, but in loving your neighbour you cling to God: therefore death cannot deprive you of your neighbour.—If, therefore, you have lost everything of erotic love and friendship, if you have never had any of this happiness— in loving your neighbour you still have the best left.

Love to one's neighbour has the very perfection of the eternal. Is it really perfection belonging to love that its object is the superior, the remarkable, the unique? I should think that this would be a perfection belonging to the object, and the perfection of the object would evoke a subtle suspicion concerning the perfection of the love. Is it an excellence in your love that it can love *only* the extraordinary, the rare? I should think it would be a merit belonging to the extraordinary and the rare that it is extraordinary and rare, but not a merit of the love for it. Are you not of the same opinion? Have you never meditated upon God's love? If it were love's merit to love the extraordinary, then God would be—if I dare say so—perplexed, for to him the extraordinary does not exist at all. The merit of being able to love *only* the extraordinary is therefore more like an accusation, not against the extraordinary nor against love, but against the love which can love *only* the extraordinary. Is it the merit of a man's delicate health that he can feel well in *only* one place in the world, sur- rounded by every favourable condition? When you see a person who has thus arranged matters in life, what is it you praise? No doubt the comfortableness of his surroundings. But have you not noticed that every word eulogising this magnificence really sounds like a joke on the poor fellow who can live *only* in this luxurious environment? Consequently, perfection in the object is not perfection in the love. Precisely because one's neighbour has none of the excellences which the beloved, a friend, a cultured person, an admired one, and a rare and extraordinary one have in high degree—for that very reason love to one's neighbour has all the perfections which love to a beloved one, a friend, a cultured person, an admired one, a rare and extraordinary one, does not have. Let men debate as much as they wish about which object of love is the most perfect—there can never be any doubt that love to one's neighbour is the most perfect love. All other love, therefore, is imperfect in that there are two questions and thereby a certain duplicity: there is first a question about the object and then about the love, or there is a question about both the object and the love. But concerning love to one's neighbour there is only one question, that about love. And there is only one answer of the eternal: this is genuine love, for love to one's neighbour is not related as a type to other types of love. Erotic love is determined by the object; friendship is determined by the object; only love to one's neighbour is determined by love. Since one's neighbour is every man, unconditionally every man, all distinctions are indeed removed from the object. Therefore genuine love is recognisable by this, that its object is without any of the more definite qualifications of difference, which means that this love is recognisable only by love. Is not this the highest perfection? Insofar as love can and may be recognised by something else, then this something else, in the relationship itself, is like a suspicion about the love, that it is not comprehensive enough and therefore not in an eternal sense infinite. This something else, unconscious to love itself, is a disposition to morbidity. In this suspicion, therefore, lies hidden the anxiety which makes erotic love and friendship dependent upon their objects, the anxiety which can kindle jealousy, the anxiety which can bring one to despair. But love to one's neighbour does not contain a suspicion about the relationship and therefore cannot become suspiciousness in the one who loves. Yet this love is not proudly independent of its object. Its equality does not appear in love's proudly turning back into itself, indifferent towards the object. No, its equality appears in love's humbly turning itself outwards, embracing all, yet loving everyone in particular but no one in partiality.

Let us consider what has already been developed, that in a human being love is a need, is the expression of riches. In fact, the deeper this need is, the greater are the riches; if the need is infinite, then the riches are also infinite. If a man's love-need is to love one single person, it must be said, even if one concedes that this need is riches, that he really needs this person. On the other hand, if the love-need in a man is to love all, there is a real need, and it is so great that it could almost produce its own object of love. In the first case the emphasis is on the speciality of the object, in the second on the essentiality of the need, and only in this latter sense is need an expression of riches. Only in this latter sense are the object of love and the love-need related equally in an infinite way, for the first person is the best person and every human being is one's neighbour, or, in the sense of *speciality* there is no object of love; whereas in the infinite sense every human being is the object of love. When one feels the need of talking with one particular person, he really needs this person; but when this need of conversing is so great that he must speak, so that if he were transported to a desert island or put in solitary confinement and the need of conversing were so great that every human being was the special person he wanted to talk with—then the need would be riches. For him in whom there is love to his neighbour, love is a need, the deepest need. He does not have need of men just to have someone to love, but he needs to love men. Yet there is no pride or haughtiness in this wealth, for God is the middle term and the "shall" of the eternal binds and guides the great need so that it does not run wild and turn into pride. But there are no limits to the objects of love, for one's neighbour is all men, unconditionally every human being.

Therefore he who in truth loves his neighbour loves also his enemy. The distinction *friend or enemy* is a distinction in the object of love, but the object of love to one's neighbour is without distinction. One's neighbour is the absolutely unrecognisable distinction between man and man; it is eternal equality before God— enemies, too, have this equality. Men think that it is impossible for a human being to love his enemies, for enemies are hardly able to endure the sight of one another. Well, then, shut your eyes— and your enemy looks just like your neighbour. Shut your eyes and remember the command that *you* shall love; then you are to love—your enemy? No. Then love your neighbour, for you cannot see that he is your enemy. When you shut your eyes, you do not see the distinctions of earthly existence, but enmity is also one of the distinctions of earthly existence. And when you shut your eyes, your mind is not diverted and confused just when you are to listen to the words of the command. And when your mind is not disturbed and confused by looking at the object of your love and the distinction of your object, then you become all ears for the words of the command, which speak one thing and one

thing only to you, that *you* ought to love your neighbour. Now,
when your eyes are closed and you have become all ears for the
command, you are on the way of perfection in loving your
neighbour.

ANDERS NYGREN: Agape and Eros

THE FUNDAMENTAL CONTRAST BETWEEN AGAPE AND EROS

The Transvaluation of All Ancient Values

1. THE GENERAL SIGNIFICANCE OF THE TRANSVALUATION

In seeking to express the relation between
Christianity and the ancient world, Nietzsche coined the well-
known formula that Christianity meant a "transvaluation of all
ancient values". This formula contains a great deal more truth
than is generally recognized. It is also capable of a far wider application than its author had in mind. It holds good, not only with
respect to Classical antiquity, but also with respect to Judaism
and, indeed, the entire pre-Christian and non-Christian world.
The "transvaluation" is seen, above all, in the central Christian
motif, the Agape motif. Agape is like a blow in the face to both
Jewish legal piety and Hellenistic Eros-piety.

From the point of view of Jewish legal piety, it is self-
evident that God loves the righteous and the godly, and that
He does not love the unrighteous and the sinner. That is a
simple corollary of the conception of fellowship with God as
governed by the Law. But Jesus declares: "I came not to call
the righteous, but sinners" (Mark ii. 17); and the reason for
this lies in God's Agape, for by its very nature Agape means the
forgiveness of sins. Agape shatters completely the legal conception of the relationship between God and man. That is the reason for the conflict of Jesus with the Pharisees and Paul's campaign
against "the Law". Agape is the opposite of "Nomos", and therefore a denial of the foundation on which the entire Jewish scale
of values rested.

But the idea of Agape is no less opposed to the ancient
Græco-Hellenistic scale of values, of which the hall-mark is Eros.
For the Greeks it is self-evident that the gods do *not love*. Why
should they, when they possess all that they can wish? Having
no lack of anything, no unsatisfied desire, they have no need to

love; that is, they have no need to desire anything, to seek long-ingly to acquire anything. Against this, Christianity confesses its fundamental faith that "God is love". This love, however, has nothing to do with acquisitive desire, but is characterised by sac-rifice and self-giving; for it is Agape. The question, "Why should God love?" has no meaning in a Christian context. God does not love in order to obtain any advantage thereby, but quite simply because it is His nature to love—with a love that seeks, not to get, but to give. This means, in other words, that no teleological ex-planation or motivation of His love can be entertained.

It is plain that Greek thought has no place for fellowship with God in the strict sense of that term. The gods live their blessed, immortal life high above the transience and change of human existence. "A god holds no intercourse with a man", says Plato (*Symposium* 203). But in Christianity, Agape means pre-cisely fellowship between God and man instituted by God. No doubt the Greek philosophers can speak at times, in harmony with popular religious ideas, of the love of the gods for men; yet even then the contrast between ancient thought and Christianity is not lessened. We have only to ask *who* it is that is loved by the deity, and the difference at once becomes clear. Aristotle's answer to this question is as follows: "He who lives according to reason will be the special object of the deity's love. For if the gods have any care for human affairs, as men think they have, we must surely assume that they take delight in the best and that which is most akin to them—which is our reason—and that they reward those who most love and honour this. . . . But it is plain that these things are to be found supremely in the wise man. Hence he is most loved by the deity."[1] Obviously the love in question here is diametrically opposed to Christian Agape. According to Aristotle, it is only reasonable to assume that God most loves the wise man; but according to Paul, the love and election of God are the direct opposite of what we might reasonably assume. "God", he says, "chose the foolish things of the world, that He might put to shame them that are wise; and God chose the weak things of the world, that He might put to shame the things that are strong; and the base things of the world, and the things that are despised, did God choose, yea and the things that are not, that He might bring to nought the things that are" (1 Cor. i. 27 f.).

Nietzsche is therefore undoubtedly right in speaking of Christianity as a transvaluation of all ancient values; and not only so, but also as regards the meaning and content of this trans-valuation he puts his finger on the decisive point. His words are important enough to be quoted as they stand. "Modern men," he says, "hardened as they are to all Christian terminology, no longer appreciate the horrible extravagance which, for ancient taste, lay in the paradox of the formula, 'God on the Cross'. Never before had there been anywhere such an audacious inversion, never anything so terrifying, so challenging and challengeable, as this formula; it promised a transvaluation of all ancient values."[2]

Nietzsche was not the first to discover that Christianity with its "God on the Cross" means the transvaluation of all ancient values. That was realised in the earliest days of Christianity, among both its friends and its foes. "God on the Cross" —it was in this that Paul, too, saw the great transvaluation introduced by Christianity. "We preach Christ crucified," he says, "unto Jews a stumbling-block, and unto Gentiles foolishness" (1 Cor. i. 23). But "God on the Cross" is only another name for the Agape of the Cross. To the Jews it was bound to be a *skandalon*, not merely because of the difficulty they had in conceiving a crucified Messiah, but also, and above all, because the Agape of the Cross rules out the entire scheme of values on which their conception of the religious relationship was based. And to the Græco-Hellenistic mind no less, the preaching of Christ crucified and the Agape of the Cross was bound to seem foolishness. Both ethically and religiously Agape is hopelessly in conflict with the mental outlook of antiquity. From an ethical point of view, it cannot but appear as sheer unrighteousness. It conflicts with the ideal of the wise man and the notion of upward endeavour. It runs directly counter to the idea of Eros and man's ascent to the sphere of the Divine. It seems to put a premium on sin; it looks very like ethical laxity, and lenience towards those to whom no lenience should be shown. Hence, as the ancients see it, it is defective also from a religious point of view. It is, indeed, a blasphemy against God; for it represents Him as worse than human judges, who do after all take pains to secure objectivity and truth. Agape cannot but seem sheer godlessness, for it contradicts everything that is characteristic of the ancient conception of God. It conflicts with the Divine immutability, incorruptibility and eternality; for how can the Immutable descend and subject Himself to the changes and chances of human life? And it conflicts with God's *eudæmonia*, His beauty, happiness and blessedness; for what could induce Him who knows no unsatisfied desire, to leave His blessedness and self-sufficiency and go to such a length of self-emptying as to endure the death of the cross? Such in brief is the kind of criticism which in the second century was directed against the Christian idea of Agape by a Platonist like Celsus.[3]

Putting it in terms that are often used—and misused—we might say that Agape gives expression to the paradoxical and irrational nature of Christianity. In saying this, however, it is important that we should make it clear that the idea of Agape is *not* paradoxical or irrational in the sense in which those terms are commonly used. There is in many quarters today an unhealthy cult of the paradoxical and irrational, almost as if the lack of clarity and consistency were sufficient evidence of religious or Christian truth. When we describe the idea of Agape as paradoxical and irrational, we do not for a moment suggest that it contains any logical contradiction or implies a *credo quia absurdum*. The idea of Agape is by no means self-contradictory. On the contrary, it is a quite simple and clear and easily comprehensible idea. It is paradoxical and irrational only inasmuch as it means a transvaluation of all previously accepted values.

2. THE RELIGIOUS-HISTORICAL BACKGROUND OF THE TRANSVALUATION

In order to bring out the deepest meaning of the contrast between Agape and Eros, however, we must do more than simply show them to be two opposed ideas of love. Otherwise we may easily give the impression that nothing is involved but an opposition at one particular point, whereas in fact it is a universal, all-embracing opposition, touching every point. Here, therefore, we must take, if only very briefly, a wider survey.

Eros and Agape are the characteristic expressions of two different attitudes to life, two fundamentally opposed types of religion and ethics. They represent two streams that run through the whole history of religion, alternately clashing against one another and mingling with one another. They stand for what may be described as the egocentric and the theocentric attitude in religion.

In the egocentric type, the religious relationship is dominated essentially by man. The distance between man and the Divine is not insuperable. Man is akin to the Deity, or is maybe himself a Divine being, though at the moment he is confused and distracted by the things of sense that surround him. To come to himself, therefore, is to come to the Divine; and therein lies man's true end, his satisfaction and blessedness. Between the Divine and the human there is thus presupposed an unbroken continuity, and no matter how great the difference between them may be, it is but relative. Hence it is possible for man to mount up successively towards an ever-increasing likeness to God, and to draw step by step nearer the Divine.

In the theocentric type, on the other hand, everything centres in God. Between God and man there is an absolute distinction, a border-line that can never be crossed from man's side. Any thought of man's raising himself up to the Divine life is felt to be sheer titanic pride, which, so far from bringing man into a right relation to God, represents the highest degree of godlessness. The gulf that is fixed between God and man is absolute, so that man has no possibility of working his way up to the Divine level. Only God himself can bridge the gulf. Man cannot by means of Eros attain to God. Real fellowship with God is possible only if God in his Agape condescends to man.

It is the egocentric type that has generally predominated in the history of religion. From primitive beginnings it rises to the spiritual heights of Mysticism. It makes it its aim to awaken in man a longing and questing for the eternal; it seeks to induce him to turn from this transitory and corruptible life and mount up on the wings of the soul to the higher world from which the soul originates. A high-water mark of this development is reached in Platonism, which has not only a philosophical but also a thoroughly religious aspect. Religiously, the great gift of Platonism to the world is its passionate love and longing for the supersensible, the selfsubsistent, the Divine.

The opposite, theocentric, tendency has never been wholly lacking, though it has remained more in the background.[4] Not until Christianity appears does it break decisively through and claim complete supremacy. It is in its theocentric character that we see the deepest reason why Christianity necessarily involves a transvaluation of all ancient values.

Religion is fellowship with God. But two different conceptions are possible of the way in which this fellowship is brought about. It can either be thought of as achieved by the raising up of the human to the Divine—and that is the contention of egocentric religion, of Eros; or else it is held to be established by the gracious condenscension of the Divine to man—and that is the contention of theocentric religion, of Agape.

TABULATION OF THE ESSENTIAL POINTS OF CONTRAST

We have seen the contrast between Eros and Agape widen out into a fundamental opposition between two whole attitudes to life. With this we have reached the point which has all along been the main purpose of our study. We stated already in the Introduction that we were not, strictly speaking, concerned with a comparison of two isolated historical phenomena. Such a comparison would easily lead to all kinds of arbitrariness. Indeed, it is questionable whether there would be any possibility of comparison; for Eros and Agape grew up in such different circumstances that they are bound to appear incommensurable when set over against one another in their simple historical form. In this connection we may recall the saying of Wilamowitz-Moellendorff about Plato and Paul, that "they could have learnt something from one another here, but, being what they were, they would not have done so."[6] What reason is there, then, for taking Plato as the starting-point for a discussion of Paul's outlook, or Paul for a discussion of Plato's? In the present instance, however, as has been said, we are not concerned simply with two such historical individuals and their views, but with two fundamentally different attitudes which set their mark on the whole of life. We are concerned with two competing fundamental motifs, two contrary ideals, or conceptions of what life means. This entirely alters the situation, and provides much more favourable conditions for the purposes of comparison and contrast.

For a comparison to be possible, the objects to be compared must, of course, have something in common as well as their points of difference; and this appears to revive our difficulty. For what could Eros and Agape have in common? There seems in fact to be no possibility of discovering any idea common to them both which might serve as a starting-point for the comparison; for at every point the opposition between them makes itself felt. It is, however, unnecessary to look for anything common to them in that sense. What is common in a case like this, where we are dealing with fundamental motifs, is the question to which they are answers. The common question furnishes a common denominator, so to speak, for the answers, despite all differences between them. Both Eros and Agape claim to give expression to man's relation to the Divine, and both exercise a formative influence on his ethical life. It is these ultimate, universal questions that concern us here. We can speak of Eros-religion and Agape-religion, of Eros-ethics and Agape-ethics; and it is the content of these general concepts that we have to try to determine.

One further observation must be made. When we are comparing and contrasting two general attitudes to life, it is easy to slip over from the consideration of facts to an appraisal of values. The terms that are used to describe the different attitudes to life are then taken as indicative of the value attached to them. For example, when we describe the contrast between Eros and Agape by saying that Eros is egocentric love, Agape unselfish love, or that Eros means self-assertion, Agape self-sacrifice, we readily associate the idea of unselfishness and self-sacrifice with that of something estimable, and the idea of self-assertion and egocentric

conduct with that of something unestimable. It is owing to the
transvaluation wrought by Christianity that this has come to seem
natural and inevitable to us. To the men of antiquity, however,
self-assertion and egocentric conduct were not less obviously estimable. We have thus two ultimate standards of value confronting
one another here, and it is our purpose simply to describe them,
not to act as judge between them. In setting Agape and Eros side
by side, *our aim is to bring out a difference in type, not a difference in value.*

Bearing this in mind, we may now go on to ask what are
the characteristic features of the Eros-attitude and the Agape-
attitude respectively. The principal and ultimately decisive contrast between them has already been clearly brought out in the
preceding pages. In order to sum up and conclude our account
of the two fundamental motifs and their contrary tendencies, we
append here a tabular survey. The various particulars it contains
have, of course, emerged here and there in the course of our investigation, but now we are less concerned with these details as
such, than with the antithetical arrangement of them, which will
enable us to see how the difference in type is manifested
throughout.

Eros is acquisitive desire and longing.	Agape is sacrificial giving.
Eros is an upward movement.	Agape comes down.
Eros is man's way to God.	Agape is God's way to man.
Eros is man's effort: it assumes that man's salvation is his own work.	Agape is God's grace: salvation is the work of Divine love.
Eros is egocentric love, a form of self-assertion of the highest, noblest, sublimest kind.	Agape is unselfish love, it "seek- eth not its own", it gives itself away.
Eros seeks to gain its life, a life divine, immortalised.	Agape lives the life of God, therefore dares to "lose it."
Eros is the will to get and pos- sess which depends on want and need.	Agape is freedom in giving, which depends on wealth and plenty.
Eros is primarily *man's* love; God is the *object* of Eros. Even when it is attributed to God, Eros is patterned on human love.	Agape is primarily *God's* love; God *is* Agape. Even when it is attributed to man, Agape is patterned on Divine love.
Eros is determined by the quality, the beauty and worth, of its object; it is not spon- taneous, but "evoked", "moti- vated".	Agape is sovereign in relation to its object, and is directed to both "the evil and the good"; it is spontaneous, "overflow- ing," "unmotivated".

| Eros *recognises value* in its object—and loves it. | Agape loves—and *creates value in its* object. |

. . . Christian fellowship with God is distinguished from all other kinds by the fact that it depends exclusively on God's Agape. We have therefore no longer any reason to ask about either the better or worse qualities of those who are the objects of Divine love. To the question, Why does God love? there is only one right answer: Because it is His nature to love.

THE CONTENT OF THE IDEA OF AGAPE

Our inquiry has now reached the point where it is possible for us briefly to describe the content of the Christian idea of love in so far as it concerns Divine love. Its main features can be summarised in the following four points:

(1) *Agape is spontaneous and "unmotivated".* This is the most striking feature of God's love as Jesus represents it. We look in vain for an explanation of God's love in the character of the man who is the object of His love. God's love is "groundless"—though not, of course, in the sense that there is no ground for it at all, or that it is arbitrary and fortuitous. On the contrary, it is just in order to bring out the element of necessity in it that we describe it as "groundless"; our purpose is to emphasise that there are no extrinsic grounds for it. The only ground for it is to be found in God Himself. God's love is altogether *spontaneous.* It does not look for anything in man that could be adduced as motivation for it. In relation to man, Divine love is *"unmotivated".* When it is said that God loves man, this is not a judgment on what man is like, but on what God is like.

It is this love, spontaneous and "unmotivated"—having no motive outside itself, in the personal worth of men—which characterises also the action of Jesus in seeking out the lost and consorting with "publicans and sinners". It was precisely in this action, which from the point of view of legal relationships was inexplicable and indefensible, that He knew Himself carrying out the Father's work and revealing His mind and will. When fellowship with God is conceived of as a legal relationship, Divine love must in the last resort be dependent on the worth of its object. But in Christ there is revealed a Divine love which breaks all bounds, refusing to be controlled by the value of its object, and being determined only by its own intrinsic nature. According to Christianity, "motivated" love is human; spontaneous and "unmotivated" love is Divine.

This being so, we can see why Jesus was bound to attack a religious relationship conceived in legal terms. Had He been concerned only to claim a place for the idea of *love in the most general sense* within the religious relationship, He could have secured it even within the legal scheme. There was no need to smash the legal scheme in order to do that. The love for which there is room in this scheme, however, is the "motivated" love that is directed to the righteous, to those who deserve it. But Jesus is not concerned with love in this ordinary sense, but with the spontaneous, unmotivated love that is Agape; and for this there is fundamentally no place within the framework of legal order. To go back once more to the words of Jesus in Matt. ix. 17, we may say that *Agape is the new wine which inevitably bursts the old wineskins.* Now we see also why there had to be a revolutionary change of attitude towards the righteous and the sinner. If God's love were restricted to the righteous it would be evoked by its object and not spontaneous; but just by the fact that it seeks sinners, who do not deserve it and can lay no claim to it, it manifests most clearly its spontaneous and unmotivated nature.

(2) *Agape is "indifferent to value".* This does not really add anything new to what has already been said; but in order to prevent a possible misunderstanding, it is necessary to give special emphasis to one aspect of the point we have just made. When Jesus makes the righteous and sinners change places, it might at first sight appear as if this were a matter of simple transvaluation, or inversion of values; but we have already said enough to show that it is a question of something far deeper. It is not that Jesus simply reverses the generally accepted standard of values and holds that the sinner is "better" than the righteous. True as it is to say that He effected a "transvaluation of all values", yet the phrase can easily give rise to a false impression. Actually, something of far deeper import than any "transvaluation" is involved here— namely, the principle that *any thought of valuation whatsoever* is out of place in connection with fellowship with God. When God's love is directed to the sinner, then the position is clear; all thought of valuation is excluded in advance; for if God, the Holy One, loves the sinner, it cannot be because of his sin, but in spite of his sin. But when God's love is shown to the righteous and godly, there is always the risk of our thinking that God loves the man on account of his righteousness and godliness. But this is a denial of Agape—as if God's love for the "righteous" were not just as unmotivated and spontaneous as His love for the sinner! As if there were any other Divine love than spontaneous and unmotivated Agape! It is only when all thought of the worthiness of the object is abandoned that we can understand what Agape is. God's love allows no limits to be set for it by the character or conduct of man. The distinction between the worthy and the un-

worthy, the righteous and the sinner, sets no bounds to His love. "He maketh His sun to rise on the evil and the good, and sendeth rain on the just and the unjust" (Matt. v. 45).

(3) *Agape is creative.* When we seek to analyse the structure of the idea of Agape, what first attracts our attention is its spontaneous and unmotivated character. This, as we have described it above, shows that we are dealing with a love of a quite unique kind. The deepest reason for its uniqueness, however, has not yet been stated. What is ultimately decisive for the meaning of Agape can only be seen when we observe that it is *Divine* love and therefore shares in the creativeness that is characteristic of all the life of God. Agape is creative love. God does not love that which is already in itself worthy of love, but on the contrary, that which in itself has no worth acquires worth just by becoming the object of God's love. Agape has nothing to do with the kind of love that depends on the recognition of a valuable quality in its object; Agape does not recognize value, but creates it. Agape loves, and imparts value by loving. The man who is loved by God has no value in himself; what gives him value is precisely the fact that God loves him. *Agape is a value-creating principle.*

We have now reached the deepest and ultimately decisive feature of the idea of Agape—a feature which it must be said has been very much obscured in modern theology. Ever since Ritschl's time it has been common for theologians to speak of "the infinite value of the human soul" as one of the central ideals of Christianity, and to connect it with the idea of "God's fatherly love". Thus A. von Harnack, in *Das Wesen des Christentums*, claims that the teaching of Jesus as a whole can be grouped under three heads, each of such a nature as to contain the whole; and one of these he entitles "God the Father and the infinite value of the human soul."[7] To this, however, we can rightly object that the idea of "the infinite value of the human soul" is by no means a central idea of Christianity. Only a false exegesis has made it possible to find support for this idea in the oft-quoted passage: "What doth it profit a man, to gain the whole world, and forfeit his life (A.V. soul)? For what should a man give in exchange for his life (A.V. soul)?" (Mark viii. 36 f.). Moreover, Harnack's statement that "all who bear a human face are of more value than the whole world"[8] shows very clearly that the thought of an infinite value of this kind as belonging to man by nature has its roots elsewhere than in Christianity.

What chiefly interests us here, however, is the destructive effect that this idea has had on the conception of Divine love. The suggestion that man is by nature possessed of such an inalienable value, easily gives rise to the thought that it is this

matchless value on which God's love is set. Even though the
Divine spark may seem to have been wholly quenched in a man
sunk in sin, it is none the less present in "all who bear a human
face", and its potentialities are capable of being actualised in
everyone. Viewed in this light, God's forgiveness of sins means
merely that He disregards the manifold faults and failings of the
outward life and looks only at the inward, imperishable value
which not even sin has been able to destroy. His forgiving love
means that He sees and values the pearl of great price, regardless
of the defilement that happens at present to cling to it. He over-
looks the defects and imperfections and concentrates on the
essence of the personality which wins His approbation.[9]

If this interpretation of Divine forgiveness and love were
correct, God's love would not in the last resort be spontaneous and
unmotivated but would have an adequate motive in the infinite
value inherent in human nature. The forgiveness of sins would
then imply merely the recognition of an already existing value.
But it is evident enough that this is not the forgiveness of sins as
Jesus understands it. When He says, "Thy sins are forgiven thee",
this is no merely formal attestation of the presence of a value
which justifies the overlooking of faults; it is the bestowal of a
gift. Something really new is introduced, something new is taking
place. The forgiveness of sins is a *creative work of Divine power*
(ἐξουσία) which Jesus knows Himself called to carry out on earth,
and which can be put on a level with other Divine miracles, such
as His healing of the paralytic (Mark ii. 5-12).

(4) *Agape is the initiator of fellowship with God.* Not
only does Agape determine the essential and characteristic content
of Christian fellowship with God, but in virtue of its creative
nature it is also important for the initiation of that fellowship.
In the relations between God and man the initiative in establishing fellowship lies with Divine Agape. If we consider the implications of the idea of Agape, it becomes very plain that all the
other ways by which man seeks to enter into fellowship with God
are futile. This is above all true of the righteous man's way of
meritorious conduct, but it is no less true of the sinner's way of
repentance and amendment. Repentance and amendment are no
more able than righteousness to move God to love.

In this connection also the advent of Agape is completely
revolutionary. Hitherto the question of fellowship with God had
always been understood as a question of the way by which man
could come to God. But now, when not only the way of righteousness but also that of self-abasement and amendment is rejected as
incapable of leading to the goal, it follows that *there is from
man's side no way at all that leads to God.* If such a thing as

fellowship between God and man nevertheless exists, this can only be due to God's own action; God must Himself come to meet man and offer him His fellowship. There is thus no way for man to come to God, but only a way for God to come to man: the way of Divine forgiveness, Divine love.

Agape is God's way to man.

NOTES

1. *Eth. Nic.*, X., viii., 9. *Cf.* H. Meyer, *Platon und die aristotelische Ethik*, 1919, pp. 187 f.

2. *Jenseits von Gut und Böse*, Drittes Haupstück, 46. Nietzsche can well be described as the modern exponent of Paul's statement in 1 Cor. i. 23. His worship of antiquity opened his eyes to the immense and fundamental difference between antiquity and Christianity, a difference which in the interests of apologetics there has all too often been a readiness to obscure.

3. For an impression of the way in which an ancient mind, in no way "hardened to all Christian terminology", reacted to the idea of Agape, we cannot do better than turn to Celsus. "What great deeds", he asks, "did Jesus perform as being a God? Did he put his enemies to shame, or bring to a ridiculous conclusion what was designed against him? . . : If not before, yet why not now, at least, does he not give some manifestation of his divinity, and free himself from this reproach, and take vengeance upon those who insult both him and his Father?" (Origen, *Contra Celsum*, II., 33 ff.). We have only to listen to questions like these to realise in a flash how completely contrary the ancient sense of values is to the Agape of Christianity. *Cf.* K. Holl, *Urchristentum und Religionsgeschichte*, 1925, pp. 19 f.: "Celsus with his characteristic acuteness of vision has seen this point too in Christianity, and he never tires of pointing out to Christians the absurdity, the contemptibleness, the revoltingness of their conception of God. Every other religion has some regard for itself, and admits only respectable, cultivated, irreproachable people into its fellowship; but Christianity runs after the riffraff of the streets. As if it were positively a bad thing to have committed no sin, or as if God were a robber chief who gathered criminals around him! In this, Celsus was only expressing the objection that every Greek or Roman must have felt against Christianity. That 'the Deity has dealings only with the pure', was for them a sacred, inviolable axiom."

4. It appears in the Old Testament, of course, but it is present in other religions as well. *Cf.* A. Nygren, *Det bestående i kristendomen*, 1922, pp. 38 f., and *Försoningen, en Guds gärning*, 1932, p. 19.—*Translator's note.*

5. See above, pp. 34 ff.

6. *Platon, I.*, 1919, p. 384.

7. A. v. Harnack, *Das Wesen des Christentums*, 1913, pp. 33 and 40 ff.; E.T., *What is Christianity?* pp. 51 and 63 ff.

8. *Op. cit.*, p. 43; E.T., p. 67.

9. *Cf.* the similar argument in F. C. Krarup, *Livsforstaaelse*, 1915, pp. 97 ff.

LEO TOLSTOY: Master and Man

STAGGERING UP to the sledge, Vassili grasped hold of it and stood for a long time without moving as he endeavoured to steady himself and regain his breath. There was nothing to be seen of Nikita in his old position, but in the sledge there lay something heaped with snow, which Vassili guessed to be his servant. Vassili's terrors had now vanished—or, if any were left, it was merely lest he should have a return of the horrible panic which he had experienced on the cob's back, and, still more, when he found himself left in the snowdrift. At all costs he must not give way to that panic again; and if he would avoid that, he must be up and doing something—must be occupying his thoughts with something. First of all he planted himself with his back to the wind, and unfastened his fur coat to cool himself. Then, when he had regained his breath a little, he shook the snow off his boots and left-hand mitten (the other one was hopelessly lost, and probably lying somewhere a couple of inches below the snow), and refastened his belt tightly—much as he was accustomed to do when he was about to step out of his store to buy cartloads of grain which the *muzhiks* had brought. This done, he set about exerting himself. The first thing which it occurred to him to do was to disentangle the cob's leg, and, the halter thus freed, he tied Brownie up to the rim of the splashboard where he had been tied before. Next, he had just gone behind the cob to straighten the crupper, sacking and saddle-piece on his back, when he saw something stir in the sledge, and then the head of Nikita emerge from beneath the snow which covered it. The frozen man raised himself a little —though evidently with a great effort—and made a strange gesture with his hand in front of his face, as though he were brushing away a fly. As he did this he seemed to Vassili to be saying something—probably Vassili's name—so the latter left the sacking unstraightened and stepped up to the sledge.

"How is it with you now?" he asked, "and what are you trying to say?"

"Only that I—I am dying," answered Nikita with difficulty and in gasps. "Give my wages to the little lad or to the wife—it does not matter which."

"Are you frozen, then?" said Vassili.

"Yes—and dying; I know it quite well," replied Nikita in a choking voice, and still fluttering his hand before his face as though to brush away a fly. "Pardon me, for Christ's sake."

For about half a minute Vassili stood without moving and in silence. Then all at once, and with the same air of decision as marked him when he had struck hands over a good bargain, he took a step backwards, tucked up the sleeves of his coat, and began with both hands to rake the snow off Nikita and out of the sledge. This done, he unhooked his belt, opened his fur coat, pushed Nikita hastily into a straight posture, and lay down upon him in such a way that the latter should be covered, not only with the coat, but with Vassili's own warm, overheated body. With one skirt of the coat tucked between Nikita's form and the side of the sledge, and the tail of it grasped between his ankles, Vassili remained lying prone, with his head resting upon the splashboard and his ears deaf either to the movements of the cob or to the howling of the wind, but intent only on listening to Nikita's breathing. For a long time Nikita lay without moving. Then he gave a deep sigh, and stirred faintly.

"There you are, you see, and yet you talk of dying!" began Vassili. "Just you lie still and grow warm, and we—"

To his great surprise Vassili found that he could say no more, for tears were welling from his eyes and his lower jaw was working. He broke off short, and swallowed a lump in his throat.

"How absurdly weak and nervous I have made myself," he thought. Yet not only did he find this weakness far from unpleasant, but it actually gave him a sensation of joy such as he had never yet experienced.

"Yes, we shall manage it all right like this," he said to himself, conscious of a rapturous feeling of emotion. After this he lay for a long time in silence, merely wiping his eyes against the fur of the coat, and tucking back its right-hand skirt as the wind blew it up at intervals; but at length he felt as though he must communicate his joy to a fellow-creature.

"Nikita," he said.

"That is better. I am getting warm now," came from underneath him.

"Nikita, my old friend, I thought we were done for. You would have been frozen, and I—"

Once more Vassili's cheeks started quivering and his eyes filled with tears, so that he could say no more.

"No, it is no good," he said to himself. "Yet I know what I know," and he remained silent. Still he lay there. Warmth seemed to be passing into his body from Nikita below and from the fur coat above. Only the hands with which he held the skirts of the coat against Nikita's sides, and his feet, from between which the wind kept blowing the skirts away, were beginning to feel frozen. His mittenless right hand in particular felt numbed. Yet he never thought of his hands or feet—only of how he could best warm the peasant who was lying beneath him.

More than once he glanced at the cob and saw that its back was uncovered, since the sacking had now slipped off altogether and was lying on the snow. He felt as if he ought to go and cover the animal over again, yet could not make up his mind to leave Nikita, even for a moment, and thus break the spell of that rapturous joy which now possessed him. As for his terrors, they had long since fled away.

"By heavens, I am not going to be beaten!" he said to

himself with reference to his efforts to warm Nikita—speaking, indeed, in just the same boastful tone in which he had been accustomed to speak of his sales or purchases.

He lay for an hour—for two—for three, but took no heed of the passing of time. At first there danced before his vision dim pictures of the storm, of the shafts, and of the cob under its high *douga*. Then these pictures became exchanged for jumbled memories of the festival, of his wife, of the *stanovoi*, and of the candle-locker—but beneath the picture of the candle-locker lay Nikita. Then again he saw the *muzhiks* trading with him, and the white, iron-roofed walls of his house—but beneath the picture of those walls again lay Nikita. Then everything became confused. One thing ran into another, until at last these various scattered impressions came together as the colours of a rainbow merge into a beam of white light, and he fell asleep. For long he slept without dreaming, but, just before the dawn came, there came also some sleep-visions. He seemed to be standing by the candle-locker, while old mother Tikhonova was asking him for a five-copeck candle for the festival. He tried to take the candle out and give it to her, but his hands remained glued in his pockets. Then he tried to walk round the locker, but his legs refused to move, and his new, clean shoes stuck fast to the stone floor, so that he could not even raise his feet to take the shoes off.

Then suddenly the locker was not a locker at all, but a bed, and on that bed Vassili could see himself lying, face downwards—lying on his own bed at home. He was lying on the bed, and could not rise, although it was necessary for him to do so, seeing that Ivan Matveitch, the *stanovoi*, was coming to see him presently, and he must go with Ivan either to buy some timber or to put the crupper straight on the cob's back—he could not be sure which. He kept asking his wife, "Has he not come yet, Mikolovna?" and she kept answering him, "No, not yet." Then he could hear someone driving up to the steps outside. Surely it must be he? But no—the vehicle had driven past. "Is he not come yet, Mikolovna?" he asked his wife once more, and once more she replied, "No, not yet." Thus he lay and lay upon the bed, unable to rise, and ever waiting—waiting: and the waiting was at once painful and joyous. Suddenly the joy of it was filled to the full! He for whose coming he had been waiting, was now at hand and it was not Ivan Matveitch nor anyone else. Yet still it was the Man for whom he had been waiting. He entered—did that Man—and called him: and this Man who had called him cried out to him again and bade him go and lie down upon Nikita. And Vassili was glad that this Someone had come. "Yes, I will go!" he cried in his joy, and with that cry Vassili awoke.

Yes, he awoke—but awoke a very different man to what he had been when he fell asleep. He tried to rise, and could not. He tried to move his hand, and could not. He tried to move his leg, and could not. Then he tried to turn his head, but that also he could not do. This surprised him, yet in no way troubled him. Then he remembered that Nikita was lying beneath him, and that Nikita was growing warm and was coming back to life. It seemed to him that he was Nikita, and Nikita he, and that his life was no longer within himself, but within Nikita. He strained his ears till he caught the sound of breathing—yes, the faint, deep breathing of Nikita. "Nikita is alive!" he cried to himself in triumph, "and therefore so also am I!"

Then he began to think about his money, his store, his house, his sales and purchases, and Mironoff's millions. He could not understand how that man whom men called Vassili Brekhunoff could bear to interest himself in such things as he did. "That man can never have known what is the greatest thing of all," he thought of this Vassili Brekhunoff. "He can never have known what I know. Yes, I know it for certain now. At last—I KNOW!"

Once again he heard the Man calling him who had called to him before, and his whole being seemed to respond in joy and loving-kindness as he replied: "I am coming, I am coming!" For he felt that he was free at last, and that nothing could hold him further.

And, indeed, nothing further than that did Vassili Andreitch see or hear or feel in this world.

Around him the tempest still kept on. The same swirls of snow kept circling in eddies and covering the coats of the dead Vassili Andreitch and the trembling Brownie, the sledge (now almost invisible) and, stretched out upon its floor, the now reviving Nikita as he lay prone beneath the body of his dead master.

ANTON CHEKHOV: The Darling

OLENKA, the daughter of the retired collegiate assessor Plemyanikov, was sitting on the back-door steps of her house doing nothing. It was hot, the flies were nagging and teasing, and it was pleasant to think that it would soon be evening. Dark rain clouds were gathering from the east, wafting a breath of moisture every now and then.

Kukin, who roomed in the wing of the same house, was

standing in the yard looking up at the sky. He was the manager of the Tivoli, an open-air theatre.

"Again," he said despairingly. "Rain again. Rain, rain, rain! Every day rain! As though to spite me. I might as well stick my head into a noose and be done with it. It's ruining me. Heavy losses every day!" He wrung his hands, and continued, addressing Olenka: "What a life, Olga Semyonovna! It's enough to make a man weep. He works, he does his best, his very best, he tortures himself, he passes sleepless nights, he thinks and thinks and thinks how to do everything just right. And what's the result? He gives the public the best operetta, the very best pantomime, excellent artists. But do they want it? Have they the least appreciation of it? The public is rude. The public is a great boor. The public wants a circus, a lot of nonsense, a lot of stuff. And there's the weather. Look! Rain almost every evening. It began to rain on the tenth of May, and it's kept it up through the whole of June. It's simply awful. I can't get any audiences, and don't I have to pay rent? Don't I have to pay the actors?"

The next day towards evening the clouds gathered again, and Kukin said with an hysterical laugh:

"Oh, I don't care. Let it do its worst. Let it drown the whole theatre, and me, too. All right, no luck for me in this world or the next. Let the actors bring suit against me and drag me to court. What's the court? Why not Siberia at hard labour, or even the scaffold? Ha, ha, ha!"

It was the same on the third day.

Olenka listened to Kukin seriously, in silence. Sometimes tears would rise to her eyes. At last Kukin's misfortune touched her. She fell in love with him. He was short, gaunt, with a yellow face, and curly hair combed back from his forehead, and a thin tenor voice. His features puckered all up when he spoke. Despair was ever inscribed on his face. And yet he awakened in Olenka a sincere, deep feeling.

She was always loving somebody. She couldn't get on without loving somebody. She had loved her sick father, who sat the whole time in his armchair in a darkened room, breathing heavily. She had loved her aunt, who came from Brianska once or twice a year to visit them. And before that, when a pupil at the progymnasium, she had loved her French teacher. She was a quiet, kindhearted, compassionate girl, with a soft gentle way about her. And she made a very healthy, wholesome impression. Looking at her full, rosy cheeks, at her soft white neck with the black mole, and at the good naïve smile that always played on her face when something pleasant was said, the men would think, "Not so bad," and would smile too; and the lady visitors, in the middle of the conversation, would suddenly grasp her hand and exclaim, "You darling!" in a burst of delight.

The house, hers by inheritance, in which she had lived from birth, was located at the outskirts of the city on the Gypsy Road, not far from the Tivoli. From early evening till late at night she could hear the music in the theatre and the bursting of the rockets; and it seemed to her that Kukin was roaring and battling with his fate and taking his chief enemy, the indifferent public, by assault. Her heart melted softly, she felt no desire to sleep, and when Kukin returned home towards morning, she tapped on her window-pane, and through the curtains he saw her face and one shoulder and the kind smile she gave him.

He proposed to her, and they were married. And when he had a good look of her neck and her full vigorous shoulders, he clapped his hands and said:

"You darling!"

He was happy. But it rained on their wedding-day, and the expression of despair never left his face.

They got along well together. She sat in the cashier's box, kept the theatre in order, wrote down the expenses, and paid out the salaries. Her rosy cheeks, her kind naïve smile, like a halo around her face, could be seen at the cashier's window, behind the scenes, and in the café. She began to tell her friends that the theatre was the greatest, the most important, the most essential thing in the world, that it was the only place to obtain true enjoyment in and become humanised and educated.

"But do you suppose the public appreciates it?" she asked. "What the public wants is the circus. Yesterday Vanichka and I gave *Faust Burlesqued*, and almost all the boxes were empty. If we had given some silly nonsense, I assure you, the theatre would have been overcrowded. Tomorrow we'll put *Orpheus in Hades* on. Do come."

Whatever Kukin said about the theatre and the actors, she repeated. She spoke, as he did, with contempt of the public, of its indifference to art, of its boorishness. She meddled in the rehearsals, corrected the actors, watched the conduct of the musicians; and when an unfavourable criticism appeared in the local paper, she wept and went to the editor to argue with him.

The actors were fond of her and called her "Vanichka and I" and "the darling." She was sorry for them and lent them small sums. When they bilked her, she never complained to her husband; at the utmost she shed a few tears.

In winter, too, they got along nicely together. They leased a theatre in the town for the whole winter and sublet it for short periods to a Little Russian theatrical company, to a conjuror and to the local amateur players.

Olenka grew fuller and was always beaming with content-ment; while Kukin grew thinner and yellower and complained of his terrible losses, though he did fairly well the whole winter. At night he coughed, and she gave him raspberry syrup and lime water, rubbed him with eau de Cologne, and wrapped him up in soft coverings.

"You are my precious sweet," she said with perfect sin-cerity, stroking his hair. "You are such a dear."

At Lent he went to Moscow to get his company together, and, while without him, Olenka was unable to sleep. She sat at the window the whole time, gazing at the stars. She likened herself to the hens that are also uneasy and unable to sleep when their rooster is out of the coop. Kukin was detained in Moscow. He wrote he would be back during Easter Week, and in his letters discussed arrangements already for the Tivoli. But late one night, before Easter Monday, there was an ill-omened knocking at the wicket-gate. It was like a knocking on a barrel—boom, boom, boom! The sleepy cook ran barefooted, plashing through the puddles, to open the gate.

"Open the gate, please," said some one in a hollow bass voice. "I have a telegram for you."

Olenka had received telegrams from her husband before; but this time, somehow, she was numbed with terror. She opened the telegram with trembling hands and read:

"Ivan Petrovich died suddenly to-day. Awaiting propt orders for wuneral Tuesday."

That was the way the telegram was written—"wuneral"—and another unintelligible word—"propt." The telegram was signed by the manager of the opera company.

"My dearest!" Olenka burst out sobbing. "Vanichka, my dearest, my sweetheart. Why did I ever meet you? Why did I ever get to know you and love you? To whom have you abandoned your poor Olenka, your poor, unhappy Olenka?"

Kukin was buried on Tuesday in the Vagankov Cemetery in Moscow. Olenka returned home on Wednesday; and as soon as she entered her house she threw herself on her bed and broke into such loud sobbing that she could be heard in the street and in the neighbouring yards.

"The darling!" said the neighbours, crossing themselves. "How Olga Semyonovna, the poor darling, is grieving!"

Three months afterwards Olenka was returning home from mass, downhearted and in deep mourning. Beside her walked a man also returning from church, Vasily Pustovalov, the manager of the merchant Babakayev's lumber-yard. He was wearing a straw hat, a white vest with a gold chain, and looked more like a land-owner than a business man.

"Everything has its ordained course, Olga Semyonovna," he said sedately, with sympathy in his voice. "And if any one near and dear to us dies, then it means it was God's will and we should remember that and bear it with submission."

He took her to the wicket-gate, said good-bye and went away. After that she heard his sedate voice the whole day; and on closing her eyes she instantly had a vision of his dark beard. She took a great liking to him. And evidently he had been impressed by her, too; for, not long after, an elderly woman, a distant ac-quaintance, came in to have a cup of coffee with her. As soon as the woman was seated at table she began to speak about Pustovalov—how good he was, what a steady man, and any woman could be glad to get him as a husband. Three days later Pustovalov himself paid Olenka a visit. He stayed only about ten minutes, and spoke little, but Olenka fell in love with him, fell in love so desperately that she did not sleep the whole night and burned as with fever. In the morning she sent for the elderly woman. Soon after, Olenka and Pustovalov were engaged, and the wedding followed.

Pustovalov and Olenka lived happily together. He usually stayed in the lumber-yard until dinner, then went out on business. In his absence Olenka took his place in the office until evening, attending to the book-keeping and despatching the orders.

"Lumber rises twenty per cent every year nowadays," she told her customers and acquaintances. "Imagine, we used to buy wood from our forests here. Now Vasichka has to go every year to the government of Mogilev to get wood. And what a tax!" she exclaimed, covering her cheeks with her hands in terror. "What a tax!"

She felt as if she had been dealing in lumber for ever so long, that the most important and essential thing in life was lumber. There was something touching and endearing in the way she pronounced the words, "beam," "joist," "plank," "stave," "lath," "gun-carriage," "clamp." At night she dreamed of whole mountains of boards and planks, long, endless rows of wagons conveying the wood somewhere, far, far from the city. She dreamed that a whole regiment of beams, 36 ft. x 5 in., were advancing in an upright position to do battle against the lumber-yard; that the beams and joists and clamps were knocking against each other, emitting the sharp crackling reports of dry wood, that they were all falling and then rising again, piling on top of each other. Olenka cried out in her sleep, and Pustovalov said to her gently:

"Olenka my dear, what is the matter? Cross yourself."

Her husband's opinions were all hers. If he thought the room was too hot, she thought so too. If he thought business was dull, she thought business was dull. Pustovalov was not fond of amusements and stayed home on holidays; she did the same.

"You are always either at home or in the office," said her friends. "Why don't you go to the theatre or to the circus, darling?"

"Vasichka and I never go to the theatre," she answered sedately. "We have work to do, we have no time for nonsense. What does one get out of going to theatre?"

On Saturdays she and Pustovalov went to vespers, and on holidays to early mass. On returning home they walked side by side with rapt faces, an agreeable smell emanating from both of them and her silk dress rustling pleasantly. At home they drank tea with milk-bread and various jams, and then ate pie. Every day at noontime there was an appetising odour in the yard and outside the gate of cabbage soup, roast mutton, or duck; and, on fast days, of fish. You couldn't pass the gate without being seized by an acute desire to eat. The samovar was always boiling on the office table, and customers were treated to tea and biscuits. Once a week the married couple went to the baths and returned with red faces, walking side by side.

"We are getting along very well, thank God," said Olenka to her friends. "God grant that all should live as well as Vasichka and I."

When Pustovalov went to the government of Mogilev to buy wood, she was dreadfully homesick for him, did not sleep nights, and cried. Sometimes the veterinary surgeon of the regiment, Smirnov, a young man who lodged in the wing of her house, came to see her evenings. He related incidents, or they played cards together. This distracted her. The most interesting of his stories were those of his own life. He was married and had a son; but he had separated from his wife because she had deceived him, and now he hated her and sent her forty rubles a month for his son's support. Olenka sighed, shook her head, and was sorry for him.

"Well, the Lord keep you," she said, as she saw him off to the door by candlelight. "Thank you for coming to kill time with me. May God give you health. Mother in Heaven!" She spoke very sedately, very judiciously, imitating her husband. The veterinary surgeon had disappeared behind the door when she called out after him: "Do you know, Vladimir Platonych, you ought to make up with your wife. Forgive her, if only for the sake of your son. The child understands everything, you may be sure."

When Pustovalov returned, she told him in a low voice

about the veterinary surgeon and his unhappy family life; and they sighed and shook their heads, and talked about the boy who must be homesick for his father. Then, by a strange association of ideas, they both stopped before the sacred images, made genuflections, and prayed to God to send them children.

And so the Pustovalovs lived for full six years, quietly and peaceably, in perfect love and harmony. But once in the winter Vasily Andreyich, after drinking some hot tea, went out into the lumber-yard without a hat on his head, caught a cold and took sick. He was treated by the best physicians, but the malady progressed, and he died after an illness of four months. Olenka was again left a widow.

"To whom have you left me, my darling?" she wailed after the funeral. "How shall I live now without you, wretched creature that I am. Pity me, good people, pity me, fatherless and motherless, all alone in the world!"

She went about dressed in black and weepers, and she gave up wearing hats and gloves for good. She hardly left the house except to go to church and to visit her husband's grave. She almost led the life of a nun.

It was not until six months had passed that she took off the weepers and opened her shutters. She began to go out occasionally in the morning to market with her cook. But how she lived at home and what went on there, could only be surmised. It could be surmised from the fact that she was seen in her little garden drinking tea with the veterinarian while he read the paper out loud to her, and also from the fact that once on meeting an acquaintance at the post-office, she said to her:

"There is no proper veterinary inspection in our town. That is why there is so much disease. You constantly hear of people getting sick from the milk and becoming infected by the horses and cows. The health of domestic animals ought really to be looked after as much as that of human beings."

She repeated the veterinarian's words and held the same opinions as he about everything. It was plain that she could not exist a single year without an attachment, and she found her new happiness in the wing of her house. In any one else this would have been condemned; but no one could think ill of Olenka. Everything in her life was so transparent. She and the veterinary surgeon never spoke about the change in their relations. They tried, in fact, to conceal it, but unsuccessfully; for Olenka could have no secrets. When the surgeon's colleagues from the regiment came to see him, she poured tea, and served the supper, and talked to them about the cattle plague, the foot and mouth disease, and the municipal slaughter houses. The surgeon was dreadfully embarrassed, and after the visitors had left, he caught her hand and hissed angrily:

"Didn't I ask you not to talk about what you don't understand? When we doctors discuss things, please don't mix in. It's getting to be a nuisance."

She looked at him in astonishment and alarm, and asked: "But, Volodichka, what *am* I to talk about?"

And she threw her arms round his neck, with tears in her eyes, and begged him not to be angry. And they were both happy.

But their happiness was of short duration. The veterinary surgeon went away with his regiment to be gone for good, when it was transferred to some distant place almost as far as Siberia, and Olenka was left alone.

Now she was completely alone. Her father had long been dead, and his armchair lay in the attic covered with dust and minus one leg. She got thin and homely, and the people who met her on the street no longer looked at her as they had used to, nor smiled at her. Evidently her best years were over, past and gone, and a new, dubious life was to begin which it were better not to think about.

In the evening Olenka sat on the steps and heard the music playing and the rockets bursting in the Tivoli; but it no longer aroused any response in her. She looked listlessly into the yard, thought of nothing, wanted nothing, and when night came on, she went to bed and dreamed of nothing but the empty yard. She ate and drank as though by compulsion.

And what was worst of all, she no longer held any opinions. She saw and understood everything that went on around her, but she could not form an opinion about it. She knew of nothing to talk about. And how dreadful not to have opinions! For instance, you see a bottle, or you see that it is raining, or you see a muzhik riding by in a wagon. But what the bottle or the rain or the muzhik are for, or what the sense of them all is, you cannot tell—you cannot tell, not for a thousand rubles. In the days of Kukin and Pustovalov and then of the veterinary surgeon, Olenka had had an explanation for everything, and would have given her opinion freely no matter about what. But now there was the same emptiness in her heart and brain as in her yard. It was as galling and bitter as a taste of wormwood.

Gradually the town grew up all around. The Gypsy Road had become a street, and where the Tivoli and the lumber-yard had been, there were now houses and a row of side streets. How quickly time flies! Olenka's house turned gloomy, the roof rusty, the shed slanting. Dock and thistles overgrew the yard. Olenka herself had aged and grown homely. In the summer she sat on the

THE DARLING / Anton Chekhov

steps, and her soul was empty and dreary and bitter. When she caught the breath of spring, or when the wind wafted the chime of the cathedral bells, a sudden flood of memories would pour over her, her heart would expand with a tender warmth, and the tears would stream down her cheeks. But that lasted only a moment. Then would come emptiness again and the feeling, What is the use of living? The black kitten Bryska rubbed up against her and purred softly, but the little creature's caresses left Olenka untouched. That was not what she needed. What she needed was a love that would absorb her whole being, her reason, her whole soul, that would give her ideas, an object in life, that would warm her aging blood. And she shook the black kitten off her skirt angrily, saying:

"Go away! What are you doing here?"

And so day after day, year after year not a single joy, not a single opinion. Whatever Marva, the cook, said was all right.

One hot day in July, towards evening, as the town cattle were being driven by, and the whole yard was filled with clouds of dust, there was suddenly a knocking at the gate. Olenka herself went to open it, and was dumbfounded to behold the veterinarian Smirnov. He had turned grey and was dressed as a civilian. All the old memories flooded into her soul, she could not restrain herself, she burst out crying, and laid her head on Smirnov's breast without saying a word. So overcome was she that she was totally unconscious of how they walked into the house and seated themselves to drink tea.

"My darling!" she murmured, trembling with joy. "Vladimir Platonych, from where has God sent you?"

"I want to settle here for good," he told her. "I have resigned my position and have come here to try my fortune as a free man and lead a settled life. Besides, it's time to send my boy to the gymnasium. He is grown up now. You know, my wife and I have become reconciled."

"Where is she?" asked Olenka.

"At the hotel with the boy. I am looking for lodgings."

"Good gracious, bless you, take my house. Why won't my house do? Oh, dear? Why, I won't ask any rent of you," Olenka burst out in the greatest excitement, and began to cry again. "You live here, and the wing will be enough for me. Oh, Heavens, what a joy!"

The very next day the roof was being painted and the walls whitewashed, and Olenka, arms akimbo, was going about the yard superintending. Her face brightened with her old smile. Her whole being revived and freshened, as though she had awakened from a long sleep. The veterinarian's wife and child arrived. She was a thin, plain woman, with a crabbed expression. The boy Sasha, small for his ten years of age, was a chubby child, with clear blue eyes and dimples in his cheeks. He made for the kitten the instant he entered the yard, and the place rang with his happy laughter.

"Is that your cat, auntie?" he asked Olenka. "When she has little kitties, please give me one. Mamma is awfully afraid of mice."

Olenka chatted with him, gave him tea, and there was a sudden warmth in her bosom and a soft gripping at her heart, as though the boy were her own son.

In the evening, when he sat in the dining-room studying his lessons, she looked at him tenderly and whispered to herself:

"My darling, my pretty. You are such a clever child, so good to look at."

"An island is a tract of land entirely surrounded by water," he recited.

"An island is a tract of land," she repeated—the first idea asseverated with conviction after so many years of silence and mental emptiness.

She now had her opinions, and at supper discussed with Sasha's parents how difficult the studies had become for the children at the gymnasium, but how, after all, a classical education was better than a commercial course, because when you graduated from the gymnasium then the road was open to you for any career at all. If you chose to, you could become a doctor, or, if you wanted to, you could become an engineer.

Sasha began to go to the gymnasium. His mother left on a visit to her sister in Kharkov and never came back. The father was away every day inspecting cattle, and sometimes was gone three whole days at a time, so that Sasha, it seemed to Olenka, was utterly abandoned, was treated as if he were quite superfluous, and must be dying of hunger. So she transferred him into the wing along with herself and fixed up a little room for him there.

Every morning Olenka would come into his room and find him sound asleep with his hand tucked under his cheek, so quiet that he seemed not to be breathing. What a shame to have to wake him, she thought.

"Sashenka," she said sorrowingly, "get up, darling. It's time to go to the gymnasium."

He got up, dressed, said his prayers, then sat down to drink tea. He drank three glasses of tea, ate two large cracknels and half a buttered roll. The sleep was not yet out of him, so he was a little cross.

"You don't know your fable as you should, Sashenka," said

Olenka, looking at him as though he were departing on a long journey. "What a lot of trouble you are. You must try hard and learn, dear, and mind your teachers."

"Oh, let me alone, please," said Sasha.

Then he went down the street to the gymnasium, a little fellow wearing a large cap and carrying a satchel on his back. Olenka followed him noiselessly.

"Sashenka," she called.

He looked round and she shoved a date or a caramel into his hand. When he reached the street of the gymnasium, he turned around and said, ashamed of being followed by a tall, stout woman:

"You had better go home, aunt. I can go the rest of the way myself."

She stopped and stared after him until he had disappeared into the school entrance.

Oh, how she loved him! Not one of her other ties had been so deep. Never before had she given herself so completely, so disinterestedly, so cheerfully as now that her maternal instincts were all aroused. For this boy, who was not hers, for the dimples in his cheeks and for his big cap, she would have given her life, given it with joy and with tears of rapture. Why? Ah, indeed, why?

When she had seen Sasha off to the gymnasium, she returned home quietly, content, serene, overflowing with love. Her face, which had grown younger in the last half year, smiled and beamed. People who met her were pleased as they looked at her.

"How are you, Olga Semyonovna, darling? How are you getting on, darling?"

"The gymnasium course is very hard nowadays," she told at the market. "It's no joke. Yesterday the first class had a fable to learn by heart, a Latin translation, and a problem. How is a little fellow to do all that?"

And she spoke of the teacher and the lessons and the textbooks, repeating exactly what Sasha said about them.

At three o'clock they had dinner. In the evening they prepared the lessons together, and Olenka wept with Sasha over the difficulties. When she put him to bed, she lingered a long time making the sign of the cross over him and muttering a prayer. And when she lay in bed, she dreamed of the far-away, misty future when Sasha would finish his studies and become a doctor or an engineer, have a large house of his own, with horses and a carriage, marry and have children. She would fall asleep still thinking of the same things, and tears would roll down her cheeks from her closed eyes. And the black cat would lie at her side purring: "Mrr, mrr, mrr."

Suddenly there was a loud knocking at the gate. Olenka woke up breathless with fright, her heart beating violently. Half a minute later there was another knock.

"A telegram from Kharkov," she thought, her whole body in a tremble. "His mother wants Sasha to come to her in Kharkov. Oh, great God!"

She was in despair. Her head, her feet, her hands turned cold. There was no unhappier creature in the world, she felt. But another minute passed, she heard voices. It was the veterinaran coming home from the club.

"Thank God," she thought. The load gradually fell from her heart, she was at ease again. And she went back to bed, thinking of Sasha who lay fast asleep in the next room and sometimes cried out in his sleep:

"I'll give it to you! Get away! Quit your scrapping!"

O. HENRY: The Gift of the Magi

ONE DOLLAR and eighty-seven cents. That was all. And sixty cents of it was in pennies. Pennies saved one and two at a time by bulldozing the grocer and the vegetable man and the butcher until one's cheeks burned with the silent imputation of parsimony that such close dealing implied. Three times Della counted it. One dollar and eighty-seven cents. And the next day would be Christmas.

There was clearly nothing to do but flop down on the shabby little couch and howl. So Della did it. Which instigates the moral reflection that life is made up of sobs, sniffles, and smiles, with sniffles predominating.

While the mistress of the home is gradually subsiding from the first stage to the second, take a look at the home. A furnished flat at $8 per week. It did not exactly beggar description, but it certainly had that word on the lookout for the mendicancy squad.

In the vestibule below was a letter-box into which no letter would go, and an electric button from which no mortal finger could coax a ring. Also appertaining thereunto was a card bearing the name "Mr. James Dillingham Young."

The "Dillingham" had been flung to the breeze during a former period of prosperity when its possessor was being paid $30 per week. Now, when the income was shrunk to $20, the letters of "Dillingham" looked blurred, as though they were thinking seriously of contracting to a modest and unassuming D. But whenever Mr. James Dillingham Young came home and reached his flat

above he was called "Jim" and greatly hugged by Mrs. James
Dillingham Young, already introduced to you as Della. Which is
all very good.

Della finished her cry and attended to her cheeks with the
powder rag. She stood by the window and looked out dully at a
gray cat walking a gray fence in a gray backyard. Tomorrow would
be Christmas Day, and she had only $1.87 with which to buy Jim
a present. She had been saving every penny she could for months,
with this result. Twenty dollars a week doesn't go far. Expenses
had been greater than she had calculated. They always are. Only
$1.87 to buy a present for Jim. Her Jim. Many a happy hour she
had spent planning for something nice for him. Something fine
and rare and sterling—something just a little bit near to being
worthy of the honor of being owned by Jim.

There was a pier-glass between the windows of the room.
Perhaps you have seen a pier-glass in an $8 flat. A very thin and
very agile person may, by observing his reflection in a rapid
sequence of longitudinal strips, obtain a fairly accurate conception of his looks. Della, being slender, had mastered the art.

Suddenly she whirled from the window and stood before
the glass. Her eyes were shining brilliantly, but her face had lost
its color within twenty seconds. Rapidly she pulled down her hair
and let it fall to its full length.

Now, there were two possessions of the James Dillingham
Youngs in which they both took a mighty pride. One was Jim's
gold watch that had been his father's and his grandfather's. The
other was Della's hair. Had the Queen of Sheba lived in the flat
across the airshaft, Della would have let her hair hang out the
window some day to dry just to depreciate Her Majesty's jewels
and gifts. Had King Solomon been the janitor, with all his treasures piled up in the basement, Jim would have pulled out his
watch every time he passed, just to see him pluck at his beard
from envy.

So now Della's beautiful hair fell about her rippling and
shining like a cascade of brown waters. It reached below her knee
and made itself almost a garment for her. And then she did it up
again nervously and quickly. Once she faltered for a minute and
stood still while a tear or two splashed on the worn red carpet.

On went her old brown jacket; on went her old brown hat.
With a whirl of skirts and with the brilliant sparkle still in her
eyes, she fluttered out the door and down the stairs to the street.

Where she stopped the sign read: "Mme. Sofronie. Hair
Goods of All Kinds." One flight up Della ran, and collected her-
self, panting. Madame, large, too white, chilly, hardly looked the
"Sofronie."

"Will you buy my hair?" asked Della.

"I buy hair," said Madame. "Take yer hat off and let's have a sight at the looks of it."

Down rippled the brown cascade.

"Twenty dollars," said Madame, lifting the mass with a practised hand.

"Give it to me quick," said Della.

Oh, and the next two hours tripped by on rosy wings. Forget the hashed metaphor. She was ransacking the stores for Jim's present.

She found it at last. It surely had been made for Jim and no one else. There was no other like it in any of the stores, and she had turned all of them inside out. It was a platinum fob chain simple and chaste in design, properly proclaiming its value by substance alone and not by meretricious ornamentation—as all good things should do. It was even worthy of The Watch. As soon as she saw it she knew that it must be Jim's. It was like him. Quietness and value—the description applied to both. Twenty-one dollars they took from her for it, and she hurried home with the 87 cents. With that chain on his watch Jim might be properly anxious about the time in any company. Grand as the watch was, he sometimes looked at it on the sly on account of the old leather strap that he used in place of a chain.

When Della reached home her intoxication gave way a little to prudence and reason. She got out her curling irons and lighted the gas and went to work repairing the ravages made by generosity added to love. Which is always a tremendous task, dear friends—a mammoth task.

Within forty minutes her head was covered with tiny, close-lying curls that made her look wonderfully like a truant schoolboy. She looked at her reflection in the mirror long, carefully, and critically.

"If Jim doesn't kill me," she said to herself, "before he takes a second look at me, he'll say I look like a Coney Island chorus girl. But what could I do—oh! what could I do with a dollar and eighty-seven cents?"

At 7 o'clock the coffee was made and the frying-pan was on the back of the stove hot and ready to cook the chops.

Jim was never late. Della doubled the fob chain in her hand and sat on the corner of the table near the door that he always entered. Then she heard his step on the stair way down on the first flight, and she turned white for just a moment. She had a habit of saying little silent prayers about the simplest every-day things, and now she whispered: "Please God, make him think I am still pretty."

The door opened and Jim stepped in and closed it. He

looked thin and very serious. Poor fellow, he was only twenty-two
—and to be burdened with a family! He needed a new overcoat
and he was without gloves.

Jim stopped inside the door, as immovable as a setter at
the scent of quail. His eyes were fixed upon Della, and there was
an expression in them that she could not read, and it terrified her.
It was not anger, nor surprise, nor disapproval, nor horror, nor
any of the sentiments that she had been prepared for. He simply
stared at her fixedly with that peculiar expression on his face.

Della wriggled off the table and went for him.

"Jim, darling," she cried, "don't look at me that way. I had
my hair cut off and sold it because I couldn't have lived through
Christmas without giving you a present. It'll grow out again—you
won't mind, will you? I just had to do it. My hair grows awfully
fast. Say 'Merry Christmas!' Jim, and let's be happy. You don't
known what a nice—what a beautiful, nice gift I've got for you."

"You've cut off your hair?" asked Jim, laboriously, as if he
had not arrived at that patent fact yet even after the hardest
mental labor.

"Cut it off and sold it," said Della. "Don't you like me just
as well, anyhow? I'm me without my hair, ain't I?"

Jim looked about the room curiously.

"You say your hair is gone?" he said, with an air almost of
idiocy.

"You needn't look for it," said Della. "It's sold, I tell you—
sold and gone, too. It's Christmas Eve, boy. Be good to me, for it
went for you. Maybe the hairs of my head were numbered," she
went on with a sudden serious sweetness, "but nobody could ever
count my love for you. Shall I put the chops on, Jim?"

Out of his trance Jim seemed quickly to wake. He enfolded
his Della. For ten seconds let us regard with discreet scrutiny
some inconsequential object in the other direction. Eight dollars
a week or a million a year—what is the difference? A mathemati-
cian or a wit would give you the wrong answer. The magi brought
valuable gifts, but that was not among them. This dark assertion
will be illuminated later on.

Jim drew a package from his overcoat pocket and threw
it upon the table.

"Don't make any mistake, Dell," he said, "about me. I
don't think there's anything in the way of a haircut or a shave or
a shampoo that could make me like my girl any less. But if you'll
unwrap that package you may see why you had me going a while
at first."

White fingers and nimble tore at the string and paper.
And then an ecstatic scream of joy; and then, alas! a quick

feminine change to hysterical tears and wails, necessitating the immediate employment of all the comforting powers of the lord of the flat.

For there lay The Combs—the set of combs, side and back, that Della had worshipped for long in a Broadway window. Beautiful combs, pure tortoise shell, with jewelled rims—just the shade to wear in the beautiful vanished hair. They were expensive combs, she knew, and her heart had simply craved and yearned over them without the least hope of possession. And now, they were hers, but the tresses that should have adorned the coveted adornments were gone.

But she hugged them to her bosom, and at length she was able to look up with dim eyes and a smile and say: "My hair grows so fast, Jim!"

And then Della leaped up like a little singed cat and cried, "Oh, oh!"

Jim had not yet seen his beautiful present. She held it out to him eagerly upon her open palm. The dull precious metal seemed to flash with a reflection of her bright and ardent spirit.

"Isn't it a dandy, Jim? I hunted all over town to find it. You'll have to look at the time a hundred times a day now. Give me your watch. I want to see how it looks on it."

Instead of obeying, Jim tumbled down on the couch and put his hands under the back of his head and smiled.

"Dell," said he, "let's put our Christmas presents away and keep 'em a while. They're too nice to use just at present. I sold the watch to get the money to buy your combs. And now suppose you put the chops on."

The magi, as you know, were wise men—wonderfully wise men—who brought gifts to the Babe in the manger. They invented the art of giving Christmas presents. Being wise, their gifts were no doubt wise ones, possibly bearing the privilege of exchange in case of duplication. And here I have lamely related to you the uneventful chronicle of two foolish children in a flat who most unwisely sacrificed for each other the greatest treasures of their house. But in a last word to the wise of these days let it be said that of all who give gifts these two were the wisest. Of all who give and receive gifts, such as they are wisest. Everywhere they are wisest. They are the magi.

3. *THE MATURITY OF LOVE*

In love, as in other aspects of human behavior, there is always the discrepancy between the potential and the actual. If we speak of the maturity of love as the state where there is fusion of the self with the other, or what we may call "love as community," we must acknowledge that its full attainment is rare and that its progress is marked by backward steps, what the psychologists call "regressions." Nevertheless, it is a clear goal of man; it seeks to transcend the good of both the lover and the beloved in a community of love that raises both to higher levels of feeling and being. Here too, however, if the goal is set beyond one's capacity, if the desired transcendence envisages self-sacrifice rather than mutual fulfillment there may be derangements that end in pathology.

THE GOSPEL OF ST. MATTHEW: Sermon on the Mount

He taught them, saying:

Blessed are the poor in spirit: for theirs is the kingdom of heaven.

Blessed are the meek; for they shall possess the land.

Blessed are they that mourn: for they shall be comforted.

Blessed are they that hunger and thirst after justice: for they shall have their fill.

Blessed are the merciful: for they shall obtain mercy.

Blessed are the clean of heart: for they shall see God.

Blessed are the peacemakers: for they shall be called the children of God.

Blessed are they that suffer persecution for justice' sake: for theirs is the kingdom of heaven.

Blessed are ye when they shall revile you and persecute you and speak all that is evil against you, untruly, for my sake:

Be glad and rejoice, for your reward is very great in heaven.

For so they persecuted the prophets that were before you.

Matthew 5:17–19.

BARUCH SPINOZA: Love and Freedom*

X. In so far as men are affected one towards the other with envy or any other emotion of hatred they are contrary reciprocally, and consequently they are the more to be feared the more power they have than the other individuals of nature.

XI. Minds are conquered not by arms, but by love and magnanimity.

XII. It is above all things useful to men that they unite their habits of life (*consuetudines*) and bind themselves together with such bonds by which they can most easily make one individual of them all, and to do those things especially which serve for the purpose of confirming friendship.

XIII. But for this skill and vigilance are required. For men are varied (for those are rare who live according to the rules prescribed by reason), and moreover they are generally envious and more prone to revenge than pity. It is a matter, therefore, of considerable force of mind to regard each one according to his disposition and to contain oneself and not imitate the emotions of others. But those who cavil at men and prefer rather to reprobate vices than to inculcate virtues, and who do not solidify but unloosen the minds of men—these, I say, are a nuisance both to themselves and to others. Wherefore many, owing to too great impatience of mind and a false zeal for religion, have preferred to live among beasts rather than among men: just as children or youths who cannot bear with equanimity the reproaches of their parents, run away to enlist and choose the inconveniences of war and the command of a tyrant rather than the conveniences of home and paternal admonition, and who will bear any kind of burden provided they may thereby spite their parents.

XIV. Therefore, although men are as a rule governed in everything by their desire or lust, yet from their common society or association many more advantages than disadvantages arise or follow. Wherefore it is but right to bear the injuries arising therefrom with equanimity, and to be zealous for those who serve to keep peace and friendship.

XV. The things which give birth to harmony or peace are those which have reference to justice, equity, and honourable dealing. For men are ill pleased not only when a thing is unjust or iniquitous, but also when it is disgraceful or when any one despises the customs received among them. But for attracting love those things are especially necessary which relate to religion and piety. . . .

XVI. Harmony or peace is often born of fear, but then it

* Reprinted from *The Strength of the Emotions*.

264

is not trustworthy. Moreover, fear arises from weakness of the mind, and therefore does not appertain to the use of reason: nor does compassion, although it seems to bear in it a sort of piety.

XVII. Men, moreover, are won over by open-handedness (*largitas*), especially those who have not the wherewithal to purchase what is necessary for sustaining life. However, to give aid to every poor man is far beyond the reach of the wealth and power of every private man. For the riches of a private man are far too little for such a thing. Moreover, the ability and facility of approach of every man are far too limited for him to be able to unite all men to himself in friendship: for which reason the care of the poor is incumbent on society as a whole, and relates to the general advantage only.

XVIII. In accepting benefits and returning thanks our duty must be wholly different: concerning which see Note, Prop. 70, and Note, Prop. 71, Part IV.

XIX. Moreover, meretricious love, that is, the lust of generation, which arises from beauty, and absolutely all love which acknowledges any other cause than freedom of the mind, passes easily into hatred, unless—what is still worse—it be a sort of madness, and then more discord than harmony is fostered (see Coroll., Prop. 31, Part III.).

XX. As for what concerns matrimony, it is certain that it is in concord with reason if the desire of uniting bodies is engendered not from beauty alone, but also from the love of bearing children and wisely educating them: and moreover, if the love of either of them, that is, of husband or wife, has for its cause not only beauty, but also freedom of mind.

RAINER MARIA RILKE: Letter to a Young Poet

Rome, May 14th, 1904

MY DEAR MR. KAPPUS,

Much time has gone by since I received your last letter. Do not hold that against me; first it was work, then interruptions and finally a poor state of health that again and again kept me from the answer, which (so I wanted it) was to come to you out of quiet and good days. Now I feel somewhat better again (the opening of spring with its mean, fitful changes was very trying here too) and come to greet you, dear Mr. Kappus, and to tell you (which I do with all my heart) one thing and another in reply to your letter, as well as I know how.

You see—I have copied your sonnet, because I found that

it is lovely and simple and born in the form in which it moves with such quiet decorum. It is the best of those of your poems that you have let me read. And now I give you this copy because I know that it is important and full of new experience to come upon a work of one's own again written in a strange hand. Read the lines as though they were someone else's, and you will feel deep within you how much they are your own.

It was a pleasure to me to read this sonnet and your letter often; I thank you for both.

And you should not let yourself be confused in your solitude by the fact that there is something in you that wants to break out of it. This very wish will help you, if you use it quietly, and deliberately and like a tool, to spread out your solitude over wide country. People have (with the help of conventions) oriented all their solutions toward the easy and toward the easiest side of the easy; but it is clear that we must hold to what is difficult; everything in Nature grows and defends itself in its own way and is characteristically and spontaneously itself, seeks at all costs to be so and against all opposition. We know little, but that we must hold to what is difficult is a certainty that will not forsake us; it is good to be solitary, for solitude is difficult; that something is difficult must be a reason the more for us to do it.

To love is good, too: love being difficult. For one human being to love another: that is perhaps the most difficult of all our tasks, the ultimate, the last test and proof, the work for which all other work is but preparation. For this reason young people, who are beginners in everything, cannot yet know love: they have to learn it. With their whole being, with all their forces, gathered close about their lonely, timid, upward-beating heart, they must learn to love. But learning-time is always a long, secluded time, and so loving, for a long while ahead and far on into life, is— solitude, intensified and deepened loneness for him who loves. Love is at first not anything that means merging, giving over, and uniting with another (for what would a union be of something unclarified and unfinished, still subordinate—?), it is a high inducement to the individual to ripen, to become something in himself, to become world, to become world for himself for another's sake, it is a great exacting claim upon him, something that chooses him out and calls him to vast things. Only in this sense, as the task of working at themselves ("to hearken and to hammer day and night"), might young people use the love that is given them. Merging and surrendering and every kind of communion is not for them (who must save and gather for a long, long time still), is the ultimate, is perhaps that for which human lives as yet scarcely suffice.

But young people err so often and so grievously in this:

that they (in whose nature it lies to have no patience) fling themselves at each other, when love takes possession of them, scatter themselves, just as they are, in all their untidiness, disorder, confusion. . . . And then what? What is life to do to this heap of half-battered existence which they call their communion and which they would gladly call their happiness, if it were possible, and their future? Thus each loses himself for the sake of the other and loses the other and many others that wanted still to come. And loses the expanses and the possibilities, exchanges the approach and flight of gentle, divining things for an unfruitful perplexity out of which nothing can come any more, nothing save a little disgust, disillusionment and poverty, and rescue in one of the many conventions that have been put up in great number like public refuges along this most dangerous road. No realm of human experience is so well provided with conventions as this: life-preservers of most varied invention, boats and swimming-bladders are here; the social conception has managed to supply shelters of every sort, for, as it was disposed to take love-life as a pleasure, it had also to give it an easy form, cheap, safe and sure, as public pleasures are.

It is true that many young people who love wrongly, that is, simply with abandon and unsolitarily (the average will of course always go on doing so), feel the oppressiveness of a failure and want to make the situation in which they have landed viable and fruitful in their own personal way—; for their nature tells them that, less even than all else that is important, can questions of love be solved publicly and according to this or that agreement; that they are questions, intimate questions from one human being to another, which in any case demand a new, special, *only* personal answer—: but how should they, who have already flung themselves together and no longer mark off and distinguish themselves from each other, who therefore no longer possess anything of their own selves, be able to find a way out of themselves, out of the depth of their already shattered solitude?

They act out of common helplessness, and then, if, with the best intentions, they try to avoid the convention that occurs to them (say, marriage), they land in the tentacles of some less loud, but equally deadly conventional solitude; for then everything far around them is—convention; where people act out of a prematurely fused, turbid communion, *every* move is convention: every relation to which such entanglement leads has its convention, be it ever so unusual (that is, in the ordinary sense immoral); why, even separation would here be a conventional step, an impersonal chance decision without strength and without fruit.

Whoever looks seriously at it finds that neither for death,

which is difficult, nor for difficult love has any explanation, any
solitude, any solution, any hint or way yet been discerned; and
for these two problems that we carry wrapped up and hand on
without opening, it will not be possible to discover any general
rule resting in agreement. But in the same measure in which we
begin as individuals to put life to the test, we shall, being individuals, meet these great things at closer range. The demands
which the difficult work of love makes upon our development are
more than life-size, and as beginners we are not up to them. But
if we nevertheless hold out and take this love upon us as burden
and apprenticeship, instead of losing ourselves in all the light and
frivolous play, behind which people have hidden from the most
earnest earnestness of their existence—then a little progress and
an alleviation will perhaps be perceptible to those who come long
after us; that would be much.

We are only just now beginning to look upon the relation
of one individual person to a second individual objectively and
without prejudice, and our attempts to live such associations have
no model before them. And yet in the changes brought about by
time there is already a good deal that would help our timorous
novitiate.

The girl and the woman, in their new, their own unfolding, will but in passing be imitators of masculine ways, good and
bad, and repeaters of masculine professions. After the uncertainty
of such transitions it will become apparent that women were only
going through the profusion and the vicissitude of those (often
ridiculous) disguises in order to cleanse their own most characteristic nature of the distorting influences of the other sex.
Women, in whom life lingers and dwells more immediately, more
fruitfully and more confidently, must surely have become fundamentally riper people, more human people, than easygoing man,
who is not pulled down below the surface of life by the weight
of any fruit of his body, and who, presumptuous and hasty, under-
values what he thinks he loves. This humanity of woman, borne
its full time in suffering and humiliation, will come to light when
she will have stripped off the conventions of mere femininity in
the mutations of her outward status, and those men who do not
yet feel it approaching today will be surprised and struck by it.
Some day (and for this, particularly in the northern countries,
reliable signs are already speaking and shining), some day there
will be girls and women whose name will no longer signify merely
an opposite of the masculine, but something in itself, something
that makes one think, not of any complement and limit, but only
of life and existence: the feminine human being.

This advance will (at first much against the will of the

outstripped men) change the love-experience, which is now full of error, will alter it from the ground up, reshape it into a relation that is meant to be of one human being to another, no longer of man to woman. And this more human love (that will fulfill itself, infinitely considerate and gentle, and kind and clear in binding and releasing) will resemble that which we are preparing with struggle and toil, the love that consists in this, that two solitudes protect and border and salute each other.

And this further: do not believe that that great love once enjoined upon you, the boy, was lost; can you say whether great and good desires did not ripen you at the time, and resolutions by which you are still living today? I believe that that love remains so strong and powerful in your memory because it was your first deep being-alone and the first inward work you did on your life.—All good wishes for you, dear Mr. Kappus!

Yours:

RAINER MARIA RILKE

MIGUEL DE UNAMUNO: Love, Suffering, Pity*

> CAIN: Let me, or happy or unhappy, learn
> To anticipate my immortality.
> LUCIFER: Thou didst before I came upon thee.
> CAIN: How?
> LUCIFER: By suffering.
>
> BYRON: *Cain*, Act II., Scene I.

THE MOST tragic thing in the world and in life, readers and brothers of mine, is love. Love is the child of illusion and the parent of disillusion; love is consolidation in desolation; it is the sole medicine against death, for it is death's brother.

> *Fratelli, a un tempo stesso, Amore e Morte*
> *Ingeneró la sorte,*

as Leopardi sang.

Love seeks with fury, through the medium of the beloved, something beyond, and since it finds it not, it despairs.

Whenever we speak of love there is always present in our memory the idea of sexual love, the love between man and woman, whose end is the perpetuation of the human race upon the earth. Hence it is that we never succeed in reducing love either to a purely intellectual or to a purely volitional element, putting

* Reprinted from *The Tragic Sense of Life.*

aside that part in it which belongs to the feeling, or, if you like, to the senses. For, in its essence, love is neither idea nor volition; rather it is desire, feeling; it is something carnal in spirit itself. Thanks to love, we feel all that spirit has of flesh in it.

Sexual love is the generative type of every other love. In love and by love we seek to perpetuate ourselves, and we perpetuate ourselves on the earth only on condition that we die, that we yield up our life to others. The humblest forms of animal life, the lowest of living beings, multiply by dividing themselves, by splitting into two, by ceasing to be the unit which they previously formed.

But when at last the vitality of the being that multiplies itself by division is exhausted, the species must renew the source of life from time to time by means of the union of two wasting individuals, by means of what is called, among protozoaria, conjugation. They unite in order to begin dividing again with more vigour. And every act of generation consists in a being's ceasing to be what it was, either wholly or in part, in a splitting up, in a partial death. To live is to give oneself, to perpetuate oneself, and to perpetuate oneself and to give oneself is to die. The supreme delight of begetting is perhaps nothing but a foretaste of death, the eradication of our own vital essence. We unite with another, but it is to divide ourselves; this most intimate embrace is only a most intimate sundering. In its essence, the delight of sexual love, the genetic spasm, is a sensation of resurrection, of renewing our life in another, for only in others can we renew our life and so perpetuate ourselves.

Without doubt there is something tragically destructive in the essence of love, as it presents itself to us in its primitive animal form, in the unconquerable instinct which impels the male and the female to mix their being in a fury of conjunction. The same impulse that joins their bodies, separates, in a certain sense, their souls; they hate one another, while they embrace, no less than they love, and above all they contend with one another, they contend for a third life, which as yet is without life. Love is a contention, and there are animal species in which the male maltreats the female in his union with her, and others in which the female devours the male after being fertilized by him.

It has been said that love is a mutual selfishness; and, in fact, each one of the lovers seeks to possess the other, and in seeking his own perpetuation through the instrumentality of the other, though without being at the time conscious of it or purposing it, he thereby seeks his own enjoyment. Each one of the lovers is an immediate instrument of enjoyment and a mediate instrument of perpetuation, for the other. And thus they are tyrants and slaves, each one at once the tyrant and slave of the other.

Is there really anything strange in the fact that the deepest religious feeling has condemned carnal love and exalted virginity? Avarice, said the Apostle, is the root of all evil, and the reason is because avarice takes riches, which are only a means, for an end; and therein lies the essence of sin, in taking means for ends, in not recognizing or in disesteeming the end. And since it takes enjoyment for the end, whereas it is only the means and not perpetuation, which is the true end, what is carnal love but avarice? And it is possible that there are some who preserve their virginity in order the better to perpetuate themselves, and in order to perpetuate something more human than the flesh.

For it is the suffering flesh, it is suffering, it is death, that lovers perpetuate upon the earth. Love is at once the brother, son, and father of death, which is its sister, mother, and daughter. And thus it is that in the depth of love there is a depth of eternal despair, out of which spring hope and consolation. For out of this carnal and primitive love of which I have been speaking, out of this love of the whole body with all its senses, which is the animal origin of human society, out of this loving-fondness, rises spiritual and sorrowful love.

This other form of love, this spiritual love, is born of sorrow, is born of the death of carnal love, is born also of the feeling of compassion and protection which parents feel in the presence of a stricken child. Lovers never attain to a love of self abandonment, of true fusion of soul and not merely of body, until the heavy pestle of sorrow has bruised their hearts and crushed them in the same mortar of suffering. Sensual love joined their bodies but disjoined their souls; it kept their souls strangers to one another; but of this love is begotten a fruit of their flesh—a child. And perchance this child, begotten in death, falls sick and dies. Then it comes to pass that over the fruit of their carnal fusion and spiritual separation and estrangement, their bodies now separated and cold with sorrow but united by sorrow their souls, the lovers, the parents, join in an embrace of despair, and then is born, of the death of the child of their flesh, the true spiritual love. Or rather, when the bond of flesh which united them is broken, they breathe with a sigh of relief. For men love one another with a spiritual love only when they have suffered the same sorrow together when through long days they have ploughed the stony ground bowed beneath the common yoke of a common grief. It is then that they know one another and feel one another, and feel with one another in their common anguish, they pity one another and love one another. For to love is to pity; and if bodies are united by pleasure, souls are united by pain.

And this is felt with still more clearness and force in the seeding, the taking root, and the blossoming of one of those tragic loves which are doomed to contend with the diamond-hard laws of Destiny—one of those loves which are born out of due time and season, before or after the moment, or out of the normal mode in which the world, which is custom, would have been willing to welcome them. The more barriers Destiny and the world and its law interpose between the lovers, the stronger is the impulse that urges them towards one another, and their happiness in loving one another turns to bitterness, and their unhappiness in not being able to love freely and openly grows heavier, and they pity one another from the bottom of their hearts; and this common pity, which is their common misery and their common happiness, gives fire and fuel to their love. And they suffer their joy, enjoying their suffering. And they establish their love beyond the confines of the world, and the strength of this poor love suffering beneath the yoke of Destiny gives them intuition of another world where there is no other law than the liberty of love—another world where there are no barriers because there is no flesh. For nothing inspires us more with hope and faith in another world than the impossibility of our love truly fructifying in this world of flesh and of appearances.

And what is maternal love but compassion for the weak, helpless, defenceless infant that craves the mother's milk and the comfort of her breast? And woman's love is all maternal.

To love with the spirit is to pity, and he who pities most loves most. Men aflame with a burning charity towards their neighbours are thus enkindled because they have touched the depth of their own misery, their own apparentiality, their own nothingness, and then, turning their newly opened eyes upon their fellows, they have seen that they also are miserable, apparential, condemned to nothingness, and they have pitied them and loved them.

Man yearns to be loved, or, what is the same thing, to be pitied. Man wishes others to feel and share his hardships and his sorrows. The roadside beggar's exhibition of his sores and gangrened mutilations is something more than a device to extort alms from the passer-by. True alms is pity rather than the pittance that alleviates the material hardships of life. The beggar shows little gratitude for alms thrown to him by one who hurries past with averted face; he is more grateful to him who pities him but does not help than to him who helps but does not pity, although from another point of view he may prefer the latter. Observe with what satisfaction he relates his woes to one who is moved by the story of them. He desires to be pitied, to be loved.

Woman's love, above all, as I have remarked, is always compassionate in its essence—maternal. Woman yields herself to the lover because she feels that his desire makes him suffer. Isabel had compassion upon Lorenzo, Juliet upon Romeo, Francesca upon Paolo. Woman seems to say: "Come, poor one, thou shalt not suffer so for my sake!" And therefore is her love more loving and purer than that of man, braver and more enduring.

Pity, then, is the essence of human spiritual love, of the love that is conscious of being love, of the love that is not purely animal, of the love, in a word, of a rational person. Love pities, and pities most when it loves most.

Reversing the terms of the adage *nihil volitum quin præcognitum*, I have told you that *nihil cognitum quin prævolitum*, that we know nothing save what we have first, in one way or another, desired; and it may even be added that we can know nothing well save what we love, save what we pity.

As love grows, this restless yearning to pierce to the uttermost and to the innermost, so it continually embraces all that it sees, and pities all that it embraces. According as you turn inwards and penetrate more deeply into yourself, you will discover more and more your own emptiness, that you are not all that you are not, that you are not what you would wish to be, that you are, in a word, only a nonentity. And in touching your own nothingness, in not feeling your permanent base, in not reaching your own infinity, still less your own eternity, you will have a wholehearted pity for yourself, and you will burn with a sorrowful love for yourself—a love that will consume your so-called self-love, which is merely a species of sensual self-delectation, the self-enjoyment, as it were, of the flesh of your soul.

Spiritual self-love, the pity that one feels for oneself, may perhaps be called egotism; but nothing could be more opposed to ordinary egoism. For this love or pity for yourself, this intense despair, bred of the consciousness that just as before you were born you were not, so after your death you will cease to be, will lead you to pity—that is, to love—all your fellows and brothers in this world of appearance, these unhappy shadows who pass from nothingness to nothingness, these sparks of consciousness which shine for a moment in the infinite and eternal darkness. And this compassionate feeling for other men, for your fellows, beginning with those most akin to you, those with whom you live, will expand into a universal pity for all living things, and perhaps even for things that have not life but merely existence. That distant star which shines up there in the night will some day be quenched and will turn to dust and will cease to shine and cease to exist. And so, too, it will be with the whole of the star-strewn heavens. Unhappy heavens!

And if it is grievous to be doomed one day to cease to be,

perhaps it would be more grievous still to go on being always oneself, and no more than oneself, without being able to be at the same time other, without being able to be at the same time everything else, without being able to be all.

If you look at the universe as closely and as inwardly as you are able to look—that is to say, if you look within yourself; if you not only contemplate but feel all things in your own consciousness, upon which all things have traced their painful impression—you will arrive at the abyss of the tedium, not merely of life, but of something more: at the tedium of existence, at the bottomless pit of the vanity of vanities. And thus you will come to pity all things; you will arrive at universal love.

In order to love everything, in order to pity everything, human and extra-human, living and non-living, you must feel everything within yourself, you must personalize everything. For everything that it loves, everything that it pities, love personalizes. We only pity—that is to say, we only love that which is like ourselves and in so far as it is like ourselves, and the more like it is the more we love; and thus our pity for things, and with it our love, grows in proportion as we discover in them the likenesses which they have with ourselves. Or, rather, it is love itself, which of itself tends to grow, that reveals these resemblances to us. If I am moved to pity and love the luckless star that one day will vanish from the face of heaven, it is because love, pity, makes me feel that it has a consciousness, more or less dim, which makes it suffer because it is no more than a star, and a star is doomed one day to cease to be. For all consciousness is consciousness of death and of suffering.

Consciousness (*conscientia*) is participated knowledge, is co-feeling, and co-feeling is com-passion. Love personalizes all that it loves. Only by personalizing it can we fall in love with an idea. And when love is so great and so vital, so strong and so overflowing, that it loves everything, then it personalizes everything and discovers that the total All, that the Universe, is also a Person possessing a Consciousness, a Consciousness which in its turn suffers, pities, and loves, and therefore is consciousness. And this Consciousness of the Universe, which love, personalizing all that it loves, discovers, is what we call God. And thus the soul pities God and feels itself pitied by Him; loves Him and feels itself loved by Him, sheltering its misery in the bosom of the eternal and infinite misery, which, in eternalizing itself and infinitizing itself, is the supreme happiness itself.

God is, then, the personalization of the All; He is the eternal and infinite Consciousness of the Universe—Consciousness taken captive by matter and struggling to free himself from it.

We personalize the All in order to save ourselves from Nothingness; and the only mystery really mysterious is the mystery of suffering.

Suffering is the path of consciousness, and by it living beings arrive at the possession of self-consciousness. For to possess consciousness of oneself, to possess personality, is to know oneself and to feel oneself distinct from other beings, and this feeling of distinction is only reached through an act of collision, through suffering more or less severe, through the sense of one's own limits. Consciousness of oneself is simply consciousness of one's own limitation. I feel myself when I feel that I am not others; to know and to feel the extent of my being is to know at what point I cease to be, the point beyond which I no longer am.

And how do we know that we exist if we do not suffer, little or much? How can we turn upon ourselves, acquire reflective consciousness, save by suffering? When we enjoy ourselves we forget ourselves, forget that we exist; we pass over into another, an alien being, we alienate ourselves. And we become centred in ourselves again, we return to ourselves, only by suffering.

> *Nessun maggior dolore*
> *che ricordarsi del tempo felice*
> *nella miseria*

are the words that Dante puts into the mouth of Francesca da Rimini (*Inferno*, v., 121-123); but if there is no greater sorrow than the recollection in adversity of happy bygone days, there is, on the other hand, no pleasure in remembering adversity in days of prosperity.

"The bitterest sorrow that man can know is to aspire to do much and to achieve nothing" (πολλὰ φρονέοττα μηδενὸς χρατέειν)—so Herodotus relates that a Persian said to a Theban at a banquet (book ix., chap. xvi.). And it is true. With knowledge and desire we can embrace everything, or almost everything; with the will nothing, or almost nothing. And contemplation is not happiness —no! not if this contemplation implies impotence. And out of this collision between our knowledge and our power pity arises.

We pity what is like ourselves, and the greater and clearer our sense of its likeness with ourselves, the greater our pity. And if we may say that this likeness provokes our pity, it may also be maintained that it is our reservoir of pity, eager to diffuse itself over everything, that makes us discover the likeness of things with ourselves, the common bond that unites us with them in suffering.

Our own struggle to acquire, preserve, and increase our own consciousness makes us discover in the endeavours and movements and revolutions of all things a struggle to acquire, preserve, and increase consciousness, to which everything tends. Beneath the actions of those most akin to myself, of my fellow-men, I feel —or, rather, I co-feel—a state of consciousness similar to that which lies beneath my own actions. On hearing my brother give a cry of pain, my own pain awakes and cries in the depth of my consciousness. And in the same way I feel the pain of animals, and the pain of a tree when one of its branches is being cut off, and I feel it most when my imagination is alive, for the imagination is the faculty of intuition, of inward vision.

Proceeding from ourselves, from our own human consciousness, the only consciousness which we feel from within and in which feeling is identical with being, we attribute some sort of consciousness, more or less dim, to all living things, and even to the stones themselves, for they also live. And the evolution of organic beings is simply a struggle to realize fullness of consciousness through suffering, a continual aspiration to be others without ceasing to be themselves, to break and yet to preserve their proper limits.

And this process of personalization or subjectivization of everything external, phenomenal, or objective, is none other than the vital process of philosophy in the contest of life against reason and of reason against life. . . .

Is all this true? And what is truth? I in my turn will ask, as Pilate asked—not, however, only to turn away and wash my hands, without waiting for an answer.

Is truth in reason, or above reason, or beneath reason, or outside of reason, in some way or another? Is only the rational true? May there not be a reality, by its very nature, unattainable by reason, and perhaps, by its very nature, opposed to reason? And how can we know this reality if reason alone holds the key to knowledge?

Our desire of living, our need of life, asks that that may be true which urges us to self-preservation and self-perpetuation, which sustains man and society; it asks that the true water may be that which assuages our thirst, and because it assuages it, that the true bread may be that which satisfies our hunger, because it satisfies it.

The senses are devoted to the service of the instinct of preservation, and everything that satisfies this need of preserving ourselves, even though it does not pass through the senses, is nevertheless a kind of intimate penetration of reality in us. Is the process of assimilating nutriment perhaps less real than the process of knowing the nutritive substance? It may be said that to eat a loaf of bread is not the same thing as seeing, touching, or tasting it; that in the one case it enters into our body, but not therefore into our consciousness. Is this true? Does not the loaf of bread that

I have converted into my flesh and blood enter more into my consciousness than the other loaf which I see and touch, and of which I say: "This is mine"? And must I refuse objective reality to the bread that I have thus converted into my flesh and blood and made mine when I only touch it?

There are some who live by air without knowing it. In the same way, it may be, we live by God and in God—in God the spirit and consciousness of society and of the whole Universe, in so far as the Universe is also a society.

God is felt only in so far as He is lived; and man does not live by bread alone, but by every word that proceedeth out of the mouth of God (Matt. iv. 4; Deut. viii. 3).

And this personalization of the all, of the Universe, to which we are led by love, by pity, is the personalization of a person who embraces and comprehends within himself the other persons of which he is composed.

The only way to give finality to the world is to give it consciousness. For where there is no consciousness there is no finality, finality presupposing a purpose. And, as we shall see, faith in God is based simply upon the vital need of giving finality to existence, of making it answer to a purpose. We need God, not in order to understand the *why*, but in order to feel and sustain the ultimate *wherefore*, to give a meaning to the Universe.

And neither ought we to be surprised by the affirmation that this consciousness of the Universe is composed and integrated by the consciousnesses of the beings which form the Universe, by the consciousnesses of all the beings that exist, and that nevertheless it remains a personal consciousness distinct from those which compose it. Only thus is it possible to understand how in God we live, move, and have our being. That great visionary, Emanuel Swedenborg, saw or caught a glimpse of this in his book on Heaven and Hell (*De Cœlo et Inferno*, lii.), when he tells us: "An entire angelic society appears sometimes in the form of a single angel, which also it hath been granted me by the Lord to see. When the Lord Himself appears in the midst of the angels, He doth not appear as encompassed by a multitude, but as a single being in angelic form. Hence it is that the Lord in the Word is called an angel, and likewise that an entire society is so called. Michael, Gabriel, and Raphael are nothing but angelical societies, which are so named from their functions."

May we not perhaps live and love—that is, suffer and pity—in this all-enveloping Supreme Person—we, all the persons who suffer and pity and all the beings that strive to achieve personality, to acquire consciousness of their suffering and their limitation? And are we not, perhaps, ideas of this total Grand Consciousness, which by thinking of us as existing confers existence upon us? Does not our existence consist in being perceived and felt by God? And, further on, this same visionary tells us, under the form of images, that each angel, each society of angels, and the whole of heaven comprehensively surveyed, appear in human form, and in virtue of this human form the Lord rules them as one man.

"God does not think, He creates; He does not exist, He is eternal," wrote Kierkegaard (*Afslutende uvidenskabelige Efterskrift*); but perhaps it is more exact to say with Mazzini, the mystic of the Italian city, that "God is great because His thought is action" (*Ai giovani d'Italia*), because with Him to think is to create, and He gives existence to that which exists in His thought by the mere fact of thinking it, and the impossible is the unthinkable by God. Is it not written in the Scriptures that God creates with His word—that is to say, with His thought—and that by this, by His Word, He made everything that exists? And what God has once made does He ever forget? May it not be that all the thoughts that have ever passed through the Supreme Consciousness still subsist therein? In Him, who is eternal, is not all existence eternalized?

Our longing to save consciousness, to give personal and human finality to the Universe and to existence, is such that even in the midst of a supreme, an agonizing and lacerating sacrifice, we should still hear the voice that assured us that if our consciousness disappears, it is that the infinite and eternal Consciousness may be enriched thereby, that our souls may serve as nutriment to the Universal Soul. Yes, I enrich God, because before I existed He did not think of me as existing, because I am one more—one more even though among an infinity of others—who, having really lived, really suffered, and really loved, abide in His bosom. It is the furious longing to give finality to the Universe, to make it conscious and personal, that has brought us to believe in God, to wish that God may exist, to create God, in a word. To create Him, yes! This saying ought not to scandalize even the most devout theist. For to believe in God is, in a certain sense, to create Him, although He first creates us.[1] It is He who in us is continually creating Himself.

We have created God in order to save the Universe from nothingness, for all that is not consciousness and eternal consciousness, conscious of its eternity and eternally conscious, is nothing more than appearance. There is nothing truly real save that which feels, suffers, pities, loves, and desires, save consciousness; there is nothing substantial but consciousness. And we need God in order to save consciousness; not in order to think existence, but in order to live it; not in order to know the why and how of it, but in order to feel the wherefore of it. Love is a contradiction if there is no God.

NOTES

1. In the translation it is impossible to retain the play upon the verbs *crear*, to create, and *creer*, to believe: *"Porque creer en Dios es en cierto modo crearle, aunque El nos cree antes."*—J. E. C. F.

ROLLO MAY: A Preface to Love*

. . . To be capable of giving and receiving mature love is as sound a criterion as we have for the fulfilled personality. But by that very token it is a goal gained only in proportion to how much one has fulfilled the prior condition of becoming a person in one's own right. Thus this whole book, not just this section, might be called a "preface to love."

In the first place it should be noted that love is actually a relatively rare phenomenon in our society. As everyone knows, there are a million and one kinds of relationships which are *called* love: we do not need to list all of the confusions of "love" with sentimental impulses and every kind of oedipal and "back to mother's arms" motifs as they appear in the romantic songs and the movies. No word is used with more meanings than this term, most of the meanings being dishonest in that they cover up the real underlying motives in the relationship. But there are many other quite sound and honest relationships called love—such as parental care for children and vice versa, or sexual passion, or the sharing of loneliness; and again the startling reality often discovered when one looks underneath the surface of individuals' lives in our lonely and conformist society, is how little the component of love is actually involved even in these relationships.

Most human relationships, of course, spring from a mixture of motives and include a combination of different feelings. Sexual love in its mature form between a man and woman is generally a blend of two emotions. One is "eros"—the sexual drive toward the other, which is part of the individual's need to fulfill himself. Two and a half millennia ago Plato pictured "eros" as the drive of each individual to unite with the complement to himself—the drive to find the other half of the original "androgyne," the mythological being who was both man and woman. The other

* Reprinted from *Man's Search for Himself.*

element in mature love between man and woman is the affirmation of the value and worth of the other person, which we include in our definition of love given below.

But granted the blending of motives and emotions, and granted that love is not a simple topic, the most important thing at the outset is to call our emotions by their right names. And the most constructive place to begin learning how to love is to see how we fail to love. We shall have made a start, at least, when we recognize our situation as that of the young man in Auden's *The Age of Anxiety:*

> So, learning to love, at length he is taught
> To know he does not.

Our society is, as we have seen, the heir of four centuries of competitive individualism, with power over others as a dominant motivation; and our particular generation is the heir of a good deal of anxiety, isolation and personal emptiness. These are scarcely good preparations for learning how to love.

When we look at the topic on the level of national relations, we come to similar conclusions. It is easy enough to slide into the comforting sentiment, "Love will solve all." To be sure, it is obvious that this distraught world's political and social problems cry out for the attitudes of empathy, imaginative concern, love for the neighbor and "the stranger." Elsewhere I have pointed out that what our society lacks is the experience of community, based on socially valuable work and love—and lacking community we fall into its neurotic substitute, the "neurosis of collectivism."[1] But it is not helpful to tell people, *ipso facto*, that they should love. This only promotes hypocrisy and sham, of which we have a good deal too much in the area of love already. Sham and hypocrisy are greater deterrents to learning to love than is outright hostility, for at least the latter may be honest and can then be worked with. Simply the proclaiming of the point that the world's hostilities and hatreds would be overcome if only people could love invites more hypocrisy; and furthermore, we have learned in our dealings with Russia how crucial it is to lead from strength, and to meet authoritarian sadism directly and realistically. Certainly every new act in international relations which affirms the values and needs of other nations and groups, as did the Marshall Plan, should be welcomed with rejoicing. At least we are learning at long last that we must affirm other nations' existence for our own sheer survival. But though such lessons are great gains, we cannot thereby conclude that occasional actions of this kind are a proof that we have learned—on the political level—to love. So, again, we shall make our most useful contribution to a world in dire need of concern for the neighbor and stranger if we begin by trying to make ourselves as individuals able to love. Lewis Mumford has remarked, "As with peace, those who call for love loudest often express it least. To make ourselves capable of loving, and ready to receive love, is the paramount problem of integration; indeed the key to salvation."

So great is the confusion about love in our day that it is even difficult to find [people] agreed upon definitions of what love is. We define love as *a delight in the presence of the other person and an affirming of his value and development as much as one's own.* Thus there are always two elements to love—that of the worth and good of the other person, and that of one's own joy and happiness in the relation with him.

The capacity to love presupposes self-awareness, because love requires the ability to have empathy with the other person, to appreciate and affirm his potentialities. Love also presupposes freedom; certainly love which is not freely given is not love. To "love" someone because you are not free to love someone else, or because you happen by the accident of birth to be in some family relation to him, is not to love. Furthermore, if one "loves" because one cannot do without the other, love is not given by choice; for one could not choose not to love. The hallmark of such unfree "love" is that it does not discriminate: it does not distinguish the "loved" person's qualities or his being from the next person's. In such a relation you are not really "seen" by the one who purports to love you—you might just as well be someone else. Neither the one who loves nor the loved one act as *persons* in such relationships; the former is not a subject operating with some freedom, and the latter is significant chiefly as an object to be clung to.

There are all kinds of dependence which in our society—having so many anxious, lonely and empty persons in it—masquerade as love. They vary from different forms of mutual aid or reciprocal satisfaction of desires (which may be quite sound if called by their right names), through the various "business" forms of personal relationships to clear parasitical masochism. It not infrequently happens that two persons, feeling solitary and empty by themselves, relate to each other in a kind of unspoken bargain to keep each other from suffering loneliness. Matthew Arnold describes this beautifully in *Dover Beach:*

> Ah, love, let us be true
> To one another! for the world, which seems
> To lie before us like a land of dreams,
> So various, so beautiful, so new,
> Hath really neither joy, nor love, nor light,
> Nor certitude, nor peace, nor help for pain;
> And we are here as on a darkling plain. . . .

But when "love" is engaged in for the purpose of vanquishing loneliness, it accomplishes its purpose only at the price of increased emptiness for both persons.

Love, as we have said, is generally confused with dependence: but in point of fact, you can love only in proportion to your capacity for independence. Harry Stack Sullivan has made the startling statement that a child cannot learn "to love anybody before he is pre-adolescent. You can get him to sound like it, to act so you can believe it. But there is no real basis and if you stress it you get queer results, many of which become neuroses."[2] That is to say, until this age the capacity for awareness and affirmation of other persons has not matured enough for love. As an infant and child he is quite normally dependent on his parents, and he may in fact be very fond of them, like to be with them, and so forth. Let parents and children frankly enjoy the happiness such a relationship makes possible. But it is very healthy and relieving for parents, in the respect of reducing their need to play god and their tendency to arrogate to themselves complete importance in nature's scheme for the child's life, to note how much more spontaneous warmth and "care" the child shows in dealing with his teddy bear or doll or, later on, his real dog than he shows in his relations with human beings. The bear or doll make no demands on him; he can project into them all he likes, and he does not have to force himself beyond his degree of maturity to empathize with their needs. The live dog is an intermediate step between the inanimate objects and human beings. Each step— from dependence, through dependability to interdependence— represents the developmental stage of the child's maturing capacity for love.

One of the chief things which keeps us from learning to love in our society, as Erich Fromm and others have pointed out, is our "marketplace orientation." We use love for buying and selling. One illustration of this is in the fact that many parents expect that the child love them as a repayment for their taking care of him. To be sure, a child will learn to pretend to certain acts of love if the parents insist on it; but sooner or later it turns out that a love demanded as a payment is no love at all. Such love is a "house built upon sand" and often collapses with a crash when the children have grown into young adulthood. For why does the fact that the parent has supported or protected a child, sent him to camp and later to college, have anything necessarily to do with his loving the parent? It could as logically be expected that the son should love the city traffic policeman on the corner who protects him from trucks or the army mess sergeant who gets him his food when he is in the army.

A deeper form of this demand is that the child should love the parent because the parent has sacrificed for him. But sacrifice may be simply another form of bargaining and may have nothing to do in motivation with an affirmation of the other's values and development.

We receive love—from our children as well as others—not in proportion to our demands or sacrifices or needs, but roughly in proportion to our own capacity to love. And our capacity to love depends, in turn, upon our prior capacity to be persons in our own right. To love means, essentially, to give; and to give requires a maturity of self-feeling. Love is shown in the statement of Spinoza's we have quoted above, that truly loving God does not involve a demand for love in return. It is the attitude referred to by the artist Joseph Binder: "To produce art requires that the artist be able to love—that is to give without thought of being rewarded."

We are not talking about love as a "giving *up*" or self-abnegation. One gives only if he has something to give, only if he has a basis of strength within himself from which to give. It is most unfortunate in our society that we have had to try to purify love from aggression and competitive triumph by identifying it with weakness. Indeed, this inoculation has been so much of a success that the common prejudice is that the weaker people are, the more they love; and that the strong man does not *need* to love! No wonder tenderness, that yeast without which love is as soggy and heavy as unrisen bread, has been generally scorned, and often separated out of the love experience.

What was forgotten was that tenderness goes along with strength: one can be gentle as he is strong; otherwise tenderness and gentleness are masquerades for clinging. The Latin origin of our words is nearer the truth—"virtue," of which love is certainly one, comes from the root *vir*, "man" (here in the sense of masculine strength), from which the word "virility" is also derived.

Some readers may be questioning, "But does one not *lose* himself in love?" To be sure, in love as in creative consciousness, it is true that one is merged with the other. But this should not be called "losing one's self"; again like creative consciousness, it is the highest level of fulfillment of one's self. When sex is an expression of love, for example, the emotion experienced at the moment of orgasm is not hostility or triumph, but *union* with the other person. The poets are not lying to us when they sing of the ecstasy in love. As in creative ecstasy, it is that moment of self-realization when one temporarily overleaps the barrier between one identity and another. It is a giving of one's self and a finding of one's self at once. Such ecstasy represents the fullest interdependence in human relations; and the same paradox applies as in creative consciousness—one can merge one's self in ecstasy only as one has gained the prior capacity to stand alone, to be a person in one's own right.

We do not mean this discussion to be a counsel of perfection. Nor is it meant to rule out or depreciate all of the other kinds of positive relationships, such as friendship (which may also be an important aspect of parent-child relations), various degrees of interchange of human warmth and understanding, the sharing of sexual pleasure and passion, and so on. Let us not fall into the error so common in our society of making love in its ideal sense all-important, so that one has only the alternatives of admitting he has never found the "pearl of great price" or resorting to hypocrisy in trying to persuade himself that all of the emotions he does feel are "love." We can only repeat: we propose calling the emotions by their right names. Learning to love will proceed most soundly if we cease trying to persuade ourselves that to love is easy, and if we are realistic enough to abandon the illusory masquerades for love in a society which is always talking about love but has so little of it.

NOTES

1. See Rollo May, *The Meaning of Anxiety*. New York, Ronald Press, 1950, Chapter 5.
2. In Dr. Sullivan's paper in *Culture and Personality*, ed. Sargent and Smith, New York, 1949, p. 194.

MARTIN C. D'ARCY: Human and Divine*

Wisely hath Helen done in setting the Cross above the Kings' heads that the Cross of Christ may be adored in Kings.
St. Ambrose on St. Helen

> Its nostrils snuffed the air and sought repose
> The while its glances, keen, uncircumscribed,
> Projecting pictures into space,
> Brought a blue saga-cycle to a close.
>   The Unicorn *by* R. M. Rilke

Salva me ex ore leonis, et a cornibus unicornium.

Enough material has now been collected to see the shape which love always takes. We begin with the distinction

* Reprinted from *The Mind and Heart of Love*.

which it is easiest to make, selfish and unselfish love. All admit
this, and it is sufficiently clear and obvious for all to use in every-
day judgements about others and to rely on in biographies and
historical criticism. Immediately, however, we take it seriously and
inquire into its ultimate truth we meet difficulties. Selfishness is
only a vice if it means an undue regard for self; unselfishness is
only a virtue if it is countered by self-respect. The two loves,
therefore, so far from being opposites appear to require the presence of each other. We do not blame a man for seeking to develop
his mind and will, for asserting his claims on occasions, so long as
he is not exclusively bent on promoting his own interests. Similarly, we admire a person who is self-sacrificing, but we are shocked
by those who show no trace of self-respect and are prepared to
throw away their honour for some belief or cause.

But if this be so, a problem arises. The two loves seem to
go hand in hand, but we do not know on what terms they are
disposed to be friendly; we are ignorant of their relative rank and
of their roots in human nature; we may even wonder whether
they are so ultimately different as they seem to be. Nor can the
problem be set on one side as academic, as if it were always
happily settled in practice. I have tried to show in preceding
chapters how the great movements in history and art and philosophy and religion are influenced by the preference for one or other
of these loves, and that it is vastly important to know where we
stand with regard to them. The two loves appear in every place
of history like the Lion and the Unicorn fighting round the town.
They take, however, such different names and appeal to such
diverse motives in us that we usually fail to see the underlying
identity, and it is because we are thus distracted that we fail also
to have any coherent idea of what these loves are and how they
are related. It is for this reason that I have taken apparently dis-
parate kinds of examples and by holding them up to the light
tried to show their interconnection. The very thinkers who had
made them a subject for examination may help too by unwittingly
disclosing more than they themselves notice.

The words Eros and Agape, which have come into favour
recently and are in their very names suggestive, were used both
by de Rougemont and Nygren to delineate two forms of loving.
They gave a beginning, especially as de Rougemont was directly
concerned with a romantic movement in history and Nygren with
a religious one. The advantage of this is that as they started from
different angles, their evidence can be taken as independent. On
a first impression their conclusions seem to clash, but on a closer
look a remarkable resemblance reveals itself. De Rougemont was
engaged in a study of the troubadours and the Provençal romantic

movement. He was struck by the fact that, at the very moment
when the Church was establishing Christian manners and morals,
the so-called courtly or chivalric songs and tales were idealizing a
love which was the antithesis of Christian marriage and the Christian sacramental view of life. The most typical example of this
love is to be found in the story of Tristram and Isolde. De Rougemont describes its features as follows: it stood in doctrine for
mystical union, in its theoretical application for woeful human
love, and in its historical fulfilment for hedonism and for a rare
and despised passion. Christian love, on the other hand, as he
understands it, stood for communion, for love of our neighbour
and blissful marriage, and in its historical fulfilment for painful
clashes and a strong passion. He calls the first Eros and the second
Agape.

     So far there might not seem to be anything which threw an
unexpected light on the love of self and the love of others. Once,
however, de Rougemont develops his theme, we listen to a strange
and fascinating story. The opposition of Eros and Agape is not a
light one, due to an historical accident; it goes down to the roots
of human nature and is coeval with man. Eros is the dark passion,
man's beguiler and destroyer. It is the Delilah or, in the language
of romance, the witch Lilith. Romance is a form of escape; it
breaks loose from the control of reason; it soars up in emotion
and crashes to its death. Some time or other in the theme of Eros
the death note will be heard; man in love with death and with
the dark goddess, and singing of the night when his soul will be
fused with the object of his passion. This passion makes itself felt
in the medieval courtly tales, but it is not peculiar to them; it
belongs to a philosophy and religion which can be traced back
to the pre-Christian Indo-European religions which swept into the
lands of the Mediterranean and strove to rival Christianity. Defeated, these beliefs were not extinguished. As the centuries succeed one another the followers of them betray their presence in a
succession of heresies or rival theories. These theories can be
summed up in the name, Gnosticism, and they all have this in
common that the material world is evil, that the soul which has
fallen or descended from the divine substance, the spiritually
One, longs to escape back from the world and to be immersed
again in the divine, and that it must as a consequence hate the
body and all things associated with the body, such as marriage.
This view, which has such close associations with Neo-Platonism
and the mystical element in the worship of Eleusis and Isis, lies
behind Manicheanism, Priscillianism and Catharism. Now, as de
Rougemont points out, there is ample evidence that this philosophy, under the name of Catharism, was prevalent in Spain and

spread across the Pyrenees through Southern France, even to Italy, just at the time that the Provençal songs and tales were written. What more likely then than that the ideas so obviously in conflict with the doctrines of Christianity came from the implacable rival of Christianity, the Gnostic religious philosophy. Thus the romantic development in Europe, with its cult of the dark passion, its antipathy to reason and its cult of death and mysticism, is traced back to Neo-Platonism and the religions of Asia. And it is this kind of love which de Rougemont calls Eros.

Far different at first sight is Nygren's account. De Rougemont thinks of Eros as unrestrained and passionate, hedonistic, and to that extent selfish, but also bent on self-destruction and fusion of its identity with the dark godhead. To Nygren it is the rational man, the natural man of the Scriptures, who relies upon himself and is fundamentally egocentric, who is moved by Eros. Eros belongs to the Greek way of life, and the Greek is the pagan of the Areopagus to whom the Christian teaching of St. Paul was folly. Greek philosophy makes man the measure of truth, and the perfection of man consists in his possessing truth. Eros is, therefore, equivalent to self-love. The Christian love, which Nygren calls Agape, does not negotiate with this self-love at all; it discards it utterly. God does everything; He is Agape, and freely, without any regard for the deserts of human beings, he initiates a corresponding Agape in them. He takes them out of themselves altogether, and inspires in them in place of self-love, a non-natural love for Himself and for their neighbours. No self-love is left. Pure Christianity, therefore, teaches Agape without any taint of Eros. But, as his book tries to prove, Christian theology proved unequal to the task of keeping the faith pure. Slowly at first, and then more rapidly as the Church came to esteem Greek thought, Eros returned. The Scholastic philosophy reeks of Plato and Aristotle and self-love is put alongside the love of God and the love of one's neighbour. Hence arose false problems about the relation of self-love to the love of God and of others.

Whereas, then, de Rougemont considers Eros to be unrestrained and passionate, and, apparently, more inclined to self-effacement than to self-regard, Nygren defines it as an Hellenic ideal, as intellectual, self-complacent and possessive, as, in short, irretrievably egocentric. Agape, on the other hand, in Nygren's view, is so theocentric as to leave nothing human in it, while de Rougemont sees in it something which irradiates reason and everything human. By God's love, as the latter says, "every human relation has been given a new *direction* in being given a new *meaning*." It is strange that two such penetrating observers should come to such strikingly different conclusions, and on a subject,

too, about which every human being from his own experience has
a tale to tell. On one point, however, they concur—Eros is somehow connected with the growth of Neo-Platonism. One thinks
that the dark passion took philosophical shape when in its journey from the East it encountered Greek thought; the other is
convinced that the egocentric philosophy of Greece soared up into
a mystical religion when it encountered the mystery religions of
the East. The only difference here is one of stress; the result is the
same, except that de Rougemont limits the enemies of Agape to
Gnosticism, while Nygren includes the whole of Hellenic philosophy and religion. This is very suggestive. It looks as if both
writers had by a too-exclusive attention to one feature or other of
Eros and Agape drawn apart. What they have positively to say is
valuable, but their conclusions sin by omission.

This conjecture is verified when we look at their omissions.
De Rougemont has many happy intuitions to give us on the nature
of both Agape and Eros. Nevertheless, his account of Eros becomes
at important points too vague. He calls it hedonistic, and this implies that it is selfish, but he does not show how this idea of Eros
is compatible with the one which he is more inclined to emphasize, namely, that of self-extinction. Again, he is concerned to
show that Eros is a dark passion which makes its victim dash himself against the bars of reason and all that is human. As a result
he seems to leave no place for reason in Eros. What is lawful and
good and reasonable is felt to belong to Agape. But Agape, which,
as is clear, from *Passion and Society*, is equivalent to the supernatural love of God, has now to carry too much. Human nature is
impoverished at the expense of grace. Eros must include the best
in man, which is his reason and will and all the ideal possessive
love of which it is capable. To right the balance, therefore, Eros
should stand for both the ecstatic, irrational and self-effacing mood
of love and the rational, self-assertive and possessive form, as they
are found in human experience; and Agape for God's special love
and man's response to it as inspirited and energized by it.

But if de Rougemont overbalances on one side, Nygren
leans too heavily to the other. Instead of Eros being little else than
a dark passion, it is now identified with the highest activities of
man, the pursuit of truth and the possession of the good. Eros is
the Greek ideal, and Agape has no relation to human reason or
ideals. Instead of doing the work of reason, as in de Rougemont,
Agape dispenses with it, and this is to take everything human out
of Agape. Man does nothing and God does all. Self-regard and
self-perfection completely disappear. But Nygren does not seem
to see that what he says takes us away from Christianity and leads
directly to the ideal of mystic fusion which so repels him. If man

can do nothing, then extreme quietism is his lot, a question which must end in man being swallowed up in union with the godhead. At times Nygren does seem to be uncomfortable at the starkness of his view. He has to eviscerate passages of the New Testament of all meaning, to deny the words, "as many as received him, he gave them power," to reject the virtue of hope, and to brand even the first Christian writers as semi-pagan. To redress the balance, therefore, we are bound to accept some self-love as legitimate, to admit some place for Greek and any other kind of true thinking. Agape will be God's love, which takes the initiative and gives the power to men to be "the sons of God." On the one side, then, there will be man with a passion which seeks for deliverance from himself and simultaneously a just regard for himself and his own perfection; and on the other God who respects man's integrity while lifting him up into a new relation of love with Himself. With such a correction of both views the violent dissimilarities vanish. De Rougemont and Nygren are looking at the same scene and seeing the same problem, which they both describe in terms of Eros and Agape. What each has to say is valuable. De Rougemont brings out the truth that man has a love which does not end with himself. Outside the Christian dispensation that love has a habit of revolting against reason and rushing off now to lose the self in some trance and ecstasy, now to practise self-immolation in dark, mysterious rites. Nygren, by contrast, shows, despite his dislike of it, how potent and all-pervading is self-love. The self is irresistibly borne along by the desire to perfect its own being. The Greeks realized this and taught mankind the value of human nature, the splendour of reason. In their eyes the ideal of life consisted in a beholding of what is most lovely and true, and in the possessing the good. "You and I," as Mgr. Ronald Knox has written, "have each of us an I that is very dear to us, a self which we think much more important than anything else in the world, which we are determined at all costs to keep safe and comfortable if we can. Our natural instinct is to set up a great capital I in front of our minds and worship it." Any theory of life which neglects this natural self-love is bound to fail. Nygren notices it and then neglects it. He notices, too, that it is in our intellectual activity that our self-love reaches its full expression. The intellect is like a spider's web which draws all into its net; but unlike a spider, it has no need to slay its victims; its happiness is in thought, in the forms or replicas of the reality outside which it can contemplate independently of the hurly-burly of actual existences.

Nygren, then, presents us with self-love and its most powerful instrument, the human reason; de Rougemont presents us with a romantic and ecstatic love, which is either irrational or ill

at ease at the superior claims upon it of reason. One love takes and
possesses; the other love likes to be beside itself and give. One is
masculine, the other is feminine. The two are necessary for one
another, and together they tell us what we are and whither we are
going. To neglect either is to court death. If the self becomes
entirely self-centred a monstrous egoism follows, but as the self
is now living on its own conceit and without external nourishment, the inflation is followed by collapse, a period of melancholia
and death. If, following the opposite line, the self abandons itself
to ecstatic love, it moves like a moth to the candle, or passively,
like the musk rose, it gives forth a stronger perfume in the dark
to entice the robber visitant of the night. It has chosen to be a
victim, to die of love and to find its sole joy in self-immolation.
That these are not fantastic images or wild spectres is proved by
the successive diseases of human thought and passion. The to-and-
fro movement between egoism and anti-personal philosophies
adequately sums up the history of thought, and it corresponds
with alternating emphases on individualism or general welfare in
politics and social ideals and personal or pantheistic ideals in religion. So long as the two loves are on speaking terms we can enjoy
the small quarrels, the bickerings, the taking of sides in favour,
let us say, of romance against classicism, liberal competition
against security, activity against passivity in prayer, moral asceticism against mystical union.

The two must never be separated. Self-love is perhaps the
quicker to move us in practice; we are all of us, in fact, sensitive
about ourselves, conceited and proud, ambitious and determined
to have our way. No matter how uneducated a man may be, how
stupid and empty-headed, he is sure to deliver his judgement as
if it were final when he is amongst his friends in pubs or at home.
So close are we to ourselves that we can hardly help making
ourselves the centre round which the whole of past and future,
as well as present history revolves. The world and its events
matter to us in the degree they touch our own fate or our likes
and dislikes. The old man is perturbed because the world is
moving towards a future condition, a hundred years hence, which
he does not like. The world a hundred years away is the world
of which he is an inhabitant now, and his "now" takes no account
of lapse of years and the short span he has to live. Everything
naturally seems relative to the I. Even the "planners" for the
future think and work as if they could rest on the Sabbath Day
and see that their work was good. But if the "I" seeps into all
activities it does not do to admit it, and so in theory, if not in
practice, selfless love receives more notice. We like to think of
ourselves and of others as disinterested and working to ideals

which will bring no personal benefit. This love is less ready to hand, and in truth may steal on us unawares. At times, indeed, we would not like to confess to its presence. When we seek to hide our identity in a crowd or are swept away by some herd passion; when we slay the very self we love or bow down before some idol, we have become victims of this love. This form of Eros can make us happy slaves of Circe or Calypso and dance madly to strange rhythms. It tells us of greater themes than that by which our little life is led; it purges us of that restless individuality which we have unduly prized, and plunges us into the abyss where alone night is the illumination. Were we swayed by this sole and single love there could be no return to selfhood and personal life. But fortunately for us the two loves are both ours. Self-regarding love can easily be an evil and but another name for selfishness; but it has a necessary and noble function. It will be appeased by nothing less than self-perfection; it demands that we remain persons; and that is why at the level of human life the monistic or pantheistic solution spells degradation. Between persons there is mutual enhancement. In true loving we receive and give, and in the relation of the self with God we receive life and receive it more abundantly.

If this be so we must inquire more profoundly into the meaning and extent of these two loves and also into their mutual relation. Now the principle of give and take which is illustrated in human loving seems to belong to a wider field and indeed to be coterminous with life. Were it the place, it might be even possible to show that a twofold movement governs everything. Here such an idea can be no more than a suggestion which to some may be helpful while to others it may sound so vague and metaphorical as to be spurious. In all that exists we presuppose or else discover activity and passivity, the positive and the negative, energy and inertia, an up and a down or a rise and fall, a coming-to-be and a passing away. In living things this principle is exemplified in the struggle for existence, and in the evolution of species. A living thing has a whole apparatus for self-preservation, and nevertheless it may be so constituted that it propagates and promotes the continuation of the species by entire subjection, a subjection so complete that it entails sometimes its own death. The splitting up into different genders marks clearly the contrast between the two loves or desires. It does not matter whether in any particular species the male or the female be dominant; it is sufficient that one of them be dominant and possessive, the other passive and possessed. In the brute creation the two desires or impulses or instincts (the name does not matter in this regard) are more obvious because they approach our own experience and can therefore more easily be judged. The male is dominant, self-assertive and violent; the female is responsive to his pleasures, but looks instinctively beyond its mate to offspring and the continuation of the species. Eric Gill, in an amusing essay, pointed out how "finery is for the male in all creatures except the human," and he argues that "by the design of divine Providence vanity has been from the beginning the virtue of male creatures. That he should take a pride in his physical condition and appearance is a necessity for the male, and vanity is designed for his advancement."[1] Vanity and pride are in man merely the exaggerations of a disposition natural to him; in women they are perverse. "Man is, on the whole, a more reasonable creature than woman, and vanity, his proper accomplishment, may safely be left in his care without fear of its running away with him." A woman's glory is not in brute strength nor in domination. She does not win her victories by "hitting and having." "Behold as the eyes of servants are on the hands of their masters, as the eyes of the handmaid are on the hands of their mistress; so are our eyes unto the Lord, our God, until he have mercy on us."

But there are vital differences between the "taking and receiving" of men and that of beasts. The typical brute male has no limit to his taking except the repletion of his appetite, and he gathers round him a submissive herd. The female again may be quite indifferent to her own fate; she may give or forfeit all. She may be compelled to commit *felo de se*. But a human being is of another order, an order which is summed up in the name of "person." He can never be a means, and he can never allow either of these two loves uncontrolled supremacy. He is forbidden Sabine rapes. Every human being has within him both the love of taking and of giving. Now his new spiritual unity includes all the instincts and impulses of the animal order; we shall expect, therefore, to see a new orientation of these impulses, of the old desires and loves, at his best a perfect sublimation of them, and a partial retrogression to them at his worst. As we have seen in preceding chapters, in the evidence from the mystery religions, mythology and the cartoons of the unconscious, this expectation is verified. The self on its lower levels contains the impulses to brutality and power, together with those of servility and self-immolation. The images of the dark goddess, of death, jostle with those of Moloch and the Minotaur.

But what were blind and crude passions are chastened and reformed into loves and human *motifs*, when they are owned by persons endowed with reason and will. Moreover, the truly human and spiritual level in man will have its characteristic expression of these two loves; they will both disclose what he is, and they will in partnership formulate the ideal of man and help him to attain it. The caution contained in this last sentence is very necessary because it safeguards us from the error of Nygren, the mystical theories of an Aldous Huxley, for instance, and even the too narrow ideal of Greek philosophy. Nygren rejected the self-regarding love, and as a result mutilated the idea of a person. Aldous Huxley again, following an Eastern tradition of mystical thought, will not have anything human in the final mystical union with the Absolute which he preaches. A true and genuine self-regard which is inherent in every human person is needed to prevent such a mystical union stultifying itself in pure absorption. On the other hand, the Greeks gave such an exclusive attention to the ideal of self-perfection that they made it very difficult to understand how love for God and for another person could be disinterested. Both the loves, as we now see, must be active and co-operative. A person as an end in himself, independent and unique and self-owning, cannot surrender himself so entirely as to deny or maim his own personal perfection. Nevertheless, he too is swayed by a love which takes him outside himself to other persons whom he has no right to possess, and to God to whom he owes everything. We must look at the whole of man, and leave nothing out, if we would understand him, and set his love in the right perspective.

Man, therefore, like every other living thing, is moved both by a desire to take and possess all for himself, and at the same time to give himself and throw away his private interests and even his life. In the brute creation the life of the individual is not of such importance as to create a real problem. The individual is sacrificed. But in the case of a rational creature like man, endowed with reason and with a corresponding urge and duty to himself, the individual cannot be sacrificed or bartered away. He cannot suffer the loss of his own soul for any good whatsoever. Moreover, as we have seen, it is in the activity of mind that man rises above the animal world and asserts himself. On the spiritual level it is the mind which represents the love of self, which is dominating, regulative and possessive. It is useful at this point to change over from the language of Eros and Agape to that of animus and anima. The animus is masculine; it is man as rational, whereas the anima is the self, exclusive of reason, but with a special reference to its spiritual aspect. Now if everything moves by its nature to conserve itself and to be more itself, and if reason, the differentiating activity of man, is of its very essence self-regarding, it is very difficult to see how the other love can enter into a person's life. Its counterpart in the animal world could be so insouciant of the self's claims as to make it a mere means to some other object and even sacrifice its life. A person cannot allow this to happen; he must never be a means and "at the mill with slaves." As Claudel's story shows, animus is determined to be master in his own house and to make anima into an obedient housewife. Many a thinker has dreamt this dream in past ages, and at times a civilization has feasted on the hope of a noble humanism, when reason should spread throughout society and all should be happy in a neat world of enlightened self-interest. But to judge by the lessons of history, anima is sure to prove refractory and to go roaming. The romantic movement, the phases of mysticism and irrationalism, bear witness to this. The only answer, the only true harmony, as preceding chapters attempted to show, must be sought in religion—in the communion of anima with its divine lover. But even this will fail unless, as in the Christian religion, the divine lover befriends animus as well, and gives power to the unavailing soul to be led to the altar with God.

The distinction just made between animus and anima prepares us for an answer to the problem of the relative status of the two loves. From a natural and human standpoint the animus or reasonable side of man would seem to have the headship. It is the masculine and regulative principle, which we are inclined to think of as the proximate ground of our independence and self-sufficiency. It is natural for every living organism to live its own life according to its nature. It would be absurd if a man made a mechanical instrument and put into it parts which interfered with the perfection of the instrument. In a human body we assume that every part of it has some relation to the whole life and well-being of the body; a malignant growth, for instance, is not normal. What more natural, then, than to take as an axiom that man's activities have for an end his well-being and that the intellect, *par excellence*, is the instrument of self-realization. No doubt, in the light of what has been said previously, a reader will notice that the argument assumes what has to be proved and that a word like "nature" is ambiguous. But he will at the same time agree with the Greek philosophers in making this principle of self-realization and self-determination the corner-stone of any constructive philosophy of human nature.

But if there were no other principle, and if this principle of self-love were totally true, then a grave difficulty would arise. For we should have to ask how it is possible to love others for themselves and how we can love God more than ourselves. Nygren stuck at this difficulty and resolved it by clearing away love of self. The Christian philosophers refused to act in this Procrustean way. Their evidence, like Nygren's, is important in its avowal of the presence of two loves, the one egocentric, the other ecstatic. Of their attempts at a solution several examples have already been given. They put the problem in the form of the question: How can man love God more than himself? Rousselot replied in terms of an analogy of the relation of a part to the whole; Gilson developed the Thomistic idea of man as the image of God. Both of these writers gave the primacy to the act of the intellect and tried to show how self-perfection turns into the disinterested love of God. The intellect, they admit, is essentially self-regarding, in that it feeds the self with reality as known; it translates that external reality into the limited idea of it which a human being can grasp and possess; and yet somehow at the end the self gives up the ghost and finds God in place of itself.

The weakness of this view is that the intellect is by its very nature possessive, and no matter how delicate any posture of it may be, no matter how incidentally disinterested its desire, it keeps a taint of selfishness. That this is so is shown by the way its advocates try to explain our love for others. They admit that in the experience of this love the self is entirely preoccupied with the other, but they are bound to say that at bottom the other is loved because he is a kind of "second self." (*Vide* Appendix at end of Chapter Two). It is for this reason that some writers look elsewhere than to the intellect for a solution or look for another kind of love. Burnaby accuses Nygren of leaving out Philia, the love, that is, which persons have for one another. De Régnon and Descoqs and others see something special in the love of *persons*. This special love which persons have for one another has been developed by a modern school of theologians. The gist of its teaching is given in the following passage: "To man the world is twofold, in accordance with his twofold attitude. He perceives what exists round about him—simply things, and beings as things, and what happens round about him—simply events and actions as events; things consisting of qualities, events of moment; things entered in the graph of place, events in that of time; things and events bounded by other things and events, measured by them, comparable with them: he perceives an ordered and detached world. . . . It is your object, remains it as long as you wish, and remains a total stranger, within you and without. You perceive it, take it to yourself as the 'truth,' and it lets itself be taken; but it does not give itself to you. Only concerning it may you make yourself 'understood' with others; it is ready, though attached to everyone in a different way, to be an object common to you all. But you cannot meet others in it. . . ."[2]

"Or on the other hand man meets what exists and becomes as what is over against him, always simply a *single* being and each thing simply as being. What exists is opened to him in happenings, and what happens affects him as what is. . . . It cannot be surveyed, and if you wish to make it capable of survey you lose it. It comes, and comes to bring *you* out; you can make it into an object for yourself, to experience and to use; you must continually do this—and as you do it you have no more present. Between you and it there is mutual giving; you say *Thou* to it and give yourself to it, and it says *Thou* to you and gives itself to you."

Hence it is that the relation of an I to a Thou is quite different from the relation of an I to an object or thing—and true love is always an I and Thou relation. "Love does not cling to the I in such a way as to have the Thou only for its 'content,' its object; but love is *between* I and Thou. The man who does not know this, with his very being know this, does not know love. . . ."

In this account there is a mixture of truth and fiction. The truth which it contains is expressed more soberly and philosophically by Descoqs and Hunter Guthrie and others. They too lay stress on the difference between the "things" which the mind makes its own and persons we greet. They would call the former the world of essences, and it is the domain and happy hunting ground of the intellect, the food of self-regarding love. Man being such by nature that he must live for his own preservation, development and perfection, is drawn to things in so far as they are suitable to his nature. A human being, just because the mark which differentiates him from the brute is his mind, will find the specific perfection of his being in growth of knowledge, in the vision of truth. When a person grows in knowledge he comes to know more and more and to unify his discoveries within his mind. All the creatures of the universe come trooping aboard into his ark, and there they are named and docketed and understood in their relationship to one another. It may be that some objects seem far superior to others and throw light upon the meaning of many of the others; it may be that some object dazzles the eyes and is too great to creep inside the ark. If it does accept the invitation it will have to send a substitute or viceroy who is not too tall to cross the threshold. But certainly with regard to the material world the mind is able to make its own, to bring into the unity of its being, all that it sees. It can understand their meaning, grasp their nature and essence and "become all things." This is to possess truth, to have a body of knowledge which conforms with things as they are, to enjoy a viewpoint which does not distort reality. But notice that however true a knowledge I possess of the things or persons outside me, that thing or person is not my possession. He or it goes on existing and dancing and suffering; I know the meaning or nature, but the existence of that thing or person escapes the mind.

This is why Buber talks of true love being a salute or address, a salutation of another I, and makes what is in fact too sharp a distinction between "It" and "I" and the work of the mind and the act of loving. De Régnon and Descoqs and Hunter Guthrie for their part do not exaggerate the divisions in the self, but they admit a distinction between nature and person. By nature we are bound to consult the wellbeing of ourselves first, and we are inclined to give the regency to the intellect and to subject all other powers of the soul under it. But, as we know now, anima is always restless when under too severe duress of the intellect, for it has another love. This other love is the love which a human person as a person has for God, from whom he has his existence, and for others as persons. It is not egocentric because a person always spells a relation, and in that personal relation the centrifugal love finds vent.

The two kinds of love, therefore, which we distinguish as "taking and giving," masculine and feminine, centripetal and centrifugal, which are contained in Eros and Agape and expressed in part by animus and anima, are now seen in the new distinction of nature and person, or better still in that of essence and existence. The metaphysics of essence and existence and nature and person under the skilful treatment of Hunter Guthrie and others gives us a more profound idea of diversities of love, and acts like a floodlight on the picture of it. But as there are many who are only irritated by the technical language of philosophy, I do not propose to repeat the argument of the last chapter. Its conclusions, in short, come to this: that desire or love directs all the activities of the soul, the intellect as much as the will; that intellectual desire represents the movement of the essential self, and will the movement of the existential self; that the movement of the essential self is self-regarding and that of the existential self towards God and other existing persons. We must not, however, think of the two loves as separate and independent within the one self, even though, in order to bring out their distinct characteristics, we have to treat them as if they were alone. In choosing examples from the animal world there is no grave consequence which follows from our taking them apart, but in human persons they come together so as to make the very warp and woof of personality. When we use the word "person" we do think of something which makes a human being his very self in his independence and singularity; and at the same time the word "person" seems to imply a relation. In other words, a person is one who owns himself and is very much an "I," and at the same time, instead of being turned inward in deadly introspection, like an idiot, he takes up a position in the world of reality and is aware of positive relations of equality or dependence or love with one or more other living beings. He has both a self-regarding love and a disinterested love. As an essence he is proud, as an existence he is dependent. He is an absolute on a finite scale, a solitary who feels "angst" and is full of grandeur and *misère*. This is the nemesis of a finite personality.

The secret of the two loves is, therefore, as so many of the writers we have quoted—Burnaby, Descoqs, Buber, Scheler and Hunter Guthrie—insist, to be found in persons and in the relation of persons. As has been appositely written: "Nothing is more intimate to our selves than this mysterious I who is the underlying subject of our acts and the term beyond which one cannot go in the line of willing. 'I' and 'Me,' and that is all. But what a mystery! See how this absolute and this incommunicable being cannot find peace in itself. It will seek—and it is not some *other thing* which it will seek, for things cannot interest it nor satisfy it—it will seek *another* I, which it will long to make its own in order to discover itself there and to lose itself. And this second I and this second Me is nevertheless also an absolute and incommunicable. It matters not. Irresistibly they will go the one to the other, for they live for one another. The person is absolute, yes, but it is also relative. Is there contradiction here? No, only mystery; the mystery of love which will not be satisfied with the intellectual likeness of its object, but desires it to live as it is in itself and to live with a life which is at the same time the life of one and the life of the other. To be a person is to be essentially in search of a person. Love presupposes knowledge, but it can to some degree do without it; what it needs is the living and actual being itself. For a person there must be a person." ("La Recherche de la Personne," by P. Philippe de la Sainte Trinité, in the *Études Carmelitaines*, April 1936.)

How then can we work out a conclusion of the two loves in the light of what has been said about a person? Within a person we can roughly distinguish what he has, his nature, his humanity, and what he is. The foundation of self-love is in the nature, and therefore it tends in the higher reaches of the soul to rely upon the intellect and to regard all else except itself as things. We can advance a high theory of love by making full use of this natural love, but the keynote of it will always be possessiveness. Our neighbours will be loved like to ourselves; they will be as it were another self; they will give us the noblest of joys. But that which makes us finally to be this self-enclosed being, isolated from all others, living and growing, expectant and attendant on what is not ourselves, is our existent being. We are not now in a play at one remove from hard reality, we are in that swirl of reality, and we must swim or drown. And it is in this condition, when we have been plunged into life, that we first discover others and salute them and address them as persons; as beings and persons who are most decidedly not ourselves, who demand of us that we treat them as beings who possess their own inalienable individuality and perfection. We are drawn to them not as being in any sense our own; it is just because they cannot be exploited or used or partitioned out that we attend to them for what they are in themselves. And here something new happens. In loving things there is only a one-way street of love. We take and hold; the thing is ours or we lose ourselves in something bigger and disappear, and that is all. But in the relation of persons there is a return of love. Both are active and the mode of taking is to receive from another, and the more one gives the more one is likely to receive. I live by his life and he lives by mine.

This is the new law of love, and the old prescriptions will not suit it. I do not and cannot ask the question whether I am ultimately loving myself first for the simple reason that when loving another I cannot get any benefit unless I give my love to that other. The less I consider any gain to self and the more I give freely and without second thoughts, the better for me and my love. I live by another's bounty as he lives by mine. This is perfect love on earth between persons, but, alas! a word of caution is needed. There are two impediments at least to its perfect fruition. The first is that, however much lovers in the act of loving deny it, there is no certainty of equality of giving and taking, no surety that love will be returned; and secondly, there is a barrier which no human person can cross. The fine point in personality must always remain untouched. We share but in part, and we are left lonely. It is at the poignant moments when we realize this that we are most tempted to do a forbidden thing—to hand ourselves over utterly and to go into the dark that we may be lost to ourselves and fused with the other. Many times we have seen the menace of this temptation and the disasters which follow on total surrender. The anima has deserted the animus, the existential self has cut itself off from the essential self and is in love with death. Strangely enough, but consistently with the true notion of personality, the relation between persons disappears and is succeeded by that between a person and a thing. No mutual love keeps both lovers in their own lovely and loved station and being. The lover becomes like a moth which dashes itself against the hot lamp; the mystic loses his identity by absorption in some impersonal Absolute.

This temptation reminds us of the indissoluble unity in the self of the two loves and the need for both of them to be operative. A person, as we argued in the last chapter, has to include both the human essence and the existence of that essence if it is to be properly and adequately defined. The self-regarding love preserves the integrity of the self and prevents the other love from getting out of hand and being too prodigal. There is a constant threat against the rights and independence of man in modern society; he is with difficulty able to call his body and his soul his own. For that reason it is just that those who love man should recall to him his proper dignity and ceaselessly proclaim that a State exists to give fuller scope for personal life and not to subordinate personal life to itself. Personal life suffers both by the constant conditioning to which it is subject, and also, though this is less obvious, by an appeal to its so-called better nature to belong to some movement or to espouse some cause. This second danger is more insidious because it comes under the disguise of an ideal, and may well be a genuine ideal. The interest of the anima is enlisted just because the cause is altruistic. Now, as we all know, causes and ideals draw men together and often bring the best out of them: without them good fellowship is impossible and life is anarchic. But as modern movements have shown, if proof be needed, youth can be easily seduced and lose its reason and interior virtue. It loses its power of judgement and worships before an idol.

In human affairs, therefore, the self-regarding love, which stands for reason and judgement and watches over and commands progress in self-perfection, must ever be active and even take precedence over the love of self-effacement. We have to say, what doth it profit to save the whole world and suffer the loss of our souls? Our true love is tested by our honour; it grows more pure the higher we set our own personal standard. The truth of this will become more apparent if we reflect that we are from birth to death, from the moment of our existence, absolutes who must be treated as persons; whereas we are from the point of view of our nature only in process of self-realization.[3] Our first duty is to belong to Him from whom comes our existent self, but what seems to be the most obvious and pressing duty is to direct the steps of our own advance aright, to struggle for existence and growth and be what our inward monitor tells us we ought to be. In the comparison of the relative roles of the two loves, the problem of living has been perforce simplified. In fact we have so kaleidoscopic a self at first that we have deliberately to attend to what we are and practise self-discipline and self-knowledge; and then lest this inner look become distorted and set up a habit of morbid introspection, we have to divert ourselves by care for what is around us. In ringing these changes for the sake of our spiritual health, we play within the two great loves and make a practical judgement how far we, in accordance with our weakness or strength, should commit ourselves to one or other of them. Some men are said to be introverts and others extroverts, and there is an infinite variety of talent and character among men; hence it would be ridiculous to try to prescribe any one mixture of self-love and disinterested love for all alike. But what no one can neglect is a sense of personal dignity. We start, as I have said, as existing persons with a nature of our own which we have to cherish and develop. This self-regard must act as a brake upon the other love, on the tendency of anima to trust itself and its experience independently of reason. The anima, especially in an age when reason is in disrepute, simmers in revolt against its collaborator. It accuses the reason of dealing with abstractions and essences, whereas it touches what is real and has its own criteria. It is true that experience is needed to correct theory, especially when our external senses can verify what has been thought. But experience left to itself can be irrational, illusory and deadly. The champion and coming victor in the struggle for self-perfection is the intellect, the godlike reason, which looks before and after, which contemplates the beloved and sees itself in intuition one with that beloved. It is the eye of truth and it detects the impostor.

The intellect has in all our descriptions of it been placed on the side of self-regarding love, as indeed its proper expression in the spiritual order. The reason for saying this is that the mind is possessive; it is concerned with essences and natures and meanings and by it the soul becomes all things in its own spiritual fashion. But as the self is one in both its loves and operates as one the mind cannot allow love to betray it. Both self-love and disinterested love have to be kept straight by truth, and by truth is meant here what conforms with the essential nature of the self and the whole order of being to which it belongs. The mind serves our loves by spotting for them and reporting, by testing and judging. We have to know ourselves and to know something of the various objects and persons we meet in our life. Love runs ahead and may have its own guarantees and signs, and were our condition perfect these might suffice. But in our struggle and wanderings in search of our one Love and of ourselves we are at the mercy of a disordered imagination, heady passions and unruly impulses, and we are at the mercy of the cunning stranger, the congenial and the novel. Were our loves enlightened we could say: ama et fac quod vis. But it is not until the searchlight of truth has played upon the many shapes which hold our attention and the many loves which beckon to us, that we can give ourselves wholeheartedly to another in personal friendship. The law of personal friendship is, as has been said, that we give what we are and we receive from the other. The law holds and does distinguish this relation from all other relations, whether of gain or loss. A person is such that he would, while remaining himself and having a never-dry fount to draw from, give himself to another. The other likewise because he is a person gives and has no thought of gain. Thus each makes up to the other in abundance the sacrifice and the apparent loss. A new circuit of love begins where two complete one another and live together in one. This is the law and the ideal, but a flaming sword cuts it off from perfection and prevents the longed-for consummation. The solitariness of the self is not overcome, and there is no sure guarantee of the lastingness and worth of the love. And it is here that the mind comes in not as a pander but as a priest. It establishes the friendship on truth; on the knowledge of the genuine character of the loved person's response and his or her worth. Only on truth can friendship be founded, on the certainty that the honour and fairness of the self will not be menaced. When this is known, and only when this is known, can the lover freely and wholeheartedly give of himself without looking back. The interests of the self are then safe in other's hands.

NOTES

1. *Art Nonsense* by Eric Gill.
2. *I and Thou* by Martin Buber.
3. The point of this distinction is brought out by the paradoxical fact that at any moment we are so fully ourselves that we can commit ourselves here and now by a decision which may settle the whole of our future, end our lives and decide our eternal destiny; and this, though we are still young, in many ways unformed and just growing into habits which may change our character considerably.

LEO TOLSTOY: What Men Live By

"We know that we have passed from death unto life, because we love the brethren. He that loveth not his brother abideth in death.

But whoso hath this world's good, and seeth his brother have need, and shutteth up his bowels of compassion from him, how dwelleth the love of God in him?

My little children, let us not love in word, neither in tongue, but in deed and in truth.

Beloved, let us love one another, for love is of God, and every one that loveth is born of God, and knoweth God.

He that loveth not knoweth not God: for God is love.

No man hath seen God at any time. If we love one another God dwelleth in us.

God is love; and he that dwelleth in love dwelleth in God, and God in him.

If a man say, I love God, and hateth his brother, he is a liar: for he that loveth not his brother whom he hath seen, how can he love God whom he hath not seen?"   (1 JOHN iii. and iv.)

A COBBLER and his wife and children had lodgings with a peasant. He owned neither house nor land, and he supported himself and his family by shoemaking.

Bread was dear and labor was poorly paid, and whatever he earned went for food.

The cobbler and his wife had one shuba[1] between them, and this had come to tatters, and for two years the cobbler had been hoarding in order to buy sheepskins for a new shuba.

When autumn came, the cobbler's hoard had grown; three paper rubles lay in his wife's box, and five rubles and twenty kopeks more were due the cobbler from his customers.

One morning the cobbler betook himself to the village to get his new shuba. He put on his wife's wadded nankeen jacket over his shirt, and outside of all a woolen kaftan. He put the three-ruble note in his pocket, broke off a staff, and after breakfast he set forth.

He said to himself, "I will get my five rubles from the peasants, and that with these three will buy pelts for my shuba."

The cobbler reached the village and went to one peasant's; he was not at home, but his wife promised to send her husband with the money the next week, but she could not give him any money. He went to another, and this peasant swore that he had no money at all; but he paid him twenty kopeks for cobbling his boots.

The cobbler made up his mind to get the pelts on credit. But the fur-dealer refused to sell on credit.

"Bring the money," said he; "then you can make your choice; but we know how hard it is to get what is one's due."

And so the cobbler did not do his errand, but he had the twenty kopeks for cobbling the boots, and he took from a peasant an old pair of felt boots to mend with leather.

At first the cobbler was vexed at heart; then he spent the twenty kopeks for vodka, and started to go home. In the morning he had felt cold, but after having drunk the brandy he was warm enough even without the shuba.

The cobbler was walking along the road, striking the frozen ground with the staff which he had in one hand, and swinging the felt boots in the other, and thus he talked to himself.

"I am warm even without a shuba," said he. "I drank a glass, and it dances through all my veins. And so I don't need a sheepskin coat. I walk along, and all my vexation is forgotten. What a fine fellow I am! What do I need? I can get along without the shuba. I don't need it at all. There's one thing: the wife will feel bad. Indeed, it is too bad; here I have been working for it, and now to have missed it! You just wait now! if you don't bring the money, I will take your hat, I vow I will! What a way of doing things! He pays me twenty kopeks at a time! Now what can you do with twenty kopeks? Get a drink; that's all! You say, 'I am poor!' But if you are poor, how is it with me? You have a house and cattle and everything; I have nothing but my own hands. You raise your own grain, but I have to buy mine, when I can, and it costs me three rubles a week for food alone. When I get home now, we shall be out of bread. Another ruble and a half of outgo! So you must give me what you owe me."

By this time the cobbler had reached the chapel at the cross-roads, and he saw something white behind the chapel.

It was already twilight, and the cobbler strained his eyes, but he could not make out what the object was.

"There never was any such stone there," he said to himself. "A cow? But it does not look like a cow! The head is like a man's; but what is that white? And why should there be any man there?"

He went nearer. Now he could see plainly. What a strange thing! It was indeed a man, but was he alive or dead? sitting there stark naked, leaning against the chapel, and not moving.

The cobbler was frightened. He said to himself, "Some one has killed that man, stripped him, and flung him down there. If I go near, I may get into trouble."

And the cobbler hurried by.

In passing the chapel he could no longer see the man; but after he was fairly beyond it, he looked back, and saw that the man was no longer leaning against the chapel, but was moving, and apparently looking after him.

The cobbler was still more scared by this, and he said to himself, "Shall I go back to him or go on? If I go back to him, there might something unpleasant happen; who knows what sort of a man he is? He can't have gone there for any good purpose. If I went to him, he might spring on me and choke me, and I could not get away from him; and even if he did not choke me, why should I try to make his acquaintance? What could be done with him, naked as he is? I can't take him with me, and give him my own clothes! That would be absurd."

And the cobbler hastened his steps. He had already gone some distance beyond the chapel, when his conscience began to prick him.

He stopped short.

"What is this that you are doing, Semyon?" he asked himself. "A man is perishing of cold, and you are frightened, and hurry by! Are you so very rich? Are you afraid of losing your money? Aï, Sema! That is not right!"

Semyon turned and went back to the man.

II

Semyon went back to the man, looked at him, and saw that it was a young man in the prime of life; there were no bruises visible on him, but he was evidently freezing and afraid; he was sitting there, leaning back, and he did not look at Semyon; apparently he was so weak that he could not lift his eyes.

Semyon went up close to him, and suddenly the man seemed to revive; he lifted his head and fastened his eyes on Semyon.

And by this glance the man won Semyon's heart.

He threw the felt boots down on the ground, took off his belt and laid it on the boots, and pulled off his kaftan.

"There's nothing to be said," he exclaimed. "Put these on! There now!"

Semyon put his hand under the man's elbow, to help him, and tried to lift him. The man got up.

And Semyon saw that his body was graceful and clean, that his hands and feet were comely, and that his face was agreeable. Semyon threw the kaftan over his shoulders. He could not get his arms into the sleeves. Semyon found the place for him, pulled the coat up, wrapped it around him, and fastened the belt.

He took off his tattered cap, and was going to give it to the stranger, but his head felt cold, and he said to himself, "The whole top of my head is bald, but he has long curly hair."

So he put his hat on again.

"I had better let him put on my boots."

He made him sit down and put the felt boots on him.

After the cobbler had thus dressed him, he said: "There now, brother, just stir about, and you will get warmed up. All these things are in other hands than ours. Can you walk?"

The man stood up, looked affectionately at Semyon, but was unable to speak a word.

"Why don't you say something? We can't spend the winter here. We must get to shelter. Now, then, lean on my stick, if you don't feel strong enough. Bestir yourself!"

And the man started to move. And he walked easily, and did not lag behind. As they walked along the road Semyon said, "Where are you from, if I may ask?"

"I do not belong hereabouts."

"No; I know all the people of this region. How did you happen to come here and get to that chapel?"

"I cannot tell you."

"Some one must have treated you outrageously."

"No one has treated me outrageously. God has punished me."

"God does all things, but you must have been on the road bound for somewhere. Where do you want to go?"

"It makes no difference to me."

Semyon was surprised. The man did not look like a male-factor, and his speech was gentle, but he seemed reticent about himself.

And Semyon said to himself, "Such things as this do not happen every day." And he said to the man, "Well, come to my house, though you will find it very narrow quarters."

As Semyon approached the yard, the stranger did not lag behind, but walked abreast of him. The wind had arisen, and searched under Semyon's shirt, and as the effect of the wine had now passed away, he began to be chilled to the bone. He walked along and began to snuffle, and he muffled his wife's jacket closer around him, and he said to himself, "That's the way you get a shuba! You go after a shuba, and you come home without your kaftan! yes, and you bring with you a naked man—besides, Matriona won't take kindly to it!"

And as soon as the thought of Matriona occurred to him, he began to feel downhearted.

But as soon as his eyes fell on the stranger, he remembered what a look he had given him behind the chapel, and his heart danced with joy.

III

Semyon's wife had finished her work early. She had chopped wood, brought water, fed the children, taken her own supper, and was now deliberating when it would be best to mix some bread, "today or tomorrow?"

A large crust was still left. She said to herself, "If Semyon gets something to eat in town, he won't care for much supper, and the bread will last till tomorrow."

Matriona contemplated the crust for some time, and said, "I am not going to mix any bread. There's just enough flour to make one more loaf. We shall get along till Friday."

Matriona put away the bread, and sat down at the table to sew a patch on her husband's shirt.

She sewed, and thought how her husband would be buying sheepskins for the shuba.

"I hope the fur-dealer will not cheat him. For he is as simple as he can be. He, himself, would not cheat anybody, but a baby could lead him by the nose. Eight rubles is no small sum. You can get a fine shuba with it. Perhaps not one tanned, but still a good one. How we suffered last winter without any shuba! Could not go to the river nor anywhere! And whenever he went outdoors, he put on all the clothes, and I hadn't anything to wear. He is late in getting home. He ought to be here by this time. Can my sweetheart have got drunk?"

Just as these thoughts were passing through her mind the door-steps creaked: some one was at the door. Matriona stuck in the needle, and went to the entry. There she saw that two men had come in,—Semyon, and with him a strange peasant, without a cap and in felt boots.

Matriona perceived immediately that her husband's breath smelt of liquor.

"Now," she said to herself, "he has gone and got drunk."

And when she saw that he had not his kaftan on, and wore only her jacket, and had nothing in his hands, and said nothing, but only simpered, Matriona's heart failed within her.

"He has drunk up the money, he has been on a spree with this miserable beggar; and, worse than all, he has gone and brought him home!"

Matriona let them pass by her into the cottage; then she herself went in; she saw that the stranger was young, and that he had on their kaftan. There was no shirt to be seen under the kaftan; and he wore no cap.

As soon as he went in, he paused, and did not move and did not raise his eyes.

And Matriona thought, "He is not a good man; his conscience troubles him."

Matriona scowled, went to the oven, and watched to see what they would do.

Semyon took off his cap and sat down on the bench good-naturedly.

"Well," said he, "Matriona, can't you get us something to eat?"

Matriona muttered something under her breath.

She did not offer to move, but as she stood by the oven she looked from one to the other and kept shaking her head.

Semyon saw that his wife was out of sorts and would not do anything, but he pretended not to notice it, and took the stranger by the arm.

"Sit down, brother," said he; "we'll have some supper."

The stranger sat down on the bench.

"Well," said Semyon, "haven't you cooked anything?"

Matriona's anger blazed out.

"I cooked," said she, "but not for you. You are a fine man! I see you have been drinking! You went to get a shuba, and you have come home without your kaftan. And, then, you have brought home this naked vagabond with you. I haven't any supper for such drunkards as you are!"

"That'll do, Matriona; what is the use of letting your tongue run on so? If you had only asked first: 'What kind of a man . . .'"

"You just tell me what you have done with the money!"

Semyon went to his kaftan, took out the bill, and spread it out.

"Here's the money, but Trifonof did not pay me; he promised it tomorrow."

Matriona grew still more angry, "You didn't buy the new shuba, and you have given away your only kaftan to this naked vagabond whom you have brought home!"

She snatched the money from the table, and went off to hide it away, saying "I haven't any supper. I can't feed all your drunken beggars!"

"Hey there! Matriona, just hold your tongue! First you listen to what I have to say . . ."

"Much sense should I hear from a drunken fool! Good reason I had for not wanting to marry such a drunkard as you are. Mother gave me linen, and you have wasted it in drink; you went to get a shuba, and you spent it for drink."

Semyon was going to assure his wife that he had spent only twenty kopeks for drink; he was going to tell her where he had found the man; but Matriona would not give him a chance to speak a word; it was perfectly marvelous, but she managed to speak two words at once! Things that had taken place ten years before—she called them all up.

Matriona scolded and scolded; then she sprang at Semyon, and seized him by the sleeve.

"Give me back my jacket! It's the only one I have, and you took it from me and put it on yourself. Give it here, you miserable dog! bestir yourself, you villain!"

Semyon began to strip off the jacket. As he was pulling his arms out of the sleeves, his wife gave it a twitch and split the jacket up the seams. Matriona snatched the garment away, threw it over her head, and started for the door. She intended to go out, but she paused, and her heart was pulled in two directions,—she wanted to vent her spite, and she wanted to find what kind of a man the stranger was.

IV

Matriona paused, and said, "If he were a good man, then he would not have been naked; why, even now, he hasn't any shirt on; if he had been engaged in decent business, you would have told where you discovered such an elegant fellow!"

"Well, I was going to tell you. I was walking along, and there, behind the chapel, this man was sitting, stark naked, and half frozen to death. It is not summer, mind you, for a naked man! God brought me to him, else he would have perished. Now what could I do? Such things don't happen every day. I took and dressed him, and brought him home with me. Calm your anger. It's a sin, Matriona; we must all die."

Matriona was about to make a surly reply, but her eyes fell on the stranger, and she held her peace.

The stranger was sitting motionless on the edge of the bench, just as he had sat down. His hands were folded on his knees, his head was bent on his breast, his eyes were shut, and he kept frowning, as if something stifled him.

Matriona made no reply.

Semyon went on to say, "Matriona, can it be that God is not in you?"

Matriona heard his words, and glanced again at the stranger, and suddenly her anger vanished. She turned from the door, went to the corner where the oven was, and brought the supper.

She set a bowl on the table, poured out the kvas,[2] and put on the last of the crust. She gave them the knife and the spoons.

"Have some victuals," she said.

Semyon touched the stranger.

"Draw up, young man," said he.

Semyon cut the bread and crumbled it into the bowl, and they began to eat their supper. And Matriona sat at the end of the table, leaned on her hand, and gazed at the stranger. And Matriona began to feel sorry for him, and she took a fancy to him.

And suddenly the stranger brightened up, ceased to frown, lifted his eyes to Matriona, and smiled.

After they had finished their supper, the woman cleared off the things, and began to question the stranger "Where are you from?"

"I do not belong hereabouts."

"How did you happen to get into this road?"

"I cannot tell you."

"Who maltreated you?"

"God punished me."

"And you were lying there stripped?"

"Yes; there I was lying all naked, freezing to death, when Semyon saw me, had compassion on me, took off his kaftan, put it on me, and bade me come home with him. And here you have fed me, given me something to eat and to drink, and have taken pity on me. May the Lord requite you!"

Matriona got up, took from the window Semyon's old shirt which she had been patching, and gave it to the stranger; then she found a pair of drawers and gave them also to him.

"There now," said she, "I see that you have no shirt. Put these things on, and then lie down wherever you please, in the loft or on the oven."

The stranger took off the kaftan, put on the shirt, and went to bed in the loft. Matriona put out the light, took the kaftan, and lay down beside her husband.

Matriona covered herself up with the skirt of the kaftan, but she lay without sleeping; she could not get the thought of the stranger out of her mind.

When she remembered that he had eaten her last crust, and that there was no bread for the morrow, when she remembered that she had given him the shirt and the drawers, she felt disturbed; but then came the thought of how he had smiled at her, and her heart leaped within her.

Matriona lay a long time without falling asleep, and when she heard that Semyon was also awake, she pulled up the kaftan, and said, "Semyon!"

"Ha?"

"You ate up the last of the bread, and I did not mix any more. I don't know how we shall get along tomorrow. Perhaps I might borrow some of neighbor Malanya."

"We shall get along; we shall have enough."

The wife lay without speaking. Then she said, "Well, he seems like a good man; but why doesn't he tell us about himself?"

"It must be because he can't."

"Siom!"[3]

"Ha?"

"We are always giving; why doesn't some one give to us?"

Semyon did not know what reply to make. He said, "You have talked enough!"

Then he turned over and went to sleep.

V

In the morning Semyon woke up.

His children were still asleep; his wife had gone to a neighbor's to get some bread. The stranger of the evening before, dressed in the old shirt and drawers, was sitting alone on the bench, looking up. And his face was brighter than it had been the evening before. And Semyon said, "Well, my dear, the belly asks for bread, and the naked body for clothes. You must earn your own living. What do you know how to do?"

"There is nothing that I know how to do."

Semyon was amazed, and he said, "If one has only the mind to, men can learn anything."

"Men work, and I will work."

"What is your name?"

"Mikhaïla."

"Well, Mikhaïla, if you aren't willing to tell about yourself, that is your affair; but you must earn your own living. If you will work as I show you, I will keep you."

"The Lord requite you! I am willing to learn; only show me what to do."

Semyon took a thread, drew it through his fingers, and showed him how to make a waxed end.

"It does not take much skill . . . look . . ."

Mikhaïla looked, and then he also twisted the thread between his fingers; he instantly imitated him, and finished the point.

Semyon showed him how to make the welt. This also Mikhaïla immediately understood. The shoemaker likewise showed him how to twist the bristle into the thread, and how to use the awl; and these things also Mikhaïla immediately learned to do.

Whatever part of the work Semyon showed him he imitated him in, and in two days he was able to work as if he had been all his life a cobbler. He worked without relaxation, he ate little, and when his work was done he would sit silent, looking up. He did not go on the street, he spoke no more than was absolutely necessary, he never jested, he never laughed.

The only time that he was seen to smile was on the first evening, when the woman got him his supper.

VI

Day after day, week after week, rolled by for a whole year. Mikhaïla lived on in the same way, working for Semyon.

And the fame of Semyon's apprentice went abroad; no one, it was said, could make such neat, strong boots as Semyon's apprentice, Mikhaïla. And from all around people came to Semyon to have boots made, and Semyon began to lay up money.

One winter's day, as Semyon and Mikhaïla were sitting at their work, a sleigh drawn by a troïka drove up to the cottage, with a jingling of bells.

They looked out of the window; the sleigh stopped in front of the cottage; a footman jumped down from the box and opened the door. A barin[4] in a fur coat got out of the sleigh, walked up to Semyon's cottage, and mounted the steps. Matriona hurried to throw the door wide open.

The barin bent his head and entered the cottage; when he drew himself up to his full height, his head almost touched the ceiling; he seemed to take up nearly all the room.

Semyon rose and bowed; he was surprised to see the barin. He had never before seen such a man.

Semyon himself was thin, the stranger was spare, and Matriona was like a dry chip; but this man seemed to be from a different world. His face was ruddy and full, his neck was like a bull's; it seemed as if he were made out of cast-iron.

The barin got his breath, took off his shuba, sat down on the bench, and said, "Which is the master shoemaker?"

Semyon stepped out, saying, "I, your honor."

The barin shouted to his footman, "Hey, Fedka,[5] bring me the leather."

The young fellow ran out and brought back a parcel. The barin took the parcel and laid it on the table.

"Open it," said he.

The footman opened it.

The barin touched the leather with his finger, and said to Semyon, "Now listen, shoemaker. Do you see this leather?"

"I see it, your honor," said he.

"Well, do you appreciate what kind of leather it is?"

Semyon felt of the leather, and said, "That's good leather."

"Indeed it's good! Fool that you are! you never in your life saw such before! German leather. It cost twenty rubles."

Semyon was startled. He said, "Where, indeed, could we have seen anything like it?"

"Well, that's all right. Can you make from this leather a pair of boots that will fit me?"

"I can, your honor."

The barin shouted at him, " 'Can' is a good word. Now just realize whom you are making those boots for, and out of what kind of leather. You must make a pair of boots, so that when the year is gone they won't have got out of shape, or ripped. If you can, then take the job and cut the leather; but if you can't, then don't take it and don't cut the leather. I will tell you beforehand, if the boots rip or wear out of shape before the year is out, I will have you locked up; but if they don't rip or get out of shape before the end of the year, then I will give you ten rubles for your work."

Semyon was frightened, and was at a loss what to say.

He glanced at Mikhaïla. He nudged him with his elbow, and whispered, "Had I better take it?"

Mikhaïla nodded his head, meaning, "You had better take the job."

Semyon took Mikhaïla's advice; he agreed to make a pair of boots that would not rip or wear out of shape before the year was over.

The barin shouted to his footman, ordered him to take the boot from his left foot; then he stretched out his leg, "Take the measure!"

Semyon cut off a piece of paper seventeen inches long, smoothed it out, knelt down, wiped his hands nicely on his apron, so as not to soil the barin's stockings, and began take the measure.

Semyon took the measure of the sole, he took the measure of the instep; then he started to measure the calf of the leg, but the paper was not long enough. The leg at the calf was as thick as a beam.

"Look out; don't make it too tight around the calf!"

Semyon was going to cut another piece of paper. The barin sat there, rubbing his toes together in his stockings, and looking at the inmates of the cottage; he caught sight of Mikhaïla.

"Who is that yonder?" he asked; "does he belong to you?"

"He is a master workman. He will make the boots."

"Look here," says the barin to Mikhaïla, "remember that they are to be made so as to last a whole year."

Semyon also looked at Mikhaïla; he saw that Mikhaïla was paying no attention, but was standing in the corner, as if he saw some one there behind the barin. Mikhaïla gazed and gazed, and suddenly smiled, and his whole face lighted up.

"What a fool you are, showing your teeth that way! You had better see to it that the boots are ready in time."

And Mikhaïla replied, "They will be ready as soon as they are needed."

"Very well."

The barin drew on his boot, wrapped his shuba round him, and went to the door. But he forgot to stoop, and so struck his head against the lintel.

The barin stormed and rubbed his head; then he got into his sleigh and drove off. After the barin was gone Semyon said, "Well, he's as solid as a rock! You could not kill him with a mallet. His head almost broke the doorpost, but it did not seem to hurt him much."

And Matriona said, "How can they help getting fat, living as they do? Even death does not carry off such a nail as he is."

VII

And Semyon said to Mikhaïla, "Now, you see, we have taken this work, and we must do it as well as we can. The leather is expensive, and the barin gruff. We must not make any blunder. Now, your eye has become quicker, and your hand is more skilful, than mine; there's the measure. Cut out the leather, and I will be finishing up those vamps."

Mikhaïla did not fail to do as he was told; he took the barin's leather, stretched it out on the table, doubled it over, took the knife, and began to cut.

Matriona came and watched Mikhaïla as he cut, and she was amazed to see what he was doing. For she was used to cobbler's work, and she looked and saw that Mikhaïla was not cutting the leather for boots, but in rounded fashion.

Matriona wanted to speak, but she thought in her own mind, "Of course I can't be expected to understand how to make boots for gentlemen; Mikhaïla must understand it better than I do; I will not interfere."

After he had cut out the work, he took his waxed ends and began to sew, not as one does in making boots, with double threads, but with one thread, just as slippers are made.

Matriona wondered at this also, but still she did not like to interfere. And Mikhaïla kept on steadily with his work.

It came time for the nooning; Semyon got up, looked, and saw that Mikhaïla had been making slippers out of the barin's leather. Semyon groaned.

"How is this?" he asked himself. "Mikhaïla has lived with me a whole year, and never made a mistake, and now he has made such a blunder! The barin ordered thick-soled boots, and he has been making slippers without soles! He has ruined the leather. How can I make it right with the barin? We can't find such leather."

And he said to Mikhaïla, "What is this you have been doing? . . . My dear fellow, you have ruined me! You know the barin ordered boots, and what have you made?"

He was in the midst of his talk with Mikhaïla when a

knock came at the rapper; some one was at the door. They looked out of the window, some one had come on horseback, and was fastening the horse. They opened the door. The same barin's footman came walking in.

"Good-day."

"Good-day to you; what is it?"

"My mistress sent me in regard to a pair of boots."

"What about the boots?"

"It is this. My barin does not need the boots; he has gone from this world."

"What is that you say?"

"He did not live to get home from your house; he died in the sleigh. When the sleigh reached home, we went to help him out, but there he had fallen over like a bag, and there he lay stone dead, and it took all our strength to lift him out of the sleigh. And his lady has sent me, saying: 'Tell the shoemaker of whom your barin just ordered boots from leather which he left with him—tell him that the boots are not needed, and that he is to make a pair of slippers for the corpse out of that leather just as quick as possible.' And I was to wait till they were made, and take them home with me. And so I have come."

Mikhaïla took the rest of the leather from the table and rolled it up; he also took the slippers, which were all done, slapped them together, wiped them with his apron, and gave them to the young man. The young man took them.

"Good-by, friends! Good luck to you!"

VIII

Still another year, and then two more passed by, and Mikhaïla had now been living five years with Semyon. He lived in just the same way as before. He never went anywhere, he kept his own counsels, and in all that time he smiled only twice—once when Matriona gave him something to eat, and the other time when he smiled on the barin.

Semyon was more than contented with his workman, and he no longer asked him where he came from; his only fear was lest Mikhaïla should leave him.

One time they were all at home. The mother was putting the iron kettles on the oven, and the children were playing on the benches and looking out of the window. Semyon was pegging away at one window, and Mikhaïla at the other was putting lifts on a heel.

One of the boys ran along the bench toward Mikhaïla, leaned over his shoulder, and looked out of the window.

"Uncle Mikhaïla, just look! a merchant's wife is coming to our house with some little girls. And one of the little girls is a cripple."

The words were scarcely out of the boy's mouth before Mikhaïla threw down his work, leaned over toward the window, and looked out-of-doors. And Semyon was surprised. Never before had Mikhaïla cared to look out, but now his face seemed soldered to the window; he was looking at something very intently.

Semyon also looked out of the window: he saw a woman coming straight through his yard; she was neatly dressed; she had two little girls by the hand; they wore shubkas,[6] and kerchiefs over their heads. The little girls looked so much alike that it was hard to tell them apart, except that one of the little girls was lame in her foot; she limped as she walked.

The woman came into the entry, felt about in the dark, lifted the latch, and opened the door. She let the two little girls go before her into the cottage, and then she followed.

"How do you do, friends?"

"Welcome! What can we do for you?"

The woman sat down by the table; the two little girls clung to her knee; they were bashful.

"These little girls need to have some goatskin shoes made for the spring."

"Well, it can be done. We don't generally make such small ones; but it's perfectly easy, either with welts or lined with linen. This here is Mikhaïla; he's my master workman."

Semyon glanced at Mikhaïla and saw that he had thrown down his work, and was sitting with his eyes fastened on the little girls.

And Semyon was amazed at Mikhaïla. To be sure the little girls were pretty; they had dark eyes, they were plump and rosy, and they wore handsome shubkas and kerchiefs; but still Semyon could not understand why he gazed so intently at them, as if they were friends of his.

Semyon was amazed, and he began to talk with the woman, and to make his bargain. After he had made his bargain, he began to take the measures. The woman lifted on her lap the little cripple, and said, "Take two measures from this one; make one little shoe from the twisted foot, and three from the well one. Their feet are alike; they are twins."

Semyon took his tape, and said in reference to the little cripple, "How did this happen to her? She is such a pretty little girl. Was she born so?"

"No; her mother crushed it."

Matriona joined the conversation; she was anxious to learn

who the woman and children were, and so she said, "Then you aren't their mother?"

"No, I am not their mother; I am no relation to them, good wife, and they are no relation to me at all; I adopted them."

"If they are not your children, you take good care of them."

"Why shouldn't I take good care of them? I nursed them both at my own breast. I had a baby of my own, but God took him. I did not take such good care of him as I do of these."

"Whose children are they?"

IX

The woman became confidential, and began to tell them about it.

"Six years ago," said she, "these little ones were left orphans in one week; the father was buried on Tuesday, and the mother died on Friday. Three days these little ones remained without their father, and then their mother followed him. At that time I was living with my husband in the country: we were neighbors; we lived in adjoining yards. Their father was a peasant, and worked in the forest at wood-cutting. And they were felling a tree, and it caught him across the body. It hurt him all inside. As soon as they got him out, he gave his soul to God, and that same week his wife gave birth to twins—these are the little girls here. There they were, poor and alone, no one to take care of them, either grandmother or sister.

"She must have died soon after the children were born. For when I went in the morning to look after my neighbor, as soon as I entered the cottage, I found the poor thing dead and cold. And when she died she must have rolled over on this little girl. . . . That's the way she crushed it, and spoiled this foot.

"The people got together, they washed and laid out the body, they had a coffin made, and buried her. The people were always kind. But the two little ones were left alone. What was to be done with them? Now I was the only one of the women who had a baby. For eight weeks I had been nursing my firstborn, a boy. So I took them for the time being. The peasants got together; they planned and planned what to do with them, and they said to me, 'Marya, you just keep the little girls for a while, and give us a chance to decide.'

"So I nursed the well one for a while, but did not think it worth while to nurse the deformed one. I did not expect that she was going to live. And, then, I thought to myself, why should the little angel's soul pass away? and I felt sorry for it. I tried to nurse her, and so I had my own and these two besides; yes, I had three children at the breast. But I was young and strong, and I had good food! And God gave me so much milk in my breasts that I had enough and to spare. I used to nurse two at once and let the third one wait. When one had finished, I would take up the third. And so God let me nurse all three; but when my boy was in his third year, I lost him. And God never gave me any more children. But we began to be in comfortable circumstances. And now we are living with the trader at the mill. We get good wages and live well. But we have no children of our own. And how lonely it would be, if it were not for these two little girls! How could I help loving them? They are to me like the wax in the candle!"

And the woman pressed the little lame girl to her with one arm, and with the other hand she tried to wipe the tears from her cheeks.

And Matriona sighed, and said, "The old saw isn't far wrong, 'Men can live without father and mother, but without God one cannot live.' "

While they were thus talking together, suddenly a flash of lightning seemed to irradiate from that corner of the cottage where Mikhaïla was sitting. All looked at him; and, behold! Mikhaïla was sitting there with his hands folded in his lap, and looking up and smiling.

X

The woman went away with the children, and Mikhaïla arose from the bench and laid down his work; he took off his apron, made a low bow to the shoemaker and his wife, and said, "Farewell, friends; God has forgiven me. Do you also forgive me?"

And Semyon and Matriona perceived that it was from Mikhaïla that the light had flashed. And Semyon arose, bowed low before Mikhaïla, and said to him, "I see, Mikhaïla, that you are not a mere man, and I have no right to detain you nor to ask questions of you. But tell me one thing: when I had found you and brought you home, you were sad; but when my wife gave you something to eat, you smiled on her, and after that you became more cheerful. And then when the barin ordered the boots, why did you smile a second time, and after that become still more cheerful; and now when this woman brought these two little girls, why did you smile for the third time and become perfectly radiant? Tell me, Mikhaïla, why was it that such a light streamed from you, and why you smiled three times?"

And Mikhaïla said, "The light blazed from me because I had been punished, but now God has forgiven me. And I smiled the three times because it was required of me to learn three of God's truths, and I have now learned the three truths of God. One truth I learned when your wife had pity on me, and so I smiled; the second truth I learned when the rich man ordered the boots, and I smiled for the second time; and now that I have seen the little girls, I have learned the third and last truth, and I smiled for the third time."

And Semyon said, "Tell me, Mikhaïla, why God punished you, and what were the truths of God, that I, too, may know them."

And Mikhaïla said, "God punished me because I disobeyed Him. I was an angel in heaven, and I was disobedient to God. I was an angel in heaven, and the Lord sent me to bring back the soul of a certain woman. I flew down to earth and I saw the woman lying alone—she was sick—she had just borne twins, two little girls. The little ones were sprawling about near their mother, but their mother was unable to lift them to her breast. The mother saw me; she perceived that God had sent me after her soul; she burst into tears, and said, 'Angel of God, I have just buried my husband; a tree fell on him in the forest and killed him. I have no sister, nor aunt, nor mother to take care of my little ones; do not carry off my soul; let me bring up my children myself, and nurse them and put them on their feet. It is impossible for children to live without father or mother.'

"And I heeded what the mother said; I put one child to her breast, and laid the other in its mother's arms, and I returned to the Lord in heaven. I flew back to the Lord, and I said, 'I cannot take the mother's soul. The father has been killed by a tree, the mother has given birth to twins, and begs me not to take her soul; she says, ' "Let me bring up my little ones; let me nurse them and put them on their feet. It is impossible for children to live without father and mother." I did not take the mother's soul.'

"And the Lord said, 'Go and take the mother's soul, and thou shalt learn three lessons: Thou shalt learn *what is in men*, and *what is not given unto men*, and *what men live by*. When thou shalt have learned these three lessons, then return to heaven.'

"And I flew down to earth and took the mother's soul. The little ones fell from her bosom. The dead body rolled over on the bed, and fell on one of the little girls and crushed her foot. I rose above the village and was going to give the soul to God, when a wind seized me, my wings ceased to move and fell off, and the soul arose alone to God, and I fell back to earth."

XI

And Semyon and Matriona now knew whom they had clothed and fed, and who it was that had been living with them, and they burst into tears of dismay and joy; and the angel said, "I was there in the field naked and alone. Hitherto I had never known what human poverty was; I had known neither cold nor hunger, and now I was a man. I was famished, I was freezing, and I knew not what to do. And I saw across the field a chapel made for God's service. I went to God's chapel, thinking to get shelter in it. But the chapel was locked, and I could not enter. And I crouched down behind the chapel, so as to get shelter from the wind. Evening came; I was hungry and chilled, and ached all over. Suddenly I heard a man walking along the road, with a pair of boots in his hand, and talking to himself. I now saw for the first time since I had become a man the face of a mortal man, and it filled me with dismay, and I tried to hide from him. And I heard this man asking himself how he should protect himself from cold during the winter, and how get food for his wife and children. And I thought, 'I am perishing with cold and hunger, and here is a man whose sole thought is to get a shuba for himself and his wife and to furnish bread for their sustenance. It is impossible for him to help me.'

"The man saw me and scowled; he seemed even more terrible than before; then he passed on. And I was in despair. Suddenly I heard the man coming back. I looked up, and did not recognize that it was the same man as before; then there was death in his face, but now it had suddenly become alive, and I saw that God was in his face. He came to me, put clothes on me, and took me home with him.

"When I reached his house, a woman came out to meet us, and she began to scold. The woman was even more terrible to me than the man; a dead soul seemed to proceed forth from her mouth, and I was suffocated by the stench of death. She wanted to drive me out into the cold, and I knew that she would die if she drove me out. And suddenly her husband reminded her of God. And instantly a change came over the woman. And when she had prepared something for me to eat, and looked kindly on me, I looked at her, and there was no longer anything like death about her; she was now alive, and in her also I recognized God.

"And I remembered God's first lesson: '*Thou shalt learn what is in men.*'

"And I perceived that LOVE was in men. And I was glad because God had begun to fulfil His promise to me, and I smiled for the first time. But I was not yet ready to know the whole. I could not understand what was not given to men, and what men lived by.

"I began to live in your house, and after I had lived with you a year the man came to order the boots which should be strong enough to last him a year without ripping or wearing out of shape. And I looked at him, and suddenly perceived behind his back my comrade, the Angel of Death. No one besides myself saw this angel; but I knew him, and I knew that before the sun should go down he would take the rich man's soul. And I said to myself: 'This man is laying his plans to live another year, and he knows not that ere evening comes he will be dead.'

"And I realized suddenly the second saying of God: *'Thou shalt know what is not given unto men.'*

"And now I knew what was in men. And now I knew also what was not given unto men. It is not given unto men to know what is needed for their bodies. And I smiled for the second time. I was glad because I saw my comrade, the angel, and because God had revealed unto me the second truth.

"But I could not yet understand all. I could not understand what men live by, and so I lived on, and waited until God should reveal to me the third truth also. And now in the sixth year the little twin girls have come with the woman, and I recognized the little ones, and I remembered how they had been left. And after I had recognized them, I thought, 'The mother besought me in behalf of her children, because she thought that it would be impossible for children to live without father and mother, but another woman, a stranger, has nursed them and brought them up.'

"And when the woman caressed the children that were not her own, and wept over them, then I saw in her the living God, and knew *what people live by.* And I knew that God had revealed to me the last truth, and had pardoned me, and I smiled for the third time."

XII

And the angel's body became manifest, and he was clad with light so bright that the eyes could not endure to look on him, and he spoke in clearer accents, as if the voice proceeded not from him, but came from heaven.

And the angel said, "I have learned that every man lives, not through care of himself, but by love.

"It was not given to the mother to know what her children needed to keep them alive. It was not given the rich man to know what he himself needed, and it is not given to any man to know whether he will need boots for daily living, or slippers for his burial.

"When I became a man, I was kept alive, not by what thought I took for myself, but because a stranger and his wife had love in their hearts, and pitied and loved me. The orphans were kept alive, not because other people deliberated about what was to be done with them, but because a strange woman had love for them in her heart, and pitied them and loved them. And all men are kept alive, not by their own forethought, but because there is LOVE IN MEN.

"I knew before that God gave life to men, and desired them to live; but now I know something above and beyond that.

"I have learned that God does not wish men to live each for himself, and therefore He has not revealed to them what they each need for themselves, but He wishes them to live in union, and therefore He has revealed to them what is necessary for each and for all together.

"I have now learned that it is only in appearance that they are kept alive through care for themselves, but that in reality they are kept alive through love. *He who dwelleth in love, dwelleth in God, and God in him, for God is Love.*"

And the angel sang a hymn of praise to God, and the cottage shook with the sound of his voice.

And the ceiling parted, and a column of fire reached from earth to heaven. And Semyon and his wife and children fell prostrate on the ground. And pinions appeared on the angel's shoulders, and he soared away to heaven.

And when Semyon opened his eyes, the cottage was the same as it had ever been, and there was no one in it save himself and his family.

NOTES

1. Fur or sheepskin outside garment.
2. Fermented drink made of rye meal or soaked bread-crumbs.
3. Diminutive of Semyon, or Simon.
4. The ordinary title of any landowner or noble.
5. Diminutive of Feodor, Theodore.
6. Little fur garments.

PART TWO

THE PATHOLOGIES OF LOVE

When the pathologies of love were first scientifically studied the emphasis was on their sexual aspects. Sadistic and masochistic behavior, homosexuality, exhibitionism, voyeurism, fetishism, transvestism, impotence and frigidity and other forms of inhibited or withheld love—all were indiscriminately lumped together as "perversions," "aberrations," "sexual anomalies," etc. Gradually it came to be understood that other manifestations such as anti-social attitudes, extremes of egoism, dependence, alienation, hypochondria and other irrational fears, manias, phobias, addictions, withdrawal, self-abasement, etc., were, perhaps, even more meaningful symptoms of disorders of love. It is significant that in the writings of the Marquis de Sade, whose name has since served to classify the pathology called sadism, *the cruelties described are frequently dissociated from a sexual partner or a sexual act; and that, similarly, in the writings of von Sacher-Masoch, whose name has been used for the contrasting and complementary type of pathology, sexual pleasure in suffering, it is emotional torments such as humiliation, betrayal and rejection that figure even more than the floggings used as preliminaries to intercourse, in procuring the gratifying pains sought by the victim.*

Revealing clues have come in the study of disturbed chil-

*dren where it was possible to see these pathologies in their early
stages and sometimes in the process of formation. The manifestations were more often social than sexual, the symptoms appearing
in the classroom, in home relationships, and in group play. They
included overaggressiveness or excessive shyness or causeless rebellion. It became clear from these and related studies that the
understanding of sexual pathology requires a larger frame, that,
in fact, its symptoms were related to more comprehensive
pathologies of love.*

*From this there was but a step to the new concept, now
gaining ground in all fields of study concerned with human behavior, the concept of the pathologies of love as deficiencies of
growth. At first the step was taken by extending sexual terms.
Oral, anal, and genital eroticism were applied to non-sexual
behavior but with continued sexual implications. Gradually, however, the emphasis was reversed and sexual pathologies were
viewed as disorders of love in the broadest sense and as disorders
in the growth of the capacity for love.*

*To return to the terms we have found most serviceable
here—if in a person's development there is no advance beyond
need-love, he may mature physically but not emotionally. In his
relations he may remain a child, dependent, demanding, able to
take but not to give. He is likely, sooner or later, to show recognizable pathological traits like narcissism, sadism, egoism, exhibitionism or homosexuality rooted in domination. If, similarly,
there is no advance beyond gift-love, if he can only give and fears
to take, masochistic traits may appear, self-abasement, homosexuality rooted in submission, and associated pathologies of
behavior.*

*Seldom, however, is the picture a clear one. There are no
sharp borders in human growth, no limit to the varieties and sub-
tleties of human relationships. The result is a confusing diversity
of forms and shades. But where studies are pursued far enough
they almost unfailingly reveal early deficiencies or distortions in
the person's background which malformed his development and
arrested his growth toward that mutual giving and taking, that
reciprocity of need and fullness that mark mature love.*

I

Love and Personal Disorder

CARLO LEVI: Love Sacred and Profane*

Nor may I listen to him who reasons not upon my death.[1]

OUT OF the forest, into the bright light bestowed by a smile of eyes benign—what mortal mood is this, what bitter sense of death? Why does death alone seem company to love, why must the world be fled, and why the chains and the renouncement? To romantic lovers, whose love despairs of anything but mystic fusion, death is the one attainment left for love; it is the blackness of the woods returning, filled with uncertain spasms and distant tremors, and the remote fanfare of the king's hunt. Eternal night without a shape or shore, such is love's own and sacred indistinction: and the beloved face is of the shades of night. For total fusion knows no freedom, will, or gods—only the blind compulsion of deep primeval darkness.

Of another death speaks the humanistic poet, a willing death, a sacrifice, a servitude of love. No more fears of darkness, nor blowing winds of hell: but waters clear, green meadows, and light of days serene. Though even here, in the shades of laurels, a death lies hidden, like a snake amid flowers and grass.

It was woman, indeed, who brought the world out of the black northern forests, peopled by monsters and sullen hierarchies. The damsel had waited for many a century upon her reef, guarded by feudal dragons, pining for the bold warrior who would come and break her chains: him, in turn, she made a free man. Troubadours of Provence and poets of the *Dolce Stil Nuovo*, the sweet new style, had placed her on the altars, the star and goddess of their rhymes: but the burden of their songs was the human and

* Reprinted from *Of Fear and Freedom.*

the free, and not the divine. Barbarous male gods gave way before
the smiling Grace: the tongues were loosened and freed from religious reverence, changing their accents and sounds. Femininity's
advent had given the world a new dimension, a perspective which
renovated thought and syntax, language and painting. The greatest of revolutions was flourishing, like all revolutions, under a
benign female deity. Europe returned to womanhood; and the
deity's signs were, in truth, nothing but memories from the former days of feudal gods. Free courts of love were superseding the
cruel courts of lords, and retaining solely their name and ceremonial; and it is singular that "courtship," "courting," "courtesy,"
derive from the usages of male and heroic times. The sacred
hierarchies of vassalage come to an end when amorous vassalage
is chosen. The inarticulate yell of hunter-kings gives way to feminine speech and human sweetness. Who could

> For such a wild and barbarous delight
> Forsake the ladies' pleasurable light?[2]

Thereafter, even the memory vanishes of the old gods, and
love profane runs free and sensual in the cities and through the
fields, where the priest of Varlungo, amid chestnuts and onions
new, lies with fair Monna Belcolore.[3] Free are the tongues, not
hidden any more in the obscurity of sacred Latin; free the pursuits of commerce, no longer shameful nor forbidden, but open
now to every Christian; free are the arts and crafts from Byzantine
indifference; free, the relations between men, from symbols, hierarchies and serfdom. And man felt evermore inclined to a personal separate life, to a world impelled by interests and ambitions,
resting entirely upon earth, and without gods. However, after the
first happy flowering of a creative and impassioned liberty, Italian
society broke up into a thousand distinct atoms, partaking no
more in the sacred community, but intent with barren appetite
of life, upon the merchant's endeavors, the interests of cold reason
and the exercise of love. Thence, an impression of void and of
peril—and also, from too much liberty, a sense of precariousness
and the dread of happiness itself. From these vague and human
fears new religions were taking shape—be it that the new lords
and masters were reasserting the sacred nature of their strength,
or that men of letters and artists were idolizing beauty, so that
Giotto and Boccaccio, the most free of spirits, already show the
first Latin signs of the coming academies. And man, who had
found himself again, himself and his woman, feels the need of
excluding her, once more, and of making her a goddess—for the
burden of an uncertain liberty weighs upon him. No more a
generical goddess of womanhood, Beatrix of freedom and felicity;

but a particular divinity, with a name all her own, with her own eyes and hair and face. And, being a deity, she is a stranger and enemy:

> So fierce was she, this enemy of mine,
> And her I saw, her very heart was wounded.[4]

Not freedom any more, but religion is now the basis for relationship with the adored enemy, and her we owe the sacrifice of self. This is the way to servitude of love, a willing servitude in the beginning:

> Then did I wander, when the ancient gates
> Of liberty were shut and locked before me
> . . . .
> Free at the start upon the path of sorrow
> Yet now, alas, in bondage to another
> Must go my soul, which sinnéd only once.[5]

There is an initial sin—idolatry. But this sin once accepted, the servitude and death which ensue are only natural, for they alone confirm Laura's divinity, while giving truth and certainty to love. It is a wandering, a meandering through labyrinths, a failure to recognize one's own face, a renouncement of world and life, a continuous self-offering, a will to die, which save, however, both the idol and the believer, and which become eternal law and sacred scripture to the new religion of love. Without such religion, the thousand rites and interdictions, the spell of servitude and enchantment, would have no meaning—and they have none, indeed, in the unspeakable vortex of sacred love, and none in the pure sensuousness of love profane, and none in free love's creative comprehension. Weariness of liberty, unsatisfied senses, fear of the indistinctness of human communion generate the religion of love. And despite the tears and the wailing, sacrifice seems a lesser evil than the peril of freedom in the midst of passion:

> Sighing for that which never would return
> I said: The burden and the chains of serfdom
> Were sweeter than this wandering alone.[6]

Petrarch, this greater Cézanne, under the same skies of Provence, was feeling and summing up the days of liberty gone by and the needs of the new religion: needs of the inmost soul, entirely human terrors, idolatrous quest of salvation.

This historical experience, which we find manifesting itself throughout the centuries and made eternal in art, is equal to the single experience of every man in its various phases, and in the various aspects of each phase. Sacred love, in its limitless power, is anarchy and does not allow any act, but solely a need, indefinite and lethal: such love cannot turn to any particular woman, but only dwell in its own self, in this chaotic oneness from which it proceeds and to which it tends to return. This unbounded potency is impotence. Here man is panting to be one with woman, with all women, in the entirety of an undifferentiated sexuality, in the complete surrender of fusion: the lover is unable to tell himself from his love or to set amorous bounds to the person beloved. And therefore, the gods of this terror must be themselves sexually indeterminate and double, or conversely—excessively male and female. Hence, in the most ancient mythologies, hermaphrodite and mutable deities coexist with other gods, consisting entirely of sex, erection and orgasm. The essential rite of these religions is *castration*, and, in a more civilized way, chastity—or the measureless blind embraces in the temples of India and Egypt, of Phoenicia and Syria, which correspond, in an opposite sense, to castration and chastity.

Circumcision may also be considered, from this point of view, as an equivalent for castration—and one should not be astonished at this additional meaning: each of these ritual acts may really have an infinite number of coexisting meanings, for infinite, also, are the terrors and the gods.

In order to know that these ambiguous deities, which are both day and night, summer and winter, sun and moon, man and woman, compel us to the sacrifice of abstinence and castration—each of us need only look inside himself. Blushing cheeks are evidence enough, without resorting to the thousands of observations made by psychiatrists and biologists, to the thousands of novels and tragedies which tell with infinite variety of moods the same romance of sacred terror and religious sacrifice. The impotence peculiar to youth is a religious defense against a premature communion, which would mean the loss of self. If a person has not yet acquired a distinct shape, how could he possibly unite with another one without melting away, or even perceive the other one's existence? Love and liberty are born together.

All things considered, sacred love is an impossibility: it leads to death even before the start. Such love, made religion, prevents its own fulfilment and thus procures salvation from that death. A voiceless abyss where all seeds are mingled, a shoreless sea which no eye may behold, a crossing from which no living soul ever returns—this is sacred love: deep black waters.

Nevertheless, in these waters, somebody is preening himself and smiling at himself, somebody who is everybody: Narcissus. Man is not yet adult; he is not free enough to recognize the *other*: but the need of love is born already, a need which makes one's own self appear as the other, and which turns inward the groping of desire. Inside, where there is nothing but waters and depth, Narcissus thinks to find another self, responding to his smile, another self which may be loved as an equal, and not dreaded like a woman or a god. But this other one is merely an image, an aerial fantasy—and this embrace too, is mortal.

Narcissus has always existed, even before the Greeks made him into a graceful myth: he is eternal. But the time which truly fits him best is that in which a vital yearning for liberty and love is thwarted or not yet fully grown: therefore, the seventeenth century, the *seicento*, lifts the sign of Narcissus upon its banners in Caravaggio's style, and reacts to the Counter-Reformation by shrinking into its own self, by retiring into its innermost depth, mirrored in the sensuous curves of the baroque. This was a time like our own, of prisons and youthful solitude:

> From my solitudes I come,
> To my solitudes I go,
> For, to stay with my own self,
> My thoughts are company enough.[7]

Not in this solitude, still anarchical, but in another and democratic one, in the midst of the numberless crowd, stands the man who is too grown up, who is entirely segregated, limited and individual, entirely out of touch with the indefinite common, deprived of sacred powers and sacred terrors, and living without freedom and without gods. Others are present, of course, but inaccessible, because there no longer exists the tie that could unite them in mutual comprehension. Human relations are wholly external, and very easy, because they are non-existent. Modesty, restraint, truthfulness, chastity, impotence make no sense any more, and there are no more interdictions, or servitude, except the bonds of interest and usage. Even reality is gone; profane love is no love, and it does not lead to a death only because it proceeds from a death. Miserable are the triumphs of the individual:

> Old ones also are his pleasure
> For the boast of a full measure . . .[8]

until the terror of his own barrenness drives him again into idolatry. One single and definite woman becomes the goddess of a private cult; and rarely indeed does she attain, by grace of poetry, the level of the divine. Servitude of love requires its own rites and mutilations, its own hatreds and wars: to nurture his idol, the worshipper must give his life away, while wounding and despising the deity itself. The rite that fits this religion of love is *sadism*: without the double sacrifice of self and of the idol beloved, worship vanishes and love is possible no more. Hence, the offences and injuries, the deceits and lies and blows, the mortifications and murders. A definite person is made sacred, because of her very definiteness and limitation: the entire world, therefore, must shrink to these limits, must lose its freedom and universality, and become this single object of love. In this confined horizon and idolatrous wretchedness, in the sweetness of these chains, the narrower the space in the accepted prison, the more one feels inclined to totally adore. In such a drying up and shriveling of the soul every self-inflicted mutilation seems holy, every humiliation and abasement acceptable in order to reach a complete religious fixation. Circe, the divine magician, goes on and on eternally taking from her adorers their likeness of men and turning them into beasts, into dogs and swine; and they, barking and grunting, express their joy and delight.

As the worshipper offers to his deity the sacrifice of his own human nature, so the idol itself must also be sacrificed: and it is a true idol only if downtrodden, offended, restricted, diminished. Not only does the beloved forsake her quality as a person, but even her appearance and the integrity of her shape—shrinking to a material part, to a leg, to a head of hair, to a breast, to a gown, to a mere object. And the love focused upon this object turns into a cruel revenge for all that has been lost. Even further than that: the idol-object ceases to have any connection with the person beloved, and becomes a fetishistic symbol, one of the thousands which psychoanalysts have so carefully classified. The more limited and precise and corporeal this symbolic object, the greater its divine potency: a glove, a picture, an excrement become irresistible, irreplaceable amorous deities, absolute tyrants.

Thus, in the private and tender and daily field of love, we are confronted with the same vicissitudes as in the field of the relationship between man and the state. Outside the freedom of a person completed, able therefore to conceive the other, to identify itself with the other in a common human nature, there is nothing but a sacred death in primeval indistinction, or a death profane in barren distinctness. Between the two impossible opposites of sacred love and love profane, any attempt at religious salvation is nothing but castration or sadism, puritanism or libertinage, extremes born of one single process. Between these two coincident extremes forever oscillate religious lovers. It is the old problem of spirit and body, which have contended since the very inception of time. The historical transition between the reign of the *Roi Soleil* and the Regency, or between the Victorian era and Lawrence's priapic revolution, is taking place continually and without hope of salvation in every man, incapable of freedom, who has made of his affections an idol, and offered sacrifices and offered up his self.

Love is not only the elementary human relationship, the first discovery of the world, the touchstone of liberty, it is also procreation, family, and therefore society and state. The point of interest here is not how love may exist, but how it may serve the greater deities of the fathers, of the clan, the tribe, the state. And certainly it is love, in its free and individual nature, which must be sacrificed to these gods. When the father is god, there is no room for love: woman is a slave, not an equal. The gravest offence is adultery, solely because it means a betrayal of God (jealousy is a divine sentiment, an impious deed, a siding with the enemy, with a stranger, with another god). Therefore, the adulterous woman is sacred, deserving of death, untouchable. Only a god son, who does not know of foreign deities, can look upon her with pity, and send her home alive. The father chooses brides for his sons, and sells his daughters as mere commodities. Jacob finds in his bed a woman he does not want, and pays with seven years of servitude for the wife of his choice, thus rendering homage to the divine authority of his father Laban: and only as a girl in love could Laban's daughter, portending a more exalted God, steal for love's sake the deities of the father, humble herself in hiding them, and sit upon them, in the camel's saddle.

For the tribe, ancient or modern, that worships not a familiar but a collective god, women are common property: adultery and sacrilege is only that which is committed outside the tribe, there where another sacred animal holds its sway. In the tribe too, but even more so in the paternal state, women have no gods of their own, and are ruled solely by the deities of their menfolk. Women may therefore be ravished by the foe, and even if born at home, they always remain strangers, because they take part in the rites only as victims. Love is impossible when it is thus turned into servitude. What counts is not the certitude of love, but that of matrimony, of children, of the family. Woman is sacrificed to the father-god. The mythical founders of cities have no human father; they are the sons of gods, of sacred virgins, of animals. They never could have separated from a true father to establish another patrician city-state: therefore their birth must be mysterious. So that Jesus might speak of love, he had to be a son without a father—and his voice truly opened locked doors. But the divine fathers and the divine States live eternally, and jealously claim, throughout eternity, the slavery of woman and the sacrifice of love.

NOTES

1. *Nè mi lece ascoltar chi non ragiona
   della mia morte.*
   (Francesco Petrarca—*Canzoniere*)
2. *per ana sì selvaggia dilettanza
   lasciar le donne a lor gaia sembianza?*
   (Dante Alighieri—*Rime*)
3. From Boccaccio's *Decamerone*.
4. *era si forte la nemica mia
   e lei vid' io ferita in mezzo 'l core.*
   (F. Petrarca—*Canzoniere*)
5. *allora errai quando l'antica strada
   di libertà mi fu precisa e tolta*

   . . . . . .

   *allor corse al suo mal libera e sciolta
   ora a posta d'altrui convien che vada
   l'anima, che peccò solò una volta.*
   (F. Petrarca—*Canzoniere*)
6. *onde più volte sospirando indietro
   dissi: Ohimè! il giogo e le catene e i ceppi
   eran più dolci che l'andare sciolto.*
   (F. Petrarca—*Canzoniere*)
7. *de mis soledades vengo
   a mis soledades voy
   porqué, para estar con migo
   me bastan mis pensamientos.*
   (Lope de Vega)
8. *delle vecchie fa conquista
   pel piacer di porle in lista*
   (Lorenzo Da Ponte—Libretto of Mozart's *Don Juan*)

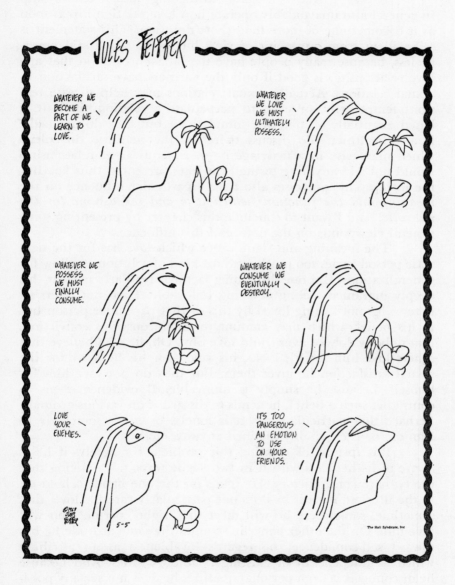

KAREN HORNEY: Neurosis and Love*

ALL THE factors disturbing human relationship in general also unavoidably operate in a love relationship as soon as it becomes one of more than short duration. This statement is self-evident from our point of view but needs to be said nevertheless, because many people have the fallacious notion that any love relationship is good if only the partners have satisfaction in sexual relations. Actually sexual relations may help to ease tensions temporarily, or even to perpetuate a relationship if it is based essentially on neurotic foundations, but they do not make it any healthier. To discuss therefore the neurotic difficulties which may arise in a marriage or in an equivalent relationship would not add anything to the principles presented thus far. But the intrapsychic processes also have a particular influence on the *meaning and the functions which love and sex assume for the neurotic*. And I want to conclude this chapter by presenting some general viewpoints on the nature of this influence.

The meaning and significance which *love* has for the neurotic person varies too much with his kind of solution to allow for generalizations. But one disturbing factor is regularly present: his deeply ingrained feeling of being unlovable. I am not referring here to his not feeling loved by this or that particular person but to his belief, which may amount to an unconscious conviction, that nobody does or ever could love him. Oh, he may believe that others love him for his looks, his voice, for his help, or for the sexual satisfaction he gives them. But they do not love him for himself, because he simply is unlovable. If evidence seems to contradict such a belief, he tends to discard it on various grounds. Perhaps that particular person is lonely, or needs somebody to lean on, or is charitably inclined anyway, etc.

But instead of tackling this problem concretely—if he is aware of it—he deals with it in two vague ways, not noticing that the two are contradictory. He tends on the one hand to hold on to the illusion, even if he does not particularly care for love, that sometime, somewhere he will meet the "right" person who will love him. On the other hand he assumes the same attitude he has toward self-confidence: he regards lovableness as an attribute which is independent of existing likable qualities. And because he disconnects it from personal qualities he does not see any possibility of its changing with his future development. He tends therefore to assume a fatalistic attitude and to regard his unlovableness as a mysterious but unalterable fact.

* Reprinted from *Neurosis and Human Growth*.

The self-effacing type becomes most easily aware of his disbelief in being lovable and, as we have seen, is the one who tries hardest to cultivate in himself likeable qualities, or at least the appearance thereof. But even he, with his absorbing interest in love, does not spontaneously go to the root of the question: what exactly is it that gives him the conviction of unlovableness?

It springs from three main sources. One of them is the impairment of the neurotic's own capacity to love. This capacity is bound to be impaired because of all the factors we discussed in this chapter: his being too wrapped up in himself, his being too vulnerable, too afraid of people, etc. This connection between feeling lovable and being ourselves able to love, although fairly often recognized intellectually, has a deep, vital meaning to very few of us. Yet in fact, if our capacity to love is well developed, we are not bothered about the question of whether or not we are lovable. Nor is it then of crucial importance whether or not we are actually loved by others.

The second source of the neurotic's feeling of being unlovable is his self-hate and its externalization. As long as he is unacceptable to himself—indeed hateworthy or contemptible—he cannot possibly believe that anybody else could love him.

These two sources, both strong and omnipresent in neurosis, account for the feeling of unlovableness not being easily removed in therapy. We can see its existence in a patient and can examine its consequences for his love life. But it can diminish only to the extent that these sources become less potent.

A third source contributes less directly but is important to mention for other reasons. It lies in the neurotic's expecting more of love than it can at best give (the "perfect love"), or expecting something different from what it can give (it cannot, for instance, relieve him of his self-hate). And since no love he does get can fulfill his expectations, he tends to feel that he is not "really" loved.

The particular kind of expectations of love varies. Generally speaking it is the fulfillment of many neurotic needs, often in themselves contradictory, or—in the case of the self-effacing type—of all his neurotic needs. And this fact of love being put into the service of neurotic needs makes it not only desirable but badly needed. Thus we find in love life the same incongruity that exists with regard to human relations in general: an increased need and a decreased capacity for it.

It is probably as little accurate to make a too neat distinction between love and sex as it is to link them up too closely (Freud). Since, however, in neuroses sexual excitement or desires more often than not are separate from a feeling of love, I want to make a few special comments on the role which *sexuality* plays in them. Sexuality retains in neuroses the functions it naturally has as a means of physical satisfaction and of intimate human contact. Also sexual well-functioning adds in many ways to the feeling of self-confidence. But in neuroses all these functions are enlarged and take on a different coloring. Sexual activities become not only a release of sexual tensions but also of manifold nonsexual psychic tensions. They can be a vehicle to drain self-contempt (in masochistic activities) or a means to act out self-torment by sexual degrading or tormenting of others (sadistic practices). They form one of the most frequent ways of allaying anxiety. The individuals themselves are unaware of such connections. They may not even be aware of being under a particular tension, or of having anxiety, but merely experience a rising sexual excitement or desire. But in analysis we can observe these connections accurately. A patient may for instance come closer to experiencing his self-hate, and suddenly there emerge plans or fantasies of sleeping with some girl. Or he may talk about some weakness in himself which he profoundly despises, and have sadistic fantasies of torturing somebody weaker than he is.

Also the natural sexual functions of establishing an intimate human contact frequently assume greater proportions. This is a well-known fact about detached people for whom sexuality may be the only bridge to others, but it is not restricted to being an obvious substitute for human closeness. It shows also in the haste with which people may rush into sexual relations, without giving themselves a chance to find out whether they have anything in common or a chance to develop a liking and understanding. It is possible of course that an emotional relatedness may evolve later on. But more often than not it does not do so because usually the initial rush itself is a sign of their being too inhibited to develop a good human relationship.

Lastly the normal relation between sexuality and self-confidence shifts to one between sexuality and pride. Sexual functioning, being attractive or desirable, the choice of a partner, the quantity or variety of sexual experiences—all become a matter of pride more than of wishes and enjoyment. The more the personal factor in love relations recedes and the purely sexual ones ascend, the more does the unconscious concern about lovableness shift to a conscious concern about attractiveness.[1]

These increased functions which sexuality assumes in neuroses do not necessarily lead to more extensive sexual activities than in the comparatively healthy person. They may do so, but they may also be responsible for greater inhibitions. A comparison with the healthy individual is difficult anyway because of the great variations, even within the range of the "normal," in sexual excitability, in intensity and frequency of sexual desires, or in forms of sexual expressions. There is however one significant difference. In a way similar to that which we discussed with regard to imagination[2] sexuality is put in the service of neurotic needs. For this reason it often assumes an *undue* importance, in the sense of an importance stemming from nonsexual sources. Furthermore, for the same reason, sexual functions can be easily disturbed. There are fears, there is a whole host of inhibitions, there is the intricate problem of homosexuality, and there are perversions. Finally, because sexual activities (including masturbation and fantasies) and their particular forms are determined—or at least partly determined—by neurotic needs or taboos, they are often compulsive in nature. All of these factors may result in the neurotic patient's having sexual relations not because he wants them but because he should please his partner; because he must have a sign of being wanted or loved; because he must allay some anxiety; because he must prove his mastery and potency, etc. Sexual relations, in other words, are less determined by his real wishes and feelings than by the drive to satisfy some compulsive needs. Even without any intention to degrade the partner, the latter ceases to be an individual and becomes a sexual "object" (Freud).[3]

How in detail the neurotic deals with these problems varies within such a wide range that I cannot even try here to outline the possibilities. *The special difficulties existing toward love and sex are after all only one expression of his total neurotic disturbances.* The variations in addition are so manifold because in kind they depend not only upon the individual's neurotic character structure but also on the particular partners he has had or still has.

This may seem like a superfluous qualification because we have learned through our analytic knowledge that there is more often than formerly was assumed an unconscious choice of partners. The validity of this concept can indeed be shown over and over again. But we have tended to go to the other extreme and assume that every partner is of the individual's choosing; and this generalization is not valid. It needs qualifications in two directions. We must first raise the question as to who does the "choosing." Properly speaking, the word "choice" presupposes a capacity to choose and a capacity to know the partner who is chosen. Both capacities are curtailed in the neurotic. He is able to choose only to the extent to which his picture of others is not distorted by the many factors we have discussed. In this strict sense there is no choice worth the name, or at least very little of it. What is meant by the term "choice of a partner" is the person's feeling attracted on the ground of his outstanding neurotic needs: his pride, his needs to dominate or to exploit, his need to surrender, etc.

But even in this qualified sense the neurotic has not much chance to "choose" a partner. He may marry because it is the thing to do; and he may be so remote from himself and so detached from others that he marries a person whom he just happens to know a little better than others or who happens to want to marry him. His estimate of himself may be so low, because of his self-contempt, that he simply cannot approach those persons of the other sex who—if only for neurotic reasons—would appeal to him. Adding to these psychological restrictions the factual ones of his often knowing very few available partners, we realize how much is left to incidental circumstances.

Instead of trying to do justice to the endless variations of erotic and sexual experiences resulting from these manifold factors involved, I shall merely indicate certain general tendencies operating in the neurotic's attitudes toward love and sex. *He may tend to exclude love* from his life. He may minimize or deny its significance or even its existence. Love then does not appear to him as desirable but is rather to be avoided or to be despised as a self-deceptive weakness.

Such a tendency to exclude love operates in a quiet but determined fashion in the resigned, detached type. Individual differences within this group mostly concern his attitude toward sexuality. He may have removed the actual possibility not only of love, but also of sex, so far from his personal life that he lives as if they did not exist or had no meaning for him personally. Toward the sexual experiences of others he feels neither envy nor disapproval, but may have considerable understanding for them if they are in some trouble.

Others may have had a few sexual relations in their younger years. But these did not penetrate through the armor of their detachment, were not too meaningful, and faded out without leaving a desire for further experiences.

For another detached person sexual experiences are important and enjoyable. He may have had them with many different people but always—consciously or unconsciously—was on his guard not to form any attachment. The nature of such transient sexual contacts depends on many factors. Among others the prevalence of expansive or self-effacing trends is relevant. The lower his estimate of himself, the more will these contacts be restricted to persons beneath his own social or cultural level, as for instance to prostitutes.

Again, others may happen to get married and may even be able to maintain a decent though distant relationship, provided the partner is likewise detached. If such a person marries somebody with whom he has not much in common, he may characteristically put up with the situation and try to abide by his duties as a husband and father. Only if the partner is too aggressive, violent, or sadistic to allow the detached person to withdraw inwardly may the latter either try to get out of the relationship or go to pieces under it.

The arrogant-vindictive type excludes love in a more militant and destructive way. His general attitude toward love usually is a derogating, debunking one. With respect to his sexual life there seem to be two principal possibilities. Either his sexual life is strikingly poor—he may merely have occasional sexual contacts for the main purpose of releasing physical or psychic tensions—or sexual relations may be important to him, provided he can give free range to his sadistic impulses. In this case he may either engage in sadistic sexual activities (which may be most exciting to him and give him satisfaction) or he may be stilted and overcontrolled in his sexual relations but treat his partner in a general sadistic fashion.

Another general tendency with regard to love and sex is also in the direction of excluding love—and sometimes also sex—from the actual life but giving it a *prominent place in his imagination.* Love then becomes a feeling so exalted and so celestial that any realistic fulfillment seems by comparison shallow and indeed despicable. E. T. A. Hoffmann, who has masterly described this aspect in the *Tales of Hoffmann,* calls love "that longing for infinity which weds us to Heaven." It is a delusion planted in our soul "through the cunning of man's hereditary enemy . . . that through love, through the pleasure of the flesh, there could be achieved on earth that which exists in our hearts as a heavenly promise only." Love therefore can be realized in fantasy only. Don Juan, in his interpretation, is destructive to women because "every betrayal of a loved bride, every joy destroyed by a fierce blow struck at the lover . . . represents an exalted triumph over that hostile monster and raises the seducer forever above our narrow life, above nature, above the Creator."

A third and last possibility to be mentioned here is an *overemphasis placed on love and sex in actual life.* Love and sex then constitute the main value of life and are glorified accordingly. We can distinguish here roughly between the conquering and the surrendering love. The latter evolves logically from the self-effacing solution and was described in that context. The former occurs in the narcissistic type, if for particular reasons his drive for mastery has focused upon love. His pride then is invested in being the ideal lover and in being irresistible. Women who are easily available do not appeal to him. He must prove his mastery by conquering those who, for whatever reasons, are difficult to attain. The conquest may consist in the consummation of the sexual act or he may aim at complete emotional surrender. When these aims are achieved his interest recedes.

NOTES

1. *Cf.* discussion of self-contempt in Chapter 5.
2. See Chapter 1.
3. Approaching the subject from the viewpoint of sex-morality, the English philosopher John Macmurray in his *Reason and Emotion*, Faber and Faber Ltd., London, 1935, makes emotional sincerity the criterion for the value of sexual relations.

HAVELOCK ELLIS: Erotic Symbolism*

LOOKED AT broadly, all the sexual deviations are examples of erotic symbolism, for in every case it will be found that some object or act that for the normal human being has little or no erotic value has assumed such value; that is to say, it has become a *symbol* of normal love. Moreover, erotic symbolism comes into play even in the more refined forms of normal love, for these involve a tendency to concentrate amorous attention on some special points in the beloved person, such points being themselves unimportant but acquiring a symbolic value. . . .

The extent of erotic symbolism is seen when we attempt to group and classify the phenomena which may be brought under this head. Such phenomena may be conveniently arranged in three great classes, on the basis of the objects which arouse them.

1. PARTS OF THE BODY— (A). *Normal:* Hand, foot, breasts, nates, hair, secretions and excretions, odor (ophresiolagnia). (B). *Abnormal:* Lameness, squinting, pitting of smallpox, etc., Paidophilia, or the sexual love of children,[1] presbyophilia, or the love of the aged, and necrophilia, or the attraction for corpses, may be included under this head, as well as the excitement caused by animals (erotic zoophilia).

2. INANIMATE OBJECTS— (A). *Garments:* Gloves, shoes and stockings and garters, aprons, handkerchiefs, underlinen. (B). *Im-*

* Reprinted from *Psychology of Sex.*

personal Objects: Here may be included all the various objects that may accidentally acquire the power of exciting sexual feeling in auto-erotism. Pygmalionism (iconolagnia) or the sexual attraction of statues, may also be included.

3. ACTS AND ATTITUDES— (A). *Active:* Whipping, cruelty, exhibitionism, mutilation and murder. (B). *Passive:* Being whipped, experiencing cruelty. Personal odors and the sound of the voice may also be included under this head. (C). *Scoptophilia or Mixoscopia or voyeurism:* including objects and scenes found to be sexually stimulating; the vision of climbing, swinging, etc.; the acts of urination and defecation (urolagnia and coprolagnia); the coitus of animals.

It will be seen that there is a vast range of kind and degree in the deviations of the sexual impulse. At one end we find the innocent and amiable attraction which his mistress's glove or slipper may possess for the lover—an attraction which has been felt by the finest and sanest minds—and at the other end the random murderous outrages of a Jack the Ripper. But we have to remember that there is at no point any definite frontier, and that by insensible gradations the systematic arrangement of sexual deviations can be seen to pass from the harmless mania to the murderous outrage. So that even when we are not dealing with the criminal or medico-legal field, but are mainly concerned with the psychology of the normal sex-life, we cannot avoid the consideration of deviations, for at one end they all come within the normal range.

Most of the extremes of symbolism are chiefly found in men. They are so rare in women that Krafft-Ebing stated, even in the late editions of his *Psychopathia Sexualis*, that he knew of no cases of erotic fetichism in women. They do, however, occur occasionally, even in well-marked forms. In its normal form erotic symbolism is undoubtedly quite common in women, and, as Moll points out, even the general fascination exerted on women by the soldier's uniform is probably due to the action of a symbolism of courage. But it also occurs in abnormal forms. There is indeed one form of erotic fetichism—kleptolagnia or erotic kleptomania —which in its typical form, occurs almost exclusively in women.

EROTIC FETICHISM

The most typical of the erotic symbolisms is constituted by erotic fetichism, a term devised by Binet in 1888. Even an erotic symbolism such as exhibitionism may be fetichistic, and every fetich is a symbol. The number of objects—not only parts of the body but inanimate things—which may acquire special erotic significance is practically infinite. There is indeed nothing that may not take on such significance. That is why the legal attempt to suppress "obscenity," regarded (according to the judicially recognized definition) as a tendency to "deprave and corrupt those whose minds are open to such immoral influences," is completely unworkable. Thus Dr. Jelliffe's patient, Zenia X, wrote that sex symbols became insistent at the age of thirteen and fourteen: "From this time on, though more fully in later years since the struggle has been more consciously sexual and thus more violent, I have been surrounded by symbols, particularly of the phallus: a garden hose in use or a jet of water, pears particularly or other elongated fruits, long pendant catkins, the pistil in the center of a flower, a stick or stick-shaped object thrust into a round hole, the lobe of the ear with which I have toyed since birth, my teeth, and my tongue which I have nervously pressed against them until weary, a finger which seemingly in order to suppress a sudden sexual thought I have many times pointed before me and then in quick correction have drawn in and folded within the others, the thumb which again involuntarily in a repressive effort is folded close within the fingers, certain letters of the alphabet. These are some of the symbols which have beset me on every hand, thrusting themselves continually before me, to remind me of the phallus or of the actual contact of the organs male and female."

The manifold complexity of sexual symbols is again brought out in a case described by Marcinowski, a highly intelligent married woman of 27, who was neurotic with slight germs of morbid deviation. The symbols were apt to occur in her dreams which she was skilful in interpreting; ships in haven were often the symbol of coitus, as was sailing in a ship; water was the symbol of the mother's body (connected with early ideas that the bladder was associated with coitus); to die (being self-abandonment) is to be in love; a knife is a phallic symbol; worms and snakes are small masculine organs; the horse and the dog are sexual symbols (she had once kissed a dog's penis), as are doves; a railway engine (attractive to her from childhood) is a symbol of the penis, as is also a tree and a banana; to kill equals coitus (she had sometimes had sadistic fancies); many fish are symbols of coitus; rain, urine, and tears are symbols of semen; wanting to urinate is for her a form of sexual excitement.

Most of these symbols are liable to occur anywhere and to anyone. The necessary conditions for a symbol to become a fetich seem to be a special predisposition, no doubt usually of neuropathic nature, though this is by no means always obvious, and a strong impression by which the object is poignantly presented to consciousness at a moment of strong sexual excitement, this event often occurring before or about puberty. The accidental association without the predisposition will scarcely suffice to evoke a fetich (except in slight degree), for such accidental associations are constantly occurring. Hirschfeld has argued that a fetich is frequently the real expression of the individual's special temperament. The soldier's red coat acts like a fetich on the servant girl because it is a symbol of the martial and virile character which appeals to her, and it may well be that in many less obvious cases the fetich really expresses ideals based on individual idiosyncrasy. But in most cases this cannot be proved, and is often indeed scarcely susceptible of proof on account of the neutral character of the fetich. A boy admires a woman who one day urinates in his presence so that he catches a glimpse of her abundant pubic hair, and such hair henceforth becomes an almost indispensable fetich to him; a youth is lying on the floor when a charming girl playfully places her foot on him, continuing to play with him thus until sexual excitement occurs, and he becomes a lifelong foot-fetichist.

Such fetichisms are, in a slight degree, entirely normal. Every lover becomes specially attracted to some individual feature of the beloved or to some of the various articles that come in contact with her. But this tendency becomes abnormal when it is exclusive or generalized, and it becomes a definite deviation when the fetich itself, even in the absence of the person, becomes completely adequate not only to arouse tumescence, but to evoke detumescence, so that there is no desire at all for sexual intercourse.

In milder though definitely abnormal cases, the subject himself devises the appropriate treatment by taking care that his fetich is set, as it were, in the ante-chamber to courtship, so that it shall not cause any arrest or deviation of the emotions it arouses. In more serious cases the fetichist often derives so much gratification from his perversion, and finds this gratification so easy, that he has no wish to become normal. In some cases fetichism leads to various anti-social offenses, especially to the theft of the desired fetich, such as shoes, handkerchiefs, or wearing apparel. Without leading to criminal actions it may prove annoying from the undue sexual excitement caused, as in the case of a young woman for whom eyeglasses or spectacles were a fetich, and who experienced excitement whenever she saw them worn, even by a woman. In such cases hypnotism was formerly resorted to, sometimes with success.

There are certain forms of erotic fetichism which are apt to be complicated in their psychological bearings. This is notably the case as regards foot-fetichism, which, under the conditions of civilization whereby the foot is usually seen clothed, becomes shoe-fetichism. There would seem to be an almost natural basis for foot-fetichism in the tendency to a worldwide association of the foot with the sexual organs. Even among the Jews the "foot" was used as a euphemism for the sexual organs, and we read, for instance, in Isaiah of "the hair of the feet," meaning the pubic hair. In widely separated parts of the world, moreover, the foot has been a center of modesty. It was so even in Spain, and Peyron noted in 1777 that the feminine custom of concealing the feet was only then passing out of fashion, and "a woman who shows her feet is no longer ready to give her favors," as, it may be added, she was also in classic Rome. Even for the normal lover the foot is one of the most attractive parts of the body. Stanley Hall found that among the parts specified as most admired in the other sex by young men and women who answered a *questionnaire* the feet came fifth (after the eyes, hair, stature, and size). Other observers, however, like Hirschfeld, have found the hand a much more frequent fetich than the foot. Infants are peculiarly interested in the foot, primarily in their own. Moreover, in many parts of the world, notably China, some parts of Siberia, as well as ancient Rome and medieval Spain, a certain degree of foot-fetichism has been recognized.

It is not usual for the normal lover, in most civilized countries today, to attach primary importance to the foot, such as he frequently attaches to the eyes. In a small but not inconsiderable minority of persons, however, the foot or the shoe becomes the most attractive part of a woman, and in some morbid cases the woman herself is regarded as a comparatively unimportant appendage to her foot or her shoes. Restif de la Bretonne furnishes an interesting example of foot-fetichism in a writer of considerable importance; in his case the fetichism was well marked, but it was never extreme, and the shoe, however attractive, was not an adequate substitute for the woman.

Eccentric as foot-fetichism may appear, it is thus simply the reemergence, by a pseudo-atavism or arrest of development, of a mental or emotional impulse which was probably experienced by our forefathers, and is often traceable among young children today. The occasional reappearance of this bygone impulse and the stability which it may acquire are thus conditioned by the sensitive reaction of an abnormally nervous and usually precocious organism to influences which, among the average and ordinary population of Europe today, are either never felt or quickly outgrown, or strictly subordinated in the highly complex crystallizations which the course of love and the process of tumescence create within us. An interesting case was elaborately psycho-analyzed by L. Binswanger: Gerda, as a child, had acquired the habit of sitting on her heels with her shoe pressed against the vulva and anus. This would cause excitement in these erogenic zones and she would find pleasure in urinating (perhaps as a form of detumescence). The shoe became her friend and lover and darling, to be carefully protected and guarded from the eyes of others. The foot and especially the shod foot became blended with all her sexual ideas, the representative of the phallus, and even, as among primitive peoples, the symbol of all fertility. On this foundation phobias and other symptoms in time developed, to some extent overlying and diminishing the original mani-festations.

It may be added that this is by no means true of foot-fetichism only. In some other fetichisms a seemingly congenital predisposition is even more marked. This is not only the case as regards hair-fetichism, fur-fetichism, etc. In many cases of fetich-isms of all kinds not only is there no record of any commencement in a definite episode (an absence which may be accounted for by the supposition that the original incident has been forgotten), but it would seem in some cases that the fetichism developed very slowly. In this sense, although we cannot speak of foot-fetichism as strictly atavism, it may be seen to arise on a congenital basis. We may, with Garnier, regard the congenital element as essential.

This congenital element of erotic symbolism is worth not-ing because more than any other form of sexual deviation the fetichisms are those which are least clearly conditioned by inborn states of the organism and most frequently aroused by seemingly accidental associations or shocks in early life. Inversion is some-times so fundamentally ingrained in the individual's constitution that it arises and develops in spite of the strongest influences in a contrary direction. But a fetichism, while it tends to occur in sensitive, nervous, timid, precocious individuals—that is to say, individuals of more or less neuropathic heredity—can usually, though not always, be traced to a definite starting point in the shock of some sexually emotional episode in early life. . . .

Krafft-Ebing regarded shoe-fetichism as, in large measure, a more or less latent form of masochism, the foot or the shoe being the symbol of the subjection and the humiliation which the mas-ochist feels in the presence of the beloved object. Moll, more cor-rectly, states that the connection is "very frequent." This was also the opinion of Garnier, who was, however, careful to point out that there are many cases in which no such connection can be traced.

While we may properly admit the frequency of the connection we must be cautious in making any general attempt to amalgamate masochism and foot-fetichism. In the broad sense in which erotic symbolism is here understood, both masochism and foot-fetichism may be coordinated as symbolisms; for the masochist his self-humiliating impulses are the symbol of ecstatic adoration; for the foot-fetichist his mistress's foot or shoe is the concentrated symbol of all that is most beautiful and elegant and feminine in her personality. But if in this sense they are coördinated, they often remain entirely distinct. Masochism, indeed, merely simulates foot-fetichism; for the masochist the boot is not strictly a symbol, it is only an instrument which enables him to carry out his impulse; the true sexual symbol for him is not the boot, but the emotion of self-subjection. For the foot-fetichist, on the other hand, the foot or the shoe is not a mere instrument, but a true symbol, the focus of his worship, an idealized object which he is content to contemplate or reverently touch. He himself usually has no impulse to any self-degrading action, nor the slightest emotion of subjection. It may be noted that in the typical case of foot-fetichism which is presented to us in the person of Restif de la Bretonne he repeatedly speaks of "subjugating" the woman for whom he feels this fetichistic adoration, and mentions that even when still a child he especially admired a delicate and fairy-like girl in this respect because she seemed to him easier to subdue. His attitude throughout life was active and masculine, not masochistic. . . .

STUFF-FETICHISMS AND EROTIC ZOOPHILIA

It is now necessary, without entirely leaving the field of fetichism, to touch on a special group of sexual symbols in which the association of contiguity with the human body is usually absent: the various methods by which animals, or animal products, or the sight of animal copulation, may arouse sexual desire in human persons. Here we encounter a symbolism mainly founded on association by resemblance; the animal sexual act recalls the human sexual act; the animal becomes the symbol of the human being.

The group of phenomena we are here concerned with includes several sub-divisions. There is, first, the more or less sexual pleasure sometimes experienced, especially by young persons, in the sight of copulating animals. This has been termed *Mixoscopic Zoophilia;* it falls within the range of normal variation. Then we have the cases in which the contact of animals, stroking, etc., produces sexual excitement or gratification; this is a sexual fetichism in the narrow sense, and is by Krafft-Ebing termed *Zoophilia*

Erotica. We have, further, the class of cases in which a real or simulated sexual intercourse with animals is desired. Such cases do not involve fetichism in the narrow sense, but they come within the sphere of erotic symbolism, as here understood. This class falls into two divisions: one in which the individual is fairly normal, but belongs to a low grade of culture; the other in which he may belong to a more refined social class, but a psychopathic condition is present. In the first case we may properly apply the simple term bestiality (it is called sodomy in some countries, but this is incorrect as well as confusing, and to be avoided), in the second case it may perhaps be better to use the term *Zooerastia,* proposed by Krafft-Ebing.

Among children, both boys and girls, it is common to find that the copulation of animals is a mysteriously fascinating spectacle. It is inevitable that this should be so, for the spectacle is more or less clearly felt to be the revelation of a secret which has been concealed from them. It is, moreover, a secret of which they feel intimate reverberations within themselves, and even in perfectly innocent and ignorant children the sight may produce an obscure sexual excitement. It would seem that this occurs more frequently in girls than in boys. Even in adult age, it may be added, women are liable to experience the same kind of emotion in the presence of such spectacles. In the sixteenth century, both in England and France, the ladies of royal and aristocratic circles would almost openly go to enjoy such spectacles. In more modern times such sights are regarded as both prurient and morbid, and for ill-balanced minds no doubt are so.

While the contemplation of animal coitus is an easily intelligible and in early life, perhaps, an almost normal symbol of sexual emotion, there is another sub-division of this group of animal fetichisms which forms a natural transition from the fetichisms which have their center in the human body: the *stuff-fetichism* or the sexual attraction exerted by various tissues, perhaps always of animal origin. Here we are in the presence of a somewhat complicated phenomenon. In part we have, in a considerable number of cases, the sexual attraction of feminine garments, for all such tissues are liable to enter into the dress. In part, also, we have a sexual deviation of tactile sensibility, for in a considerable proportion of these cases it is the touch sensations which are potent in arousing the erotic impulse. But in part, also, it would seem, we have here the conscious or sub-conscious presence of an animal fetich, and it is notable that perhaps all these stuffs, and especially fur, which is by far the commonest of the groups, are distinctively animal products. We may perhaps regard the fetich of feminine hair—a much more important and common

fetich, indeed, than any of the stuff-fetichisms—as a link of transition. Hair is at once an animal and a human product, while it may
be separated from the body and possesses the qualities of a stuff.
Krafft-Ebing remarks that the senses of touch, smell, and hearing,
as well as sight, seem to enter into the attraction exerted by hair.

As a sexual fetich hair belongs strictly to the group of parts
of the body; but since it can be removed from the body and is sexually effective as a fetich in the absence of the person to whom it
belongs, it is on a level with the garments which may serve in a
similar way, with shoes or handkerchiefs or gloves. Psychologically, hair-fetichism presents no special problem, but the wide
attraction of hair—it is sexually the most generally noted part of
the feminine body after the eyes—and the peculiar facility with
which when plaited it may be removed have long rendered hair-
fetichism a condition of special medico-legal interest.

The hair-despoiler (*Coupeur des nattes* or *Zopfab-schnei-
der*), however modern fashions may have diminished his activities,
might formerly have been found in any civilized country, though
the most carefully studied cases occurred in Paris. Such persons
are usually of nervous temperament and bad heredity; the attraction of hair occasionally develops in early life; sometimes the morbid impulse only appears in later life after fever. The fetich may
be either flowing hair or braided hair, but is usually one or the
other, and not both. Sexual excitement and ejaculation may be
produced in the act of touching or cutting off the hair, which is
subsequently, in many cases, used for masturbation. As a rule the
hair-despoiler is a pure fetichist, no element of sadistic pleasure
entering into his feelings.

The stuff-fetiches are most usually fur and velvet; feathers,
silk, and leather also sometimes exerting this influence; they are
all, it will be noted, animal substances. The most interesting is
probably fur, the attraction of which is not uncommon in association with passive algolagnia. As Stanley Hall showed, the fear of
fur, as well as the love of it, is by no means uncommon in childhood; it may appear in infancy and in children who have never
come in contact with animals. It is noteworthy that in most cases
of uncomplicated stuff-fetichism the attraction apparently arises
on a congenital basis, as it appears in persons of nervous or sensitive temperament at an early age and without being attached to
any definite or causative incident. The sexual excitation is nearly
always produced by touch rather than by sight. If the specific
sexual sensations may be regarded as a special modification of tick-
lishness, the erotic symbolism in the case of these stuff-fetichisms
would seem to be a more or less congenital deviation of ticklish-
ness in relation to specific animal contacts.

A further degree of deviation in this direction is reached in erotic *zoophilia*, as exemplified in a case recorded by Krafft-Ebing. In this case a congenital neuropath, of good intelligence but delicate and anemic, with feeble sexual powers, had a great love of domestic animals, especially dogs and cats, from an early age; when petting them he experienced sexual emotions, although he was innocent in sexual matters. At puberty he realized the nature of his feelings and tried to break himself of his habits. He succeeded, but then began erotic dreams accompanied by images of animals, and these led to masturbation associated with ideas of a similar kind. At the same time he had no wish for any sort of intimate intercourse with animals, and was indifferent as to the sex of the animals which attracted him; his sexual ideas were normal. Such a case seems to be one of fetichism on a tactile basis, and thus forms a transition between the stuff-fetichisms and the complete perversion of sexual attraction toward animals.

Krafft-Ebing considered that this is radically distinct from erotic *zoophilia*. This view cannot be accepted. Bestiality and *zooerastia* merely present in a more marked and profoundly perverted form a further degree of the same phenomenon which we meet with in erotic *zoophilia*; the difference is that they occur either in more insensitive or in more markedly psychopathic persons. It is, however, somewhat doubtful whether we can always or even usually distinguish between *zooerastia* and bestiality, for it seems probable that in most cases of ordinary bestiality some slight traces of mental anomaly might be found, if such cases always were, as they should be, properly investigated. As Moll remarks, it is often hardly possible to draw a sharp line between vice and disease.

We here reach the grossest and most frequent perversion in the group: bestiality or the impulse to attain sexual gratification by intercourse, or other close contact, with animals. In seeking to comprehend this deviation it is necessary to divest ourselves of the attitude towards animals which is the inevitable outcome of refined civilization and urban life. Most sexual deviations, if not in large measure the actual outcome of civilized life, easily adjust themselves to it. Bestiality (except in one form to be noted later) is, on the other hand, the sexual anomaly of dull, insensitive, and unfastidious peasants. It flourishes among primitive peoples and rural communities. It is the vice of the clodhopper who is unattractive to women or inapt to court them. In some stages of culture it is not a vice at all. Thus, when in Sweden at the end of the thirteenth century it was first made an offense by the Swedish pagan provincial laws, it was still only as an offense against the owner of the animal, who was entitled to compensation. Among still simpler peoples such as the Salish of British Columbia, animals are regarded as no lower in the scale of life than human beings, and in some respects superior, so that there is no place for our conception of "bestiality.". . .

EXHIBITIONISM

Another symbolistic manifestation of the sexual impulse, serious in adult life, may occur innocently, and not abnormally, in childhood. This is exhibitionism. Several writers have pointed out that at puberty, and even in adolescence, an impulse of ostentation extending to the developing organs of sex (in girls more especially to the breasts) is not uncommon. It is a common infantile tendency which seems perfectly natural. Freud refers to the exhilaration even very young children experience in nakedness; they love to dance about naked before going to bed, often raising their little garments, even before strangers, a reminiscence, as Freud views it, of a lost Paradisiacal state, to become later in exhibitionists a morbid obsession, and often even normally re-asserted after puberty in a definite though restrained form. Putnam thought that the frequency with which we dream of being in an insufficiently dressed state reveals a latent exhibitionism, though this view I cannot accept: it is overlooked that during sleep we actually are in such a state. Sometimes in childhood it is a mutual practice (even to the age of twelve) as a manifestation of simple interest in the sexual organs; it is often also due to an impulse of mischief or rebellion, though, when persistent, it may have an obscure sexual cause, and be the sign of an irritation desiring unknown relief, a kind of vicarious masturbation, to be dealt with in the same manner as ordinary masturbation. In adults exhibitionism is more definitely a symbol of coitus, and its forms fall into several groups.

First described and named by Lasègue in 1877, exhibitionism is thus a form of erotic symbolism in which an adequate equivalent of coitus is found in the simple act of deliberately exhibiting the sexual organ to persons of the opposite sex, usually by preference to young and presumably innocent persons, often children. It would appear to be a not infrequent phenomenon, and most women, once or more in their lives, especially when young, have encountered a man who has thus deliberately exposed himself before them. It is indeed the commonest sexual offense, and Norwood East found that of 291 sexual offenders received for trial or on remand at Brixton Prison as many as 101 were cases of "indecent exposure," though it must be added that sexual offenders were, altogether, only about 4 per cent. of the total number of prisoners.

The exhibitionist, though often a young and apparently vigorous man, is satisfied with the mere act of self-exhibition and the emotional reaction which that act produces; he seldom makes demands on the woman to whom he exposes himself; he seldom speaks, he makes no effort to approach her; as a rule, he fails even to display the signs of sexual excitation. He seldom masturbates; his desires are completely gratified by the act of exhibition and by the emotional reaction he supposes that it arouses in the woman. He departs satisfied and relieved.

Various classifications of exhibitionism have been put forward; thus Maeder recognized three forms; (1) the *infantile*, to gaze and to be gazed at being normal in childhood; (2) the *senile*, which is a method of sexual excitement in the impotent; and (3) exhibitionism as a *method of sexual invitation*, which may occur in fairly normal persons of defective virility. This classification may not be complete, but it rightly insists on the element of sexual weakness, which is significant in exhibitionism, and on the fact that the aberration has a normal basis in the common actions of childhood. Krafft-Ebing divided exhibitionists into four clinical groups: (1) acquired states of mental weakness with cerebral or spinal disease clouding consciousness and at the same time causing impotence; (2) epileptics in whom the act is an abnormal organic impulse performed in a state of imperfect consciousness; (3) a somewhat allied group of neurasthenic cases; (4) periodical impulsive cases with deep hereditary taint. This classification is not altogether satisfactory. Norwood East for practical purposes divided exhibitionists into two main groups: the *psychopathic* (about two-thirds of the whole with "visionaries" and mental defectives predominating), and the *depraved* (who have a vicious motive and include the remaining one-third). Most cases fall into one or other of two mixed groups (1) cases in which there is more or less congenital abnormality, but otherwise a fair or even complete degree of mental integrity; they are usually young adults, they are more or less conscious of the end they wish to attain, and it is often only with a severe struggle that they yield to their impulses; (2) cases in which the beginnings of mental or nervous disorder or alcoholic degeneration have diminished the sensibility of the higher centers; these subjects are sometimes old men (clergymen, etc.) whose lives have been absolutely correct; they are often only vaguely aware of the nature of the satisfaction they are seeking, and frequently no struggle precedes the manifestation; with rest and restorative treatment the health may be improved and the acts cease. It is in the first class of cases alone that there is a developed sexual anomaly. In the cases of the second class there is a more or less definite sexual intention, but it is only just conscious, and the emergence of the impulse is due not to its strength but to the weakness, temporary or permanent, of the higher inhibiting centers. Of this alcohol is a common cause, either by causing real mental confusion or by liberating latent tendencies; Norwood East remarks that the decreased consumption of alcohol in England has been accompanied by decrease in the number of convictions for indecent exposure (in England and Wales in 1913, 866 men were so convicted, in 1923 and among a larger population only 548).

Epileptic cases, with loss of consciousness during the act, can only be regarded as presenting a pseudo-exhibitionism. They are not so common as is sometimes supposed; Norwood East found none in a series of 150 cases (though epileptics were among them) and remarks that in his experience these cases are not as frequent as they are dramatic. It is undoubtedly true that cases of real or apparent exhibitionism may occur in epileptics as was clearly shown by Pelanda in Verona many years ago. We must not, however, too hastily conclude that because these acts occur in epileptics they are necessarily unconscious acts. When the act of pseudo-exhibitionism is truly epileptic, it has no psychic sexual content, and it will certainly be liable to occur under all sorts of circumstances, when the patient is alone or in a miscellaneous concourse of people. It corresponds exactly to the cases in which epileptics sometimes carry out the act of urination, during a psychic attack, in an apparently purposive but really unconscious manner. Such an act is automatic, unconscious, and involuntary; the spectators are not even perceived; it cannot be an act of exhibitionism, for the act of exhibition implies deliberate and conscious intention. Whenever, on the other hand, the place and the time are evidently chosen deliberately—a quiet spot, the presence of only one or two young women or children—it is difficult to admit that we are in the presence of a fit of epileptic unconsciousness, even when the subject is known to be epileptic.

Excluding these epileptic pseudo-exhibitionists, who, from the legal point of view, are clearly irresponsible, it must still be remembered that in exhibitionism there is usually either a high degree of mental abnormality on a neuropathic basis, or else actual disease. This is true to a greater extent in exhibitionism than in almost any other form of sexual perversion. No subject of exhibitionism should be sent to prison without expert medical examination. Hirschfeld believes that the exhibitionist is never mentally normal. In some cases the impulse to exhibitionism may be overcome or may pass away. This result is more likely to come about in those cases in which exhibitionism has been largely conditioned by chronic alcoholism or other influences tending to destroy the inhibiting and restraining action of the higher centers, which may be overcome by hygiene and treatment. When it occurs in youth it tends to be spontaneously outgrown, as in the youthful Rousseau who records that as a boy he once or twice displayed his nates to girls at a distance. When traveling through Moravia many years ago I noted a young woman who had been bathing in a stream near the railway line and as the train passed turned her back to it and raised her chemise. (Here we have to bear in mind the ancient method of exorcism by displaying the nates, later degenerating into a way of showing contempt especially practiced by women.) True exhibitionism is rare in the female except in childhood. As Douglas Bryan puts it, women in exhibitionism treat the whole body as a penis to be exposed.

Exhibitionism is an act which, on the face of it, may seem nonsensical or meaningless, but it is wildly extravagant to regard it as necessarily an inexplicable act of madness, such as it was once, if not still, frequently treated both by writers on insanity and on sexual perversion, even though in its extreme form it may be associated with either.

We must regard exhibitionism as fundamentally a symbolic act based on a perversion of courtship. The exhibitionist, if a male, displays the organ of sex to a feminine witness, and in the shock of modest sexual shame by which she reacts to that spectacle he finds a gratifying similitude of the normal emotions of coitus. He feels that he has effected a psychic defloration.

Exhibitionism is thus analogous, and indeed related, to the impulse felt by many persons to perform indecorous acts or tell indecent stories before young and innocent persons of the opposite sex. This also is a kind of exhibitionism, the gratification it causes lying exactly, as in physical exhibitionism, in the emotional confusion which it is felt to arouse, though we cannot accept the view of Näcke that exhibitionism is simply a form of sadism and the satisfaction felt only due to the horror aroused. The two kinds of exhibitionism may be combined in the same person.

It is of interest to point out that the sexual symbolism of active flagellation is very closely analogous to this symbolism of exhibitionism. The flagellant approaches a woman with the rod (itself a symbol of the penis and in some countries bearing names which are also applied to that organ) to inflict on an intimate part of her body the signs of blushing and the spasmodic movements which are associated with sexual excitement, while at the same time she feels, or the flagellant imagines that she feels, the corresponding emotions of delicious shame. It is an even closer mimicry of the sexual act than the exhibitionist attains, for the latter fails to secure the consent of the woman nor does he enjoy any intimate contact with her naked body. The difference is connected with the fact that the active flagellant is usually a more virile and normal person than the exhibitionist. There is, however, only analogy here and not identity; we must not regard the exhibitionist (as is sometimes done) as a sadist. In the majority of cases the exhibitionist's sexual impulse is feeble, and he may even be suffering from an early stage of general paralysis, senile dementia, or other enfeebling cause of mental disorganization, such as chronic alcoholism. Sexual feebleness is further indicated by the fact that the individuals selected as witnesses are frequently mere children.

Psychologically the exhibitionist's act is not so inexplicable as on the surface it may appear. He is usually a shy and timid person, sometimes of rather infantile constitution; and his act is a violent reaction against his disposition. Fetichists are also apt to be similarly shy and reserved, and Hirschfeld has insisted that there is frequently an element of fetichism in the exhibitionist. He would indeed recognize two factors as present in all these cases: (1) an endogenous and neurotic, and (2) an exogenous factor which is usually fetichistic. It is never the face that excites the exhibitionist but, much more usually, the legs, which is why, Hirschfeld believes, the spectacle of children and schoolgirls so often induces these acts, as they are most likely to display naked legs.

The reaction aroused by the act may fall into one of three groups: (1) the girl is frightened and runs away; (2) she is indignant and abuses the culprit; (3) she is pleased or amused, and laughs or smiles. It is the last reaction which affords the exhibitionist most satisfaction.

It seems probable that a form of erotic symbolism somewhat similar to exhibitionism is to be found in the rare cases in which sexual gratification is derived from throwing ink, acid, or other defiling liquids on women's white dresses. Moll, Thoinot, Hirschfeld, and others have recorded cases of this kind. Thoinot considers that in these cases the fleck is the fetich. That is an incorrect account of the matter. The white garments in most cases probably constitute the primary fetich, but that fetich becomes more acutely realized, and at the same time both parties are thrown into an emotional state which to the fetichist becomes a mimicry of coitus, by the act of defilement. We may perhaps connect with this phenomenon the attraction which muddy shoes often exert over the shoe fetichist. Restif de la Bretonne associated his love of neatness in women with his attraction to the feet, the part, he remarks, least easy to keep clean.

Garnier applied the term *sadi-fetichism* to active flagellation and many similar manifestations such as we are here concerned with, on the ground that they are hybrids which combine the morbid adoration for a definite object with the impulse to exercise a more or less degree of violence. From the standpoint of the conception of erotic symbolism I have adopted there is no need for this term. There is here no hybrid combination of two unlike mental states. We are simply concerned with states of erotic symbolism, more or less complete, more or less complex.

The conception of exhibitionism as a process of erotic symbolism involves a conscious or unconscious attitude of attention in the exhibitionist's mind to the psychic reaction of the woman towards whom his display is directed. He seeks to cause an emotion which, probably in most cases, he desires should be pleasurable. But from one cause or another his finer sensibilities are inhibited or in abeyance, and he is unable to estimate accurately either the impression he is likely to produce or the general results of his action, or else he is moved by a strong impulsive obsession which overpowers his judgment. In many cases he has good reason for believing that his act will be pleasurable rather than the reverse, and frequently finds complacent witnesses among low-class servant girls, etc.

But the exhibitionist usually wishes to produce more than a mere titillated amusement; he seeks a powerful effect which must be emotional whether or not it is pleasurable. There is sometimes an evident effort—on the part of a weak, vain, and effeminate man—to produce a maximum of emotional effect. The attempt to heighten the emotional shock is also seen in the fact that the exhibitionist may choose a church as the scene of his exploits, not during service, for he always avoids a concourse of people, but perhaps towards evening when there are only a few kneeling women scattered through the edifice. The church is chosen, from no impulse to commit a sacrilegious outrage—which, as a rule, the exhibitionist does not feel his act to be—but because it really presents the conditions most favorable to the act and the effects desired, "just what is necessary," as one such said, "for an exchange of impressions." "What are they thinking? What do they say to each other about me? Oh, how I should like to know!" A patient of Garnier's, who haunted churches for this purpose, made the significant statement: "Why do I like going to churches? I can scarcely say. *But I know that it is only there that my act has its full importance.* The woman is in a devout frame of mind, and she must see that such an act in such a place is not a joke in bad taste or a disgusting obscenity; *that if I go there it is not to amuse myself; it is more serious than that!* I watch the effect produced on the faces of the ladies to whom I show my organs. I wish to

see them express a profound joy, I wish, in fact, that they may be
forced to say to themselves: *How impressive Nature is when thus
seen!*" It is clear that we have here a trace of the same feeling
which inspired ancient phallic worship, a feeling which is, indeed,
sometimes found today, as Stanley Hall and others have pointed
out, in youths at adolescence, as well as in women, though it is
normally under restraint and merely exists as a certain pride in
the possession of the fully developed male or female attributes.

That is why exhibitionism is in its most nearly normal
forms a youthful manifestation. Norwood East found that as many
as 57 of his 150 cases, over one-third, were below 25 years of age,
the number gradually diminishing at successive later ages, while
the great majority of the whole number are unmarried. That also
is why so important a group (40 in Norwood East's cases) can be
termed "visionaries." That is to say they are cultivating youthful
fantasies of abnormal courtship, though, as East remarks, "in not
a few one is reminded of the courtships of the farmyard and the
love-antics and 'showing off' indulged in by certain animals."

It is a pseudo-atavism that this phallicism is openly manifested by the exhibitionist. There is no true emergence of an
ancestrally inherited instinct, but, by the paralysis or inhibition
of the finer and higher feelings current in civilization, the exhibitionist is placed on the same mental level as the man of a more
primitive age, and he thus presents the basis on which the impulses belonging to a lower culture may naturally take root and
develop. When the hereditary neuropathic disturbance is not too
profound there is often, under favorable conditions, a gratifying
and complete return to normal conduct.

It will be seen that the exhibitionist is but carrying one
stage further—as so often happens with sexual deviations—a sexual
manifestation which has a primitive foundation, and within duly
controlled limits and under proper conditions might even be
considered legitimate. He is often simply a too reckless narcissist.
But under our present-day social conditions his conduct, however
natural at its roots, cannot be tolerated; it may lead to nervous or
hysterical symptoms in the innocent girl who is subjected to it;
and the interference of the police is rightly called for.

But what is to be done with the exhibitionist when he is
brought before the magistrate? As Norwood East states, in a large
proportion of cases the courts now themselves call for a report on
the mental state. The problem has become a difficult one with the
more intelligent view of sexual deviations which is tending to
prevail. A small punishment has no effect; a severe one would be
unjust and equally ineffective; unless the offender is well-to-do
he cannot be sent to an institution for expert investigation and

treatment. I may here quote a letter from a friend who is a magistrate and a man of distinguished ability. "At quarter sessions yesterday there was a case of a man, a laborer, who had been repeatedly convicted of indecent exposure. The sentence was six months' hard labor. The difficulty seems to be twofold. One, there is, so far as we know, no place where such a man can be sent for detention and treatment, and two, as the prison doctor would only say the man was sub-normal and would not certify, we had no power over him. The result is that a healthy man of 38, who may well live to be 68, will in six months be let loose and as likely as not repeat his offense. He had a very good army record. Other justices were much concerned about the case and I was cheered to notice that the feeling of the Bench was much against sending such a man to prison. The only alternative was to release him. Happily we are past the stage of flogging which is of course provided for under the Statute and would certainly have been inflicted two or three years ago."

Another magistrate, who is a physician and psycho-therapist, writes to me in this connection: "I have seen a good many such cases on the Bench; they are very sad indeed. Some I have managed to get off; others had to take their punishment 'according to the law.' There is no doubt that the majority need psycho-therapeutic treatment, being mental cases rather than criminal offenders. Many are genuinely horrified at their own practise which they strenuously try to control. Much propaganda is necessary to effect a change in the conventional outlook."

With regard to the therapeutic treatment, I should like to point out that it is most likely to prove effective if carried out in connection with a sun-bathing camp on nudist lines of the kind now becoming widely recognized and accepted. If the exhibitionist is often simply a narcissist of unusually pronounced type, presenting impulses which are not necessarily anti-social, and indeed, under some conditions socially recognizable, to give him an opportunity for their legitimate manifestation is to confer upon him a new power of self-control. An exhibitionist who is encouraged to practice nudity among men and women who, being themselves completely nude, accept him as a matter of course is at once to gratify his narcissistic desires so far as they are innocent and to deprive them of their morbid intensity. If his impulses cannot be restrained within innocent limits, he faces the certainty that he will be deprived of the privilege conferred upon him. A wholesome and socializing channel is provided for an impulse which otherwise becomes isolating and degrading.

The first advice to give to an exhibitionist who has not yet attracted the attention of the police is that he should never go out alone. Hirschfeld, who recognizes the importance of this rule, remarks that the advice is always taken in good part, for the exhibitionist tends to be in terror of his own impulses. When he is actually arrested and brought before the magistrate, the sensible and humane course on a first offense is to dismiss him with a warning on condition that he seeks medical advice. In many large towns there are now special clinics which are at the disposal of magistrates, police surgeons, and social workers at a negligible cost, and these should be oftener used. On the second offense there should be compulsory detention for at least a month in a Home for examination and treatment. This is in line with the opinion of Forel that exhibitionists are not dangerous, and (unless when weak-minded) should not be detained for more than a short period for treatment in a mental home.

ALGOLAGNIA (SADISM AND MASOCHISM)

Algolagnia is a convenient term (devised by Schrenck-Notzing) to indicate the connection between sexual excitement and pain, without reference to its precise differentiation into active and passive forms. The active form is commonly called *sadism*, after the Marquis de Sade (1740–1814), who illustrated it slightly in his life and largely in his books. The passive form is called masochism, after the Austrian novelist Sacher-Masoch (1836–1895), who has repeatedly described this sexual deviation, which he himself manifested, in his novels. Sadism is generally defined as sexual emotion associated with the wish to inflict pain, physical or moral, on the object of the emotion. Masochism is sexual emotion associated with the desire to be physically subjugated and morally humiliated by the person arousing the emotion. When fully developed, the actions which constitute the algolagnia—whether active or passive, whether real, simulated, symbolic, or only imagined—constitute in themselves an adequate gratification of the sexual impulse, and, in the last degree, insure detumescence without the need for coitus.

The desirability of using the term algolagnia is shown by the existence of manifestations in this group which do not conveniently fall within the sphere of either sadism or masochism. Thus Krafft-Ebing and Moll refused to accept passive flagellation as masochistic, regarding it as simply a physical stimulant; so it may be; but in many cases it is definitely masochistic, active flagellation definitely sadistic. In either case there is an association of sexual emotion with pain. Thus the term "algolagnia" conveniently covers phenomena which are not always easy to include either under sadism or masochism.

Definitionally this merging of sadism with masochism is inconvenient, but psychologically it is sound. Masochism, as Freud put it, is sadism turned round on to the self. That indeed is the chief ground on which it is desirable to group sadism and masochism together under one heading. Clinically, they often exist separately, but there is no clear line of demarcation between them, and though it may be rare to find an element of sadism in the pure masochist, it is common to find an element of masochism in the sadist. Even de Sade himself was not a pure sadist, but had in him distinct elements of masochism clearly revealed in his works. The active and passive elements may be closely united, if not really identical. Thus a subject of mainly active algolagnia, for whom the whip is a stimulating fetich, writes: "My reaction is to the *active* side of the act. I have developed a slight interest for the passive side, but am convinced that this depends upon a semi-sub-conscious inversion or transference of the act, so that, though applied to me, it is imagined sub-consciously as applied by me to someone else." It is interesting to note, also, that while the masochist may sometimes seem masculine and robust in general temperament, the sadist is frequently a timid, delicate, and feminine personality. Thus Riedel, a sadist youth studied by Lacassagne (and finally sent to an asylum) who killed another boy, had voluptuous ideas of blood from the age of four and liked to play at killing, was of infantile physical development, very timid and delicate, modest (so that he could not urinate in the presence of another person), very religious, hating obscenity and immorality, and with a pleasant childlike face and expression. But the love of blood and murder was an irresistible obsession, and its gratification produced immense emotional relief. Another sadistic French youth, studied by A. Marie (and also sent to an asylum), was of similar temperament, very timid, easily blushing, unable to look even children in the eye, or to make advances to women, or to urinate in the presence of others. . . .

All love, as the old English writer, Robert Burton, long since said, is a kind of slavery. The lover is his mistress's servant; he must be ready to undertake all sorts of risks, to encounter many dangers, to fulfill many unpleasant duties, in order to serve her and to gain her favor. Romantic poetry is full of evidence of this attitude of the lover. The further back we go among savages, towards primitive conditions, the more marked, on the whole, becomes this subjection of the lover in courtship and the severity of the trials he must undergo to win his mistress's favor. Among animals, the same thing is witnessed in a still cruder form; the male must exert his energies in the highest to win the female and he often returns maimed and bleeding from contests with a successful rival. Alike to suffer pain and to inflict pain is an incidental if not essential part of courtship. The female, on her part, is inextricably mixed up in the same process, either by sympathetic or reciprocal influences. And if in the process of courtship the wooer is her slave and she is able to view with pleasure the sufferings she is the cause of, alike to successful and unsuccessful wooers, she in turn becomes subjugated to her mate and later to her offspring, receiving her full share of the pain which the sexual process involves. Sometimes even in the course of courtship the female suffers pain, as among many birds when the male at mating time falls into a state of sexual frenzy, and the more passive female suffers: thus the chaffinch is a rough wooer, though as the female becomes submissive he is said to become gentle and considerate. The love-bite, again, is an animal as well as human device, and horses, donkeys, etc., gently bite the female before coitus.

That the infliction of pain is a sign of love is a widespread idea both in ancient and modern times. Lucian makes a woman say: "He who has not rained blows on his mistress and torn her hair and her garments is not yet in love." The same idea, that for a man to beat his sweetheart is an appreciated sign of love, occurs in one of Cervantes's *Exemplary Novels*, "Rinconete and Cortadillo." And a patient of Janet's said of her husband: "He does not know how to make me suffer a little. One cannot love a man who does not make one suffer a little." Reversely, Millamant says in Congreve's *Way of the World*, "One's cruelty is one's power."

But algolagnic manifestations are more than a mere atavistic exaggeration of normal manifestations of courtship. They are, especially in organically feeble organisms, the manifestation of an instinctive attempt to re-inforce the sexual impulse. The incidental emotions of courtship, *viz.*, anger and fear, are themselves stimulants to sexual activity. It thus becomes possible to invoke anger or fear artificially in order to strengthen a failing sexual impulse. The most convenient method of doing this is by the action of pain: if the pain is inflicted we are in the presence of sadism, if suffered in the presence of masochism, if simply witnessed we are in an intermediate stage which may be tinged with either sadism or masochism according to the direction of the sympathies of the algolagnic spectator. From this point of view the sadist and the masochist alike merely use pain as a method of drawing on a great reservoir of primitive emotion, which imparts energy to a feeble sexual impulse.

When we understand the foundations on which algolagnic deviations rest, we see that they have only an accidental and not an essential association with cruelty. It is not the desire to be cruel which impels the sadist, however cruel he may be in actual fact. He wishes to arouse his own flagging emotions, and in order to do so he in many cases arouses the emotions of his victim; the most potent method of doing so he knows of is to give her pain. But he frequently desires that she shall feel this pain as pleasure. Even in the sphere of normal love a man will often inflict small pains or hardships on the woman he loves, and all the time be anxious that she should like them, or even experience pleasure in them. The sadist merely goes a step further, and (as in one recorded case) sticks pins into the girl while insisting that she shall all the time wear a smiling face; it is not his wish to be cruel, he would prefer to give pleasure, though he is content with the mere appearance of the victim's pleasure. Even when the sadist goes so far as to kill his victim he is moved not by the desire to cause death, but to shed blood, so securing the emotional stimulus which is imparted almost universally by the spectacle of shed blood, and Leppmann has acutely observed that in sadistic crimes it is usual to find the wound in those parts of the body, like the neck or the abdomen, which will lead to the maximum shedding of blood.

Similarly the masochist has no wish to suffer cruelty. In that slight degree of passive algolagnia which Krafft-Ebing, Moll, and others regard as simply a heightened degree of a normal attitude and entitle "sexual subjection" (*Hörigheit*), there need be no serious violence, either physical or psychic, but only a complacent acceptance of the caprices and domination of the beloved person. There is no clear line of demarcation between sexual subjection and masochism—apart from the important fact that in sexual subjection the normal impulse to coitus remains, while in masochism it tends to be replaced by the perverse impulse—and the masochist retains the same pleasure, and even in many cases ecstasy, as he experiences the manifold ill-treatment he desires. This ill-treatment may involve the reality, or the simulacrum, of a great many actions: binding and fettering, trampling, semi-strangulation, the performance of menial duties and tasks commonly felt to be disgusting by the beloved person, verbal abuse, etc. For the masochist such acts have become the equivalent of coitus, and the idea of cruelty, and in most cases even pain, never enters. If we bear this in mind the elaborate hypotheses which some psychologists (even Freud) have ingeniously constructed to explain masochism are seen to be completely unnecessary.

NOTES

1. Paidophilia is sometimes regarded as a separate deviation. Medico-legally it is convenient so to regard it. I am, however, inclined to agree with Leppmann,

who has carefully studied sexual outrages on children, that, psychologically, there is no definite deviation on a congenital basis involving an exclusive sexual attraction to unripe girls. It may easily be associated with impotent senility. Otherwise it occurs either as an occasional luxurious specialty of a few over-refined persons, or, more commonly, as part of a general indiscriminating sexual tendency in the weak-minded. So far as it has any psychological definition, it may perhaps best be regarded as resembling the symbolisms.

WESTON LA BARRE: Perverse and Neurotic Love*

THE FACT that human sexual roles are partly learned means that human individuals, unlike wild animals, can sometimes learn wrong answers to the Riddle of the Sphinx. For example, the homosexual woman appears to have resolved the Riddle wrongly as: "She may love (women), but not love the one (father) whom she loves (and hence she cannot love men)." Or she may continue, as initially, to love women: "She may love (women sexually) but not love (dependently) the one whom she loves (mother)." For some males too, because of the child's inordinate fear of the father's categorical imperative, there come other biologically wrong answers to the Riddle. This may be either because the boy remains fixed in an outmoded dependency relationship with his dominating or over-protective mother and does not dare the rewards of a more dangerous manhood; or it may be because the permitted dependent love of the child for his mother becomes contaminated with sexualized love, and then the terror of the father forces the son to repress all love of women and to masquerade instead as a lover of men, whom he really destructively hates. The homosexual man believes that "He may love (men, in a variety of non-adaptive ways), but not love the one (mother) whom he loves (dependently and/or sexually)." He has, however, mistaken a mere object-taboo of a single specific person, his mother, for a generalized aim-taboo of a whole sex, i.e., the heterosexual love of women—which is a grievous denotative confusion. And he has also been confused about the modes and the means of love—which is a grievous connotative confusion, both symbolically and psychiatrically.

The perverse and the neurotic, therefore, contrive behavior that is in a sense "adaptive." But the behavior is adaptive not to the new biological roles of the adult in his new family-of-procreation, but adaptive rather to a childish misconception of roles, which is rooted in his old family-of-origin. For the homosexual, even in anthropoids, obviously "loves" out of fear and hatred and

* Reprinted from *The Human Animal*.

frustration; sporadic homosexual behavior in infra-primate animals we can only view as trial-and-error learning or *faute de mieux*. By a merely pseudo-effeminizing or meretricious infantilizing of himself, the homosexual also defrauds and unmans or effeminizes the other male. An examination of the various perverse methods of loving establishes this point clearly. The illogic of his answers to the Riddle is quite plain.

Now the biologist is quite prepared to accept any kind of organic behavior, however bizarre—if it is adaptive. For example, in *Ceratias holboelli*, a curious deep-sea fish in which it is difficult for the sexes to find each other, there is a vascular connection between the female and the parasitic male, the latter receiving bountiful nourishment for further growth and maturity—in order to fertilize the female. This extraordinary behavior is obviously adaptive biologically. But neurotic behavior is "adaptive" only psychologically, and adaptive only to a misconceived view of biological roles. For it is difficult to see how a "love" based on fear, destructive hatred, and frustration of one's own and others' essential biological nature can be adaptive. To rob someone of his or her love of the other sex, and hence to rob them also of paternity or maternity, is doubly to rob the individual of his full human potentiality. The biologist is therefore forced to conclude that behavior which is non-adaptive biologically, but only adaptive psychologically, is properly not his concern but the psychiatrist's; that homosexuality among humans is not a genuine variety of love but a dishonest and desperate neurotic game, arising from tragic unsuccess in escaping from the family-of-origin to a family-of-procreation. Neither biologist nor psychiatrist can accept the views of literary apologists from Plato to Gide that homosexuality is a "normal" abnormality. For the normal process is clear. A girl becomes a woman by an identification with her mother and through a mysterious change in the sex of her original love object. A boy must become a man by similarly admiring manliness—in a rival he may hate or envy—through the mysterious love of male *logos*, not of physical males. When he begins to discover this logos or pattern in himself, he gives up wishing to destroy the father, but instead identifies with him and wishes to become like the father, in admiration of things masculine that comes out later as a normal adult manly self-confidence.

The psychiatrists, no doubt rightly, tell us that there is no neurosis without some basic libidinal role-misidentification. In this lies the value of their explanations of psychopathy for a biologically oriented understanding of the human animal. Their findings also fit in exactly with those of the physical anthropologist. For the family is the factory of human sexuality. The process is very largely one of individual life-history, post-natal, and conditioned. Psychologists agree that man's very sexuality is not furnished with instinctive channelings. It is, in fact, the dependent human child's very lability, ductility, and eductability which make the socialization process possible. Man does not have completely structured sexual instincts which fit him soon to adult animal life. The only "instincts" he is born with, such as the grasping and the sucking reflexes, are minimally and specifically those that fit him to the condition of the human infant. And the cultural anthropologist agrees with them all: for he is aware that man either invents his own responses, or accepts those invented for him.

JULES MICHELET: Hysteria*

MADELEINE WAS born at Rouen in 1607, and was left an orphan at nine years old. At twelve she was bound apprentice to a tradeswoman of the city, a worker in linen. The Confessor of the establishment, a Franciscan, was absolute master of the house, the linen-worker, who was chiefly employed in making nun's robes, depending wholly on the Church's patronage. The monk made the apprentice girls, who were drugged probably with belladonna and other Wizards' potions, believe he was taking them to the "Sabbath" and marrying them to the great devil Dagon. He had his will of three of them, and Madeleine, at fourteen, made the fourth.

She was filled with ardent piety, especially towards St. Francis. A Franciscan convent had just been founded at Louviers by a lady of Rouen, widow of the *King's Procureur* Hennequin, hanged for malversation. The lady hoped by this good work to do something for the salvation of her husband's soul, and with this view consulted a holy man, an aged priest by name Father David, who superintended the new foundation. Outside the gates of the town, buried in the woods surrounding Louviers, the convent, a poor place gloomily situated, and established under such tragic circumstances, seemed a fit place for the austere life. David himself was known by a strange, violent book he had composed against the abuses that disgraced the Religious Houses, the *Fouet des Paillards* (A Whip for Wantons), as it was called.[1] Nevertheless, this stern moralist had some very curious notions as to what constituted purity. He was an *Adamite*, preaching the nudity Adam practised in his innocence. Obedient to his teaching, the Sisters

* Reprinted from *The Sorceress.*

of the convent at Louviers, by way of subjugating and humiliating the novices and breaking them in to discipline, required (no doubt in summer-time) these young Eves to resume the condition of our first mother. They made them take exercise in this state in certain private gardens, and even appear so in chapel. Madeleine, who had succeeded at sixteen in being received as a novice, was too proud (too pure-minded perhaps so far) to submit to this strange way of living. She incurred the displeasure of the authorities and was scolded for having endeavoured, at Communion, to hide her bosom with the altar-cloth.

She was equally reluctant to unveil her soul, and would not confess to the Lady Superior . . . ,—a usual practice in convents and one that the Abbesses found greatly to their liking. She preferred to entrust the care of her soul to the old priest, David, who separated her from the other Sisters,—while he returned the compliment by entrusting his body to her when he was ill. He did not hide from her his private, inner doctrine, the conventual theory of *Illuminism:* "The body cannot contaminate the soul; we must, by means of sin, which makes us humble and cures our pride, kill sin," etc. The nuns, saturated with these doctrines, and unobtrusively putting them in practice among themselves, appalled Madeleine with their abominable doings (p. 41 and elsewhere). She withdrew and kept apart from the rest, living in the outer purlieus of the convent, having secured the post of *tourière.*[2]

She was eighteen when David died. His advanced age can scarcely have allowed him to go very far with Madeleine, but the curé Picart, his successor, pursued her with ardent importunity. At confession he spoke of nothing but love, and made her Sacristaness, that he might be able to be with her alone in the convent chapel. She did not like him; but the Sisters forbade her any other confessor, for fear of her divulging their little mysteries. This put her completely in Picart's hands. He assailed her when she was ill, when she was almost on her deathbed; moreover, he assailed her through her fears, leading her to believe that David had handed on to him certain diabolical talismans. Last of all, he assailed her through her feelings of compassion, shamming sick himself and beseeching her to visit him in his room. From that moment he was her master, and it would seem, confused her wits with magic potions. She dreamed of the Witches' Sabbath, fancied herself carried off thither in his company, where she was at once altar and victim. And it is only too true she was so in sad reality!

But Picart was not satisfied with the barren pleasures of the "Sabbath," but, defying scandalous tongues, boldly got her with child.

The nuns, whose turpitude he knew, were afraid of him.

Besides which they were bound to him by their worldly interests; it was his credit, his energy, the alms and gifts he attracted from all quarters, which had enriched their convent. He was even now building them a great church. The affair of Loudun has sufficiently shown what were the ambitions and mutual rivalries of these Houses and the jealous eagerness they displayed to out-vie one another. Picart, in virtue of the goodwill of rich patrons, found himself promoted to the rôle of benefactor and sacred founder of the convent. "Dear heart," he declared to Madeleine, " 'tis I am building this magnificent church. After my death you will see wonders. . . . Will you not do as I wish?"

He was a great lord, and carried things with a high hand. He paid down a dowry for her, and from a mere lay Sister raised her to the position of a full-blown Sister, so that, being no longer in charge of the turning-box, and living within the convent itself, she might conveniently be delivered or contrive abortion, as the case might be. Provided with certain drugs, and possessed of certain secrets, convents could dispense with the necessity of calling in medical aid. Madeleine declares (*Examination*, p. 13) she bore several children. What became of these infants she does not say.

Picart, already an oldish man, dreaded Madeleine's fickleness, fearing she might form a new connexion with some other confessor, to whom she could pour out her remorse. He adopted a hateful means of attaching her irrevocably to himself. He made her swear an oath pledging herself *to die when he should die, and be with him where he should go.* The poor, faint-hearted creature endured agonies of terror. Would he drag her with him into the tomb? would he set her in Hell alongside of himself? She fully believed herself a lost soul. She became his chattel, his familiar spirit bound to do his will, and he used her and abused her for every vile purpose. He prostituted her in a fourfold orgy, carried out with his vicar Boullé and another woman. He made use of her to win over the other nuns by a magic talisman. The sacred wafer, dipped in Madeleine's blood and buried in the convent garden, was a sure way of agitating their senses and eluding their wits.

It was the very same year that Urbain Grandier was burned, and all France was talking of nothing else but the devils of Loudun. The Penitentiary of Evreux, who had been one of the actors in that drama, brought back appalling accounts of what had occurred to Normandy. Madeleine felt herself *possessed*, assailed, battered, by devils; a cat with fiery eyes pursued her with amorous advances. Little by little other Sisters caught the contagion, and began to experience strange, supernatural stirrings.

Madeleine had asked help of a Capuchin, and later on of the Bishop of Evreux. The Lady Superior, who could not but be aware of the fact, was rather glad than otherwise, seeing the glory and riches a similar affair had brought to the Convent of Loudun. But for six years the Bishop was deaf to all such appeals, being no doubt afraid of Richelieu, who was trying at the time to initiate a reform of the Religious Houses.

His wish was to put an end to all these scandals. Only at his death and that of Louis XIII., in the general confusion that followed, under the Queen and Mazarin, did the priests really take up their dealings with the supernatural again, and resume their struggle with the Devil. Picart was dead, and interference looked less hazardous now in an affair in which that dangerous man might have involved many others in his own guilt. To fight the visions of Madeleine, another visionary of the same sort was sought for, and soon found. A certain Anne of the Nativity was introduced into the convent, a woman of sanguine and hysterical temperament, on occasion shown, a savage and half a madwoman, actually insane enough to believe her own lies. It was a stand-up fight, regularly arranged like a bout between two bulldogs; and the pair fell to sacrificing each other with outrageous calumnies. Anne declared she saw the Devil standing stark naked by Madeleine's side. Madeleine swore that she had seen Anne at the Witches' Sabbath, along with the Lady Superior, the Mother Delegate, and the Mother of the Novices. Not that there was a single novel feature; it was all a *réchauffé* of the two famous cases at Aix and Loudun. Both had the printed reports of those trials, and followed them slavishly, without a trace of discrimination or originality.

The accuser Anne and her devil Leviathan had the countenance of the Penitentiary of Evreux, one of the chief actors in the Loudun affair. By his advice the Bishop of Evreux orders the exhumation of Picart's body, so that his corpse being removed from the neighbourhood of the convent may remove the devils along with it. Madeleine, condemned without a hearing, is to be degraded, and examined to discover on her body the satanic sign-manual. Her veil and robe are torn off her wretched body, which is left to be the butt of an unworthy curiosity, ready to pry into her very vitals to find excuse to send her to the stake. The Sisters would entrust to no hands but their own this cruel search, in itself a terrible punishment. These virgin nuns, in the guise of matrons, verified her condition, whether pregnant or no, then shaved her in every part of her person, and pricking with their needles, driving them deep in the quivering flesh, sought if there was anywhere a spot insensible to pain, as the devil's mark is bound to be.

But every stab hurt; failing the crowning triumph of proving her a Witch, at any rate they had the satisfaction of gloating over her tears and cries of agony.

But Anne was not satisfied yet; on the testimony of her devil, the Bishop condemned Madeleine, whom the examination vindicated from the suspicions entertained, to be immured in an *in pace* for life. Her removal, it was alleged, would calm the other nuns. But it was not so. The Devil raged only the more furiously; and a score of the Sisters were soon screaming, prophesying, and struggling.

The sight attracted the curious in crowds from Rouen, and even from Paris. A young surgeon of the latter city, Yvelin by name, had already been a spectator of the farce perpetrated at Loudun, and now came to watch the one at Louviers. He was accompanied by a magistrate, a very clear-headed man and an Assistant Counsellor at Rouen. They devoted a steady and persevering attention to the matter, establishing themselves in the town and studying the phenomena systematically for seventeen days.

From the very first day they detected the imposture. A conversation they had had with the Penitentiary on entering the town was repeated to them (as a special revelation) by the devil in possession of Anne of the Nativity. On every occasion they accompanied the crowd to the convent garden. The scene and its accessories were extremely striking; the shades of night, the torches, the trembling and smoky lights, all produced effects which had been lacking at Loudun. The mode of procedure, however, was of the simplest; one of the *possessed* would declare, "You will find a talisman at such and such a spot in the garden." A hole was dug at the place indicated, and the charm duly discovered. Unfortunately, Yvelin's friend, the sceptical magistrate, refused to quit the side of the principal performer, the nun Anne. On the very edge of an excavation they were going to open up, he grasps her hand, and opening the fingers, finds the talisman (a little black thread) concealed there, which she was on the point of throwing into the hole.

Exorcists, Penitentiary, priests, and Capuchins, who were all present, were covered with confusion. The intrepid Yvelin, on his own authority, commenced an inquiry and saw to the bottom of the whole thing. Among fifty-two nuns there were, he declared, six *under possession*, diabolic or otherwise, who would seem to have deserved a taste of discipline. Seventeen others, *under a spell*, were merely victims, a troop of young women affected by the morbid excitement characteristic of cloister life. He details the symptoms with precision; the girls are otherwise normal, but hysterical, suffering from extreme disturbances and derangements of the womb, to all intents and purposes lunatic and deranged. Nervous contagion had destroyed their wits, and the very first thing to do is to isolate them from each other.

NOTES

1. See Floquet, *Parl. de Normandie*, vol. v. p. 636.
2. *i.e.* the nun who attends to the turning-box of a convent, by means of which communication is kept up with the outside world.

HONORÉ DE BALZAC: A Passion in the Desert

"THE WHOLE show is dreadful," she cried, coming out of the menagerie of M. Martin. She had just been looking at that daring speculator "working with his hyena"—to speak in the style of the program.

"By what means," she continued, "can he have tamed these animals to such a point as to be certain of their affection for——."

"What seems to you a problem," said I, interrupting, "is really quite natural."

"Oh!" she cried, letting an incredulous smile wander over her lips.

"You think that beasts are wholly without passions?" I asked her. "Quite the reverse; we can communicate to them all the vices arising in our own state of civilization."

She looked at me with an air of astonishment.

"Nevertheless," I continued, "the first time I saw M. Martin, I admit, like you, I did give vent to an exclamation of surprise. I found myself next to an old soldier with the right leg amputated, who had come in with me. His face had struck me. He had one of those intrepid heads, stamped with the seal of warfare, and on which the battles of Napoleon are written. Besides, he had that frank good-humored expression which always impresses me favorably. He was without doubt one of those troopers who are surprised at nothing, who find matter for laughter in the contortions of a dying comrade, who bury or plunder him quite light-heartedly, who stand intrepidly in the way of bullets; in fact, one of those men who waste no time in deliberation, and would not hesitate to make friends with the devil himself. After looking very attentively at the proprietor of the menagerie getting out of his box, my companion pursed up his lips with an air of mockery and contempt, with that peculiar and expressive twist which superior people assume to show they are not taken in. Then when I was expatiating on the courage of M. Martin, he smiled, shook his head knowingly, and said, 'Well known.'

"How 'well known'?" I said. "If you would only explain to me the mystery I should be vastly obliged."

"After a few minutes, during which we made acquaintance, we went to dine at the first *restaurateur's* whose shop caught our eye. At dessert a bottle of champagne completely refreshed and brightened up the memories of this odd old soldier. He told me his story, and I said he had every reason to exclaim, 'Well known.' "

When she got home, she teased me to that extent and made so many promises, that I consented to communicate to her the old soldier's confidences. Next day she received the following episode of an epic which one might call "The Frenchman in Egypt."

During the expedition in Upper Egypt under General Desaix, a Provençal soldier fell into the hands of the Mangrabins, and was taken by these Arabs into the deserts beyond the falls of the Nile.

In order to place a sufficient distance between themselves and the French army, the Mangrabins made forced marches, and only rested during the night. They camped round a well overshadowed by palm trees under which they had previously concealed a store of provisions. Not surmising that the notion of flight would occur to their prisoner, they contented themselves with binding his hands, and after eating a few dates, and giving provender to their horses, went to sleep.

When the brave Provençal saw that his enemies were no longer watching him, he made use of his teeth to steal a scimitar, fixed the blade between his knees, and cut the cords which prevented using his hands; in a moment he was free. He at once seized a rifle and dagger, then taking the precaution to provide himself with a sack of dried dates, oats, and powder and shot, and to fasten a scimitar to his waist he leaped onto a horse, and spurred on vigorously in the direction where he thought to find the French army. So impatient was he to see a bivouac again that he pressed on the already tired courser at such speed that its flanks were lacerated with his spurs, and at last the poor animal died, leaving the Frenchman alone in the desert. After walking some time in the sand with all the courage of an escaped convict, the soldier was obliged to stop, as the day had already ended. In spite of the beauty of an oriental sky at night, he felt he had not strength enough to go on. Fortunately he had been able to find a small hill, on the summit of which a few palm trees shot up into the air; it was their verdure seen from afar which had brought hope and consolation to his heart. His fatigue was so great that he lay down upon a rock of granite, capriciously cut out like a camp-bed; there he fell asleep without taking any precaution to defend himself while he slept. He had made the sacrifice of his life. His last thought was one of regret. He repented having left the Mangrabins, whose nomad life seemed to smile on him now that he was afar from them and without help. He was awakened by the sun, whose pitiless rays fell with all their force on the granite and produced an intolerable heat—for he had had the stupidity to place himself inversely to the shadow thrown by the verdant majestic heads of the palm trees. He looked at the solitary trees and shuddered—they reminded him of the graceful shafts crowned with foliage which characterize the Saracen columns in the cathedral of Aries.

But when, after counting the palm trees, he cast his eye around him, the most horrible despair was infused into his soul. Before him stretched an ocean without limit. The dark sand of the desert spread farther than sight could reach in every direction, and glittered like steel struck with a bright light. It might have been a sea of looking-glass, or lakes melted together in a mirror. A fiery vapor carried up in streaks made a perpetual whirlwind over the quivering land. The sky was lit with an oriental splendor of insupportable purity, leaving naught for the imagination to desire. Heaven and earth were on fire.

The silence was awful in its wild and terrible majesty. Infinity, immensity, closed in upon the soul from every side. Not a cloud in the sky, not a breath in the air, not a flaw on the bosom of the sand, ever moving in diminutive waves; the horizon ended as at sea on a clear day, with one line of light, definite as the cut of a sword.

The Provençal threw his arms around the trunk of one of the palm trees, as though it were the body of a friend, and then in the shelter of the thin straight shadow that the palm cast upon the granite, he wept. Then sitting down he remained as he was, contemplating with profound sadness the implacable scene, which was all he had to look upon. He cried aloud, to measure the solitude. His voice, lost in the hollows of the hill, sounded faintly, and aroused no echo—the echo was in his own heart. The Provençal was twenty-two years old;—he loaded his carbine.

"There'll be time enough," he said to himself, laying on the ground the weapon which alone could bring him deliverance.

Looking by turns at the black expanse and the blue expanse, the soldier dreamed of France—he smelt with delight the gutters of Paris—he remembered the towns through which he had passed, the faces of his fellow-soldiers, the most minute details of his life. His southern fancy soon showed him the stones of his beloved Provence, in the play of the heat which waved over the spread sheet of the desert. Fearing the danger of this cruel mirage, he went down the opposite side of the hill to that by which he had come up the day before. The remains of a rug showed that this place of refuge had at one time been inhabited; at a short distance he saw some palm trees full of dates. Then the instinct which binds us to life awoke again in his heart. He hoped to live long enough to await the passing of some Arabs, or perhaps he might hear the sound of cannon; for at this time Bonaparte was traversing Egypt.

This thought gave him new life. The palm tree seemed to bend with the weight of the ripe fruit. He shook some of it down. When he tasted this unhoped-for manna, he felt sure that the palms had been cultivated by a former inhabitant—the savory, fresh meat of the dates was proof of the care of his predecessor. He passed suddenly from dark despair to an almost insane joy. He went up again to the top of the hill, and spent the rest of the day in cutting down one of the sterile palm trees, which the night before had served him for shelter. A vague memory made him think of the animals of the desert; and in case they might come to drink at the spring, visible from the base of the rocks but lost farther down, he resolved to guard himself from their visits by placing a barrier at the entrance of his hermitage.

In spite of his diligence, and the strength which the fear of being devoured asleep gave him, he was unable to cut the palm in pieces, though he succeeded in cutting it down. At eventide the king of the desert fell; the sound of its fall resounded far and wide, like a sign in the solitude; the soldier shuddered as though he had heard some voice predicting woe.

But like an heir who does not long bewail a deceased parent, he tore off from this beautiful tree the tall broad green leaves which are its poetic adornment, and used them to mend the mat on which he was to sleep.

Fatigued by the heat and his work, he fell asleep under the red curtains of his wet cave.

In the middle of the night his sleep was troubled by an extraordinary noise; he sat up, and the deep silence around him allowed him to distinguish the alternative accents of a respiration whose savage energy could not belong to a human creature.

A profound terror, increased still further by the darkness, the silence, and his waking images, froze his heart within him. He almost felt his hair stand on end, when by straining his eyes to their utmost he perceived through the shadows two faint yellow lights. At first he attributed these lights to the reflection of his own pupils, but soon the vivid brilliance of the night aided him gradually to distinguish the objects around him in the cave, and he beheld a huge animal lying but two steps from him. Was it a lion, a tiger, or a crocodile?

The Provençal was not educated enough to know under what species his enemy ought to be classed; but his fright was all the greater, as his ignorance led him to imagine all terrors at once; he endured a cruel torture, noting every variation of the breathing close to him without daring to make the slightest movement. An odor, pungent like that of a fox, but more penetrating, profounder—so to speak—filled the cave, and when the Provençal became sensible of this, his terror reached its height, for he could not longer doubt the proximity of a terrible companion, whose royal dwelling served him for shelter.

Presently the reflection of the moon, descending on the horizon, lit up the den, rendering gradually visible and resplendent the spotted skin of a panther.

The lion of Egypt slept, curled up like a big dog, the peaceful possessor of a sumptuous niche at the gate of an hotel; its eyes opened for a moment and closed again; its face was turned toward the man. A thousand confused thoughts passed through the Frenchman's mind; first he thought of killing it with a bullet from his gun, but he saw there was not enough distance between them for him to take proper aim—the shot would miss the mark. And if it were to wake!—the thought made his limbs rigid. He listened to his own heart beating in the midst of the silence, and cursed the two violent pulsations which the flow of blood brought on, fearing to disturb that sleep which allowed him time to think of some means of escape.

Twice he placed his hand on his scimitar, intending to cut off the head of his enemy; but the difficulty of cutting the stiff, short hair compelled him to abandon this daring project. To miss would be to die for *certain*, he thought; he preferred the chances of fair fight, and made up his mind to wait till morning; the morning did not leave him long to wait.

He could now examine the panther at ease; its muzzle was smeared with blood.

"She's had a good dinner," he thought, without troubling himself as to whether her feast might have been on human flesh. "She won't be hungry when she gets up."

It was a female. The fur on her belly and flanks was glistening white; many small marks like velvet formed beautiful bracelets round her feet; her sinuous tail was also white, ending with black rings; the overpart of her dress, yellow like unburnished gold, very lissom and soft, had the characteristic blotches in the form of rosettes, which distinguish the panther from every other feline species.

This tranquil and formidable hostess snored in an attitude as graceful as that of a cat lying on a cushion. Her blood-stained paws, nervous and well-armed, were stretched out before her face, which rested upon them, and from which radiated her straight, slender whiskers, like threads of silver.

If she had been like that in a cage, the Provençal would doubtless have admired the grace of the animal, and the vigorous contrasts of vivid color which gave her robe an imperial splendor; but just then his sight was troubled by her sinister appearance.

The presence of the panther, even asleep, could not fail to produce the effect which the magnetic eyes of the serpent are said to have on the nightingale.

For a moment the courage of the soldier began to fail before this danger, though no doubt it would have risen at the mouth of a cannon charged with shell. Nevertheless, a bold thought brought daylight to his soul and sealed up the source of the cold sweat which sprang forth on his brow. Like men driven to bay who defy death and offer their body to the smiter, so he, seeing in this merely a tragic episode, resolved to play his part with honor to the last.

"The day before yesterday the Arabs would have killed me perhaps," he said; so considering himself as good as dead already, he waited bravely, with excited curiosity, his enemy's awakening.

When the sun appeared, the panther suddenly opened her eyes; then she put out her paws with energy, as if to stretch them and get rid of cramp. At last she yawned, showing the formidable apparatus of her teeth and pointed tongue, rough as a file.

"A regular *petite maîtresse*," thought the Frenchman, seeing her roll herself about so softly and coquettishly. She licked off the blood which stained her paws and muzzle, and scratched her head with reiterated gestures full of prettiness. "All right, make a little toilet," the Frenchman said to himself, beginning to recover his gaiety with his courage; "we'll say good morning to each other presently," and he seized the small, short dagger which he had taken from the Mangrabins. At this moment the panther turned her head toward the man and looked at him fixedly without moving.

The rigidity of her metallic eyes and their insupportable luster made him shudder, especially when the animal walked toward him. But he looked at her caressingly, staring into her eyes in order to magnetize her, and let her come quite close to him;

then with a movement both gentle and amorous, as though he were caressing the most beautiful of women, he passed his hand over her whole body, from the head to the tail, scratching the flexible vertebrae which divided the panther's yellow back. The animal waved her tail voluptuously, and her eyes grew gentle; and when for the third time the Frenchman accomplished this interesting flattery, she gave forth one of those purrings by which our cats express their pleasure; but this murmur issued from a throat so powerful and so deep, that it resounded through the cave like the last vibrations of an organ in a church. The man, understanding the importance of his caresses, redoubled them in such a way as to surprise and stupefy his imperious courtesan. When he felt sure of having extinguished the ferocity of his capricious companion, whose hunger had so fortunately been satisfied the day before, he got up to go out of the cave; the panther let him go out, but when he had reached the summit of the hill she sprang with the lightness of a sparrow hopping from twig to twig, and rubbed herself against his legs, putting up her back after the manner of all the race of cats. Then regarding her guest with eyes whose glare had softened a little, she gave vent to that wild cry which naturalists compare to the grating of a saw.

"She is exacting," said the Frenchman, smilingly.

He was bold enough to play with her ears; he caressed her belly and scratched her head as hard as he could.

When he saw that he was successful, he tickled her skull with the point of his dagger, watching for the right moment to kill her, but the hardness of her bones made him tremble for his success.

The sultana of the desert showed herself gracious to her slave; she lifted her head, stretched out her neck, and manifested her delight by the tranquillity of her attitude. It suddenly occurred to the soldier that to kill this savage princess with one blow he must poignard her in the throat.

He raised the blade, when the panther, satisfied no doubt, laid herself gracefully at his feet, and cast up at him glances in which, in spite of their natural fierceness, was mingled confusedly a kind of good-will. The poor Provençal ate his dates, leaning against one of the palm trees, and casting his eyes alternately on the desert in quest of some liberator and on his terrible companion to watch her uncertain clemency.

The panther looked at the place where the date stones fell, and every time that he threw one down her eyes expressed an incredible mistrust.

She examined the man with an almost commercial prudence. However, this examination was favorable to him, for when he had finished his meager meal she licked his boots with her powerful rough tongue, brushing off with marvellous skill the dust gathered in the creases.

"Ah, but when she's really hungry!" thought the Frenchman. In spite of the shudder this thought caused him, the soldier began to measure curiously the proportions of the panther, certainly one of the most splendid specimens of its race. She was three feet high and four feet long without counting her tail; this powerful weapon, rounded like a cudgel, was nearly three feet long. The head, large as that of a lioness, was distinguished by a rare expression of refinement. The cold cruelty of a tiger was dominant, it was true, but there was also a vague resemblance to the face of a sensual woman. Indeed, the face of this solitary queen had something of the gaiety of a drunken Nero: she had satiated herself with blood, and she wanted to play.

The soldier tried if he might walk up and down, and the panther left him free, contenting herself with following him with her eyes, less like a faithful dog than a big Angora cat, observing everything, and every movement of her master.

When he looked around, he saw, by the spring, the remains of his horse; the panther had dragged the carcass all that way; about two-thirds of it had been devoured already. The sight reassured him.

It was easy to explain the panther's absence, and the respect she had had for him while he slept. The first piece of good luck emboldened him to tempt the future, and he conceived the wild hope of continuing on good terms with the panther during the entire day, neglecting no means of taming her, and remaining in her good graces.

He returned to her, and had the unspeakable joy of seeing her wag her tail with an almost imperceptible movement at his approach. He sat down then, without fear, by her side, and they began to play together; he took her paws and muzzle, pulled her ears, rolled her over on her back, stroked her warm, delicate flanks. She let him do whatever he liked, and when he began to stroke the hair on her feet she drew her claws in carefully.

The man, keeping the dagger in one hand, thought to plunge it into the belly of the too-confiding panther, but he was afraid that he would be immediately strangled in her last convulsive struggle; besides, he felt in his heart a sort of remorse which bid him respect a creature that had done him no harm. He seemed to have found a friend, in a boundless desert; half unconsciously he thought of his first sweetheart, whom he had nicknamed "Mignonne" by way of contrast, because she was so atrociously jealous that all the time of their love he was in fear of the knife with which she had always threatened him.

This memory of his early days suggested to him the idea of making the young panther answer to this name, now that he began to admire with less terror her swiftness, suppleness, and softness. Toward the end of the day he had familiarized himself with his perilous position; he now almost liked the painfulness of it. At last his companion had got into the habit of looking up at him whenever he cried in a falsetto voice, "Mignonne."

At the setting of the sun Mignonne gave, several times running, a profound melancholy cry. "She's been well brought up," said the light-hearted soldier; "she says her prayers." But this mental joke only occurred to him when he noticed what a pacific attitude his companion remained in. "Come, *ma petite blonde*, I'll let you go to bed first," he said to her, counting on the activity of his own legs to run away as quickly as possible, directly she was asleep, and seek another shelter for the night.

The soldier waited with impatience the hour of his flight, and when it had arrived he walked vigorously in the direction of the Nile; but hardly had he made a quarter of a league in the sand when he heard the panther bounding after him, crying with that saw-like cry more dreadful even than the sound of her leaping.

"Ah!" he said, "then she's taken a fancy to me; she has never met any one before, and it is really quite flattering to have her first love." That instant the man fell into one of those movable quicksands so terrible to travellers and from which it is impossible to save onself. Feeling himself caught, he gave a shriek of alarm; the panther seized him with her teeth by the collar, and, springing vigorously backward, drew him as if by magic out of the whirling sand.

"Ah, Mignonne!" cried the soldier, caressing her enthusiastically; "we're bound together for life and death—but no jokes, mind!" and he retraced his steps.

From that time the desert seemed inhabited. It contained a being to whom the man could talk, and whose ferocity was rendered gentle by him, though he could not explain to himself the reason for their strange friendship. Great as was the soldier's desire to stay upon guard, he slept.

On awakening he could not find Mignonne; he mounted the hill, and in the distance saw her springing toward him after the habit of these animals, who cannot run on account of the extreme flexibility of the vertebral column. Mignonne arrived, her jaws covered with blood; she received the wonted caress of her companion, showing with much purring how happy it made her. Her eyes, full of languor, turned still more gently than the day before toward the Provençal who talked to her as one would to a tame animal.

"Ah! Mademoiselle, you are a nice girl, aren't you? Just look at that! so we like to be made much of, don't we? Aren't you ashamed of yourself? So you have been eating some Arab or other, have you? that doesn't matter. They're animals just the same as you are; but don't you take to eating Frenchmen, or I shan't like you any longer."

She played like a dog with its master, letting herself be rolled over, knocked about, and stroked, alternately; sometimes she herself would provoke the soldier, putting up her paw with a soliciting gesture.

Some days passed in this manner. This companionship permitted the Provençal to appreciate the sublime beauty of the desert; now that he had a living thing to think about, alternations of fear and quiet, and plenty to eat, his mind became filled with contrast and his life began to be diversified.

Solitude revealed to him all her secrets, and enveloped him in her delights. He discovered in the rising and setting of the sun sights unknown to the world. He knew what it was to tremble when he heard over his head the hiss of a bird's wing, so rarely did they pass, or when he saw the clouds, changing and many-colored travellers, melt one into another. He studied in the night time the effect of the moon upon the ocean of sand, where the simoom made waves swift of movement and rapid in their change. He lived the life of the Eastern day, marvelling at its wonderful pomp; then, after having revelled in the sight of a hurricane over the plain where the whirling sands made red, dry mists and death-bearing clouds, he would welcome the night with joy, for then fell the healthful freshness of the stars, and he listened to imaginary music in the skies. Then solitude taught him to unroll the treasures of dreams. He passed whole hours in remembering mere nothings, and comparing his present life with his past.

At last he grew passionately fond of the panther; for some sort of affection was a necessity.

Whether it was that his will powerfully projected had modified the character of his companion, or whether, because she found abundant food in her predatory excursions in the desert, she respected the man's life, he began to fear for it no longer, seeing her so well tamed.

He devoted the greater part of his time to sleep, but he was obliged to watch like a spider in its web that the moment of his deliverance might not escape him, if any one should pass the line marked by the horizon. He had sacrificed his shirt to make a flag with, which he hung at the top of a palm tree, whose foliage he had torn off. Taught by necessity, he found the means of keeping it spread out, by fastening it with little sticks; for the wind might not be blowing at the moment when the passing traveller was looking through the desert.

It was during the long hours, when he had abandoned hope, that he amused himself with the panther. He had come to learn the different inflections of her voice, the expressions of her eyes; he had studied the capricious patterns of all the rosettes which marked the gold of her robe. Mignonne was not even angry when he took hold of the tuft at the end of her tail to count her rings, those graceful ornaments which glittered in the sun like jewelry. It gave him pleasure to contemplate the supple, fine outlines of her form, the whiteness of her belly, the graceful pose of her head. But it was especially when she was playing that he felt most pleasure in looking at her; the agility and youthful lightness of her movements were a continual surprise to him; he wondered at the supple way in which she jumped and climbed, washed herself and arranged her fur, crouched down and prepared to spring. However rapid her spring might be, however slippery the stone she was on, she would always stop short at the word "Mignonne."

One day, in a bright mid-day sun, an enormous bird coursed through the air. The man left his panther to look at this new guest; but after waiting a moment the deserted sultana growled deeply.

"My goodness! I do believe she's jealous," he cried, seeing her eyes become hard again; "the soul of Virginie has passed into her body; that's certain."

The eagle disappeared into the air, while the soldier admired the curved contour of the panther.

But there was such youth and grace in her form! she was beautiful as a woman! the blond fur of her robe mingled well with the delicate tints of faint white which marked her flanks.

The profuse light cast down by the sun made this living gold, these russet markings, to burn in a way to give them an indefinable attraction.

The man and the panther looked at one another with a look full of meaning; the coquette quivered when she felt her friend stroke her head; her eyes flashed like lightning—then she shut them tightly.

"She has a soul," he said, looking at the stillness of this queen of the sands, golden like them, white like them, solitary and burning like them.

"Well," she said, "I have read your plea in favor of beasts; but how did two so well adapted to understand each other end?"

"Ah, well! you see, they ended as all great passions do end—by a misunderstanding. For some reason *one* suspects the other of treason; they don't come to an explanation through pride, and quarrel and part from sheer obstinacy."

"Yet sometimes at the best moments a single word or a look is enough—but anyhow go on with your story."

"It's horribly difficult, but you will understand, after what the old villain told me over his champagne.

"He said—'I don't know if I hurt her, but she turned round, as if enraged, and with her sharp teeth caught hold of my leg—gently, I daresay; but I, thinking she would devour me, plunged my dagger into her throat. She rolled over, giving a cry that froze my heart; and I saw her dying, still looking at me without anger. I would have given all the world—my cross even, which I had not got then—to have brought her to life again. It was as though I had murdered a real person; and the soldiers who had seen my flag, and were come to my assistance, found me in tears.'

" 'Well sir,' he said, after a moment of silence, 'since then I have been in war in Germany, in Spain, in Russia, in France; I've certainly carried my carcass about a good deal, but never have I seen anything like the desert. Ah! yes, it is very beautiful!'

" 'What did you feel there?' I asked him.

" 'Oh! that can't be described, young man. Besides, I am not always regretting my palm trees and my panther. I should have to be very melancholy for that. In the desert, you see, there is everything, and nothing.'

" 'Yes, but explain——'

" 'Well,' he said, with an impatient gesture, 'it is God without mankind.' "

II

The Unloved Child

M. F. ASHLEY MONTAGU: The Privation of Love*

> I on my part have come to regard the desire to love, to give,
> and "to be good" or "co-operative" as influencing the appetites from
> their very first thwartings.
> —Ian D. Suttie[1]

> All men are born good. He who loses his goodness and yet lives
> is lucky to escape.
> —Confucius

LOVE IS RECIPROCAL

THE INFANT soon learns that in order to be
satisfied, in order to be loved, he too must love, he must satisfy
the requirements of others, he must cooperate. He learns that he
must gracefully give up or postpone the satisfaction of certain
desires if he is to achieve satisfaction in others, and if he is to
retain the love of those whose love he needs. This, too, is at once
a recognizable adult pattern of behavior which takes its origin in
these early experiences. From the beginning this pattern of behavior provides the most important means by which the socialization of the organism is achieved—first, through love as a feeling
of belongingness (security), and second, through love as authority, the authority of the affectionate tie. "I belong to this family,
and it is because these people love me that I belong. I like to
'belong,' therefore I must obey them and retain their love so that
I may continue to belong." This is what the child resolves for
himself though he may never give conscious expression to the
thought. The relationships of his family life condition his personal relationships throughout his life. "They are loaded with
affection and carry the burden of giving to each a *place*—a sense
of belonging, a meaning to the process of arriving and being."[2]

* Reprinted from *The Direction of Human Development.*

381

Outside the family, as a "grown-up," the approval (love) of one's fellows is secured by conforming to the standards of the group. This is the family pattern repeated on a less intensive but more extensive scale. To conform means the willingness to forego certain satisfactions in order to obtain others, to suffer a certain amount of deprivation and thwarting of satisfactions as a discipline which may ultimately lead to what are socially esteemed as greater rewards. Conflict, repression, and aggressiveness are the consequences of those experiences both in the family and in the group.

THE PRIVATION OF LOVE

The importance of love in the early social development of the infant cannot be overemphasized. Its significance can best be understood when we consider a disease from which, but half a century ago, more than half the children in their first year of life regularly died.[3] This disease was known as *marasmus*, from the Greek word meaning "wasting away." The disease was also known as infantile atrophy or debility. When studies were undertaken to track down its cause, it was discovered that it was generally babies in the "best" homes and hospitals who were most often its victims, babies who were apparently receiving the best and most careful physical attention, while babies in the poorest homes, with a good mother, despite the lack of hygienic physical conditions, often overcame the physical handicaps and flourished. What was wanting in the sterilized environment of the babies of the first class and was generously supplied in babies of the second class was mother love. This discovery is responsible for the fact that hospitals today endeavor to keep the infant for as short a period as possible. The best place for the infant is with its mother, and if its own mother is not available, with a warm foster mother, for what the infant must have is love. Drs. Ruth and Harry Bakwin, pediatricians of great experience, make the following point:

The effect of residence in a hospital manifests itself by a fairly well-defined clinical picture. A striking feature is the failure to gain properly, despite the ingestion of diets which are entirely adequate for growth in the home. Infants in hospitals sleep less than others and they rarely smile or babble spontaneously. They are listless and apathetic and look unhappy. The appetite is indifferent and food is accepted without enthusiasm. The stools tend to be frequent and, in sharp contrast with infants cared for in the home, it is unusual for 24 hours to pass without an evacuation. Respiratory infections which last only a day or two in the home are prolonged and may persist for weeks and months. Return to the home results in defervescence [disappearance of fever] within a few days and a prompt and striking gain in weight.[4]

MOTHER-LOVE

The emotional deprivation suffered by infants in hospitals may do vastly more damage than the physical condition which brought them there. The infant can suffer no greater loss than the privation of its mother's love, for it would seem that the satisfaction of the generalized feeling of dependency, in itself a basic need, is best accomplished through mother-love. An old Egyptian proverb says that since God could not be everywhere He created mothers. The fact seems to have been more than glimpsed long ago that because the mother is the person usually most profoundly interested in the welfare of her infant it is from her that the infant is most likely to receive the supports and reassurances which love bestows. This is not to say that some other person could not do as much for it. There is every reason to believe that devoted foster mothers or nurses have often successfully taken the place of the actual mother in giving the infant all the love that it required. Normally, however, the infant receives its love from the person best qualified to give it, the mother.

Let us observe what is likely to happen to the infant who is separated from his mother shortly after birth. A typical and early case is one described by Dr. Margaret Ribble.

Little Bob was born in the maternity hospital where the writer was making studies of infants at the time. He was a full-term child and weighed six pounds three ounces at birth. During the two weeks stay in the hospital the baby was breast fed and there was no apparent difficulty with his body functions. The mother, a professional woman, had been reluctant about breast feeding because she wished to take up her work as soon as possible after the baby was born, but she yielded to the kindly encouragement of the hospital nurses, and the feeding was successful. Both mother and child were thriving when they left the hospital.

On returning home the mother found that her husband had suddenly deserted her—the climax of an unhappy and maladjusted marriage relationship. She discovered soon after that her milk did not agree with the baby. As is frequently the case, the deep emotional reaction had affected her milk secretion. The infant refused the breast and began to vomit. Later he was taken to the hospital and the mother did not call to see him. At the end of a month she wrote that she had been seriously ill and asked the hospital to keep the child until further notice.

In spite of medical attention and skillful feeding, this baby remained for two months at practically the same weight. He was in a crowded ward and received very little personal attention. The busy nurses had no time to take him up and work with him as a mother would, by changing his position and making him comfortable at frequent intervals. The habit of finger sucking developed, and gradually the child became what is known as a ruminator, his food coming up and going down with equal ease. At the age of two months he weighed five pounds. The baby at this time was transferred to a small children's hospital, with the idea that this institution might be able to give him more individual care. It became apparent that the mother had abandoned the child altogether.

When seen by the writer, this baby actually looked like a seven months' foetus yet he had also a strange appearance of oldness. His arms and legs were wrinkled and wasted, his head large in proportion to the rest of his body, his chest round and flaring widely at the base over an enormous liver. His breathing was shallow, he was generally inactive, and his skin was cold and flabby. He took large quantities of milk but did not gain weight since most of it went through him with very little assimilation and with copious discharges of mucus from his intestines. The baby showed at this time the pallor which in our study we have found typical of infants who are not mothered, although careful examination of his blood did not indicate a serious degree of anemia. He was subject to severe sweating, particularly during sleep. A thorough study showed no indication of tuberculosis. The child's abdomen was large and protruding, but this proved to be due to lax intestinal muscles and consequent distention with gas and to a greatly enlarged and distended liver, which was actually in proportion to that of the foetus. There was no evidence of organic disease, but growth and development were definitely at a standstill, and it appeared that the child was gradually slipping backward to lower and lower levels of body economy and function.

The routine treatment of this hospital for babies who are not gaining weight is to give them concentrated nursing care. They are held in the nurses' laps for feeding and allowed at least half an hour to take the bottle. From time to time their position in the crib is changed and when possible the nurse carries them about the ward for a few minutes before or after each feeding. This is the closest possible approach to mothering in a busy infants' ward. Medical treatment consists of frequent injections of salt solution under the skin to support the weakened circulation in the surface of the body.

With this treatment the child began to improve slowly. As his physical condition became better, it was possible for our research group to introduce the services of a volunteer "mother" who came to the hospital twice daily in order to give him some of the attention he so greatly needed. What she actually did was to hold him in her lap for a short period before his 10 A.M. and 6 P.M. feedings. She was told that he needed love more than he needed medicine, and she was instructed to stroke the child's head gently and speak or sing softly to him and walk him about. Her daily visits were gradually prolonged until she was spending an hour twice a day, giving the baby this artificial mothering. The result was good. The child remained in the hospital until he was five months of age, at which time he weighed nine pounds. All rumination and diarrhea had stopped, and he had become an alert baby with vigorous muscular activity. His motor coordinations were of course retarded. Although he held up his head well and looked about, focusing his eyes and smiling in response to his familiar nurses, he could not yet grasp his own bottle or turn himself over, as is customary at this age. The finger sucking continued, as is usually the case with babies who have suffered early privation.

In accordance with the new hospital procedure, as soon as the child's life was no longer in danger, he was transferred to a good, supervised foster home in order that he might have still more individual attention. Under this regime, his development proceeded well and gradually he mastered such functions as sitting, creeping, and standing. His speech was slow in developing, however, and he did not walk until after the second year. The general health of this child is now excellent at the end of his third year; also his "I.Q." is high on standard tests, but his emotional life is deeply damaged. With any change in his routine or with a prolonged absence of the foster mother, he goes into a state which is quite similar to a depression. He becomes inactive, eats very little, becomes constipated and extremely pale. When his foster mother goes away, he usually reacts with a loss of body tone and alertness, rather than with a definite protest. His emotional relationship to the foster mother is receptive, like that of a young infant, but he makes little response to her mothering activities except to function better when she is there. He has little capacity to express affection, displays no initiative in seeking it, yet fails to thrive without it. This lack of response makes it difficult for the foster mother to show him the affection which he so deeply needs. Without the constant friendly explanations of the situation from the visiting nurse, she would probably have given up the care of the child.[5]

THE INSTITUTION CHILD

Recent research indicates that to a greater or less extent the history of the emotional development of Little Bob represents the pattern of the history of most mother-separated infants. The history of this unmothered child is by no means extreme, but it does illustrate, rather strikingly, the effects upon the newborn and infant of the absence of those stimulations which are provided by the mother's love. Without those stimulations the psychosomatic effects upon the child are often disastrous. Such a child may be emotionally crippled for life. As adults such children remain fixated at their early dependent infantile level, they demand affection but cannot return it. In this particular field intensive research is now being pursued.[6] What is required are studies which will not only inquire into the personality development of unmothered children, though this is indispensable, but it is also highly desirable to discover the variation in mothering which different mothers have given their children, and to inquire into exactly the amount and quality of mothering the person has received from the mother and how much from nurses and other persons.

Studies are also required on the variations in the kind of mothering the same mother gives her child over the course of the years. A mother may be good for her child for the first year but not for the second, or she may be good for the first two years but not for the next few years, and so on in all possible combinations and permutations. This is a problem which has thus far received no attention.

Studies carried out on children who have spent their infancy in institutions lead to the following conclusion, in the words of one of the earliest investigators in this field:

[Such infants] undergo an isolation type of experience with resulting isolation type of personality, characterized by unsocial behavior, hostile aggression, lack of patterns for giving and receiving affection, inability to understand and accept limitations, much insecurity in adapting to environment. These children present delays in development and intensification as well as prolongation of behavior manifestations at these levels. At the time of the transfer [to a foster home], the children are at a stage when they can form only partial love attachments; hostility and aggression are at a peak; egocentricity is marked, and they do not recognize the individuality and needs of others. They are unprepared for and unequal to the demands and limitations of a family setting. They are exposed to attention and affection far in excess of anything they have previously known, and react excessively either by extravagant behavior, negativism or both.[7]

The work of Goldfarb originally, as well as that of others since, has demonstrated conclusively that the institutionally reared child is characterized by a personality which is strikingly less differentiated than that of the home-reared child. Such children are markedly more passive and apathetic, as a consequence, presumably, of their highly routinized experience. Motivation and ambition are lacking. Language retardation is severe and persists well into adolescence. Aggressive behavior and instability of emotional response are usual, and deficiencies of inhibition the rule. Such children are restless, aimless in their behavior, unreflective, and lacking in persistence. The impoverished social environment of the institution, the lack of a dynamic and varied social experience, is reflected in the inability of the institutionalized child to develop meaningful reciprocal human relationships. The absence of the loving attention, affection, and stimulation of the family with its human protecting and supporting ties in the experience of such children, leads to a marked insecurity with a resulting hunger for attention and affection. In the younger children attention-seeking behavior is particularly marked, and this is usually combined with hostile, overtly aggressive acts. Eventually, the conflict between the hunger for affection and the inability to respond to normal human relationships is resolved by a more consistent defense of emotional isolation, resulting in apathetic social responses and a pattern of withdrawal from life's tasks.[8]

Such children, while they may improve following adoption into a family, never fully recover from the effects of their early deprivations. It is not difficult to recognize such persons as adults. The basic personality defects are congealed at a level of extreme immaturity. By the age of three years the damage has usually been so effectively done as to affect the institution child for the rest of his life. This does not mean that all institution children are so affected or those that have been cannot substantially recover.[9]

As Goldfarb points out, "Under normal circumstances, early dependency becomes the constructive basis for the development of a growing and secure sense of independence. In other words, independence is a positive and mature adaptation based on a secure grasp of the self in relation to other people. This is to be differentiated from the isolation reaction of the institution group, for the latter reaction represents defensive adaptation to a confused, hazy, and thus fearful grasp of one's relationship to the world of people and things as well as to inadequate methods for meeting reality."[10]

The dependency needs normally satisfied by the mother are in institution children *inadequately* satisfied, and the result is a more or less serious failure of development of the affective life of the person. Such children suffer conspicuously from what David Levy has called "primary affect hunger," which he defines as "a state of privation due primarily to a lack of maternal affection, with a resulting need, as of food in a state of starvation."[11]

It is important to note that *inadequate* satisfaction of the dependency needs, *not* complete deprivation, is sufficient to produce this failure of affective development. It appears that the damage done is related to the degree of privation suffered by the infant. For example, rejected children will show very similar symptoms to institution children. The differences, however, are significant, depending on variables that have been operative or not upon such children.

The deprivation situation is characterized by a marked poverty of affective and social stimulation. In the institution child this is further reinforced by the handicapping barrenness and narrowness of the institution environment. The world of things and of people, of experience, as something lived or undergone is flattened out, and severely limited. The interstimulation of family relationships in all their manifold aspects is lost. And as Goldfarb so well puts it, "The institution child thus establishes no specific identifications and engages in no meaningful reciprocal relationships with the people. The basic motivations to normal maturation and differentiation of personality are absent. Paucity in content and organization of both intellect and feeling follow. The ego structure is primitive and undeveloped . . . Both the 'I' of the inner life, and the 'It' of the outer life, are crippled."[12]

On the other hand, while the rejected child may suffer from a greater or less degree of affective deprivation, the horizon of its experience is usually not nearly as limited as that of the institution child. It is perhaps for this reason that the rejected child does not usually exhibit any defects in abstract thinking as does the institution child. He is more anxious than the latter, more ambitiously purposeful, and possesses a much greater capacity for insight. He therefore usually responds to treatment, whereas the institution child rarely and with much greater difficulty effectively responds.

It is possible that there are some homes in which the rejection of a child has been so extreme as to produce symptoms in it of deprivation identical with those of the institution child. This is an area of social pathology which requires further investigation.

René Spitz has paid particular attention to the child which has been confined to an institution during its first year of life. Infants in two different institutions were simultaneously studied. These institutions were well organized in all physical respects: in housing, asepsis, food, and hygiene. Infants were admitted to both shortly after birth.

The institutions differed in but one factor: in the amount of emotional interchange offered. In the first institution, called "Nursery," the infants were looked after by their own mothers. In the second institution, called "Foundlinghome," the children were raised from the third month by overworked nursing personnel, one nurse caring for from eight to twelve children. The absence or presence of emotional interchange between mother and child formed the one independent variable in the comparison of the two groups.

The response to this variable showed up in many ways, but perhaps most comprehensively in the developmental quotient, which represents a measure of the total development of six sectors of the personality: mastery of perception, of bodily functions, of social relations, of memory and imitation, of manipulative ability, and of intelligence. Toward the end of the first year though the "Foundlinghome" infants had a developmental quotient of 124 to start with, whereas "Nursery" had a developmental quotient of 101.5, the deprived "Foundlinghome" infants sink to a D.Q. of 72, while the "Nursery" infants rise to 105. By the end of the second year the D.Q. had fallen in the "Foundlinghome" group to the amazing low of 45, corresponding to a mental age of about 10 months. As Spitz remarks:

> We have here an impressive example of how the absence of one psychosocial factor, that of emotional interchange with the mother, results in a complete reversal of a developmental trend. . . .
> It should be realized that the factor which was present in the first case, but eliminated in the second, is the pivot of all development in the first year. It is the mother-child relation. By choosing this factor as our independent variable we were able to observe its vital importance. While the children in "Nursery" developed into normal healthy toddlers, a two-year observation of "Foundlinghome" showed that the emotionally starved children never learned to speak, to walk, to feed themselves. With one or two exceptions in a total of 91 children, those who survived were human wrecks who behaved either in the manner of agitated or of apathetic idiots.[13]

The mortality rates in the two institutions were striking and significant. During five years of observation involving 239 children who had been institutionalized for one year or more, "Nursery" did not lose a single child through death, whereas in "Foundlinghome" 37 per cent of children died during a two-years observation period. Death, Spitz remarks, is but an extreme consequence of the general physical and psychological decline, which affects children completely starved of emotional interchange.

A large proportion of the children deprived of mother-love show various degrees of depression, in which the main presenting system is a great increase in the exhibition of the emotions of displeasure. Spitz has called this condition "anaclitic depression." In this condition anxiety reactions to the point of panic will occur upon the appearance of a strange person or some ordinary toy. Such children will scream by the hour, often with accompaniments of tears, heavy salivation, severe perspiration, convulsive trembling, dilation of the pupils, and so on.

In 19 children exhibiting the clear-cut symptoms of anaclitic depression the mother had in each case been removed from the child somewhere between the sixth and eighth month for a practically unbroken period of three months, during which the child did not see its mother at all, or saw her at most once a week.

The separation had been unavoidable, and before it the mother had had full charge of the infant, and, indeed, had spent more time with it than is usually the case at home. In the course of four to six weeks following the mother's removal each child developed the symptoms described above. No child whose mother was not removed developed these symptoms. When within a period not more than three months after the removal of the mother she was restored to the child, the recovery of all normal faculties was spectacular. Where, as in the "Foundlinghome" children, the mother was not restored no intervention of any kind was effective in bringing these children out of their depression.[14]

The central importance of the mother or of a mother-substitute for the proper psychosomatic development of the child could not be more dramatically emphasized than by Spitz's findings.[15]

Reference has been made to the important findings of Beres and Obers on a group of young adults and adolescents who had experienced extreme deprivation in infancy. Their findings in every way corroborate those of Spitz and other workers, but more importantly they hold out some hope, if not for the complete recovery of such deprived human beings, then at least for the possibility of considerable rehabilitation.

When we survey our cases [the authors write], in the attempt to find any correlations that will permit understanding of the causes of modifications of psychic structure that we noted, we are impressed rather by the individual variations. Changes occur with or without psychotherapy; changes occur early and later in life; in some cases changes take the form of continuous improvement, in others of fluctuation in symptomatology. It becomes obvious that available data do not permit any positive correlations at this time. . . .

The implications for therapy are evident. The therapeutic nihilism which has characterized the approach to these cases is not warranted if we limit the aim of therapy to increasing of ego functioning to the level of social adjustment. The most important single therapeutic factor we believe to be the opportunity for the development of a close stable relationship to an adult person, whether in a placement situation, a casework relationship or in psychotherapy. In this sense, we have been working in the tradition of Aichorn[16] who emphasized the importance of the transference relationship in the treatment of his "wayward youth." The treatment of these cases requires a flexible and a patient approach which must utilize the combined skills of caseworker and psychiatrist. To this extent the therapy of such cases would be very difficult to carry out except with the facilities of a social agency.[17]

Complete recovery is far from being claimed as a possibility for such cases, and while our purpose in this section has been to point out the importance of maternal love for the healthy development of the child, and the extremely damaging effects which follow upon the deprivation of such love, it is important not to leave the reader with a sense of the hopelessness of the lot of such emotionally deprived children. As Beres and Obers point out, there are indications that much can be achieved by and for them. Further therapeutic research in this field is urgently needed.[18]

Holman, in a study of 200 children in England, found that separation from the parents had significantly adverse effects upon the development of the child only when that separation was early and permanent. Temporary separation, either before or after the age of four, was not found to be associated with behavior disturbances, nor was permanent separation which began in the fifth year of life or later. Interestingly enough, Holman found that early separation from the father was no less adverse in its effects than permanent early separation from the mother.[19] Incidentally, Holman found that hostility and ill-treatment from parents had a more damaging effect upon the development of the children than ambivalence.

NOTES

1. Ian D. Suttie, *The Origins of Love and Hate*, New York, Julian Press, 1953, p. 42.

2. James Plant, *Personality and the Cultural Pattern*, New York, The Commonwealth Fund, 1937, p. 267.

3. As late as the second decade of this century the death rate for infants under 1 year of age in various foundling institutions throughout the United States was nearly 100 per cent! See H. D. Chapin, "A plea for accurate statistics in infants' institutions," *Transactions of the American Pediatric Society*, vol. 27, 1915, p. 180.

4. Ruth M. Bakwin and Harry Bakwin, *Psychologic Care During Infancy and Childhood*, New York, Appleton-Century, 1942, p. 295.

5. Margaret Ribble, *The Rights of Infants*, New York, Columbia University Press, 1943, pp. 4–7.

6. See John Bowlby, *Maternal Care and Mental Health*, New York, Columbia University Press, 1951.

7. Lawson G. Lowrey, "Personality distortion and early institutional care," *American Journal of Orthopsychiatry*, vol. 10, 1940, pp. 576–585.

8. For an important series of research findings on the personality of the institutionalized child see William Goldfarb, "The effects of early institutional care on adolescent personality," *Journal of Experimental Education*, vol. 12, 1943, pp. 106–129; also the following papers by the same author, "Infant rearing and problem behavior," *American Journal of Orthopsychiatry*, vol. 13, 1943, pp. 249–265; "The effects of early institutional care on adolescent personality (graphic Rorschach data)," *Child Development*, vol. 14, 1943, pp. 213–223; "Infant rearing as a factor in foster home replacement," *American Journal of Orthopsychiatry*, vol. 14, 1944, pp. 162–166; (with Bruno Klopfer) "Rorschach characteristics of 'Institution Children,'" *Rorschach Research Exchange*, vol. 8, 1944, pp. 92–100; "Psychological privation in infancy and subsequent adjustment," *American Journal of Ortho-*

psychiatry, vol. 15, 1945, pp. 247–255; "Effects of psychological deprivation in infancy and subsequent stimulation," *American Journal of Psychiatry*, vol. 102, 1945, pp. 18–33.

9. F. Bodman, et al., "The social adaptation of institution children," *Lancet*, vol. 258, 1950, pp. 173–176; M. Castle, "Institution and non-institution children at school," *Human Relations*, vol. 7, 1954, pp. 349–366.

10. William Goldfarb, "The effects of early institutional care on adolescent personality," *loc. cit.*, p. 128.

11. David M. Levy, "Primary affect hunger," *American Journal of Psychiatry*, vol. 94, 1937, pp. 643–652.

12. William Goldfarb, "Psychological privation in infancy and subsequent adjustment," *loc. cit.*, p. 254.

13. René A. Spitz, "The role of ecological factors in emotional development," *Child Development*, vol. 20, 1949, pp. 145–155; René A. Spitz, "Hospitalism," *The Psychoanalytic Study of the Child*, vol. 1, New York, International Universities Press, 1945, pp. 53–74; René A. Spitz, "Hospitalism: A follow-up report," *The Psychoanalytic Study of the Child*, vol. 2, New York, International Universities Press, 1947, pp. 113–117; René A. Spitz, "Are parents necessary?" in *The March of Medicine, 1947*, New York, Columbia University Press, 1948, pp. 37–53; René A. Spitz, "Anaclitic depression," *The Psychoanalytic Study of the Child*, vol. 2, *loc. cit.*, pp. 313–342; René A. Spitz, "Autoerotism," *The Psychoanalytic Study of the Child*, vol. 3/4, New York, International Universities Press, 1949, pp. 85–120.

14. René A. Spitz, "Anaclitic depression," *loc. cit.*, p. 331.

15. See R. A. Spitz, "The psychogenic diseases of infancy," *The Psychoanalytic Study of the Child*, vol. 6, New York, International Universities Press, 1951, pp. 255–275. See also L. Bender and H. Yarnell, "An observation nursery: A study of 250 children in the Psychiatric Division of Bellevue Hospital," *American Journal of Psychiatry*, vol. 97, 1941, pp. 1158–1174; Harry Bakwin, "Loneliness in infants," *American Journal of Diseases of Children*, vol. 63, 1942, pp. 30–40; H. Edelston, "Separation anxiety in young children," *Genetic Psychology Monographs*, vol. 28, 1943, pp. 3–95; Harry Bakwin, "Emotional deprivation in infants," *Journal of Pediatrics*, vol. 35, 1949, pp. 512–521; Adrian H. Vander Veer, "The unwanted child," Publication of the Illinois League for Planned Parenthood, April 10, 1940, pp. 3–12; Eustace Chesser, *Unwanted Child*, London, Rich & Cowan, 1948; Percival M. Symonds, *The Dynamics of Parent-Child Relationships*, New York, Bureau of Publications, Columbia University, 1949.

16. August Aichhorn, *Wayward Youth*, New York, Viking Press, 1935.

17. David Beres and Samuel J. Obers, "The effects of extreme deprivation in infancy on psychic structure in adolescence: A study in ego developments," *The Psychoanalytic Study of the Child*, vol. 5, New York, International Universities Press, 1950, pp. 212–235.

18. Along these lines see Beata Rank and Dorothy Macnaughton, "A clinical contribution to early ego development," *The Psychoanalytic Study of the Child*, vol. 5, *loc. cit.*, pp. 53–73.

19. Portia Holman, "Some factors in the aetiology of maladjustment in children," *Journal of Mental Science*, vol. 99, 1953, pp. 654–688; see also Leo Bartmeier, "The contribution of the father to the mental health of the family," *American Journal of Psychiatry*, vol. 110, 1953, pp. 277–280; O. Spurgeon English and Florence Foster, *Fathers Are Parents Too*, New York, Putnam, 1951.

BRUNO BETTELHEIM: The Children*

      . . . Although emotions a child originally felt about his parents are continually being transferred to staff mem-

* Reprinted from *Love Is Not Enough*.

bers, this always happens in diluted form. To some degree, too, the behaviour of adults at the School serves to counteract the anxiety a child felt about these very emotions. The difference between a counselor at the school and a child's mother gives the child a feeling of security at the School because he is safe there from his mother's interference, while the mother is safe from the possible consequences of his hostility.

After nearly five months at the School, Emily expressed all this as she began to communicate some of her feelings. In talking to the psychiatrist she was comparing her regular counselors, particularly her counselor Joan and a new substitute counselor whom we shall call Marilyn. Emily had brought with her to this interview a candy stick which she now unwrapped, saying it was a present from Joan. Then she added, "She becares me." When asked what this meant, she answered, "She becares me, she doesn't love me." Asked what love meant, Emily answered, "Love means to hug me and kiss me and carry me and put me down." After a pause she added, "Parents do it. Counselors becare you. They give you clothes and candy. Joan becares me. Marilyn loves me. My parents don't becare me, they're not counselors."

In these and similar remarks Emily expressed some of the reasons for her autistic withdrawal at home, but also, in a way, why it became possible for her to come out of her shell at the School and make some contacts with others. Parents, according to her, love and hug you and put you down—and from other remarks Emily made, one might add, not as the child wants things but as it pleases the parent. Counselors at the School take care of the child when the child shows a need and without the child having to give something in return. That is what Emily meant by "becaring" a child.

The new and inexperienced substitute counselor, she felt, came too close to her for comfort, imposed emotions on Emily (who was not ready for them) by cuddling her and carrying her around. This close contact, which she called love, was more than she could accept at the time and it overpowered her physically and emotionally. She was ready to be "becared," to take advantage of the care given her, but as yet she could only do so as long as no one expected her to love in return.

Experience at the School shows that of all possible relationships, the one to parental figures is formed last. This notwithstanding the fact that for one particular child or another, the same counselor may have represented first a slavey or a "sucker," good only to be taken advantage of, then a hated older sibling, and finally a much desired older friend.

The difficulty in forming parental relationships, and the

time element involved in their formation, was nicely demonstrated by the statement of one eight-year-old after having been at the School for eighteen months. Speaking of me, he told his counselor: "First I had no use for him, I didn't even know when he was around. Then, about a year ago, I was terribly scared of him; when he even looked at me, I shivered. Now I like him a lot and I don't like it if he goes on one of his trips."[1]

This child, whose relationship to his father was one of the most disturbing elements in his previous life, was able to take significant steps in integration during his initial stay at the School because he was not forced to cope with those emotional problems which an attachment to a parental figure might have revived. During the second period of his adjustment, his guilt feelings were so great that forcing him into closeness to a father figure would have overpowered him with fear and guilt. Only in the latter phases of his adjustment was he able to master parental relations realistically and to take advantage of the added protection and security which only they can provide. But even then he could express his feelings only to the figure of an older sibling.

After so much has been said about how unsuitable it is for a treatment center to be organized along the lines of a home, it should be stressed that such institutions are very adequate for children whose ability to form ties to parental figures has remained unimpaired. Such children are soon able to transfer to them the positive ties they had once formed to their parents. But then there is no need for them to be placed in a special school for emotionally disturbed children. . . .

There is no such thing as a typical child, and selecting any one of them to serve as a first example is even more difficult when writing about an institution that prides itself on considering each child as a distinct individual. But if one child must serve as an introduction, then the problems we faced with Lucille are as good as any others.

Lucille was not yet six when she entered the School. Her life history included placements in two children's homes—one of them a treatment institution—and three foster homes, none of which were able to cope with her or her problems. Between placements there were always times when she lived with her unmarried mother who was highly unbalanced. All the treatment efforts that were made in her behalf at two psychiatric clinics also failed to improve her disturbance. Among other things, psychiatric examination revealed schizophrenic tendencies, extreme hyperactivity and disorders of thinking. The symptoms which were most troublesome in her various placements were her uncontrollable temper tantrums and her sex delinquency. Before she was five years old she was already approaching strange men on the street, demanding attention from them, being extremely provocative toward them sexually, and making efforts to fondle them.

When I first saw her she approached me on all fours and was barking like a puppy. Then she jumped at me, and tried first to bite and then to touch me in the genital region. Any conversation with her then was impossible because she immediately escaped into delusional talk. Later, when we began to understand her life experiences and her reactions to them, we realized that in playing the provocative puppy she was not acting out any phantasy play, but was repeating a scene she had enacted many times before in reality, often with pleasurable results for herself. Actually, she was trying realistically to please and amuse me as she had once amused a series of "fathers" she had "attracted" to the mother by her novel performances.

These fathers would usually begin by feeding her candy and handling her while she sat on her mother's lap, and then push her off when they were ready to take over. A frequent observation of the sex act formed her most impressive life experience and much later, when we could quiet her down enough to play with her, it became apparent, for example, that playing house (to her knowledge) meant the following sequence of events: the mother feeds the baby, who is then thrown into a corner while male and female puppets jump violently upon one another.[2]

For a child suffering from an anxiety neurosis, such play might have been a sadistic interpretation of the sex act, the repetition of a primal scene she had experienced as extremely upsetting, because it showed parents in a relationship so different from the usual one. In Lucille's case, however, the play represented not the most unusual part of her knowledge of how parents live with one another, but all she knew in the world of the relations between parents. Hers was a true and not a distorted picture of her parents' behaviour, or of those who took the place of parents in her life. An immediate "working through" of these traumatic experiences would have led to nothing since nothing was buried beyond them.

For Lucille, there was a long process of learning about normal human relationships that had to come before any efforts could be made to help her place her experiences in a more normal context. She had to learn first of all about what normal adult relationships to one another (and to a child) should be like, before she was ready to work through her childhood recollections, which she had neither repressed nor conceived of as unusual.

As a matter of fact, the greatest difficulties of the majority of our children have not come about through repressive or defensive mechanisms that interfere with the normal process of living. Although some also suffer from having had too much to repress, and although all of them have worked out pathological defenses for themselves, the most important reason for their inability to get along in the world is their having failed to organize their personalities from the very beginning. It is not that they have deviately organized personalities, but that their personalities are not sufficiently organized. In most cases, their living experiences have failed to coalesce and stayed fragmentary to such a degree that no more than the rudiments of personalities have developed.

Some children show such a total lack of repression that they are hardly socialized at all. Others have failed so completely in their defensive efforts that they have given up entirely trying to get along in this world; they have withdrawn from it totally, including an unwillingness to speak, or to eat. Hence our main task is to bring some intelligible order into chaos. The reorganization of disjointed personalities is secondary, and by comparison a much simpler task, but it comes only much later, if at all.

In helping to bring order into the child's personality we rely mainly on his desire to get along in a world that provides him with ample satisfaction of all, or almost all, of his needs and not only the ones that are commonly accepted by adults as legitimate. We feel that before anything else a child has to be utterly convinced that—contrary to his past experiences—this world can be a pleasant one, before he can feel any impulse to get along in it. Once such a desire has sprung up and has really become part of his personality, then and only then can we also expect him to accept and to come to terms with the less pleasant aspects of life.

This, incidentally, is the way the normal child learns, or should learn how to put up with displeasure. As an infant (and before birth) all his needs are presumably satisfied. But only after many months of experiencing the world as something relatively satisfying do we expect him to learn to control some of his behaviour, even if that seems an unpleasant task.

The satisfaction of a child's wants must become the means which will induce him to form a positive relation to the adults who provide for his well being. Then, to the satisfaction of the child's needs, is added the unique gratifying experience that only a genuine human relationship can offer. The relation to this person eventually challenges the child to change his personality at least in part in the image of the person or persons who are now so important to him. He identifies with them, as we say, and this identification is often the starting point for the organization of his personality. Those aspects of the adult's personality with which the child identifies then form the nucleus around which he organizes his talents, his interests, his desires and his temperament, all of which have until now been chaotic and undeveloped.

But the bringing of order into chaos must also be preceded by the experience of living in an orderly world. Living day in and day out among adults who provide the child with images of reasonable and orderly living becomes a challenge to him to take up their pattern, first in his external and then in his internal life. Nor must the idea of orderliness be imposed on him by force. It must be so presented that the child himself begins to realize that this way of life is more sensible and more to his advantage. Sooner or later then it will also help him to feel that it might be better for him to organize his inner life sensibly, too.

This is quite different from the analysis of the transference relationship which is the recognized tool of the prevalent schools of psychotherapy. This method, of course, presupposes the earlier existence of relationships that can be transferred. But since many of our children have never had the previous experience of a meaningful relation, we must rely at the School on real, honest-to-goodness relationships. For example, Lucille had experienced nothing in her previous life that was suitable as a basis for forming new relationships, nor any that had ever made life worth living for her. In order to rehabilitate her we had to provide her with the entirely new experience of satisfying human relationships. Only then could she evolve the frame of reference which led her to an understanding of the world around her and of her past experiences. In her case no obstacles to her understanding of the world had to be removed, other than those which originated in correctly interpreted past experiences. But these had not only been mostly upsetting, they had all been chaotic, and therefore so was her world. No child will try to understand or otherwise try to come to grips with a world that seems utterly senseless. First, the world had to begin to look pleasant and orderly to Lucille before she could feel any desire to become a pleasant person herself, and to organize her inner chaotic strivings. In many similar cases our task is to provide new experiences that will allow ordering of the actual world rather than doing away with misinterpretations of past experiences that interfere with the development of a correct world picture.

Since so many of our children have never before been a partner in a satisfying human relationship, they are unable, at first, to form personal relations of any kind. Even children who because of overpowering pressure have been forced into seeming submission and at first show "polite" behaviour, later reveal that the politeness was only a screen behind which lay a hatred of all other persons which kept them from forming relations. Later, as they felt the security of the School, this screen evaporated and their hatred appeared. Like Lucille, they barked or they growled at us, not in a seductive way but aggressively. They could only scream, but not talk.

Richard, an eleven-year-old, overanxious and compulsively clean boy, later told us: "My mother used to wash my mouth with soap when I used bad words, but along with the bad ones she washed away all the good words, too." Richard hardly spoke to us at all for many weeks. If he had to communicate he would scream at us and there were very few things he shouted that did not end with the repeated exclamation "kill, kill," most often "kill the Doctor" (meaning me). He called himself "the Killer," and instead of painting his name on his closet as other children do, he painted in huge red letters the word "Killer." During this time he held long growling conversations with his teddy bear whom he totally controlled, as he himself had been totally controlled in the past. This teddy bear he made the executor of all his hatred.[3] Although he quickly took ample advantage of the satisfactions we offered, it was many months before he was ready to talk to us, and many more before he was able to form even one meaningful human relation. . . .

Since, or perhaps because, the new child's relations to adults are badly damaged, most newcomers are much more interested in other children than in adults. While they may remain indifferent for some time to all adults, or at best take a ruthless advantage of them, they are immediately fascinated by group life, whether positively or negatively. For a time some behave as though they were entirely engulfed by it. Hence, a few remarks on the group may precede a discussion of the new child's first concrete experiences.

In the minds of the children their dormitory group is the most important of all; it is their "family" unit. In order to preserve it as much as possible as an organic unity, we try not to add more than one new child at a time, and not to add another before the previous newcomer has become a well integrated member of the group. This does not mean that the children of such a group function always, or even most of the time, as a unified group. On the contrary, the coherence of the group often reveals itself best in the child's ability to venture out from its security to new areas of living. What is important to each child is that he knows that his group is an always available haven of security for him. Through his positive relations to the other children and adults, or the willingness of adults to take ill humour without retaliation, the child can always replenish the emotional energy he expends on his ventures into the outside world.

A new child tends to roam from group to group because he has not yet found security in his personal relations, and hence one association is as good—or more accurately, as bad—as another. In addition, he is afraid to commit himself emotionally to any one set of persons. Then comes a time when the group support is very needed and very important, because the child is still so insecure with all outsiders that he sticks to the group all the time, or at least to those of its members who are not otherwise emotionally engaged. Later, when the child feels secure in his group, he will leave it for moments at a time, but only if other children of his group are in sight. And finally he will leave it more frequently, to form shortlived associations outside of it from which he returns periodically to the security of the group.

It is often through the members of a coherent group that the new child gets his first inkling of the climate of living that characterizes the School. This happens less because of his desire to understand, than because the others are ready to form relations with him, to take him into the group. The newcomer is usually indifferent and frequently inimical to the group. His past life has taught him to expect the worst of others, and so he does. But the group—without forcing itself on him—genuinely welcomes him, which is contrary to past experiences and often a real "shock," because it is so unexpected a challenge to reexamine his picture of the world and his relations to other children. The group, for its part, tries to help the new child to become one of them not because it is the nice thing to do or because adults suggest it, but out of an inner necessity: the presence of an outsider makes them uncomfortable so they wish to make him an insider.

This is true, of course, only if the group can exist undisturbed by new additions for a considerable length of time. Otherwise, the frequent changes do not allow for the development of a group climate which is strong enough to take in the newcomer. If the various members of a group still feel unsure of one another, the newcomer is either hated because of the additional threat that his coming implies, or he is wooed as a potential ally and hence not received as a person, but used as a tool.

In a way, the reception of a newcomer into the group is a test of its coherence, a test of the security which the children of the group find in one another. To the casual observer, groups that have reached different stages in group integration may seem to function on the same level of coherence so long as they remain undisturbed. But as soon as a newcomer enters, they react differently. In the least coherent, and hence least secure group, the children will turn against the newcomer, either by behaving as if they are so much of an ingroup that there is no chance for an outsider to ever become one of them, by allowing various children to compete for his friendship, or by being openly hostile to him.

Children of a better integrated group may make a show of ingroup "belonging," of a coherence much greater than it actually is; they will go out of their way to make the newcomer join them in a hurry. They behave either as if they were accepting him as a practical test of their mutual coherence (the newcomer's eagerness to join is needed in maintaining the fiction that they are an integrated group), or as if to convince themselves through a show of coherence that the addition of a child is no threat to their mutual security.

A truly well integrated group will meet the newcomer with friendly indifference. The children who form such a group feel so secure that they can take the newcomer or leave him. If he wants to join, well and good; if not, that's all right with them, too. If a newcomer is introduced into such a group the children will explain to him what they are doing and invite him to join in, but otherwise they go on pretty much as they were. By and large they let the newcomer alone and show respect for his privacy, which is precisely what the children of a less integrated group are unable to do.

To the new child, too, the casual reception he gets from the coherent group is most reassuring—and so are the casual remarks of an "old-timer"—while the obvious overtures by members of a less coherent group will add to his insecurity. If *they* do not know where they stand with one another, how can he hope to find his place within their group? Moreover, he will recognize their interest in him for what it is: the desire to gain favour with him for their own benefit, or to overcome the anxiety his arrival has created.

Similarly, a welcoming party for the newcomer is successful in setting him at ease only if he is not made the center of the party but just a participant like everyone else. The purpose of such a party is to take the edge off everyone's uneasiness rather than to make the newcomer immediately and artificially a bona fide member of the group. The party in "honour" of a newcomer with him as the center of attention is sometimes advocated to help a new child feel "at home," but this we have found less desirable. The honour may flatter his narcissism, but narcissism will be least useful in gaining him membership in the group. Moreover, it arouses some justified fears about later being able to live up to the exceptional position such a party seems to raise him to. The awakening after the party will be all the ruder if his first experience in the group was that of being its most important member.

Thus, a party with the newcomer as the central person is undesirable in terms of the way he experiences it.

From the point of view of the new child's acceptance by the rest of the children these parties are even less desirable. In reality, it is the old members of the group who are entitled to special attention because they are being asked to take in a newcomer and also to share the adult group leaders with him. The addition of a new child means actual hardship for them and they cannot be expected to be happy about his coming as a return for his being imposed on them.

Arranging a party with the new child as the center of attention is often an effort on the part of the arranging adult to deny the real distribution of hardship, if not to turn it into its opposite. Knowing that the difficult task of adjusting to a child is being imposed on the group, some adults behave as if that were an enjoyable event, thus denying the hardship they impose on the children. Statements such as "we're all so glad to have you join us" only convince members of the old group that their interests are being betrayed. The adult, instead of protecting the group's interest against the newcomer, seems then to identify with the interests of the newcomer instead of the ones he knows longer and better.

We find it preferable to admit openly that the addition of the newcomer is a painful imposition on the old group members, one that we regret and for which we apologize. We explain why such things are unavoidable because of the mechanics of the institution and we make it clear that the party is given much more for the old members than for the new one. If, besides the other fun of the party, each child (as well as the newcomer) receives a toy, their loss is in part compensated, or at least symbolically so, by the adult and the School.

A party arranged for all children of the group rather than just the newcomer is also more acceptable to a new child who has formed no relationships as yet, because he feels that it does not oblige him, as a party in his honour might do. This was obvious from the behaviour of Alice, aged eight, who suffered from deep-seated anxieties that had kept her withdrawn from all contact with reality. Her personal withdrawal she had covered up most of her life by "goody-goody" behaviour, interrupted by occasionally violent and dangerous attacks against her mother and a younger sister whom she hated even more.

At the party we gave on her arrival she ate very little as if she wanted to show us that she knew very well she didn't belong yet. Candy that was offered to her she put in her pocket, as if to tell us she was not ready to share bed and board with us, or that she knew perfectly well she was still without status in the group. She might also have been testing to see if such taking of food was allowed. (Other children at these parties test to see if they can overeat or waste food.)

After the party the rest of the children paid little attention to Alice although she made her bid for it by talking about her family. Since the others hardly knew her, this subject was a topic of no interest to them. Finally, she announced to anyone who would listen that she was very fond of her little sister. But this kind of talk was too much for Priscilla, who had also hated a younger sister violently and had also tried to cover up her feelings at one time by overt expressions of love. Priscilla, from her own experiences, may also have sensed the insincerity in Alice's statement. Since she had learned by now to admit to her real emotions, she told Alice casually that she, for one, was *not* fond of her sister. Alice looked at the counselor, expected disapproval of such an impolite denial of social conventions. But nothing further was said and Alice felt that in spite of her statement, her true emotions had been understood and shared by Priscilla and perhaps even by the counselor. She responded by putting her toys away in her toy chest, a first gesture of her feeling at home.[4]

As with many other children, Alice used her first day to explore the School in its relation to her dominant feelings of being unloved and uncared for. She wondered who would fix her things when they got broken, and whether her toys would be safe. Then she asked who would buy her shoes, and when Lucille told her that the counselor would, and that she herself had just gotten new shoes the day before, Alice remarked that her father had promised her a new pair but had never gotten around to getting them for her. That such criticism of her father was taken as a matter of course and that the counselor made no effort to reassure her or to make excuses for her father gave her the courage to state other complaints about her parents. For one thing, she had lost a tooth, she said, and put it under her pillow but had never gotten her dime from the Blue Fairy.

When she awoke the next morning, Alice began further testing to see if the counselor would protect other children—and by implication, herself—against malice and practical jokes. She eyed a sleepy-looking child in a bed near her own and suggested to the counselor: "Tell her her mother's here, that'll make her get up." When the counselor replied she would do no such thing, she became bolder about criticizing her mother by making the apparently irrelevant comment that she was ashamed of her mother.[5]

Thus within the first twenty-four hours, Alice had brought

some of her main problems out pretty directly—her fear that she would never be properly cared for, that her mother was inadequate to the degree that she had to be ashamed of her and that her father was unreliable in his promises. All these she could state more or less openly after the lie about her sister had fallen flat and after she saw that the expression of true feelings was supported at the School even when it violated politeness and conventions. In becoming frank about stating her feelings it was also a comfort to know that her counselor would prevent her from acting dangerously hostile toward other children and thus protect her from things she was afraid she might do if there was no one to control her hostility.

Alice's entry into the School was made easier by her placement in a rather well integrated group where all other children felt so secure with each other that they were free to support her in expressing her feelings. But the placement of Paul, aged ten, was due to an emergency (several suicidal and at least one homicidal attempt) and could not wait for an opening in a group that had already developed an adequate coherence. Things were off to a bad start as soon as the counselor had shown him around the house and introduced him to the other boys in his dormitory group. Bob (aged eight) felt he could not rely on the support of his group with the threat of a new child coming up, because he was not established in it very well himself. His own insecurity, plus the age difference, made him afraid of competition from a ten-year-old boy, so he tried from the beginning to put Paul "in his place."

In a superior tone he asked Paul if he had brought his ice skates along since the children planned to go skating after the party. Paul was taken aback and felt badly about not having ice skates, or about not knowing how to skate, or both. "I forgot to bring mine," he said, and at the same time he took hold of the counselor's hand as though looking for support when he thus found his dignity attacked. She kept hold of his hand and asked him to sit down beside her, but he refused to sit with the others at the "party" table, and seated himself at a small one where she joined him from time to time. Apart from the others, he pretended to read comics, but actually he watched very carefully to see what went on. When the other boys offered him food, he declined, saying he wasn't very hungry. Toward the end of the party the children spontaneously formed a band and marched around the room singing. Paul hummed the tune but did not join them, though he waved his pop bottle in time to the music.[6]

Thus while the children in this group were not secure enough with one another to make Paul feel safe about joining

them, his freedom to observe their behaviour gave him some inkling of the atmosphere of the School. Soon after the party he
retired to his bed, but remained watchful. When he saw another
boy begin to suck his thumb after getting into bed, Paul left his
own bed under the pretext of fetching something, but actually
in order to walk past the other child, trying very hard to be casual
about it. When he was sure he had seen right, that nobody seemed
to care if a big boy sucked his thumb, he returned to his bed and
put his thumb in his mouth with relief.[7]

Thus, by observing other children who, if not further
ahead in overcoming their difficulties are at least further ahead
in not being afraid to enjoy themselves, the new child arrives at
some feeling of what the School has to offer.

The less secure the children of a group are, the less they
are able to mitigate the anxieties of a new child and the more it
becomes up to the adult to convey to the new child that he is now
living in a setting where his needs will be satisfied wherever possible. This is more difficult because the emotionally disturbed
child, as I have said, trusts adults even less than other children.
He must be helped in beginning to recognize that his dread of the
world of adults is not wholly justified, that not all adults misunderstand him, or wish him ill.

Sometimes the expression of the child's need and his testing of adults are so direct that even during the first day (or days)
of his stay it is possible to provide him with experiences that will
make his defenses against legitimate needs start to crumble. After
that he can permit himself satisfaction of at least some of the
desires which have so far remained frustrated. This satisfaction
does not always lead directly to good personal relations in severely
disturbed children, and nothing would be wronger than to expect
that it could. On the contrary, just because a child may quickly
feel secure about the satisfaction of some of his instinctual needs,
he may dare to reveal the severity of his emotional disturbance
more openly. But this means he will also be freer about showing
his negativism, his distorted ideas about others and their actions,
about the world and also himself. Newly gained feelings of
strength and security are often spent in more vigorous acting out.
In a way, though, this augurs well for their eventually being
brought into the context of a personal relation: the child no
longer acts out secretly and in isolation, but in the presence of a
significant adult; or he directs against that person the negativism
which is no longer bottled up inside.

Paul, before coming to the School, had made all his destructive attempts when no adult was present. But within a month
after enrollment, he had brought his self-destructive tendencies

into a social context, and then expressed them mainly in symbolic ways. He no longer tried to destroy himself or others, but what was worn next to his or their bodies. First, he tried to set his own pajamas on fire and when he was stopped from doing that, he made a heap of the other children's pajamas a few days later and tried to burn them. But both efforts were made only after he was sure that his counselor would immediately be available, and after she extinguished the small fires he experienced obvious relief.[8]

Sometimes the new child's behaviour is so threatening to even a coherent group that the children draw away from the new-comer and then the School has to be interpreted mainly by adults. Of course, it cannot be said too often that emotionally disturbed children do not trust any verbal statements. Adult actions they trust somewhat more, but most convincing is the feeling-tone con-veyed by the act. Nevertheless, the behaviour of adults remains a poor substitute for the conviction that is carried by the statements and behaviour of other children. Still, we must often rely on our-selves when the new child's behaviour is such as to forcefully alienate the group.

Mary on her first day, is a case in point. This child was nine years old when she came to the School, and while her behav-iour showed psychotic features, it was rather her asocial actions that had led to her placement. These included stealing, violent attacks against children and repellant cruelty to animals. As soon as Mary was introduced to her group, Grace, one of the others in the group, did her best to make Mary feel at home. She asked her a few questions and when these brought no response she seemed to sense that a new child could not be expected to reveal personal matters if she herself did not take the initiative. So she told Mary that her parents were dead.

This broke the ice for a moment and Mary replied that she herself had been living with an aunt. Then Grace volunteered that things weren't bad here, much better than in a foster home she had lived in where she had been kicked around. To this Mary replied with high glee and a nasty smile that she had once hit a girl over the head with a lead pipe so badly that many stitches had to be taken in the child's head (a true statement) and that the children here had better watch out and not cross her. This atti-tude perturbed the other children enough to have them draw away from her.[9]

Fortunately, the security the others had already gained at the institution and with one another sufficed to keep them from being frightened by Mary. Therefore, they did not need to react with a show of how dangerous they could be, as children in a less secure group might have done. But her behaviour was enough for them to wish to steer clear of her and they left her strictly alone which, of course, did not make Mary feel any more at home.

Since this avenue of coming to terms with the School was now closed, it was up to a counselor to try to show Mary in some practical way, and despite her great negativism toward adults, what the attitude of the School is toward children. As the counselor was taking her around the School, Mary showed some interest in the paints she discovered in the play room. At the same time she told the counselor how once, when the painters were redecorating her home, she had started to play with the paint but then got it all over herself and got a bad licking. The counselor made no attempt to assure her that such behaviour was accepted at the School (a statement Mary would either have considered untrue or an effort to play up to her because she was so dangerous) ; she merely told Mary that these paints she could use right away if she wanted to.[10]

Gingerly, Mary took up the paints, but soon she became more courageous, and asked what would happen if she got paint on herself. The counselor told her "nothing," that she would just wipe it off, and she showed her how easily you can do that with turpentine. At that, Mary dipped her fingers all the way into the paint jar and made blotches all over her arm. Then she held out the arm for the counselor to wipe. While this was being done, she asked, "What do you do to girls who stink like turpentine?" at which the counselor only laughed. Thus reassured she opened up with a long stream of questions—who took care of the children and who did what with them and when—ending up with some questions about playing with clay, though despite encouragement, she hadn't the courage to try it that first day.

Mary, on her original visit to the School, had been encouraged to ask questions but there was nothing she had wanted to ask. Only after a concrete experience had shown her that we understand children, did it make sense to her to listen to what we had to say. Previously she had shown no interest in learning about the School. Perhaps she preferred not to be talking to strangers about what she had on her mind; perhaps she had no interest in talking with us because she did not trust us to tell her the truth; or it may have been just her extreme general negativism to adults. Now, as she listened, what impressed her the most about life at the School was the assurance that she could rest or go to sleep whenever she wanted to. This statement she tested immediately by retiring to her bed. Once there she seemed relieved enough, but probably because she felt the need to retire from temptation after she had given in to it by soiling herself with paint and by overcoming her negativism about asking questions freely.

Since we respected her right to behave negatively and to avoid contact with us, the immediate sequence to this incident did not happen until approximately a month later. Although in chronology it does not belong to the first encounter, psychologically it belongs so closely to her first experience at the School that it may be mentioned here.

When Mary next consented to go with her counselor to the playroom, she painted the face of an unhappy little girl, and when her counselor asked who this was, she indicated clearly that it was a picture of herself. But then she added that the girl had no name, that she was just any girl, "a girl without any name." Her feeling seemed to be that she had no personal identity of her own.[11]

After thus revealing one of her more serious problems, she immediately withdrew again from all contact with her counselor and fell back into solitary eating. But since she did this in the counselor's presence, she was able to re-establish contact after eating awhile because the fact that her behaviour was not criticized brought back some confidence, if not in herself then at least in the School. Then she asked the counselor to read her a story she knew very well. It was the story of a caterpillar (in Mary's words, "an ugly worm") who after many adventures turned into a butterfly. Midway through the story her tension rose and she said, "Do you know what happens in the end?" "Yes," the counselor said, "but why don't you tell me?" So Mary told her excitedly how the ugly, unhappy worm turns into a beautiful, happy butterfly. It was the first time she had shown any positive emotion and it was as if she had hope now that some day she herself might be changed from a nameless, just-any-girl, into a happy, distinct individual.

To be able to believe that, at least for a moment, to believe that she could become a distinct person, that satisfaction and happiness might be available to her, was really the beginning of progress in treatment. This was really Mary's first day of being "in the School;" before that she was never more than physically present. Thus, in a way, it was her first day of "living" there, although she had been there some thirty days and nights.

While the true beginning of Mary's life at the School was removed by one month from the day of her arrival, it is possible, with other children to create this experience at the very beginning of their stay.

Frank (aged eleven), was an acting-out delinquent whose behaviour was traceable to early and continued deprivation due to placement in inadequate and ever-changing foster homes.

When his mother finally married again and established a suitable home his attitudes had become so asocial that he was constantly at odds with society. One of his efforts to compensate for many past disappointments took the form of overeating, which resulted in obesity.

His parents' efforts to have him lose weight by dieting were interpreted by him as due to dislike on their part. During his first meal at the School he announced that it was important for him to reduce and he asked the counselor not to serve him too much and to remind him to watch his diet. He was told matter-of-factly that he could eat as much or as little as he pleased, that it was entirely up to him, and that we had no wish to influence him either way. As it turned out, he hardly touched his food. The counselor assured him that it was all right with her, except that he would probably get hungry later on if he ate nothing at all. This apparently convinced him that she meant it when she said he could eat as much as he liked, and he fell on his food wolfishly. He requested four helpings of the main fare and five of the dessert, and after he had eaten most of that, he asked "Is that all we have to eat?" He was given another helping, after which he was ready to admit he had had enough.[12]

On the same day Frank set about learning how far he could go in the use of "bad" language. Although his own talk was full of obscenity, he criticized other children, saying: "You swear an awful lot here." Then he turned to the counselor and asked, "How come you let them talk like that? Don't you stop them?" She told him she saw no reason for interfering, but then he wanted to know, "Is it because you can't stop them?" (Only weakness, he felt, could explain why it went by unpunished.) On this very first day Frank also wanted assurance about enuresis and asked what would happen if he ever wet his bed. When his counselor told him, "nothing," except that his sheets would be changed, he asked to be wakened in the middle of the night. This request she refused, although he pestered for a promise of some kind, and when he saw that she meant what she said, as in the case of his food, he was vastly relieved.[13]

Next, with surprise, he investigated the stuffed animals which he noticed on the beds of the other children. "That's kind of funny, isn't it?" he said. "All of them having stuffed animals. That's like babies, isn't it?"

From the very beginning, Frank was exploring to find out whether satisfaction of his special needs (such as the need to overeat) was available to him, and whether these things took precedence in our minds over abstract norms (how much a boy of his age "should" eat); it was also important to him to find out if the free and honest expression of his feelings (through "bad" language) was possible, or whether he had to hide his true feelings behind pretense and "polite" language. Moreover, he found out that his infantile or neurotic tendencies (bedwetting) were taken for granted as legitimate needs, or legitimate in terms of his disturbance. The fact that he and the others could play with stuffed animals may have told him vaguely that children at the School can be childish or mature as they wish, or as their emotional need may be, and that they need not conform to standards of maturity out of line with their emotional development of the moment.

Unlike many of the children who come to the School, protection against parental interference was not a major worry with Frank and therefore he was not at all curious about it. As a runaway child he knew the answer to the problem of too much parental or adult interference. He had his symptomatic behaviour: he could truant. Children whose personality structure does not permit them to eliminate parental control by acting out or by running away but who, for example, must swallow their hostility, seek assurance first and foremost that we intend to protect them from their parents. Until they feel safe on that score they cannot permit themselves to do any exploring at all. Without that assurance it makes little difference whether or not we allow them to satisfy those asocial or infantile (but nevertheless real enough) needs, pleasures which their parents always frowned on or frankly prohibited.

Hank, a seven-year-old negativistic boy, had retaliated for years against what he experienced as parental rejection by aggression and violent temper tantrums. With these tools he had successfully intimidated his parents and other children—so much so that neither public nor private schools could keep him. From earliest infancy the parents had enforced, among other things, a rigid regime of cleanliness and "good" behaviour, and had exercised pressure for prematurely grown-up ways. So it is understandable that his first concern at the School was to investigate those aspects of living which had always placed him under greatest stress.

First he wanted to know how much safety there was at the School from parental control. From the moment he came, he expressed his resentment of his mother, but in doing so he showed how he rebelled against her control, and at the same time submitted to it. As with all other children when they come to the School, we asked him what he would like to be called. He said, "Hank, not Henry" and then added that he hated the name Henry because that was what his mother liked to call him.

When he was taken up to see his dormitory, he said he pre-

ferred to sleep in the upper bunk of a double decker bed, because
his mother always thought he might fall out of an upper bunk
and would want him to sleep in a lower one. When he saw the
stuffed animals, he immediately defended himself from the temptation to childish enjoyment. "Oh, no," he said, "none of that stuff
for me—I'm grown up; I don't like stuffed animals!"

His anxiety about cleanliness showed itself immediately.
The bathrooms are adjacent to the dormitories, which most children accept without any ado. But Hank said he wished his bathroom were right in the same room with his bed, and for some time
he pretended it was, so central an issue for him were the functions
served by the bathroom.

As he unpacked his tooth brush that first day, he told the
counselor, "You know, I love to brush my teeth." She laughed
a little, and gave him to understand she was not very convinced.
So he repeated his statement. Then, as it brought no response, he
switched to some innocuous topic, but after a few minutes of
small talk, he asked her, "What happens around here if you don't
brush your teeth?" She told him we were not very concerned about
it but that his teeth might get dirty, and he admitted, "That's
right, they might. But I still forget to brush my teeth sometimes."
She assured him that all boys sometimes forget to brush their
teeth, and with that he was apparently satisfied.[14]

Yet in spite of this conversation, no real contact had been
established. Hank remained very distant, as if the counselor and
the other children did not really exist. The next evening, when
he was in the tub, he began to tell her that he usually quarreled
with his mother when she made him take his bath. As he told her
of these things, he went through a ritualistic soaping, rubbing,
and rinsing of each separate part of his body, washing each one
several times. "I have to do a very close inspection job," he said,
"because I don't like to take chances." She assured him no one was
going to inspect how well he cleaned himself, but it made no
impression. "Oh, but I can't take it easy," he said, "my mother
told me not to." The counselor continued to assure him without
pressing the point, to which he replied, "Oh, but my mother
might move in here with me, and then she'd see." The counselor
promised him that was entirely impossible, but he was still un-
convinced. "Well, Mother might come as a counselor," he said.
"You never can tell."[15]

Since he had no faith in her statements as yet, he kept asking other children if it was true that parents never visited the
School. It was only after they had all told him repeatedly that
visits from parents are rare, that the children are told about them
beforehand, and that parents never enter the part of the building

the children live in that he allowed himself to become less compulsive about his washing. Then his anxieties about cleanliness and elimination and his numerous other compulsions slowly gave way to more natural behaviour and he became more relaxed.

Hank maintained his distance until the end of his second day at the School. That night, at bedtime, the counselor read him a story, then sang him a few songs and finally brought him his night snack. When he saw the food appear, he unbent at last. "Gee," he said, "three things we get when we go to bed—stories, songs and something to eat." This time there was real contact between counselor and child. He then asked her to buy him a stuffed animal and she promised he would have it the next day. That night, Hank fell asleep in a matter of minutes though his long history in insomnia and night terrors was to reappear again and again before he knew genuine night rest.[16]

While it is true that Hank's compulsions and the most asocial expressions of his fears and hostility disappeared very soon, basically his anxious and hostile personality structure could change only very slowly. In general, the assuring and protective environment of the School soon permits the child to give up his pathological defenses against early fixations. For this reason, it was possible for Hank to relinquish his bathing ritual when the necessary assurance was offered in the very situation in which it began. But undoing his strong anal fixations and starting him on the path to changing his personality did not happen as dramatically as his giving up of defensive behaviour. The reason may be that the compulsive defense of the bathing ritual was externally imposed by the parent rather than one that was developed spontaneously by the child.

Similarly, the parentally imposed pretension that one is grown up at seven and no longer wishes to play with childish toys (or that one loves to brush one's teeth), are given up rather quickly, as were Frank's pretended wish to diet. But these do not really imply progress in personality integration. Instead they should be viewed as necessary steps in treatment which need to be taken before important changes in the child's personality can take place.

NOTES

1. Participant observer: Ronnie Dryovage.
2. Participant observer: Florence White.
3. Participant observer: Patty Pickett.
4. Participant observer: Joan Little.

5. Participant observer: Joan Little.
6. Participant observer: Gayle Shulenberger.
7. Incidentally, although Paul had begun on his very first night to return to primitive forms of satisfaction, he soon became frightened and felt we were dangerously indulgent. He complained for some time that we were spoiling him and asked the counselor not to permit him or the others what he felt to be undesirable behaviour, such as messing with food or wasting it, or getting presents too often.
8. Participant observer: Gayle Shulenberger.
9. Participant observer: Joan Little.
10. Participant observer: Gayle Shulenberger.
11. Participant observer: Gayle Shulenberger.
12. Participant observer: Patty Pickett.
13. Participant observer: *Idem.*
14. Participant observer: Ronnie Dryovage.
15. Participant observer: *Idem.*
16. Participant observer: Ronnie Dryovage.

BERNARD BRESSLER: Dreams and Early Memories*

. . . During the initial phase of the analysis, the patient continued to maintain the myth of her mother's irreplaceable goodness. Frequently, when she spoke of her mother, the patient wept, for she missed the dead woman very much, and recalled a repetitious dream about her mother returning only to leave shortly. It soon became clear that the patient's limitless sense of her mother's goodness served both to deny her own deeply repressed rage over the birth of her rival and to seduce her mother into giving her the love the patient felt she never received from that time on.

Objectively it can be said that the parent was neither the most Holy Mother of consciousness nor the carnivorous witch of the deep unconscious, though she did entertain certain personality quirks. Not only had she frequently informed the patient that during her first pregnancy she wanted a dark haired boy but, for some reason or other, was ashamed of the patient's red hair and would often buy hats to disguise the objectionable carrot-top. This served to make the patient feel rejected. In addition, the mother was not a good sex informant. She failed to prepare the patient adequately about her menstrual period and, in addition, when the patient was about eight or nine, typical of the women of her generation, the mother pointed to a feeble-minded girl, whom the patient knew, saying, "That's what will happen to you if you play with yourself."

However, the mother was a much freer individual than the patient. When the patient was fifteen the mother married a

* Reprinted from *"First Dreams in Analysis."*

second husband, a bishop in the Mormon church. Shortly after the marriage, the patient found a contraceptive in her mother's bedroom and was quite surprised about it. When the mother offered to talk about it, however, the patient refused to listen.

During the analysis proper, the patient denied knowing anything about sex until she was 18 years old, although she could identify feelings at an earlier age which she later realized were sexual. The sadomasochistic nature of her sexual fantasies became clear in the transference. For example, she remembered a girl cousin who fell on a nail which stuck in her vagina and injured her badly. This, to the patient, was like having intercourse. After a dream in which the patient became aware of sexual feelings towards the analyst, she remembered how she had almost died after having her tonsils removed and that, at six also, she had broken her arm as a result of a fall. The patient interpreted both events as punishment meted out by her murderous, castrating mother who was bent on destroying her child because she had had sexual feelings towards her father. In passing, it can be noted that the patient fell quite often; her fear and proclivity seemed to be her way of preventing and acting out a traumatically repressed memory.

Significantly, the patient had no real relationship with a man prior to the mother's death. Subsequently, though the patient had superficial contact with men, her first and only other sexual involvement prior to the one initiated just before entering treatment, was a rather narcissistic, phallic man whose Don Juan personality resembled her father's. At no time, however, was there a question of marriage either on her part or his. Despite this father resemblance, the over-all relationship was almost a direct mother and child representation, with the patient taking care of him in the same way she had taken care of her mother—and, in the same way she had wanted to be taken care of. Moreover, since the patient was completely frigid their sexual relationship was meaningless. They used to go to a hotel or motel and she would insist on a darkened room—thereby darkening her face as her mother had once done with the hat; he would then have intercourse with her, in a rather perfunctory fashion.

Needless to say, the patient's deep fixation on an introjected, annihilating mother figure prevented her from experiencing orgasm. "In the ecstasy of orgasm," Deutsch[1] points out, "the woman experiences herself as a helpless child—abandoned to her love partner—a deep experience in which her ego becomes the child she conceives in her fantasy and with which she will continue to identify herself when the fantasy comes true."

Regression in the service of the ego was impossible for the

patient since, due to her rage over her sister's birth, the patient's unconscious image of herself was that of a cannibalistic infant, ready to eat or to be eaten. To allow an eclipse of consciousness was subliminally similar to inviting her own death.

For a fuller insight into the problem, I would like to cite an example Deutsch gives of a woman who reversed the process, an obsessional neurotic who

. . . constantly tormented herself with feelings of guilt; she accused herself of having caused the deaths of various relatives by acts of negligence. After she married and overcame the first difficulties of coitus, she achieved full orgastic gratification. But after achieving the orgastic eclipse of consciousness, she was seized by a fear of never being able to awaken from this state. During each following coitus she compulsively watched herself in order 'not to go too far,' and as a result became frigid. The destructive elements intensified her masochistic readiness and transformed her pleasure into a fear of death. Usually, such a fear of death is mobilized during childbirth or during the expectation of childbirth.

. . . In addition, the patient was impelled to discuss her irregular menstrual period—her concern over her disorderly menses running through the analysis like a red thread or (umbilical) cord. The patient not only returned to this problem in her verbal communications; her body seemed to speak a language of its own. She appeared able to have or not to have a period as her unconscious saw fit—with excessive flow, extreme pain and the passing of clots, and sometimes even having two periods in one month.

It was as though her body defended itself against the accusations of an archaic and punitive superego—or, stepping into its own primitive conception of a pregenital ogre, became itself the murderous mother punishing her child. . . .

Gradually, the patient attained symptomatic relief and her menstrual periods became regular, almost completely without pain; the menorrhagia and metrorrhagia disappeared. Further, now that on one level at least her mother was no longer the murderous creature of childhood fantasy, the patient began to think of marrying her boyfriend who was, under the circumstances, the best possible choice.

NOTES

1. Deutsch, H.: The Psychology of the Sexual Act. *Psychology of Women,* Vol. II. New York: Grune & Stratton, 1945.

AUGUST AICHHORN: The Delinquent*

WE DO not always have to go so deeply into our problem to discover the original causes of dissocial outbreaks as was necessary in the cases described in the last chapter. Nor do we always need to uncover these first causes before we start our work of re-education. It suffices at first to make sure of the direction in which they lie. The course of the treatment will of itself lead us into the deeper underlying causes of the delinquency.

I shall now tell you about a boy in our institution whose difficulties became clear after a single interview because of our psychoanalytic understanding. However, I shall not try at the present time to differentiate between the immediate precipitating cause and the deeper motives. My intention is to show you how the psychoanalytically trained worker looks at the situation, and how he draws his conclusions.

From the case history, we learned that the boy was a seventeen-year-old carpenter's helper, and had been learning his trade in his father's shop. Here he had repeatedly stolen considerable amounts of denatured alcohol and some lumber. The father had first tried threats and then severity, entirely without effect. The parents were troubled about him and hoped a period in our institution would influence him for the better.

I was struck by the statement in the history that he had urinated into the empty bottles in order to conceal the theft of the denatured alcohol. We could pass over this point as something accidental, and be satisfied with the explanation that it was easy for him to cover up the theft in this way since urine has the same color as denatured alcohol. But let us look for other possible reasons. Why did he do just this? We need the knowledge that we have gained from psychoanalysis to help us answer this question. While reading the history, I recalled the analysis of a neurotic patient in which there had been a similar situation, where the act of urinating into a bottle had meant revenge on his father, carried out by the same organ with which he felt his father had injured him. It occurred to me that this action might have the same meaning for this dissocial boy. Perhaps I have aroused your antagonism with this assumption and you may repudiate this explanation as absurd or unacceptable. But you must suspend judgment and consider the facts. When you learn to look at things differently you will not raise immediate objections but will say that perhaps it could be so. We do not yet know whether our assumption is true or not; we must first observe the boy in the institution and talk with him.

* Reprinted from *Wayward Youth*.

A much more important and serious argument against the interpretation of single incidents like this is the danger of drawing too general conclusions from them. If we try to spare ourselves a thorough examination of the boy himself we shall go astray; we may easily overlook facts and arrive at false conclusions. We must approach the situation without prejudice and preconceived ideas, and consider carefully all that he has to say. It was only a fortunate coincidence that enabled me, through my experience with the neurotic case, to gain a clue to the significance of this boy's behavior.

When this boy came, a big, husky, overgrown youth, I received him myself, as I did all newly admitted boys. After this I had no direct contact with him for a period in which I left him to adjust himself to the environment. The reasons for this mode of procedure will be clearer when we discuss the subject of the relationship which must be established between the child and the worker or counsellor. About two weeks after the boy's admission, a nice-looking young woman of about twenty-five came to ask about him. Up to this time, I had not yet had a long talk with him. However, I had kept in touch with the people in contact with him and I knew what he was doing. I took it for granted that the girl was his sister and was surprised to find that she was his stepmother. From his counsellor I learned that he often talked of his stepmother in his group and had already written her two letters. I had no idea of their content as we did not read our charges' letters, and they could write when and to whom they pleased. The woman was willing to talk freely about her stepson, and spoke understandingly about him in spite of all the difficulties he had made at home. When she told me how the neighbors held her responsible for the behavior of the boy—because that is always the way with stepmothers—she cried and got very much excited that she should be so blamed. She said that she was not a bad stepmother, that she treated the boy well, that he would say so too, because he liked her. When I asked her how she knew that he liked her so much, she became embarrassed and hesitated. When I pressed her for an answer, she said that it would be so easy for me to misunderstand and that I might suspect something for which there were no grounds. I assured her that I would think nothing of the sort, that I would listen attentively and that her cooperation would be very important for the real understanding of the boy. Thereupon she related: "When we go along the street together he often turns to me and says, 'See, Mother, how people look at us.' That makes me think that he considers himself a grown-up man. He has written me twice to come to visit him and in both letters he asked me to wear my brown dress so that the boys could see it." I asked her if she had the dress on. "Yes, I must give him some pleasure." We talked of other things, of her relationship to the boy and to his father, which seemed throughout normal and pleasant. Returning to the subject of her relationship to the boy, she said that he had often told her to let him know when she needed money and then he would sell his father's lumber and bring the money to her. She had never taken any from him and had not known of the actual stealing for a long time. She had always felt that this talk was only joking. It was she, however, who first learned of his misdemeanors. All her efforts to influence him for the better were in vain so that she finally decided to tell his father. He was unable to influence the boy either with mildness or severity. The boy became more troublesome and more hostile toward his father. Because of the stealing, they were afraid to try to get him another job. It therefore seemed necessary to place him in an institution. The woman became gradually more confidential and said spontaneously that she had always felt that the boy had more feeling for her than children usually have for a stepmother. For this reason she could not understand why he did not change his behavior in response to her admonitions, and she came to doubt his real feeling for her. There had been no question of a more intimate relationship between them. I felt certain of this not only from my impression of the woman herself but also because of the way in which she gave this information. She had been married to the boy's father for three years. She was a friend of his mother, and long before her death had been a frequent visitor in the house. The boy was twelve when her friendship with his mother began. Even at that time she had found him an alert, pleasing boy who often showed her a kind of childish tenderness.

We can easily imagine the conflict into which this boy was thrown. During his adolescence a woman appears in the household who is not enough older to be excluded as a love object. He directs his libidinal strivings toward her. The relationship goes on peacefully for two years; nothing improper happens; he has for her the normal tender feelings of an adolescent. We can assume that, had his mother lived, this woman, who later became his stepmother, would have been only one stage in his development; but the father marries her when she was still an object of adoration to the boy. He is at puberty, a period in which the unconscious erotic feelings can come very close to breaking through into consciousness. Such erotic expressions were now no longer permissible and must be repressed. This brought the boy into an unbearable relationship to his father. The father had not only taken the loved one away from his son, but now forces her on him as a mother. This aroused hate and aggression against the father. Thus the dissocial behavior of the boy becomes understandable. It is analogous to the neurotic symptom which has its motivation in unconscious sexual wishes.

The neighbors were right. The stepmother was a cause of the boy's misdemeanors, but not in the way they thought and not in a sense which she and the boy could comprehend.

We shall conclude the discussion of the causes of dissocial behavior here and take up other questions of remedial training, breaking away from the usual procedure of interpolating theoretical explanations. I shall now give a continuous report of a case from the time the boy was brought to me to the point at which we might consider him adjusted. The theoretical considerations in this case we shall leave to the end. We shall not concern ourselves too deeply with the causes of the delinquency but shall consider more in detail the process of treatment.

A factory foreman brought his seventeen-year-old son into the child-guidance clinic because he wanted to put him in an institution. The boy was at this time apprenticed to a shoemaker. From the father we learned certain important facts. Until the previous summer the son had been a good boy who made no trouble at home or in the shop. One day he asked his father for some money, saying that he could get the leather to make himself a pair of shoes cheap. He obtained the money but failed to come home that night, and the family learned the next day that he had not been at the shop. Since such a thing had never happened before, the family was very much concerned, feared that he had met with an accident or had been attacked. They reported his disappearance to the police and inquired about him daily at headquarters. Six days later his mother received word that he had been picked up penniless by the police in another city and was already on his way home. The family was overjoyed at his return, but this pleasure was soon forgotten in the distress over his subsequent behavior. The boy would not talk. He refused to tell his father why he had left his work or where he had spent the week. He became more obdurate and defiant, and would say nothing more than that he had been to Graz, the city in which he had been picked up. His father became excited, a great scene occurred, and finally he gave his son a severe beating. After this, things went from bad to worse. The boy would not work, stayed away from home, hung about the streets or in cafés all day, and stayed out later and later at night. As if this were not enough, he continued to get money out of his father and his employer. His father punished him with increasing severity in the hope of changing his behavior. Since this only made him worse and drove him further from his family, his mother began to take his part and persuaded her husband to be more gentle with him. This method brought only temporary improvement, and finally his mother's patience was exhausted and his father reverted once more to force. Severity and kindness were tried alternately several times, but the boy only acted worse. The father concluded his remarks to me with the following words: "You can't imagine how awful it is. We've tried to be good to him and we've tried being strict and beating him, but nothing helps. We don't know what to do next. Perhaps if he goes into an institution, they can make something out of him."

Up to this point the father had confined his talk to a description of his son's behavior and of his efforts to improve him. He had told us nothing of himself nor of the family relationships. Since such knowledge was indispensable to our insight into the problem, I turned the conversation in this direction. The family consisted of the father, the stepmother, a brother two years older who was about to enter the university, and a stepsister of five. The father had been married to the stepmother for twelve years and the five-year-old girl was a child of this marriage. The relationship between the parents, as well as the economic situation, was good. That the boy could have any feeling of inferiority in relation to the older brother seemed to the father out of the question, as the two had always been treated alike and had got along well together until this one began to behave so badly. Now they quarrelled all the time. The father thought that the stepsister was so much younger that there could be no question of jealousy of her. He did not pay much attention to her, was neither very affectionate with her nor unpleasant to her. The father was bitter, and complained that the change in the boy had completely disturbed what had formerly been a peaceful, happy family life. They used to sit around in the evening reading aloud, singing, or playing. Now when he got home at night he heard nothing except his son's misdemeanors, and he often had to go out on the street to look for him. The son had begun to learn the trade of shoemaker against his father's wishes. He had failed in the seventh grade and had refused to repeat the year. All arguments with him were in vain. He insisted on becoming a shoemaker like the stepmother's father. I inquired about the boy's relationship to girls, wondering if that could offer any explanation for his first running away. The father stated definitely that he knew his son's attitude toward girls and that this was impossible. When I asked how he explained this sudden change, he said, "Either the devil's got into him or he's gone crazy."

"Then he would not belong in our institution," I remarked.

The father answered, "Oh, you must not take that remark literally, but this has all happened so suddenly."

I talked to the boy alone. He was a very thin young man who looked somewhat older than his seventeen years. He was well-dressed. The following is a part of the conversation, given verbatim.

"Do you know where you are?"

"No."

"In the child-guidance clinic of the Juvenile Court."

"Oh yes. My father wants to put me in a reform school."

"Your father has told me what has happened and I'd like to help you."

"It's no use." He shrugged his shoulders and turned away.

"Certainly it's no use, if you don't want help."

"You can't help me."

"I know you don't have much confidence in me; we don't know each other yet."

"Not that, but anyway it's no use." He showed the same hopeless, unco-operative air.

"Are you willing to talk to me?"

"Why not?"

"I must ask you various questions and I'll make you a proposition."

"What?" The tone betrayed expectation.

"That you don't answer any question you don't like."

"How do you mean?" He was astonished and incredulous.

"The questions you don't like you need not answer or you may tell me it's none of my business."

"Why do you say that?"

"Because I'm not a detective nor a policeman and I don't need to know everything. Anyway you wouldn't tell me the truth if I asked questions you didn't like."

"How do you know that?"

"Because that is what everybody does and you are no exception. I wouldn't tell everything either to someone whom I'd met for the first time."

"But if I talk and tell you lies, will you know that too?"

"No, but that would be too bad. And anyway it isn't necessary because I don't want to force you to answer me."

"At home they always said if I'd talk, nothing bad would happen to me, but when I did it was always much worse. So I quit talking."

"But here it's a little different. I'll be satisfied with what you are willing to tell. But I'd like to be sure you are telling me the truth."

"Good."

"You agree?" I offered him my hand which he took eagerly.

"Agreed."

You will understand this type of introduction and its purpose better when we take up the question of the emotional contact between the worker and the patient. You will soon see what a good relationship I had established with him.

"What grade were you in when you left school?"

"Seventh."

"Why didn't you go further in school?"

"I failed in three subjects and didn't want to go any more."

"Did your father agree to that?"

"He would have liked it better if I had repeated the grade."

"How did you happen to take up shoemaking?"

"My grandfather is a shoemaker and I wanted to be one too."

"I'm not interested in knowing all about your troubles, but how did they begin? Why did you go to Graz?"

"I don't know."

"There must be some reason, though, why you went there. You might just as well have chosen another city."

"I really don't know."

"But it's not so long ago, not even a year. Think a little; maybe it will occur to you."

"Perhaps because my brother went there a year ago with a holiday group." Here he hesitated and became silent.

"Don't you want to tell me something more?" I asked this question after a pause during which I had noticed that the boy was having a battle with himself and was unable to come to a conclusion. He looked me straight in the eyes, then bowed his head, and shaken with sobs, said:

"If you promise you won't tell my father, I'll tell you something."

"Here's my hand on it." He took my hand and shook it vigorously.

"I wanted to kill myself."

"When?"

"Last summer."

"Before you got the money from your father or afterwards?"

"Before."

"Why?"

"My brother went away with mother to visit an aunt, and since I was an apprentice I had to stay at home. I went to work for a week. Then I laid off for three days and suddenly got afraid my father would find it out. Then I wanted to kill myself."

"Did you try to kill yourself?"

"No. I thought I'd go away and never come back. I got the money from my father and started off. When the money was all gone, I didn't know what to do and came back home. At home there was an awful row and since then everything's been all wrong."

"How do you get along with your brother?"

"All right; we used to get along better, but now he is on father's side."

"Do you think the other children are treated better at home than you?"

"No!"

"Doesn't it matter to you that your brother is getting educated and that you are a shoemaker's apprentice?" To this question he made no reply.

He went on to report the following facts. He was four when his mother died. His father remarried a year later. His stepmother was much attached to her father, the shoemaker, who according to the boy must have been a very understanding man. The tender attachment he had had to his own mother he transferred very quickly to the stepmother. The relationship to his father also had been good until the previous year. Despite his present antagonism to his father, he described him as a good man who stayed at home in the evenings, went seldom to beer taverns, and spent a great deal of time with his children. There was no great financial strain.

It is interesting to note how the boy justified the money episode. His father gave the brother money for the trip with his mother; therefore he had a right to the same amount. Had he told his father his true reason for wanting the money, of course it would have been refused. Consequently, he lied. It was not yet clear why he held his father responsible for his becoming a shoemaker. He said: "Father should have known better than I. I was dumb. A fourteen-year-old boy doesn't know what he wants to be. My father should have made me repeat the seventh grade. If he'd only insisted, then I would have obeyed and today I'd still be in school."

After a while I asked him if he thought it was possible for him and his father to come to some understanding. I offered to help. He was skeptical, but not so reluctant as at first. He said,

"Oh, I've talked to my father time and again. It's no use." I tried to make him see that his father could not understand him as long as he did not know what he was really thinking. He might let me try to explain to the father. He released me from my promise to say nothing.

The boy went into the next room and sent his father to me. I had to talk with his father a long time before I could make him see that, without knowing it and without meaning to, he had lived with his son and had not been able to understand him. I told him also what the boy had suffered as a result of this situation. At first he listened in astonishment and shook his head incredulously; then he became indignant. Finally, as he began to understand, he was unable to restrain his tears. He apologized and said that he had not wept so since he was a child. I reassured him by saying that it was a natural reaction to such a realization and that I took it as proof of his affection for the boy. He calmed himself and was in such a conciliatory mood that I thought it was an opportune moment to begin to effect an understanding between father and son.

I must interpolate something here in order to avoid a misunderstanding. I have told you that it is wrong in a situation of conflict to induce a compromise by talking each of the participants into conceding a little. What I attempted here with this boy and his father does not contradict my former statement. This talking things over accomplished the purpose in that it enabled the son to tell his father what motivated his conduct and it thereby restored his lost relationship to his father. This placed the formerly good relationship upon a more secure basis.

So I called the boy back. I started the conversation along these lines and then left them alone, feeling that a third person would only prove a hindrance. After about twenty minutes, I came back to find them both red-eyed and silent. The father said in answer to my look of astonishment, "It's no use, he won't talk." I know that the mentor dare not let himself get angry and I know that I should have been able to understand the father's emotional situation, but I was angry and disappointed in him. I had worked with him for over two hours to show him how the situation had arisen and had tried to show him what he must do to bring the poor boy back into a sympathetic relation to him, and now he was behaving like this! Without looking at the father, I went over to the boy, put my hand on his head, and said, "Never mind, one doesn't always have to talk. Two people can understand each other without saying a word." At that the boy began to cry violently. I do not know just how it happened or who took the initiative, but the next minute they were in each other's arms. I must admit that I too was not untouched by the scene. After things were a little calmer, I wanted to get the boy out of the way in order to say something important to the father, so I sent him out to buy me some cigarettes. I made it as clear as I could to the father that such a first reconciliation was far from being the end of the conflict. He could expect that his son would prove even more troublesome in the near future. Since there was no time then for a longer interview, I advised him to come back to me as soon as his son misbehaved again in order to consult me before he undertook any disciplinary measures. At the boy's suggestion, we arranged that he and the father should go straight from me to his employer so that he could get back to work that afternoon. The boy seemed relieved and pleased. Father and son went away arm in arm as though a lasting harmony had been established.

Early the next morning I found the father in despair, waiting for me at the door of the clinic. He poured out a flood of complaints. "It's no use. We can't do a thing with that boy. He must go to the reform school. You saw how broken-up he was yesterday, and now it's the same old story again. Kindness doesn't work with him."

I asked calmly, "But what's the matter?" You will understand that I was not especially disturbed. I had told him the day before that something more was bound to happen. I was surprised, however, that it had happened so quickly. The father continued, "We went away entirely reconciled. On the way I gave him a good talking-to, to the effect that he must keep on being good now since I had forgiven him. He listened and said nothing, so that I had to keep myself in hand not to get angry again. I didn't give his employer any explanation because he thinks that the boy was sick. Instead of beginning work in the afternoon as he should have, he went bumming around until late that night."

You will remember that I had sent the boy out for cigarettes in order to call the father's attention to the fact that backsliding was to be expected. Now it had occurred. Although the father should have been prepared for this by my talk, he had lost control of himself, had reproached his son severely, and had jeopardized what we had achieved on the preceding day. It is understandable that the father's participation made the boy seem to play the role of the "ungrateful prodigal." Such critical situations are usually misunderstood by parents and often by educators. Since the real situation is seldom properly recognized, we find ourselves on the wrong track, and endanger the success of all our pedagogical efforts.

What occurs in these dissocial young people has a great deal to do with unconscious guilt feelings. We shall go into that later. However, we can now clarify some of the determining factors. It is comprehensible that a boy who has been accustomed to severe punishment for his misdemeanors should feel distrustful when the punishing person, the father, suddenly shows a right-about-face attitude. This change is not trusted and is therefore put to further tests; confidence is established only when the boy is convinced that the punishment is really abandoned. The dissocial youth is not satisfied when he gets kind and gentle treatment from his superiors; he aggravates them through increasingly annoying behavior. Instead of understanding this, the parents may take this behavior as proof that he cannot be influenced through kindness and consideration. They begin again with severity, and soon the old situation is restored, and no improvement can be expected. However, if the father shows real understanding and does not let himself make the mistake of falling back into the old attitude, then a critical situation arises for the youth. The antagonistic conduct, motivated by defiance of the father, has no longer any meaning. When the dissocial behavior begins as an expression of distrust, it is as though the child said to the parents, "Treat me the way you used to." You will understand this better when we discuss the aggressive type in Chapter Eight.

It is only when the provocative behavior fails to achieve its aim that this pattern which supports the delinquency breaks down. Then gradually the manifestations of delinquency recede. The period of time necessary for this is indefinite; it varies according to how deeply the motivation is anchored in the unconscious. We are dealing here with a process which I have often observed but for which no adequate theory has been worked out. Such a theory can be evolved only when a sufficient number of such cases has been analyzed.

Let us go back to our case. I now saw that the father because of his emotional situation could not be counted on as a therapeutic helper and that I must work without him. I learned that the boy was at present at work and asked the father to send him to meet me that evening. I often have young people who work come to meet me on my way home in the evening. He met me punctually and was cordial though not communicative. He belonged to that group of people who talk little, but who are pleased to have someone with them. I asked him how he was and how he had got along with his work the past two days. He lied to me with a glib assurance about everything he had done the day before whereas I knew that he had not been in the workshop. We mentioned his father and he remarked that I really did not know his father. When I asked what he meant, he said, "You think he's a lot better than he really is." "Is he so bad then?" "No, but he is not good to me. He nagged me all the way home yesterday. He said I had to be good now that he'd forgiven me."

We have here an indication why the boy had reverted to his former behavior so quickly. The father, who tried to talk him into something, seemed to him not to be the understanding person he had appeared in our interview. He had forced the boy back again into a bad position. As we talked, we walked slowly along the street. It began to rain and I thought I had better take a trolley. He was unwilling to leave me and came along. Among other things, we talked about music, whereupon he lost some of his reticence and told me that his family was musical; his father played the violin, his brother the piano, and he himself the flute. When we reached his transfer point where I urged him to leave, he remained, saying he would go the whole way home with me. Just before we got out, he asked me when and where we could meet again. I gave him an appointment for three days later, whereupon he said, "That's too far off. Can't it be sooner?" I said, "Yes, if you want to meet me tomorrow evening at seven on Blank Street." He went with me to my door and said, "Please give my regards to your wife." My wife had never been mentioned; he did not even know that I was married, but took it for granted. I stood by the door watching him as he walked away. After about fifty steps, he turned and raised his hat and I did likewise. This was repeated several times, until he reached the corner. The next evening he was there right on the dot. He proposed that we walk rather than ride so that we need not part so soon. Walking this distance took about an hour. Again he did not talk much but he invited me to come to his house some evening to hear some music. It was not certain that his father would play, but his brother had already promised to accompany him on the piano. I said that I was a very severe musical critic and that he and his brother must really get up a good program before they could expect me to come. You will understand that I wanted to turn his own impulse to account pedagogically and I therefore utilized this interest, which would keep him occupied at home over a long period of time.

Since I was very busy during this period I could give him only a half hour three times a week and this had to be on my way home in the evening. If I were going to be able to achieve anything remedial with him under such unfavorable circumstances, he must develop some strong emotional feeling for me. It was not wise to question him directly. The only way I could appraise his feelings was to put them to the test, and so I told him to come to meet me two hours earlier than I could be there. When I got there, he was gone. I learned that he had waited more than an hour and a half. He was not irritated when he left, but had left a request that I should let him know when and where we might meet again. We met the next day. I decided to praise him for his long wait as soon as a good opportunity presented itself. I did not have long to wait. He was friendly, did not reproach me, but on the contrary said he understood that I had a great deal to do and could not always keep appointments. Again we walked. He talked about his employer and told me jubilantly of some new work which had been entrusted to him. Through it all, I could see clearly a new feeling of his own importance. He talked also of the disagreeable things in the shop. Another worker was jealous of him and was cross and grouchy if he whistled a tune, something he had of late especially enjoyed. Then he began to talk about home. He became particularly expansive over the musical program. He was very pleased with his brother, who was co-operating with him very well. This showed me the direction in which I could reward him. I thought it well to settle on a date, but since I wanted things to become a little more stable at home I put it off until Sunday, two weeks following. He was very happy to know that I would come on a certain day and was not impatient that he had to wait so long. We walked along in silence; he was lost in his thoughts and I was busy watching him. After a while I asked him what he was thinking about. He was embarrassed and did not want to tell me. When I pressed him, he said that it was really too stupid, he was not thinking about anything in particular, perhaps I'd only laugh at him if he told me but things were always like that with him. At first something would seem very important to him; he could not express it to his own satisfaction, he could only intimate it. If the other person did not show any interest, he would suddenly feel he had made too much fuss about something unimportant and would be embarrassed and unable to open his mouth. I made him understand that I did not expect anything remarkable from him and if it cost him too much effort he should remain silent. We went a little further and then he began timidly, "If my father were only like you, I would never have done all those things." I took that as an opening for talking about his relationship to his father. What he said was in substance only what we already know. The next three interviews were concerned mostly with various members of the family and in many points they clarified his relationship to his father.

One Saturday, after a week's separation, he turned up beaming. His pay had been raised a third. This was even more surprising since he had already received a slight increase in pay two weeks before. This, in addition to the fact that he had been entrusted with more important work, shows us that he had developed a new attitude toward his work. We see too that it can be materially advantageous to reach an inner equilibrium. The employer had certainly not raised his pay out of love for the boy nor out of interest in his re-education. As a matter of fact he was ignorant that any such remedial training was going on. I would like to make it clear here that, as a matter of principle, I do not make any contact with the employer or the place of work. However helpful that might prove at times, it is too dangerous to risk as it may only bring the youth into a more difficult position. Employers and fellow-workers could thus learn things which, in case of trouble, they could use against the youth.

Now to the Sunday visit! The family were all at home. The boy was greatly excited and I tried to put him at ease by asking them to begin. They played better than one would have expected. The boy was on fire with enthusiasm. I let him see plainly that I was pleased, but did not overdo my appreciation. The situation was natural; the whole family was happy, as I could read in their faces, and they were more than cordial to me. During a short pause, we sat around the table discussing various things, the mother's household affairs, the father's work, and the like, but nothing was said about his son's former or present behavior. I stayed for nearly three hours.

The father, pleased with the outcome, came with me part of the way home. He was just as enthusiastic now as he had been despairing several weeks before. And just as then I had to curb his despair because all was not lost, so now I had to curb his enthusiasm because all was not yet won. Unpleasant surprises were not yet excluded. He said, "It seems like a dream to me that I could have been so discouraged that I wanted to put that boy in an institution. I didn't know what else to do. It's just like old times now. He works regularly and his employer told me he was completely satisfied with him. He comes home in the evening promptly, gets out his flute, and the two boys play together for hours. We're really a united family again. I can't tell you how happy I am that everything is all right once more."

The next evening I met the boy again. I did not have much time for him as I had an appointment. He went on the streetcar with me, talked over details of my visit, and closed with, "I went to bed right afterwards and I had to think it all over again, it was so nice." We continued meeting a few weeks longer, and though he walked all the way home with me, he did not come into my house because I wished to avoid that. Our meetings were interrupted by my vacation. During such a period, I do not give up the relationship already established but I keep in touch with the boy through letters. I exert myself to avoid everything that will weaken the transference at a time when it is pedagogically effective. A long separation without correspondence would constitute such a disturbing factor. That this relationship must be broken off later is obvious, but this question will be taken up in another chapter. He was an enthusiastic letter writer. He wrote at least once a week, and if I replied immediately, twice. In one of these letters he reported that his mother and sister had gone to visit relatives. The mother had wanted to hire a woman to help with the housework while she was gone but he had thought this unnecessary and had offered to keep house himself. He told me about the bachelor housekeeping and how his father and brother must take orders from him. If they did not behave, he made a scene, and his father gave in more quickly than his brother, with whom he often had to be severe. Gradually the letters became cooler in tone although they arrived as frequently as before. When I came home, I let him know and he came to our next appointment with his old enthusiasm. He asked how I was and seemed pleased when I told him that we could meet in our usual way two days later. He did not come but wrote me a note excusing himself and asking if we could postpone the meeting until two days later. I agreed but he failed to turn up again and sent no excuse. I was not annoyed by his not coming. However, I cannot say that I was pleased with his release from me because it seemed to have occurred too quickly. I became a little anxious about him and feared that he had fallen back into his old ways. I was far from thinking that a permanent result had been accomplished. I wrote to him and received an immediate reply. He said that things were going well and that at present he was working overtime in the evening and therefore could not meet me. In a few weeks the rush would be over and he would be glad to see me again. By chance I met his father and he spoke with approbation of the excellent behavior of the boy and said he hoped it would continue.

For several weeks I did not see him. At Christmas he came to see me, sent me a card at New Year's, and then I did not hear from him for many weeks. In the spring I met him by chance in the streetcar. He was in the best of spirits. For the next year and a half I had letters from him now and then, especially at holiday times. As far as his retraining went, the task was finished. He continued to do well for three years. We must recognize, however, that this boy had many other adjustments to make, among them a satisfactory heterosexual relationship.

Without an analysis of this boy, we can never be sure of the real reasons for the delinquency; we can only point to possible or apparent causal factors. The surprising features in this case, which are certainly not convincing without analysis, are the quickness and permanence of the therapy. To the psychoanalyst, it is clear that this therapeutic result was accomplished through the transference. The question whether permanent results can in general be obtained in this way will be taken up later.

It seemed clear that we were dealing in this case with an act of revenge against the father. The boy felt inferior to the brother because as a student he had advantages which were denied an apprentice. Yet it is not entirely clear why at seventeen he reproached his father and made him responsible for the fact that he had become a shoemaker, when at fourteen he had put up such a stubborn resistance against his father's wish to keep him in school. We know from both the father and the son that the job of shoemaker's apprentice was not agreeable to the boy. At that time, the incentive to be a shoemaker's apprentice must have been stronger than the wish to continue in school. This incentive later disappeared. A sixteen-year-old boy is no longer in the same psychological situation as a fourteen-year-old. We must therefore try to reconstruct the psychological situation of the boy when he began his apprenticeship. One of his statements gives us a clue. As we stood at my door the first evening he said, "Please give my regards to your wife." This is not just a chance remark nor one called forth by mere politeness as we had never spoken of my wife. Either he had noticed my wedding ring or he took it for granted that I was married. In any case, my marriage was a fact to this boy: else he would not have sent his greetings to my wife. This assumption is further understandable since he had put me in the place of his father. We recall how he said to me later, "If my father acted toward me the way you do, then I wouldn't have done these things." It is in this connection that we can understand that the greetings to my wife were in reality for his mother. When such utterances come forth without any demonstrable external stimulus, they come out of the unconscious and must somehow involve a great deal of affect. Can we assume that there was such a strong tie to his mother? She had been dead for a long time and the stepmother had long been a member of the family circle. We might risk this possible conclusion because we can find some grounds for it. In the first place a feminine habitus, an anxious, shy behavior, had already made us think of an infantile incestuous tie. The relationship to his stepmother was very good, as we learned first from his father, then from the boy, and finally from our own observation. His love for his own mother he seemed to have transferred completely to his stepmother. The infantile incestuous tie was still in operation, the wave of repression in adolescence was stronger than normal—that is to say, he had not succeeded in giving up his love object within the family in favor of one outside. We see the same attitude to women in this boy that we did in the other youth; he turns away from them. In such cases the father remains the unconscious rival for the mother's love. The antagonism is repressed because one must love one's father. When, because of this repressed and unconscious antagonism and rivalry, the boy refused to go to school, he achieved satisfaction for his unconscious desire for revenge against his father. He knew that this would upset his father, particularly since he was a chief clerk and wished his son to have a similar position. The boy was not satisfied, however, with being unwilling to study; he went further and became a shoemaker like the stepmother's father. We know that the stepmother was tenderly attached to her own father. If the boy became a shoemaker, then he would force his stepmother to value him more than she did *his* own father; even as much as she did *her* father. We now realize that the father's efforts to keep him at his studies would have proved in vain even if he had not failed in school.

Two years later, when the dissocial behavior began, he was in a different psychological state. We can imagine that the affective motive which had led him to be a shoemaker had been weakened by the unpleasant experience of being an apprentice. This must have been hard for a child of middle-class family who undoubtedly felt himself socially degraded, especially since he went to the workshop directly out of school. Furthermore he was always comparing himself with his student brother. The brother's vacation in a camp had made a deep impression on him. His sacrifice for his stepmother, that he became a shoemaker, was also in vain; she took his brother, not him, to visit her relatives. It would be comprehensible if hate had sprung up in him against his stepmother and had found an outlet in aggression toward her. But we see nothing of this. We must remember in this connection that between the time of leaving school and becoming an apprentice, and the time of running away when he was sixteen, two years had elapsed. During this period he had lived through an interval of puberty and was in another developmental phase. Although the power of repression was still strong, the surge of libido had markedly strengthened his masculine aggression. He had no conscious hate feelings against his mother which would have been the case had the incestuous tie to her not abated. The loosening of this tie makes an approach to his father possible. He had actually tried to return to his father. He induced his father to give him money, and rationalized this by the fact that his brother had been given traveling money also. This gave him the same relationship to the father that the brother had. That he chose an objectionable way to bring himself closer to his father does not alter the fact. He did not recognize that he had taken an unfortunate path; he realized only that he had failed. We can imagine the conscious and unconscious struggle that raged in the boy: the disagreeable experiences as an apprentice, the father's disapproval of his being a shoemaker, the effort to hold his father as love object although his father had repulsed him and was at the same time a rival for the love of the stepmother; the futility of the sacrifice for his stepmother, and finally the feeling that the way back to his father was barricaded against him. It is not surprising that the boy, who saw his whole life plan disturbed, should think about killing himself. That he only carried his suicidal intentions out symbolically in the running away was due to his self-love, in psychoanalytical terms, his narcissism. This enabled him after much hesitation to find a way out of his torment.

This case demonstrates what we can learn about the causes of dissocial behavior without going deeply into the matter as in a psychoanalysis.

HENRY JAMES: The Pupil

THE POOR young man hesitated and procrastinated: it cost him such an effort to broach the subject of terms, to speak of money to a person who spoke only of feelings and, as it were, of the aristocracy. Yet he was unwilling to take leave, treating his engagement as settled, without some more conventional glance in that direction than he could find an opening for in the manner of the large, affable lady who sat there drawing a pair of soiled *gants de Suède* through a fat, jewelled hand and, at once pressing and gliding, repeated over and over everything but the thing he would have liked to hear. He would have liked to hear the figure of his salary; but just as he was nervously about to sound that note the little boy came back—the little boy Mrs. Moreen had sent out of the room to fetch her fan. He came back without the fan, only with the casual observation that he couldn't find it. As he dropped this cynical confession he looked straight and hard at the candidate for the honour of taking his education in hand. This personage reflected, somewhat grimly, that the first thing he should have to teach his little charge would be to appear to address himself to his mother when he spoke to her—especially not to make her such an improper answer as that.

When Mrs. Moreen bethought herself of this pretext for getting rid of their companion, Pemberton supposed it was precisely to approach the delicate subject of his remuneration. But it had been only to say some things about her son which it was better that a boy of eleven shouldn't catch. They were extravagantly to his advantage, save when she lowered her voice to sigh, tapping her left side familiarly: "And all over-clouded by *this*, you know—all at the mercy of a weakness——!" Pemberton gathered that the weakness was in the region of the heart. He had known the poor child was not robust: this was the basis on which he had been invited to treat, through an English lady, an Oxford acquaintance, then at Nice, who happened to know both his needs and those of the amiable American family looking out for something really superior in the way of a resident tutor.

The young man's impression of his prospective pupil, who had first come into the room, as if to see for himself, as soon as Pemberton was admitted, was not quite the soft solicitation the visitor had taken for granted. Morgan Moreen was, somehow, sickly without being delicate, and that he looked intelligent (it is true Pemberton wouldn't have enjoyed his being stupid) only added to the suggestion that, as with his big mouth and big ears he really couldn't be called pretty, he might be unpleasant. Pemberton was modest—he was even timid; and the chance that his small scholar might prove cleverer than himself had quite figured, to his nervousness, among the dangers of an untried experiment. He reflected, however, that these were risks one had to run when one accepted a position, as it was called, in a private family; when as yet one's University honours had, pecuniarily speaking, remained barren. At any rate, when Mrs. Moreen got up as if to intimate that, since it was understood he would enter upon his duties within the week she would let him off now, he succeeded, in spite of the presence of the child, in squeezing out a phrase about the rate of payment. It was not the fault of the conscious smile which seemed a reference to the lady's expensive identity, if the allusion did not sound rather vulgar. This was exactly because she became still more gracious to reply: "Oh! I can assure you that all that will be quite regular."

Pemberton only wondered, while he took up his hat, what "all that" was to amount to—people had such different ideas. Mrs. Moreen's words, however, seemed to commit the family to a pledge definite enough to elicit from the child a strange little comment, in the shape of the mocking, foreign ejaculation "Oh, là-là!"

Pemberton, in some confusion, glanced at him as he walked slowly to the window with his back turned, his hands in his pockets and the air in his elderly shoulders of a boy who didn't play. The young man wondered if he could teach him to play, though his mother had said it would never do and that this was why school was impossible. Mrs. Moreen exhibited no discomfiture; she only continued blandly: "Mr. Moreen will be delighted to meet your wishes. As I told you, he has been called to London for a week. As soon as he comes back you shall have it out with him."

This was so frank and friendly that the young man could only reply, laughing as his hostess laughed: "Oh! I don't imagine we shall have much of a battle."

"They'll give you anything you like," the boy remarked unexpectedly, returning from the window. "We don't mind what anything costs—we live awfully well."

"My darling, you're too quaint!" his mother exclaimed, putting out to caress him a practised but ineffectual hand. He slipped out of it, but looked with intelligent, innocent eyes at Pemberton, who had already had time to notice that from one moment to the other his small satiric face seemed to change its time of life. At this moment it was infantine; yet it appeared also to be under the influence of curious intuitions and knowledges. Pemberton rather disliked precocity, and he was disappointed to find gleams of it in a disciple not yet in his teens. Nevertheless he divined on the spot that Morgan wouldn't prove a bore. He would prove on the contrary a kind of excitement. This idea held the young man, in spite of a certain repulsion.

"You pompous little person! We're not extravagant!" Mrs. Moreen gaily protested, making another unsuccessful attempt to draw the boy to her side. "You must know what to expect," she went on to Pemberton.

"The less you expect the better!" her companion interposed. "But we *are* people of fashion."

"Only so far as *you* make us so!" Mrs. Moreen mocked, tenderly. "Well, then, on Friday—don't tell me you're superstitious—and mind you don't fail us. Then you'll see us all. I'm so sorry the girls are out. I guess you'll like the girls. And, you know, I've another son, quite different from this one."

"He tries to imitate me," said Morgan to Pemberton.

"He tries? Why, he's twenty years old!" cried Mrs. Moreen.

"You're very witty," Pemberton remarked to the child— a proposition that his mother echoed with enthusiasm, declaring that Morgan's sallies were the delight of the house. The boy paid no heed to this; he only inquired abruptly of the visitor, who was surprised afterwards that he hadn't struck him as offensively forward: "Do you *want* very much to come?"

"Can you doubt it, after such a description of what I shall hear?" Pemberton replied. Yet he didn't want to come at all; he was coming because he had to go somewhere, thanks to the collapse of his fortune at the end of a year abroad, spent on the system of putting his tiny patrimony into a single full wave of experience. He had had his full wave, but he couldn't pay his hotel bill. Moreover, he had caught in the boy's eyes the glimpse of a far-off appeal.

"Well, I'll do the best I can for you," said Morgan; with which he turned away again. He passed out of one of the long windows; Pemberton saw him go and lean on the parapet of the terrace. He remained there while the young man took leave of his mother, who, on Pemberton's looking as if he expected a farewell from him, interposed with: "Leave him, leave him; he's so strange!" Pemberton suspected she was afraid of something he might say. "He's a genius—you'll love him," she added. "He's much the most interesting person in the family." And before he could invent some civility to oppose to this, she wound up with: "But we're all good, you know!"

"He's a genius—you'll love him!" were words that recurred to Pemberton before the Friday, suggesting, among other things, that geniuses were not invariably lovable. However, it was all the better if there was an element that would make tutorship absorbing: he had perhaps taken too much for granted that it would be dreary. As he left the villa after his interview, he looked up at the balcony and saw the child leaning over it. "We shall have great larks!" he called up.

Morgan hesitated a moment; then he answered, laughing: "By the time you come back I shall have thought of something witty!"

This made Pemberton say to himself: "After all he's rather nice."

II

On the Friday he saw them all, as Mrs. Moreen had promised, for her husband had come back and the girls and the other son were at home. Mr. Moreen had a white moustache, a confiding manner and, in his buttonhole, the ribbon of a foreign order—bestowed, as Pemberton eventually learned, for services. For what services he never clearly ascertained: this was a point— one of a large number—that Mr. Moreen's manner never confided. What it emphatically did confide was that he was a man of the world. Ulick, the firstborn, was in visible training for the same profession—under the disadvantage as yet, however, of a buttonhole only feebly floral and a moustache with no pretensions to type. The girls had hair and figures and manners and small fat feet, but had never been out alone. As for Mrs. Moreen, Pemberton saw on a nearer view that her elegance was intermittent and her parts didn't always match. Her husband, as she had promised, met with enthusiasm Pemberton's ideas in regard to a salary. The young man had endeavoured to make them modest, and Mr. Moreen confided to him that *he* found them positively meagre. He further assured him that he aspired to be intimate with his children, to be their best friend, and that he was always looking out for them. That was what he went off for, to London and other places—to look out; and this vigilance was the theory of life, as well as the real occupation, of the whole family. They all looked out, for they were very frank on the subject of its being necessary. They desired it to be understood that they were earnest people, and also that their fortune, though quite adequate for earnest people, required the most careful administration. Mr. Moreen, as the parent bird, sought sustenance for the nest. Ulick found sustenance mainly at the club, where Pemberton guessed that it was usually served on green cloth. The girls used to do up their hair and their frocks themselves, and our young man felt appealed to to be glad, in regard to Morgan's education, that, though it must naturally be of the best, it didn't cost too much. After a little he *was* glad, forgetting at times his own needs in the interest inspired by the child's nature and education and the pleasure of making easy terms for him.

During the first weeks of their acquaintance Morgan had been as puzzling as a page in an unknown language—altogether different from the obvious little Anglo-Saxons who had misrepresented childhood to Pemberton. Indeed the whole mystic volume in which the boy had been bound demanded some practice in translation. To-day, after a considerable interval, there is something phantasmagoric, like a prismatic reflection or a serial novel, in Pemberton's memory of the queerness of the Moreens. If it were not for a few tangible tokens—a lock of Morgan's hair, cut by his own hand, and the half-dozen letters he got from him when they were separated—the whole episode and the figures peopling it would seem too inconsequent for anything but dreamland. The queerest thing about them was their success (as it appeared to him for a while at the time), for he had never seen a family so brilliantly equipped for failure. Wasn't it success to have kept him so hatefully long? Wasn't it success to have drawn him in that first morning at *déjeuner*, the Friday he came—it was enough to *make* one superstitious—so that he utterly committed himself, and this not by calculation or a *mot d'ordre*, but by a happy instinct which made them, like a band of gipsies, work so neatly together? They amused him as much as if they had really been a band of gipsies. He was still young and had not seen much of the world—his English years had been intensely usual; therefore the reversed conventions of the Moreens (for they had their standards) struck him as topsyturvy. He had encountered nothing like them at Oxford; still less had any such note been struck to his younger American ear during the four years at Yale in which he had richly supposed himself to be reacting against Puritanism. The reaction of the Moreens, at any rate, went ever so much further. He had thought himself very clever that first day in hitting them all off in his mind with the term "cosmopolite." Later, it seemed feeble and colourless enough—confessedly, helplessly provisional.

However, when he first applied it to them he had a degree of joy—for an instructor he was still empirical—as if from the apprehension that to live with them would really be to see life. Their sociable strangeness was an intimation of that—their chatter of tongues, their gaiety and good humour, their infinite dawdling (they were always getting themselves up, but it took forever, and Pemberton had once found Mr. Moreen shaving in the drawing-room), their French, their Italian and, in the spiced fluency, their cold, tough slices of American. They lived on macaroni and coffee (they had these articles prepared in perfection), but they knew recipes for a hundred other dishes. They overflowed with music and song, were always humming and catching each other up, and had a kind of professional acquaintance with continental cities. They talked of "good places" as if they had been strolling players. They had at Nice a villa, a carriage, a piano and a banjo, and they went to official parties. They were a perfect calendar of the "days" of their friends, which Pemberton knew them, when they were indisposed, to get out of bed to go to, and which made the week larger than life when Mrs. Moreen talked of them with Paula and Amy. Their romantic initiations gave their new inmate at first an almost dazzling sense of culture. Mrs. Moreen had translated something, at some former period—an author whom it made Pemberton feel *borné* never to have heard of. They could imitate Venetian and sing Neapolitan, and when they wanted to say something very particular they communicated with each other in an ingenious dialect of their own—a sort of spoken cipher, which Pemberton at first took for Volapuk, but which he learned to understand as he would not have understood Volapuk.

"It's the family language—Ultramoreen," Morgan explained to him drolly enough; but the boy rarely condescended to use it himself, though he attempted colloquial Latin as if he had been a little prelate.

Among all the "days" with which Mrs. Moreen's memory

was taxed she managed to squeeze in one of her own, which her friends sometimes forgot. But the house derived a frequented air from the number of fine people who were freely named there and from several mysterious men with foreign titles and English clothes whom Morgan called the princes and who, on sofas with the girls, talked French very loud, as if to show they were saying nothing improper. Pemberton wondered how the princes could ever propose in that tone and so publicly: he took for granted cynically that this was what was desired of them. Then he acknowledged that even for the chance of such an advantage Mrs. Moreen would never allow Paula and Amy to receive alone. These young ladies were not at all timid, but it was just the safeguards that made them so graceful. It was a houseful of Bohemians who wanted tremendously to be Philistines.

In one respect, however, certainly, they achieved no rigour —they were wonderfully amiable and ecstatic about Morgan. It was a genuine tenderness, an artless admiration, equally strong in each. They even praised his beauty, which was small, and were rather afraid of him, as if they recognised that he was of a finer clay. They called him a little angel and a little prodigy and pitied his want of health effusively. Pemberton feared at first that their extravagance would make him hate the boy, but before this happened he had become extravagant himself. Later, when he had grown rather to hate the others, it was a bribe to patience for him that they were at any rate nice about Morgan, going on tiptoe if they fancied he was showing symptoms, and even giving up somebody's "day" to procure him a pleasure. But mixed with this was the oddest wish to make him independent, as if they felt that they were not good enough for him. They passed him over to Pemberton very much as if they wished to force a constructive adoption on the obliging bachelor and shirk altogether a responsibility. They were delighted when they perceived that Morgan liked his preceptor, and could think of no higher praise for the young man. It was strange how they contrived to reconcile the appearance, and indeed the essential fact, of adoring the child with their eagerness to wash their hands of him. Did they want to get rid of him before he should find them out? Pemberton was finding them out month by month. At any rate, the boy's relations turned their backs with exaggerated delicacy, as if to escape the charge of interfering. Seeing in time how little he had in common with them (it was by *them* he first observed it—they proclaimed it with complete humility), his preceptor was moved to speculate on the mysteries of transmission, the far jumps of heredity. Where his detachment from most of the things they represented had come from was more than an observer could say—it certainly had burrowed under two or three generations.

As for Pemberton's own estimate of his pupil, it was a good while before he got the point of view, so little had he been prepared for it by the smug young barbarians to whom the tradition of tutorship, as hitherto revealed to him, had been adjusted. Morgan was scrappy and surprising, deficient in many properties supposed common to the *genus* and abounding in others that were the portion only of the supernaturally clever. One day Pemberton made a great stride: it cleared up the question to perceive that Morgan *was* supernaturally clever and that, though the formula was temporarily meagre, this would be the only assumption on which one could successfully deal with him. He had the general quality of a child for whom life had not been simplified by school, a kind of homebred sensibility which might have been bad for himself but was charming for others, and a whole range of refinement and perception—little musical vibrations as taking as picked-up airs—begotten by wandering about Europe at the tail of his migratory tribe. This might not have been an education to recommend in advance, but its results with Morgan were as palpable as a fine texture. At the same time he had in his composition a sharp spice of stoicism, doubtless the fruit of having had to begin early to bear pain, which produced the impression of pluck and made it of less consequence that he might have been thought at school rather a polyglot little beast. Pemberton indeed quickly found himself rejoicing that school was out of the question: in any million of boys it was probably good for all but one, and Morgan was that millionth. It would have made him comparative and superior—it might have made him priggish. Pemberton would try to be school himself—a bigger seminary than five hundred grazing donkeys; so that, winning no prizes, the boy would remain unconscious and irresponsible and amusing—amusing, because, though life was already intense in his childish nature, freshness still made there a strong draught for jokes. It turned out that even in the still air of Morgan's various disabilities jokes flourished greatly. He was a pale, lean, acute, undeveloped little cosmopolite, who liked intellectual gymnastics and who, also, as regards the behaviour of mankind, had noticed more things than you might suppose, but who nevertheless had his proper playroom of superstitions, where he smashed a dozen toys a day.

III

At Nice once, towards evening, as the pair sat resting in the open air after a walk, looking over the sea at the pink western lights, Morgan said suddenly to his companion: "Do you like it—you know, being with us all in this intimate way?"

"My dear fellow, why should I stay if I didn't?"

"How do I know you will stay? I'm almost sure you won't, very long."

"I hope you don't mean to dismiss me," said Pemberton.

Morgan considered a moment, looking at the sunset. "I think if I did right I ought to."

"Well, I know I'm supposed to instruct you in virtue; but in that case don't do right."

"You're very young—fortunately," Morgan went on, turning to him again.

"Oh yes, compared with you!"

"Therefore, it won't matter so much if you do lose a lot of time."

"That's the way to look at it," said Pemberton accommodatingly.

They were silent a minute; after which the boy asked: "Do you like my father and mother very much?"

"Dear me, yes. They're charming people."

Morgan received this with another silence; then, unexpectedly, familiarly, but at the same time affectionately, he remarked: "You're a jolly old humbug!"

For a particular reason the words made Pemberton change colour. The boy noticed in an instant that he had turned red, whereupon he turned red himself and the pupil and the master exchanged a longish glance in which there was a consciousness of many more things than are usually touched upon, even tacitly, in such a relation. It produced for Pemberton an embarrassment; it raised, in a shadowy form, a question (this was the first glimpse of it), which was destined to play as singular and, as he imagined, owing to the altogether peculiar conditions, an unprecedented part in his intercourse with his little companion. Later, when he found himself talking with this small boy in a way in which few small boys could ever have been talked with, he thought of that clumsy moment on the bench at Nice as the dawn of an understanding that had broadened. What had added to the clumsiness then was that he thought it his duty to declare to Morgan that he might abuse him (Pemberton) as much as he liked, but must never abuse his parents. To this Morgan had the easy reply that he hadn't dreamed of abusing them; which appeared to be true: it put Pemberton in the wrong.

"Then why am I a humbug for saying I think them charming?" the young man asked, conscious of a certain rashness.

"Well—they're not your parents."

"They love you better than anything in the world—never forget that," said Pemberton.

"Is that why you like them so much?"

"They're very kind to me," Pemberton replied, evasively.

"You *are* a humbug!" laughed Morgan, passing an arm into his tutor's. He leaned against him, looking off at the sea again and swinging his long, thin legs.

"Don't kick my shins," said Pemberton, while he reflected: "Hang it, I can't complain of them to the child!"

"There's another reason, too," Morgan went on, keeping his legs still.

"Another reason for what?"

"Besides their not being your parents."

"I don't understand you," said Pemberton.

"Well, you will before long. All right!"

Pemberton did understand, fully, before long; but he made a fight even with himself before he confessed it. He thought it the oddest thing to have a struggle with the child about. He wondered he didn't detest the child for launching him in such a struggle. But by the time it began the resource of detesting the child was closed to him. Morgan was a special case, but to know him was to accept him on his own odd terms. Pemberton had spent his aversion to special cases before arriving at knowledge. When at last he did arrive he felt that he was in an extreme predicament. Against every interest he had attached himself. They would have to meet things together. Before they went home that evening, at Nice, the boy had said, clinging to his arm:

"Well, at any rate you'll hang on to the last."

"To the last?"

"Till you're fairly beaten."

"*You* ought to be fairly beaten!" cried the young man, drawing him closer.

IV

A year after Pemberton had come to live with them Mr. and Mrs. Moreen suddenly gave up the villa at Nice. Pemberton had got used to suddenness, having seen it practised on a considerable scale during two jerky little tours—one in Switzerland the first summer, and the other late in the winter, when they all ran down to Florence and then, at the end of ten days, liking it much less than they had intended, straggled back in mysterious depression. They had returned to Nice "for ever," as they said; but this didn't prevent them from squeezing, one rainy, muggy May night, into a second-class railway-carriage—you could never tell by which class they would travel—where Pemberton helped them to stow away a wonderful collection of bundles and bags. The explanation of this manœuvre was that they had determined to spend the summer "in some bracing place"; but in Paris they dropped into a small furnished apartment—a fourth floor in a third-rate avenue, where there was a smell on the staircase and the *portier* was hateful—and passed the next four months in blank indigence.

The better part of this baffled sojourn was for the preceptor and his pupil, who, visiting the Invalides and Notre Dame, the Conciergerie and all the museums, took a hundred remunerative rambles. They learned to know their Paris, which was useful, for they came back another year for a longer stay, the general character of which in Pemberton's memory to-day mixes pitiably and confusedly with that of the first. He sees Morgan's shabby knickerbockers—the everlasting pair that didn't match his blouse and that as he grew longer could only grow faded. He remembers the particular holes in his three or four pairs of coloured stockings.

Morgan was dear to his mother, but he never was better dressed than was absolutely necessary—partly, no doubt, by his own fault, for he was as indifferent to his appearance as a German philosopher. "My dear fellow, you *are* coming to pieces," Pemberton would say to him in sceptical remonstrance; to which the child would reply, looking at him serenely up and down: "My dear fellow, so are you! I don't want to cast you in the shade." Pemberton could have no rejoinder for this—the assertion so closely represented the fact. If however the deficiencies of his own wardrobe were a chapter by themselves he didn't like his little charge to look too poor. Later he used to say: "Well, if we are poor, why, after all, shouldn't we look it?" and he consoled himself with thinking there was something rather elderly and gentlemanly in Morgan's seediness—it differed from the untidiness of the urchin who plays and spoils his things. He could trace perfectly the degrees by which, in proportion as her little son confined himself to his tutor for society, Mrs. Moreen shrewdly forbore to renew his garments. She did nothing that didn't show, neglected him because he escaped notice, and then, as he illustrated this clever policy, discouraged at home his public appearances. Her position was logical enough—those members of her family who did show had to be showy.

During this period and several others Pemberton was quite aware of how he and his comrade might strike people; wandering languidly through the Jardin des Plantes as if they had nowhere to go, sitting, on the winter days, in the galleries of the Louvre, so splendidly ironical to the homeless, as if for the advantage of the *calorifère* [hot-air stove]. They joked about it sometimes: it was the sort of joke that was perfectly within the boy's compass. They figured themselves as part of the vast, vague, hand-to-mouth multitude of the enormous city and pretended they were proud of their position in it—it showed them such a lot of life and made them conscious of a sort of democratic brotherhood. If Pemberton could not feel a sympathy in destitution with his small companion (for after all Morgan's fond parents would never have let him really suffer), the boy would at least feel it with him, so it came to the same thing. He used sometimes to wonder what people would think they were—fancy they were looked askance at, as if it might be a suspected case of kidnapping. Morgan wouldn't be taken for a young patrician with a preceptor—he wasn't smart enough; though he might pass for his companion's sickly little brother. Now and then he had a five-franc piece, and except once, when they bought a couple of lovely neckties, one of which he made Pemberton accept, they laid it out scientifically in old books. It was a great day, always spent on the quays, rummaging among the dusty boxes that garnish the parapets. These were occasions that helped them to live, for their books ran low very soon after the beginning of their acquaintance. Pemberton had a good many in England, but he was obliged to write to a friend and ask him kindly to get some fellow to give him something for them.

If the bracing climate was untasted that summer the young man had an idea that at the moment they were about to make a push the cup had been dashed from their lips by a movement of his own. It had been his first blow-out, as he called it, with his patrons; his first successful attempt (though there was little other success about it), to bring them to a consideration of his impossible position. As the ostensible eve of a costly journey the moment struck him as a good one to put in a signal protest—to present an ultimatum. Ridiculous as it sounded he had never yet been able to compass an uninterrupted private interview with the elder pair or with either of them singly. They were always flanked by their elder children, and poor Pemberton usually had his own little charge at his side. He was conscious of its being a house in which the surface of one's delicacy got rather smudged; nevertheless he had kept the bloom of his scruple against announcing to Mr. and Mrs. Moreen with publicity that he couldn't go on longer without a little money. He was still simple enough to suppose Ulick and Paula and Amy might not know that since his arrival he had only had a hundred and forty francs; and he was magnanimous enough to wish not to compromise their parents in their eyes. Mr. Moreen now listened to him, as he listened to every one and to everything, like a man of the world, and seemed to appeal to him—though not of course too grossly—to try and be a little

more of one himself. Pemberton recognised the importance of the
character from the advantage it gave Mr. Moreen. He was not
even confused, whereas poor Pemberton was more so than there
was any reason for. Neither was he surprised—at least any more
than a gentleman had to be who freely confessed himself a little
shocked, though not strictly, at Pemberton.

"We must go into this, mustn't we, dear?" he said to his
wife. He assured his young friend that the matter should have
his very best attention; and he melted into space as elusively as if,
at the door, he were taking an inevitable but deprecatory precede-
ence. When, the next moment, Pemberton found himself alone
with Mrs. Moreen it was to hear her say: "I see, I see," stroking
the roundness of her chin and looking as if she were only hesi-
tating between a dozen easy remedies. If they didn't make their
push Mr. Moreen could at least disappear for several days. During
his absence his wife took up the subject again spontaneously, but
her contribution to it was merely that she had thought all the
while they were getting on so beautifully. Pemberton's reply to
this revelation was that unless they immediately handed him a
substantial sum he would leave them for ever. He knew she would
wonder how he would get away, and for a moment expected her
to inquire. She didn't, for which he was almost grateful to her, so
little was he in a position to tell.

"You won't, you know you won't—you're too interested,"
she said. "You *are* interested, you know you are, you dear, kind
man!" She laughed, with almost condemnatory archness, as if it
were a reproach (but she wouldn't insist), while she flirted a
soiled pocket-handkerchief at him.

Pemberton's mind was fully made up to quit the house
the following week. This would give him time to get an answer
to a letter he had despatched to England. If he did nothing of
the sort—that is, if he stayed another year and then went away
only for three months—it was not merely because before the
answer to his letter came (most unsatisfactory when it did arrive),
Mr. Moreen generously presented him—again with all the precautions of a man of the world—three hundred francs. He was exasperated to find that Mrs. Moreen was right, that he couldn't
bear to leave the child. This stood out clearer for the very reason
that, the night of his desperate appeal to his patrons, he had seen
fully for the first time where he was. Wasn't it another proof of
the success with which those patrons practised their arts that they
had managed to avert for so long the illuminating flash? It descended upon Pemberton with a luridness which perhaps would
have struck a spectator as comically excessive, after he had returned to his little servile room, which looked into a close court

where a bare, dirty opposite wall took, with the sound of shrill clatter, the reflection of lighted back-windows. He had simply given himself away to a band of adventurers. The idea, the word itself, had a sort of romantic horror for him—he had always lived on such safe lines. Later it assumed a more interesting, almost a soothing, sense: it pointed a moral, and Pemberton could enjoy a moral. The Moreens were adventurers not merely because they didn't pay their debts, because they lived on society, but because their whole view of life, dim and confused and instinctive, like that of clever colour-blind animals, was speculative and rapacious and mean. Oh! they were "respectable," and that only made them more *immondes*. The young man's analysis of them put it at last very simply—they were adventurers because they were abject snobs. That was the completest account of them—it was the law of their being. Even when this truth became vivid to their in-genious inmate he remained unconscious of how much his mind had been prepared for it by the extraordinary little boy who had now become such a complication in his life. Much less could he then calculate on the information he was still to owe to the extraordinary little boy.

<h2 style="text-align:center">v</h2>

But it was during the ensuing time that the real problem came up—the problem of how far it was excusable to discuss the turpitude of parents with a child of twelve, of thirteen, of four-teen. Absolutely inexcusable and quite impossible it of course at first appeared; and indeed the question didn't press for a while after Pemberton had received his three hundred francs. They produced a sort of lull, a relief from the sharpest pressure. Pemberton frugally amended his wardrobe and even had a few francs in his pocket. He thought the Moreens looked at him as if he were almost too smart, as if they ought to take care not to spoil him. If Mr. Moreen hadn't been such a man of the world he would perhaps have said something to him about his neckties. But Mr. Moreen was always enough a man of the world to let things pass—he had certainly shown that. It was singular how Pemberton guessed that Morgan, though saying nothing about it, knew something had happened. But three hundred francs, espe-cially when one owed money, couldn't last for ever; and when they were gone—the boy knew when they were gone—Morgan did say something. The party had returned to Nice at the beginning of the winter, but not to the charming villa. They went to an hotel, where they stayed three months, and then they went to another hotel, explaining that they had left the first because they had waited and waited and couldn't get the rooms they wanted. These apartments, the rooms they wanted, were generally very splendid; but fortunately they never *could* get them—fortunately, I mean, for Pemberton, who reflected always that if they had got them there would have been still less for educational expenses. What Morgan said at last was said suddenly, irrelevantly, when the moment came, in the middle of a lesson, and consisted of the apparently unfeeling words: "You ought to *filer*, you know—you really ought."

Pemberton stared. He had learnt enough French slang from Morgan to know that to *filer* meant to go away. "Ah, my dear fellow, don't turn me off!"

Morgan pulled a Greek lexicon toward him (he used a Greek-German), to look out a word, instead of asking it of Pemberton. "You can't go on like this, you know."

"Like what, my boy?"

"You know they don't pay you up," said Morgan, blushing and turning his leaves.

"Don't pay me?" Pemberton stared again and then feigned amazement. "What on earth put that into your head?"

"It has been there a long time," the boy replied, continuing his search.

Pemberton was silent, then he went on: "I say, what are you hunting for? They pay me beautifully."

"I'm hunting for the Greek for transparent fiction," Morgan dropped.

"Find that rather for gross impertinence, and disabuse your mind. What do I want of money?"

"Oh, that's another question!"

Pemberton hesitated—he was drawn in different ways. The severely correct thing would have been to tell the boy that such a matter was none of his business and bid him go on with his lines. But they were really too intimate for that; it was not the way he was in the habit of treating him; there had been no reason it should be. On the other hand Morgan had quite lighted on the truth—he really shouldn't be able to keep it up much longer; therefore why not let him know one's real motive for forsaking him? At the same time it wasn't decent to abuse to one's pupil the family of one's pupil; it was better to misrepresent than to do that. So in reply to Morgan's last exclamation he just declared, to dismiss the subject, that he had received several payments.

"I say—I say!" the boy ejaculated, laughing.

"That's all right," Pemberton insisted. "Give me your written rendering."

Morgan pushed a copybook across the table, and his companion began to read the page, but with something running in his head that made it no sense. Looking up after a minute or two he found the child's eyes fixed on him, and he saw something strange in them. Then Morgan said: "I'm not afraid of the reality."

"I haven't yet seen the thing that you *are* afraid of—I'll do you that justice!"

This came out with a jump (it was perfectly true), and evidently gave Morgan pleasure. "I've thought of it a long time," he presently resumed.

"Well, don't think of it any more."

The child appeared to comply, and they had a comfortable and even an amusing hour. They had a theory that they were very thorough, and yet they seemed always to be in the amusing part of lessons, the intervals between the tunnels, where there were waysides and views. Yet the morning was brought to a violent end by Morgan's suddenly leaning his arms on the table, burying his head in them and bursting into tears. Pemberton would have been startled at any rate; but he was doubly startled because, as it then occurred to him, it was the first time he had ever seen the boy cry. It was rather awful.

The next day, after much thought, he took a decision and, believing it to be just, immediately acted upon it. He cornered Mr. and Mrs. Moreen again and informed them that if, on the spot, they didn't pay him all they owed him, he would not only leave their house, but would tell Morgan exactly what had brought him to it.

"Oh, you *haven't* told him?" cried Mrs. Moreen, with a pacifying hand on her well-dressed bosom.

"Without warning you? For what do you take me?"

Mr. and Mrs. Moreen looked at each other, and Pemberton could see both that they were relieved and that there was a certain alarm in their relief. "My dear fellow," Mr. Moreen demanded, "what use *can* you have, leading the quiet life we all do, for such a lot of money?"—an inquiry to which Pemberton made no answer, occupied as he was in perceiving that what passed in the mind of his patrons was something like: "Oh, then, if we've felt that the child, dear little angel, has judged us and how he regards us, and we haven't been betrayed, he must have guessed—and, in short, it's *general!*" an idea that rather stirred up Mr. and Mrs. Moreen, as Pemberton had desired that it should. At the same time, if he had thought that his threat would do something towards bringing them round, he was disappointed to find they had taken for granted (how little they appreciated his delicacy!) that he had already given them away to his pupil. There was a mystic

uneasiness in their parental breasts, and that was the way they
had accounted for it. None the less his threat did touch them; for
if they had escaped it was only to meet a new danger. Mr. Moreen
appealed to Pemberton, as usual, as a man of the world; but his
wife had recourse, for the first time since the arrival of their
inmate, to a fine *hauteur*, reminding him that a devoted mother,
with her child, had arts that protected her against gross mis-
representation.

"I should misrepresent you grossly if I accused you of
common honesty!" the young man replied; but as he closed the
door behind him sharply, thinking he had not done himself much
good, while Mr. Moreen lighted another cigarette, he heard Mrs.
Moreen shout after him, more touchingly:

"Oh, you do, you *do*, put the knife to one's throat!"

The next morning, very early, she came to his room. He
recognised her knock, but he had no hope that she brought him
money; as to which he was wrong, for she had fifty francs in her
hand. She squeezed forward in her dressing-gown, and he received
her in his own, between his bath-tub and his bed. He had been
tolerably schooled by this time to the "foreign ways" of his hosts.
Mrs. Moreen was zealous, and when she was zealous she didn't
care what she did; so she now sat down on his bed, his clothes
being on the chairs, and, in her preoccupation, forgot, as she
glanced round, to be ashamed of giving him such a nasty room.
What Mrs. Moreen was zealous about on this occasion was to
persuade him that in the first place she was very good-natured to
bring him fifty francs, and, in the second, if he would only see it,
he was really too absurd to expect to be *paid*. Wasn't he paid
enough, without perpetual money—wasn't he paid by the comfortable, luxurious home that he enjoyed with them all, without
a care, an anxiety, a solitary want? Wasn't he sure of his position,
and wasn't that everything to a young man like him, quite unknown, with singularly little to show, the ground of whose exorbi-
tant pretensions it was not easy to discover? Wasn't he paid, above
all, by the delightful relation he had established with Morgan—
quite ideal, as from master to pupil—and by the single privilege
of knowing and living with so amazingly gifted a child, than
whom really—she meant literally what she said—there was no
better company in Europe? Mrs. Moreen herself took to appealing
to him as a man of the world; she said "Voyons, mon cher," and
"My dear sir, look here now"; and urged him to be reasonable,
putting it before him that it was really a chance for him. She
spoke as if, according as he *should* be reasonable, he would prove
himself worthy to be her son's tutor and of the extraordinary
confidence they had placed in him.

After all, Pemberton reflected, it was only a difference of
theory, and the theory didn't matter much. They had hitherto
gone on that of remunerated, as now they would go on that of
gratuitous, service; but why should they have so many words
about it? Mrs. Moreen, however, continued to be convincing;
sitting there with her fifty francs she talked and repeated, as
women repeat, and bored and irritated him, while he leaned
against the wall with his hands in the pockets of his wrapper,
drawing it together round his legs and looking over the head of
his visitor at the grey negations of his window. She wound up with
saying: "You see I bring you a definite proposal."

"A definite proposal?"

"To make our relations regular, as it were—to put them
on a comfortable footing."

"I see—it's a system," said Pemberton. "A kind of blackmail."

Mrs. Moreen bounded up, which was what the young man
wanted.

"What do you mean by that?"

"You practise on one's fears—one's fears about the child if
one should go away."

"And, pray, what would happen to him in that event?"
demanded Mrs. Moreen, with majesty.

"Why, he'd be alone with *you*."

"And pray, with whom *should* a child be but with those
whom he loves most?"

"If you think that, why don't you dismiss me?"

"Do you pretend that he loves you more than he loves *us*?"
cried Mrs. Moreen.

"I think he ought to. I make sacrifices for him. Though
I've heard of those *you* make, I don't see them."

Mrs. Moreen stared a moment; then, with emotion, she
grasped Pemberton's hand. "*Will* you make it—the sacrifice?"

Pemberton burst out laughing. "I'll see—I'll do what I can
—I'll stay a little longer. Your calculation is just—I *do* hate
intensely to give him up; I'm fond of him and he interests me
deeply, in spite of the inconvenience I suffer. You know my situation perfectly; I haven't a penny in the world, and, occupied as
I am with Morgan, I'm unable to earn money."

Mrs. Moreen tapped her undressed arm with her folded
bank-note. "Can't you write articles? Can't you translate, as *I* do?"

"I don't know about translating; it's wretchedly paid."

"I am glad to earn what I can," said Mrs. Moreen virtu-
ously, with her head high.

"You ought to tell me who you do it for." Pemberton

paused a moment, and she said nothing; so he added: "I've tried to turn off some little sketches, but the magazines won't have them—they're declined with thanks."

"You see then you're not such a phœnix—to have such pretensions," smiled his interlocutress.

"I haven't time to do things properly," Pemberton went on. Then as it came over him that he was almost abjectly good-natured to give these explanations he added: "If I stay on longer it must be on one condition—that Morgan shall know distinctly on what footing I am."

Mrs. Moreen hesitated. "Surely you don't want to show off to a child?"

"To show *you* off, do you mean?"

Again Mrs. Moreen hesitated, but this time it was to produce a still finer flower. "And *you* talk of blackmail!"

"You can easily prevent it," said Pemberton.

"And *you* talk of practising on fears," Mrs. Moreen continued.

"Yes, there's no doubt I'm a great scoundrel."

His visitor looked at him a moment—it was evident that she was sorely bothered. Then she thrust out her money at him. "Mr. Moreen desired me to give you this on account."

"I'm much obliged to Mr. Moreen; but we have no account."

"You won't take it?"

"That leaves me more free," said Pemberton.

"To poison my darling's mind?" groaned Mrs. Moreen.

"Oh, your darling's mind!" laughed the young man.

She fixed him a moment, and he thought she was going to break out tormentedly, pleadingly: "For God's sake, tell me what *is* in it!" But she checked this impulse—another was stronger. She pocketed the money—the crudity of the alternative was comical— and swept out of the room with the desperate concession: "You may tell him any horror you like!"

VI

A couple of days after this, during which Pemberton had delayed to profit by Mrs. Moreen's permission to tell her son any horror, the two had been for a quarter of an hour walking together in silence when the boy became sociable again with the remark: "I'll tell you how I know it; I know it through Zénobie."

"Zénobie? Who in the world is *she*?"

"A nurse I used to have—ever so many years ago. A charming woman. I liked her awfully, and she liked me."

"There's no accounting for tastes. What is it you know through her?"

"Why, what their idea is. She went away because they didn't pay her. She did like me awfully, and she stayed two years. She told me all about it—that at last she could never get her wages. As soon as they saw how much she liked me they stopped giving her anything. They thought she'd stay for nothing, out of devotion. And she did stay ever so long—as long as she could. She was only a poor girl. She used to send money to her mother. At last she couldn't afford it any longer, and she went away in a fearful rage one night—I mean of course in a rage against *them*. She cried over me tremendously, she hugged me nearly to death. She told me all about it," Morgan repeated. "She told me it was their idea. So I guessed, ever so long ago, that they have had the same idea with you."

"Zénobie was very shrewd," said Pemberton. "And she made you so."

"Oh, that wasn't Zénobie; that was nature. And experience!" Morgan laughed.

"Well, Zénobie was a part of your experience."

"Certainly I was a part of hers, poor dear!" the boy exclaimed. "And I'm a part of yours."

"A very important part. But I don't see how you know that I've been treated like Zénobie."

"Do you take me for an idiot?" Morgan asked. "Haven't I been conscious of what we've been through together?"

"What we've been through?"

"Our privations—our dark days."

"Oh, our days have been bright enough."

Morgan went on in silence for a moment. Then he said: "My dear fellow, you're a hero!"

"Well, you're another!" Pemberton retorted.

"No, I'm not; but I'm not a baby. I won't stand it any longer. You must get some occupation that pays. I'm ashamed, I'm ashamed!" quavered the boy in a little passionate voice that was very touching to Pemberton.

"We ought to go off and live somewhere together," said the young man.

"I'll go like a shot if you'll take me."

"I'd get some work that would keep us both afloat," Pemberton continued.

"So would I. Why shouldn't *I* work? I ain't such a *crétin*!"

"The difficulty is that your parents wouldn't hear of it," said Pemberton. "They would never part with you; they worship the ground you tread on. Don't you see the proof of it? They don't dislike me; they wish me no harm; they're very amiable people; but they're perfectly ready to treat me badly for your sake."

The silence in which Morgan received this graceful sophistry struck Pemberton somehow as expressive. After a moment Morgan repeated: "You *are* a hero!" Then he added: "They leave me with you altogether. You've all the responsibility. They put me off on you from morning till night. Why, then, should they object to my taking up with you completely? I'd help you."

"They're not particularly keen about my being helped, and they delight in thinking of you as *theirs*. They're tremendously proud of you."

"I'm not proud of them. But you know *that*," Morgan returned.

"Except for the little matter we speak of they're charming people," said Pemberton, not taking up the imputation of lucidity, but wondering greatly at the child's own, and especially at this fresh reminder of something he had been conscious of from the first—the strangest thing in the boy's large little composition, a temper, a sensibility, even a sort of ideal, which made him privately resent the general quality of his kinsfolk. Morgan had in secret a small loftiness which begot an element of reflection, a domestic scorn not imperceptible to his companion (though they never had any talk about it), and absolutely anomalous in a juvenile nature, especially when one noted that it had not made this nature "old-fashioned," as the word is of children—quaint or wizened or offensive. It was as if he had been a little gentleman and had paid the penalty by discovering that he was the only such person in the family. This comparison didn't make him vain; but it could make him melancholy and a trifle austere. When Pemberton guessed at these young dimnesses he saw him serious and gallant, and was partly drawn on and partly checked, as if with a scruple, by the charm of attempting to sound the little cool shallows which were quickly growing deeper. When he tried to figure to himself the morning twilight of childhood, so as to deal with it safely, he perceived that it was never fixed, never arrested, that ignorance, at the instant one touched it, was already flushing faintly into knowledge, that there was nothing that at a given moment you could say a clever child didn't know. It seemed to him that *he* both knew too much to imagine Morgan's simplicity and too little to disembroil his tangle.

The boy paid no heed to his last remark; he only went on: "I should have spoken to them about their idea, as I call it, long ago, if I hadn't been sure what they would say."

"And what would they say?"

"Just what they said about what poor Zénobie told me—
that it was a horrid, dreadful story, that they had paid her every
penny they owed her."

"Well, perhaps they had," said Pemberton.

"Perhaps they've paid you!"

"Let us pretend they have, and *n'en parlons plus.*"

"They accused her of lying and cheating," Morgan insisted
perversely. "That's why I don't want to speak to them."

"Lest they should accuse me, too?"

To this Morgan made no answer, and his companion, looking down at him (the boy turned his eyes, which had filled, away),
saw that he couldn't have trusted himself to utter.

"You're right. Don't squeeze them," Pemberton pursued.
"Except for that, they *are* charming people."

"Except for *their* lying and *their* cheating?"

"I say—I say!" cried Pemberton, imitating a little tone of
the lad's which was itself an imitation.

"We must be frank, at the last; we *must* come to an understanding," said Morgan, with the importance of the small boy who
lets himself think he is arranging great affairs—almost playing at
shipwreck or at Indians. "I know all about everything," he added.

"I daresay your father has his reasons," Pemberton observed, too vaguely, as he was aware.

"For lying and cheating?"

"For saving and managing and turning his means to the
best account. He has plenty to do with his money. You're an
expensive family."

"Yes, I'm very expensive," Morgan rejoined, in a manner
which made his preceptor burst out laughing.

"He's saving for *you*," said Pemberton. "They think of
you in everything they do."

"He might save a little——" The boy paused. Pemberton
waited to hear what. Then Morgan brought out oddly: "A little
reputation."

"Oh, there's plenty of that. That's all right!"

"Enough of it for the people they know, no doubt. The
people they know are awful."

"Do you mean the princes? We mustn't abuse the princes."

"Why not? They haven't married Paula—they haven't
married Amy. They only clean out Ulick."

"You *do* know everything!" Pemberton exclaimed.

"No, I don't, after all. I don't know what they live on, or
how they live, or *why* they live! What have they got and how did
they get it? Are they rich, are they poor, or have they a *modeste
aisance*? Why are they always chiveying about—living one year

like ambassadors and the next like paupers? Who are they, anyway, and what are they? I've thought of all that—I've thought of
a lot of things. They're so beastly worldly. That's what I hate
most—oh, I've *seen* it! All they care about is to make an appearance and to pass for something or other. What do they want to
pass for? What *do* they, Mr. Pemberton?"

"You pause for a reply," said Pemberton, treating the
inquiry as a joke, yet wondering too, and greatly struck with the
boy's intense, if imperfect, vision. "I haven't the least idea."

"And what good does it do? Haven't I seen the way people
treat them—the 'nice' people, the ones they want to know? They'll
take anything from them—they'll lie down and be trampled on.
The nice ones hate that—they just sicken them. You're the only
really nice person we know."

"Are you sure? They don't lie down for me!"

"Well, you shan't lie down for them. You've got to go—
that's what you've got to do," said Morgan.

"And what will become of you?"

"Oh, I'm growing up. I shall get off before long. I'll see
you later."

"You had better let me finish you," Pemberton urged,
lending himself to the child's extraordinarily competent attitude.

Morgan stopped in their walk, looking up at him. He had
to look up much less than a couple of years before—he had grown,
in his loose leanness, so long and high. "Finish me?" he echoed.

"There are such a lot of jolly things we can do together
yet. I want to turn you out—I want you to do me credit."

Morgan continued to look at him. "To give you credit—
do you mean?"

"My dear fellow, you're too clever to live."

"That's just what I'm afraid you think. No. no; it isn't fair
—I can't endure it. We'll part next week. The sooner it's over the
sooner to sleep."

"If I hear of anything—any other chance, I promise to go,"
said Pemberton.

Morgan consented to consider this. "But you'll be honest,"
he demanded; "you won't pretend you haven't heard?"

"I'm much more likely to pretend I have."

"But what can you hear of, this way, stuck in a hole with
us? You ought to be on the spot, to go to England—you ought to
go to America."

"One would think you were *my* tutor!" said Pemberton.

Morgan walked on, and after a moment he began again:
"Well, now that you know that I know and that we look at the
facts and keep nothing back—it's much more comfortable, isn't it?"

"My dear boy, it's so amusing, so interesting, that it surely will be quite impossible for me to forgo such hours as these."

This made Morgan stop once more. "You *do* keep something back. Oh, you're not straight—*I* am!"

"Why am I not straight?"

"Oh, you've got your idea!"

"My idea?"

"Why, that I probably shan't live, and that you can stick it out till I'm removed."

"You *are* too clever to live!" Pemberton repeated.

"I call it a mean idea," Morgan pursued. "But I shall punish you by the way I hang on."

"Look out or I'll poison you!" Pemberton laughed.

"I'm stronger and better every year. Haven't you noticed that there hasn't been a doctor near me since you came?"

"*I'm* your doctor," said the young man, taking his arm and drawing him on again.

Morgan proceeded, and after a few steps he gave a sigh of mingled weariness and relief. "Ah, now that we look at the facts, it's all right!"

VII

They looked at the facts a good deal after this; and one of the first consequences of their doing so was that Pemberton stuck it out, as it were, for the purpose. Morgan made the facts so vivid and so droll, and at the same time so bald and so ugly, that there was fascination in talking them over with him, just as there would have been heartlessness in leaving him alone with them. Now that they had such a number of perceptions in common it was useless for the pair to pretend that they didn't judge such people; but the very judgment, and the exchange of perceptions, created another tie. Morgan had never been so interesting as now that he himself was made plainer by the sidelight of these confidences. What came out in it most was the soreness of his characteristic pride. He had plenty of that, Pemberton felt—so much that it was perhaps well it should have had to take some early bruises. He would have liked his people to be gallant, and he had waked up too soon to the sense that they were perpetually swallowing humble-pie. His mother would consume any amount, and his father would consume even more than his mother. He had a theory that Ulick had wriggled out of an "affair" at Nice: there had once been a flurry at home, a regular panic, after which they all went to bed and took medicine, not to be accounted for on any other supposition. Morgan had a romantic imagination, fed by poetry and history, and he would have liked those who "bore his name" (as he used to say to Pemberton with the humour that made his sensitiveness manly) to have a proper spirit. But their one idea was to get in with people who didn't want them and to take snubs as if they were honourable scars. Why people didn't want them more he didn't know—that was people's own affair; after all they were not superficially repulsive—they were a hundred times cleverer than most of the dreary grandees, the "poor swells" they rushed about Europe to catch up with. "After all, they *are* amusing—they are!" Morgan used to say, with the wisdom of the ages. To which Pemberton always replied: "Amusing—the great Moreen troupe? Why, they're altogether delightful; and if it were not for the hitch that you and I (feeble performers!) make in the *ensemble*, they would carry everything before them."

What the boy couldn't get over was that this particular blight seemed, in a tradition of self-respect, so undeserved and so arbitrary. No doubt people had a right to take the line they liked; but why should *his* people have liked the line of pushing and toadying and lying and cheating? What had their forefathers—all decent folk, so far as he knew—done to them, or what had *he* done to them? Who had poisoned their blood with the fifth-rate social ideal, the fixed idea of making smart acquaintances and getting into the *monde chic*, especially when it was foredoomed to failure and exposure? They showed so what they were after; that was what made the people they wanted not want *them*. And never a movement of dignity, never a throb of shame at looking each other in the face, never any independence or resentment or disgust. If his father or his brother would only knock some one down once or twice a year! Clever as they were they never guessed how they appeared. They were good-natured, yes—as good-natured as Jews at the doors of clothing-shops! But was that the model one wanted one's family to follow? Morgan had dim memories of an old grandfather, the maternal, in New York, whom he had been taken across the ocean to see, at the age of five: a gentleman with a high neckcloth and a good deal of pronunciation, who wore a dress-coat in the morning, which made one wonder what he wore in the evening, and had, or was supposed to have, "property" and something to do with the Bible Society. It couldn't have been but that *he* was a good type. Pemberton himself remembered Mrs. Clancy, a widowed sister of Mr. Moreen's, who was as irritating as a moral tale and had paid a fortnight's visit to the family at Nice shortly after he came to live with them. She was "pure and refined," as Amy said, over the banjo, and had the air of not knowing what they meant and of keeping something back. Pemberton judged that what she kept back was an approval of many of their ways; therefore it was to be supposed that she too was of a good type, and that Mr. and Mrs. Moreen and Ulick and Paula and Amy might easily have been better if they would.

But that they wouldn't was more and more perceptible from day to day. They continued to "chivey," as Morgan called it, and in due time became aware of a variety of reasons for proceeding to Venice. They mentioned a great many of them—they were always strikingly frank, and had the brightest friendly chatter, at the late foreign breakfast in especial, before the ladies had made up their faces, when they leaned their arms on the table, had something to follow the *demitasse*, and, in the heat of familiar discussion as to what they "really ought" to do, fell inevitably into the languages in which they could *tutoyer*. Even Pemberton liked them, then; he could endure even Ulick when he heard him give his little flat voice for the "sweet sea-city." That was what made him have a sneaking kindness for them— that they were so out of the workaday world and kept him so out of it. The summer had waned when, with cries of ecstasy, they all passed out on the balcony that overhung the Grand Canal; the sunsets were splendid—the Dorringtons had arrived. The Dorringtons were the only reason they had not talked of at breakfast; but the reasons that they didn't talk of at breakfast always came out in the end. The Dorringtons, on the other hand, came out very little; or else, when they did, they stayed—as was natural—for hours, during which periods Mrs. Moreen and the girls sometimes called at their hotel (to see if they had returned) as many as three times running. The gondola was for the ladies; for in Venice too there were "days," which Mrs. Moreen knew in their order an hour after she arrived. She immediately took one herself, to which the Dorringtons never came, though on a certain occasion when Pemberton and his pupil were together at St. Mark's—where, taking the best walks they had ever had and haunting a hundred churches, they spent a great deal of time—they saw the old lord turn up with Mr. Moreen and Ulick, who showed him the dim basilica as if it belonged to them. Pemberton noted how much less, among its curiosities, Lord Dorrington carried himself as a man of the world; wondering too whether, for such services, his companions took a fee from him. The autumn, at any rate, waned, the Dorringtons departed, and Lord Verschoyle, the eldest son, had proposed neither for Amy nor for Paula.

One sad November day, while the wind roared round the old palace and the rain lashed the lagoon, Pemberton, for exercise and even somewhat for warmth (the Moreens were horribly frugal about fires—it was a cause of suffering to their inmate), walked up and down the big bare *sala* with his pupil. The

scagliola floor was cold, the high battered casements shook in the
storm, and the stately decay of the place was unrelieved by a parti-
cle of furniture. Pemberton's spirits were low, and it came over
him that the fortune of the Moreens was now even lower. A blast
of desolation, a prophecy of disaster and disgrace, seemed to draw
through the comfortless hall. Mr. Moreen and Ulick were in the
Piazza, looking out for something, strolling drearily, in mackintoshes, under the arcades; but still, in spite of mackintoshes, unmistakable men of the world. Paula and Amy were in bed—it
might have been thought they were staying there to keep warm.
Pemberton looked askance at the boy at his side, to see to what
extent he was conscious of these portents. But Morgan, luckily
for him, was now mainly conscious of growing taller and stronger
and indeed of being in his fifteenth year. This fact was intensely
interesting to him—it was the basis of a private theory (which,
however, he had imparted to his tutor) that in a little while he
should stand on his own feet. He considered that the situation
would change—that, in short, he should be "finished," grown up,
producible in the world of affairs and ready to prove himself of
sterling ability. Sharply as he was capable, at times, of questioning
his circumstances, there were happy hours when he was as superficial as a child; the proof of which was his fundamental assumption
that he should presently go to Oxford, to Pemberton's college,
and, aided and abetted by Pemberton, do the most wonderful
things. It vexed Pemberton to see how little, in such a project,
he took account of ways and means: on other matters he was so
sceptical about them. Pemberton tried to imagine the Moreens at
Oxford, and fortunately failed; yet unless they were to remove
there as a family there would be no *modus vivendi* for Morgan.
How could he live without an allowance, and where was the
allowance to come from? He (Pemberton) might live on Morgan;
but how could Morgan live on him? What was to become of him
anyhow? Somehow, the fact that he was a big boy now, with better
prospects of health, made the question of his future more difficult.
So long as he was frail the consideration that he inspired seemed
enough of an answer to it. But at the bottom of Pemberton's
heart was the recognition of his probably being strong enough to
live and not strong enough to thrive. He himself, at any rate, was
in a period of natural, boyish rosiness about all this, so that the
beating of the tempest seemed to him only the voice of life and
the challenge of fate. He had on his shabby little overcoat, with
the collar up, but he was enjoying his walk.

It was interrupted at last by the appearance of his mother
at the end of the *sala*. She beckoned to Morgan to come to her,
and while Pemberton saw him, complacent, pass down the long

vista, over the damp false marble, he wondered what was in the air. Mrs. Moreen said a word to the boy and made him go into the room she had quitted. Then, having closed the door after him, she directed her steps swiftly to Pemberton. There *was* something in the air, but his wildest flight of fancy wouldn't have suggested what it proved to be. She signified that she had made a pretext to get Morgan out of the way, and then she inquired—without hesitation—if the young man could lend her sixty francs. While, before bursting into a laugh, he stared at her with surprise, she declared that she was awfully pressed for the money; she was desperate for it—it would save her life.

"Dear lady, *c'est trop fort!*" Pemberton laughed. "Where in the world do you suppose I should get sixty francs, *du train dont vous allez?*"

"I thought you worked—wrote things, don't they pay you?"

"Not a penny."

"Are you such a fool as to work for nothing?"

"You ought surely to know that."

Mrs. Moreen stared an instant, then she coloured a little. Pemberton saw she had quite forgotten the terms—if "terms" they could be called—that he had ended by accepting from herself; they had burdened her memory as little as her conscience. "Oh, yes, I see what you mean—you have been very nice about that; but why go back to it so often?" She had been perfectly urbane with him ever since the rough scene of explanation in his room, the morning he made her accept *his* "terms"—the necessity of his making his case known to Morgan. She had felt no resentment, after seeing that there was no danger of Morgan's taking the matter up with her. Indeed, attributing this immunity to the good taste of his influence with the boy, she had once said to Pemberton: "My dear fellow; it's an immense comfort you're a gentleman." She repeated this, in substance, now. "Of course you're a gentleman—that's a bother the less!" Pemberton reminded her that he had not "gone back" to anything; and she also repeated her prayer that, somewhere and somehow, he would find her sixty francs. He took the liberty of declaring that if he could find them it wouldn't be to lend them to *her*—as to which he consciously did himself injustice, knowing that if he had them he would certainly place them in her hand. He accused himself, at bottom and with some truth, of a fantastic, demoralised sympathy with her. If misery made strange bedfellows it also made strange sentiments. It was moreover a part of the demoralisation and of the general bad effect of living with such people that one had to make rough retorts, quite out of the tradition of good manners. "Morgan, Morgan, to what pass have I come for you?" he pri-

vately exclaimed, while Mrs. Moreen floated voluminously down
the *sala* again, to liberate the boy; groaning, as she went, that
everything was too odious.

Before the boy was liberated there came a thump at the
door communicating with the staircase, followed by the appari-
tion of a dripping youth who poked in his head. Pemberton
recognised him as the bearer of a telegram and recognised the
telegram as addressed to himself. Morgan came back as, after
glancing at the signature (that of a friend in London), he was
reading the words: "Found jolly job for you—engagement to
coach opulent youth on own terms. Come immediately." The
answer, happily, was paid, and the messenger waited. Morgan,
who had drawn near, waited too, and looked hard at Pemberton;
and Pemberton, after a moment, having met his look, handed him
the telegram. It was really by wise looks (they knew each other so
well) that, while the telegraph-boy, in his waterproof cape, made
a great puddle on the floor, the thing was settled between them.
Pemberton wrote the answer with a pencil against the frescoed
wall, and the messenger departed. When he had gone Pemberton
said to Morgan:

"I'll make a tremendous charge; I'll earn a lot of money
in a short time, and we'll live on it."

"Well, I hope the opulent youth will be stupid—he probably will—" Morgan parenthesised, "and keep you a long time."

"Of course, the longer he keeps me the more we shall have
for our old age."

"But suppose *they* don't pay you!" Morgan awfully suggested.

"Oh, there are not two such——!" Pemberton paused, he
was on the point of using an invidious term. Instead of this he
said "two such chances."

Morgan flushed—the tears came to his eyes. "*Dites toujours*,
two such rascally crews!" Then, in a different tone, he added:
"Happy opulent youth!"

"Not if he's stupid!"

"Oh, they're happier then. But you can't have everything,
can you?" the boy smiled.

Pemberton held him, his hands on his shoulders. "What
will become of *you*, what will you do?" He thought of Mrs.
Moreen, desperate for sixty francs.

"I shall turn into a man." And then, as if he recognised all
the bearings of Pemberton's allusion: "I shall get on with them
better when you're not here."

"Ah, don't say that—it sounds as if I set you against them!"

"You do—the sight of you. It's all right; you know what

I mean. I shall be beautiful. I'll take their affairs in hand; I'll marry my sisters."

"You'll marry yourself!" joked Pemberton; as high, rather tense pleasantry would evidently be the right, or the safest, tone for their separation.

It was, however, not purely in this strain that Morgan suddenly asked: "But I say—how will you get to your jolly job? You'll have to telegraph to the opulent youth for money to come on."

Pemberton bethought himself. "They won't like that, will they?"

"Oh, look out for them!"

Then Pemberton brought out his remedy. "I'll go to the American Consul; I'll borrow some money of him—just for the few days, on the strength of the telegram."

Morgan was hilarious. "Show him the telegram—then stay and keep the money!"

Pemberton entered into the joke enough to reply that, for Morgan, he was really capable of that; but the boy, growing more serious, and to prove that he hadn't meant what he said, not only hurried him off to the Consulate (since he was to start that evening, as he had wired to his friend), but insisted on going with him. They splashed through the tortuous perforations and over the humpbacked bridges, and they passed through the Piazza, where they saw Mr. Moreen and Ulick go into a jeweller's shop. The Consul proved accommodating (Pemberton said it wasn't the letter, but Morgan's grand air), and on their way back they went into St. Mark's for a hushed ten minutes. Later they took up and kept up the fun of it to the very end; and it seemed to Pemberton a part of that fun that Mrs. Moreen, who was very angry when he had announced to her his intention, should charge him, grotesquely and vulgarly, and in reference to the loan she had vainly endeavoured to effect, with bolting lest they should "get something out" of him. On the other hand he had to do Mr. Moreen and Ulick the justice to recognise that when, on coming in, *they* heard the cruel news, they took it like perfect men of the world.

VIII

When Pemberton got at work with the opulent youth, who was to be taken in hand for Balliol, he found himself unable to say whether he was really an idiot or it was only, on his own part, the long association with an intensely living little mind that made him seem so. From Morgan he heard half-a-dozen times: the boy

wrote charming young letters, a patchwork of tongues, with indulgent postscripts in the family Volapuk and, in little squares
and rounds and crannies of the text, the drollest illustrations—
letters that he was divided between the impulse to show his present disciple, as a kind of wasted incentive, and the sense of something in them that was profanable by publicity. The opulent
youth went up, in due course, and failed to pass; but it seemed to
add to the presumption that brilliancy was not expected of him
all at once that his parents, condoning the lapse, which they good-
naturedly treated as little as possible as if it were Pemberton's,
should have sounded the rally again, begged the young coach to
keep his pupil in hand another year.

The young coach was now in a position to lend Mrs.
Moreen sixty francs, and he sent her a post-office order for the
amount. In return for this favour he received a frantic, scribbled
line from her: "Implore you to come back instantly—Morgan
dreadfully ill." They were on the rebound, once more in Paris—
often as Pemberton had seen them depressed he had never seen
them crushed—and communication was therefore rapid. He wrote
to the boy to ascertain the state of his health, but he received no
answer to his letter. Accordingly he took an abrupt leave of the
opulent youth and, crossing the Channel, alighted at the small
hotel, in the quarter of the Champs Elysées, of which Mrs. Moreen
had given him the address. A deep if dumb dissatisfaction with
this lady and her companions bore him company: they couldn't
be vulgarly honest, but they could live at hotels, in velvety
entresols, amid a smell of burst pastilles, in the most expensive
city in Europe. When he had left them, in Venice, it was with an
irrepressible suspicion that something was gong to happen; but
the only thing that had happened was that they succeeded in
getting away. "How is he? where is he?" he asked of Mrs. Moreen;
but before she could speak, these questions were answered by the
pressure round his neck of a pair of arms, in shrunken sleeves,
which were perfectly capable of an effusive young foreign squeeze.

"Dreadfully ill—I don't see it!" the young man cried. And
then, to Morgan: "Why on earth didn't you relieve me? Why
didn't you answer my letter?"

Mrs. Moreen declared that when she wrote he was very
bad, and Pemberton learned at the same time from the boy that
he had answered every letter he had received. This led to the
demonstration that Pemberton's note had been intercepted. Mrs.
Moreen was prepared to see the fact exposed, as Pemberton perceived, the moment he faced her, that she was prepared for a good
many other things. She was prepared above all to maintain that
she had acted from a sense of duty, that she was enchanted she

had got him over, whatever they might say; and that it was useless of him to pretend that he didn't *know*, in all his bones, that his place at such a time was with Morgan. He had taken the boy away from them and now he had no right to abandon him. He had created for himself the gravest responsibilities; he must at least abide by what he had done.

"Taken him away from you?" Pemberton exclaimed indignantly.

"Do it—do it, for pity's sake; that's just what I want. I can't stand *this*—and such scenes. They're treacherous!" These words broke from Morgan, who had intermitted his embrace, in a key which made Pemberton turn quickly to him, to see that he had suddenly seated himself, was breathing with evident difficulty and was very pale.

"*Now* do you say he's not ill—my precious pet?" shouted his mother, dropping on her knees before him with clasped hands, but touching him no more than if he had been a gilded idol. "It will pass—it's only for an instant; but don't say such dreadful things!"

"I'm all right—all right," Morgan panted to Pemberton, whom he sat looking up at with a strange smile, his hands resting on either side of the sofa.

"Now do you pretend I've been treacherous—that I've deceived?" Mrs. Moreen flashed at Pemberton as she got up.

"It isn't *he* says it, it's I!" the boy returned, apparently easier, but sinking back against the wall; while Pemberton, who had sat down beside him, taking his hand, bent over him.

"Darling child, one does what one can; there are so many things to consider," urged Mrs. Moreen. "It's his *place*—his only place. You see *you* think it is now."

"Take me away—take me away," Morgan went on, smiling to Pemberton from his white face.

"Where shall I take you, and how—oh, *how*, my boy?" the young man stammered, thinking of the rude way in which his friends in London held that, for his convenience, and without a pledge of instantaneous return, he had thrown them over, of the just resentment with which they would already have called in a successor, and of the little help as regarded finding fresh employment that resided for him in the flatness of his having failed to pass his pupil.

"Oh, we'll settle that. You used to talk about it," said Morgan. "If we can only go, all the rest's a detail."

"Talk about it as much as you like, but don't think you can attempt it. Mr. Moreen would never consent—it would be so precarious," Pemberton's hostess explained to him. Then to Morgan she explained: "It would destroy our peace, it would break our hearts. Now that he's back it will be all the same again. You'll have your life, your work and your freedom, and we'll all be happy as we used to be. You'll bloom and grow perfectly well, and we won't have any more silly experiments, will we? They're too absurd. It's Mr. Pemberton's place—every one in his place. You in yours, your papa in his, me in mine—*n'est-ce pas, chéri?* We'll all forget how foolish we've been, and we'll have lovely times."

She continued to talk and to surge vaguely about the little draped, stuffy *salon*, while Pemberton sat with the boy, whose colour gradually came back; and she mixed up her reasons, dropping that there were going to be changes, that the other children might scatter (who knew?—Paula had her ideas), and that then it might be fancied how much the poor old parent-birds would want the little nestling. Morgan looked at Pemberton, who wouldn't let him move; and Pemberton knew exactly how he felt at hearing himself called a little nestling. He admitted that he had had one or two bad days, but he protested afresh against the iniquity of his mother's having made them the ground of an appeal to poor Pemberton. Poor Pemberton could laugh now, apart from the comicality of Mrs. Moreen's producing so much philosophy for her defence (she seemed to shake it out of her agitated petticoats, which knocked over the light gilt chairs), so little did the sick boy strike him as qualified to repudiate any advantage.

He himself was in for it, at any rate. He should have Morgan on his hands again indefinitely; though indeed he saw the lad had a private theory to produce which would be intended to smooth this down. He was obliged to him for it in advance; but the suggested amendment didn't keep his heart from sinking a little, any more than it prevented him from accepting the prospect on the spot, with some confidence moreover that he would do so even better if he could have a little supper. Mrs. Moreen threw out more hints about the changes that were to be looked for, but she was such a mixture of smiles and shudders (she confessed she was very nervous), that he couldn't tell whether she were in high feather or only in hysterics. If the family were really at last going to pieces why shouldn't she recognise the necessity of pitching Morgan into some sort of lifeboat? This presumption was fostered by the fact that they were established in luxurious quarters in the capital of pleasure; that was exactly where they naturally *would* be established in view of going to pieces. Moreover didn't she mention that Mr. Moreen and the others were enjoying themselves at the opera with Mr. Granger, and wasn't *that* also precisely where one would look for them on the eve of a smash? Pemberton gathered that Mr. Granger was a rich, vacant American—a big bill with a flourishy heading and no items; so that one of Paula's "ideas" was probably that this time she had really done it, which was indeed an unprecedented blow to the general cohesion. And if the cohesion was to terminate what was to become of poor Pemberton? He felt quite enough bound up with them to figure, to his alarm, as a floating spar in case of a wreck.

It was Morgan who eventually asked if no supper had been ordered for him; sitting with him below, later, at the dim, delayed meal, in the presence of a great deal of corded green plush, a plate of ornamental biscuit and a languor marked on the part of the waiter. Mrs. Moreen had explained that they had been obliged to secure a room for the visitor out of the house; and Morgan's consolation (he offered it while Pemberton reflected on the nastiness of lukewarm sauces) proved to be, largely, that this circumstance would facilitate their escape. He talked of their escape (recurring to it often afterwards), as if they were making up a "boy's book" together. But he likewise expressed his sense that there was something in the air, that the Moreens couldn't keep it up much longer. In point of fact, as Pemberton was to see, they kept it up for five or six months. All the while, however, Morgan's contention was designed to cheer him. Mr. Moreen and Ulick, whom he had met the day after his return, accepted that return like perfect men of the world. If Paula and Amy treated it even with less formality an allowance was to be made for them, inasmuch as Mr. Granger had not come to the opera after all. He had only placed his box at their service, with a bouquet for each of the party; there was even one apiece, embittering the thought of his profusion, for Mr. Moreen and Ulick. "They're all like that," was Morgan's comment; "at the very last, just when we think we've got them fast, we're chucked!"

Morgan's comments, in these days, were more and more free; they even included a large recognition of the extraordinary tenderness with which he had been treated while Pemberton was away. Oh, yes, they couldn't do enough to be nice to him, to show him they had him on their mind and make up for his loss. That was just what made the whole thing so sad, and him so glad, after all, of Pemberton's return—he had to keep thinking of their affection less, had less sense of obligation. Pemberton laughed out at this last reason, and Morgan blushed and said: "You know what I mean." Pemberton knew perfectly what he meant; but there were a good many things it didn't make any clearer. This episode of his second sojourn in Paris stretched itself out wearily, with

their resumed readings and wanderings and maunderings, their
potterings on the quays, their hauntings of the museums, their
occasional lingerings in the Palais Royal, when the first sharp
weather came on and there was a comfort in warm emanations,
before Chevet's wonderful succulent window. Morgan wanted to
hear a great deal about the opulent youth—he took an immense
interest in him. Some of the details of his opulence—Pemberton
could spare him none of them—evidently intensified the boy's
appreciation of all his friend had given up to come back to him;
but in addition to the greater reciprocity established by such a
renunciation he had always his little brooding theory, in which
there was a frivolous gaiety too, that their long probation was
drawing to a close. Morgan's conviction that the Moreens couldn't
go on much longer kept pace with the unexpended impetus with
which, from month to month, they did go on. Three weeks after
Pemberton had rejoined them they went on to another hotel, a
dingier one than the first; but Morgan rejoiced that his tutor had
at least still not sacrificed the advantage of a room outside. He
clung to the romantic utility of this when the day, or rather the
night, should arrive for their escape.

For the first time, in this complicated connection, Pemberton felt sore and exasperated. It was, as he had said to Mrs.
Moreen in Venice, *trop fort*—everything was *trop fort*. He could
neither really throw off his blighting burden nor find in it the
benefit of a pacified conscience or of a rewarded affection. He had
spent all the money that he had earned in England, and he felt
that his youth was going and that he was getting nothing back
for it. It was all very well for Morgan to seem to consider that
he would make up to him for all inconveniences by settling himself upon him permanently—there was an irritating flaw in such
a view. He saw what the boy had in his mind; the conception
that as his friend had had the generosity to come back to him he
must show his gratitude by giving him his life. But the poor
friend didn't desire the gift—what could he do with Morgan's
life? Of course at the same time that Pemberton was irritated he
remembered the reason, which was very honourable to Morgan
and which consisted simply of the fact that he was perpetually
making one forget that he was after all only a child. If one dealt
with him on a different basis one's misadventures were one's own
fault. So Pemberton waited in a queer confusion of yearning and
alarm for the catastrophe which was held to hang over the house
of Moreen, of which he certainly at moments felt the symptoms
brush his cheek and as to which he wondered much in what form
it would come.

Perhaps it would take the form of dispersal—a frightened

sauve qui peut, a scuttling into selfish corners. Certainly they were less elastic than of yore; they were evidently looking for something they didn't find. The Dorringtons hadn't reappeared, the princes had scattered; wasn't that the beginning of the end? Mrs. Moreen had lost her reckoning of the famous "days"; her social calendar was blurred—it had turned its face to the wall. Pemberton suspected that the great, the cruel, discomfiture had been the extraordinary behaviour of Mr. Granger, who seemed not to know what he wanted, or, what was much worse, what *they* wanted. He kept sending flowers, as if to bestrew the path of his retreat, which was never the path of return. Flowers were all very well, but—Pemberton could complete the proposition. It was now positively conspicuous that in the long run the Moreens were a failure; so that the young man was almost grateful the run had not been short. Mr. Moreen, indeed, was still occasionally able to get away on business, and, what was more surprising, he was also able to get back. Ulick had no club, but you could not have discovered it from his appearance, which was as much as ever that of a person looking at life from the window of such an institution; therefore Pemberton was doubly astonished at an answer he once heard him make to his mother, in the desperate tone of a man familiar with the worst privations. Her question Pemberton had not quite caught; it appeared to be an appeal for a suggestion as to whom they could get to take Amy. "Let the devil take her!" Ulick snapped; so that Pemberton could see that not only they had lost their amiability, but had ceased to believe in themselves. He could also see that if Mrs. Moreen was trying to get people to take her children she might be regarded as closing the hatches for the storm. But Morgan would be the last she would part with.

One winter afternoon—it was a Sunday—he and the boy walked far together in the Bois de Boulogne. The evening was so splendid, the cold lemon-coloured sunset so clear, the stream of carriages and pedestrians so amusing and the fascination of Paris so great, that they stayed out later than usual and became aware that they would have to hurry home to arrive in time for dinner. They hurried accordingly, arm-in-arm, good-humoured and hungry, agreeing that there was nothing like Paris after all and that after all, too, that had come and gone they were not yet sated with innocent pleasures. When they reached the hotel they found that, though scandalously late, they were in time for all the dinner they were likely to sit down to. Confusion reigned in the apartments of the Moreens (very shabby ones this time, but the best in the house), and before the interrupted service of the table (with objects displaced almost as if there had been a scuffle, and a great wine stain from an overturned bottle), Pemberton could

not blink the fact that there had been a scene of proprietary
mutiny. The storm had come—they were all seeking refuge. The
hatches were down—Paula and Amy were invisible (they had
never tried the most casual art upon Pemberton, but he felt that
they had enough of an eye to him not to wish to meet him as
young ladies whose frocks had been confiscated), and Ulick appeared to have jumped overboard. In a word, the host and his
staff had ceased to "go on" at the pace of their guests, and the air
of embarrassed detention, thanks to a pile of gaping trunks in the
passage, was strangely commingled with the air of indignant
withdrawal.

When Morgan took in all this—and he took it in very
quickly—he blushed to the roots of his hair. He had walked, from
his infancy, among difficulties and dangers, but he had never seen
a public exposure. Pemberton noticed, in a second glance at him,
that the tears had rushed into his eyes and that they were tears of
bitter shame. He wondered for an instant for the boy's sake,
whether he might successfully pretend not to understand. Not
successfully, he felt, as Mr. and Mrs. Moreen, dinnerless by their
extinguished hearth, rose before him in their little dishonoured
salon, considering apparently with much intensity what lively
capital would be next on their list. They were not prostrate, but
they were very pale, and Mrs. Moreen had evidently been crying.
Pemberton quickly learned however that her grief was not for the
loss of her dinner, much as she usually enjoyed it, but on account
of a necessity much more tragic. She lost no time in laying this
necessity bare, in telling him how the change had come, the bolt
had fallen, and how they would all have to turn themselves about.
Therefore cruel as it was to them to part with their darling she
must look to him to carry a little further the influence he had so
fortunately acquired with the boy—to induce his young charge to
follow him into some modest retreat. They depended upon him,
in a word, to take their delightful child temporarily under his
protection—it would leave Mr. Moreen and herself so much more
free to give the proper attention (too little, alas! had been given)
to the readjustment of their affairs.

"We trust you—we feel that we can," said Mrs. Moreen
slowly rubbing her plump white hands and looking, with com-
punction, hard at Morgan, whose chin, not to take liberties, her
husband stroked with a tentative paternal forefinger.

"Oh, yes; we feel that we can. We trust Mr. Pemberton
fully, Morgan," Mr. Moreen conceded.

Pemberton wondered again if he might pretend not to
understand; but the idea was painfully complicated by the immediate perception that Morgan had understood.

"Do you mean that he may take me to live with him—for ever and ever?" cried the boy. "Away, away, anywhere he likes?"

"For ever and ever? *Comme vous-y-allez!*" Mr. Moreen laughed indulgently. "For as long as Mr. Pemberton may be so good."

"We've struggled, we've suffered," his wife went on; "but you've made him so your own that we've already been through the worst of the sacrifice."

Morgan had turned away from his father—he stood looking at Pemberton with a light in his face. His blush had died out, but something had come that was brighter and more vivid. He had a moment of boyish joy, scarcely mitigated by the reflection that, with his unexpected consecration of his hope—too sudden and too violent; the thing was a good deal less like a boy's book—the "escape" was left on their hands. The boyish joy was there for an instant, and Pemberton was almost frightened at the revelation of gratitude and affection that shone through his humiliation. When Morgan stammered "My dear fellow, what do you say to *that*?" he felt that he should say something enthusiastic. But he was still more frightened at something else that immediately followed and that made the lad sit down quickly on the nearest chair. He had turned very white and had raised his hand to his left side. They were all three looking at him, but Mrs. Moreen was the first to bound forward. "Ah, his darling little heart!" she broke out; and this time, on her knees before him and without respect for the idol, she caught him ardently in her arms. "You walked him too far, you hurried him too fast!" she tossed over her shoulder at Pemberton. The boy made no protest, and the next instant his mother, still holding him, sprang up with her face convulsed and with the terrified cry "Help, help! he's going, he's gone!" Pemberton saw, with equal horror, by Morgan's own stricken face, that he *was* gone. He pulled him half out of his mother's hands, and for a moment, while they held him together, they looked, in their dismay, into each other's eyes. "He couldn't stand it, with his infirmity," said Pemberton—"the shock, the whole scene, the violent emotion."

"But I thought he *wanted* to go to you!" wailed Mrs. Moreen.

"I *told* you he didn't, my dear," argued Mr. Moreen. He was trembling all over, and he was, in his way, as deeply affected as his wife. But, after the first, he took his bereavement like a man of the world.

III

The Unloving: Egoism

OVID: Echo and Narcissus*

THEY say that Jove, disposed to mirth as he and Juno
  sat
A-drinking nectar after meat in sport and pleasant rate,
Did fall a-jesting with his wife, and said: 'A greater
  pleasure
In Venus' games ye women have than men beyond all
  measure.'
She answered, no. To try the truth, they both of them
  agree
The wise Tiresias in this case indifferent judge to be,
Who both the man's and woman's joys by trial under-
  stood,
For finding once two mighty snakes engend'ring in a
  wood,
He struck them overthwart the backs, by means whereof
  behold
(As strange a thing to be of truth as ever yet was told)
He being made a woman straight, seven winter lived so.
The eighth he finding them again did say unto them tho:
'And if to strike ye have such power as for to turn their
  shape
That are the givers of the stripe, before you hence
  escape,
One stripe now shall I lend you more.' He struck them
  as beforne
And straight returned his former shape in which he
  first was born.
Tiresias therefore being ta'en to judge this jesting strife,

* Reprinted from *The Metamorphoses*.

470

Gave sentence on the side of Jove; the which the queen
    his wife
Did take a great deal more to heart than needed, and
    in spite
To wreak her teen upon her judge, bereft him of his
    sight;
But Jove (for to the gods it is unlawful to undo
The things which other of the gods by any means have
    do)
Did give him sight in things to come for loss of sight of
    eye,
And so his grievous punishment with honour did supply.
By means whereof within a while in city, field, and town
Through all the coast of Aonie was bruited his renown,
And folk to have their fortunes read that daily did resort,
Were answered so as none of them could give him mis-
    report.
    The first that of his soothfast words had proof in all
        the realm,
    Was freckled Liriope, whom sometime surprised in his
        stream
The flood Cephisus did enforce. This lady bare a son
Whose beauty at his very birth might justly love have
    won.
Narcissus did she call his name; of whom the prophet
    sage,
Demanded if the child should live to many years of age,
Made answer: 'Yea, full long, so that himself he do not
    know.'
The soothsayer's words seemed long but vain, until the
    end did show
His saying to be true indeed by strangeness of the rage
And strangeness of the kind of death that did abridge
    his age;
For when years three times five and one he fully lived
    had,
So that he seemed to stand between the state of man
    and lad,
The hearts of divers trim young men his beauty 'gan
    to move,
And many a lady fresh and fair was taken in his love.
But in that grace of Nature's gift such passing pride
    did reign
That to be touched of man or maid he wholly did dis-
    dain.

A babbling nymph that Echo hight, who hearing others
      talk
By no means can restrain her tongue but that it needs
      must walk,
Nor of herself hath power to 'gin to speak to any wight,
Espied him driving into toils the fearful stags of flight.
This Echo was a body then and not an only voice,
Yet of her speech she had that time no more than now
      the choice,
That is to say, of many words the latter to repeat.
The cause thereof was Juno's wrath, for when that with
      the feat
She might have often taken Jove in dalliance with his
      dames,
And that by stealth and unbewares in midst of all his
      games,
This elf would with her tattling talk detain her by the
      way
Until that Jove had wrought his will, and they were
      fled away;
The which when Juno did perceive she said with wrath-
      ful mood:
'This tongue that hath deluded me shall do thee little
      good,
For of thy speech but simple use hereafter shalt thou
      have.'
The deed itself did straight confirm the threat'nings
      that she gave.
Yet Echo of the former talk doth double oft the end
And back again with just report the words erst spoken
      send.
   Now when she saw Narcissus stray about the forest
      wide,
   She waxed warm and step for step fast after him she
      hied.
The more she followed after him and nearer that she
      came,
The hotter ever did she wax as nearer to her flame,
Like as the lively brimstone doth which dipped about a
      match
And put but softly to the fire, the flame doth lightly
      catch.
O Lord, how often would she fain, if Nature would
      have let,
Entreated him with gentle words some favour for to get!

But Nature would not suffer her nor give her leave to
'gin.
Yet (so far forth as she by grant at Nature's hand could
win)
Aye ready with attentive ear she hearkens for some
sound
Whereto she might reply her words, from which she is
not bound.
By chance the stripling being strayed from all his com-
pany
Said: 'Is there anybody nigh?' Straight Echo an-
swered: 'I.'
Amazed he casts his eye aside, and looketh round about,
And 'Come' (that all the forest rang) aloud he calleth
out.
And 'Come,' saith she; he looketh back, and seeing no
man follow
'Why fliest?' he crieth once again, and she the same
doth hollow.
He still persists, and wondering much what kind of
thing it was
From which that answering voice by turn so duly seemed
to pass,
Said: 'Let us join.' She, by her will desirous to have said,
'In faith with none more willingly at any time or stead,'
Said: 'Let us join.' And standing somewhat in her own
conceit
Upon these words she left the wood, and forth she
yeadeth straight
To coll the lovely neck for which she longed **had so**
much.
He runs his way, and will not be embraced of no such,
And saith: 'I first will die ere thou shalt take of me thy
pleasure.'
She answered nothing else thereto but 'take of me thy
pleasure.'
Now when she saw herself thus mocked, she gat her to
the woods,
And hid her head for very shame among the leaves and
buds;
And ever since she lives alone in dens and hollow caves.
Yet stuck her love still to her heart, through which she
daily raves
The more for sorrow of repulse. Through restless cark
and care

Her body pines to skin and bone, and waxeth wondrous
    bare.
The blood doth vanish into air from out of all her veins,
And nought is left but voice and bones: the voice yet
    still remains:
Her bones they say were turned to stones. From thence
    she lurking still
In woods, will never show her head in field nor yet on
    hill.
Yet is she heard of every man: it is her only sound,
And nothing else that doth remain alive above the
    ground.
Thus had he mocked this wretched nymph and many
    more beside
That in the waters, woods, and groves, or mountains
    did abide.
Thus had he mocked many men, of which one, mis-
    content
To see himself deluded so, his hands to heaven up bent,
And said: 'I pray to God he may once feel fierce Cupid's
    fire
As I do now, and yet not joy the thing he doth desire.'
The goddess Rhamnuse, who doth wreak on wicked
    people take,
Assented to his just request for ruth and pity's sake.
    There was a spring withouten mud as silver clear and
      still,
    Which neither shepherds, nor the goats that fed upon
      the hill,
Nor other cattle troubled had, nor savage beast had
    stirred,
Nor branch, nor stick, nor leaf of tree, nor any fowl
    nor bird.
The moisture fed and kept aye fresh the grass that
    grew about,
And with their leaves the trees did keep the heat of
    Phoebus out.
The stripling weary with the heat and hunting in the
    chase,
And much delighted with the spring and coolness of
    the place,
Did lay him down upon the brim, and as he stooped low
To staunch his thirst, another thirst of worse effect did
    grow,
For as he drank, he chanced to spy the image of his face,

The which he did immediately with fervent love em-
brace.
He feeds a hope without cause why, for like a foolish
noddy
He thinks the shadow that he sees to be a lively body.
Astraughted like an image made of marble stone he lies,
There gazing on his shadow still with fixed staring eyes.
Stretched all along the ground, it doth him good to see
His ardent eyes which like two stars full bright and
shining be,
And eke his fingers, fingers such as Bacchus might
beseem,
And hair that one might worthily Apollo's hair it deem.
His beardless chin and ivory neck, and eke the perfect
grace
Of white and red indifferently bepainted in his face.
All these he wond'reth to behold, for which, as I do
gather,
Himself was to be wondered at, or to be pitied rather.
He is enamoured of himself for want of taking heed,
And where he likes another thing he likes himself in-
deed;
He is the party whom he woos, and suitor that doth woo,
He is the flame that sets on fire, and thing that burneth
too.
O Lord, how often did he kiss that false, deceitful thing!
How often did he thrust his arms midway into the spring
To have embraced the neck he saw and could not catch
himself!
He knows not what it was he saw, and yet the foolish elf
Doth burn in ardent love thereof. The very selfsame
thing
That doth bewitch and blind his eyes, increaseth still
his sting.
Thou fondling, thou, why dost thou raught the fickle
image so?
The thing thou seekest is not there, and if aside thou go
The thing thou lovest straight is gone. It is none other
matter
That thou dost see than of thyself the shadow in the
water.
The thing is nothing of itself; with thee it doth abide,
With thee it would depart if thou withdrew thyself
aside.

No care of meat could draw him thence, nor yet desire
    of rest,
But lying flat against the ground, and leaning on his
    breast,
With greedy eyes he gazeth still upon the falsed face,
And through his sight is wrought his bane. Yet for a
    little space
He turns and sets himself upright, and holding up his
    hands
With piteous voice unto the wood that round about
    him stands
Cries out and says: 'Alas, ye woods, and was there ever
    any
That loved so cruelly as I! You know: for unto many
A place of harbour have you been, and fort of refuge
    strong.
Can you remember any one in all your time so long
That hath so pined away as I? I see and am full fain,
Howbeit that I like and see, I cannot ye attain:
So great a blindness in my heart through doting love
    doth reign.
And for to spite me more withal, it is no journey far,
No drenching sea, no mountain high, no wall, no lock,
    no bar,
It is but even a little drop that keeps us two asunder.
He would be had, for look! how oft I kiss the water
    under,
So oft again with upward mouth he riseth toward me,
A man would think to touch at least I should yet
    able be.
It is a trifle in respect that lets us of our love.
What wight soever that thou art come hither up above.
O peerless piece, why dost thou me thy lover thus de-
    lude?
Or whither fliest thou of thy friend thus earnestly
    pursued?
Ywis I neither am so foul nor yet so grown in years
That in this wise thou shouldst me shun. To have me to
    their feres
The nymphs themselves have sued ere this; and yet, as
    should appear,
Thou dost pretend some kind of hope of friendship by
    the cheer,
For when I stretch mine arms to thee, thou stretchest
    thine likewise,

And if I smile thou smilest too: and when that from
    mine eyes
The tears do drop, I well perceive the water stands in
    thine.
Like gesture also dost thou make to every beck of mine,
And as by moving of thy sweet and lovely lips, I ween,
Thou speakest words although mine ears conceive not
    what they been.
It is myself I well perceive, it is mine image sure,
That in this sort deluding me this fury doth procure.
I am enamoured of myself, I do both set on fire
And am the same that swelteth too, through impotent
    desire.
What shall I do? Be wooed or woo? Whom shall I woo
    therefore?
The thing I seek is in myself, my plenty makes me poor.
O would to God I for a while might from my body part!
This wish is strange to hear a lover wrapped all in smart
To wish away the thing the which he loveth as his heart.
My sorrow takes away my strength. I have not long to
    live,
But in the flower of youth must die. To die it doth
    not grieve,
For that by death shall come the end of all my grief
    and pain.
I would this youngling whom I love might longer life
    obtain:
For in one soul shall now delay we steadfast lovers
    twain.'
    This said in rage he turns again unto the foresaid
        shade,
    And rores the water with the tears and slobb'ring that
        he made
    That through his troubling of the well his image 'gan
        to fade;
Which when he saw to vanish so: 'Oh, whither dost
    thou fly?
Abide I pray thee heartily,' aloud he 'gan to cry.
'Forsake me not so cruelly that loveth thee so dear,
But give me leave a little while my dazzled eyes to cheer
With sight of that which for to touch is utterly denied,
Thereby to feed my wretched rage and fury for a tide.'
As in this wise he made his moan, he stripped off his
    coat
And with his fist outrageously his naked stomach smote.

A ruddy colour where he smote rose on his stomach
    sheer,
Like apples which do partly white and striped red
    appear,
Or as the clusters ere the grapes to ripeness fully come,
An orient purple here and there begins to grow on some.
Which things as soon as in the spring he did behold
    again,
He could no longer bear it out, but fainting straight for
    pain,
As lithe and supple wax doth melt against the burning
    flame,
Or morning dew against the sun that glareth on the
    same;
Even so by piecemeal being spent and wasted through
    desire,
Did he consume and melt away with Cupid's secret fire.
His lively hue of white and red, his cheerfulness and
    strength,
And all the things that liked him did wanze away at
    length,
So that in fine remained not the body which of late
The wretched Echo loved so, who when she saw his state,
Although in heart she angry were and mindful of his
    pride,
Yet rueing his unhappy case, as often as he cried
'Alas!' she cried 'Alas!' likewise with shirl redoubled
    sound.
And when he beat his breast, or struck his feet against
    the ground,
She made like noise of clapping too. These are the words
    that last
Out of his lips, beholding still his wonted image passed:
'Alas, sweet boy, beloved in vain, farewell.' And by
    and by
With sighing sound the selfsame words the Echo did
    reply.
With that he laid his weary head against the grassy
    place,
And death did close his gazing eyes that wondered at
    the grace
And beauty which did late adorn their master's heavenly
    face.
And afterward when into hell received was his sprite,

He goes me to the Well of Styx, and there both day and
     night
Stands tooting on his shadow still as fondly as before.
The water-nymphs, his sisters, wept and wailed for him
     sore,
And on his body strewed their hair clipped off and shorn
     therefore.
The wood-nymphs also did lament, and Echo did re-
     bound
To every sorrowful noise of theirs with like lamenting
     sound.
The fire was made to burn the corse, and waxen tapers
     light.
A hearse to lay the body on with solemn pomp was
     dight,
But as for body none remained: instead thereof they
     found
A yellow flower with milk-white leaves new sprung upon
     the ground.

FRANCIS BACON: Self-love*

NARCISSUS IS said to have been extremely beautiful and comely, but intolerably proud and disdainful; so that,
pleased with himself, and scorning the world, he led a solitary life
in the woods; hunting only with a few followers, who were his
professed admirers, among whom the nymph Echo was his constant attendant. In this method of life it was once his fate to
approach a clear fountain, where he laid himself down to rest,
in the noonday heat; when, beholding his image in the water, he
fell into such a rapture and admiration of himself, that he could
by no means be got away, but remained continually fixed and
gazing, till at length he was turned into a flower, of his own name,
which appears early in the spring, and is consecrated to the
infernal deities, Pluto, Proserpine, and the Furies.

This fable seems to paint the behaviour and fortune of
those, who, for their beauty, or other endowments, wherewith
nature (without any industry of their own) has graced and
adorned them, are extravagantly fond of themselves: for men of
such a disposition generally affect retirement, and absence from

* Reprinted from *The Works of Francis Bacon.*

public affairs; as a life of business must necessarily subject them to many neglects and contempts, which might disturb and ruffle their minds: whence such persons commonly lead a solitary, private, and shadowy life; see little company, and those only such as highly admire and reverence them; or, like an echo, assent to all they say.

And they who are depraved, and rendered still fonder of themselves by this custom, grow strangely indolent, inactive, and perfectly stupid. The Narcissus, a spring flower, is an elegant emblem of this temper, which at first flourishes, and is talked of, but when ripe, frustrates the expectation conceived of it.

And that this flower should be sacred to the infernal powers, carries out the allusion still further; because men of this humour are perfectly useless in all respects: for whatever yields no fruit, but passes, and is no more, like the way of a ship in the sea, was by the ancients consecrated to the infernal shades and powers.

DENIS DE ROUGEMONT: Don Juan*

WHEN HE strides on stage, glittering in silk and gold, the heroic seducer at his proudest, we are tempted to see in him only the natural fire of desire, a kind of vehement and somehow innocent animality. But Nature has never produced anything like this.

We sense there is something demonic about him, almost a polemic of defiant wickedness: the hand extended to the Commendatore in the last act of Mozart's opera. Now this is not the animal but the man, and not prior to but after morality. There is no Don Juan among the "noble savages" or the "primitives" we hear about. Don Juan presupposes a society encumbered with exact rules which it prefers to infringe rather than throw off.

In the intoxication of anarchy he thrives on, this *grand seigneur* never forgets his rank. His natural mood is scorn; nothing is further from nature. Consider how he treats women: incapable of possessing them, he first violates them morally in order to subjugate the animal part of their being; and no sooner has he taken than he rejects them, as if he sought the fact of the crime rather than the gratifications of pleasure. A perpetual polemicist, he happens to be completely determined by the good and the just—against them. If the laws of morality did not exist, he would invent them in order to violate them. Which is what suggests to us

* Reprinted from *Love Declared.*

the spiritual nature of his secret, so carefully masked by the pretext of instinct. On the summits of the mind in revolt, we shall
see Nietzsche renew this mortal challenge a hundred years later.

But need we seek so far? Isn't the "perfectly natural"
search for desire's intensity enough to explain this frenzy of in-
constancy? Then Don Juan would be the man of the first encounter, of the most exciting victory. "Novelty is the tyrant of our
soul," wrote the old Casanova. But it is already no longer the
voluptuary who speaks thus. The true sensualist's joys lie beyond
those moments Don Juan flees as soon as they are within his
grasp.

Must we resort to the indiscreet doctors of the School of
Vienna? A splendid opportunity for them, and one they have not
missed. For them, too, Don Juan is the contrary of what we suppose; he suffers from a secret anxiety bordering on impotence.
And it is true that the man who yields to that superficial attraction which almost every pretty woman can exert over almost
every man does not suggest the image of health. But in this insolent fury, in this gay and querulous swagger, how can we see
nothing more than weakness and deficiency?

Perhaps we might go further, applying spiritual criteria?
For instance, Don Juan might be the type of man who does not
achieve that personal level where what is unique in a human
being can be manifested. Why can he desire only novelty in a
woman? And why does he seek the new, something new at any
price, whatever it may be? The man who seeks is the man who
has not, but perhaps also the man who *is not*. The man who has,
lives by his possession and does not abandon it for the Uncertain
—that is, if he truly possesses. Don Juan might be the man who
cannot love, because loving is first of all choosing, and to choose
one must *be*, and Don Juan has no being. But the contrary is no
less likely: Don Juan seeking everywhere his ideal, his "type" of
female beauty (unconscious memory of his mother)—too quickly
seduced by the most fleeting resemblance, always disappointed
by the reality as soon as he approaches it, already dashing off toward other appearances, ever more agonized and cruel. What if
he found his "type"! I can imagine the metamorphosis. We see
him stop short, suddenly change expression, lower his head, grow
somber, as though suddenly turning shy, and fascinated for the
first time by lover's revelation, transform himself into the image
of Tristan.

But he will not find his type. He is Don Juan because we
know he cannot find it, either impotent to attach himself, or impotent to release himself from an obsessive image. Hence his
apparent power, his *furia*, his dionysiac rhythm.

Now if Don Juanism is a passion of the mind and not, as

we used to think, an instinctual exultation, everything suggests that this passion is not *always* linked to sex. One even wonders if sensuality, in fact, is not the very realm in which Don Juan reveals himself as least dangerous. (Let us here define danger as what can compromise a certain social equilibrium which it is the purpose of manners to maintain, that equilibrium being, moreover, either good or bad.) This is because the desire for novelty and perpetual change, once the insatiable mind provokes it, becomes a threat to life. In diverting this passion toward pleasure, society manages to afford it satisfactions which exhaust it, without endangering the established order by unproductive expenditures.

Of course Don Juan is a cheat—in fact that is how he lives (the faro table was Casanova's great financial resource: a symbol he explains many times over). But constant cheating is less dangerous than the sudden defection of an honest man. We are on guard, and we know the system, which is at every point related to the rules of the game. Let us imagine a more secret Don Juanism, a faro table where one puts invisible "values" on the cards instead of clinking coins. Then the cheating ceases to be a vulgar and profitable manipulation. It can become the heroic act of an honesty without scruples, still considered criminal because it institutes, with subversive rigor, a new order.

Nietzsche took his stand in opposition to the age. And the adversary he chose is the spirit of inertia, our natural weight, our natural faculty for falling back into habit. The immoralist, like the moralist, is a vigilant enemy of instinct: for if he glorifies it, it is in a polemical spirit; it is because he wants to assault nature in a new way.

He proceeds from challenge to challenge, first aroused then exasperated by the adversary's silence or cowardice. Ideas turn themselves inside out at the mind's whim: no truth can any longer endure. Men surrender or fall into doubt at the first blandishment of a scientific hypothesis. No longer is there a faith which affirms and maintains by virtue of the absurd. How tired one grows of winning at every throw, merely by denying rules no one now dares call inviolable! Who would die these days for a virtue whose goal no one knows? And look how quickly all these venerable truths have yielded! Soon only God and his Son will be left. Already "the moral God is refuted." What will the Other One say? In the biography of the Don Juan of truths, this is the moment of the Commendatore's invitation! Yet God says nothing. He does not accept the challenge. Nietzsche waits, in the vacant night of the peaks. When dawn comes, it is only another earthly dawn. No one has spoken. God is dead!

Nietzsche wanted to *violate* the secret of each idea, of each belief, of each value; and their swift defeat renders them all contemptible after the first possession. Why should he linger over them? They were exciting for the mind only by the false virtue that was attributed to them. But once they have betrayed the vulgarity they have in common, victory loses all its savor. Now he must destroy the new values he had invented for the struggle. He must disgustedly reject what he had so impetuously desired, must turn the laugh on the followers, the successors, the disciples emboldened by another's glowing triumph, who already suppose they can abuse his victims.

Mille e tre truths have surrendered, and not one has been able to hold him.

What do "contradictions" matter! It is not in order to construct a system that he disputes, denounces, and destroys; it is for the joy of intellectual rape. As Don Juan pursues the image of the Mother, Nietzsche pursues the obscure and obsessive image of a Truth that will not surrender but possess him forever, worthy at last of his true passion! He unrelentingly hunts down everything that moves, everything that stops, everything that appears to resist. Brief pleasures—the interval of an aphorism, a lightning flash that is always disappointing: it is not *she* whom he has just possessed. O hatred of their feeble truths! Truth is dead! Will she live again?

For if this God is dead forever, love is now impossible. He must *invent* a love which at least permits him to hate everything that fades, that yields, all the shamelessness and lethargy of the world.

It is at the point of dionysiac fury where joy in destruction turns to pain, and in the agony of a power annihilated by its own success, that Nietzsche suddenly encounters the fascinating idea of the Eternal Return. Confronting the Sils-Maria rock, we see him stop short, change expression, and for the first time lower his head and adore. Everything will eternally return to this moment, to this instant! Eternity is the return of time; and no longer the victory over time. But in time, he said, God has died. If God is dead, then he must have lived? God will live again, eternally! Thus Nietzsche becomes the Tristan of a destiny he can possess only by a love that is eternally *distant*.

A cheat, Don Juan makes love without loving. If he triumphs, it is by violating the truth of human beings. Nietzsche sets up values which destroy the old rules, but which are valid only because of these rules and insofar as they are felt to violate them. Should he succeed in imposing them, they would lose their meaning, since the system that measured them would no longer exist. Beyond good and evil, beyond the rules of the game, a passion must reveal itself; either death or eternal life. So Don Juan must vanish (for Don Juan won only by cheating, and if there are no longer any rules, one can no longer cheat).

Here perhaps is the key to the mystery: *in respecting all the rules, we could never do anything but lose.* Then: either we shall be damned, or else we shall receive our pardon. But Nietzsche and Don Juan do not believe in pardon, so they are either obliged to win during the time-span of their lives—hence the cheating; or else they must deny the end of time, the final reckoning, the last judgment—hence the notion of the Eternal Return.

As I was speaking of these things to a friend: "I used to know," she said, "a married man with whom I flirted to no purpose, and as we separated he said: 'I'm adding you to my list of the *mille e tre.*' They were the women he had not had, out of faithfulness to his own wife."

Where is the cheating here? In the challenge, instituted at the heart of the rule?

JACQUES CASANOVA: Memoirs

MADAME LEBEL was one of the ten or twelve women for whom in my happy youth I cherished the greatest affection. She had all the qualities to make a man a good wife, if it had been my fate to experience such felicity. But perhaps I did well not to tie myself down with irrevocable bonds, though now my independence is another name for slavery. But if I had married a woman of tact, who would have ruled me unawares to myself, I should have taken care of my fortune and have had children, instead of being lonely and penniless in my old age.

But I must indulge no longer in digressions on the past which cannot be recalled, and since my recollections make me happy I should be foolish to cherish idle regrets.

I calculated that if I started directly I should get to Lausanne an hour before Madame Lebel, and I did not hesitate to give her this proof of my regard. I must here warn my readers, that, though I loved this woman well, I was then occupied with another passion, and no voluptuous thought mingled with my desire of seeing her. My esteem for her was enough to hold my passions in check, but I esteemed Lebel too, and nothing would have induced me to disturb the happiness of this married pair. . . .

I knocked at Madame Dubois's door at five o'clock, almost

dying with hunger. Her surprise was extreme, for she did not know that her daughter was going to meet me at her house. Without more ado I gave her two louis to get us a good supper.

At seven o'clock, Madame Lebel, her husband, and a child of eighteen months, whom I easily recognized as my own, arrived. Our meeting was a happy one indeed; we spent ten hours at table, and mirth and joy prevailed. At day-break she started for Soleure, where Lebel had business. M. de Chavigni had desired to be remembered most affectionately to me. Lebel assured me that the ambassador was extremely kind to his wife, and he thanked me heartily for having given such a woman up to him. I could easily see that he was a happy husband, and that his wife was as happy as he.

My dear housekeeper talked to me about my son. She said that nobody suspected the truth, but that neither she nor Lebel (who had faithfully kept his promise, and had not consummated the marriage for the two months agreed upon) had any doubts.

"The secret," said Lebel to me, "will never be known, and your son will be my sole heir, or will share my property with my children if I ever have any, which I doubt." . . .

I passed three hours in telling them of all the adventures I had during the twenty-seven months since we had seen one another. As to their history, it was soon told; it had all the calm which belongs to happiness.

Madame Lebel was as pretty as ever, and I could see no change in her, but I was no longer the same man. She thought me less lively than of old, and she was right. The Renaud had blasted me, and the pretended Lascaris had given me a great deal of trouble and anxiety. . . .

The next day, the eve of my dinner party, I ordered a repast in which no expense was to be spared. I did not forget to tell the landlord to get me the best wines, the choicest liqueurs, ices, and all the materials for a bowl of punch. I told him that we should be six in number, for I foresaw that M. Tronchin would dine with us. I was right; I found him at his pretty house ready to receive us, and I had not much trouble in inducing him to stay. In the evening I thought it as well to tell the syndic and his three friends about it in Helen's presence, while she, feigning ignorance, said that her mother had told her they were going somewhere or other to dinner.

"I am delighted to hear it," said I; "it must be at M. Tronchin's."

My dinner would have satisfied the most exacting *gourmet*, but Hedvig was its real charm. She treated difficult theological questions with so much grace, and rationalised so skilfully, that

though one might not be convinced it was impossible to help
being attracted. I have never seen any theologian who could treat
the most difficult points with so much facility, eloquence, and
real dignity, and at dinner she completed her conquest of myself.
M. Tronchin, who had never heard her speak before, thanked me
a hundred times for having procured him this pleasure, and being
obliged to leave us by the call of business he asked us to meet
again in two days' time.

I was much interested during the dessert by the evident
tenderness of the pastor for Helen's mother. His amorous eloquence grew in strength as he irrigated his throat with champagne, Greek wine, and eastern liqueurs. The lady seemed
pleased, and was a match for him as far as drinking was concerned, while the two girls and myself only drank with sobriety.
However, the mixture of wines, and above all the punch, had
done their work, and my charmers were slightly elevated. Their
spirits were delightful, but rather pronounced. I took this favourable opportunity to ask the two aged lovers if I might take the
young ladies for a walk in the garden by the lake, and they told
us enthusiastically to go and enjoy ourselves. We went out arm
in arm, and in a few minutes we were out of sight of everyone.

"Do you know," said I to Hedvig, "that you have made a
conquest of M. Tronchin?"

"Have I? The worthy banker asked me some very silly
questions."

"You must not expect everyone to be able to contend with
you."

"I can't help telling you that your question pleased me
best of all. A bigoted theologian at the end of the table seemed
scandalized at the question and still more at the answer."

"And why?"

"He says I ought to have told you that a deity could not
impregnate a woman. He said that he would explain the reason
to me if I were a man, but being a woman and a maid he could
not with propriety expound such mysteries. I wish you would tell
me what the fool meant."

"I should be very glad, but you must allow me to speak
plainly, and I shall have to take for granted that you are acquainted with the physical conformation of a man."

"Yes, speak as plainly as you like, for there is nobody to
hear what we say; but I must confess that I am only acquainted
with the peculiarities of the male by theory and reading. I have
no practical knowledge. I have seen statues, but I have never seen
or examined a real live man. Have you, Helen?"

"I have never wished to do so."

"Why not? It is good to know everything."

"Well, Hedvig, your theologian meant to say that a god was not capable of this."

"What is that?"

"Give me your hand."

"I can feel it, and have thought it would be something like that; without this provision of nature man would not be able to fecundate his mate. And how could the foolish theologian maintain that this was an imperfection?"

"Because it is the result of desire, Hedvig, and it would not have taken place in me if I had not been charmed with you, and if I had not conceived the most seducing ideas of the beauties that I cannot see from the view of the beauties I can see. Tell me frankly whether feeling that did not give you an agreeable sensation."

"It did, and just in the place where your hand is now. Don't you feel a pleasant tickling there, Helen, after what the gentleman has been saying to us?"

"Yes, I feel it, but I often do, without anything to excite me."

"And then," said I, "nature makes you appease it . . . thus?"

"Not at all."

"Oh, yes!" said Hedvig. "Even when we are asleep our hands seek that spot as if by instinct, and if it were not for that solace I think we should get terribly ill."

As this philosophical discourse, conducted by the young theologian in quite a professional manner, proceeded, we reached a beautiful basin of water, with a flight of marble steps for bathers. Although the air was cool our heads were hot, and I conceived the idea of telling them that it would do them good to bathe their feet, and that if they would allow me I would take off their shoes and stockings.

"I should like to so much," said Hedvig.

"And I too," said Helen.

"Then sit down, ladies, on the first step."

They proceeded to sit down and I began to take off their shoes, praising the beauty of their legs, and pretending for the present not to want to go farther than the knee. When they got into the water they were obliged to pick up their clothes, and I encouraged them to do so.

"Well, well," said Hedvig, "men have thighs too."

Helen, who would have been ashamed to be beaten by her cousin, was not backward in shewing her legs.

"That will do, charming maids," said I, "you might catch cold if you stayed longer in the water."

They walked up backwards, still holding up their clothes for fear of wetting them, and it was then my duty to wipe them dry with all the handkerchiefs I had. This pleasant task left me at freedom to touch and see, and the reader will imagine that I did my best in that direction. The fair theologian told me I wanted to know too much, but Helen let me do what I liked with such a tender and affectionate expression that it was as much as I could do to keep within bounds. At last, when I had drawn on their shoes and stockings, I told them that I was delighted to have seen the hidden charms of the two prettiest girls in Geneva.

"What effect had it on you?" asked Hedvig.

"I daren't tell you to look, but feel, both of you."

"Do you bathe, too."

"It's out of the question, a man's undressing takes so much trouble."

"But we have still two hours before us, in which we need not fear any interruption."

This reply gave me a foretaste of the bliss I had to gain, but I did not wish to expose myself to an illness by going into the water in my present state. I noticed a summer-house at a little distance, and feeling sure that M. Tronchin had left the door open, I took the two girls on my arm and led them there without giving them any hint of my intentions. The summer-house was scented with vases of *pot-pourri* and adorned with engravings; but, best of all, there was a large couch which seemed made for repose and pleasure. I sat down on it between my two sweethearts, and as I caressed them I told them I was going to shew them something they had never seen before, and without more ado I displayed to their gaze the principal agent in the preservation of the human race. They got up to admire it, and taking a hand of each one I procured them some enjoyment, but in the middle of their labours an abundant flow of liquid threw them into the greatest astonishment.

"That," said I, "is the Word which makes men."

"It's beautiful!" cried Helen, laughing at the term "word."

"I have a word too," said Hedvig, "and I will shew it to you if you will wait a minute."

"Come, Hedvig, and I will save you the trouble of making it yourself, and will do it better."

"I daresay, but I have never done it with a man."

"No more have I," said Helen.

Placing them in front of me I gave them another ecstacy. We then sat down, and while I felt all their charms I let them touch me as much as they liked till I watered their hands a second time.

We made ourselves decent once more, and spent half an hour in kisses and caresses, and I then told them that they had made me happy only in part, but that I hoped they would make my bliss complete by presenting me with their maidenheads. I shewed them the little safety-bags invented by the English in the interests of the fair sex. They admired them greatly when I explained their use, and the fair theologian remarked to her cousin that she would think it over. We were now close friends, and soon promised to be something more; and we walked back and found the pastor and Helen's mother strolling by the side of the lake....

I did not see Helen that evening, but I saw her the next day at her mother's house, for I was in mere politeness bound to thank the old lady for the honour she had done me. She gave me a most friendly reception, and introduced me to two very pretty girls who were boarding with her. They might have interested me if I had been stopping long in Geneva, but as it was Helen claimed all my attraction.

"To-morrow," said the charming girl, "I shall be able to get a word with you at Madame Tronchin's dinner, and I expect Hedvig will have hit on some way for you to satisfy your desires."

The banker gave us an excellent dinner. He proudly told me that no inn-keeper could give such a good dinner as a rich gentleman who has a good cook, a good cellar, good silver plate, and china of the best quality. We were twenty of us at table, and the feast was given chiefly in honour of the learned theologian and myself, as a rich foreigner who spent money freely. M. de Ximenes, who had just arrived from Ferney was there, and told me that M. de Voltaire was expecting me, but I had foolishly determined not to go....

Hedvig shone in solving the questions put to her by the company....

After dinner everybody crowded round this truly astonishing girl, so that I had no opportunity of whispering my love. However, I went apart with Helen, who told me that the pastor and his niece were going to sup with her mother the following day.

"Hedvig," she added, "will stay the night and sleep with me as she always does when she comes to supper with her uncle. It remains to be seen if you are willing to hide in a place I will shew you at eleven o'clock tomorrow, in order to sleep with us. Call on my mother at that hour to-morrow, and I will find an opportunity of shewing you where it is. You will be safe though not comfortable, and if you grow weary you can console yourself by thinking that you are in our minds."

"Shall I have to stay there long?"

"Four hours at the most. At seven o'clock the street door is shut, and only opened to anyone who rings."

"If I happen to cough while I am in hiding might I be heard?"

"Yes, that might happen."

"There's a great hazard. All the rest is of no consequence; but no matter, I will risk all for the sake of so great happiness."

In the morning I paid the mother a visit, and as Helen was escorting me out she shewed me a door between the two stairs.

"At seven o'clock," said she, "the door will be open, and when you are in put on the bolt. Take care that no one sees you as you are entering the house."

At a quarter to seven I was already a prisoner. I found a seat in my cell, otherwise I should neither have been able to lie down or to stand up. It was a regular hole, and I knew by my sense of smell that hams and cheeses were usually kept there; but it contained none at present, for I felt all round to see how the land lay. As I was cautiously stepping round I felt my foot encounter some resistance, and putting down my hand I recognized the feel of linen. It was a napkin containing two plates, a nice roast fowl, bread, and a second napkin. Searching again I came across a bottle and a glass. I was grateful to my charmers for having thought of my stomach, but as I had purposely made a late and heavy meal I determined to defer the consumption of my cold collation till a later hour.

At nine o'clock I began, and as I had neither a knife nor a corkscrew I was obliged to break the neck of the bottle with a brick which I was fortunately able to detach from the mouldering floor. The wine was delicious old Neuchâtel, and the fowl was stuffed with truffles, and I felt convinced that my two nymphs must have some rudimentary ideas on the subject of stimulants. I should have passed the time pleasantly enough if it had not been for the occasional visits of a rat, who nearly made me sick with his disgusting odour. I remembered that I had been annoyed in the same way at Cologne under somewhat similar circumstances.

At last ten o'clock struck, and I heard the pastor's voice as he came downstairs talking; he warned the girls not to play any tricks together, and to go to sleep quietly. That brought back to my memory M. Rose leaving Madame Orio's house at Venice twenty-two years before; and reflecting on my character I found myself much changed, though not more reasonable; but if I was not so sensible to the charms of the sex, the two beauties who were awaiting me were much superior to Madame Orio's nieces.

In my long and profligate career in which I have turned the heads of some hundreds of ladies, I have become familiar with all the methods of seduction; but my guiding principle has been never to direct my attack against novices or those whose prejudices were likely to prove an obstacle except in the presence of another woman. I soon found out that timidity makes a girl averse to being seduced, while in company with another girl she is easily conquered; the weakness of the one brings on the fall of the other. Fathers and mothers are of the contrary opinion, but they are in the wrong. They will not trust their daughter to take a walk or go to a ball with a young man, but if she has another girl with her there is no difficulty made. I repeat, they are in the wrong; if the young man has the requisite skill their daughter is a lost woman. A feeling of false shame hinders them from making an absolute and determined resistance, and the first step once taken the rest comes inevitably and quickly. The girl grants some small favour, and immediately makes her friend grant a much greater one to hide her own blushes; and if the seducer is clever at his trade the young innocent will soon have gone too far to be able to draw back. Besides the more innocence a girl has, the less she knows of the methods of seduction. Before she has had time to think, pleasure attracts her, curiosity draws her a little farther, and opportunity does the rest.

For example, I might possibly have been able to seduce Hedvig without Helen, but I am certain I should never have succeeded with Helen if she had not seen her cousin take liberties with me which she no doubt thought contrary to the feelings of modesty which a respectable young woman ought to have.

Though I do not repent of my amorous exploits, I am far from wishing that my example should serve for the perversion of the fair sex, who have so many claims on my homage. I desire that what I say may be a warning to fathers and mothers, and secure me a place in their esteem at any rate.

Soon after the pastor had gone I heard three light knocks on my prison door. I opened it, and my hand was folded in a palm as soft as satin. All my being was moved. It was Helen's hand, and that happy moment had already repaid me for my long waiting.

"Follow me on tiptoe," she whispered, as soon as she had shut the door; but in my impatience I clasped her in my arms, and made her feel the effect which her mere presence had produced on me, while at the same time I assured myself of her docility. "There," she said, "now come upstairs softly after me."

I followed her as best I could in the darkness, and she took me along a gallery into a dark room, and then into a lighted one which contained Hedvig almost in a state of nudity. She came to me with open arms as soon as she saw me, and, embracing me

ardently, expressed her gratitude for my long and dreary imprisonment.

"Divine Hedvig," I answered, "if I had not loved you
madly I would not have stayed a quarter of an hour in that dismal
cell, but I am ready to spend four hours there every day till I
leave Geneva for your sake. But we must not lose any time; let
us go to bed."

"Do you two go to bed," said Helen; "I will sleep on the
sofa."

"No, no," cried Hedvig, "don't think of it; our fate must
be exactly equal."

"Yes, darling Helen," said I, embracing her; "I love you
both with equal ardour, and these ceremonies are only wasting
the time in which I ought to be assuring you of my passion.
Imitate my proceedings. I am going to undress, and then I shall
lie in the middle of the bed. Come and lie beside me, and I'll
shew you how I love you. If all is safe I will remain with you till
you send me away, but whatever you do do not put out the light."

In the twinkling of an eye, discussing the theory of shame
the while with the theological Hedvig, I presented myself to
their gaze in the costume of Adam. Hedvig blushed and parted
with the last shred of her modesty, citing the opinion of St.
Clement Alexandrinus that the seat of shame is in the shirt.
I praised the charming perfection of her shape, in the hope of
encouraging Helen who was slowly undressing herself; but an
accusation of mock modesty from her cousin had more effect than
all my praises. At last this Venus stood before me in a state of
nature, covering her most secret parts with her hand, and hiding
one breast with the other, and appearing woefully ashamed of
what she could not conceal. Her modest confusion, this strife
between departing modesty and rising passion, enchanted me.

Hedvig was taller than Helen; her skin was whiter, and
her breasts double the size of Helen's; but in Helen there was
more animation, her shape was more gently moulded, and her
breast might have been the model for the Venus de Medicis.

She got bolder by degrees, and we spent some moments in
admiring each other, and then we went to bed. Nature spoke out
loudly, and all we wanted was to satisfy its demands. With much
coolness I made a woman of Hedvig, and when all was over she
kissed me and said that the pain was nothing in comparison with
the pleasure.

The turn of Helen (who was six years younger than
Hedvig) now came, but the finest fleece that I have ever seen was
not won without difficulty. She was jealous of her cousin's success,
and held it open with her two hands; and though she had to

submit to great pain before being initiated into the amorous mysteries, her sighs were sighs of happiness, as she responded to my ardent efforts. Her great charms and the vivacity of her movements shortened the sacrifice, and when I left the sanctuary my two sweethearts saw that I needed repose.

The altar was purified of the blood of the victims, and we all washed, delighted to serve one another.

Life returned to me under their curious fingers, and the sight filled them with joy. I told them that I wished to enjoy them every night till I left Geneva, but they told me sadly that this was impossible.

"In five or six days time, perhaps, the opportunity may recur again, but that will be all."

"Ask us to sup at your inn to-morrow," said Hedvig; "and maybe, chance will favour the commission of a sweet felony."

I followed this advice.

I overwhelmed them with happiness for several hours, passing five or six times from one to the other before I was exhausted. In the intervals, seeing them to be docile and desirous, I made them execute Aretin's most complicated postures, which amused them beyond words. We kissed whatever took our fancy, and just as Hedvig applied her lips to the mouth of the pistol, it went off and the discharge inundated her face and her bosom. She was delighted, and watched the process to the end with all the curiosity of a doctor. The night seemed short, though we had not lost a moment's time, and at daybreak we had to part. I left them in bed and I was fortunate enough to get away without being observed.

I slept till noon, and then having made my toilette I went to call on the pastor, to whom I praised Hedvig to the skies. This was the best way to get him to come to supper at Balances the next day.

"We shall be in the town," said I, "and can remain together as long as we please, but do not forget to bring the amiable widow and her charming daughter."

He promised he would bring them both.

In the evening I went to see the syndic and his three friends, who naturally found me rather insensible to their charms. I excused myself by saying that I had a bad headache. I told them that I had asked the young theologian to supper, and invited the girls and the syndic to come too; but, as I had foreseen, the latter would not hear of their going as it would give rise to gossip.

I took care that the most exquisite wines should form an important feature of my supper. The pastor and the widow were both sturdy drinkers, and I did my best to please them. When I saw that they were pretty mellow and were going over their old recollections, I made a sign to the girls, and they immediately went out as if to go to a retiring-room. Under pretext of shewing them the way I went out too, and took them into a room telling them to wait for me.

I went back to the supper-room, and finding the old friends taken up with each other and scarcely conscious of my presence, I gave them some punch, and told them that I would keep the young ladies company; they were looking at some pictures, I explained. I lost no time, and shewed them some extremely interesting sights. These stolen sweets have a wonderful charm. When we were to some extent satisfied, we went back, and I plied the punch-ladle more and more freely. Helen praised the pictures to her mother, and asked her to come and look at them.

"I don't care to," she replied.

"Well," said Helen, "let us go and see them again."

I thought this stratagem admissible, and going out with my two sweethearts I worked wonders. Hedvig philosophised over pleasure, and told me she would never have known it if I had not chanced to meet her uncle. Helen did not speak; she was more voluptuous than her cousin, and swelled out like a dove, and came to life only to expire a moment afterwards. I wondered at her astonishing fecundity; while I was engaged in one operation she passed from death to life fourteen times. It is true that it was the sixth time with me, so I made my progress rather slower to enjoy the pleasure she took in it.

EMILIA PARDO BAZÁN: Sister Aparición

THROUGH THE low, double grille of the convent of the Sisters of St. Clare in S——— I saw a prostrate nun praying. She lay in front of the high altar, her face against the floor, her arms outstretched, and her body absolutely immobile. She seemed no more alive than the supine statues of a queen and a princess whose alabaster sepulchers adorned the chancel. Suddenly the nun sat up, no doubt to breathe, and I could see her. It was evident that she must have been very beautiful in her younger years, as one can see that ruined walls were once a splendid palace. The nun could as easily have been eighty as ninety; her face had the yellow pallor of the dead, and her trembling head, sunken mouth, and white eyebrows indicated that she had reached an age at which the passage of time is no longer noted.

The remarkable thing about that spectral face, which was no longer of this world, was its eyes. Defying time, they still preserved their fire, their intense blackness, and a violently impassioned and dramatic expression. They had a look that once seen could never be forgotten. Such volcanic eyes would be inexplicable in a nun who had entered the convent offering God an innocent heart. They spoke of a stormy past; they gave off the light of some tragic memory. I was consumed by curiosity, but without hope of ever learning the secret of the nun. Chance, however, took it upon itself to satisfy my desire to the full.

That same evening, at the round dining-table of the inn, I struck up an acquaintance with an elderly gentleman, very talkative and wide awake, one of those who love to give a stranger information. Flattered by my interest, he threw open the files of his wonderful memory. I had no more than mentioned the Convent of St. Clare and alluded to the impression the eyes of the old nun had made on me than my guide burst out, "Ah, Sister Aparición! Yes indeed, yes indeed. There is certainly something about her eyes. Her history is written there. Believe me or not, those furrows in her cheeks, which, seen close, look like canals, were plowed by her tears. Weeping for forty years! A lot of salt water could fall in that length of time. And yet the water never dimmed the embers of her eyes. Poor Sister Aparición! I can tell you the story of her life better than anybody else, for my father knew her as a girl, and I even believe he courted her a little. They say she was like a goddess.

"Sister Aparición was called Irene before she took the veil. Her parents were of good family. They had several children, but the others died, and they concentrated all their love and indulgence on Irene, their only child. The town where she was born was A———. And destiny, which begins to weave the rope with which to hang us from the sheets of our cradle, willed it that this same town should be the birthplace of the famous poet—"

I gave a cry and, taking the words out of the mouth of the narrator, pronounced the glorious name of the author of *The Fallen Archangel*, perhaps the most genuine representative of the romantic fever; a name that carries in its accents an edge of contemptuous arrogance, of scornful disdain or bitter irony, and of despairing, blasphemous nostalgia. That name and the look of the nun became fused in my imagination, though as yet I knew nothing of the link between them, but already sensing, by their union, one of those dramas of the heart which flow living blood.

"That is he," repeated my informant, "the famous Juan de Camargo, the pride of the village of A———. It has neither mineral springs, nor a miracle-working saint, nor a cathedral, nor

Roman inscriptions, nor anything of interest to show visitors, but it proudly points out in its square, 'This is the house where Camargo was born.' "

"Ah," I interrupted, "now I see. Sister Aparición—Irene, I mean—fell in love with Camargo, he paid no attention to her, and she entered the convent to forget—"

"Just a minute," exclaimed the narrator, smiling, "just a minute. If that were all there was to it, it would just be an every-day occurrence and hardly worth the trouble of telling. No, there is a lot more to Sister Aparición's case than that. Be patient and you shall hear it all.

"As a child, Irene had seen Juan de Camargo a thousand times without ever talking to him, because he was already a young man, and very aloof and withdrawn; he did not even have anything to do with the other lads in the village. When Irene was coming into flower, Camargo, an orphan, was already studying law in Salamanca, and he came to the village only to visit his guardian during vacations. One summer, as he was returning to A———, the student happened to look up at Irene's window and noticed the girl, who had her eyes fixed on him, eyes that could take the heart out of a man's breast, two black suns, for you've seen what they're still like. Camargo reined in his hired horse to drink his fill of that incredible beauty. But the girl, blushing like a poppy, drew back from the window and closed it with a bang. That same night Camargo, who had already begun to publish his verses in short-lived literary journals, wrote a beautiful poem describing the effect the sight of Irene had produced in him as he entered his village. And wrapping the paper on which it was written around a stone, when night had fallen he threw it at Irene's window. The glass broke, and the girl picked up the paper and read the poem, not once, but a hundred, a thousand times; she drank it in, steeped herself in it. Nevertheless, that poem, which is not in-cluded in Camargo's collected works, was not a declaration of love, but a strange mixture of lament and imprecation. The poet lamented the fact that the purity and beauty of the girl in the window were not for him, who was accursed. If he should come near her, he would blast the lily. After this incident of the poem, Camargo gave no indication that he remembered there was such a person as Irene, and in October he left for Madrid. This was the beginning of the feverish period of his life, his political adventures and his literary activities.

"From the time Camargo left, Irene became sadder with every day that passed, until she became really sick. Her parents did everything they could to raise her spirits. They took her for a time to Badajoz; they had her meet young men, go to dances. She had admirers, her ears rang with praises, but her state of mind and her health got no better.

"She could think of nothing but Camargo, to whom what Byron said of Laura was applicable: that those who saw him did not see him in vain; that his recollection was ever present in the memory, for men like him defy disdain and neglect. Even Irene did not think she was in love; she believed herself to be the victim of a spell contained in that poem, so somber, so strange. Beyond doubt she had what is now called an obsession, and at every moment she saw before her Camargo, pale, stern, his curling hair shadowing his thoughtful brow. Irene's parents, seeing their daughter wasting away with some mysterious ailment, decided to take her to the capital, where there were not only excellent doctors to consult, but many distractions.

"By the time Irene reached Madrid, Camargo was famous. His haughty, fiery verses, impassioned and electric, had created a school of imitators; his adventures and exploits were the talk of the day. He had surrounded himself with a gang of ne'er-do-wells, witty, careless Bohemians, who invented new escapades every night, sometimes carrying on orgiastic carousals of which certain blasphemous, libertine poems make mention, though some critics insist these are not really Camargo's. The drunken revels and libertine orgies alternated with sessions of the Masonic lodges and revolutionary meetings; Camargo was already paving the way for his exile. Irene's provincial, ingenuous family knew nothing of all this; and when they met the poet in the street, they greeted him warmly, for after all he came from home.

"Camargo, struck anew by the beauty of the girl, and noting that the sight of him brought the color back to her beautiful, pale cheeks, accompanied them and promised to come to visit them. The poor country mice were flattered by his attentions, and their satisfaction grew when they noticed that a few days later, when Camargo had fulfilled his promise, Irene began to revive. Unaware of the scandals that surrounded his name, it seemed to them that he might be a possible son-in-law, and they allowed him to repeat his visits.

"I can see by the expression on your face that you think you can guess the ending. You are mistaken. Irene, fascinated, beside herself as though she had drunk some magic philter, nevertheless for six months refused to visit Camargo in his home. The chaste resistance of the girl made him the butt of his friends' jokes, and pride, which is the poisoned root of certain romantic attitudes, such as those of Byron and Camargo, led him to make a bet, a satanic, diabolical revenge. He pleaded, he coaxed, he grew cold, he aroused her jealousy, he threatened suicide—in a word, he employed every snare until Irene, overpowered, finally agreed to the dangerous assignation. Thanks to a miracle of courage and decorum, she came away pure and unsullied, and Camargo was the victim of such jeers that he was beside himself with rage.

"At the second meeting Irene's powers were exhausted; her will bowed, and she succumbed. And when, confused and tremulous, she lay with closed eyes in the arms of her infamous lover, he, letting out a roar of laughter, pulled the cords of a curtain, and Irene saw eight or ten young men devouring her with lascivious eyes, while they laughed and clapped their hands ironically.

"Leaping to her feet, and without dressing herself, hair loose and shoulders bare, she plunged down the stairs and into the street. She reached her home followed by a crowd of street urchins, who flung stones and mud at her. She absolutely refused to say where she had been or what had happened to her. My father heard about it because he happened to know one of those with whom Camargo had made his bet. Irene suffered an attack of brain fever and her life was despaired of. When she recovered she entered this convent—as far as possible from A———. Her penitence has horrified the nuns; incredible fasts, mixing her bread with ashes, going three days without tasting water, praying through the winter nights barefoot and on her knees; scourging herself, wearing a ring about her neck, a crown of thorns under her coif, a belt of nails about her waist. . . .

"The thing that most impressed her companions, who consider her a saint, was her continuous weeping. They say— though it is probably just a story—that once she filled a washbasin with tears. Then suddenly one day her eyes became dry, without one tear, and glittering as you saw them. This happened over twenty years ago. The devout believe this was the sign of God's forgiveness. Nevertheless, Sister Aparición does not believe that she has been pardoned, for, old as she is, she still fasts and prostrates and scourges herself."

"She is doing penance for two," I answered, surprised that my chronicler's penetration had failed to grasp this point. "Do you think Sister Aparición has forgotten the unhappy soul of Camargo?"

GEORGE SAND: Letter to Alfred de Musset

15-17 April, 1834.

. . . . Never, never believe, Alfred, that I could be happy if I thought I had lost your heart. Whether I have been mistress or mother to you, what does that matter? Whether I have inspired you by love or by friendship, whether I have been happy or unhappy with you—nothing of this affects the present state of my mind. I know that I love you, that is all. . . . To watch over you, to keep you from all harm, from all friction; to surround you with distractions and pleasures, that is the need which awakens regret in me since I lost you. Why has a task so sweet, a task which I should have undertaken so joyfully, become little by little so bitter, and then suddenly impossible? What fate has intervened to turn my remedies into poisons? How is it that I, who would have given all my vitality to give you a night's repose and peace, have become a torment, a scourge, a spectre to you? When these atrocious memories besiege me (and at what hour do they leave me in peace?), I go nearly mad, I soak my pillow with tears; I hear in the silence of the night your voice calling me. Who will call me now? Who will need me to keep watch? How am I to use up the strength which I had accumulated for you and which now turns against me? Oh, my child, my child! How much I need your tenderness and your forgiveness! Never ask me for mine, and never say you have wronged me: how did I know? I remember nothing except that we have been very unhappy and have parted; but I know, I feel, that all our lives we shall love one another from our heart, from our intelligence, and that we shall by a holy affection try to cure ourselves mutually of the ills that we have each suffered for the other.

Alas, no! we were not to blame; we obeyed our destiny, for our natures, more impulsive than others', prevented us living the life of ordinary lovers; but we were born to know and to love each other, be sure of that. Had it not been for your youth and the weakness which your tears produced in me one morning, we should have remained brother and sister. . . .

You were right, our embraces were an incest, but we knew it not; we threw ourselves innocently and sincerely into each other's arms. Well now, have those embraces left us a single remembrance which is not chaste and holy? On a day of fever and delirium you reproached me with never having made you feel the pleasures of love. I shed tears at that, but now I am well content that there should have been something true in that speech.

I am well content that those pleasures have been more austere, more veiled than any you will find elsewhere. At least you, in the arms of other women, will not be reminded of me. But when you are alone, when you feel the need to pray and to shed tears, you will think of your George, of your true comrade, of your sick-nurse, of your friend, of something better than that. For the sentiment which unites us is combined of so many things, that it can compare to none other. The world will never understand it at all; so much the better. We love each other and we can snap our fingers at it.

Good-bye, good-bye, my dearest little one. Write me very often, I beg of you. Oh that I knew you arrived safe and sound in Paris! Remember that you have promised to take care of yourself. Good-bye, my Alfred, love your George. Send me, I beg, twelve pairs of glacé gloves, six yellow and six of colour. Send me, above all, the verses you have made. All, I have not a single one!

FRITZ WITTELS: Narcissa*

A CERTAIN woman had a promiscuous sex life and always experienced an orgasm until her marriage. Yet she never knew the full experience of being head over heels in love. She rather despised her sex partners, behaving very much like a feminine Don Juan, dropping her beaus shortly after she had given them everything, or what some conceited men thought to be everything. She liked them asking her on their knees for continuation of an affair that had begun so promisingly and orgiastically. She refused to continue and enjoyed this kind of sex life both ways: the enthusiastic beginning and her own superiority in denying herself later. A particular pattern of hers was to take men away from other women. Once she had succeeded in that, the affair lost most of its interest to her. Freud called this pattern the presence of an injured third person, perhaps a married woman whose husband she took, perhaps even her own older sister, whom she deprived of a beau.

However, life does not consist of sex only. One gets older, one experiences disappointments, one feels that one should get married. So she considered several men for this purpose, but most of them knew better than to marry a woman more or less spoiled for a lasting marital relationship, too much Narcissa, as we have called this type in a previous chapter. When she finally succeeded

* Reprinted from *Sex Habits of American Women.*

in finding a man who would propose to her, but whom she did not really love—she never had really loved anybody in her life—she married him and to her consternation experienced no orgasm with her husband.

One thing becomes perfectly clear in this example: the damage cannot possibly be in this woman's sex organ, it is in her personality. Her sex life was based on the opposite of truth and fidelity; the marriage certificate made the difference; not, of course, the slip of paper that she knew was lying safely in her drawer, but the idea of belonging for good to a man with the prerogatives of a husband. To him she would not surrender.

FLANDERS DUNBAR: Frigidity*

IT IS important that the Fallopian tubes through which the ovum or egg finds its way to the uterus remain open. For a long time it was thought that only an infection or some other injury could close them. It is now know that there are many ways of producing a muscle spasm in these tubes, just as one may temporarily close a rubber hose by stepping on it. An emotional crisis or shock may close these tubes just as it may make one clench one's fist. If this happens at the time of ovulation, which occurs only once a month, the ovum may die before it has made contact with the sperm cell. Conception will be impossible until the next month, and if again and again the same thing happens, the woman may decide that she has blocked tubes and is therefore sterile.

Young Mrs. R. had such spasms. She had married at twenty, and wanted to start a family right away. After three years, she came to her doctor in great distress. She had read that most couples conceive a child within the first year unless they take contraceptive measures. She also had read that many conditions which cause infertility can be corrected if treated early. So she wanted a complete set of tests. The first test, which was to discover whether or not her tubes were open, showed them closed. She was tested again after ovulation had occurred. The tubes were found to be open. The obvious conclusion was that the muscles contracted involuntarily at the time of ovulation. It developed that Mrs. R. had acquired in girlhood a considerable anxiety over the dangers and discomforts of pregnancy. This is not unusual in circles where a favorite subject of conversation among older women is "the ter-

* Reprinted from *Mind and Body*.

rible time poor so-and-so had" in delivery. After Mrs. R. grew up
and married, she shrugged off her fears—at least she thought so—
and assured her doctor, her husband and herself: "There's nothing I want so much as a baby."

Her involuntary nervous system, because of her buried
fear, contradicted her conscious desire. Some women in these circumstances develop a headache or nausea to last for the brief
period of ovulation. They thus avoid intercourse during the only
time they can conceive, although they keep repeating their desire
for children. Other wives suddenly are "too tired." Still others
manage to plan a little trip away from home and husband. Sometimes involuntary muscle spasm temporarily seems all that is
needed to prevent conception.

Gynecologists have noticed that frequently their patients
become pregnant immediately after taking the test which proves
whether or not the tubes are open. This seems to happen as often
when the report is negative as when it is positive. The explanation would appear to be that the test itself has removed or relieved
the emotional tension which caused sterility. It should be added
that in other women the test has been found to aggravate the
tension.

Sometimes frigid women bear children reluctantly; sometimes frigid women have difficulty in becoming pregnant. But it
should be remembered that a great many non-frigid women are
as relatively infertile for other reasons.

For many centuries it was believed that sterility was entirely a female disorder. Any man capable of intercourse was supposed by that fact to be fertile. History is full of barren wives who
were put aside or killed or perhaps tolerated by their husbands,
but it was seldom supposed that the men had any share in the
couple's sterility. At the end of the seventeenth century a major
political crisis in England was caused by the fact that King William and Queen Mary had no child to inherit the throne. The
monarch still had great power in those days, and the growth of
Parliament's authority owed much to this couple's childlessness,
for the crown passed to Mary's sister, Anne, an invalid without
much personality or intelligence who had to rely upon her ministers. During their lifetime, the childlessness of William and
Mary was a matter of much concern to all the statesmen of Europe
and therefore was widely commented upon. The wife was young,
healthy, vigorous. The husband had been asthmatic all his life,
racked with digestive disorders, so neurotic that he was described
by his admirers as very uncertain in his temper and generally so
frail that for thirty years he was supposed to be at death's door.
Furthermore, he never had produced a child by any of his mis-

tresses. Yet not even his bitterest enemies—and he had many—suggested seriously that he might be responsible for the couple's sterility.

In recent years it has been found that childlessness is due to defects in the male quite as often as in the female. Dr. Rock, through whose fertility clinic several thousand apparently sterile couples have passed, finds that in about one-third of his cases both partners are infertile.

As attention was turned to the father as a potential factor in the woman's apparent sterility, the age-old problem of impotence was seen in a new light. It has been known for a long time that physiological treatment of impotence is relatively ineffective, but now the effectiveness of emotional difficulties in impotence is coming to be understood. Impotence may have almost the same emotional background as tubal spasm in the female and is readily cured by alleviation of emotional conflict. . . .

HAVELOCK ELLIS: Auto-eroticism: The Daydream*

THOUGH BY no means easy to detect, these elaborate and more or less erotic daydreams are everywhere not uncommon in young men and especially in young women. Each individual has his own particular dream, which is always varying and developing, but, except in very imaginative persons, to no great extent. Such a daydream is often founded on a basis of pleasurable personal experience, and developed on that basis. It may involve an element of perversity, even though that element finds no expression in real life. It is, of course, fostered by sexual abstinence. Most usually there is little attempt to realize it. It does not necessarily lead to masturbation, though it sometimes causes some sexual congestion or even spontaneous sexual orgasm.

The daydream is a strictly private and intimate experience, not only from its very nature, but also because it occurs in images which the subject finds great difficulty in translating into language, even when willing to do so. In other cases it is elaborately dramatic or romantic in character, the hero or heroine passing through many experiences before attaining the erotic climax of the story. The climax tends to develop in harmony with the subject's growing knowledge or experience; at first merely a kiss, it may develop into any refinement of voluptuous gratification. The daydream may occur alike in normal and abnormal persons.

* Reprinted from *Psychology of Sex.*

Rousseau, in his *Confessions*, describes such dreams, in his case combined with masochism and masturbation. Raffalovich refers to the process by which in sexual inverts the vision of a person of the same sex, perhaps seen in the street or the theater, is evoked in solitary reveries, producing a kind of "psychic onanism," whether or not it leads on to physical manifestations.

Although daydreaming of this kind has until recent times been little studied, since it loves secrecy and solitude, and has seldom been counted of sufficient interest for scientific inquisition, it is really a process of considerable importance, and occupies a large part of the auto-erotic field. It is frequently cultivated by refined and imaginative young men and women who lead a chaste life and would be repelled by masturbation. In such persons, under such circumstances, it must be considered as strictly normal, the inevitable outcome of the play of the sexual impulse. No doubt it may often become morbid, and is never a healthy process when indulged in to excess, as it is liable to be by refined young people with artistic impulses, to whom it is in the highest degree seductive and insidious. Though the daydream is far from always colored by sexual emotion, yet it is a significant indication of its really sexual origin that, as I have been informed by persons of both sexes, even in these apparently non-sexual cases it frequently ceases on marriage.

FËDOR DOSTOEVSKY: The Christmas Tree and the Wedding

THE OTHER day I saw a wedding. . . . But no! I would rather tell you about a Christmas tree. The wedding was superb. I liked it immensely. But the other incident was still finer. I don't know why it is that the sight of the wedding reminded me of the Christmas tree. This is the way it happened:

Exactly five years ago, on New Year's Eve, I was invited to a children's ball by a man high up in the business world, who had his connections, his circle of acquaintances, and his intrigues. So it seemed as though the children's ball was merely a pretext for the parents to come together and discuss matters of interest to themselves, quite innocently and casually.

I was an outsider, and, as I had no special matters to air, I was able to spend the evening independently of the others. There was another gentleman present who like myself had just stumbled upon this affair of domestic bliss. He was the first to attract my attention. His appearance was not that of a man of birth or high family. He was tall, rather thin, very serious, and well dressed. Apparently he had no heart for the family festivities. The instant he went off into a corner by himself the smile disappeared from his face, and his thick dark brows knitted into a frown. He knew no one except the host and showed every sign of being bored to death, though bravely sustaining the rôle of thorough enjoyment to the end. Later I learned that he was a provincial, had come to the capital on some important, brain-racking business, had brought a letter of recommendation to our host, and our host had taken him under his protection, not at all *con amore*. It was merely out of politeness that he had invited him to the children's ball.

They did not play cards with him, they did not offer him cigars. No one entered into conversation with him. Possibly they recognised the bird by its feathers from a distance. Thus, my gentleman, not knowing what to do with his hands, was compelled to spend the evening stroking his whiskers. His whiskers were really fine, but he stroked them so assiduously that one got the feeling that the whiskers had come into the world first and afterwards the man in order to stroke them.

There was another guest who interested me. But he was of quite a different order. He was a personage. They called him Julian Mastakovich. At first glance one could tell he was an honoured guest and stood in the same relation to the host as the host to the gentleman of the whiskers. The host and hostess said no end of amiable things to him, were most attentive, wining him, hovering over him, bringing guests up to be introduced, but never leading him to any one else. I noticed tears glisten in our host's eyes when Julian Mastakovich remarked that he had rarely spent such a pleasant evening. Somehow I began to feel uncomfortable in this personage's presence. So, after amusing myself with the children, five of whom, remarkably well-fed young persons, were our host's, I went into a little sitting-room, entirely unoccupied, and seated myself at the end that was a conservatory and took up almost half the room.

The children were charming. They absolutely refused to resemble their elders, notwithstanding the efforts of mothers and governesses. In a jiffy they had denuded the Christmas tree down to the very last sweet and had already succeeded in breaking half of their playthings before they even found out which belonged to whom.

One of them was a particularly handsome little lad, dark-eyed, curly-haired, who stubbornly persisted in aiming at one with his wooden gun. But the child that attracted the greatest attention was his sister, a girl of about eleven, lovely as a Cupid. She was quiet and thoughtful, with large, full, dreamy eyes. The children had somehow offended her, and she left them and walked into the same room that I had withdrawn into. There she seated herself with her doll in a corner.

"Her father is an immensely wealthy business man," the guests informed each other in tones of awe. "Three hundred thousand rubles set aside for her dowry already."

As I turned to look at the group from which I heard this news item issuing, my glance met Julian Mastakovich's. He stood listening to the insipid chatter in an attitude of concentrated attention, with his hands behind his back and his head inclined to one side.

All the while I was quite lost in admiration of the shrewdness our host displayed in the dispensing of the gifts. The little maid of the many-rubled dowry received the handsomest doll, and the rest of the gifts were graded in value according to the diminishing scale of the parents' stations in life. The last child, a tiny chap of ten, thin, red-haired, freckled, came into possession of a small book of nature stories without illustrations or even head and tail pieces. He was the governess's child. She was a poor widow, and her little boy, clad in a sorry-looking little nankeen jacket, looked thoroughly crushed and intimidated. He took the book of nature stories and circled slowly about the children's toys. He would have given anything to play with them. But he did not dare to. You could tell he already knew his place.

I like to observe children. It is fascinating to watch the individuality in them struggling for self-assertion. I could see that the other children's things had tremendous charm for the red-haired boy, especially a toy theatre, in which he was so anxious to take a part that he resolved to fawn upon the other children. He smiled and began to play with them. His one and only apple he handed over to a puffy urchin whose pockets were already crammed with sweets, and he even carried another youngster pickaback—all simply that he might be allowed to stay with the theatre.

But in a few moments an impudent young person fell on him and gave him a pummelling. He did not dare even to cry. The governess came and told him to leave off interfering with the other children's games, and he crept away to the same room the little girl and I were in. She let him sit down beside her, and the two set themselves busily in dressing the expensive doll.

Almost half an hour passed, and I was nearly dozing off, as I sat there in the conservatory half listening to the chatter of the red-haired boy and the dowered beauty, when Julian Mastakovich entered suddenly. He had slipped out of the drawing-room under cover of a noisy scene among the children. From my secluded corner it had not escaped my notice that a few moments before he had been eagerly conversing with the rich girl's father, to whom he had only just been introduced.

He stood still for a while reflecting and mumbling to himself, as if counting something on his fingers.

"Three hundred—three hundred—eleven—twelve—thirteen —sixteen—in five years! Let's say four per cent—five times twelve—sixty, and on these sixty——. Let us assume that in five years it will amount to—well, four hundred. Hm—hm! But the shrewd old fox isn't likely to be satisfied with four per cent. He gets eight or even ten, perhaps. Let's suppose five hundred, five hundred thousand, at least, that's sure. Anything above that for pocket money—hm—"

He blew his nose and was about to leave the room when he spied the girl and stood still. I, behind the plants, escaped his notice. He seemed to me to be quivering with excitement. It must have been his calculations that upset him so. He rubbed his hands and danced from place to place, and kept getting more and more excited. Finally, however, he conquered his emotions and came to a standstill. He cast a determined look at the future bride and wanted to move toward her, but glanced about first. Then, as if with a guilty conscience, he stepped over to the child on tip-toe, smiling, and bent down and kissed her head.

His coming was so unexpected that she uttered a shriek of alarm.

"What are you doing here, dear child?" he whispered, looking around and pinching her cheek.

"We're playing."

"What, with him?" said Julian Mastakovich with a look askance at the governess's child. "You should go into the drawing-room, my lad," he said to him.

The boy remained silent and looked up at the man with wide-open eyes. Julian Mastakovich glanced round again cautiously and bent down over the girl.

"What have you got, a doll, my dear?"

"Yes, sir." The child quailed a little, and her brow wrinkled.

"A doll? And do you know, my dear, what dolls are made of?"

"No, sir," she said weakly, and lowered her head.

"Out of rags, my dear. You, boy, you go back to the drawing-room, to the children," said Julian Mastakovich, looking at the boy sternly.

The two children frowned. They caught hold of each other and would not part.

"And do you know why they gave you the doll?" asked Julian Mastakovich, dropping his voice lower and lower.

"No."

"Because you were a good, very good little girl the whole week."

Saying which, Julian Mastakovich was seized with a paroxysm of agitation. He looked round and said in a tone faint, almost inaudible with excitement and impatience:

"If I come to visit your parents will you love me, my dear?"

He tried to kiss the sweet little creature, but the red-haired boy saw that she was on the verge of tears, and he caught her hand and sobbed out loud in sympathy. That enraged the man.

"Go away! Go away! Go back to the other room, to your playmates."

"I don't want him to. I don't want him to! You go away!" cried the girl. "Let him alone! Let him alone!" She was almost weeping.

There was a sound of footsteps in the doorway. Julian Mastakovich started and straightened up his respectable body. The red-haired boy was even more alarmed. He let go the girl's hand, sidled along the wall, and escaped through the drawing-room into the dining-room.

Not to attract attention, Julian Mastakovich also made for the dining-room. He was red as a lobster. The sight of himself in a mirror seemed to embarrass him. Presumably he was annoyed at his own ardour and impatience. Without due respect to his importance and dignity, his calculations had lured and pricked him to the greedy eagerness of a boy, who makes straight for his object —though this was not as yet an object; it only would be so in five years' time. I followed the worthy man into the dining-room, where I witnessed a remarkable play.

Julian Mastakovich, all flushed with vexation, venom in his look, began to threaten the red-haired boy. The red-haired boy retreated farther and farther until there was no place left for him to retreat to, and he did not know where to turn in his fright.

"Get out of here! What are you doing here? Get out, I say, you good-for-nothing! Stealing fruit, are you? Oh, so, stealing fruit! Get out, you freckle face, go to your likes!"

The frightened child, as a last desperate resort, crawled quickly under the table. His persecutor, completely infuriated, pulled out his large linen handkerchief and used it as a lash to drive the boy out of his position.

Here I must remark that Julian Mastakovich was a somewhat corpulent man, heavy, well-fed, puffy-cheeked, with a paunch and ankles as round as nuts. He perspired and puffed and panted. So strong was his dislike (or was it jealousy?) of the child that he actually began to carry on like a madman.

I laughed heartily. Julian Mastakovich turned. He was utterly confused and for a moment, apparently, quite oblivious of his immense importance. At that moment our host appeared in the doorway opposite. The boy crawled out from under the table and wiped his knees and elbows. Julian Mastakovich hastened to carry his handkerchief, which he had been dangling by the corner, to his nose. Our host looked at the three of us rather suspiciously. But, like a man who knows the world and can readily adjust himself, he seized upon the opportunity to lay hold of his very valuable guest and get what he wanted out of him.

"Here's the boy I was talking to you about," he said, indicating the red-haired child. "I took the liberty of presuming on your goodness in his behalf."

"Oh," replied Julian Mastakovich, still not quite master of himself.

"He's my governess's son," our host continued in a beseeching tone. "She's a poor creature, the widow of an honest official. That's why, if it were possible for you—"

"Impossible, impossible!" Julian Mastakovich cried hastily. "You must excuse me, Philip Alexeyevich, I really cannot. I've made inquiries. There are no vacancies, and there is a waiting list of ten who have a greater right—I'm sorry."

"To bad," said our host. "He's a quiet, unobtrusive child."

"A very naughty little rascal, I should say," said Julian Mastakovich, wryly. "Go away, boy. Why are you here still? Be off with you to the other children."

Unable to control himself, he gave me a sidelong glance. Nor could I control myself. I laughed straight in his face. He turned away and asked our host, in tones quite audible to me, who that odd young fellow was. They whispered to each other and left the room, disregarding me.

I shook with laughter. Then I, too, went to the drawing-room. There the great man, already surrounded by the fathers and mothers and the host and the hostess, had begun to talk eagerly with a lady to whom he had just been introduced. The lady held the rich little girl's hand. Julian Mastakovich went into fulsome praise of her. He waxed ecstatic over the dear child's beauty, her talents, her grace, her excellent breeding, plainly laying himself out to flatter the mother, who listened scarcely able to restrain tears of joy, while the father showed his delight by a gratified smile.

The joy was contagious. Everybody shared in it. Even the children were obliged to stop playing so as not to disturb the conversation. The atmosphere was surcharged with awe. I heard the mother of the important little girl, touched to her profoundest depths, ask Julian Mastakovich in the choicest language of courtesy, whether he would honour them by coming to see them. I heard Julian Mastakovich accept the invitation with unfeigned enthusiasm. Then the guests scattered decorously to different parts of the room, and I heard them, with veneration in their tones, extol the business man, the business man's wife, the business man's daughter, and, especially, Julian Mastakovich.

"Is he married?" I asked out loud of an acquaintance of mine standing beside Julian Mastakovich.

Julian Mastakovich gave me a venomous look.

"No," answered my acquaintance, profoundly shocked by my—intentional—indiscretion.

Not long ago I passed the Church of ———. I was struck by the concourse of people gathered there to witness a wedding. It was a dreary day. A drizzling rain was beginning to come down. I made my way through the throng into the church. The bridegroom was a round, well-fed, pot-bellied little man, very much dressed up. He ran and fussed about and gave orders and arranged things. Finally word was passed that the bride was coming. I pushed through the crowd, and I beheld a marvellous beauty whose first spring was scarcely commencing. But the beauty was pale and sad. She looked distracted. It seemed to me even that her eyes were red from recent weeping. The classic severity of every line of her face imparted a peculiar significance and solemnity to her beauty. But through that severity and solemnity, through the sadness, shone the innocence of a child. There was something inexpressibly naïve, unsettled and young in her features, which, without words, seemed to plead for mercy.

They said she was just sixteen years old. I looked at the bridegroom carefully. Suddenly I recognised Julian Mastakovich, whom I had not seen again in all those five years. Then I looked at the bride again.—Good God! I made my way, as quickly as I could, out of the church. I heard gossiping in the crowd about the bride's wealth—about her dowry of five hundred thousand rubles—so and so much for pocket money.

"Then his calculations were correct," I thought, as I pressed out into the street.

IV

*The Flight from the Other:
Homosexuality*

JEAN-PAUL SARTRE: Genet—Criminal and Saint*

HE IS fifteen years old.[1] He has become what
they wanted him to be: a hardened thief. The authorities examine the case and decide that his apprenticeship is over and that it
is high time to send him to his post. They take him and throw
him into jail and from there into a reformatory. The matter is
settled. It does not require much imagination to guess what he
suffered. Thus far, his exile has been only a moral one. Now he
is being confined. They are cloistering him, they are cutting him
off from the universe. The doors have closed upon him. He contemplates with terror the new world in which it has been decided
that he is to pass his life and that other society which will henceforth be his. Firmly resolved to be submissive to nothing, bent on
willing the fate which he has been assigned, he is about to decide
to adapt himself to his new existence. But before he has had time
to catch his breath, "the miracle of horror" has already occurred
that other society of castoffs, of dregs that excremental society
rejects him.

"I suffered cruelly, I experienced the shame of having my
head cropped, of being garbed in an unspeakable outfit, of being
assigned to that vile place. I knew the contempt of the other inmates, who were stronger or more evil than I."

Condemned by Good, scorned by Evil, he is driven to the
confines of two enemy societies which shuttle him back and forth.
His sense of shame increases. His bourgeois ways, which he has
not quite lost, cause him to feel cruelly the humiliation of being
shorn and being dressed in an unspeakable outfit. But if he wants
to find comfort in the thought that he has willed Evil with all the

* Reprinted from *Saint Genet*.

consequences that it entails, then he must admit to himself that
he has found something more evil than himself. He is too young,
too soft, too weak, too cowardly. Which means, above all: too
gentle and too conscious. The truth of the matter is what Green
Eyes will later say to Lefranc: "You're not our kind." They
badger him, they insult him, they brutalize him. He becomes a
butt.

"I was sixteen years old. . . . I kept no place in my heart
where the feeling of my innocence could dwell. I recognized myself as being the coward, the traitor, the thief, the homo that they
saw in me. . . . With a little patience and reflection, I discovered
within myself sufficient reason for being called by those names.
It appalled me to realize that I was composed of filth. I became
abject."

How could he be loved? By whom? They spit in his face.
He dares to gaze upon the meanest and handsomest hoodlums,
but he has not the audacity to want them to love him. He knows
only too well that he is not lovable. The passionate decision to
will his destiny imparts a kind of cynical and brutal realism to all
his thoughts, all his desires, even to his dreams. Even in his
dreams he endeavors, as Descartes says, "to conquer himself rather
than fortune." And besides, those glamorous boys are not meant
for loving. Surrounded by a court of admirers, they are the handsome object of everyone's attention. They are absolute ends, and as
such they gather and fix upon themselves all the scattered love that
floats within the four walls. They are, by nature, the beloved.
Genet immediately effects one of the extraordinary reversals at
which he is an old hand. While deciding, in accordance with the
discipline he elaborated a few years earlier, "to say yea from the
bottom of his heart to every charge brought against him," he
makes a zealous effort to love those who despise him. Precisely
because he is alone and wretched, because he is dying to be suc-
cored, to be comforted, because he has a fabulous need to *receive*
love, he decides to *give* it. He adores all those cruel, handsome
children who plague him mercilessly, he adores them, he servilely
submits to their desires, he becomes a doormat. Since he is unable
to be the beloved, he will become the lover. A strange operation,
in which the most abject humility disguises the most stiff-necked
pride, in which the most utter love masks the most corrosive
hatred. If we succeed in grasping the meaning of this, we shall be
very close to deciphering Genet's secret: his passive homosexuality.

Not that it is to be dated from this new choice. He himself
has informed us that, as far as he remembers, he felt his first
homosexual desire—a quite innocent desire aroused by a handsome child on a bicycle—at the age of ten. He has even written

that his homosexuality preceded his stealing and that the latter was merely a consequence of the former. But we cannot follow him in this. I can very well imagine that it flatters his self-esteem to trace his pilferings, which are more external and vulgar, and which might, after all, have sprung from the occasion, to a deeper, more singular, more autonomous taste. But since, by his own confession, he stole before having relations with boys, even before desiring their caresses, we cannot help but regard his claim as merely the effect of a pious wish: if he wanted to support it, he would have to project his homosexuality, without proof, as some kind of metaphysical virtue beyond his memories. I quite recognize that at the present time he is more essentially a homosexual than a thief. But what does that prove? One of the constant characteristics of the psychic life is the fact that later determinations act upon earlier ones, envelop them and endow them with a new meaning. At present, Genet is perhaps a thief because he is a homosexual. But he became a homosexual because he was a thief. A person is not born homosexual or normal. He becomes one or the other, according to the accidents of his history and to his own reaction to these accidents. I maintain that inversion is the effect of neither a prenatal choice nor an endocrinian malformation nor even the passive and determined result of complexes. It is an outlet that a child discovers when he is suffocating.

Genet's early states of sexual agitation—those he experienced before entering the reformatory—must be regarded as rehearsals, experiences and experiments, not as manifestations of a bent. Can any man maintain that he never dreamed, in childhood, of caressing a playmate? And what of it! And even if there were an actual exchange of caresses, would that be a reason to speak of homosexuality? It is only afterward that these tentative efforts take on meaning. When the individual definitively takes one path rather than another, "the retrospective illusion" then detects in them the premonitory signs of disorder or decides to regard them only as inconsequential deviations. Inversely, our inventions are mainly decisions and clarifications. What we think we discover in a moment of special insight is what we have been inventing for years, bit by bit, absent-mindedly as it were, without being completely involved. Following close upon his early thefts and his original crisis, Genet's homosexual desires were at first merely "experiments just to see," attempts to discover, on the periphery of his fundamental decision, a safety exit. But if he desired boys, he did so with a kind of innocence. The passage which we quoted above makes this quite clear: applying to his new state the severe discipline which he had elaborated five years earlier, "I recognized myself," he says, ". . . as being the *homo* that they saw in me. . . . With a little patience and reflection, I discovered within myself sufficient reason for being called by that name." This means that he had never previously considered himself an invert. The illumination which establishes himself in his own eyes as a "homo" cannot be distinguished from the will to become one, that is, to give his past a meaning and a name and to consider it the preformation of his future. Deciding both to be the lover and to claim the insulting name of homo, Genet *learns*, by this very decision, that he has always been an invert. By the same token he realizes that the safety exit merges with the main exit: to want to be *the* thief and to decide that he will be a homosexual are one and the same thing. If his first sexual experiments had not been games, even if shared, and dreams, he would have realized this earlier. In any case, the will to Evil is primary, and, even though he may claim the contrary, Genet is well aware of this. Let us bear in mind, rather, Querelle, his hero: if he decides to be caught by Norbert, he does so after having killed and because he has killed.

As a result of his original crisis and of the ensuing decision, Genet finds himself immersed in a situation that might be called prehomosexual. Even if he had never subsequently slept with a man or dreamed of doing so, he was marked, set off. He would have remained, like so many others, a Vestal of homosexuality. Like the trim, smart, nimble, graceful banker whom everyone took for a fairy and who was always getting involved in long-drawn-out affairs with women without even suspecting the existence of forbidden love, until a chance debauch revealed it to him at the age of forty and thereupon changed him retrospectively into *what he was*. Sexually, Genet is first of all a raped child. This first rape was the gaze of the other, who took him by surprise, penetrated him, transformed him forever into an object. Let there be no misunderstanding: I am not saying that his original crisis *resembles* a rape, I say that it *is* one. The events which strike us take place at the same time on all levels of our mental life and express themselves, on each level, in a different language. An actual rape can become, in our conscience, an iniquitous and yet ineluctable condemnation and, vice versa, a condemnation can be felt as a rape. Both acts transform the guilty person into an object, and if, in his heart, he feels his objectification as a shameful thing, he feels it in his sex as an act of coitus to which he has been subjected. Genet has now been deflowered; an iron embrace has made him a woman. All that is left for him is to put up with *being*. He is the village whore; everyone can have him at will. Undressed by the eyes of the decent folk as women are by those of males, he carries his fault as they do their breasts and behind.

Many women loathe their backside, that blind and public mass which belongs to everyone before belonging to them. When they are grazed from behind, their excitement and their shame will mount together. The same holds for Genet. Having been caught stealing *from behind,* his back opens when he steals; it is with his back that he awaits human gazes and catastrophe. Why be surprised if, after that, he feels more like an object by virtue of his back and behind and if he has a kind of sexual reverence for them? The guilty child has been unmasked, possessed, and it is as a culprit that he will experience excitement and desire. And since he wills to become what they have made him, that is, an object, this willing will have repercussions even in the way he feels his body and the erection of his penis. To the man who makes himself a hunter, his penis is a knife, but to the one who becomes an object, it is a still life, a *thing,* which hardens only so as to give a better grip and to become easier to handle. It is typical that Proust, who was a homosexual, never called the penis a sword or a scythe, as do our village Lotharios, but a "clamp."[2] The turgescence that the male feels as the aggressive stiffening of a muscle will be felt by Genet as the blossoming of a flower. Whether it be the swelling up of an inert air chamber or the unsheathing of a sword, nothing is decided in advance: the entire choice which one makes of oneself gives its meaning to this inner perception. One man feels his transcendence in his penis; another, his passivity. And, in point of fact, it is quite true that an erection is a hardening, a spurt, but it is also true that this induration is undergone. The raw fact is ambiguous; the meaning depends on the individual. But the male swoops down on the female, carries her off, subjects her and feeds her. The very way in which he makes love reflects his economic situation and his pride in earning his living. Where do you expect Genet to get his pride? He does not earn his living, he loses it. Parasite of a society that denies him salvation through action, excluded from all undertakings, where would he find that mixture of oppressive imperialism and generosity which at present characterizes manly sexuality? The male rarely wishes to seduce by his physical qualities. He has received them, not made them. He makes his woman love him for his power, his courage, his pride, his aggressiveness, in short he makes her desire him as a faceless force, a pure power to do and take, not as an object agreeable to the touch. He seeks in submissive eyes the reflection of his infinite freedom. But the acts of Genet, who does nothing, who undoes, who acts only in order to be, are effectual only in appearance. They reveal not his force but his essence. They are *gestures.* He says about Divine: "She tried for male gestures . . . whistled, put her hands into her pockets, and this whole performance was carried out so unskillfully that in the course of a single evening she seemed to be four or five characters at the same time." Divine is himself. He displays himself, he makes himself an object. That being so, how could he take? And what need has he of a woman, that other object which competes with him? All they could do would be to dance in front of each other, each wanting to be taken, not to take, to be seen, not to look.

This priority, in the subject itself, of the object over the subject leads, as we see, to amorous passivity, which, when it affects a male, inclines him to homosexuality.

In short, Genet decides to *realize* his being and knows that he cannot achieve this result unaided. He therefore resorts to the mediation of others. This means that he makes of his objectivity for others the *essential* and of his reality-for-himself the inessential. What he desires is to be manipulated passively by the Other so as to become an object in his own eyes. Any man who places his truth in his Being-for-the-Other finds himself in a situation which I have called prehomosexual. And this is the case, for example, of many actors, even if they enjoy sleeping only with women.

But in the case of Genet there is something else; he is inclined to homosexuality by other factors. Before there was any sexual determination, Genet reacted to his condemnation by effecting an ethical and generalized inversion. He was, as he has said, turned inside-out like a glove. Since he has been cast into nothingness, it is from nothingness alone that he wishes to derive. He is a monster, the exception to the rule, the improbable, in fact the impossible. He is an undesirable, born not of man but of some incubus. He cannot found a family. Thus, he has not only been exiled from the fields, woods and springs, he has been excluded *from his own nature.* We bathe in our life, in our blood, in our sperm. Our body is a dense water that carries us along; we have only to let ourselves go. A lowly Venus who is hardly to be distinguished from digestion, from respiration, from the beating of our heart, gently inclines us toward woman. We have only to trust her. The servant goddess will attend to everything, to our pleasure and to the species. But Genet *is dead.* His life is no more *natural* than his birth, it haunts a corpse. He hangs on only by power of will. If he pays any attention to the muted sensations which come to him from his organs, he feels impossible and falls into astonishment. He does not find within himself any of those powerful instincts that support the desires of the decent man. He knows only the death instinct. His sexual desires will be phantoms, as his life itself is a phantom. Whatever their object, they are condemned in advance. He is *forbidden from the beginning* to desire.

All societies castrate the maladjusted. This castration can be actually physical or can be achieved by persuasion. The result is the same. The desire of Genet, who is condemned, outside of nature, impossible, becomes a desire for the impossible and for what is against nature. And since this outcast child is only an appearance, his sexuality itself must be a sham, a trick of nothingness. None of the ordinary sources can determine it; it does not emanate from universal nature; it does not have its roots there. The fact is, it is up in the air, a pure, diabolical imitation of the legitimate movements of our senses. In assuming his situation, Genet takes his stand on absolute particularity; he will derive only from himself. This upheaval affects even his sexuality. His contorted desire, sharp and nervous, derives only from itself. It can have no natural relationship with its object. And since Genet's sincerity is the demand for artifice, his excitement will be all the more sincere insofar as he feels more artificial, more free. He does not know abandon, swooning. If he lets himself go, he falls into a pit. Thus, *he does not abandon himself* to sexuality. On the contrary, it appears at the maximum of tension. At the height of passion it retains a taste of ashes and freedom. And since negative freedom and Evil are one and the same, his sexual life is a new field which opens out to his perversity. Desire of nothingness, nothingness of desire, exhausting effort of the entire being, sterile, rootless and aimless, Genet's sexual desire contains within itself a fierce demand for its autonomy and singularity, in defiance of the rules, in defiance of nature, in defiance of life of the species and in defiance of society. It will reflect him completely in the realm of the flesh.

Such is the situation that has been created for him. And though it inclines him strongly to homosexuality, it does not yet determine whether Genet will be a boy queen or a girl queen. It is here that the aforementioned upheaval occurs. Genet, who is the butt of the young big shots of the reformatory, is metamorphosed into a lover, that is, into a woman. But why? We have seen what the beloved gains in playing his role: he is magnified in the lover's heart. He is sheltered, saved. But what of the lover? Why does he demand disgust and rebuffs, the other's indifference, the tortures of jealousy and, in the end, the despair that comes from the certainty of not being loved? And yet he must have something to gain by this. What is behind it all? For Genet, the answer is clear: love is a magical ceremonial whereby the lover steals the beloved's being in order to incorporate it into himself:

"The earliest form of love that I remember is my desire *to be* a pretty boy . . . whom I saw going by."[3]

The earliest, perhaps. But Genet adopted it later. Divine

says to Gabriel: "You're myself," and Gabriel, decent chap that
he is, smiles fatuously without realizing that his blood is being
sucked from him. And the lieutenant's passionate, fierce love of
Querelle is the desire to take away his penis and testicles and
graft them on himself. . . .

No doubt it is essential that the pimps have muscles. In
the presence of a powerful build, Genet swoons and melts with
love, excited by the simple display of virile strength, but these
muscles serve no purpose. Too aristocratic to work, the beloved
are too lazy to want to achieve the kind of athletic distinction of
which the lover might be proud; and too serious as well, too absorbed in their austere and egotistical dances; and as for fighting,
they are too cowardly. In fact, if we are to believe Genet's accounts, the stronger they are the more cowardly they are. Darling
is a coward, Green Eyes is a coward, Bulkaen, Paulo and Stilitano
are cowards. Far from reproaching them with this cowardice,
Genet delights in it. If he is threatened, it does not even occur
to him to take refuge under their wing. Those powerful arms are
not meant for protecting him. Quite the contrary, Darling and
Green Eyes snicker when the girl queens tear each other to pieces
for love of them. The Germans rape Riton in front of Erik's eyes
without the latter's making a move to defend him. No, the
muscles are for display. They impart a quiet and terrible power
to movements, they are the signs of transcendence. But only the
signs, for the pimp never does anything. They are the epaulettes
and gold braid which manifest his right to command. Above all,
their compact solidity is the symbol of the criminal's absolute
density, his impenetrability: muscles and frame represent the
being of this appearance, the opacity of the initself. Impenetrable
and tough, bulky, tense, rocky, the pimp will be defined by his
rigidity. His body, drawn upward by the muscles, seems a penis
taut with the desire to pierce, to bore, to split, rising toward the
sky "with the cruel and sudden sharpness of a steeple puncturing
a cloud of ink." *Rigidity*, word dear to Genet, both moral and
sexual, designating the tension of his soul, his hatred of all abandon, and the fatal force that drives the criminal to his destruction.
Rigidity: Destiny is a giant penis, the man is utterly a sex organ
and the organ becomes a man. "The big, inflexible, strict pimps,
their cocks in full bloom—I no longer know whether they are lilies
or whether lilies and cocks are not totally they." Genet's pansexualism is going to find this muscular and sexual stiffness everywhere. The child Querelle, at the foot of one of the two massive
towers that defend the port of La Rochelle, experienced "a feeling
both of power and impotence. First of pride, pride at knowing
that so high a tower is the symbol of his virility . . . and, at the

same time, he had a feeling of quiet humility in the presence of the serious and incomparable potency of some indefinable male." When Genet describes the relationship of a girl queen to a male, he uses a comparison which recurs constantly, that of a spiral rolling about an upright rigidity. And this image evolves to the point of becoming a sexual motif which is reproduced by Nature everywhere. First, there is the *spectacle:*

"The girl queens are huddled together and chattering and cheeping around the boy queens who are straight, motionless and vertiginous, as motionless and silent as branches."

Then, the *gesture:*

"All the queens imparted to their bodies a tendril-like movement and fancied they were enlacing this handsome man, that they were twining around him."

Then, the *metaphor:*

"Round some, more upright, more solid than the others, twined dematis, convolvulus, nasturtium, little pimps too, tortuous."

Finally, the sexual pattern creeps into the perception: the sky in the middle of palaces becomes "the column of azure round which twines the marble."

But, inversely, this pansexualism is panmoralistic. Not a touch of sensuality in this universe. The penis is made of *metal;* Paulo's is a cannon. What excites Genet about a prick is never the flesh of which it is composed but its power of penetration, its mineral hardness. It is a drill, a pile driver, it will be a dagger, "a torture machine." The sex organ and the muscles are of the same nature: rods, iron bars, steel claws whose function is to subdue him in spite of himself, to support, by means of a foreign constraint, his will to be enslaved. Genet, as we have seen, loathes gratuitousness. To submit voluntarily would be pointless. That is what "normal" lovers do when they yield to the will of their mistresses. And they always retain the feeling that this submission is an act, that they are the masters. Genet's excitement requires that the servitude be effective, imposed. In order for him to feel that he belongs to the Other and that through this surrender he becomes the Other in his own eyes, the strength of the beloved must force him to the floor. Let the male violate him, bully him, beat him. Above all, he himself must not be able to break his chains on pain of death. Gorgui kills his mistress who wanted to leave him, Divine fears that Gorgui may kill "her." Erik despises the executioner because the latter has not killed him. Armand excites Genet more than anyone else because "his muscular power, visible in the shape of the skull and the base of the neck, further proclaimed, and imposed, these detestable qualities. It made them sparkle." Genet reads his fate in this muscularity, a horrible destiny of docility. Desire immediately reduces him to submission. But what is his desire if not dizziness? And what is dizziness if not a fall that is felt in advance and mimed in his flesh, the fall into the Other's heart from the top of the cliff that stands against the sky? The movement is relative. This penis rises up with the speed of Genet's fall, and the deeper the abyss into which Genet falls, the more dizzying is its height. At the bottom of the precipice the lover finds the corpse of the beloved who has fallen there before him: the fist that makes Genet grovel before the pimp is one and the same as the Fatality that drives the latter to death. Thus, this universe of strongholds, minarets and bell towers, this phallic bristling of nature, is the vision of a man who is falling and who sees high walls rising above him and hiding the sun. Genet's sexuality is the dynamism of the fall, the gravity of Evil felt in the flesh. Bachelard would say that he has an "Icarus complex." In this sense, the sexual act proper represents the religious ceremony, which makes it possible to gather into an instant the infiniteness of daily submission. Genet undergoes Armand's brutality, his exigencies; he begs, steals and prostitutes himself for him; he laces his shoes, lights his cigarettes. All these jobs take time and patience. Servitude is a long-term undertaking; it is broken up into a thousand particular dislikes which conceal the whole. In order for him to enjoy them, there must be a violent contraction, a spasm which sums up everything in a moment, in short a *festival,* which is a kind of *sacred time* that emerges cyclically amidst profane time and endows the latter with new force. The sexual act is the festival of submission;[4] it is also the ritual renewal of the feudal contract whereby the vassal becomes his lord's liegeman. . . .

Sensual pleasure is rigorously excluded from this ceremony. The beauty which Genet serves is inflexibly severe. The male never caresses the girl queen. If he touches her, it is only to place her roughly in a position that will heighten his pleasure. What rightfully reverts to Genet is the suffering which is flight, which is self-hatred. He boldly demands it as his share. He says of an adolescent who is possessed by a pimp: "He desired only an increase of pain so as to lose himself in it." And another of his characters cries out, while being taken: "Kill me!" Even the orgasm is denied the lover, at least during intercourse. Or rather it is the lover himself who denies himself the right to ejaculate. If, out of kindness (which, be it added, is very rare) , the beloved makes an effort to give him pleasure, he declines. Riton gently pushes Erik's hand away because "It was normal that Erik get pleasure from Riton, who was younger than he, and normal that Riton serve Erik." The lover, who is the beloved's slave, takes his pleasure alone, afterward, and hides himself to do so. Divine goes to finish off in the toilet—and quite likely he does not choose this unclean place at random—or else quickly and ashamedly masturbates behind Our Lady's back. The lover's pleasure is the upbeat. It is glossed over. It is already the moment of separation, of solitude. The downbeat is the pleasure of the beloved. They both exhaust themselves, amidst violence and pain, in serving it; they both sacrifice themselves so that the absolute, namely, the male's orgasm, may come into being. Thus, it is both true and false that Genet gets no pleasure during intercourse. *There is* pleasure within him, deep in his martyrized flesh; only, it is the other who gets it. But the Other is his own Nature, himself as he is changed into himself. Little by little, as the thrusts which are tearing him apart become increasingly brutal, Genet begins to feel, deep inside him, the gradual birth of a phantom of pleasure, an urgent absence, *his* gratification insofar as he is the Other, his pleasure as *other pleasure*, an absolute begotten by his body, a pleasure which the movements of his loins cause the beloved to bring forth and which finally emerges beneath the sky, an autonomous and self-sufficient reality. Thus, the supreme moment of coitus is not that of abandon to natural plenitude, of letting go, of release of tension, of satisfied expectation. Quite the contrary, it is at the maximum of tension; his whole body grows taut and offers itself as a receptacle for the pleasure which grazes him, which inhabits him, which blossoms in the darkness of his bowels and of which he will never experience anything but the *reverse*, that is, suffering. Suffering is the necessary complement of the other's pleasure; he enjoys it as pleasure insofar as he is other. We are thus back at the generalized inversion that characterizes Evil, the will that is eager—since he is denied everything—to seize upon privation as the mark of plenitude, to be filled by emptiness. His pain is imaginary pleasure. He grows tense, gives himself, pants, swoons, in short makes all the movements and moans of a woman who is coming. In the case of the latter, however, this behavior accompanies the orgasm, it is its expression and effect, whereas in Genet it is a magical attitude that aims at *treating suffering as pleasure*. He imitates abandon at the price of extreme tension, he cries aloud and tosses about so that the pleasure he receives may become, in the eyes of invisible witnesses, the meaning of his attitudes. No one is more active than this homosexual who is called a passive homosexual. I would compare him to the frigid woman who strains against herself in an effort to feel an absent ecstasy. But there is a fundamental difference between them. The latter is actually rebelling against her frigidity. The phantom of pleasure which she finally attains seems to her only a makeshift. Genet, lord of Evil, deliberately substitutes appearance for being. He *could* give himself the orgasm, and refuses it. If he pursues this imaginary gratification, it is not in defiance of its unreality but because of it. The frigid wife looks forward to a stroke of luck, to a late awakening of her senses. Genet looks forward *to nothing*. At the core of the sexual act we find a mad desire for the impossible. The two stages of the sexual act both involve a structure of make-believe. The downbeat is a real presence of the Other, a felt visitation and a virtual presence of pleasure; the upbeat of masturbation is a real presence of pleasure, but accompanied by fantasy: Divine masturbates while thinking of Our Lady, but Our Lady has come out of Divine and forgotten him. In the last analysis, it is this creative tension which is the goal. At the moment when he charges the Other with crushing his consciousness and shattering it, Genet, emperor of sham, remains a free and exasperated consciousness which supports, all by itself, an imaginary world. The highest moment of this consciousness is that in which it becomes a consciousness which forgets itself, a consciousness aware of forgetting itself, just as the highest moment of the criminal's life is that of his death. The summit of pride is the abyss of humility. It is when his God visits him that Genet, inverted mystic, is at the height of solitude.

This savage and contorted life, this exalted affirmation of the impossible, is followed by death, like the instant of beheading. Are not the "white flowers" which come out of the beloved's penis sisters of the red flowers which sprang from the decapitated body of Pilorge? The orgasm is the paradoxical instant of the most intense pleasure and of the end of pleasure. Within Genet the beloved dies. Genet senses this death and accompanies it. He suddenly relaxes, expands, "sinks into darkness," dies with the other's death: he swoons. Thus, beneath the constructions of his will, we find the foundation of his basic anxieties and his humble desire for suicide, a desire which is forever being rejected, repressed, forever being reborn. Indeed, it frequently happens that our most constantly repudiated primary desires give consistency and flesh to the acts of will that contradict them most, and there is thus a double determination of the most important acts of our life, which thus admit of two opposite interpretations. The dizziness that overcomes Genet in the presence of a handsome male certainly expresses this extraordinarily complex construction which causes Genet to choose to be the other and to find his destiny in the stately tragedy of capital punishment. But at the same time, this infinite fall is, in an obscure, in a muted way, a kind of leave which he grants himself: leave to die.

NOTES

1. In *Miracle of the Rose*, Genet writes: "When I was taken to the Mettray Reformatory, I was fifteen years and seventeen days old. . . ."
2. Another homosexual has called it "a slug" in an excellent but unpublishable short story.
3. Cf. Cocteau, *Le Grand Écart* (*OEuvres complètes*, I, 15): "Ever since childhood he had felt the desire to be those whom he found beautiful, not to be loved by them."
4. At least such is its manifest aspect. We shall see later that it also represents the passion and ritual murder of the beloved.

SIMONE DE BEAUVOIR: The Lesbian*

THE LESBIAN could readily accept the loss of her femininity if in doing so she gained a successful virility; though she can employ artificial means of deflowering and possessing her loved one, she is none the less a castrate and may suffer acutely from the realization of that fact. She is unfulfilled as a woman, impotent as a man, and her disorder may lead to psychosis. One patient said to Dalbiez:[1] "If I only had something to penetrate with, it would be better." Another wished that her breasts were rigid. The lesbian will often try to compensate for her virile inferiority by an arrogance, an exhibitionism, by which, in fact, an inner disequilibrium is betrayed. Sometimes, again, she will succeed in establishing with other women a type of relation quite analogous to those which a "feminine" man or a youth still uncertain of his virility might have with them. A very striking case of this kind is that of "Count Sandor" reported by Krafft-Ebing.[2] By means of the expedient just mentioned, this woman had attained a state of equilibrium, which was destroyed only by the intervention of society.

Sarolta came of a titled Hungarian family known for its eccentricities. Her father had her reared as a boy, calling her Sandor; she rode horseback, hunted, and so on. She was under such influences until, at thirteen, she was placed in an institution. A little later she fell in love with an English girl, pretending to be a boy, and ran away with her. At home again, later, she resumed the name Sandor and wore boy's clothing, while being carefully educated. She went on long trips with her father, always in male attire; she was addicted to sports, drank, and visited brothels. She felt particularly drawn toward actresses and other such detached women, preferably not too young but "feminine" in nature. "It delighted me," she related, "if the passion

* Reprinted from *The Second Sex*.

of a lady was disclosed under a poetic veil. All immodesty in a woman was disgusting to me. I had an indescribable aversion to female attire—indeed, for everything feminine, but only in so far as it concerned me; for, on the other hand, I was all enthusiasm for the beautiful sex." She had numerous affairs with women and spent a good deal of money. At the same time she was a valued contributor to two important journals.

She lived for three years in "marriage" with a woman ten years older than herself, from whom she broke away only with great difficulty. She was able to inspire violent passions. Falling in love with a young teacher, she was married to her in an elaborate ceremony, the girl and her family believing her to be a man; her father-in-law on one occasion noticed what seemed to be an erection (probably a priapus); she shaved as a matter of form, but servants in the hotel suspected the truth from seeing blood on her bedclothes and from spying through the keyhole.

Thus unmasked, Sandor was put in prison and later acquitted, after thorough investigation. She was greatly saddened by her enforced separation from her beloved Marie, to whom she wrote long and impassioned letters from her cell.

The examination showed that her conformation was not wholly feminine: her pelvis was small and she had no waist. Her breasts were developed, her sexual parts quite feminine but not maturely formed. Her menstruation appeared late, at seventeen, and she felt a profound horror of the function. She was equally horrified at the thought of sexual relations with the male; her sense of modesty was developed only in regard to women and to the point that she would feel less shyness in going to bed with a man than with a woman. It was very embarrassing for her to be treated as a woman, and she was truly in anguish at having to wear feminine clothes. She felt that she was "drawn as by a magnetic force toward women of twenty-four to thirty." She found sexual satisfaction exclusively in caressing her loved one, never in being caressed. At times she made use of a stocking stuffed with oakum as a priapus. She detested men. She was very sensitive to the moral esteem of others, and she had much literary talent, wide culture, and a colossal memory.

Sandor was not psychoanalyzed, but a number of salient points emerge from the simple statement of the facts. It would appear that without a "masculine protest," quite spontaneously, she always thought of herself as a man, thanks to her upbringing and her natural constitution; the manner in which her father included her in his traveling and in his life evidently had a decisive influence. Her mannishness was so well established that she showed no ambivalence in regard to women; loving them like a man, she did not feel herself compromised by them; she loved them in a purely dominating, active way, without accepting reciprocal attentions. But it is remarkable that she "detested men" and that she liked older women especially. This suggests that she had a *masculine* Œdipus complex in regard to her mother; she retained the childish attitude of the very little girl who, forming a couple with her mother, nourishes the hope of protecting her and some day dominating her.

It often happens that when the child has felt a lack of maternal affection, she is haunted all her life by the need for it: reared by her father, Sandor must have dreamed of a loving and dear mother, whom she sought, later, in other women; that explains her profound envy of other men, bound up with her respect, her "poetic" love, for detached women and older women, who seemed in her eyes to bear a sacred character. Her attitude toward women was precisely that of Rousseau with Mme de Warens, of the young Benjamin Constant with Mme de Charrière: sensitive and "feminine" adolescents, they also turned to motherly mistresses. We frequently meet with the lesbian, more or less markedly of this type, who has never identified herself with her mother—because she either admired or detested her too much—but who, while declining to be a woman, wishes to have around her the soft delight of feminine protection; from the warm shelter of that womb she can emerge into the outer world with mannish boldness; she behaves like a man, but as a man she is fragile, weak, and this makes her desire an older mistress; the pair will correspond to that well-known heterosexual couple: matron and adolescent.[3]

The psychoanalysts have strongly emphasized the importance of the early relations established between the homosexual woman and her mother. There are two cases in which the adolescent girl finds difficulty in escaping her mother's influence: if she has been too lovingly watched over by an anxious mother, or if she has been maltreated by a "bad mother," who has inspired in the girl a deep sense of guilt. In the first case their relation often verges upon homosexuality: they sleep together, caress each other, or indulge in breast kisses; the young girl will later seek the same happiness in other arms. In the second case she will feel keenly the need for a "good mother," who will protect her from the first and ward off the curse she feels has been placed upon her. One of Havelock Ellis's subjects, who had detested her mother throughout her childhood, describes the love she felt at sixteen for an older woman, as follows:[4]

I felt like an orphaned child who had suddenly acquired a mother, and through her I began to feel less antagonistic to grown people and to feel the first respect I had ever felt for what they said. . . . My love for her was perfectly pure, and I thought of hers as simply maternal. . . . I liked her to touch me and she sometimes held me in her arms or let me sit on her lap. At bedtime she used to come and say good-night and kiss me upon the mouth.

If the older woman is so inclined, the younger will be delighted to abandon herself to more ardent embraces. She will ordinarily assume the passive role, for she wishes to be dominated, protected, cradled, and caressed like a small child. Whether such relations remain platonic or become physical, they frequently have the character of a true amorous passion. But from the very fact that they form a classic stage in adolescent development, it is clear that they are insufficient to explain a definite choice of homosexuality. In them the young girl seeks at once a liberation and a security that she could find also in masculine arms. After having passed through the period of amorous enthusiasm, the younger woman often feels toward the older the same ambivalent sentiment that she felt toward her mother; she submits to her influence while desiring to escape from it; if her friend insists on holding her, she will remain for a time her "captive";[5] but she finally escapes, after bitter scenes or in friendly fashion; having done with adolescence, she feels ripe for the life of a normal woman. To become a confirmed lesbian she must either refuse— like Sandor—to accept her femininity or let it flower in feminine arms. This is to say that fixation on the mother is not by itself enough to explain inversion. And this condition may indeed be chosen for quite other reasons. The woman may discover or foresee through complete or partial experiences that she will not derive pleasure from heterosexual relations, that only another woman can fully provide it: to the woman who makes a religion of her femininity, especially, the homosexual embrace may prove most satisfying.

It is most important to emphasize the fact that refusal to make herself the object is not always what turns woman to homosexuality; most lesbians, on the contrary, seek to cultivate the treasures of their femininity. To be willing to be changed into a passive object is not to renounce all claim to subjectivity: woman hopes in this way to find self-realization under the aspect of herself as a thing; but then she will be trying to find herself in her otherness, her alterity. When alone she does not succeed in really creating her double; if she caresses her own bosom, she still does not know how her breasts seem to a strange hand, nor how they are felt to react under a strange hand; a man can reveal to her the existence of her flesh *for herself*—that is to say, as she herself perceives it, but not what it is *to others*. It is only when her fingers trace the body of a woman whose fingers in turn trace her body that the miracle of the mirror is accomplished. Between man and woman love is an act; each torn from self becomes other: what fills the woman in love with wonder is that the languorous passivity of her flesh should be reflected in the male's impetuosity; the narcissistic woman, however, recognizes her enticements but dimly in the man's erected flesh. Between women love is contemplative; caresses are intended less to gain possession of the other than gradually to re-create the self through her; separateness is abolished, there is no struggle, no victory, no defeat; in exact reciprocity each is at once subject and object, sovereign and slave; duality becomes mutuality. Says Colette in *Ces plaisirs:* "The close resemblance gives certitude of pleasure. The lover takes delight in being sure of caressing a body the secrets of which she knows, and whose preferences her own body indicates to her." And Renée Vivien's poem (from *Sortilèges*) expresses the same idea: "Our bodies are made alike . . . Our destiny the same . . . In you I love my child, my darling, and my sister."

This mirroring may assume a maternal cast; the mother who sees herself and projects herself in her daughter often has a sexual attachment for her; she has in common with the lesbian the longing to protect and cradle a soft carnal object in her arms. Colette brings out this analogy when she writes in *Vrilles de la vigne* as follows: "You will delight me, bending over me, when, with your eyes filled with maternal concern, you seek in your passionate one the child you have not borne"; and Renée Vivien enlarges on the same sentiment in another of her poems: ". . . And my arms were made the better to shelter you . . . Like a warm cradle where you shall find repose."

In all love—sexual or maternal—exist at once selfishness and generosity, desire to possess the other and to give the other all; but the mother and the lesbian are similar especially in the degree to which both are narcissistic, enamored respectively in the child or the woman friend, each of her own projection or reflection.

But narcissism—like the mother fixation—does not always lead to homosexuality, as is proved, for example, in the case of Marie Bashkirtsev, in whose writings no trace of affection for women is to be found. Cerebral rather than sensual, and extremely conceited, she dreamed from childhood of being highly regarded by men: she was interested only in what could add to her renown. A woman who idolizes herself alone and whose aim is success in general is incapable of a warm attachment to other women; she sees in them only enemies and rivals.

The truth is that there is never a single determining factor; it is always a matter of a choice, arrived at in a complex total situation and based upon a free decision; no sexual fate governs the life of the individual woman: her type of eroticism, on the contrary, expresses her general outlook on life.

Environmental circumstances, however, have a considerable influence on the choice. Today the two sexes still live largely separated lives: in boarding schools and seminaries for young women the transition from intimacy to sexuality is rapid; lesbians are far less numerous in environments where the association of girls and boys facilitates heterosexual experiences. Many women who are employed in workshops and offices, surrounded by women, and who see little of men, will tend to form amorous friendships with females: they will find it materially and morally simple to associate their lives. The absence or difficulty of heterosexual contacts will doom them to inversion. It is hard to draw the line between resignation and predilection: a woman can devote herself to women because man has disappointed her, but sometimes man has disappointed her because in him she was really seeking a woman.

NOTES

1. *La Méthode psychanalytique et la doctrine freudienne.*
2. *Psychopathia Sexualis* (English translation, Physicians and Surgeons Book Co., 1931), p. 428.
3. Like the Marschallin and Octavian in Richard Strauss's opera *Der Rosenkavalier.*—Tr.
4. *Studies in the Psychology of Sex*, Vol. II, Part 2, p. 238.
5. As in Dorothy Baker's novel *Trio*, otherwise quite superficial.

MAY E. ROMM: Fetishism and Homosexuality*

A PROFESSIONAL man in his late twenties had a hair fetishism. He was married, had one child, and sought treatment because his difficulties had become too great a burden to his wife. In addition he also suffered from anxieties in his professional and in his social life. Though the patient had achieved relative financial success completely on his own merit, he felt that he was intellectually inferior, and that his success was due to luck rather than to personal accomplishment. Headaches, indigestion, weakness, fatigue and pruritis ani were frequent symptoms. He was slovenly in his dress and habits and had to force himself to observe ordinary bodily hygiene. He indulged in compulsive habits that were obnoxious to him: he picked his nose and ate the secreta; he surreptitiously smeared saliva and nasal secretions on his clothes or on the upholstery of his car; he frequently

* Reprinted from *"Some Dynamics in Fetishism."*

scratched his scalp and face and when scabs formed, he picked them off and put them in his mouth.

The patient's immediate problem was his interest in women's hair. The only way in which he could get a satisfactory orgasm was to cut his wife's hair during the forepleasure stage, or at times after intercourse had started. His wife at first submitted to these demands but she became more and more disturbed by the performance and by her subsequent ludicrous appearance. The patient was, moreover, compelled to have his own hair cut several times a week, and looked longingly into the windows of every barber shop he passed, hoping to see a woman having her hair cut. He spent a great deal of time traveling to remote sections of the city to have his hair cut by women barbers. His reaction to having his hair cut was not orgastic; it relieved him of generalized tension. He indulged almost daily in masturbation during which he fantasied he was cutting a woman's hair.

He had a specification for the woman's coiffure: bangs covering the forehead, the back hair falling to the shoulders, soft and feminine. Magazine pictures of women so coiffured were cut out and saved. He made progressive demands that his wife keep changing her coiffure to make it conform to his fetishistic ideal. He even suggested to his feminine employees that they wear their hair in this fashion. Occasionally his masturbatory fantasies centered about the cutting of men's hair.

The patient's earliest recollection was of his mother washing her hair. When drying her hair in the sun she would throw it over her face. He was both fascinated and horrified at not being able to see her face, and relieved when it was again visible. Her hair combings held a great fascination for him. At the age of four he and a playmate cut each other's hair. His mother was indignant, punished him and refused to trim his hair, saying that he would have to remain 'funny' until his hair grew. The patient was heartsick. Shortly thereafter he was caught rubbing mud in a girl's hair and was punished. At the age of five, after attending school for several days, he informed his mother that he wanted to stay at home. The mother insisted that he go, dressed him in a white suit and sent him out of the house. He walked as far as the gate where he had an attack of uncontrollable diarrhea and ran into the house shrieking. His mother considered the diarrhea a symptom of illness, comforted him, bathed him and put him to bed. She was very solicitous and tender toward him for several days. With great emotion the patient said that this was the first time he ever received any real attention or semblance of love from his mother.

Until he was about twelve his mother cut the patient's hair

with a bowl in a Dutch bob fashion so that his forehead was covered with bangs. As he grew older he resented the feminine appearance of his haircut. Although he was ten years old when his sister was born he had a complete amnesia for his mother's pregnancy, and had no recollection of his reaction to his sister until she was three years old and was wearing bangs.

At the age of eleven the patient asked his parents to explain the difference between a boy and a girl. They were embarrassed and evaded the question. Later his older brother told him that a girl is the same in front as a boy is behind. He dated his pruritis ani from that period. At the age of thirteen his father discussed sex with him and told him he must never indulge in masturbation which he said was dangerous and wicked, and he must never get a girl into trouble. The patient took these admonitions seriously and avoided masturbation until the age of nineteen. While he feared venereal disease, he was even more fearful of impregnating a woman. His first sexual experience at twenty-one was with a prostitute much older than himself. He was impotent and reacted with a feeling of shame and inadequacy.

As a young child the patient felt unwanted and unloved. He was fascinated by his mother's hair and was intrigued by his father's wavy hair. He was jealous of a male cousin, two years his senior, who lived with the family and who had what he described as 'beautiful locks'. His own hair was straight and unruly. He recalled that his parents bemoaned the fact that he was the only member of the family whose hair was unattractive. He had great curiosity about his father's pubic hair. He resented the thought of his parents' sexual relationship and either witnessed or visualized the primal scene before he was six.

The patient described his own personality as very passive; he was fearful of people and was always willing to give much more than he expected in return. His choice of girls during his late teens and early twenties indicated that he sought out those who were aggressive and who had beautiful blonde hair. Several women with whom he had sexual relations admitted to him that they were essentially homosexual. This information disturbed him very little, if at all. His libidinal attention was centered on their hair. The knowledge that the woman he courted lacked interest in heterosexuality relieved him of the responsibility of gratifying her sexually.

He seemed to be very considerate, kind and generous toward his wife, but when cutting her hair he occasionally had the fantasy of gouging out pieces of her scalp. On one occasion he resented what he considered her dominance and asked if she would let him shave her head. When she refused, he thought how nice it would be if he could shave her head and his own and his hair would grow faster; in that way he could get ahead of her. As his compulsion to cut his wife's hair closer and closer to the scalp became more intense, he became more sensitive about her appearance and was angry that she was not ingenious in utilizing a hat or a bandana to cover her head. She retorted that as long as he mutilated her he should be exposed to the embarrassment of her appearance.

After the patient had been in analysis three months, he stated that since fetishism was an illness he felt justified in indulging it until he was cured; his acceptance of treatment was proof of his good faith in wanting to be cured. As this was obviously an attempt to coerce the analyst into approving the patient's mutilation of his wife, he was told that he would not get censure or approval or permission from the analyst and that he was trying to use the analysis as his superego. He reacted with apparent calm and understanding. The following day he came completely shaved. He had been under extreme tension the night before and had used a dozen razor blades to shave every bit of hair from his scalp and body, a procedure which occupied most of the night. This was a reaction to his wife's refusal to let him clip her hair close to the scalp. He had a feeling that both the analyst and his wife were against him. As he left the analyst's office, he went to the lavatory and collapsed. He dragged himself into the waiting room, pale, tremulous, perspiring profusely. He was brought back to the office, helped to the couch and, after being given some water, regained his composure and was able to go home. The following day his associations disclosed that he wanted to make sure that no matter what he did he would not be dismissed from analysis. His collapse had been an unconscious somatic reaction which, in addition to self-punishment for his misdeed, had the secondary gain of playing on the sympathy of the analyst, as he had previously played on the sympathy of his mother when she forced him to start for school. He wanted from the analyst the same love and tenderness he had received from his mother after the attack of diarrhea. There was a curious lack of concern about his ludicrous and rather frightening appearance which lasted for weeks. He registered an equanimity occasionally seen in patients who have survived a serious surgical procedure.

The patient spent hours trying to fathom what he regarded as his passivity and cowardice. He could not reconcile it with the fact that at the age of eighteen he courted danger to such an extent that he became a hero in the eyes of the group with whom he traveled.

He recalled that at fourteen, while taking a walk with a

girl of the same age, he insisted on clipping a lock of her hair, explaining that he was demonstrating how the barber should cut her hair. During adolescence he occasionally had his hair cut as frequently as three times a day. His pleasure was marred when the barber used clippers; the thrill was in the sensation he experienced as the scissors cut his hair. It was obvious that the haircutting had an exhibitionistic element for, whenever his hair was cut so close to the head that he was ashamed of his appearance, he would invariably leave his hat somewhere.

For weeks after he had shaved his head the patient had difficulty in attaining an emission. Until his hair grew, he was occasionally impotent. He laughingly said that even his unconscious could not accept the shaving of his head; like Samson, he was devoid of power when his hair was cut off. He said he wanted to be a tower of strength, but feared to be strong lest he use it as a weapon against others.

Although the patient complained that he left a great many things undone and was tortured by his inefficiency, he actually had a desire and a need to bring things to completion. He dreamed he was on top of a hill with two other men, one of whom whipped out a pistol and shot and killed the other. The patient was a bystander among a group of twelve people. In his associations he was the man who did the shooting and the man who was shot. The number twelve, being a dozen, represented completion. In shooting a man he defied the authority represented by his father whom he dreaded. By being killed he punished himself for having shaved his head and for his death wishes. He tried to settle all scores in the one dream.

The patient related that frequently during intercourse he removed some of his wife's vaginal secretion and surreptitiously put it in her hair. He asked whether he was displacing her genitals to her scalp. After a second episode of shaving himself—his chest axillary and pubic hair—he masturbated with a sense of feeling clean. He recalled how disgusted he was as a child when he saw the combings of his mother's hair accumulated in a container. He said that statues of females without pubic hair gave him the impression of emasculated males. For him, sex and dirt were synonymous. Removing hair from one's body was equivalent to cleanliness, although it also represented castration.

After a scene with his wife when she cried after permitting him to cut her hair, he dreamed he saw his mother nude with her hair falling below her shoulders, a repetitive dream from the age of fourteen. The patient saw a close resemblance in his wife's and his mother's physical appearance. He asked whether in cutting his wife's hair he was attempting to take his mother out of his wife.

Since until the age of fourteen he had had a Dutch bob and had always wanted his wife to have a similar one, he wondered whether he did not seek a wife in his own image. He connected his narcissism with extreme fear of homosexuality.

During the period in which the fetish was dominant, the patient's demands on his wife became bolder. He finally asked if she would permit him to shave her head, and then would wear a wig. She refused to answer that request and the patient became so tense he burst into tears. Extremely angry, he accused her of dominating and emasculating him. He was amazed that he, who had always considered himself so meek and gentle, suddenly fantasied he was having a fight with his wife in which he seized her, pinned her down on the bed and hacked at her hair. She wriggled out of his grasp, grabbed his testicles and tried to tear them off. He believed this fantasy demonstrated how insecure and ambivalent he was. In an attempt to relieve his severe tension he struggled between the wish to be a dominant male, aggressive and sadistic toward his wife, and the desire to give up his masculinity, be castrated by his wife and thus return to a state of impotence, passivity and helplessness. He needed proof that people loved him, and wanted to feel he could do anything he wished to his wife, particularly what was unacceptable to her, and that she would still love him. On one occasion when his wife consented to let him cut her hair, he went to the bathroom to get the scissors and almost fainted. He was frightened at the thought of what he could do with scissors.

While complaining that the analysis was interfering with his freedom to indulge his fetishism, the patient suddenly became angry and said he did not want to be dependent on the analyst or anyone else, but wanted to cure himself. He stated that he masturbated in order not to depend on another for sexual gratification. He never wanted a partner in business because he wished to control every situation. He had started the practice of law with his father but shortly thereafter put his father on an allowance and dismissed him. He was afraid to trust anyone.

The patient now began to be aware of his father's influence in his life. He recalled his overwhelming curiosity about his father's body, and his sexual excitement when his father took him into his bed for Sunday naps. He became irate as he speculated about the possibility that his father had fondled him provocatively, trying desperately to displace the blame to his father.

At times the patient would fantasy during masturbation that he was able to take his penis in his mouth and in so doing he would be a complete circle. At this period he dreamed that he was looking at his body and discovered he had breasts like a woman and male genitals. He discussed his envy of women who had the exclusive function of conception and childbirth. He wanted to be a fusion of male and female. In a dream his penis was in his pocket and he could attach it to his body at will; he imagined how frightened his wife would be if she were to see his body without his genitals: he would then have her in his power—he could be a male and grant her intercourse or he could be a female and give her nothing.

He frequently dreamed of his wife as a monster towering over him, and would waken frightened. He dreamed that his wife came into the room with her hair hanging below her shoulders, like his mother's hair in his adolescent dream. As she leaned over him he had an orgasm. Dreams of castration were often followed by dreams wherein his penis was a destructive weapon which could injure the woman by hurting or poisoning her and needed sterilization and medical attention to make it harmless. He associated to this the fantasy that if he could obtain sexual gratification by cutting a woman's hair, he could save her from the possible harm which might occur if they had intercourse.

When the patient reported several dreams in which he was interested in a woman's hair and his own feet, he noted that he kept his attention as far as possible from the region of the genitals. He wondered why he had not developed a shoe fetishism. Dreams of intense aggression, in which he saw people run over and mutilated, recalled memories of sadistic acts, as a ten-year-old child, of killing rabbits and cats.

While he had a very sensitive need for his wife's sexual compliance, all desire left him whenever his wife indicated any sexual drive. After a period of considerable improvement, the patient had a relapse into fetishistic domination which he believed was a reaction to his recently increased aggression. He said that if he shaved his head he would be like a helpless baby whom his mother, his wife and the analyst would love: in pictures of the Madonna and Child, the Child, he said, is always hairless. This identification with the Christ Child gave him a virgin mother, a denial that she ever had intercourse with his father. This led to the memory of a primal scene he vaguely recalled witnessing, when he was about six years old, which reactivated the pain he felt then at the thought of his mother being sexually violated by his father. He remembered an impulse in childhood to become a priest. The Greek priest, in his cassock with his hair flowing over his shoulders, represented to him a neuter person, celibate and bisexual. His distrust of everyone he attributed mostly to the disappointment consequent to his discovery of the sexual relationship between his parents. The mother, who was supposed to be an angel, turned out to be human and carnal. His father, who should have been tender toward him, displayed cruelty when he was six years old by pinning him down and forcing him to swallow castor oil, while his mother, who should have protected him, did not interfere. He considered his marriage a failure because his wife would not accede to all his unreasonable demands. The analyst failed him because he was only one among her other patients. All that was left to him was masturbation during which his fantasy could create anything he wanted. He could not trust himself because, while he wanted to be a kind and good person, his fantasies were sadistic. He was despondent.

The patient's more permanent improvement began after he released a great deal of aggression toward his father whom he represented in dreams as a vicious dog, a dangerous lion and a cruel person. He dreamed that a thief came to steal his wife's fur coat which he had bought her recently. The patient had a gun in his hand and shot the thief. He associated the fur coat with hair. He felt that the thief was either his father who stole his mother from him, or the analyst who was trying to cure him and so was taking his fetish away from him. This was followed by a dream in which the patient went to a jewelry store and asked the clerk to exchange a small round watch for an elongated man's watch. The clerk was very pleasant to him and said he would exchange it, but the employer, a big, mean man, was very angry and forbade the exchange. There was a violent quarrel between the employer and the patient, but the clerk handed him the watch he wanted. As he was leaving the shop he was attacked by a curly-haired black dog from which he escaped by skilfully slamming the door in the dog's face. The kind, understanding clerk represented the analyst; the employer and the dog, his father who frightened him about sex and forbade him any pleasure. The round watch was his femininity, the long watch his penis. His father castrated him and insisted that he be a passive, feminine person. The analyst restored his masculinity.

His scoptophilia as a child included an interest in looking at his feces as well as his great need to see the genitals of both parents. For years he had the impression, when he was dissatisfied with himself, that his feces had a putrid odor. He connected his anger with putrefaction. Whenever he felt socially, financially or sexually insecure, he developed flatulence and diarrhea. He not only felt physically relieved by copious evacuations, but the fetid odor and the sound of expelling flatus produced in him a feeling of pleasure and triumph which seemed to dissipate his anxiety.

His guilt was intense for his curiosity about his parents' sexual relationship. He dreamed of seeing his father making a speech to an audience. Suddenly he noticed that his father's penis was exposed. He was delighted to see his father humiliated and wondered whether he should tell him how ludicrous he appeared but decided against it. The dream gratified the infantile wish to see his father's penis, and he realized that his intense hatred of his father had underneath it a great desire to love him and be loved by him in return. He felt that if he had had a sympathetic father he would have been able to have more friends; that he would not have rebelled so much against authority, and that he would neither have had to cringe nor want to dominate.

After spending an afternoon with his parents, he dreamed of experiencing great pleasure in the anticipation of his mother getting into bed with him. She climbed into his bed, and he was intrigued by her long flowing hair. There was a great deal of love-making (forepleasure). Suddenly he heard someone coming. He jumped up to investigate and discovered a man with a flashlight coming up the stairs. The patient felt paralyzed with fear but hailed the man. The intruder, with a smile on his face, walked past the patient into the bathroom and began unscrewing parts of the toilet.

The woman in the dream was both his mother and his wife. The man with the flashlight represented his father. After the initial shock and fear he felt that his snooping father was no longer a threat to him since the woman in bed with him was his wife. The toilet was associated with his anality and homosexuality which were connected with the relationship to his father.

After several years of analysis, this patient achieved a genital relationship with his wife, indulging in masturbation only when his wife was menstruating. He developed an adequate self-esteem, his relationship with his friends, family and employees becoming much freer and more pleasurable. He became so much more productive in his work that his income came to exceed his greatest expectations. On rare occasions, when under environmental stress, he had fetishistic fantasies with no impulse to act them out. He retained a more than usual interest in his wife's hairdress.

CONCLUSIONS

The development of this patient's fetishism began before the age of four. It was directly connected with his interest in his mother's hair. His mother fostered his interest in hair by cutting his hair herself until puberty. As an infant his fascination with his mother's hair when, in drying it, it covered her face was apparently accompanied by both pleasure and fear: when her hair

covered her face he felt a sense of loss; when her face was uncovered, he was reassured. At four, he was scolded and ridiculed
for cutting his hair in a game played with another child. He
realized that cutting one's own or another's hair could represent
pleasurable excitement and punishment for either or both parties
involved: his sadomasochistic reaction was established. Cutting
his own hair represented castration, the neuter gender, and relig-
iosity, as exemplified by the shaved crown of the priest, and the
bald head of the Christ Child. When he identified himself with
the latter he denied his own and his parents' sexuality. He was
then born exclusively of the mother, and the father did not exist.
His infantile aggression toward his father was unresolved from
early childhood, partially a projection of his ambivalence deriving
from his unresolved erotic relationship with him. Failing to
sublimate it, he repressed all tender feelings for him, rationalizing
his alienation as a rejection; hence, during the first year of his
analysis he estimated his father's rôle in his life as unimportant,
believing that his father had no tender emotion toward him, and
had used him to gratify his sadistic aggression. Unable to identify
himself with his father and thus share the mother's love, he
wanted his mother exclusively for himself. His repetitive dream
of his nude mother coming into his room with her hair flowing
over her shoulders excluded the father. In the last dream reported,
his mother and his wife are almost equivalent. It is interesting to
note, in relegating his father to the bathroom, that he frequently
described his father's character as penurious (anal).

In his unsuccessful attempts to make a genital sexual
adaptation, his fixation to his mother had to be denied to avoid
the incest taboo, and to permit sexual function. This compromise
expressed itself in requiring bangs which represented masculinity
and was a defense from incest; the flowing, back hair, which was
a feminine equivalent, defended him from homosexuality. This
conflict created severe tension which resulted in aggression and
sadism toward his love object. He attempted to solve this problem
by removing all hair from the woman. When he had the impulse
to clip or shave his wife's hair, and had sadistic fantasies of
gouging out pieces of her scalp, he forestalled the sadistic and
criminal trend by displacing the aggression to himself, by shaving
his own head and body, thus castrating himself, avoiding the
aggression toward his wife, and sufficiently punishing himself to
neutralize his guilt. The secondary gain was the expectation of
sympathy from the analyst who then represented his mother.

In the course of his analysis, whenever the analyst represented a good, indulgent love object, his relationship toward his
wife, parents and friends was tolerant and tender; whenever the

analyst became the forbidding parental authority, the patient's tension mounted and his fetishistic needs became intensified. With analysis of the transference, his ego became stronger, and he assumed responsibility for his behavior and began functioning on an adult object relationship.

Might such an intense acting out as the shaving of the patient's body and his subsequent collapse have been defenses against homicidal drives, fears of suicide, or a psychotic episode? Did the patient act out suicide or a psychosis to avoid an aggressive attack? Was his collapse a reaction to the unconscious realization of what the act of shaving his entire body represented? Could this episode have been avoided by a different method of analytic technique? Was his ego too weak to face the interpretation that, like a child, he wanted the analyst, whom he identified with a parental figure, to grant him permission to indulge his fetishistic cravings? It is obvious that he felt rejected and unloved by the analyst. He felt compelled to defy her and then react with guilt and a need for self-punishment.

The patient's homosexual drive exerted sufficient pressure to find expression in masturbatory fantasies, anal itching, anger toward and emotional rejection of his father, and in a strong attachment to a male friend. By seeking in the female a combination of masculine and feminine, his ego strove to avoid both homosexuality and incest.[1] He revealed that haircutting represented two wishes—to cut off the woman's hair and to discover that she did not have a penis; also to cut off her hair in the hope that he might find the penis.[2] Fearing both, he would frequently withdraw from relationships with women and indulge in intensive masturbation, seeking reassurance against castration in the tactile sensation. He repeatedly emphasized his scoptophilia in regard to his own feces and his father's genitals, among his memories of childhood. After he dreamed during analysis about seeing his father's genitals, masturbation began to lose its compulsive character.

Since the prognosis in severe perversions is guarded, the degree of integration of this patient's personality is gratifying. The analysis was a long one; six hundred and sixty-two hours over a period of six years with several purposeful interruptions which were helpful to him. These 'vacations from analysis', as the patient termed them, occurred in the last two years of treatment when, while maintaining the improvement he had made, he developed resistances that made his analysis unproductive. It developed that these were resistances to awareness of homosexual feelings and fantasies about his father. He would rationalize that he was functioning adequately and could maintain himself without further help. After several months, he would on his own initiative resume the analysis with increased impetus and productivity. His fear of rejection was dissolved by the analyst's readiness to resume with him when he indicated his desire for further help. On his return he invariably concentrated on his relationship with his father and his fear of homosexuality. As this homosexuality was analyzed, he realized how he had isolated himself from relationships which he thought might involve tender emotions. His preference for bisexuality became clear to him and with this clarification many of his defenses dissolved. The psychological energy which went into his projective defenses became available for constructive activity.

NOTES

1. Freud: *Three Contributions to the Theory of Sex*. New York: Nervous and Mental Disease Monographs, 1930.
2. Payne, S. M.: *Some Observations on the Ego Development of the Fetishist*. Int. J. Psa., XX, 1939, pp. 161–170.

PETRONIUS: The Satyricon*

WHILE I WAS in Asia on business, I was staying at a private home in Pergamum. During my pleasant stay there I enjoyed most comfortable accommodations and cultural surroundings. In addition, my host had a son of remarkable beauty. Naturally, I got the idea of becoming the boy's lover without the knowledge of his father. Whenever, at dinner, the subject of pederasty came up I feigned being vehemently scandalized and claimed that I did not want to even hear such obscene talk. The result was that everyone at the table, the boy's mother above all, looked upon me as a man of profound philosophical virtue. I assumed the role of protector of the boy lest any seducers should enter the home. I led him to the gymnasium, I supervised his studies, I became his teacher in studies and in virtue.

One day we were resting in the dining room. Because of excessive celebration on the holiday we didn't even have strength to go upstairs to our bedrooms. Somewheres around midnight I noticed that the boy was still awake. In subdued tones I uttered a prayer to Venus "O goddess," I said, "if I can only kiss this boy and he does not notice it I will give him a pair of doves tomor-

* Freely translated by Ed.

row." The boy heard the value I put on this pleasure and started to snore. I drew close to the pretender and stole a few kisses. I was quite pleased with this beginning. Early the next morning I got up, I obtained the pair of doves and brought them back to the expectant boy. Thus was my vow fulfilled.

The next night the situation was similar. But this time I changed my prayer. "O goddess, if I may embrace this boy with a wandering hand and he does not feel it I will give him two superb fighting cocks." When he heard this the boy got closer to me. I think he was afraid that I might fall asleep. I quickly indulged him and enjoyed the pleasures of his whole body—I stopped before the supreme culmination. The next day I made him overjoyed with the gifts I had vowed.

On the third night I had a further opportunity. I got up and softly spoke to the boy who was scarcely asleep. "Immortal gods, if I may have the fullest and most desired relations with this sleeping boy, I will give him tomorrow the finest Macedonian horse in return for this happiness. But only if he doesn't feel anything." The boy never slept so soundly. First, I embraced his milk-white body and kissed him passionately and finally I achieved the climax of my wishes. He waited for me the next day in his room as was his wont. It's a good bit easier, you know, to buy doves and fighting cocks than to buy a horse. And furthermore, I was somewhat afraid that my extravagance might appear suspicious. I took a walk for a few hours and when I came back it was with nothing more than a kiss for the boy. He embraced me while he looked around. "Where's the horse, sir?" he said.

Although for the time being this shut the door on my pleasures, I did get my opportunity again. A few days later, a similar situation arose. When I knew that his father was asleep, I asked the boy to resume relations with me. I said all the things that frustrated love dictates. He was angry. All he said was: "You either go to sleep or I'll tell my father." There's nothing so difficult, however, that somebody with desires like mine can't overcome. When he said, "I'll wake my father" I simply went over and took my pleasure from him. He didn't resist very much. Evidently he wasn't displeased at my advances. He did complain that he had been deceived and that he had become the laughing-stock of his friends (apparently he had boasted about my kindness). "I'm not like you" he said. "To prove it, you can do it again if you want." So I took my pleasure with him again, at his invitation, and soon fell asleep. The boy was not satisfied with this repeat performance. So he woke me from my sleep and asked "Wouldn't you like to do something?" His suggestion was in no way unwelcome. With tremendous exertion on my part I gave the boy what he wanted. And exhausted I fell asleep again. Scarcely an hour went by before he began to poke me. "Why don't we do it again," he said. I was totally annoyed at his waking me and I used his own words on him. "You either go to sleep or I'll tell your father on you."

OSCAR WILDE: Letter to Lord Alfred Douglas

[January–March 1897]   *H.M. Prison, Reading*
DEAR BOSIE, After long and fruitless waiting I have determined to write to you myself, as much for your sake as for mine, as I would not like to think that I had passed through two long years of imprisonment without ever having received a single line from you, or any news or message even, except such as gave me pain.

Our ill-fated and most lamentable friendship has ended in ruin and public infamy for me, yet the memory of our ancient affection is often with me, and the thought that loathing, bitterness and contempt should for ever take that place in my heart once held by love is very sad to me: and you yourself will, I think, feel in your heart that to write to me as I lie in the loneliness of prison-life is better than to publish my letters without my permission or to dedicate poems to me unasked, though the world will know nothing of whatever words of grief or passion, of remorse or indifference you may choose to send as your answer or your appeal.

I have no doubt that in this letter in which I have to write of your life and of mine, of the past and of the future, of sweet things changed to bitterness and of bitter things that may be turned into joy, there will be much that will wound your vanity to the quick. If it prove so, read the letter over and over again till it kills your vanity. If you find in it something of which you feel that you are unjustly accused, remember that one should be thankful that there is any fault of which one can be unjustly accused. If there be in it one single passage that brings tears to your eyes, weep as we weep in prison where the day no less than the night is set apart for tears. It is the only thing that can save you. If you go complaining to your mother, as you did with reference to the scorn of you I displayed in my letter to Robbie, so that she may flatter and soothe you back into self-complacency or conceit, you will be completely lost. If you find one false excuse for yourself, you will soon find a hundred, and be just what you were before. Do you still say, as you said to Robbie in your answer, that I *"attribute unworthy motives"* to you? Ah! you had no motives in life. You had appetites merely. A motive is an intellectual aim. That you were *"very young"* when our friendship began? Your defect was not that you knew so little about life, but that you knew so much. The morning dawn of boyhood with its delicate bloom, its clear pure light, its joy of innocence and expectation you had left far behind. With very swift and running feet you had passed from Romance to Realism. The gutter and the things that live in it had begun to fascinate you. That was the origin of the trouble in which you sought my aid, and I, so unwisely according to the wisdom of this world, out of pity and kindness gave it to you. You must read this letter right through, though each word may become to you as the fire or knife of the surgeon that makes the delicate flesh burn or bleed. Remember that the fool in the eyes of the gods and the fool in the eyes of man are very different. One who is entirely ignorant of the modes of Art in its revolution or the moods of thought in its progress, of the pomp of the Latin line or the richer music of the vowelled Greek, of Tuscan sculpture or Elizabethan song may yet be full of the very sweetest wisdom. The real fool, such as the gods mock or mar, is he who does not know himself. I was such a one too long. You have been such a one too long. Be so no more. Do not be afraid. The supreme vice is shallowness. Everything that is realised is right. Remember also that whatever is misery to you to read, is still greater misery to me to set down. To you the Unseen Powers have been very good. They have permitted you to see the strange and tragic shapes of Life as one sees shadows in a crystal. The head of Medusa that turns living men to stone, you have been allowed to look at in a mirror merely. You yourself have walked free among the flowers. From me the beautiful world of colour and motion has been taken away.

I will begin by telling you that I blame myself terribly. As I sit here in this dark cell in convict clothes, a disgraced and ruined man, I blame myself. In the perturbed and fitful nights of anguish, in the long monotonous days of pain, it is myself I blame. I blame myself for allowing an unintellectual friendship, a friendship whose primary aim was not the creation and contemplation of beautiful things, to entirely dominate my life. From the very first there was too wide a gap between us. You had been idle at your school, worse than idle at your university. You did not realise that an artist, and especially such an artist as I am,[1] one, that is to say, the quality of whose work depends on the intensification of personality, requires for the development of his art the companionship of ideas, and intellectual atmosphere, quiet, peace, and solitude. You admired my work when it was finished: you enjoyed the brilliant successes of my first nights, and the brilliant banquets that followed them: you were proud, and quite naturally so, of being the intimate friend of an artist so distinguished: but you could not understand the conditions requisite for the production of artistic work. I am not speaking in phrases of rhetorical exaggeration but in terms of absolute truth to actual fact when I remind you that during the whole time we were together I never wrote one single line. Whether at Torquay, Goring, London, Florence or elsewhere, my life, as long as you were by my side, was entirely sterile and uncreative. And with but few intervals you were, I regret to say, by my side always.

I remember, for instance, in September '93, to select merely one instance out of many, taking a set of chambers, purely in order to work undisturbed, as I had broken my contract with John Hare for whom I had promised to write a play, and who was pressing me on the subject. During the first week you kept away. We had, not unnaturally indeed, differed on the question of the artistic value of your translation of *Salome*, so you contented yourself with sending me foolish letters on the subject. In that week I wrote and completed in every detail, as it was ultimately performed, the first act of *An Ideal Husband*. The second week you returned and my work practically had to be given up. I arrived at St. James's Place every morning at 11.30, in order to have the opportunity of thinking and writing without the interruptions inseparable from my own household, quiet and peaceful as that household was. But the attempt was vain. At twelve o'clock you drove up, and stayed smoking cigarettes and chattering till 1.30, when I had to take you out to luncheon at the Café Royal or the Berkeley. Luncheon with its *liqueurs* lasted usually till 3.30. For an hour you retired to White's. At tea-time you appeared again, and stayed till it was time to dress for dinner. You dined with me either at the Savoy or at Tite Street. We did not separate as a rule till after midnight, as supper at Willis's had to wind up the entrancing day. That was my life for those three months, every single day, except during the four days when you went abroad. I then, of course, had to go over to Calais to fetch you back. For one of my nature and temperament it was a position at once grotesque and tragic.

You surely must realise that now? You must see now that your incapacity of being alone: your nature so exigent in its persistent claim on the attention and time of others: your lack of any power of sustained intellectual concentration: the unfortunate accident—for I like to think it was no more—that you had not yet been able to acquire the "Oxford temper" in intellectual matters, never, I mean, been one who could play gracefully with ideas but had arrived at violence of opinion merely—that all these things,

combined with the fact that your desires and interests were in
Life not in Art, were as destructive to your own progress in culture as they were to my work as an artist? When I compare my
friendship with you to my friendship with such still younger men
as John Gray and Pierre Louÿs I feel ashamed. My real life, my
higher life was with them and such as they.

Of the appalling results of my friendship with you I don't
speak at present. I am thinking merely of its quality while it
lasted. It was intellectually degrading to me. You had the rudiments of an artistic temperament in its germ. But I met you
either too late or too soon, I don't know which. When you were
away I was all right. The moment, in the early December of the
year to which I have been alluding, I had succeeded in inducing
your mother to send you out of England, I collected again the
torn and ravelled web of my imagination, got my life back into
my own hands, and not merely finished the three remaining acts
of *An Ideal Husband*, but conceived and had almost completed
two other plays of a completely different type, the *Florentine
Tragedy* and *La Sainte Courtisane*, when suddenly, unbidden,
unwelcome, and under circumstances fatal to my happiness you
returned. The two works left then imperfect I was unable to take
up again. The mood that created them I could never recover.
You now, having yourself published a volume of verse, will be
able to recognise the truth of everything I have said here.
Whether you can or not it remains as a hideous truth in the very
heart of our friendship. While you were with me you were the
absolute ruin of my Art, and in allowing you to stand persistently
between Art and myself I give to myself shame and blame in the
fullest degree. You couldn't know, you couldn't understand, you
couldn't appreciate. I had no right to expect it of you at all. Your
interests were merely in your meals and moods. Your desires were
simply for amusements, for ordinary or less ordinary pleasures.
They were what your temperament needed, or thought it needed
for the moment. I should have forbidden you my house and my
chambers except when I specially invited you. I blame myself
without reserve for my weakness. It was merely weakness. One
half-hour with Art was always more to me than a cycle with you.
Nothing really at any period of my life was ever of the smallest
importance to me compared with Art. But in the case of an artist,
weakness is nothing less than a crime, when it is a weakness that
paralyses the imagination.

I blame myself again for having allowed you to bring me
to utter and discreditable financial ruin. I remember one morning in the early October of '92 sitting in the yellowing woods at
Bracknell with your mother. At that time I knew very little of

your real nature. I had stayed from a Saturday to Monday with you at Oxford. You had stayed with me at Cromer for ten days and played golf. The conversation turned on you, and your mother began to speak to me about your character. She told me of your two chief faults, your vanity, and your being, as she termed it, *"all wrong about money."* I have a distinct recollection of how I laughed. I had no idea that the first would bring me to prison, and the second to bankruptcy. I thought vanity a sort of graceful flower for a young man to wear; as for extravagance—for I thought she meant no more than extravagance—the virtues of prudence and thrift were not in my own nature or my own race. But before our friendship was one month older I began to see what your mother really meant. Your insistence on a life of reckless profusion: your incessant demands for money: your claim that all your pleasures should be paid for by me whether I was with you or not: brought me after some time into serious monetary difficulties, and what made the extravagances to me at any rate so monotonously uninteresting, as your persistent grasp on my life grew stronger and stronger, was that the money was really spent on little more than the pleasures of eating, drinking, and the like. Now and then it is a joy to have one's table red with wine and roses, but you outstripped all taste and temperance. You demanded without grace and received without thanks. You grew to think that you had a sort of right to live at my expense and in a profuse luxury to which you had never been accustomed, and which for that reason made your appetites all the more keen, and at the end if you lost money gambling in some Algiers Casino you simply telegraphed next morning to me in London to lodge the amount of your losses to your account at your bank, and gave the matter no further thought of any kind.

When I tell you that between the autumn of 1892 and the date of my imprisonment I spent with you and on you more than £5000 in actual money, irrespective of the bills I incurred, you will have some idea of the sort of life on which you insisted. Do you think I exaggerate? My ordinary expenses with you for an ordinary day in London—for luncheon, dinner, supper, amusements, hansoms and the rest of it—ranged from £12 to £20, and the week's expenses were naturally in proportion and ranged from £80 to £130. For our three months at Goring my expenses (rent of course included) were £1340. Step by step with the Bankruptcy Receiver I had to go over every item of my life. It was horrible. *"Plain living and high thinking"*[2] was, of course, an ideal you could not at that time have appreciated, but such extravagance was a disgrace to both of us. One of the most delightful dinners I remember ever having had is one Robbie and I had together in a little Soho café, which cost about as many shillings as my dinners to you used to cost pounds. Out of my dinner with Robbie came the first and best of all my dialogues.[3] Idea, title, treatment, mode, everything was struck out at a 3 franc 50 c. *table-d'hôte*. Out of the reckless dinners with you nothing remains but the memory that too much was eaten and too much was drunk. And my yielding to your demands was bad for you. You know that now. It made you grasping often: at times not a little un-scrupulous: ungracious always. There was on far too many occa-sions too little joy or privilege in being your host. You forgot —I will not say the formal courtesy of thanks, for formal cour-tesies will strain a close friendship—but simply the grace of sweet companionship, the charm of pleasant conversation, that τερπνὸν κακόν as the Greeks called it, and all those gentle humanities that make life lovely, and are an accompaniment to life as music might be, keeping things in tune and filling with melody the harsh or silent places. And though it may seem strange to you that one in the terrible position in which I am situated should find a difference between one disgrace and another, still I frankly admit that the folly of throwing away all this money on you, and letting you squander my fortune to your own hurt as well as to mine, gives to me and in my eyes a note of common profligacy to my Bankruptcy that makes me doubly ashamed of it. I was made for other things.

But most of all I blame myself for the entire ethical deg-radation I allowed you to bring on me. The basis of character is will-power, and my will-power became absolutely subject to yours. It sounds a grotesque thing to say, but it is none the less true. Those incessant scenes that seemed to be almost physically necessary to you, and in which your mind and body grew dis-torted and you became a thing as terrible to look at as to listen to: that dreadful mania you inherit from your father, the mania for writing revolting and loathsome letters: your entire lack of any control over your emotions as displayed in your long resentful moods of sullen silence, no less than in the sudden fits of almost epileptic rage: all these things in reference to which one of my letters to you, left by you lying about at the Savoy or some other hotel and so produced in Court by your father's Counsel, con-tained an entreaty not devoid of pathos, had you at that time been able to recognise pathos either in its elements or its expression:— these, I say, were the origin and causes of my fatal yielding to you in your daily increasing demands. You wore one out. It was the triumph of the smaller over the bigger nature. It was the case of that tyranny of the weak over the strong which somewhere in one of my plays I describe as being "the only tyranny that lasts."[4]

And it was inevitable. In every relation of life with others one has to find some *moyen de vivre*. In your case, one had either to give up to you or to give up. There was no other alternative. Through deep if misplaced affection for you: through great pity for your defects of temper and temperament: through my own proverbial good-nature and Celtic laziness: through an artistic aversion to coarse scenes and ugly words: through that incapacity to bear resentment of any kind which at that time characterised me: through my dislike of seeing life made bitter and uncomely by what to me, with my eyes really fixed on other things, seemed to be mere trifles too pretty for more than a moment's thought or interest—through these reasons, simple as they may sound, I gave up to you always. As a natural result, your claims, your efforts at domination, your exactions grew more and more unreasonable. Your meanest motive, your lowest appetite, your most common passion, became to you laws by which the lives of others were to be guided always, and to which, if necessary, they were to be without scruple sacrificed. Knowing that by making a scene you could always have your way, it was but natural that you should proceed, almost unconsciously I have no doubt, to every excess of vulgar violence. At the end you did not know to what goal you were hurrying, or with what aim in view. Having made your own of my genius, my will-power, and my fortune, you required, in the blindness of an inexhaustible greed, my entire existence. You took it. At the one supremely and tragically critical moment of all my life, just before my lamentable step of beginning my absurd action, on the one side there was your father attacking me with hideous cards left at my club, on the other side there was you attacking me with no less loathsome letters. The letter I received from you on the morning of the day I let you take me down to the Police Court to apply for the ridiculous warrant for your father's arrest was one of the worst you ever wrote, and for the most shameful reason. Between you both I lost my head. My judgment forsook me. Terror took its place. I saw no possible escape, I may say frankly, from either of you. Blindly I staggered as an ox into the shambles. I had made a gigantic psychological error. I had always thought that my giving up to you in small things meant nothing: that when a great moment arrived I could reassert my will-power in its natural superiority. It was not so. At the great moment my will-power completely failed me. In life there is really no small or great thing. All things are of equal value and of equal size. My habit—due to indifference chiefly at first— of giving up to you in everything had become insensibly a real part of my nature. Without my knowing it, it had stereotyped my temperament to one permanent and fatal mood. That is why, in the subtle epilogue to the first edition of his essays, Pater says that "Failure is to form habits."[5] When he said it the dull Oxford people thought the phrase a mere wilful inversion of the somewhat wearisome text of Aristotelian *Ethics,* but there is a wonderful, a terrible truth hidden in it. I had allowed you to sap my strength of character, and to me the formation of a habit had proved to be not Failure merely but Ruin. Ethically you had been even still more destructive to me than you had been artistically.

The warrant once granted, your will of course directed everything. At a time when I should have been in London taking wise counsel, and calmly considering the hideous trap in which I had allowed myself to be caught—the booby-trap as your father calls it to the present day—you insisted on my taking you to Monte Carlo, of all revolting places on God's earth, that all day, and all night as well, you might gamble as long as the Casino remained open. As for me—baccarat having no charms for me—I was left alone outside to myself. You refused to discuss even for five minutes the position to which you and your father had brought me. My business was merely to pay your hotel expenses and your losses. The slightest allusion to the ordeal awaiting me was regarded as a bore. A new brand of champagne that was recommended to us had more interest for you.

On our return to London those of my friends who really desired my welfare implored me to retire abroad, and not to face an impossible trial. You imputed mean motives to them for giving such advice, and cowardice to me for listening to it. You forced me to stay to brazen it out, if possible, in the box by absurd and silly perjuries. At the end, I was of course arrested and your father became the hero of the hour: more indeed than the hero of the hour merely: your family now ranks, strangely enough, with the Immortals: for with that grotesqueness of effect that is as it were a Gothic element in history, and makes Clio the least serious of all the Muses, your father will always live among the kind pure-minded parents of Sunday-school literature, your place is with the Infant Samuel, and in the lowest mire of Malebolge I sit between Gilles de Retz and the Marquis de Sade.

Of course I should have got rid of you. I should have shaken you out of my life as a man shakes from his raiment a thing that has stung him. In the most wonderful of all his plays[6] Æschylus tells us of the great Lord who brings up in his house the lion-cub, the λέοντος ἴνιν, and loves it because it comes bright-eyed to his call and fawns on him for its food: φαιδρωπὸς ποτὶ χεῖρα, σαίνων τε γαστρὸς ἀνάγκαις. And the thing grows up and shows the nature of its race, ἦθος τὸ πρόσθε τοκήων, and destroys the lord and his house and all that he possesses. I feel that I was such a one as he. But my fault was, not that I did not part from you, but that I parted from you far too often. As far as I can make out I ended my friendship with you every three months regularly, and each time that I did so you managed by means of entreaties, telegrams, letters, the interposition of your friends, the interposition of mine, and the like to induce me to allow you back. When at the end of March '93 you left my house at Torquay I had determined never to speak to you again, or to allow you under any circumstances to be with me, so revolting had been the scene you had made the night before your departure. You wrote and telegraphed from Bristol to beg me to forgive you and meet you. Your tutor,[7] who had stayed behind, told me that he thought that at times you were quite irresponsible for what you said and did, and that most, if not all, of the men at Magdalen were of the same opinion. I consented to meet you, and of course I forgave you. On the way up to town you begged me to take you to the Savoy. That was indeed a visit fatal to me. . . .

NOTES

1. Wilde originally wrote "was."
2. Wordsworth, "Sonnet written in London, September 1802."
3. Almost certainly "The Decay of Lying."
4. *A Woman of No Importance*, Act III.
5. In the "Conclusion" to his *Studies in the History of the Renaissance* (1873). The "Conclusion" was omitted from the second edition (1877) but restored in the third (1888), where this sentence is altered to "In a sense it might even be said that our failure is to form habits."
6. *Agamemnon*. The words quoted occur in lines 717–728.
7. Campbell Dodgson.

SAPPHO: To Anactoria

SOME SAY that the fairest thing upon the dark earth is a host of foot-soldiers, and others again a fleet of ships, but for me it is my beloved. And it is easy to make anyone understand this.

When Helen saw the most beautiful of mortals, she chose for best that one, the destroyer of all the house of Troy, and thought not much of children or dear parent but was led astray by love to bestow her heart far off for woman is ever easy to lead astray when she thinks of no account what is near and dear.

Even so, Anactoria, you do not remember, it seems, when she is with you, one the gentle sound of whose footfall I would rather hear and the brightness of whose shining face I would rather see than all the chariots and mail-clad footmen of Lydia.

I know that in this world man cannot have the best yet to pray for a part of what was once shared is better than to forget it.

DJUNA BARNES: Night Watch*

THE STRANGEST "salon" in America was Nora's. Her house was couched in the centre of a mass of tangled grass and weeds. Before it fell into Nora's hands the property had been in the same family two hundred years. It had its own burial ground, and a decaying chapel in which stood in tens and tens mouldering psalm books, laid down some fifty years gone in a flurry of forgiveness and absolution.

It was the "paupers" salon for poets, radicals, beggars, artists, and people in love; for Catholics, Protestants, Brahmins, dabblers in black magic and medicine; all these could be seen sitting about her oak table before the huge fire, Nora listening, her hand on her hound, the firelight throwing her shadow and his high against the wall. Of all that ranting, roaring crew, she alone stood out. The equilibrium of her nature, savage and refined, gave her bridled skull a look of compassion. She was broad and tall, and though her skin was the skin of a child, there could be seen coming, early in her life, the design that was to be the weather-beaten grain of her face, that wood in the work; the tree coming forward in her, an undocumented record of time.

She was known instantly as a Westerner. Looking at her, foreigners remembered stories they had heard of covered wagons; animals going down to drink; children's heads, just as far as the eyes, looking in fright out of small windows, where in the dark another race crouched in ambush; with heavy hems the women becoming large, flattening the fields where they walked; God so ponderous in their minds that they could stamp out the world with him in seven days.

At these incredible meetings one felt that early American history was being re-enacted. The Drummer Boy, Fort Sumter, Lincoln, Booth, all somehow came to mind; Whigs and Tories were in the air; bunting and its stripes and stars, the swarm increasing slowly and accurately on the hive of blue; Boston tea tragedies, carbines, and the sound of a boy's wild calling; Puritan

* Reprinted from *Nightwood*.

feet, long upright in the grave, striking the earth again, walking up and out of their custom; the calk of prayers thrust in the heart. And in the midst of this, Nora.

By temperament Nora was an early Christian; she believed the word. There is a gap in "world pain" through which the singular falls continually and forever; a body falling in observable space, deprived of the privacy of disappearance; as if privacy, moving relentlessly away, by the very sustaining power of its withdrawal kept the body eternally moving downward, but in one place, and perpetually before the eye. Such a singular was Nora. There was some derangement in her equilibrium that kept her immune from her own descent.

Nora had the face of all people who love the people—a face that would be evil when she found out that to love without criticism is to be betrayed. Nora robbed herself for everyone; incapable of giving herself warning, she was continually turning about to find herself diminished. Wandering people the world over found her profitable in that she could be sold for a price forever, for she carried her betrayal money in her own pocket.

Those who love everything are despised by everything, as those who love a city, in its profoundest sense, become the shame of that city, the *détraqués*, the paupers; their good is incommunicable, outwitted, being the rudiment of a life that has developed, as in man's body are found evidences of lost needs. This condition had struck even into Nora's house; it spoke in her guests, in her ruined gardens where she had been wax in every work of nature.

Whenever she was met, at the opera, at a play, sitting alone and apart, the programme face down on her knee, one would discover in her eyes, large, protruding and clear, that mirrorless look of polished metals which report not so much the object as the movement of the object. As the surface of a gun's barrel, reflecting a scene, will add to the image the portent of its construction, so her eyes contracted and fortified the play before her in her own unconscious terms. One sensed in the way she held her head that her ears were recording Wagner or Scarlatti, Chopin, Palestrina, or the lighter songs of the Viennese school, in a smaller but more intense orchestration.

And she was the only woman of the last century who could go up a hill with the Seventh Day Adventists and confound the seventh day—with a muscle in her heart so passionate that she made the seventh day immediate. Her fellow worshippers believed in that day and the end of the world out of a bewildered entanglement with the six days preceding it; Nora believed for the beauty of that day alone. She was by fate one of those people who are born unprovided for, except in the provision of herself.

One missed in her a sense of humour. Her smile was quick and definite, but disengaged. She chuckled now and again at a joke, but it was the amused grim chuckle of a person who looks up to discover that they have coincided with the needs of nature in a bird.

Cynicism, laughter, the second husk into which the shucked man crawls, she seemed to know little or nothing about. She was one of those deviations by which man thinks to reconstruct himself.

To "confess" to her was an act even more secret than the communication provided by a priest. There was no ignominy in her; she recorded without reproach or accusation, being shorn of self-reproach or self-accusation. This drew people to her and frightened them; they could neither insult nor hold anything against her, though it embittered them to have to take back injustice that in her found no foothold. In court she would have been impossible; no one would have been hanged, reproached or forgiven because no one would have been "accused." The world and its history were to Nora like a ship in a bottle; she herself was outside and unidentified, endlessly embroiled in a preoccupation without a problem.

Then she met Robin. The Denckman circus, which she kept in touch with even when she was not working with it (some of its people were visitors to her house), came into New York in the fall of 1923. Nora went alone. She came into the circle of the ring, taking her place in the front row.

Clowns in red, white and yellow, with the traditional smears on their faces, were rolling over the sawdust, as if they were in the belly of a great mother where they was yet room to play. A black horse, standing on trembling hind legs that shook in apprehension of the raised front hooves, his beautiful ribboned head pointed down and toward the trainer's whip, pranced slowly, the foreshanks flickering to the whip. Tiny dogs ran about trying to look like horses, then in came the elephants.

A girl sitting beside Nora took out a cigarette and lit it; her hands shook and Nora turned to look at her; she looked at her suddenly because the animals, going around and around the ring, all but climbed over at that point. They did not seem to see the girl, but as their dusty eyes moved past, the orbit of their light seemed to turn on her. At that moment Nora turned.

The great cage for the lions had been set up, and the lions were walking up and out of their small strong boxes into the arena. Ponderous and furred they came, their tails laid down across the floor, dragging and heavy, making the air seem full of withheld strength. Then as one powerful lioness came to the turn of the bars, exactly opposite the girl, she turned her furious great head with its yellow eyes afire and went down, her paws thrust through the bars and, as she regarded the girl, as if a river were falling behind impassable heat, her eyes flowed in tears that never reached the surface. At that the girl rose straight up. Nora took her hand. "Let's get out of here!" the girl said, and still holding her hand Nora took her out.

In the lobby Nora said, "My name is Nora Flood," and she waited. After a pause the girl said, "I'm Robin Vote." She looked about her distractedly. "I don't want to be here." But it was all she said; she did not explain where she wished to be.

She stayed with Nora until the mid-winter. Two spirits were working in her, love and anonymity. Yet they were so "haunted" of each other that separation was impossible.

Nora closed her house. They travelled from Munich, Vienna and Budapest into Paris. Robin told only a little of her life, but she kept repeating in one way or another her wish for a home, as if she were afraid she would be lost again, as if she were aware, without conscious knowledge, that she belonged to Nora, and that if Nora did not make it permanent by her own strength, she would forget.

Nora bought an apartment in the *rue du Cherche-Midi*. Robin had chosen it. Looking from the long windows one saw a fountain figure, a tall granite woman bending forward with lifted head; one hand was held over the pelvic round as if to warn a child who goes incautiously.

In the passsage of their lives together every object in the garden, every item in the house, every word they spoke, attested to their mutual love, the combining of their humours. There were circus chairs, wooden horses bought from a ring of an old merry-go-round, venetian chandeliers from the Flea Fair, stage-drops from Munich, cherubim from Vienna, ecclesiastical hangings from Rome, a spinet from England, and a miscellaneous collection of music boxes from many countries; such was the museum of their encounter, as Felix's hearsay house had been testimony of the age when his father had lived with his mother.

When the time came that Nora was alone most of the night and part of the day, she suffered from the personality of the house, the punishment of those who collect their lives together. Unconsciously at first, she went about disturbing nothing; then she became aware that her soft and careful movements were the outcome of an unreasoning fear—if she disarranged anything Robin might become confused—might lose the scent of home.

Love becomes the deposit of the heart, analogous in all

degrees to the "findings" in a tomb. As in one will be charted the taken place of the body, the raiment, the utensils necessary to its other life, so in the heart of the lover will be traced, as an indelible shadow, that which he loves. In Nora's heart lay the fossil of Robin, intaglio of her identity, and about it for its maintenance ran Nora's blood. Thus the body of Robin could never be unloved, corrupt or put away. Robin was now beyond timely changes, except in the blood that animated her. That she could be spilled of this fixed the walking image of Robin in appalling apprehension on Nora's mind—Robin alone, crossing streets, in danger. Her mind became so transfixed that, by the agency of her fear, Robin seemed enormous and polarized, all catastrophes ran toward her, the magnetized predicament; and crying out, Nora would wake from sleep, going back through the tide of dreams into which her anxiety had thrown her, taking the body of Robin down with her into it, as the ground things take the corpse, with minute persistence, down into the earth, leaving a pattern of it on the grass, as if they stitched as they descended.

Yes now, when they were alone and happy, apart from the world in their appreciation of the world, there entered with Robin a company unaware. Sometimes it rang clear in the songs she sang, sometimes Italian, sometimes French or German, songs of the people, debased and haunting, songs that Nora had never heard before, or that she had never heard in company with Robin. When the cadence changed, when it was repeated on a lower key, she knew that Robin was singing of a life that she herself had no part in; snatches of harmony as tell-tale as the possessions of a traveller from a foreign land; songs like a practised whore who turns away from no one but the one who loves her. Sometimes Nora would sing them after Robin, with the trepidation of a foreigner repeating words in an unknown tongue, uncertain of what they may mean. Sometimes unable to endure the melody that told so much and so little, she would interrupt Robin with a question. Yet more distressing would be the moment when, after a pause, the song would be taken up again from an inner room where Robin, unseen, gave back an echo of her unknown life more nearly tuned to its origin. Often the song would stop altogether, until unthinking, just as she was leaving the house, Robin would break out again in anticipation, changing the sound from a reminiscence to an expectation.

Yet sometimes, going about the house, in passing each other, they would fall into an agonized embrace, looking into each other's face, their two heads in their four hands, so strained together that the space that divided them seemed to be thrusting them apart. Sometimes in these moments of insurmountable grief

Robin would make some movement, use a peculiar turn of phrase not habitual to her, innocent of the betrayal, by which Nora was informed that Robin had come from a world to which she would return. To keep her (in Robin there was this tragic longing to be kept, knowing herself astray) Nora knew now that there was no way but death. In death Robin would belong to her. Death went with them, together and alone; and with the torment and catastrophe, thoughts of resurrection, the second duel.

Looking out into the fading sun of the winter sky, against which a little tower rose just outside the bedroom window, Nora would tabulate by the sounds of Robin dressing the exact progress of her toilet; chimes of cosmetic bottles and cream jars; the faint perfume of hair heated under the electric curlers; seeing in her mind the changing direction taken by the curls that hung on Robin's forehead, turning back from the low crown to fall in upward curves to the nape of the neck, the flat uncurved back head that spoke of some awful silence. Half narcoticized by the sounds and the knowledge that this was in preparation for departure, Nora spoke to herself: "In the resurrection, when we come up looking backward at each other, I shall know you only of all that company. My ear shall turn in the socket of my head; my eyeballs loosened where I am the whirlwind about that cashed expense, my foot stubborn on the cast of your grave." In the doorway Robin stood. "Don't wait for me," she said.

In the years that they lived together, the departures of Robin became slowly increasing rhythm. At first Nora went with Robin; but as time passed, realizing that a growing tension was in Robin, unable to endure the knowledge that she was in the way or forgotten, seeing Robin go from table to table, from drink to drink, from person to person, realizing that if she herself were not there Robin might return to her as the one who, out of all the turbulent night, had not been lived through, Nora stayed at home, lying awake or sleeping. Robin's absence, as the night drew on, became a physical removal, insupportable and irreparable. As an amputated hand cannot be disowned because it is experiencing a futurity, of which the victim is its forebear, so Robin was an amputation that Nora could not renounce. As the wrist longs, so her heart longed, and dressing she would go out into the night that she might be "beside herself," skirting the café in which she could catch a glimpse of Robin.

Once out in the open Robin walked in a formless meditation, her hands thrust into the sleeves of her coat, directing her steps toward that night life that was a known measure between Nora and the cafés. Her meditations, during this walk, were a part of the pleasure she expected to find when the walk came to an

end. It was this exact distance that kept the two ends of her life—
Nora and the cafés—from forming a monster with two heads.

Her thoughts were in themselves a form of locomotion. She
walked with raised head, seeming to look at every passer-by, yet
her gaze was anchored in anticipation and regret. A look of anger,
intense and hurried, shadowed her face and drew her mouth
down as she neared her company; yet as her eyes moved over the
façades of the buildings, searching for the sculptured head that
both she and Nora loved (a Greek head with shocked protruding
eyeballs, for which the tragic mouth seemed to pour forth tears),
a quiet joy radiated from her own eyes; for this head was remembrance of Nora and her love, making the anticipation of the
people she was to meet set and melancholy. So, without knowing
she would do so, she took the turn that brought her into this particular street. If she was diverted, as was sometimes the case, by
the interposition of a company of soldiers, a wedding or a funeral,
then by her agitation she seemed a part of the function to the
persons she stumbled against, as a moth by his very entanglement
with the heat that shall be his extinction is associated with flame
as a component part of its function. It was this characteristic that
saved her from being asked too sharply "where" she was going;
pedestrians who had it on the point of their tongues, seeing her
rapt and confused, turned instead to look at each other.

The doctor, seeing Nora out walking alone, said to himself, as the tall black-caped figure passed ahead of him under the
lamps, "There goes the dismantled—Love has fallen off her wall.
A religious woman," he thought to himself, "without the joy and
safety of the Catholic faith, which at a pinch covers up the spots
on the wall when the family portraits take a slide; take that safety
from a woman," he said to himself, quickening his step to follow
her, "and love gets loose and into the rafters. She sees her everywhere," he added, glancing at Nora as she passed into the dark.
"Out looking for what she's afraid to find—Robin. There goes
mother of mischief, running about, trying to get the world home."

Looking at every couple as they passed, into every carriage
and car, up to the lighted windows of the houses, trying to discover not Robin any longer, but traces of Robin, influences in her
life (and those which were yet to be betrayed), Nora watched
every moving figure for some gesture that might turn up in the
movements made by Robin; avoiding the quarter where she knew
her to be, where by her own movements the waiters, the people on
the terraces, might know that she had a part in Robin's life.

Returning home, the interminable night would begin. Listening to the faint sounds from the street, every murmur from
the garden, an unevolved and tiny hum that spoke of the progres-

sive growth of noise that would be Robin coming home, Nora lay
and beat her pillow without force, unable to cry, her legs drawn
up. At times she would get up and walk, to make something in
her life outside more quickly over, to bring Robin back by the
very velocity of the beating of her heart. And walking in vain,
suddenly she would sit down on one of the circus chairs that stood
by the long window overlooking the garden, bend forward, putting her hands between her legs, and begin to cry, "Oh, God! Oh,
God! Oh, God!" repeated so often that it had the effect of all
words spoken in vain. She nodded and awoke again and began to
cry before she opened her eyes, and went back to the bed and fell
into a dream which she recognized; though in the finality of this
version she knew that the dream had not been "well dreamt"
before. Where the dream had been incalculable, it was now completed with the entry of Robin.

Nora dreamed that she was standing at the top of a house,
that is, the last floor but one—this was her grandmother's room—
an expansive, decaying splendour; yet somehow, though set with
all the belongings of her grandmother, was as bereft as the nest of
a bird which will not return. Portraits of her great-uncle, Llewel-
lyn, who died in the Civil War, faded pale carpets, curtains that
resembled columns from their time in stillness—a plume and an
ink well—the ink faded into the quill; standing, Nora looked
down into the body of the house, as if from a scaffold, where now
Robin had entered the dream, lying among a company below.
Nora said to herself, "The dream will not be dreamed again." A
disc of light, which seemed to come from someone or thing standing behind her and which was yet a shadow, shed a faintly luminous glow upon the upturned still face of Robin, who had the
smile of an "only survivor," a smile which fear had married to
the bone.

From round about her in anguish Nora heard her own
voice saying, "Come up, this is Grandmother's room," yet knowing it was impossible because the room was taboo. The louder
she cried out the farther away went the floor below, as if Robin
and she, in their extremity, were a pair of opera glasses turned to
the wrong end, diminishing in their painful love; a speed that ran
away with the two ends of the building, stretching her apart.

This dream that now had all its parts had still the former
quality of never really having been her grandmother's room. She
herself did not seem to be there in person, nor able to give an invitation. She had wanted to put her hands on something in this
room to prove it; the dream had never permitted her to do so.
This chamber that had never been her grandmother's, which was,
on the contrary, the absolute opposite of any known room her

grandmother had ever moved or lived in, was nevertheless saturated with the lost presence of her grandmother, who seemed in the continual process of leaving it. The architecture of dream had rebuilt her everlasting and continuous, flowing away in a long gown of soft folds and chin laces, the pinched gatherings that composed the train taking an upward line over the back and hips in a curve that not only bent age but fear of bent age demands.

With this figure of her grandmother who was not entirely her recalled grandmother went one of her childhood, when she had run into her at the corner of the house—the grandmother who, for some unknown reason, was dressed as a man, wearing a billycock and a corked moustache, ridiculous and plump in tight trousers and a red waistcoat, her arms spread saying with a leer of love, "My little sweetheart!"—her grandmother "drawn upon" as a prehistoric ruin is drawn upon, symbolizing her life out of her life, and which now appeared to Nora as something being done to Robin, Robin disfigured and eternalized by the hieroglyphics of sleep and pain.

Waking, she began to walk again, and looking out into the garden in the faint light of dawn, she saw a double shadow falling from the statue, as if it were multiplying, and thinking perhaps this was Robin, she called and was not answered. Standing motionless, straining her eyes, she saw emerge from the darkness the light of Robin's eyes, the fear in them developing their luminosity until, by the intensity of their double regard, Robin's eyes and hers met. So they gazed at each other. As if that light had power to bring what was dreaded into the zone of their catastrophe, Nora saw the body of another woman swim up into the statue's obscurity, with head hung down, that the added eyes might not augment the illumination; her arms about Robin's neck, her body pressed to Robin's, her legs slackened in the hang of the embrace.

Unable to turn her eyes away, incapable of speech, experiencing a sensation of evil, complete and dismembering, Nora fell to her knees, so that her eyes were not withdrawn by her volition, but dropped from their orbit by the falling of her body. Her chin on the sill she knelt, thinking, "Now they will not hold together," feeling that if she turned away from what Robin was doing, the design would break and melt back into Robin alone. She closed her eyes, and at that moment she knew an awful happiness. Robin, like something dormant, was protected, moved out of death's way by the successive arms of women; but as she closed her eyes, Nora said "Ah!" with the intolerable automatism of the last "Ah!" in a body struck at the moment of its final breath.

V

Master and Slave:
Sadism-Masochism

THEODOR REIK: Masochism in Modern Man*

PHENOMENA

THE INVESTIGATOR'S first task is to answer the question: what happens? His second is to answer the question: how does it happen? To fulfill the first we have to start in our case from the phenomenological world of masochism. We shall have to seek for definite features and characteristics of this instinctual disposition, what its forms of expression have in common and what distinguishes it from other instinctual phenomena. Before undertaking such a task of sifting and sorting it is advisable to pause and state the first general impression masochistic phenomena make on the observer. One should certainly not surrender to such first impressions; yet they should not be underrated. They may be deceptive and true at the same time. These fleeting impressions, so obscure and yet so distinct, are the very ones which deserve to be retained. They keep to the surface, but the surface—correctly seen—is the extroverted inside. Every secret that man would hide will betray itself on the surface, will manifest itself on the outside.

The unprejudiced observer's first general impression of masochistic phenomena is paradoxical. The literal meaning of the word paradoxical is: contradictory, incredible, running counter to general opinion. Applied to phenomena it can only mean: something that rationally could not exist and yet is there. It is a strange phenomenon that a river should disappear and reappear on the surface of the earth many miles away. But such examples are known and are explainable. It would produce a paradoxical

* Reprinted from *Of Love and Lust.*

impression, however, if a river suddenly changed its direction and began running backward toward its source. Inconsistency, of course, is not to be confounded with absurdity. The element of antagonism, of apparently intentional contradiction, proves rather that there is a meaning in this inconsistency. The inconsistent is not nonsensical; it is merely contradictory. It does not stand outside of general belief. It takes a stand against it. It is easy to recognize that this first general impression is common to all forms of masochism. It is equally incredible and contradictory that the ego's own abasement and defeat, degradation and rejection, are aimed at in social masochism.

The impression of a paradox is due not only to the factors of aberration and queerness of the instinctual gratification. Such factors are indeed common to all perversions and yet the picture of masochism acts differently upon us. This impression must result from features which are not clear to us at first, items additional to the general character of the aberration. The impression discriminating this instinctual expression from others is best seen by a comparison. Other perversions are comparable to single participants of a hiking group who have strayed from the highway and have erroneously taken a wrong route. The masochist is comparable to a person who "intentionally" goes astray in order to reach his secret aim by a detour.

This is the first general impression gathered before scrutinizing details of the phenomena. Such an impression can be ignored—it has been ignored up till now—but it cannot be denied.

This impression of paradox must also have its psychological justification.

Are there any characteristic elements invariably common to all different forms of masochism? The sexological and psychological literature surely offers sufficient observational material to make characterization of masochistic phenomena easy. Although there might be even too much of such material I dare state that up till now not even the phenomenology of masochism has been adequately investigated. A description of the essential single features, of what is common to all masochistic forms, is still lacking.

It will be worth while to quote some examples as illustrative material. In selecting examples the primary consideration will be the fact that there can be no doubt as to their masochistic character. Neither differences of sex nor the question of whether we deal with an actual masochistic scene or with a fancied perversion are considered in this selection. From this point of view the three following examples may claim to be representative of the essentials.

A young girl has the following phantasy to which she clung

through the years with but trifling variations. It is late evening or night. In her daydream she goes through the streets to the butcher shop which has closed its shutters a long time ago. She knocks and when the butcher opens she says, "Please, I would like to be butchered." He grants her request without any fuss as though it were something quite usual and lets her in. She undresses in the rear of the big shop and lies down naked on one of the butcher's stalls. She has to lie there and wait a long time. The butcher is cutting up some calves. Once in a while one of his employees comes by, touches her body and tests her flesh like an expert testing an animal to be slaughtered. Finally the butcher himself comes. He also tests the different parts of her body, hauling her about as if she were a dead calf. Finally he grabs the butcher knife, but before he makes a cut he puts his finger into her vagina. At this moment she has an orgasm.

Let us follow up this unquestionable masochistic phantasy with another one, a man's. A man of thirty-seven, father of three children, is fully potent sexually only with the aid of varied and different phantasies. I select one at random: to an ancient barbaric idol, somewhat like the Phoenician Moloch, a number of vigorous young men are to be sacrificed at certain not too frequent intervals. They are undressed and laid on the altar one by one. The rumble of drums is joined by the songs of the approaching temple choirs. The high priest followed by his suite approaches the altar and scrutinizes each of the victims with a critical eye. They must satisfy certain requirements as to physical beauty and athletic appearance. The high priest takes the genital of each prospective victim in his hand and carefully tests its weight and form. If he does not approve of the genital, the young man will be rejected as obnoxious to the god and unworthy of being sacrificed. The high priest gives the order for the execution and the ceremony continues. With a sharp cut the young men's genitals and the surrounding parts are cut away.

The patient, who is of a decidedly visualizing type, imagines the progress of the scene very vividly. He himself is not a participant but only a spectator. Here the question might be raised whether such a phantasy is masochistic or sadistic. The phantasy first was used in masturbation and only later was invoked in intercourse with his wife. The decision as to whether the phantasy is primarily masochistic or more sadistic in character must rest on information as to the person with whom the patient identifies. In our case it is certain that the daydreamer identifies with one of the victims, usually not the one who is just being castrated but with the next, who is compelled to look on at the execution of his companion. The patient shares every intensive affect of this victim, feels his terror and anxiety with all the physical sensations since he imagines that he himself will experience the same fate in a few moments.

Rather than take the third example from the field of phantasy again I shall select an actual instance of masochistic perverse practice. A married middle-aged man visits a prostitute from time to time and enacts the following scene: on entering he asks her whether she gives "Russian lessons." The phrase is used in certain newspapers of his country to advertise masochistic practices. In the patient's imagination the term connotes the terrors of pogroms and scenes in Russian prisons which he has read about. If the girl says "yes," he gives her explicit directions as to what she must do. She must scold him in a certain manner as if he were a little boy who has been naughty. She must say that he deserves a good hiding and so on. He obediently pulls off his trousers and receives a blow on the buttocks. Sometimes the blow is superfluous since the ejaculation has already occurred. In coitus the patient is impotent.

It is not to be doubted that these three examples are representative of masochism as a perversion. It is perhaps accidental that in none of them the sensation of pain is emphasized or the perception of pain is of any importance. Even in the phantasy of the execution of the young men there is no stress on the pleasure of suffering pain; rather is the stress on the pleasure in the idea of anxiety and terror. We recall that the pleasurable excitement lay in the next victim's fright at the sight of his predecessor's castration. The castration itself appeared in the phantasy merely as a surgical operation. No stress was laid on the sensation of pain.

If we thus have excluded the pleasure in pain as an indispensable element, what remains as a common denominator? Surely everything else that hitherto was known and acknowledged as characteristic of masochism: the passive nature, the feeling of impotence and the submission to another person, the cruel, humiliating and shameful treatment by this person and the consequent sexual excitement. There is nothing new yet disclosed as characteristic or at least not yet sufficiently valued. These newly emphasized characteristics not only have to be essential. They have to claim acknowledgment as indispensable elements of masochism. Naturally they do not always appear in the same form or with the same intensity, yet they are always present. Where they are lacking we cannot speak of masochism.

JEAN-JACQUES ROUSSEAU: The Confessions

As Mademoiselle Lambercier had the affection of a mother for us, she also exercised the authority of one, and sometimes carried it so far as to inflict upon us the punishment of children when we had deserved it. For some time she was content with threats, and this threat of a punishment that was quite new to me appeared very terrible; but, after it had been carried out, I found the reality less terrible than the expectation; and, what was still more strange, this chastisement made me still more devoted to her who had inflicted it. It needed all the strength of this devotion and all my natural docility to keep myself from doing something which would have deservedly brought upon me a repetition of it; for I had found in the pain, even in the disgrace, a mixture of sensuality which had left me less afraid than desirous of experiencing it again from the same hand. No doubt some precocious sexual instinct was mingled with this feeling, for the same chastisement inflicted by her brother would not have seemed to me at all pleasant. But, considering his disposition, there was little cause to fear the substitution; and if I kept myself from deserving punishment, it was solely for fear of displeasing Mademoiselle Lambercier; for, so great is the power exercised over me by kindness, even by that which is due to the senses, that it has always controlled the latter in my heart.

The repetition of the offence, which I avoided without being afraid of it, occurred without any fault of mine, that is to say, of my will, and I may say that I profited by it without any qualm of conscience. But this second time was also the last; for Mademoiselle Lambercier, who had no doubt noticed something which convinced her that the punishment did not have the desired effect, declared that it tired her too much, and that she would abandon it. Until then we had slept in her room, sometimes even in her bed during the winter. Two days afterwards we were put to sleep in another room, and from that time I had the honour, which I would gladly have dispensed with, of being treated by her as a big boy.

Who would believe that this childish punishment, inflicted upon me when only eight years old by a young woman of thirty, disposed of my tastes, my desires, my passions, and my own self for the remainder of my life, and that in a manner exactly contrary to that which should have been the natural result? When my feelings were once inflamed, my desires so went astray that, limited to what I had already felt, they did not trouble themselves to look for anything else. In spite of my hot blood, which has been inflamed with sensuality almost from my birth, I kept myself free from every taint until the age when the coldest and most sluggish temperaments begin to develop. In torments for a long time, without knowing why, I devoured with burning glances all the pretty women I met; my imagination unceasingly recalled them to me, only to make use of them in my own fashion, and to make of them so many Mlles. Lambercier.

Even after I had reached years of maturity, this curious taste, always abiding with me and carried to depravity and even frenzy, preserved my morality, which it might naturally have been expected to destroy. If ever a bringing-up was chaste and modest, assuredly mine was. My three aunts were not only models of propriety, but reserved to a degree which has long since been unknown amongst women. My father, a man of pleasure, but a gallant of the old school, never said a word, even in the presence of women whom he loved more than others, which would have brought a blush to a maiden's cheek; and the respect due to children has never been so much insisted upon as in my family and in my presence. In this respect I found M. Lambercier equally careful; and an excellent servant was dismissed for having used a somewhat too free expression in our presence. Until I was a young man, I not only had no distinct idea of the union of the sexes, but the confused notion which I had regarding it never presented itself to me except in a hateful and disgusting form. For common prostitutes I felt a loathing which has never been effaced: the sight of a profligate always filled me with contempt, even with affright. My horror of debauchery became thus pronounced ever since the day when, walking to Little Sacconex by a hollow way, I saw on both sides holes in the ground, where I was told that these creatures carried on their intercourse. The thought of the one always brought back to my mind the copulation of dogs, and the bare recollection was sufficient to disgust me.

This tendency of my bringing-up, in itself adapted to delay the first outbreaks of an inflammable temperament, was assisted, as I have already said, by the direction which the first indications of sensuality took in my case. Busying my imagination solely with what I had actually felt, in spite of most uncomfortable effervescence of blood, I knew how to turn my desires only in the direction of that kind of pleasure with which I was acquainted, without ever going as far as that which had been made hateful to me, and which, without my having the least suspicion of it, was so closely related to the other. In my foolish fancies, in my erotic frenzies, in the extravagant acts to which they sometimes led me, I had recourse in my imagination to the assistance of the other sex, without ever thinking that it was serviceable for any purpose than that for which I was burning to make use of it.

In this manner, then, in spite of an ardent, lascivious and precocious temperament, I passed the age of puberty without desiring, even without knowing of any other sensual pleasures than those of which Mademoiselle Lambercier had most innocently given me the idea; and when, in course of time, I became a man, that which should have destroyed me again preserved me. My old childish taste, instead of disappearing, became so associated with the other, that I could never banish it from the desires kindled by my senses. This madness, joined to my natural shyness, has always made me very unenterprising with women, for want of courage to say all or power to do all, inasmuch as the kind of enjoyment, of which the other was only for me the final consummation could neither be appropriated by him who longed for it, nor guessed by her who was able to bestow it. Thus I have spent my life in idle longing, without saying a word, in the presence of those whom I loved most. Too bashful to declare my taste, I at least satisfied it in situations which had reference to it and kept up the idea of it. To lie at the feet of an imperious mistress, to obey her commands, to ask her forgiveness—this was for me a sweet enjoyment; and, the more my lively imagination heated my blood, the more I presented the appearance of a bashful lover. It may be easily imagined that this manner of making love does not lead to very speedy results, and is not very dangerous to the virtue of those who are its object. For this reason I have rarely possessed, but have none the less enjoyed myself in my own way—that is to say, in imagination. Thus it has happened that my senses, in harmony with my timid disposition and my romantic spirit, have kept my sentiments pure and my morals blameless, owing to the very tastes which, combined with a little more impudence, might have plunged me into the most brutal sensuality. . . .

The Comtesse de Menthon, the mother of one of my pupils, was a woman of great wit, and had the reputation of being equally malicious. It was reported that she had caused several quarrels, amongst others, one which had had fatal consequences for the house of Antremont. Mamma was sufficiently intimate with her to be acquainted with her character; having quite innocently taken the fancy of someone upon whom Madame de Menthon had designs, mamma was charged by her with the offence of the preference shown towards her, although she had neither sought nor accepted it; and, from that time, Madame de Menthon sought to do her rival several ill turns, none of which succeeded. By way of sample, I will relate one of the most laughable. They were together in the country, with several gentlemen of the neighbourhood, amongst whom was the suitor in question. Madame de Menthon one day told one of these gentlemen that Madame de Warens was very affected, and she had no taste, dressed badly, and kept her bosom covered like a tradesman's wife. "As for the last point," answered the gentleman, who was fond of a joke, "she has her reasons for it; I know she has a scar on her breast, just like an ugly rat, so perfectly natural that it looks as if it was moving." Hatred, like love, causes credulity. Madame de Menthon resolved to make capital out of this discovery; and one day, when mamma was playing cards with the lady's ungrateful favourite, she seized the opportunity to step behind her rival, and, almost upsetting her chair, cleverly turned back her neckerchief; but, instead of the large rat, the gentleman saw something very different, which it was easier to see than to forget, and this was certainly not what the lady had intended.

I was not calculated to attract Madame de Menthon, who only liked to see brilliant company around her; nevertheless, she paid me some attention, not on account of my personal appearance, about which she certainly did not trouble herself, but because of my supposed wit, which might have made me serviceable to her. She had a lively taste for satire, and was fond of composing songs and verses about those who displeased her. If she had found me sufficiently gifted to assist her in composing her verses, and sufficiently obliging to write them, between us we should soon have turned Chambéri upside down. These lampoons would have been traced back to their source; Madame de Menthon would have got out of it by sacrificing me, and I should, perhaps, have been imprisoned for the rest of my life, as a reward for playing the Apollo of the ladies.

Happily, nothing of the kind happened. Madame de Menthon kept me to dinner two or three times, to make me talk, and found that I was only a fool. I was conscious of this myself, and sighed over it, envying the accomplishments of my friend Venture, whereas I ought to have been grateful to my stupidity for saving me from danger. I continued her daughter's singing-master, and nothing more, but I lived peacefully, and was always welcome in Chambéri, which was far better than being considered a wit by her, and a serpent by everybody else.

Be that as it may, mamma saw that, in order to rescue me from the perils of my youth, she must treat me as a man, which she immediately proceeded to do, but in the most singular manner that ever occurred to a woman in similar circumstances. I found her manner more serious, and her utterances more moral than usual. The playful gaiety, which was usually mingled with her advice, was all at once succeeded by a sustained gravity, neither familiar nor severe, which seemed to pave the way for an explanation. After having in vain asked myself the reason of this change, I asked her, which was just what she expected. She proposed a walk in the little garden on the following day; the next morning found us there. She had taken precautions that we should be left undisturbed all day, and employed the time in preparing me for the kindness which she wished to show me, not, as another woman would have done, by artifices and coquetry, but by language full of feeling and good sense, better calculated to instruct than to seduce me, which appealed rather to my heart than to my senses. But, however admirable and useful the words she addressed to me may have been, although they were anything but cold and mournful, I did not listen to them with all the attention they deserved, and did not impress them on my memory, as I should have done at any other time. The manner in which she began, the appearance of careful preparation had disquieted me; while she was speaking, I was dreamy and distracted, thinking less of what she was saying than of what she wanted; and, as soon as I understood, which was by no means easy, the novelty of the idea, which had never once entered my head all the time I had been living with her, it so completely took possession of me, that I was no longer in a state to pay attention to what she said to me. I only thought of her, and did not listen to her.

Most instructors are liable to the perverse idea, which I have not avoided myself in my "Émile," of making young people attentive to that which they desire to impress upon them, by revealing to them the prospect of something in the highest degree attractive. Struck by the object held before him, a young man devotes his attention to that exclusively, and, leaping lightly over your introductory discourses, makes straight for the goal towards which you are leading him too slowly for his liking. If it be desired to make him attentive, he must not be allowed to go too far ahead; and it was just in this particular that mamma showed her want of judgment. With characteristic singularity, which accorded with her systematic mind, she took the superfluous precaution of attaching conditions; but, as soon as I saw their reward, I no longer listened to them, and hastened to agree to everything. I even doubt whether there is a man in the world sufficiently honest and courageous to bargain in a similar case, or a woman capable of pardoning him, if he ventured to do so. In consequence of the same singularity, she attached to the agreement the most solemn formalities, and gave me eight days to think over them, which, like a hypocrite, I assured her I did not require; for, to crown the singularity of the whole affair, I was really glad of the respite, so greatly had the novelty of these ideas struck me, and so disordered did I feel the state of my own to be, that I wanted time to set them in order.

It will be imagined that those eight days seemed eight

centuries to me; on the contrary, I could have wished that they had really lasted as long. I do not know how to describe my condition; it was a kind of fright mingled with impatience, during which I was so afraid of what I longed for, that I sometimes seriously endeavoured to think of some decent way of avoiding the promised happiness. Consider my ardent and lascivious temperament, my heated blood, my heart intoxicated with love, my vigorous health, my age. Remember that, in this condition, thirsting after women, I had never yet touched one; that imagination, need, vanity, and curiosity, all combined to devour me with the burning desire of being a man and showing myself one. Add to this, above all—for it must never be forgotten—that my tender and lively attachment to her, far from diminishing, had only become warmer every day, that I was never happy except with her; that I never left her except to think of her; that my heart was full, not only of her goodness and amiability, but of her sex, her form, her person; in a word, of her, under every aspect in which she could be dear to me. Do not imagine, that, because she was ten or twelve years older than myself, she had either grown old, or appeared so to me. During the five or six years since the first sight of her had so enchanted me, she had really altered very little, and, in my eyes, not at all. She had always appeared charming to me, and, at that time, everyone still considered her so. Her figure alone had become a little stouter. In other respects, it was the same eye, the same complexion, the same bosom, the same features, the same beautiful fair hair, the same cheerfulness, even the voice was the same, the silvery voice of youth, which always made so deep an impression upon me, that, even now, I cannot hear without emotion the tones of a pretty girlish voice.

What I had to fear in the expectation of possessing one who was so dear to me, was naturally the anticipation of it, and the inability to control my desires and imagination sufficiently to remain master of myself. It will be seen that, at an advanced age, the mere idea of certain trifling favours which awaited me in the company of the person I loved, heated by blood to such a degree that it was impossible for me to make with impunity the short journey which separated me from her. How then was it that, in the flower of my youth, I felt so little eagerness for the first enjoyment? How was it that I could see the hour approach with more pain than pleasure? How was it that, instead of the rapture which should have intoxicated me, I almost felt repugnance and fear? There is no doubt that, if I had been able to escape my happiness with decency, I should have done so with all my heart. I have promised singularities in the history of my attachment to her; this is surely one which would never have been expected.

The reader, already disgusted, is doubtless of opinion that, being already possessed by another man, she degraded herself in my eyes by distributing her favours, and that a feeling of disesteem cooled those with which she had inspired me. He is mistaken. This distribution was certainly very painful to me, as much in consequence of a very natural feeling of delicacy as because I really considered it unworthy of her and myself; but it never altered my feelings towards her, and I can swear that I never loved her more tenderly than when I had so little desire to possess her. I knew too well her modest heart and her cold temperament to think for a moment that sensual pleasure had anything to do with this abandonment of herself; I was perfectly convinced that nothing but anxiety to save me from dangers that were otherwise almost inevitable and to preserve me entirely for myself and my duties, caused her to violate a duty which she did not regard in the same light as other women, as will be shown later. I pitied her and pitied myself. I should have liked to say to her: "No, mamma, it is not necessary; I will answer for myself without that." But I did not dare to do so—first, because it was not a thing to say, and, in the second place, because in the main I felt that it was not true, and that, in reality, there was only *one* woman who could protect me against other women and secure me against temptations. Without desiring to possess her, I was very glad that she prevented me from desiring the possession of other women, to such an extent did I look upon everything as a misfortune which would draw me away from her. Our long-continued and innocent intercourse, far from weakening my feelings for her, had strengthened them, but, at the same time, had given them a different turn, which made them more affectionate, more tender perhaps, but also less sensual. Having so long called her mamma, having enjoyed with her the intimacy of a son, I had become accustomed to look upon myself as one. I believe that this was really the cause of the little eagerness I felt to possess her, although she was so dear to me. I well remember that my early feelings, without being livelier, were more sensual. At Annecy, I was intoxicated; at Chambéri, I was no longer so. I still loved her as passionately as possible; but I loved her more for her own sake than for my own, or, at least, I sought happiness with her, rather than enjoyment; she was for me more than a sister, more than a mother, more than a friend, even more than a mistress; and for that very reason she was not a mistress for me. In short, I loved her too well to desire to possess her; that is most clearly prominent in my ideas.

The day, more dreaded than wished for, at length arrived. I promised everything, and kept my word. However, I obtained it. For the first time I found myself in the arms of a woman, a woman whom I adored. Was I happy? No; I tasted pleasure. A certain unconquerable feeling of melancholy poisoned its charm; I felt as if I had been guilty of incest. Two or three times, while pressing her in ecstasy to my arms, I wetted her bosom with my tears. She, on the other hand, was neither sad nor excited; she was tender and calm. As she was by no means sensual and had not looked for enjoyment, she felt no gratification, and never experienced remorse.

I repeat it: all her faults were due to her errors, none to her passions. She was well born, her heart was pure, she loved propriety; her inclinations were upright and virtuous, her taste was refined; she was formed for an elegance of manners which she always loved but never followed, because, instead of listening to her heart, which always guided her aright, she listened to her reason, which guided her wrongly. When she was led astray by false principles, these were always belied by her real feelings; but, unfortunately, she rather prided herself on her philosophy, and the morals which she drew from it corrupted those which her heart dictated.

M. de Tavel, her first lover, was her instructor in philosophy, and the principles which he taught her were those which he found necessary, in order to seduce her. Finding her attached to her husband, devoted to her duties, always cold, calculating, and inaccessible to sensual feelings, he endeavoured to reach her by sophistries, and succeeded in convincing her that the duties, to which she was so attached, were so much catechism-nonsense, intended solely for the amusement of children; that the union of the sexes was in itself a matter of the greatest indifference; that conjugal fidelity was merely an apparent obligation, the inner morality of which only had reference to public opinion; that the husband's repose was the only rule of duty which the wife need respect, so that secret acts of unfaithfulness, being nothing to him against whom they were committed, were equally nothing to the conscience; in short, he persuaded her that the thing was nothing in itself, that only scandal called it into existence, and that every woman who appeared virtuous owed it to that alone. In this manner the wretch attained his object, by corrupting the mind of a child whose heart he had been unable to corrupt. He was punished for it by an all-devouring jealousy, being convinced that she treated him as he had persuaded her to treat her husband. I do not know whether he was mistaken in this. The minister Perret was supposed to have been his successor. All I know is, that the cold temperament of this young woman, which ought to have protected her against this system, was just what subsequently prevented her from abandoning it. She could not conceive that anyone should attach such importance to that which possessed no importance for her. She never honoured by the name of virtue an abstinence which cost her so little.

She hardly ever misused these false principles for her own sake; but she misused them for the sake of others, and that in consequence of another maxim almost equally false, but more in harmony with the goodness of her heart. She always believed that nothing attached a man so strongly to a woman as possession; and, although her love for her friends was only friendship, it was a friendship so tender, that she employed all possible means at her disposal to attach them more strongly to her. The remarkable thing is, that she nearly always succeeded. She was so truly amiable, that, the greater the intimacy in which one lived with her, the more one found fresh reasons for loving her. Another thing worthy of notice is that, after her first weakness, she rarely bestowed her favours except upon the unfortunate; persons of distinction spent their labour upon her in vain; but, if she once began to feel sympathy for a man, he must have been little deserving of love if she did not end by loving him. If she sometimes chose those who were unworthy of her, the blame rested, not on any low inclinations, which were far removed from her noble heart, but only on her too generous, too kindly, too compassionate, and too feeling disposition, which she did not always control with sufficient judgment.

If some false principles led her astray, how many admirable ones did she possess, to which she always remained constant! By how many virtues did she make up for her weaknesses, if those errors can be so called, with which the senses had so little to do! The same man, who deceived her in one point, instructed her admirably in a thousand others; and, as her passions were not so unruly as to prevent her from following her reason, she took the right path when her sophisms did not mislead her. Her motives, even in her errors, were praiseworthy; owing to her mistaken ideas, she might do wrong, but she was incapable of doing so wilfully. She abhorred duplicity and lying; she was just, fair, humane, disinterested, faithful to her word, her friends, and the duties which she regarded as such, incapable of revenge or hatred, without the least idea that there was any merit in forgiveness. Finally, to return to those qualities which less admit of excuse, without knowing how to estimate the value of her favours, she never made a common trade of them; she was lavish of them, but she never sold them, although she was always at her wit's end how to live; and I venture to assert, that if Socrates could esteem Aspasia, he would have respected Madame de Warens. . . .

I do not know whether Claude Anet was aware of the intimacy of our relations. I have reason to believe that it did not escape his notice. He was very quick-witted, but very discreet; he never said what he did not think, but he did not always say what he thought. Without giving me the least hint that he knew about it, he seemed to show by his conduct that he did. This conduct was certainly not due to any lowness of disposition, but to the fact that, having adopted his mistress's principles, he could not disapprove if she acted in accordance with them. Although no older than she was, he was so mature and serious, that he looked upon us almost as two children, who deserved to be indulged, and both of us regarded him as a man worthy of respect, whose esteem we had to conciliate. It was not until she had been unfaithful to him, that I understood the extent of the attachment that she felt for him. Since she knew that I only felt, thought and breathed through her, she showed me how much she loved him, in order that I might feel the same affection for him, and she laid less stress upon her friendship than upon her esteem for him, since this was the feeling which I was capable of sharing most fully. How often did she move our hearts, and make us embrace with tears, at the same time telling us that we were both necessary to her happiness in life! Let not those women who read this laugh maliciously. With her peculiar temperament, there was nothing suspicious about this necessity; it was solely the necessity of her heart.

ALGERNON CHARLES SWINBURNE: Dolores

(NOTRE-DAME DES SEPT DOULEURS)

COLD eyelids that hide like a jewel
    Hard eyes that grow soft for an hour;
The heavy white limbs, and the cruel
    Red mouth like a venomous flower;
When these are gone by with their glories,
    What shall rest of thee then, what remain,
O mystic and sombre Dolores,
    Our Lady of Pain?

Seven sorrows the priests give their Virgin;
    But thy sins, which are seventy times seven,
Seven ages would fail thee to purge in,
    And then they would haunt thee in heaven:

Fierce midnights and famishing morrows,
　And the loves that complete and control
All the joys of the flesh, all the sorrows
　That wear out the soul.

O garment not golden but gilded,
　O garden where all men may dwell,
O tower not of ivory, but builded
　By hands that reach heaven from hell;

O mystical rose of the mire,
　O house not of gold but of gain,
O house of unquenchable fire,
　Our Lady of Pain!

O lips full of lust and of laughter,
　Curled snakes that are fed from my breast,
Bite hard, lest remembrance come after
　And press with new lips where you pressed.
For my heart too springs up at the pressure,
　Mine eyelids too moisten and burn;
Ah, feed me and fill me with pleasure,
　Ere pain come in turn.

In yesterday's reach and to-morrow's,
　Out of sight though they lie of to-day,
There have been and there yet shall be sorrows
　That smite not and bite not in play.
The life and the love thou despisest,
　These hurt us indeed, and in vain,
O wise among women, and wisest,
　Our Lady of Pain.

Who gave thee thy wisdom? what stories
　That stung thee, what visions that smote?
Wert thou pure and a maiden, Dolores,
　When desire took thee first by the throat?
What bud was the shell of a blossom
　That all men may smell to and pluck?
What milk fed thee first at what bosom?
　What sins gave thee suck?

We sift and bedeck and bedrape us,
　Thou art noble and nude and antique;

Libitina thy mother, Priapus
   Thy father, a Tuscan and Greek.
We play with light loves in the portal,
   And wince and relent and refrain;
Loves die, and we know thee immortal,
   Our Lady of Pain.

Fruits fail and love dies and time ranges;
   Thou art fed with perpetual breath,
And alive after infinite changes,
   And fresh from the kisses of death;
Of languors rekindled and rallied,
   Of barren delights and unclean,
Things monstrous and fruitless, a pallid
   And poisonous queen.

Could you hurt me, sweet lips, though I hurt you?
   Men touch them, and change in a trice
The lilies and languors of virtue
   For the raptures and roses of vice;
Those lie where thy foot on the floor is,
   These crown and caress thee and chain,
O splendid and sterile Dolores,
   Our Lady of Pain.

There are sins it may be to discover,
   There are deeds it may be to delight.
What new work wilt thou find for thy lover,
   What new passions for daytime or night?
What spells that they know not a word of
   Whose lives are as leaves overblown?
What tortures undreamt of, unheard of,
   Unwritten, unknown?

An beautiful passionate body
   That never has ached with a heart!
On thy mouth though the kisses are bloody,
   Though they sting till it shudder and smart,
More kind than the love we adore is,
   They hurt not the heart or the brain,
O bitter and tender Dolores,
   Our Lady of Pain.

As our kisses relax and redouble,
   From the lips and the foam and the fangs

Shall no new sin be born for men's trouble,
  No dream of impossible pangs?
With the sweet of the sins of old ages
  Wilt thou satiate thy soul as of yore?
Too sweet is the rind, say the sages,
  Too bitter the core.

Hast thou told all thy secrets the last time,
  And bared all thy beauties to one?
Ah, where shall we go then for pastime,
  If the worst that can be has been done?
But sweet as the rind was the core is;
  We are fain of thee still, we are fain,
O sanguine and subtle Dolores,
  Our Lady of Pain.

By the hunger of change and emotion,
  By the thirst of unbearable things,
By despair, the twin-born of devotion,
  By the pleasure that winces and stings,
The delight that consumes the desire,
  The desire that outruns the delight,
By the cruelty deaf as a fire
  And blind as the night,

By the ravenous teeth that have smitten
  Through the kisses that blossom and bud,
By the lips intertwisted and bitten
  Till the foam has a savour of blood,
By the pulse as it rises and falters,
  By the hands as they slacken and strain,
I adjure thee, respond from thine altars,
  Our Lady of Pain. . . .

JEAN-PAUL SARTRE: Erostratus*

YOU REALLY have to see men from above. I put
out the light and went to the window: they never suspected for a
moment you could watch them from up there. They're careful of
their fronts, sometimes of their backs, but their whole effect is
calculated for spectators of about five feet eight. Who ever

* Reprinted from *Intimacy*.

thought about the shape of a derby hat seen from the seventh floor? They neglect protecting their heads and shoulders with bright colors and garish clothes, they don't know how to fight this great enemy of Humanity, the downward perspective. I leaned on the window sill and began to laugh: where was this wonderful upright stance they're so proud of: they were crushed against the sidewalk and two long legs jumped out from under their shoulders.

On a seventh floor balcony: that's where I should have spent my whole life. You have to prop up moral superiorities with material symbols or else they'll tumble. But exactly what is my superiority over men? Superiority of position, nothing more: I have placed myself above the human within me and I study it. That's why I always liked the towers of Notre-Dame, the platforms of the Eiffel Tower, the Sacré-Coeur, my seventh floor on the Rue Delambre. These are excellent symbols.

Sometimes I had to go down into the street. To the office, for example. I stifled. It's much harder to consider people as ants when you're on the same plane as they are: they *touch* you. Once I saw a dead man in the street. He had fallen on his face. They turned him over, he was bleeding. I saw his open eyes and his cockeyed look and all the blood. I said to myself, "It's nothing, it's no more touching than wet paint. They painted his nose red, that's all." But I felt a nasty softness in my legs and neck and I fainted. They took me into a drugstore, gave me a few slaps on the face and a drink. I could have killed them.

I knew they were my enemies but they didn't know it. They liked each other, they rubbed elbows; they would even have given me a hand, here and there, because they thought I was like them. But if they could have guessed the least bit of the truth, they would have beaten me. They did later, anyhow. When they got me and knew *who* I was, they gave me the works, they beat me up for two hours in the station house, they slapped me and punched me and twisted my arms, they ripped off my pants and to finish they threw my glasses on the floor and while I looked for them, on all fours, they laughed and kicked me. I always knew they'd end up beating me; I'm not strong and I can't defend myself. Some of them had been on the lookout for me for a long time: the big ones. In the street they'd bump into me to see what I'd do. I said nothing. I acted as if I didn't understand. But they still got me. I was afraid of them: it was a foreboding. But don't think I didn't have more serious reasons for hating them.

As far as that was concerned, everything went along much better starting from the day I bought a revolver. You feel strong when you assiduously carry on your person something that can explode and make a noise. I took it every Sunday, I simply put it in my pants pocket and then went out for a walk—generally along the boulevards. I felt it pulling at my pants like a crab, I felt it cold against my thigh. But little by little it got warmer with the contact of my body. I walked with a certain stiffness, I looked like a man with a hard-on, with his thing sticking out at every step. I slipped my hand in my pocket and felt the *object*. From time to time I went into a *urinoir*—even in there I had to be careful because I often had neighbors—I took out my revolver, I felt the weight of it, I looked at its black-checkered butt and its trigger that looked like a half-closed eyelid. The others, the ones who saw me from the outside, thought I was pissing. But I never piss in the *urinoirs*.

One night I got the idea of shooting people. It was a Saturday evening, I had gone out to pick up Lea, a blonde who works out in front of a hotel on the Rue Montparnasse. I never had intercourse with a woman: I would have felt robbed. You get on top of them, of course, but they eat you up with their big hairy mouth and, from what I hear, they're the ones—by a long shot— who gain on the deal. I don't ask anybody for anything, but I don't give anything, either. Or else I'd have to have a cold, pious woman who would give in to me with disgust. The first Saturday of every month I went to one of the rooms in the Hotel Duquesne with Lea. She undressed and I watched her without touching her. Sometimes I went off in my pants all by myself, other times I had time to get home and finish it. That night I didn't find her. I waited for a little while and, as I didn't see her coming, I supposed she had a cold. It was the beginning of January and it was very cold. I was desolated: I'm the imaginative kind and I had pictured to myself all the pleasure I would have gotten from the evening. On the Rue Odessa there was a brunette I had often noticed, a little ripe but firm and plump: I don't exactly despise ripe women: when they're undressed they look more naked than the others. But she didn't know anything of my wants and I was a little scared to ask her right off the bat. And then I don't care too much for new acquaintances: these women can be hiding some thug behind a door, and after, the man suddenly jumps out and takes your money. You're lucky if you get off without a beating. Still, that evening I had nerve, I decided to go back to my place, pick up the revolver and try my luck.

So when I went up to this woman, fifteen minutes later, my gun was in my pocket and I wasn't afraid of anything. Looking at her closely, she seemed rather miserable. She looked like my neighbor across the way, the wife of the police sergeant, and I was very pleased because I'd been wanting to see her naked for a long time. She dressed with the window open when the sergeant wasn't there, and I often stayed behind my curtain to catch a glimpse of her. But she always dressed in the back of the room.

There was only one free room in the Hotel Stella, on the fifth floor. We went up. The woman was fairly heavy and stopped to catch her breath after each step. I felt good: I have a wiry body in spite of my belly, and it takes more than five floors to wind me. On the fifth floor landing, she stopped and put her right hand to her heart and breathed heavily. She had the key to the room in her left hand.

"It's a long way up," she said, trying to smile at me. Without answering, I took the key from her and opened the door. I held my revolver in my left hand, pointing straight ahead through the pocket and I didn't let go of it until I switched the light on. The room was empty. They had put a little square of green soap on the washbasin, for a one-shot. I smiled: I don't have much to do with bidets and little squares of soap. The woman was still breathing heavily behind me and that excited me. I turned; she put out her lips towards me. I pushed her away.

"Undress," I told her.

There was an upholstered armchair; I sat down and made myself comfortable. It's at times like this I wish I smoked. The woman took off her dress and stopped, looking at me distrustfully.

"What's your name," I asked, leaning back.

"Renée."

"All right, Renée, hurry up. I'm waiting."

"You aren't going to undress?"

"Go on," I said, "don't worry about me."

She dropped her panties, then picked them up and put them carefully on top of her dress along with her brassiere.

"So you're a little lazybones, honey?" she asked me. "You want your little girl to do all the work?"

At the same time she took a step towards me, and, leaning her hands on the arm of the chair, tried heavily to kneel between my legs. I got up brusquely.

"None of that," I told her.

She looked at me with surprise.

"Well, what do you want me to do?"

"Nothing. Just walk. Walk around. I don't want any more from you."

She began to walk back and forth awkwardly. Nothing annoys women more than walking when they're naked. They don't have the habit of putting their heels down flat. The whore arched her back and let her arms hang. I was in heaven: there I was, calmly sitting in an armchair, dressed up to my neck, I had even kept my gloves on and this ripe woman had stripped herself naked at my command and was turning back and forth in front of me. She turned her head towards me, and, for appearance, smiled coquettishly.

"You think I'm pretty? You're getting an eyeful?"

"Don't worry about that."

"Say," she asked with sudden indignation, "do you think you're going to make me walk up and down like this very long?"

"Sit down."

She sat on the bed and we watched each other in silence. She had gooseflesh. I could hear the ticking of an alarm clock from the other side of the wall. Suddenly I told her.

"Spread your legs."

She hesitated a fraction of a second, then obeyed. I looked between her legs and turned up my nose. Then I began to laugh so hard that tears came to my eyes. I said, simply, "Look at that!"

And I started laughing again.

She looked at me, stupefied, then blushed violently and clapped her legs shut.

"Bastard," she said between her teeth.

But I laughed louder, then she jumped up and took her brassiere from the chair.

"Hey!" I said, "it isn't over. I'm going to give you fifty francs after a while, but I want my money's worth."

She picked up her panties nervously.

"I've had enough, get it? I don't know what you want. And if you had me come up here to make a fool out of me . . ."

Then I took out my revolver and showed it to her. She looked at me seriously and dropped the panties without a word.

"Walk," I told her, "walk around."

She walked around for another five minutes. Then I gave her my cane and made her do exercises. When I felt my drawers were wet I got up and gave her a fifty-franc note. She took it.

"So long," I added. "I don't think I tired you out very much for the money."

I went out, I left her naked in the middle of the room, the braissiere in one hand and the fifty-franc note in the other. I didn't regret the money I spent; I had dumbfounded her and it isn't easy to surprise a whore. Going down the stairs I thought, "That's what I want. To surprise them all." I was happy as a child. I had brought along the green soap and after I reached home I rubbed it under the hot water for a long time until there was nothing left of it but a thin film between my fingers and it looked like a mint candy someone had sucked on for a long time.

But that night I woke up with a start and I saw her face again, her eyes when I showed her my gun, and her fat belly that bounced up and down at every step.

What a fool, I thought. And I felt bitter remorse: I should have shot her while I was at it, shot that belly full of holes. That night and three nights afterward, I dreamed of six little red holes grouped in a circle about the navel.

As a result, I never went out without my revolver. I looked at people's backs, and I imagined, from their walk, the way they would fall if I shot them. I was in the habit of hanging around the Châtelet every Sunday when the classical concerts let out. About six o'clock I heard a bell ring and the ushers came to fasten back the plate glass doors with hooks. This was the beginning: the crowd came out slowly; the people walked with floating steps, their eyes still full of dreams, their hearts still full of pretty sentiments. There were a lot of them who looked around in amazement: the street must have seemed quite strange to them. Then they smiled mysteriously: they were passing from one world to another. I was waiting for them in this other world. I slid my right hand into my pocket and gripped the gun butt with all my strength. After a while, I *saw* myself shooting them. I knocked them off like clay pipes, they fell, one after the other and the panic-stricken survivors streamed back into the theatre, breaking the glass in the doors. It was an exciting game: when it was over, my hands were trembling and I had to go to Dreher's and drink a cognac to get myself in shape.

I wouldn't have killed the women. I would have shot them in the kidneys. Or in the calves, to make them dance.

I still hadn't decided anything. But I did everything just as though my power of decision had stopped. I began with minor details. I went to practice in a shooting gallery at Denfert-Rochereau. My scores weren't tremendous, but men are bigger targets, especially when you shoot point blank. Then I arranged my publicity. I chose a day when all my colleagues would be together in the office. On Monday morning. I was always very friendly with them, even though I had a horror of shaking their hands. They took off their gloves to greet you; they had an obscene way of undressing their hand, pulling the glove back and sliding it slowly along the fingers, unveiling the fat, wrinkled nakedness of the palm. I always kept my gloves on.

We never did much on Mondays. The typist from the commercial service came to bring us receipts. Lemercier joked pleasantly with her and when she had gone, they described her charms with a blasé competence. Then they talked about Lindbergh. They liked Lindbergh. I told them:

"I like the black heroes."

"Negroes?" Masse asked.

"No, black as in Black Magic. Lindbergh is a white hero. He doesn't interest me."

"Go see if it's easy to cross the Atlantic," Bouxin said sourly.

I told them my conception of the black hero.

"An anarchist," Lemercier said.

"No," I said quietly, "the anarchists like their own kind of men."

"Then it must be a crazy man."

But Masse, who had some education, intervened just then. "I know your character," he said to me. "His name is Erostratus. He wanted to become famous and he couldn't find anything better to do than to burn down the temple of Ephesus, one of the seven wonders of the world."

"And what was the name of the man who built the temple?"

"I don't remember," he confessed, "I don't believe anybody knows his name."

"Really? But you remember the name of Erostratus? You see, he didn't figure things out too badly."

The conversation ended on these words, but I was quite calm. They would remember it when the time came. For myself, who, until then, had never heard of Erostratus, his story was encouraging. He had been dead for more than two thousand years and his act was still shining like a black diamond. I began to think that my destiny would be short and tragic. First it frightened me but I got used to it. If you look at it a certain way, it's terrible but, on the other hand, it gives the passing moment considerable force and beauty. I felt a strange power in my body when I went down into the street. I had my revolver on me, the thing that explodes and makes noise. But I no longer drew my assurance from that, it was from myself: I was a being like a revolver, a torpedo or a bomb. I too, one day at the end of my somber life, would explode and light the world with a flash as short and violent as magnesium. At that time I had the same dream several nights in a row. I was an anarchist. I had put myself in the path of the Tsar and I carried an infernal machine on me. At the appointed hour, the cortège passed, the bomb exploded and we were thrown into the air, myself, the Tsar, and three gold-braided officers before the eyes of the crowd.

I now went for weeks on end without showing up at the office. I walked the boulevards in the midst of my future victims or locked myself in my room and made my plans. They fired me at the beginning of October. Then I spent my leisure working on the following letter, of which I made 102 copies:

MONSIEUR: You are a famous man and your works sell by the thousands. I am going to tell you why: because you love men. You have humanism in your blood; you are lucky. You expand when you are with people; as soon as you see one of your fellows, even without knowing him, you feel sympathy for him. You have a taste for his body, for the way he is jointed, for his legs which open and close at will, and above all for his hands: it pleases you because he has five fingers on each hand and he can set his thumb against the other fingers. You are delighted when your neighbor takes a cup from the table because there is a way of taking it which is strictly human and which you have often described in your works; less supple, less rapid than that of a monkey, but is it not so much more intelligent? You also love the flesh of man, his look of being heavily wounded with re-education, seeming to re-invent walking at every step, and his famous look which even wild beats cannot bear. So it has been easy for you to find the proper accent for speaking to man about himself: a modest, yet frenzied accent. People throw themselves greedily upon your books, they read them in a good armchair, they think of a great love, discreet and unhappy, which you bring them and that makes up for many things, for being ugly, for being cowardly, for being cuckolded, for not getting a raise on the first of January. And they say willingly of your latest book: it's a good deed.

I suppose you might be curious to know what a man can be like who does not love men. Very well, I am such a man, and I love them so little that soon I am going out and kill half a dozen of them: perhaps you might wonder why *only* half a dozen? Because my revolver has only six cartridges. A monstrosity, isn't it? And moreover, an act strictly impolitic? But I tell you I *cannot* love them. I understand very well the way you feel. But what attracts you to them disgusts me. I have seen, as you, men chewing slowly, all the while keeping an eye on everything, the left hand leafing through an economic review. Is it my fault I prefer to watch the sea-lions feeding? Man can do nothing with his face without its turning into a game of physiognomy. When he chews, keeping his mouth shut, the corners of his mouth go up and down, he looks as though he were passing incessantly from serenity to tearful surprise. You love this, I know, you call it the watchful-ness of the spirit. But it makes me sick; I don't know why; I was born like that.

If there were only a difference of taste between us I would not trouble you. But everything happens as if you had grace and

I had none. I am free to like or dislike lobster newburg, but if I do not like men I am a wretch and can find no place in the sun. They have monopolized the sense of life. I hope you will understand what I mean. For the past 33 years I have been beating against closed doors above which is written "No entrance if not a humanist." I have had to abandon all I have undertaken; I had to choose: either it was an absurd and ill-fated attempt, or sooner or later it had to turn to their profit. I could not succeed in detaching from myself thoughts I did not expressly destine for them, in formulating them: they remained in me as slight organic movements. Even the tools I used I felt belonged to them; words, for example: I wanted *my own* words. But the ones I use have dragged through I don't know how many consciences; they arrange themselves in my head by virtue of the habits I have picked up from the others and it is not without repugnance that I use them in writing to you. But this is the last time. I say to you: love men or it is only right for them to let you sneak out of it. Well, I do not want to sneak out. Soon I am going to take my revolver, I am going down into the street and see if anybody can do anything to *them*. Goodbye, perhaps it will be you I shall meet. You will never know then with what pleasure I shall blow your brains out. If not—and this is more likely—read tomorrow's papers. There you will see that an individual named Paul Hilbert has killed, in a moment of fury, six passers-by on the Boulevard Edgar-Quinet. You know better than anyone the value of newspaper prose. You understand then that I am not "furious." I am, on the contrary, quite calm and I pray you to accept, Monsieur, the assurance of my distinguished sentiments.

PAUL HILBERT

I slipped the 102 letters in 102 envelopes and on the envelopes I wrote the addresses of 102 French writers. Then I put the whole business in my table drawer along with six books of stamps.

I went out very little during the two weeks that followed. I let myself become slowly occupied by my crime. In the mirror, to which I often went to look at myself, I noticed the changes in my face with pleasure. The eyes had grown larger, they seemed to be eating up the whole face. They were black and tender behind the glasses and I rolled them like planets. The fine eyes of an artist or assassin. But I counted on changing even more profoundly after the massacre. I have seen photographs of two beautiful girls—those servants who killed and plundered their mistress. I saw their photos *before* and *after*. *Before*, their faces poised like sky flowers above piqué collars. They smelled of hygiene and appetizing honesty. A discreet curling iron had waved their hair exactly alike. And, even more reassuring than their curled hair, their collars and their look of being at the photographer's, there was their resemblance as sisters, their well considered resemblance which immediately put the bonds of blood and natural roots of the family circle to the fore. *After*, their faces were resplendent as fire. They had the bare neck of prisoners about to be beheaded. Everywhere wrinkles, horrible wrinkles of fear and hatred, folds, holes in the flesh as though a beast with claws had walked over their faces. And those eyes, always those black, depthless eyes—like mine. Yet they did not resemble one another. Each one, in her own way, bore the memory of the common crime. "If it is enough," I told myself, "for a crime which was mostly chance, to transform these orphans' faces, what can I not hope for from a crime entirely conceived and organized by myself?" It would possess me, overturning my all-too-human ugliness . . . a crime, cutting the life of him who commits it in two. There must be times when one would like to turn back, but this shining object is there behind you, barring the way. I asked only an hour to enjoy mine, to feel its crushing weight. This time, I would arrange to have everything my way: I decided to carry out the execution at the top of the Rue Odessa. I would profit by the confusion to escape, leaving them to pick up their dead. I would run, I would cross the Boulevard Edgar-Quinet and turn quickly into the Rue Delambre. I would need only 30 seconds to reach the door of my building. My pursuers would still be on the Boulevard Edgar-Quinet, they would lose my trail and it would surely take them more than an hour to find it again. I would wait for them in my room, and when I would hear the beating on the door I would re-load my revolver and shoot myself in the mouth.

I began to live more expensively; I made an arrangement with the proprietor of a restaurant on the Rue Vavin who had a tray sent up every morning and evening. The boy rang, but I didn't open, I waited a few minutes, then opened the door half-way and saw full plates steaming in a long basket set on the floor.

On October 27, at six in the evening, I had only 17 and a half francs left. I tooks my revolver and the packet of letters and went downstairs. I took care not to close the door, so as to re-enter more rapidly once I had finished. I didn't feel well, my hands were cold and blood was rushing to my head, my eyes tickled me. I looked at the stores, the Hotel de l'Ecole, the stationer's where I buy my pencils and I didn't recognize them. I wondered, "What street is this?" The Boulevard Montparnasse was full of people. They jostled me, pushed me, bumped me with their elbows or shoulders. I let myself be shoved around, I didn't have the strength to slip in between them. Suddenly I saw myself in the heart of this mob, horribly alone and little. How they could have hurt me if they wanted! I was afraid because of the gun in my pocket. It seemed to me they could guess it was there. They would look at me with their hard eyes and would say: "Hey there . . . hey . . . !" with happy indignation, harpooning me with their men's paws. Lynched! They would throw me above their heads and I would fall back in their arms like a marionette. I thought it wiser to put off the execution of my plan until the next day. I went to eat at the *Cupole* for 16 francs 80. I had 70 centimes left and I threw them in the gutter.

I stayed three days in my room, without eating, without sleeping. I had drawn the blinds and I didn't dare go near the window or make a light. On Monday, someone rang at my door. I held my breath and waited. After a minute they rang again. I went on tiptoe and glued my eye to the keyhole. I could only see a piece of black cloth and a button. The man rang again and then went away. I don't know who it was. At night I had refreshing visions, palm trees, running water, a purple sky above a dome. I wasn't thirsty because hour after hour I went and drank at the spigot. But I was hungry. I saw the whore again. It was in a castle I had built in Causses Noires, about 60 miles from any town. She was naked and alone with me. Threatening her with my revolver I forced her to kneel and then run on all fours; then I tied her to a pillar and after I explained at great length what I was going to do, I riddled her with bullets. These images troubled me so much that I had to satisfy myself. Afterwards, I lay motionless in the darkness, my head absolutely empty. The furniture began to creak. It was five in the morning. I would have given anything to leave the room, but I couldn't go out because of the people walking in the street.

Day came, I didn't feel hungry any more, but I began to sweat: my shirt was soaked. Outside there was sunlight. Then I thought "He is crouched in blackness, in a closed room, for three days. He has neither eaten nor slept. They rang and He didn't open. Soon, He is going into the street and He will kill."

I frightened myself. At six o'clock in the evening hunger struck me again. I was mad with rage. I bumped into the furniture, then I turned lights on in the rooms, the kitchen, the bathroom. I began to sing at the top of my voice. I washed my hands and I went out. It took me a good two minutes to put all the letters in the box. I shoved them in by tens. I must have crumpled a few envelopes. Then I followed the Boulevard Montparnasse as far as the Rue Odessa. I stopped in front of a haberdasher's window and when I saw my face I thought, "Tonight."

I posted myself at the top of the Rue Odessa, not far from the street lamp, and waited. Two women passed, arm in arm.

I was cold but I was sweating freely. After a while I saw three men come up; I let them by: I needed six. The one on the left looked at me and clicked his tongue. I turned my eyes away.

At seven-five, two groups, following each other closely, came out onto the Boulevard Edgar-Quinet. There was a man and a woman with two children. Behind them came three old women. I took a step forward. The woman looked angry and was shaking the little boy's arm. The man drawled,

"What a little bastard he is."

My heart was beating so hard it hurt my arms. I advanced and stood in front of them, motionless. My fingers, in my pocket, were all soft around the trigger.

"Pardon," the man said, bumping into me.

I remembered I had closed the door of the apartment and that provoked me. I would have to lose precious time opening it. The people were getting further away. I turned around and followed them mechanically. But I didn't feel like shooting them any more. They were lost in the crowd on the boulevard. I leaned against the wall. I heard eight and nine o'clock strike. I repeated to myself, "Why must I kill all these people who are dead *already?*" and I wanted to laugh. A dog came and sniffed at my feet.

When the big man passed me, I jumped and followed him. I could see the fold of his red neck between his derby and the collar of his overcoat. He bounced a little in walking and breathed heavily, he looked husky. I took out my revolver: it was cold and bright, it disgusted me, I couldn't remember very well what I was supposed to do with it. Sometimes I looked at it and sometimes I looked at his neck. The fold in the neck smiled at me like a smiling, bitter mouth. I wondered if I wasn't going to throw my revolver into the sewer.

Suddenly, the man turned around and looked at me, irritated. I stepped back.

"I wanted to ask you . . ."

He didn't seem to be listening, he was looking at my hands.

"Can you tell me how to get to the Rue de la Gaité?"

His face was thick and his lips trembled. He said nothing. He stretched out his hand. I drew back further and said:

"I'd like . . ."

Then I *knew* I was going to start screaming. I didn't want to: I shot him three times in the belly. He fell with an idiotic look on his face, dropped to his knees and his head rolled on his left shoulder.

"Bastard," I said, "rotten bastard!"

I ran. I heard him coughing. I also heard shouts and feet clattering behind me. Somebody asked, "Is it a fight?" then right after that someone shouted "Murder! Murder!" I didn't think these shouts concerned me. But they seemed sinister, like the sirens of the fire engines when I was a child. Sinister and slightly ridiculous. I ran as fast as my legs could carry me.

Only I had committed an unpardonable error: instead of going up the Rue Odessa to the Boulevard Edgar-Quinet, *I was running down it toward the Boulevard Montparnasse.* When I realized it, it was too late: I was already in the midst of the crowd, astonished faces turned toward me (I remember the face of a heavily rouged woman wearing a green hat with an aigrette) and I heard the fools in the Rue Odessa shouting "murder" after me. A hand took me by the shoulder. I lost my head then: I didn't want to die stifled by this mob. I shot twice. People began to scream and scatter. I ran into a café. The drinkers jumped up as I ran through but made no attempt to stop me, I crossed the whole length of the café and locked myself in the lavatory. There was still one bullet in my revolver.

A moment went by. I was out of breath and gasping. Everything was extraordinarily silent, as though the people were keeping quiet on purpose. I raised the gun to my eyes and I saw its small hole, round and black: the bullet would come out there; the powder would burn my face. I dropped my arm and waited. After a while they came; there must have been a crowd of them, judging by the scuffling of feet on the floor. They whispered a little and then were quiet. I was still breathing heavily and I thought they must hear me breathing from the other side of the partition. Someone advanced quietly and rattled the door knob. He must have been flattened beside the door to avoid my bullets. I still wanted to shoot—but the last bullet was for me.

"What are they waiting for," I wondered. "If they pushed against the door and broke it down *right* away I wouldn't have time to kill myself and they would take me alive." But they were in no hurry; they gave me all the time in the world to die. The bastards, they were afraid.

After a while, a voice said, "All right, open up. We won't hurt you."

There was silence and the same voice went on, "You know you can't get away."

I didn't answer, I was still gasping for breath. To encourage myself to shoot, I told myself, "If they get me, they're going to beat me, break my teeth, maybe put an eye out." I wanted to know if the big man was dead. Maybe I only wounded him . . . They were getting something ready, they were dragging something heavy across the floor. I hurriedly put the barrel of the gun in my mouth, and I bit hard on it. But I couldn't shoot, I couldn't even put my finger on the trigger. Everything was dead silent.

I threw away the revolver and opened the door.

PART THREE

THE MEANINGS OF LOVE--
TWO SUMMATIONS

The following two selections, one from the biologist Julian Huxley, the other from the psychologist Erich Fromm, are interesting summations of the problems, the nature and the varied aspects of love. They are placed here for their usefulness as a bridge between the two volumes, serving as a review of what has preceded and as an introduction to the second volume, where we turn, more directly and fully, to the experience of love.

SIR JULIAN HUXLEY: What do we Know About Love?*

THE OPENING scene of that glorious satire, *Of Thee I Sing*, reveals a party caucus with an admirable presidential candidate but no ideas. They accordingly ask the hotel chambermaid, as representative of the People, what most people are most interested in, and are unhesitatingly answered "Love". And so love becomes the chief plank in their platform.

The first thing we know about love is what the chambermaid's answer implied—that for most people it is the most absorbing and interesting subject in existence. (In 1954, the Russians, at the Second Congress of Soviet Writers, officially rediscovered this important social fact.) Love can send young people eloping to Gretna Green, break up families, reduce strong men to lovesick slaves, even lead to murder or make kings lose their thrones; it can also energize human lives, induce the writing of a great deal of verse, including some of the finest poetry, induce states of ecstasy otherwise unattainable by the great majority of men and women, and provide the substance for most of our emotional dreaming.

This statement needs two qualifications. While it applies to contemporary Western peoples and doubtless to many others, it is not true for all cultures: sometimes war or hunting may take first place. Secondly, love as a plank in the chambermaid's personal platform and as an engrossing subject of popular interest means only one kind of love—the romantic sexual kind, the fact of "being in love".

It is almost impossible to give a formal definition of anything so complex and general as love. All I can do is to indicate some of the range of meanings comprised in this one little word. There is mother-love and self-love, father-love and grandmother-love, and children's love for their parents; there is brotherly love (which gave Philadelphia its name) and love of one's country; there is being in love, and making love; one can say that a man loves his food, though good manners dictates that he should not say it himself (when I as a small boy said I would love some chicken, my great-aunt rebuked me with the Victorian rhyme "You may love a screeching owl; you may not love a roasted fowl").

Many people love dancing; there are music-lovers, art-lovers, sport-lovers, dog-lovers, bird-lovers, sun-lovers, mountain-lovers; most of us have an intense and deep-rooted love of the surroundings in which we grew up; ministers assure us that God loves us and insist that we should love God, while Jesus adjured

* Reprinted from *New Bottles for New Wine*.

us to love our enemies; and there is love of money and love of power. . . .

All these are legitimate and normal usage: in its comprehensive sense, *love* clearly includes all of them. But equally clearly, the love in which one can be or into which one can fall is for most of us somehow pre-eminent over all other kinds.

Being in love is a special case of love as a general human capacity. It is love at it's most intense, and love personally focused and directed in a very special way. Our common speech reflects this fact. We talk of *falling in love*, as if it was something outside us, into which we are precipitated suddenly, accidentally and against our will, like falling into a pond. We say that X is infatuated with Y, or bewitched by her, or madly in love. Classical mythology expressed the suddenness and the sense of compulsion in the symbol of Cupid the blind archer, whose arrows inflict a magic wound on our emotional being.

Love at first sight (though of course not universal or indeed usual) is a frequent occurrence, surprising as a fact for scientific consideration as well as to those who experience it. But even when we are in love with someone we have known for months or years, the actual falling in love has been often, perhaps usually, not a gradual process but a sudden moment. Being in love, whether we fall suddenly or grow gradually into it, always has an element of compulsion, a sense of being possessed by some extraneous and magical power. Lovers are obsessed by an image of the loved one, to whom they ascribe every virtue and merit. Outside observers of the phenomenon speak of the lover's madness; and love is proverbially blind.

The lover experiences a sense of heightened vitality and finds a new significance in life. Mere contemplation of the beloved becomes a wellspring of the highest enjoyment. The lover seeks the presence of the beloved. Merely to see her (or him) from a distance is to feast the soul as well as the eyes; and to touch her is an inspiring bliss. But when, through two hands and two pairs of eyes, the two souls can interpenetrate, an even more magical state is achieved, as described in Donne's poem *The Ecstasy*.

> . . . Our hands were firmly cémented
>   By a fast balm which thence did spring;
> Our eye-beams twisted, and did thread
>   Our eyes upon one double string. . . .
>
> As 'twixt two equal armies Fate
>   Suspends uncertain victory,
> Our souls—which to advance their state
>   Were gone out—hung 'twixt her and me.

> And whilst our souls negotiate there,
> We like sepulchral statues lay;
> All day the same our postures were,
> And we said nothing, all the day.

Modern psychology has rightly abandoned the term *soul*, because of the philosophical and theological implications that have become attached to it; but we can translate it as meaning the unitary inner core of our conscious selves and this sense of the going out of our essential being and of its interpenetrating or uniting with another being is one of the hall-marks of being in love.

This is embodied in one of the loveliest epigrams of the Greek Anthology:

> Τὴν ψυχὴν ᾿Αγάθωνα φιλῶν ἐπὶ χείλεσιν ἔσχον·
> ἦλθε γὰρ ἡ τλήμων ὡς διαβησομένη.

As I kissed Agathon, I had my soul in my lips; for the rash creature came thither as if to pass across.

For true lovers, the act of physical union is actuated not merely or indeed mainly by the desire for pleasure but for the transcendent sense of total union which it can bring. William Blake rightly rebukes the puritans who

> Call a shame and sin
> Love's temple that God dwelleth in . . .
> And render that a lawless thing
> On which the soul expands its wing.

And Robert Bridges reminds us how the lower is necessarily incorporated in the higher:—

> We see Spiritual, Mental and Animal
> To be gradations merged together in growth, . . .
> . . . And that the animal pleasure
> Runneth throughout all graces heartening all energies.

Even children may fall in sudden love, long before puberty and its hormones have actuated the full sexual urge. The classical example is Dante, who fell in love with Beatrice when she was just eight and he nearly nine. In his *Vita Nuova*—The New Life— he has left an immortal description of the event which coloured all his later existence. "At that instant, the spirit of life which dwells in the heart's most secret chamber began to tremble so violently that all the pulses of my body shook; and in trembling it said these words: 'Here is a god stronger than I, who is come to rule over me.' "

He only saw her a few more times, and she died at the age

of twenty-five. But his love dominated the rest of his life, and inspired his great work. The distinction between love and sex is very obvious here. Dante reserved his fullest and highest love for a woman whose hand he had never even touched, but had four children by the excellent wife he later married. However, before dealing further with this question, I want to say something about the evolution and development of love—its evolution in nature apart from man, and its development in individual human beings.

People sometimes ask what purpose love serves in nature. But a biologist cannot answer a question framed in terms of purpose, for purpose implies deliberate design for a conscious end, and there is no evidence of that in the natural world. To be biologically answerable, the question should run, "What functions does love perform in living organisms?" Even so, the biologist cannot give a nice simple or single answer, for among animals there are various different kinds of love, expressed in various different ways, and manifested in different degrees of clarity and intensity. There has been an evolution of love, as of every other property of life, and we must supplement our question by asking how the different kinds of love have evolved.

In many young mammals, like kittens, some adult mammals, like otters, and various adult birds, like penguins and rooks and swifts, we find something closely akin to our love of play or sport—the enjoyment of bodily performance for its own sake, irrespective of its practical utility. Among birds there is the beginning of a love of beauty, manifested in the collection of bright objects by jackdaws and magpies, and in bowerbirds by a preference for certain colours and by their deliberate painting of their bowers. The roots of love of country are shown in the attachment of many kinds of birds and mammals to their home territory, and of love of nature in such rituals as the high aerial dawn-chorus of swallows and martins.

Finally, animals show several different types of love in the restricted sense—love focused on other individuals. There is parental love, of parent for offspring; there is offspring love, of offspring for parent; there is sexual love, between actual or potential mates; and there is social love, for other individuals of the same species. The roots of social love are found in gregarious animals, and are manifested in the distress caused by solitude and the impulse to seek the company of their fellows.

Parental love is in most species only maternal. In many mammals and in all polygamous birds, the mother alone is concerned about the young—think of bears or sheep or the domestic hen. But in some fish and toads and a few birds, like emus and phalaropes, it is the male alone that looks after eggs and young; and of course in all our familiar songbirds the cock bird helps to feed the young once they have been hatched by the hen, while in birds like grebes and gannets, auks and petrels and penguins, both cock and hen share equally in incubation too. Comparatively few insects show parental love (the female earwig is one), and in those where it is most developed, namely bees and ants, it is not strictly speaking parental love but maiden-aunt love (or nurse love if you like), for it is only the neuter females, the so-called workers, that have the instinct to look after the eggs and grubs.

This brings up an important point. In animals, parental (and nurse) love is purely instinctive; not only the urge to care for the young, but also the detailed ways in which it manifests itself, depend on inborn nervous mechanisms, and do not have to be learned. Furthermore, like all instincts, parental love, though doubtless associated with strong emotions, is blind and automatic. It is a psychological mechanism which works admirably in normal conditions, but is apt to go astray in abnormal ones. Thus a worker wasp which was kept from access to food for the young was seen to satisfy its nurse-instinct by biting off the hind end of a grub and offering it to the front end!

The same blind imprisonment of instinctive behaviour within a limited situation is seen even in birds and mammals. Thus song-birds only pay attention to their young so long as they are in the nest. When a cuckoo has ejected its foster-brothers and -sisters, the parents take no notice of their cries of distress, even if they are hanging on a twig just outside the nest. And even in normal circumstances it is not the sight of the young bird as an individual that impels the parents to feed it, but merely the colour and shape of its gaping mouth: they will feed an artificial gape of painted wood (if properly made) just as readily as their own nestlings. And a cow distressed by the removal of her calf can be comforted by its skin.

The same sort of thing holds for the sexual instinct. Certain orchids get pollinated by looking and perhaps smelling like female flies: the male flies try to mate with them, and in so doing transfers the fertilizing pollen from flower to flower. Similarly many birds will attempt to mate with a stuffed dead female as readily as with a real live one—provided that it is set up in a certain pose; and the sperm for artificial insemination in cattle and horses can be obtained because the mating urge of bulls and stallions is aroused by suitable dummies as well as by live cows or mares.

But the mental life of birds, for instance, is a curious mixture, in which some types of emotional behaviour are carried out blindly, crudely, and wholly instinctively, while others depend on detailed learning. A cock robin, for instance (not the fat American robin, which is really a thrush, but our little European robin redbreast), will be automatically and irrationally stimulated to his threat-display by the sight of a red breast, whether on a live rival, a stuffed bird, or a headless and tailless dummy; but he learns the difference between his mate and all other hen robins and can recognize her individually afar off.

The robin's red breast and the gape of nestling birds are examples of what are called *releasers*—they are visual sign-stimuli which release the action of innate impulses and chains of activity, in the one case of hostility or aggression, in the other of service or affection—the beginnings of hate and of love.

In polygamous-promiscuous species like ruff and sage-grouse and blackcock, the sexes never meet except on a communal display-ground, and the males' sexual "love" is merely the urge to physical mating, expressed in violent antics serving to intimidate rivals or stimulate mates by showing off the exaggerated masculine display-plumage.

In most birds, however, there is an emotional bond between mates, and the pair stays together, either for the brood, or for the season, or, in a number of species, for life. Life-mates like to be close together even in the winter, as you may see with jackdaws. This emotional bond is clearly one of the forerunners of human married love.

In some water-birds, such as grebes, where male and female share equally the duties of incubating the eggs and feeding the young, there are elaborate ceremonies of mutual display, participated in by both mates together, and obviously highly stimulating to the emotions. What is more, some displays are not confined to the period of courtship or physical mating, but continue right through the breeding season, until the young are full-grown. Here I would say the rituals of animal love find their fullest expression.

Though from the standpoint of the species this emotional bond has been evolved for the utilitarian function of keeping the mated pair together while their joint efforts are needed for the successful rearing of their young, from that of the individual birds the ceremonies are clearly very satisfying and have emotional value in themselves.

Emotional life in animals is essentially a patchwork. Particular urges or emotions arise in particular circumstances, and usually stay in separate channels. Fear may dictate behaviour for a period, then suddenly hunger steps in, then perhaps sexual desire. Animals lack man's capacity to bring together many different urges and emotions, memories and hopes, into a single continuity of conscious life. The main exception to this, interestingly enough, concerns love. Both in the parent-offspring relation and in that between the two sexes, attraction and hostility are often combined. The primary reaction of a nestling or a brooding heron to the appearance of an adult at the nest is fear and hostility: before the arriving bird is accepted as parent or as mate, it must be recognized as such; and recognition is effected by a special "appeasing" display. This in turn forms the basis for the elaborate ceremony of nest-relief, which finally serves as an emotional bond between the mated pair.

In many birds' species, during the "courtship" period, the sight of a bird of the opposite sex often acts as a sign-stimulus releasing both hostility (as an alien intruding individual) and attraction (as a potential mate). Thus the unmated male housesparrow in possession of a nest-site endeavours to attract passing females, but if one tries to enter the nest he will attack her, and even after they have accepted each other as mates, it may be two or three days before she is allowed into her future home.

The courtship-displays of many species turn out to be ritualizations of this ambivalent emotion compounded of attraction and either hostility or fear (and show many parallels with human courtship, especially in young people). The male bird's aggressivity may be transformed into a stimulating display of masculinity and desire, and female timidity often expresses itself by reverting to infantile dependence, with adoption of the nestling's food-begging attitude.

Thus love, in the sense of positive attraction between individuals, has arisen during biological evolution in the form of a patchwork of distinct urges or drives, each serving a distinct biological function. The mechanism of each separate kind of love is largely built in to the species by heredity. For the most part, each drive is automatically activated by a sign-stimulus functioning as a releaser, a distinctive pattern of sight or sound (like the gape of the nestling for stimulating the parental feeding drive of its parents, or the "song" of male grasshoppers for the sexual approach of the female); and is expressed in a genetically predetermined set of actions (like the displays of amorous male birds). Learning by experience plays only a secondary role, or sometimes no role at all.

Further, there is little synthesis of the separate drives into a coherent or continuous mental life. However, desire is often frustrated, and attraction often compounded with hostility or fear, and the resultant conflict is reconciled in the performance of some ritualized ceremony of display. This may then be further specialized during subsequent evolution to provide more effective stimulation of the female, or be converted into a mutual ceremony serving as a bond to keep the mated pair together; and such ceremonies, especially the mutual ones, may come to have emotional value in themselves.

" 'Tis love, 'tis love that makes the world go round," sang the anonymous ballad-monger. And certainly love, in its dawning manifestations among animals, secures the perpetuation of the species and the care of offspring, lays the foundations of more or less permanent marriage unions, and may even emerge as a value in itself.

When we come to our own species, we find a certain general parallel between the process of individual development of love in man and that of its evolution in animals, but also many important differences. There is more reliance on learning by experience, less on inborn genetic mechanisms. However, two or three inborn sign-stimuli do seem to exist. One is the smile. Even a crudely grimacing model of a smiling face will elicit from an infant a smile (and the positive mood which goes with smiling and is one of the bases of enjoying and loving). And women's breasts (though, as Dr. Johnson pointed out, not feeding-bottles) will act as a powerful sign-stimulus to male sexual love.

Non-sexual loves of many kinds appear and develop in the growing child. At the outset are the simple basic desires for food and warmth and protection, soon transmuted into love of enjoyment and contentment, general satisfaction and fulfilment. Then the personal focusing of love on to the individuals that provide what is desired—first mother or nurse, then father, brothers and sisters, and other children. Then the widening of the circle of love and of personal attachment (Walt Whitman speaks of the "fluid and attaching character" that some people seem to exude); and finally, love for the beautiful or the strange, the thrilling or the significant.

These more complex loves may sometimes attain the intensity of passions. The full force of a child's emotions may be bound up with some shell or curious stone that he has found: or the experience of beauty may change his whole emotional attitude to life. Let Wordsworth speak:

> My heart leaps up when I behold
>   A rainbow in the sky:
> So was it when my life began;
> So is it now I am a man;
> So be it when I shall grow old,
>   Or let me die!
> The Child is father of the Man;

And I could wish my days to be
Bound each to each by natural piety.

Or again, in his famous Ode:

There was a time when meadow, grove and stream,
The earth, and every common sight,
            To me did seem
            Apparell'd in celestial light,
The glory and the freshness of a dream.

"The hour of splendour in the grass, of glory in the flower" may pass and fade, but the experience of love for natural beauty, of enhanced vitality and the upleaping heart, of self-transcendence in loving union with something outside onself, may change a growing human being permanently, and can enter later into his love for God, for someone of the other sex, for ideals. As one of Truman Capote's characters says, apropos of a jay's lovely blue egg that she had kept from childhood, "love is a chain of love. . . . Because you can love one thing, you can love another."

The growing child comes to love many different kinds of things in many different ways—sometimes with the self-centred desire for possession; sometimes with the self-transcending desire for unity with the object of desire, or the outgoing sense of communion in the act of experience, as with Richard Jefferies' or Thomas Traherne's mystical experiences of the beauty and wonder of nature; sometimes with the enriching of enjoyment in the full and free exercise of his faculties, physical or psychological.

And then, at puberty, there is the intrusion of the sexual impulse. The sex impulse appears as an alien power, strong, new and often frightening. The experience is all the more upsetting because the new power, though alien to our past life or present make-up, is yet within us, a part of ourselves. The central problem of adolescence is, in general, how to incorporate this intruding force into the developing personality; and in particular, how to integrate sex and love. This is especially acute because of the disharmony between man's biological nature and his social arrangements, the fact that there is a gap of years between the time when the sexual impulse emerges (and emerges at maximum strength, at least in boys, as Dr. Kinsey has shown) and the time when marriage is possible.

Adolescence is also the time when love, as distinct from sexual desire, alters its character. At puberty romantic idealism raises its head as well as sex: and another problem of adolescence is how to integrate this idealism with the hard facts of existence, and romance with the practical business of living.

Man, however, differs from all other animals in having a

brain which can and largely does bring all the various elements
of experience into contact, instead of keeping them in a series of
wholly or largely separate compartments or channels. This not
only provides the basis for conceptual thought, and so for all
man's ideas and philosophic systems, ideals and works of art and
creative imagination, but also for his battery of complex sentiments unknown in animals, such as reverence and religious awe,
moral feelings (including hate and contempt arising from moral
abhorrence), and love in its developed form.

It also, however, provides the basis for emotional or psychological conflict on a scale unknown in animals. One of the
unique characters of man is his constant subjection to mental
conflict, with the resultant necessity for making moral decisions.
Man's morality, indeed, is a necessary consequence of his inner
conflicts.

Nowhere is this better illustrated than in love. Strong
sexual desire, as well as the reverent worship of beauty, self-fulfil-
ment, and ideal aspiration, plays a part in human love. But crude
sexual desire in itself is merely lust and is universally regarded
as immoral, and to many people the sexual act appears as something dirty or disgusting.

However, love at its truest and fullest and most intense
can include in its single embrace an enormous range of emotions
and sentiments, and fuse them all, even those of baser metal, in
its crucible. It can combine humility with pride, passion with
peace, self-assertion with self-surrender; it can reconcile violence
of feeling with tenderness, can swallow up disgust in beauty and
imperfection in fulfilment, and sublimate sexual desire into joy
and fuller life.

It can, but it does not always do so. Sometimes the inhibitions of morality or romantic idealism are too strong, and the
fusion is imperfect, the reconciliation remains incomplete. This
is especially so in puritan cultures and religions imbued with a
sense of sin. St. Paul's attitude to sexual love is expressed in his
dictum that it is better to marry than to burn: tormented souls
like St Augustine and Tolstoy came to regard sexual love not as
fulfilment but as sin, and Gandhi's autobiography tells us how his
early indulgences drove him later to prescribe—for others!—self-
control and abstinence instead of the ideal of pure enjoyment, of
joy disciplined and transformed by tenderness, reverence, and
beauty.

Sometimes, indeed, love involves contradictory and un-
reconciled emotions. In one of his most famous poems, Catullus
wrote

> *Odi et amo: quare id faciam, fortasse requiris.*
> *Nescio, sed fieri sentio et excrucior.*

"I hate and love: how can that be, perhaps you ask? I know not, but so I feel, and am in torment." The hero of Somerset Maugham's *Of Human Bondage* is intellectually aware of the imperfections and indeed the unattractiveness of the girl he is in love with, but remains emotionally enslaved by her.

In love, indeed, the conflict between reason and emotion is often at highest pitch. However, though falling in love is irrational, or at least non-rational, yet love can be (though it is not always) later influenced by reason and guided by experience. Emotion in general is non-rational; it tends to all-or-nothing manifestations and is naturally resistant to the critical and balanced spirit of reason. And the emotions involved in love are so violent that this uncritical or anti-critical tendency readily overrides reason. That is why love is called blind, why it may become a kind of madness or sickness. But reason can play a part later. With time, as the emotional violence of love diminishes and rational experience accumulates, a point may suddenly be reached at which reason gains the upper hand, the deluded lover's eyes are opened, he realizes that he has been blind, and he falls out of love as he once fell in. Such experiences are useful though harsh reminders of the sad fact that emotional certitude alone is never a guarantee of rightness or truth, in religious or moral belief any more than in love: sudden religious conversion resembles falling in love in many ways, including its non-rationality.

Luckily for the human race, love often chooses aright. And then reason and emotional experience may give it eyes to see and may transform a transient madness into the highest and most enduring sanity. This rationally guided transformation and development of love has been immortally described by Wordsworth in his poem, *Perfect Woman*. It is too long for me to quote in its entirety, but you will recall how it begins with a magical, altogether non-rational moment—

> She was a Phantom of delight
> When first she gleam'd upon my sight;

how experience altered the vision—

> I saw her upon nearer view,
> A Spirit, yet a Woman too!

and how it finally transformed sudden magic into permanent serenity—

> And now I see with eye serene
> The very pulse of the machine . . .

A perfect Woman, nobly planned,
To warn, to comfort, and command;
And yet a Spirit still, and bright
With something of angelic light.

Often, however, love does not choose right the first time.
I should rather say, first love often does not choose permanently
right. Many teen-age "pashes" and "crushes", however violent at
the time, and many cases of adolescent calf-love, though often
valuable and indeed "right" in the sense of providing necessary
experience to the callow personality, are soon outgrown.

Even when it comes to marriage, many first choices are
wrong, and later ones may be much more right. The relation
between love and marriage urgently needs reconsideration. For
one thing, in our Western societies, we have become too credulous
about romantic love, just as earlier ages were too credulous about
religious faith. Both can often be blind, and then both can mislead us. For another, we have become obsessed with the rigid
moralists' stern insistence on the inviolability and indissolubility
of marriage—a religious doctrine imposed on a social bond.

The emotional certitude of being in love with someone
does not guarantee either its rightness, or its uniqueness, or its
permanence, any more than it ensures that the love shall be recip-
rocated. And the undoubted general desirability, both social and
personal, of long-enduring monogamous marriage does not pre-
clude the occasional desirability of divorce and change of mar-
riage-partner, nor justify the branding of any extra-marital love
as a grave social immorality or personal sin.

Our reconsideration should be related to the idea of
greater fulfilment. Of course conflicts will inevitably arise between greater fulfilment for onself, for one's partner, one's
children, and one's community; but they will then be better
illuminated and more readily soluble than in the light of romantic illusion, religious dogma, or static and absolute morality.

It must be remembered that love and its manifestations
differ in different societies and cultures. We find a differentiation
and development of love as part of the general cultural evolution
of man. Margaret Mead and other anthropologists have shown to
what a surprising extent cultures may differ in their general attitude to love, both sexual and parental, and in their expression
of it. Masculinity may be valued either higher or lower than femininity, ardour and passion higher or lower than coolness and
acceptance; parental love may be either indulgent or strict to children, or its expression, warm and full in early years, may be suddenly withdrawn from the child at a certain age; the attitude of

society both to pre-marital love-making and post-marital love-affairs may differ enormously.

A striking example of the evolution of love is the rise of the idea of romantic love in medieval Europe. This found an exaggerated expression in the ballads of the troubadours and the rituals of chivalry, but has left a permanent mark on our Western civilization.

Love presents, in intensive form, man's central and perennial problem—how to reconcile the claims of the individual and of society, personal desires with social aims. The problem is perhaps most acute in adolescence, for this involves a disharmony of timing: our sexual desires arise, and in males arise in fullest force, several years before marriage is desirable or possible. Different cultures have met this problem in very different ways. Thus in eighteenth-century England and nineteenth-century France it was the acknowledged thing for upper-class young men to take a mistress, while this was frowned on in Geneva and New England. In twentieth-century America, dating and petting have superseded "bundling" as the recognized formula.

Many primitive societies go further, and institutionalize adolescent love. Thus among the Masai of East Africa the boys after initiation become Moran or Warriors and live in communities with the initiated girls, sharing what seems to be a very agreeable love-life. Only after some years do they marry, and from then on, extra-marital love is severely frowned on. Their neighbours, the Kikuyu, had a somewhat similar system, in which, however, full sexual intercourse was not permitted. The same sort of arrangement prevails among the Bontocs of the Philippines, as recorded by Stewart Kilton in his *Dream Giants and Pygmies*. Here, as among country-folk in England until quite recently, adolescent love-making serves also as a try-out of fertility. A girl can only marry if she conceives; and sterile girls become "a sort of educational institution" for young boys.

In modern civilization the problem is very real and very serious. On the one hand, clearly both undisciplined indulgence and complete promiscuity in love are individually damaging, or anti-social, or both; but on the other hand, complete repression of this most powerful of impulses is equally damaging, and so is the self-reproach that the indulgence or even the mere manifestation of the impulse arouses in sensitive adolescents who have had an exaggerated sense of sin imposed on them. From another angle, it is tragic to think of millions of human beings denied the full beauty and exaltation of love precisely while their impulses are strongest and their sensibilities at their highest pitch.

No civilization has yet adequately harmonized the disharmony or provided satisfactory means of resolving the conflict. Indeed there can be no solution in the sense that there is a single definite solution to a mechanical puzzle or a mathematical problem. The problem of love, as of any other aspect of life, must be solved *ambulando*, or rather *vivendo*, in living; and the correctness of the solution is only to be measured by the fulfilment achieved, the degree to which desirable possibilities are realized and conflicting elements and interests harmonized. What is more, we can rarely expect to arrive at a satisfactory solution at the first shot: fulfilment is a process, and we have to learn it, to achieve it step by step, often making mistakes, often precipitated into new and unforeseen problems or conflicts by the solution of previous ones.

Love between the sexes can provide some of the highest fulfilments of life. It also provides an important means for the development of personality: through it we learn many necessary things about ourselves, about others, about society, and about human ideals. We must, I think, aim at a moral and religious climate of society in which the adolescent experiments of love, instead of being branded as wicked or relegated to furtive and illicit gropings, or repressed until they collapse in neurosis or explode in lust, or merely tolerated as an unpleasing necessity, are socially sanctioned and religiously sanctified, in the same sort of way as marriage is now. Adolescent affairs of the heart could be regarded as reverent experiments in love, or as trial marriages, desirable preparations for the more enduring adventure of adult marriage. Young people would assuredly continue to make mistakes, to be selfish or lustful or otherwise immoral; but matters would I am sure be better than they are now, and could not well be much worse.

In considering love we must not leave out hate, for in one sense love and hate are the positive and negative aspects of the same thing, the primary emotional reaction to another individual. This can either be one of attraction, desire, or tenderness, or one of repulsion, fear, or hostility. In this light it is easy to understand how love, especially when ardent and blind, can so readily turn into equally uncritical hate.

From the evolutionary angle, however, love and hate must be thought of as distinct. They have independent origins and are canalized and expressed in different ways. As we have seen, love in animals may have a number of separate and specific manifestations—parental, sexual, and social. The same holds for hate: it may manifest itself in fear, in avoidance, or in aggression. We have also seen how love and hate may be simultaneously aroused, as in the combination of desire and hostility in the sexual life of birds, and may then be compounded and the conflict reconciled in a new expression, in the form of a ritual display.

For the most part, however, psychological conflict is avoided in animals by means of an automatic nervous mechanism similar to that which prevents conflicting muscles from coming into action simultaneously. When, for instance, a nervous message is sent to the flexor muscles to contract and bend our arm, it is accompanied by a second message inhibiting and relaxing the extensor muscles which would straighten it. The same sort of thing often happens with more complicated reflex activities, and, as already mentioned, with animal instincts: when the fear instinct is switched into action, the hunger or the sex instinct is switched out. It may also operate in man's emotional conflicts: one of two conflicting patterns of feeling and thought may be either voluntarily and temporarily suppressed into the subconscious, or wholly and permanently repressed into the unconscious. There, however, as Freud discovered, it can still continue its nagging and produce a sense of guilt. Total and unremembered repression naturally occurs most often in infancy and early life, before experience and reason have had time to begin coping with the paralysing conflict between contradictory emotions and impulses.

The primal conflict which besets the human infant is between love and hate. He (or she) inevitably loves his mother (or mother-surrogate) as the fountainhead of his satisfactions, his security, comfort, and peace. But at times he is also angry with her, as the power which arbitrarily, it seems to him, denies him satisfaction and thwarts his impulses: and his anger calls into play what the psychologists call aggression—his battery of magic hate-phantasies and death-wishes and destructive rage-impulses.

But his hate soon comes into paralysing conflict with his love, and must be repressed. It also gives him a sense of guilt or wrongness, even from its lair in the unconscious; and this charge of primal guilt continues to exist and is built into his developing personality. When an action or impulse arouses this sense of guilt, it is automatically felt as wrong. Thus the infantile conflict between love and hate generates what we may call the individual's proto-ethical mechanism, the rudiment around which his conscience and his truly ethical sense of right and wrong are later built, rather as his embryonic notochord provided the basis for the future development of his backbone.

Of course, reason and experience, imagination and ideals also make their contributions. But the basis of conscience and ethics remains irrational and largely unconscious, as shown by the terrifying sense of sin and unworthiness which besets those

unfortunates on whom a too-heavy burden of personal guilt has
been imposed.

Consciences, in fact, are not genetically predetermined and
do not grow automatically like backbones, but need the infantile
conflict between love and hate for their origination. This is demonstrated by recent studies like those of John Bowlby and Spitz,
on children who have been brought up in impersonal institutions
or otherwise deprived of the care of a mother or personal mother-
substitute, during a critical period between one and three years
old. Many of them never develop a conscience, and grow up as
amoral beings, creatures without ethics.

The mother is thus the central figure in the evolution of
love. For one thing, maternal love always involves tenderness and
devoted care, which sexual love does not. Only when the different
kinds or components of love become blended, as they do most
thoroughly in man, though to some extent in some birds and
mammals, does sexual love come to involve tenderness as well as
desire. As Robert Bridges writes in his *Testament of Beauty*, "In
man this blind motherly attachment is the spring of his purest
affection, and of all compassion." And again, "Through mother-
hood it [self-hood] came in animals to altrustic feeling, and
thence-after in man rose to spiritual affection."

But the mother also provides the focus for the human
infant's personal emotions, both of love and hate, and in so doing
unwittingly lays the foundations of conscience, and starts the
child on its course towards high morality and spiritual ideals.

I have no space to discuss many other aspects of love—the
problem of homosexual love, for instance; or the interesting differences found by Dr. Kinsey between the development of sexual
love in men and in women; or the relations between married love
and conjugal fidelity.

But I would like to close with an affirmation of the unique
importance of love in human life—an affirmation which seems to
me essential in a tormented age like ours, where violence and disillusion have joined forces with undigested technological advance
to produce an atmosphere of cynicism and crude materialism.

Mother-love is indispensable not only for the healthy and
happy physical growth of young human beings, but for their
healthy and happy moral and spiritual growth as well. Personal
love between the sexes is not only indispensable for the physical
continuance of the race, but for the full development of the
human personality. It is part of education: through love, the self
learns to grow. Love of beauty and of all lovely and wonderful
things is equally indispensable for our mental growth and the
realization of our possibilities. It brings reverence and a sense of

transcendence into sexual and personal love, and indeed into all of life. In general, love is a positive emotion, an enlargement of life leading on towards greater fulfilment and capable of counter-acting human hate and destructive impulses.

Let the final word be that of a poet who was also a man of science—Robert Bridges.

> He [Aristotle] hath made Desire to be the prime mover of all.
> I see the emotion of saint, lovers and poets all
> To be the kindling of some personality
> By an eternizing passion; and that God's worshipper
> Looking on any beauty falleth straightway in love;
> And that love is a fire in whose devouring flames
> All earthly ills are consumed.

ERICH FROMM: The Theory of Love*

MAN IS gifted with reason; he is *life being aware of itself*; he has awareness of himself, of his fellow man, of his past, and of the possibilities of his future. This awareness of himself as a separate entity, the awareness of his own short life span, of the fact that without his will he is born and against his will he dies, that he will die before those whom he loves, or they before him, the awareness of his aloneness and separateness, of his helplessness before the forces of nature and of society, all this makes his separate, disunited existence an unbearable prison. He would become insane could he not liberate himself from this prison and reach out, unite himself in some form or other with men, with the world outside.

The experience of separateness arouses anxiety; it is, indeed, the source of all anxiety. Being separate means being cut off, without any capacity to use my human powers. Hence to be separate means to be helpless, unable to grasp the world—things and people—actively; it means that the world can invade me without my ability to react. Thus, separateness is the source of intense anxiety. Beyond that, it arouses shame and the feeling of guilt. This experience of guilt and shame in separateness is expressed in the Biblical story of Adam and Eve. After Adam and Eve have eaten of the "tree of knowledge of good and evil," after they have disobeyed (there is no good and evil unless there is freedom to disobey), after they have become human by having emancipated themselves from the original animal harmony with nature, i.e., after their birth as human beings—they saw "that they were naked

* Reprinted from *The Art of Loving*.

—and they were ashamed." Should we assume that a myth as old
and elementary as this has the prudish morals of the nineteenth-
century outlook, and that the important point the story wants to
convey to us is the embarrassment that their genitals were visible?
This can hardly be so, and by understanding the story in a Victorian spirit, we miss the main point, which seems to be the following: after man and woman have become aware of themselves
and of each other, they are aware of their separateness, and of
their difference, inasmuch as they belong to different sexes. But
while recognizing their separateness they remain strangers, because they have not yet learned to love each other (as is also
made very clear by the fact that Adam defends himself by blaming
Eve, rather than by trying to defend her). *The awareness of human separation, without reunion by love—is the source of shame.
It is at the same time the source of guilt and anxiety.*

The deepest need of man, then, is the need to overcome
his separateness, to leave the prison of his aloneness. The *absolute*
failure to achieve this aim means insanity, because the panic of
complete isolation can be overcome only by such a radical withdrawal from the world outside that the feeling of separation disappears—because the world outside, from which one is separated,
has disappeared.

Man—of all ages and cultures—is confronted with the solution of one and the same question: the question of how to overcome separateness, how to achieve union, how to transcend one's
own individual life and find at-onement. The question is the same
for primitive man living in caves, for nomadic man taking care
of his flocks, for the peasant in Egypt, the Phoenician trader, the
Roman soldier, the medieval monk, the Japanese samurai, the
modern clerk and factory hand. The question is the same, for it
springs from the same ground: the human situation, the conditions of human existence. The answer varies. The question can
be answered by animal worship, by human sacrifice or military
conquest, by indulgence in luxury, by ascetic renunciation, by obsessional work, by artistic creation, by the love of God, and by the
love of Man. While there are many answers—the record of which
is human history—they are nevertheless not innumerable. On the
contrary, as soon as one ignores smaller differences which belong
more to the periphery than to the center, one discovers that there
is only a limited number of answers which have been given, and
only could have been given by man in the various cultures in
which he has lived. The history of religion and philosophy is the
history of these answers, of their diversity, as well as of their
limitation in number.

The answers depend, to some extent, on the degree of individuation which an individual has reached. In the infant I-ness has developed but little yet; he still feels one with mother, has no feeling of separateness as long as mother is present. Its sense of aloneness is cured by the physical presence of the mother, her breasts, her skin. Only to the degree that the child develops his sense of separateness and individuality is the physical presence of the mother not sufficient any more, and does the need to overcome separateness in other ways arise.

Similarly, the human race in its infancy still feels one with nature. The soil, the animals, the plants are still man's world. He identifies himself with animals, and this is expressed by the wearing of animal masks, by the worshiping of a totem animal or animal gods. But the more the human race emerges from these primary bonds, the more it separates itself from the natural world, the more intense becomes the need to find new ways of escaping separateness.

One way of achieving this aim lies in all kinds of *orgiastic states*. These may have the form of an auto-induced trance, sometimes with the help of drugs. Many rituals of primitive tribes offer a vivid picture of this type of solution. In a transitory state of exultation the world outside disappears, and with it the feeling of separateness from it. Inasmuch as these rituals are practiced in common, an experience of fusion with the group is added which makes this solution all the more effective. Closely related to, and often blended with this orgiastic solution, is the sexual experience. The sexual orgasm can produce a state similar to the one produced by a trance, or to the effects of certain drugs. Rites of communal sexual orgies were a part of many primitive rituals. It seems that after the orgiastic experience, man can go on for a time without suffering too much from his separateness. Slowly the tension of anxiety mounts, and then is reduced again by the repeated performance of the ritual.

As long as these orgiastic states are a matter of common practice in a tribe, they do not produce anxiety or guilt. To act in this way is right, and even virtuous, because it is a way shared by all, approved and demanded by the medicine men or priests; hence there is no reason to feel guilty or ashamed. It is quite different when the same solution is chosen by an individual in a culture which has left behind these common practices. Alcoholism and drug addiction are the forms which the individual chooses in a non-orgiastic culture. In contrast to those participating in the socially patterned solution, such individuals suffer from guilt feelings and remorse. While they try to escape from separateness by taking refuge in alcohol or drugs, they feel all the more separate after the orgiastic experience is over, and thus are driven to take recourse to it with increasing frequency and intensity. Slightly different from this is the recourse to a sexual orgiastic solution. To some extent it is a natural and normal form of overcoming separateness, and a partial answer to the problem of isolation. But in many individuals in whom separateness is not relieved in other ways, the search for the sexual orgasm assumes a function which makes it not very different from alcoholism and drug addiction. It becomes a desperate attempt to escape the anxiety engendered by separateness, and it results in an ever-increasing sense of separateness, since the sexual act without love never bridges the gap between two human beings, except momentarily.

All forms of orgiastic union have three characteristics: they are intense, even violent; they occur in the total personality, mind *and* body; they are transitory and periodical. Exactly the opposite holds true for that form of union which is by far the most frequent solution chosen by man in the past and in the present: the union based on *conformity* with the group, its customs, practices and beliefs. Here again we find a considerable development.

In a primitive society the group is small; it consists of those with whom one shares blood and soil. With the growing development of culture, the group enlarges; it becomes the citizenry of a *polis*, the citizenry of a large state, the members of a church. Even the poor Roman felt pride because he could say "*civis romanus sum*"; Rome and the Empire were his family, his home, his world. Also in contemporary Western society the union with the group is the prevalent way of overcoming separateness. It is a union in which the individual self disappears to a large extent, and where the aim is to belong to the herd. If I am like everybody else, if I have no feelings or thoughts which make me different, if I conform in custom, dress, ideas, to the pattern of the group, I am saved; saved from the frightening experience of aloneness. The dictatorial systems use threats and terror to induce this conformity; the democratic countries, suggestion and propaganda. There is, indeed, one great difference between the two systems. In the democracies non-conformity is possible and, in fact, by no means entirely absent; in the totalitarian systems, only a few unusual heroes and martyrs can be expected to refuse obedience. But in spite of this difference the democratic societies show an overwhelming degree of conformity. The reason lies in the fact that there *has* to be an answer to the quest for union, and if there is no other or better way, then the union of herd conformity becomes the predominant one. One can only understand the power of the fear to be different, the fear to be only a few steps away from the herd, if one understands the depths of the need not to be separated. Sometimes this fear of non-conformity is rationalized as fear of practical dangers which could threaten the nonconformist. But actually, people *want* to conform to a much higher degree than they are *forced* to conform, at least in the Western democracies.

Most people are not even aware of their need to conform. They live under the illusion that they follow their own ideas and inclinations, that they are individualists, that they have arrived at their opinions as the result of their own thinking—and that it just happens that their ideas are the same as those of the majority. The consensus of all serves as a proof for the correctness of "their" ideas. Since there is still a need to feel some individuality, such need is satisfied with regard to minor differences; the initials on the handbag or the sweater, the name plate of the bank teller, the belonging to the Democratic as against the Republican party, to the Elks instead of to the Shriners become the expression of individual differences. The advertising slogan of "it is different" shows up this pathetic need for difference, when in reality there is hardly any left.

This increasing tendency for the elimination of differences is closely related to the concept and the experience of equality, as it is developing in the most advanced industrial societies. Equality had meant, in a religious context, that we are all God's children, that we all share in the same human-divine substance, that we are all one. It meant also that the very differences between individuals must be respected, that while it is true that we are all one, it is also true that each one of us is a unique entity, is a cosmos by itself. Such conviction of the uniqueness of the individual is expressed for instance in the Talmudic statement: "Whosoever saves a single life is as if he had saved the whole world; whosoever destroys a single life is as if he had destroyed the whole world." Equality as a condition for the development of individuality was also the meaning of the concept in the philosophy of the Western Enlightenment. It meant (most clearly formulated by Kant) that no man must be the means for the ends of another man. That all men are equal inasmuch as they are ends, and only ends, and never means to each other. Following the ideas of the Enlightenment, Socialist thinkers of various schools defined equality as abolition of exploitation, of the use of man by man, regardless of whether this use were cruel or "human."

In contemporary capitalistic society the meaning of equality has been transformed. By equality one refers to the equality of automatons; of men who have lost their individuality. *Equality today means "sameness," rather than "oneness."* It is the sameness of abstractions, of the men who work in the same jobs, who have the same amusements, who read the same newspapers, who have the same feelings and the same ideas. In this respect one must also look with some skepticism at some achievements which are usually praised as signs of our progress, such as the equality of women. Needless to say I am not speaking against the equality of women; but the positive aspects of this tendency for equality must not deceive one. It is part of the trend toward the elimination of differences. Equality is bought at this very price: women are equal because they are not different any more. The proposition of Enlightenment philosophy, *l'âme n'a pas de sexe*, the soul has no sex, has become the general practice. The polarity of the sexes is disappearing, and with it erotic love, which is based on this polarity. Men and women become the *same*, not *equals* as opposite poles. Contemporary society preaches this ideal of unindividualized equality because it needs human atoms, each one the same, to make them function in a mass aggregation, smoothly, without friction; all obeying the same commands, yet everybody being convinced that he is following his own desires. Just as modern mass production requires the standardization of commodities, so the social process requires standardization of man, and this standardization is called "equality."

Union by conformity is not intense and violent; it is calm, dictated by routine, and for this very reason often is insufficient to pacify the anxiety of separateness. The incidence of alcoholism, drug addiction, compulsive sexualism, and suicide in contemporary Western society are symptoms of this relative failure of herd conformity. Furthermore, this solution concerns mainly the mind and not the body, and for this reason too is lacking in comparison with the orgiastic solutions. Herd conformity has only one advantage: it is permanent, and not spasmodic. The individual is introduced into the conformity pattern at the age of three or four, and subsequently never loses his contact with the herd. Even his funeral, which he anticipates as his last great social affair, is in strict conformance with the pattern.

In addition to conformity as a way to relieve the anxiety springing from separateness, another factor of contemporary life must be considered: the role of the work routine and of the pleasure routine. Man becomes a "nine to fiver," he is part of the labor force, or the bureaucratic force of clerks and managers. He has little initiative, his tasks are prescribed by the organization of the work; there is even little difference between those high up on the ladder and those on the bottom. They all perform tasks prescribed by the whole structure of the organization, at a prescribed speed, and in a prescribed manner. Even the feelings are prescribed: cheerfulness, tolerance, reliability, ambition, and an ability to get along with everybody without friction. Fun is routinized in similar, although not quite as drastic ways. Books are selected by the book clubs, movies by the film and theater owners and the advertising slogans paid for by them; the rest is also uniform: the Sunday ride in the car, the television session, the card game, the social parties. From birth to death, from Monday to Monday, from morning to evening—all activities are routinized, and prefabricated. How should a man caught in this net of routine not forget that he is a man, a unique individual, one who is given only this one chance of living, with hopes and disappointments, with sorrow and fear, with the longing for love and the dread of the nothing and of separateness?

A third way of attaining union lies in *creative activity*, be it that of the artist, or of the artisan. In any kind of creative work the creating person unites himself with his material, which represents the world outside of himself. Whether a carpenter makes a table, or a goldsmith a piece of jewelry, whether the peasant grows his corn or the painter paints a picture, in all types of creative work the worker and his object become one, man unites himself with the world in the process of creation. This, however, holds true only for productive work, for work in which *I* plan, produce, see the result of my work. In the modern work process of a clerk, the worker on the endless belt, little is left of this uniting quality of work. The worker becomes an appendix to the machine or to the bureaucratic organization. He has ceased to be he—hence no union takes place beyond that of conformity.

The unity achieved in productive work is not interpersonal; the unity achieved in orgiastic fusion is transitory; the union achieved by conformity is only pseudo-unity. Hence, they are only partial answers to the problem of existence. The full answer lies in the achievement of interpersonal union, of fusion with another person, in *love*.

This desire for interpersonal fusion is the most powerful striving of man. It is the most fundamental passion, it is the force which keeps the human race together, the clan, the family, society. The failure to achieve it means insanity or destruction—self-destruction or destruction of others. Without love, humanity could not exist for a day. Yet, if we call the achievement of interpersonal union "love," we find ourselves in a serious difficulty. Fusion can be achieved in different ways—and the differences are not less significant than what is common to the various forms of love. Should they all be called love? Or should we reserve the word "love" only for a specific kind of union, one which has been the ideal virtue in all great humanistic religions and philosophical systems of the last four thousand years of Western and Eastern history?

As with all semantic difficulties, the answer can only be arbitrary. What matters is that we know what kind of union we are talking about when we speak of love. Do we refer to love as the mature answer to the problem of existence, or do we speak of those immature forms of love which may be called *symbolic union*? In the following pages I shall call love only the former. I shall begin the discussion of "love" with the latter.

Symbolic union has its biological pattern in the relationship between the pregnant mother and the foetus. They are two, and yet one. They live "together" (*symbiosis*), they need each other. The foetus is a part of the mother, it receives everything it needs from her; mother is its world, as it were; she feeds it, she protects it, but also her own life is enhanced by it. In the *psychic* symbiotic union, the two bodies are independent, but the same kind of attachment exists psychologically.

The *passive* form of the symbiotic union is that of submission, or if we use a clinical term, of *masochism*. The masochistic person escapes from the unbearable feeling of isolation and separateness by making himself part and parcel of another person who directs him, guides him, protects him; who is his life and his oxygen, as it were. The power of the one to whom one submits is inflated, may be a person or a god; he is everything, I am nothing, except inasmuch as I am part of him. As a part, I am part of greatness, of power, of certainty. The masochistic person does not have to make decisions, does not have to take any risks; he is never alone—but he is not independent; he has no integrity; he is not yet fully born. In a religious context the object of worship is called an idol; in a secular context of a masochistic love relationship the essential mechanism, that of idolatry, is the same. The masochistic relationship can be blended with physical, sexual desire; in this case it is not only a submission in which one's mind participates, but also one's whole body. There can be masochistic submission to fate, to sickness, to rhythmic music, to the orgiastic state produced by drugs or under hypnotic trance—in all these instances the person renounces his integrity, makes himself the instrument of somebody or something outside of himself; he need not solve the problem of living by productive activity.

The *active* form of symbiotic fusion is domination or, to use the psychological term corresponding to masochism, *sadism*. The sadistic person wants to escape from his aloneness and his sense of imprisonment by making another person part and parcel of himself. He inflates and enhances himself by incorporating another person, who worships him.

The sadistic person is as dependent on the submissive person as the latter is on the former; neither can live without the other. The difference is only that the sadistic person commands, exploits, hurts, humiliates, and that the masochistic person is commanded, exploited, hurt, humiliated. This is a considerable difference in a realistic sense; in a deeper emotional sense, the difference is not so great as that which they both have in common: fusion without integrity. If one understands this, it is also not surprising to find that usually a person reacts in both the sadistic and the masochistic manner, usually toward different objects. Hitler reacted primarily in a sadistic fashion toward people, but masochistically toward fate, history, the "higher power" of nature. His end—suicide among general destruction—is as characteristic as was his dream of success—total domination.[1]

In contrast to symbiotic union, mature *love* is *union under the condition of preserving one's integrity,* one's individuality. *Love is an active power in man*; a power which breaks through the walls which separate man from his fellow men, which unites him with others; love makes him overcome the sense of isolation and separateness, yet it permits him to be himself, to retain his integrity. In love the paradox occurs that two beings become one and yet remain two.

If we say love is an activity, we face a difficulty which lies in the ambiguous meaning of the word "activity." By "activity," in the modern usage of the word, is usually meant an action which brings about a change in an existing situation by means of an expenditure of energy. Thus a man is considered active if he does business, studies medicine, works on an endless belt, builds a table, or is engaged in sports. Common to all these activities is that they are directed toward an outside goal to be achieved. What is *not* taken into account is the *motivation* of activity. Take for instance a man driven to incessant work by a sense of deep insecurity and loneliness; or another one driven by ambition, or greed for money. In all these cases the person is the slave of a passion, and his activity is in reality a "passivity" because he is driven; he is the sufferer, not the "actor." On the other hand, a man sitting quiet and contemplating, with no purpose or aim except that of experiencing himself and his oneness with the world, is considered to be "passive," because he is not "doing" anything. In reality, this attitude of concentrated meditation is the highest activity there is, an activity of the soul, which is possible only under the condition of inner freedom and independence. One concept of activity, the modern one, refers to the use of energy for the achievement of external aims; the other concept of activity refers to the use of man's inherent powers, regardless of whether any external change is brought about. The latter concept of activity has been formulated most clearly by Spinoza. He differentiates among the affects between active and passive affects, "actions" and "passions." In the exercise of an active affect, man is free, he is the master of his affect; in the exercise of a passive affect, man is driven, the object of motivations of which he himself is not aware. Thus Spinoza arrives at the statement that virtue and power are one and the same.[2] Envy, jealousy, ambition, any kind of greed are passions; love is an action, the practice of a human power, which can be practiced only in freedom and never as the result of a compulsion.

Love is an activity, not a passive affect; it is a "standing in," not a "falling for." In the most general way, the active character of love can be described by stating that love is primarily *giving*, not receiving.

What is giving? Simple as the answer to this question seems to be, it is actually full of ambiguities and complexities. The most widespread misunderstanding is that which assumes that giving is "giving up" something, being deprived of, sacrificing. The person whose character has not developed beyond the stage of the receptive, exploitative, or hoarding orientation, experiences the act of giving in this way. The marketing character is willing to give, but only in exchange for receiving; giving without receiving for him is being cheated.[3] People whose main orientation is a non-productive one feel giving as an impoverishment. Most individuals of this type therefore refuse to give. Some make a virtue out of giving in the sense of a sacrfiice. They feel that just because it is painful to give, one *should* give; the virtue of giving to them lies in the very act of acceptance of the sacrifice. For them, the norm that it is better to give than to receive means that it is better to suffer deprivation than to experience joy.

For the productive character, giving has an entirely different meaning. Giving is the highest expression of potency. In the very act of giving, I experience my strength, my wealth, my power. This experience of heightened vitality and potency fills me with joy. I experience myself as overflowing, spending, alive, hence as joyous.[4] Giving is more joyous than receiving, not because it is a deprivation, but because in the act of giving lies the expression of my aliveness.

It is not difficult to recognize the validity of this principle by applying it to various specific phenomena. The most elementary example lies in the sphere of sex. The culmination of the male sexual function lies in the act of giving; the man gives himself, his sexual organ, to the woman. At the moment of orgasm he gives his semen to her. He cannot help giving it if he is potent. If he cannot give, he is impotent. For the woman the process is not different, although somewhat more complex. She gives herself too; she opens the gates to her feminine center; in the act of receiving, she gives. If she is incapable of this act of giving, if she can only receive, she is frigid. With her the act of giving occurs again, not in her function as a lover, but in that as a mother. She gives of herself to the growing child within her, she gives her milk to the infant, she gives her bodily warmth. Not to give would be painful.

In the sphere of material things giving means being rich. Not he who *has* much is rich, but he who *gives* much. The hoarder who is anxiously worried about losing something is, psychologically speaking, the poor, impoverished man, regardless of how much he has. Whoever is capable of giving of himself is rich. He experiences himself as one who can confer of himself to others. Only one who is deprived of all that goes beyond the barest necessities for subsistence would be incapable of enjoying the act of giving material things. But daily experience shows that what a person considers the minimal necessities depends as much on his character as it depends on his actual possessions. It is well known that the poor are more willing to give than the rich. Nevertheless, poverty beyond a certain point may make it impossible to give, and is so degrading, not only because of the suffering it causes directly, but because of the fact that it deprives the poor of the joy of giving.

The most important sphere of giving, however, is not that of material things, but lies in the specifically human realm. What does one person give to another? He gives of himself, of the most precious he has, he gives of his life. This does not necessarily mean that he sacrifices his life for the other—but that he gives him of that which is alive in him; he gives him of his joy, of his interest, of his understanding, of his knowledge, of his humor, of his sadness—of all expressions and manifestations of that which is alive in him. In thus giving of his life, he enriches the other person, he enhances the other's sense of aliveness by enhancing his own sense of aliveness. He does not give in order to receive; giving is in itself exquisite joy. But in giving he cannot help bringing something to life in the other person, and this which is brought to life reflects back to him; in truly giving, he cannot help receiving that which is given back to him. Giving implies to make the other person a giver also and they both share in the joy of what they have brought to life. In the act of giving something is born, and both persons involved are grateful for the life that is born for both of them. Specifically with regard to love this means: love is a power which produces love; impotence is the inability to produce love. This thought has been beautifully expressed by Marx: "Assume," he says, "*man as man*, and his relation to the world as a human one, and you can exchange love only for love, confidence for confidence, etc. If you wish to enjoy art, you must be an artistically trained person; if you wish to have influence on other people, you must be a person who has a really stimulating and furthering influence on other people. Every one of your relationships to man and to nature must be a definite expression of your *real, individual* life corresponding to the object of your will. If you love without calling forth love, that is, if your love as such does not produce love, if by means of an *expression of life* as a loving person you do not make of yourself a *loved person*, then your love is impotent, a misfortune."[5] But not only in love does giving mean receiving. The teacher is taught by his students, the actor is stimulated by his audience, the psychoanalyst is cured by his patient—provided they do not treat each other as objects, but are related to each other genuinely and productively.

It is hardly necessary to stress the fact that the ability to love as an act of giving depends on the character development of the person. It presupposes the attainment of a predominantly productive orientation; in this orientation the person has overcome dependency, narcissistic omnipotence, the wish to exploit others, or to hoard, and has acquired faith in his own human powers, courage to rely on his powers in the attainment of his goals. To the degree that these qualities are lacking, he is afraid of giving himself—hence of loving.

Beyond the element of giving, the active character of love becomes evident in the fact that it always implies certain basic elements, common to all forms of love. These are *care, responsibility, respect* and *knowledge*.

That love implies *care* is most evident in a mother's love for her child. No assurance of her love would strike us as sincere if we saw her lacking in care for the infant, if she neglected to feed it, to bathe it, to give it physical comfort; and we are impressed by her love if we see her caring for the child. It is not different even with the love for animals or flowers. If a woman told us that she loved flowers, and we saw that she forgot to water them, we would not believe in her "love" for flowers. *Love is the active concern for the life and the growth of that which we love.* Where this active concern is lacking, there is no love. This element of love has been beautifully described in the book of Jonah. God has told Jonah to go to Nineveh to warn its inhabitants that they will be punished unless they mend their evil ways. Jonah runs away from his mission because he is afraid that the people of Nineveh will repent and that God will forgive them. He is a man with a strong sense of order and law, but without love. However, in his attempt to escape, he finds himself in the belly of a whale, symbolizing the state of isolation and imprisonment which his lack of love and solidarity has brought upon him. God saves him, and Jonah goes to Nineveh. He preaches to the inhabitants as God had told him, and the very thing he was afraid of happens. The men of Nineveh repent their sins, mend their ways, and God forgives them and decides not to destroy the city. Jonah is intensely angry and disappointed; he wanted "justice" to be done, not mercy. At last he finds some comfort in the shade of a tree which God had made to grow for him to protect him from the sun. But when God makes the tree wilt, Jonah is depressed and angrily complains to God. God answers: "Thou hast had pity on the gourd for the which thou hast not labored neither madest it grow; which came up in a night, and perished in a night. And should I not spare Nineveh, that great city, wherein are more than sixscore thousand people that cannot discern between their right hand and their left hand; and also much cattle?" God's answer to Jonah is to be understood symbolically. God explains to Jonah that the essence of love is to "labor" for something and "to make something grow," that love and labor are inseparable. One loves that for which one labors, and one labors for that which one loves.

Care and concern imply another aspect of love; that of *responsibility*. Today responsibility is often meant to denote duty, something imposed upon one from the outside. But responsibility, in its true sense, is an entirely voluntary act; it is my response to the needs, expressed or unexpressed, of another human being. To be "responsible" means to be able and ready to "respond." Jonah did not feel responsible to the inhabitants of Nineveh. He, like Cain, could ask: "Am I my brother's keeper?" The loving person responds. The life of his brother is not his brother's business alone, but his own. He feels responsible for his fellow men, as he feels responsible for himself. This responsibility, in the case of the mother and her infant, refers mainly to the care for physical needs. In the love between adults it refers mainly to the psychic needs of the other person.

Responsibility could easily deteriorate into domination and possessiveness, were it not for a third component of love, *respect*. Respect is not fear and awe; it denotes, in accordance with the root of the word (*respicere* = to look at) , the ability to see a person as he is, to be aware of his unique individuality. Respect means the concern that the other person should grow and unfold as he is. Respect, thus, implies the absence of exploitation. I want the loved person to grow and unfold for his own sake, and in his own ways, and not for the purpose of serving me. If I love the other person, I feel one with him or her, but with him *as he is*, not as I need him to be as an object for my use. It is clear that respect is possible only if *I* have achieved independence; if I can stand and walk without needing crutches, without having to dominate and exploit anyone else. Respect exists only on the basis of freedom: "l'amour est l'enfant de la liberté" as an old French song says; love is the child of freedom, never that of domination.

To respect a person is not possible without *knowing* him; care and responsibility would be blind if they were not guided by knowledge. Knowledge would be empty if it were not motivated by concern. There are many layers of knowledge; the knowledge which is an aspect of love is one which does not stay at the periphery, but penetrates to the core. It is possible only when I can transcend the concern for myself and see the other person in his own terms. I may know, for instance, that a person is angry, even if he does not show it overtly; but I may know him more deeply than that; then I know that he is anxious, and worried; that he feels lonely, that he feels guilty. Then I know that his anger is only the manifestation of something deeper, and I see him as anxious and embarrassed, that is, as the suffering person, rather than as the angry one.

NOTES

1. Cf. a more detailed study of sadism and masochism in E. Fromm, *Escape from Freedom*, Reinhart & Company, New York, 1941.
2. Spinoza, *Ethics* IV, Def. 8.
3. Cf. a detailed discussion of these character orientations in E. Fromm, *Man for Himself*, Rinehart & Company, New York, 1947, Chap. III, pp. 54–117.
4. Compare the definition of joy given by Spinoza.
5. "Nationalökonomie und Philosophie," 1844, published in Karl Marx' *Die Frühschriften*, Alfred Kröner Verlag, Stuttgart, 1953, pp. 300, 301. (My translation, E. F.)